The Fruits And Fruit Trees Of America; Or, The Culture, Propagation, And Management, In The Garden And Orchard, Of Fruit Trees Generally; With Descriptions Of All The Finest Varieties Of Fruit, Native And Foreign, Cultivated In This Country

Downing, A. J. (Andrew Jackson), 1815-1852

THE

FRUITS AND FRUIT TREES

OF

AMERICA;

OR,

THE CULTURE, PROPAGATION, AND MANAGEMENT, IN THE GARDEN AND
ORCHARD, OF FRUIT TREES GENERALLY;

WITH

DESCRIPTIONS OF ALL THE FINEST VARIETIES OF FRUIT,
NATIVE AND FOREIGN, CULTIVATED IN THIS COUNTRY.

BY A. J. DOWNING.

CORRESPONDING MEMBER OF THE ROYAL BOTANIC SOCIETY OF LONDON; AND OF THE
HORTICULTURAL SOCIETIES OF BERLIN; THE LOW COUNTRIES; MASSACHU-
SETTS; PENNSYLVANIA; INDIANA; CINCINNATI. ETC.

What wondrous life is this I lead?
Ripe apples drop about my head;
The luscious clusters of the vine
Upon my mouth do crush their wine;
The nectarine and curious peach
Into my hands themselves do reach.

MARVELL.

FOURTEENTH EDITION.

NEW YORK:

JOHN WILEY, 167 BROADWAY.

1854.

TO

MARSHALL P. WILDER, Esq.,

PRESIDENT OF THE

MASSACHUSETTS HORTICULTURAL SOCIETY,

THIS VOLUME IS DEDICATED,

BY HIS FRIEND,

THE AUTHOR

PREFACE.

A M N born on the banks of one of the noblest and most fruitful rivers in America, and whose best days have been spent in gardens and orchards, may perhaps be pardoned for talking about fruit trees.

Indeed the subject deserves not a few, but many words. "Fine fruit is the flower of commodities." It is the most perfect union of the useful and the beautiful that the earth knows. Trees full of soft foliage; blossoms fresh with spring beauty; and, finally,—fruit, rich, bloom-dusted, melting, and luscious—such are the treasures of the orchard and the garden, temptingly offered to every landholder in this bright and sunny, though temperate climate.

"If a man," says an acute essayist, "should send for me to come a hundred miles to visit him, and should set before me a basket of fine summer fruit, 1 should think there was some proportion between the labour and the reward."

I must add a counterpart to this. He who owns a rood of proper land in this country, and, in the face of all the pomonal riches of the day, only raises crabs and choke-pears, deserves to lose the respect of all sensible men. The classical antiquarian must pardon one for doubting if, amid all the wonderful beauty of the golden age, there was anything to equal our delicious modern fruits—our honied Seckels, and Beurrés, our melting Rareripes. At any rate, the science of modern horticulture has restored almost everything that can be desired to give a paradisiacal richness to our fruit-gardens. Yet there are many in utter ignorance of most of these fruits, who seem to live under some ban of expulsion from all the fair and goodly productions of the garden.

Happily, the number is every day lessening. America is

young orchard, but when the planting of fruit-trees in one of the newest States numbers nearly a quarter of a million in a single year; when there are more peaches exposed in the markets of New York, annually, than are raised in all France; when American apples, in large quantities, command double prices in European markets; there is little need for entering into any praises of this soil and climate generally, regarding the culture of fruit. In one part or another of the Union every man may, literally, sit under his own vine and fig tree.

It is fortunate for an author, in this practical age, when his subject requires no explanation to show its downright and direct usefulness. When I say I heartily desire that every man should cultivate an orchard, or at least a tree, of good fruit, it is not necessary that I should point out how much both himself and the public will be, in every sense, the gainers. Otherwise I might be obliged to repeat the advice of Dr. Johnson to one of his friends. "If possible," said he, "have a good orchard. I know a clergyman of small income who brought up a family very reputably, which he chiefly fed on apple dumplings."(!)

The first object, then, of this work is to increase the taste for the planting and cultivation of fruit-trees. The second one is to furnish a manual for those who, already more or less informed upon the subject, desire some work of reference to guide them in the operations of culture, and in the selection of varieties.

If it were only necessary for me to present for the acceptance of my readers a choice garland of fruit, comprising the few sorts that I esteem of the most priceless value, the space and time to be occupied would be very brief.

But this would only imperfectly answer the demand that is at present made by our cultivators. The country abounds with collections of all the finest foreign varieties; our own soil has produced many native sorts of the highest merit; and from all these, kinds may be selected which are highly valuable for every part of the country. But opinions differ much as to the merits of some sorts. Those which succeed perfectly in one section, are sometimes ill-adapted to another. And, finally, one

needs some accurate description to know when a variety comes into bearing, if its fruit is genuine, or even to identify an indifferent
kind, in order to avoid procuring it again.   Hence the number
of varieties of fruit that are admitted here.   Little by little I
have summoned them into my pleasant and quiet court, tested
them as far as possible, and endeavoured to pass the most im-
partial judgment upon them.   The verdicts will be found in the
following pages.

From this great accumulation of names, Pomology has become an embarrassing study, and those of our readers who
are large collectors will best understand the difficulty—nay, the
impossibility of making a work like this perfect.

Towards settling this chaos in nomenclature, the exertions of
the Horticultural Society of London have been steadily directed
for the last twenty years.   That greatest of experimental gardens
contains, or has contained, nearly all the varieties of fruit, from
all parts of the world, possessing the least celebrity.   The vast
confusion of names, dozens sometimes meaning the same variety, has been by careful comparison reduced to something like
real order.   The relative merit of the kinds has been proved
and published.   In short, the horticultural world owes this Society a heavy debt of gratitude for these labours, and to the science
and accuracy of Mr. Robert Thompson, the head of its fruit-
department, horticulturists here will gladly join me in bearing
the fullest testimony.

To give additional value to these results, I have adopted in
nearly all cases, for fruits known abroad, the nomenclature of
the London Horticultural Society.   By this means I hope to
render universal on this side of the Atlantic the same standard
names, so that the difficulty and confusion which have always
more or less surrounded this part of the subject may be hereafter avoided.

These foreign fruits have now been nearly all proved in
this country, and remarks on their value in this climate, deduc-
ed from actual experience, are here given to the public.   To
our native and local fruits especial care has also been devoted.
Not only have most of the noted sorts been proved in the gar

dens here, but I have had specimens before me for comparison, the growth of no less than fourteen of the different States. There are still many sorts, nominally fine, which remain to be collected, compared, and proved; some of which will undoubtedly deserve a place in future editions. To the kindness of pomologists in various sections of the country I must trust for the detection of errors in the present volume, and for information of really valuable new varieties.*

Of the *descriptions* of fruit, some explanation may be necessary. First, is given the *standard* name in capitals, followed by the authorities—that is, the names of authors who have previously given an account of it by this title. Below this are placed, in smaller type, the various *synonymes*, or local names, by which the same fruit is known in various countries or parts of the country. Thus, on page 386, is the following:

117. FLEMISH BEAUTY. § Lind. Thomp.

Belle de Flandres.	Impératrice de France.
Bouche Nouvelle.	Boschpeer.
Bosch.	Josephine ⎱ *incorrectly*
Bosc Sire.	Fondante Du Bois ⎰ *of some.*

By this is signified, first, that FLEMISH BEAUTY is the *standard* name of the pear; secondly, that it has been previously described by Lindley and Thompson; thirdly, that the others—*synonymes*—are various local names by which the Flemish Beauty is also known in various places; and, lastly that by the two latter names—Josephine, and Fondante Du Bois—it is *incorrectly* known in some collections; these two names really belonging to other distinct pears.

It is at once apparent that one of the chief points of value of a book like this, lies in the accuracy with which these synonymous names are given—since a person might, in looking over different

* It is well to remark that many of the so-called new varieties, especially from the West, prove to be old and well known kinds, slightly altered in appearance by new soil and different climate. A new variety must possess very superior qualities to entitle it to regard, now that we have so many fine fruits in our collections.

catalogues issued here and abroad, suppose that all nine of the above are different varieties—when they are really all different names for a single pear. In this record of synonymes, I have therefore availed myself of the valuable experience of the London Horticultural Society, and added all the additional information in my own possession.

Many of the more important varieties of fruit are shown in *outline*. I have chosen this method as likely to give the most correct idea of the form of a fruit, and because I believe that the mere outline of a fruit, like a profile of the human face, will often be found more characteristic than a highly finished portrait in colour. The outlines have been nearly all traced directly from fruits grown here. *They are from specimens mostly below the average size.* It has been the custom to choose the largest and finest fruits for illustration—a practice very likely to mislead. I believe the general character is better expressed by specimens of medium size, or rather below it.

It only remains for me to present my acknowledgments to the numerous gentlemen, in various parts of the country, who have kindly furnished information necessary to the completion of the work. The names of many are given in the body of the volume. But to the following I must especially tender my thanks, for notes of their experience, or for specimens of fruits to solve existing doubts.

In Massachusetts, to Messrs. M. P. Wilder, S. G. Perkins, J. P. Cushing, B. V. French, S. Downer, and C. M. Hovey, of Boston; John C. Lee, J. M. Ives, the late Robert Manning and his son R. Manning, of Salem; and Otis Johnson, of Lynn.

In Connecticut, to Dr. E. W. Bull, of Hartford; Mr. S. Lyman, of Manchester; and the Rev. H. S. Ramsdell, of Thompson.

In New York, to Messrs. David Thomas, of Aurora; J. J. Thomas, of Macedon; Luther Tucker, and Isaac Denniston, of Albany; Alexander Walsh, of Lansingburgh; T. H. Hyatt, of Rochester; R. L. Pell, of Pelham; C. Downing, of Newburgh; and Wm. H. Aspinwall, of Staten Island.

In Ohio, to Professor Kirtland, of Cleveland ; Dr. Hildreth, of Marietta ; and Messrs. N. Longworth, C W. Elliott, and A. H. Ernst, of Cincinnati.

In Indiana, to the Rev. H. W. Beecher, of Indianapolis. In New Jersey, to Messrs. Thomas Hancock, of Burlington, and J. W. Hayes, of Newark. In Pennsylvania, to Mr. Frederick Brown, and Col. Carr, of Philadelphia. In Maryland, to Lloyd N. Rogers, Esq., of Baltimore. In Georgia, to James Camak, Esq., of Athens.

A. J. D.

HIGHLAND GARDENS, }
Newburgh, N. Y., May, 1845. }

ABBREVIATIONS AND BOOKS QUOTED.

Arboretum Britannicum, or the Trees and Shrubs of Britain, pictorially and botanically delineated, and scientifically and popularly described by J. C. Loudon London, 1845, 8 vols. 8vo.

Annales de la Société d'Horticulture de Paris.—Paris. In monthlv Nos. 8vo. from 1827 to 1845.

Annales de l'Institut de Fromont. Par le Chevalier Soulange Bodin. Paris, 8vo. 1829 to 1834, 6 vols.

Adlum. A Memoir on the cultivation of the Vine in America, and the best mode of making Wine. By John Adlum. 12mo. Washington, 1828.

Bon Jard. Le Bon Jardinier, pour l'Année 1844. Contenant des principes generaux de culture, etc. Par A. Poiteau and M. Vilmorin, Paris. 12mo.—yearly volume.

Busby. A Visit to the principal Vineyards of France and Spain. By Jas. Busby. New York, 12mo. 1835.

Bridgeman. The Young Gardener's Assistant. By Thomas Bridgeman. Tenth ed. New York, 1844, 8vo.

Baumann's Cat. Catalogue des Vegetaux en tout genre dispanible dans l'Etablissement des Frères Baumann, à Bolwiller, 1842.

Coxe. A View of the Cultivation of Fruit Trees in the United States, and of the Management of Orchards and Cider. By William Coxe.—Philadelphia, 8vo., 1817.

Chaptal. Chemistry applied to Agriculture. By John Anthony Chaptal. American ed., 12mo. Boston, 1835.

Cobbett. The American Gardener. By Wm. Cobbett. London, 1821. 12mo.

Coleman. Reports on the Agriculture of Massachusetts. By Henry Coleman. Boston, 8vo. 1840-41.

Dom. Gard. The Domestic Gardener's Manual. By John Towers. London, 1839, 8vo.

Duhamel. Traité des Arbres Fruitiers, par M. Duhamel Dumonceau. Paris, 1768, 2 vols. 4to.

Cultivator. The Cultivator, a monthly journal of Agriculture, &c., Edited by Luther Tucker. Albany, continued to the present time, 8vo.

Diel. Versuch ein Systematischen Beschreibung in Deutschland vorhandener Kernobstsorten. Von Dr. Aug. Freidr. Ad. Diel. 12mo. 24 vols. 1799—1825.

De Candolle. Physiologie Végétale, ou Exposition des Forces et des Fonctions vitales des Végétaux. Par A. P. De Candolle. Paris, 1832, 3 vols. 8vo.

—————. Prodromus Systematis Naturalıs Vegetabılıs Paris, 1818—
1830, 4 vols, 8vo.

D'Albret Cours Théorique et Pratique de la Taille des Arbres Fruitiers.
Par D'Albret Parıs, 1840, 8vo.

Forsyth A Treatise on the Culture and Management of Fruit-trees. **By**
William Forsyth, 7th ed London, 1824, 8vo.

Floy Lindley's Guide to the Orchard. American ed. with additions **by**
Michael Floy. New York, 1833, 12mo.

Fessenden. New American Gardener, containing practical dırectıons for .
the culture of Fruıts and Vegetables. By Thos. E Fessenden. Boston, 1828, 12mo

Gard. Mag. The Gardener's Magazine, conducted by J. C. Loudon, ın
monthly nos 8vo , 19 vols to 1844., London.

Gard Chron The Gardener's Chronicle, and Agricultural Gazette, edited by Professor Lındley, a weekly journal 4to 5 vols 1844 to the
present time.

Hoare. A Practical Treatise on the cultivation of the Grape Vine on
open walls By Clement Hoare. London, 1840, 12mo

Hort Soc. Cat. See *Thompson.*

Hort. Trans. Transactions of the Horticultural Society of London. London, 4to. 1815, and at intervals to the present time.

Hooker Pomona Londonensis By Wılliam Hooker. London, 1813,
4to.

Hayward The Science of Horticulture By Joseph Hayward. London,
1824, 8vo

Harris. A Report on the insects of Massachusetts injurious to Vegetation
By Dr. T. W. Harrıs. Cambridge, 1841, 8vo.

Hov. Mag. or H. M The Magazine of Horticulture, Botany and Ru-
ral Affairs. Conducted by C M Hovey. Boston, 8vo. monthly nos.
1834 to the present time.

Johnston. Lectures on Agricultural Chemistry and Geology. By Jas. W
F. Johnston. American ed New York, 12mo 2 vols. 1842.

Jard Fruit Le Jardin Fruitier, par Louıs Noısette, 2 ed Paris, 1839,
2 vols. 8vo.

Knight Varıous articles ın the London Horticultural Transactions. By
Thomas Andrew Knight, its late President.

Knoop Pomologıe ou descriptıon des Arbres Fruıtiers Par Joh. Herm
Knoop Amsterdam, 1771, Fol.

Ken. The New American Orchardist By Wıllıam Kenrick, Boston,
1844.

Kollar. A Treatise on Insects ınjurıous to Gardeners, Foresters and
Farmers. By Vıncent Kollar, Notes by Westwood London, 1840,
12mo.

Langley. Pomona, or the Fruit Garden Illustrated By Batty Langley,
London, 1729, Folio.

Loudon. An Encyclopedıa of Gardening. By J. C. Loudon. London.
1835, 1 thıck vol 8vo

—————. An Encyclopedıa of Plants. By the same. London, 1836, **1 thick
vol. 8vo.**

—————. An Encyclopedıa of Agriculture. By the same. London, **1931, 1
thick vol. 8vo.**

Loudon Hortus Britannicus. A Catalogue of all the plants in Britain, by the same. London, 8vo.

————. The Suburban Horticulturist By the same. London, 1842, 8vo.

————. The Suburban Gardener and Villa Companion. By the same London, 1838, 1842, 8vo.

————. Arboretum et Fruticetum Britannicum. By the same, 3 vols. London, 1838, 8vo.

Liebig. Organic Chemistry in its applications to Agriculture and Physiology. By Justus Liebig. American ed., Cambridge, 1844, 12mo.

Lind A Guide to the Orchard and Kitchen Garden, or an account of the Fruits and Vegetables cultivated in Great Britain. By George Lindley. London, 1831, 8vo.

Lindley. An Introduction to Botany. By John Lindley. London, 1832, 8vo.

————. An Introduction to the Natural System of Botany. By John Lindley. London, 1835, 2d ed. 8vo.

————. British Fruits. See Pomological Magazine—it is the same work.

————. The Theory of Horticulture, or an attempt to explain the Operation of Gardening upon Physiological Principles. By John Lindley. London, 8vo. 1840.

————. The same work with Notes by A. Gray and A. J. Downing. New York, 1841, 12mo.

L. or Linnæus. Species Plantarum, 5th. ed. Berlin, 1810, 5 vols. 8vo.

Lelieur. La Pomone Française, ou Traité de la Culture Française, et de la Taille des Arbres Fruitiers. Par le Compte Lelieur. Paris, 1811, 8vo.

Man. The New England Fruit Book. By R. Manning, 2d ed. enlarged by John M. Ives, Salem, 1844, 12mo.

Man. in H. M. Manning's articles in Hovey's Magazine.

Mill. The Gardener's and Botanist's Dictionary. By Philip Miller.—revised by Professor Martyn. London, 1819, 2 vols. 8vo.

Michaux. The North American Sylva, or Descriptions of the Forest Trees of the United States, Canada, &c. By A. F. Michaux. Paris, 1819, 3 vols Svo

M'Intosh. The Orchard and Fruit Garden. By Charles McIntosh. London, 1819, 12mo.

N. Duh. (The New Duhamel) Traité des Arbres Fruitiers de Duhamel. Nouvelle edition augmentée, etc. Par MM. Poiteau et Turpin, Paris. 5 vols. Folio, 1808 et seq.

Nois. See Jardin Fruitier.

New England Farmer. A weekly periodical, devoted to Agriculture, Horticulture, &c. Boston, 4to. continued to the present time.

O Duh. See Duhamel.

Pom. Mag. or P. M. The Pomological Magazine, or Figures and Descriptions of the most important varieties of Fruit cultivated in Great Britain. London, 1828, 3 vols. 8vo.

Pom. Man. The Pomological Manual. By William R. Prince. New York, 1831, 2 vols. 8vo.

Prince. A Treatise on the Vine. By William R. Prince, New York, 1830. 8vo.

Prince A short Treatise on Horticulture. By William Prince, New York, 1828, 12mo

Phillips Pomarium Britannicum ;—an Historical and Botanical Account of the Fruits known in Great Britain. By Henry Phillips, London, 1820, 8vo

Poit. or Poiteau. Pomologie Française. Recueil des plus beaux Fruits, cultivés en France. Par Poiteau. Paris, 1838, and continued in 4to. nos.

Rivers A Descriptive Catalogue of Pears, cultivated by T. Rivers. Sawbridgeworth, 1843-44, pamphlet, 8vo.

Ron. or Ronalds. Pyrus Malus Brentfordienses, or a concise description of Selected Apples, with a figure of each sort. By Hugh Ronalds, London, 1831, 4to

Ray Historia Plantarum, a John Ray, M. D., London, 3 vols. Folio, 1636—1704.

Revue Horticole Journal des Jardiniers et Amateurs. Audot, Editeur Paris, 1844, et chaque mois, 12mo.

Switzer. The Practical Fruit Gardener. By Stephen Switzer, 1724, 8vo

Torrey & Gray. A Flora of North America, containing abridged descriptions of all the known plants growing North of the Gulf of Mexico By John Torrey, M.D , and Asa Gray, M.D., New York, vol. 1st, 8vo New York, 1840, and still in progress

Thomp. A Catalogue of the Fruits Cultivated in the Garden of the Horticultural Society of London, 3d ed , London, 1842. [Prepared with great care by Robert Thompson, the head of the Fruit Department]

Thacher. The American Orchardist By James Thacher, M.D , Boston, 1822, 8vo

Van Mons. Arbres Fruitiers, ou Pomologie Belge Experimentale et Raisonnée, Par J. R. Van Mons. Louvain, 1835—1836, 2 vols. 12mo.

———. Catalogue des Arbres Fruitiers, Descriptif, Abrégé. Par J. B. **Van** Mons, Louvain, 1823.

Wilder, MSS. Manuscript notes on Fruits, by M. P. Wilder, Esq., President of the Massachusetts Horticultural Society.

FRUITS AND FRUIT TREES

CHAPTER I.

THE PRODUCTION OF NEW VARIETIES OF FRUIT.

In our survey of the culture of fruits let us begin at the beginning. Gradual amelioration, and the skilful practice of the cultivator, have so filled our orchards and gardens with good fruits, that it is necessary now to cast a look back at the types from which these delicious products have sprung.

In the tropical zone, amid the surprising luxuriance of vegetation of that great natural hothouse, nature offers to man, almost without care, the most refreshing, the most delicious, and the most nutritive fruits. The Plantain and Bananna, excellent either raw or cooked, bearing all the year, and producing upon a roof of ground the sustenance of a family; the refreshing Guava and Sapodilla; the nutritious Bread-fruit; such are the natural fruit trees of those glowing climates. Indolently seated under their shade, and finding a refreshing coolness both from their ever-verdant canopy of leaves, and their juicy fruits, it is not here that we must look for the patient and skilful cultivator.

But, in the temperate climates, nature wears a harsher and sterner aspect. Plains bounded by rocky hills, visited not only by genial warmth and sunshine, but by cold winds and seasons of ice and snow; these are accompanied by sturdy forests, whose outskirts are sprinkled with crabs and wild cherries, and festooned with the clambering branches of the wild grape. These native fruits, which at first offer so little to the eye, or the palate, are nevertheless the types of our garden varieties. Destined in these climates to a perpetual struggle with nature, it is here that we find man ameliorating and transforming her.

Transplanted into a warmer aspect, stimulated by a richer soil, reared from selected seeds, carefully pruned, sheltered and watched, by slow degrees the sour and bitter crab expands into a Golden Pippin, the wild pear loses its thorns and becomes a Bergamotte or a Beurré, the Almond is deprived of its bitterness, and the dry and flavourless Peach is at length a tempting and delicious fruit. It is thus only in the face of obstacles, in a climate where nature is not prodigal of perfections, and in the midst of thorns and sloes, that MAN THE GARDENER arises and forces nature to yield to his art.

1

These improved sorts of fruit which man every where causes to share his civilization, bear, almost equally with himself, the impress of an existence removed from the natural state. When reared from seeds they always show a tendency to return to a wilder form, and it seems only *chance* when a new seedling is equal to, or surpasses its parent. Removed from their natural form, these artificially created sorts are also much more liable to diseases and to decay. From these facts arises the fruit-garden, with its various processes of grafting, budding and other means of continuing the sort; with also its sheltered aspects, warm borders, deeper soils, and all its various refinements of art and culture.

In the whole range of cares and pleasures belonging to the garden, there is nothing more truly interesting than the production of new varieties of fruit. It is not, indeed, by sowing the seeds that the lover of good fruit usually undertakes to stock his garden and orchard with fine fruit trees. Raising new varieties is always a slow, and, as generally understood, a most uncertain mode of bringing about this result. The novice, plants and carefully watches his hundred seedling pippins, to find at last, perhaps, ninety-nine worthless or indifferent apples. It appears to him a lottery, in which there are too many blanks to the prizes. He, therefore, wisely resorts to the more certain mode of grafting from well known and esteemed sorts.

Notwithstanding this, every year, under the influences of garden culture, and often without our design, we find our fruit trees reproducing themselves; and occasionally, there springs up a new and delicious sort, whose merits tempt us to fresh trials after perfection.

To a man who is curious in fruit, the pomologist who views with a more than common eye, the crimson cheek of a peach, the delicate bloom of a plum, or understands the epithets, rich, melting, buttery, as applied to a pear, nothing in the circle of culture, can give more lively and unmixed pleasure, than thus to produce and to create—for it is a sort of creation—an entirely new sort, which he believes will prove handsomer and better than any thing that has gone before. And still more, as varieties which originate in a certain soil and climate, are found best adapted to that locality, the production of new sorts of fruit, of high merit, may be looked on as a most valuable, as well as interesting result.

Beside this, all the fine new fruits, which, of late, figure so conspicuously in the catalogues of the nurseries and fruit gardens, have not been originated at random and by chance efforts. Some of the most distinguished pomologists have devoted years to the subject of the improvement of fruit trees by seeds, and have attained if not certain results, at least some general laws, which greatly assist us in this process of amelioration. Let us therefore examine the subject a little more in detail.

In the wild state, every genus of trees consist of one or more *species*, or strongly marked individual sorts ; as, for example, the white birch and the black birch ; or, to confine ourselves more strictly to the matter in hand, the different species of cherry, the wild or bird cherry, the sour cherry, the mazzard cherry, &c. These *species, in their natural state*, exactly reproduce themselves ; to use a common phrase, they " come the same" from seed. This they have done for centuries, and doubtless will do forever, so long as they exist under natural circumstances only.

On the other hand, suppose we select one of these *species* of fruit-trees, and adopt it into our gardens. So long as we cultivate that individual tree, or any part of it, in the shape of sucker, graft, or bud, its nature will not be materially altered. It may, indeed, through cultivation, be stimulated into a more luxuriant growth ; it will probably produce larger leaves and fruit ; but we shall neither alter its fruit in texture, color or taste. It will always be identically the same.

The process of amelioration begins with a new generation, and by sowing the seeds. Some species of tree, indeed, seem to refuse to yield their wild nature, never producing any variation by seed ; but all fruit-trees and many others, are easily *domesticated*, and more readily take the impress of culture.

If we sow a quantity of seed in garden soil of the common black mazzard cherry, (*Cerasus avium*,) we shall find that, in the leaves and habit of growth, many of the seedlings do not entirely resemble the original species. When they come into bearing, it is probable we shall also find as great a diversity in the size, color and flavor of the fruit. Each of these individual plants, differing from the original type, (the mazzard,) constitutes a new *variety* ; though only a few, perhaps only one, may be superiour to the original species.

It is worthy of remark, that exactly in proportion as this reproduction is frequently repeated, is the change to a great variety of forms, or new sorts increased. It is likely indeed, that to gather the seeds from a wild mazzard in the woods, the instances of departure from the form of the original species would be very few ; while if gathered from a garden tree, itself some time cultivated, or several removes from a wild state, though still a mazzard, the seedlings will show great variety of character.

Once in the possession of a *variety*, which has *moved out* of the natural into a more domesticated form, we have in our hands the best material for the improving process. The fixed original habit of the species is broken in upon, and this variety which we have created, has always afterwards some tendency to make further departures from the original form. It is true that all or most of its seedlings will still retain a likeness to the parent, but a few will differ in some respects, and it is by seizing upon those which show symptoms of variation, that the improver of vegetable races founds his hopes.

We have said that it is a part of the character of a species to produce the same from seed. This characteristic is retained even where the *sport*, (as gardeners term it) into numberless varieties is greatest. Thus, to return to cherries, the Kentish or common pie-cherry is one species, and the small black mazzard another, and although a great number of varieties of each of these species have been produced, yet there is always the likeness of the species retained. From the first we may have the large and rich Mayduke, and from the last the sweet and luscious Black-Hearts; but a glance will show us that the duke cherries retain the distinct dark foliage, and, in the fruit, something of the same flavor, shape and color of the original species; and the heart cherries the broad leaves and lofty growth of the mazzard. So too, the currant and gooseberry are different species of the same genus; but though the English gooseberry growers have raised thousands of new varieties of this fruit, and shown them as large as hen's eggs, and of every variety of form and color, yet their efforts with the gooseberry have not produced any thing resembling the common currant.

Why do not varieties produce the same from seed? Why if we plant the stone of a Green Gage plum, will it not always produce a Green Gage? This is often a puzzling question to the practical gardener, while his every day experience forces him to assent to the fact.

We are not sure that the vegetable physiologists will undertake to answer this query fully. But in the mean time we can throw some light on the subject.

It will be remembered that our garden varieties of fruits are not natural forms. They are the artificial productions of our culture. They have always a *tendency to improve*, but they have also another and a stronger *tendency to return to a natural, or wild state*. "There can be no doubt," says Dr. Lindley, "that if the arts of cultivation were abandoned for only a few years, all the annual varieties of plants in our gardens would disappear and be replaced by a few original wild forms." Between these two tendencies, therefore, the one derived from nature, and the other impressed by culture, it is easily seen how little likely is the progeny of varieties always to reappear in the same form.

Again, our American farmers, who raise a number of kinds of Indian corn, very well know that, if they wish to keep the sorts distinct, they must grow them in different fields. Without this precaution they find on planting the seeds produced on the yellow corn plants, that they have the next season a progeny, not of yellow corn alone, but composed of every color and size, yellow, white and black, large and small, upon the farm. Now many of the varieties of fruit trees have a similar power of intermixing with each other while in blossom, by the dust or pollen of their flowers, carried through the air, by the action of bees and other causes. It will readily occur to the reader, in considering this fact, what an influence our custom of planting the different varieties of plum or of cherry together in a garden or orchard, must have upon the constancy of habit in the seedlings of such fruits.

But there is still another reason for this habit, so perplexing to the novice, who, having tasted a luscious fruit, plants, watches and rears its seedling, to find it perhaps, wholly different in most respects. This is the influence of *grafting*. Among the great number of seedling fruits produced in the United States, there is found occasionally a variety, perhaps a plum or a peach, which will nearly always reproduce itself from seed. From some fortunate circumstances in its origin, unknown to us, this sort, in becoming improved, still retains strongly this habit of the natural or wild form, and its seeds produce the same. We can call to mind several examples of this; fine fruit trees whose seeds have established the reputation in their neighborhood of fidelity to the sort. But when a *graft* is taken from one of these trees, and placed upon another stock, this grafted tree is found to lose its singular power of producing the same by seed, and becomes like all other worked trees. The stock exercises some, as yet, unexplained power, in dissolving the strong natural habit of the variety, and it becomes like its fellows, subject to the laws of its artificial life.

When we desire to raise new varieties of fruit, the common practice is to collect the seeds of the finest table fruits—those sorts whose merits are every where acknowledged to be the highest. In proceeding thus we are all pretty well aware, that the chances are generally a hundred to one against our obtaining any new variety of great excellence. Before we offer any advice on rearing seedlings let us examine briefly the practice and views of two distinguished horticulturists abroad, who have paid more attention to this subject than any other persons whatever; Dr. Van Mons of Belgium, and Thos. Andrew Knight, Esq., the late President of the Horticultural Society of London.

The Van Mons Theory.

Dr. Van Mons, Professor at Louvain, devoted the greater part of his life to the amelioration of fruits. His nurseries contained in 1823, no less than two thousand seedlings of merit. His perseverance was indefatigable, and experimenting mainly on

Pears, he succeeded in raising an immense number of new varieties of high excellence The Beurré Diel, De Louvain, Frederic of Wurtemberg, &c , are a few of the many well known sorts which are the result of his unwearied labours.

The Van Mons theory may be briefly stated as follows :

All fine fruits are artificial products ; the aim of nature, in a wild state, being only a healthy, vigorous state of the tree, and *perfect seeds* for continuing the species It is the object of cul-ture, therefore, to subdue, or enfeeble this excess of vegetation ; to lessen the coarseness of the tree ; to diminish the size of the seeds ; and to refine the quality and increase the size of the flesh or pulp

There is always a tendency in our varieties of fruit trees to return by their seeds towards a wild state.

This tendency is most strongly shown in the seeds borne by *old* fruit-trees. And " the older the tree is of any cultivated variety of Pear," says Dr. Van Mons, " the nearer will the seedlings, raised from it, approach a wild state, without however ever being able to return to that state."

On the other hand, the seeds of a young fruit tree of a good sort, being itself in the state of amelioration, have the least ten-dency to retrograde, and are the most likely to produce improved sorts.

Again, there is a certain limit to perfection in fruits. When this point is reached, as in the finest varieties, the next genera-tion will more probably produce bad fruit, than if reared from seeds of an indifferent sort, in the course of amelioration. While, in other words, the seeds of the oldest varieties of good fruit mostly yield inferiour sorts, seeds taken from recent varie-ties of bad fruit, and *reproduced uninterruptedly for several gene-rations*, will certainly produce good fruit.

With these premises, Dr. Van Mons begins by gathering his seeds from a young seedling tree, without paying much regard to its quality, except that it must be in a *state of variation ;* that is to say, a garden variety, and not a wild sort. These he sows in a seedbed or nursery, where he leaves the seedlings until they attain sufficient size to enable him to judge of their character. He then selects those which appear the most pro-mising, plants them a few feet distant in the nursery, and awaits their fruit. Not discouraged at finding most of them of mediocre quality, though differing from the parent, he gathers the first seeds of the most promising and sows them again. The next generation comes more rapidly into bearing than the first, and shows a greater number of promising traits. Gathering imme-diately, and sowing the seeds of this generation, he produces a third, then a fourth, and even a fifth generation, uninterruptedly, from the original sort. Each generation he finds to come more quickly into bearing than the previous one, (the 5th sowing of pears fruiting at 3 years,) and to produce a greater number of valuable varieties ; until in the fifth generation the seedlings are nearly all of great excellence.

Dr. Van Mons found the pear to require the longest time to attain perfection, and he carried his process with this fruit through five generations. Apples he found needed but four races, and peaches, cherries, plums, and other stone fruits, were brought to perfection in three successive reproductions from the seed.

It will be remembered that it is a leading feature in this theory that, in order to improve the fruit, we must *subdue or enfeeble* the original coarse luxuriance of the tree. Keeping this in mind, Dr. Van Mons always gathers his fruit before fully ripe, and allows them to rot before planting the seeds, in order to refine or render less wild and harsh the next generation. In transplanting the young seedlings into quarters to bear, he cuts off the tap root, and he annually shortens the leading and side branches, besides planting them only a few feet apart. All this lessens the vigour of the trees, and produces an impression upon the nature of the seeds which will be produced by their first fruit ; and, in order to continue in full force the progressive variation, he allows his seedlings to bear on their own roots.*

Such is Dr. Van Mons' theory and method for obtaining new varieties of fruit. It has never obtained much favour in England, and from the length of time necessary to bring about its results, it is scarcely likely to come into very general use here. At the same time it is not to be denied that in his hands it has proved a very successful mode of obtaining new varieties.

It is also undoubtedly true that it is a mode closely founded on natural laws, and that the great bulk of our fine varieties have originated, nominally by chance, but really, by successive reproductions from the seed in our gardens.

It is not a little remarkable that the constant springing up of fine new sorts of fruit in the United States, which is every day growing more frequent, is given with much apparent force as a proof of the accuracy of the Van Mons theory. The first colonists here, who brought with them many seeds gathered from the best old varieties of fruits, were surprised to find their seedlings producing only very inferiour fruits. These seedlings had returned by their inherent tendency almost to a wild state. By rearing from them, however, seedlings of many repeated generations, we have arrived at a great number of the finest apples,

---

* " I have found this art to consist in regenerating in a direct line of descent, and as rapidly as possible an improving variety, taking care that there be no interval between the generations. To sow, to re-sow, to sow again, to sow perpetually, in short to do nothing but sow, is the practice to be pursued, and which cannot be departed from ; and in short this is the whole secret of the art I have employed."—Van Mons' *Arbres Fruitiers*, 1. p. 223.

pears, peaches and plums   According to Dr. Van Mons, had
this process been continued *uninterruptedly*, from one generation
to the next, a much shorter time would have been necessary for
the production of first rate varieties.

To show how the practice of chance sowing works in the
other hemisphere, it is stated by one of the most celebrated of
the old writers on fruits, Duhamel of France, that he had been
in the habit of planting seeds of the finest table pears for fifty
years without ever having produced a good variety. These
seeds were from trees of old varieties of fruit.

The American gardener will easily perceive, from what we
have stated, a great advantage placed in his hands at the present
time for the amelioration of fruits by this system. He will
see that, as most of our American varieties of fruit are the result of repeated sowings, more or less constantly repeated, he
has before him almost every day a part of the ameliorating process in progress ; to which Dr. Van Mons, beginning *de novo*,
was obliged to devote his whole life. Nearly all that it is necessary for him to do in attempting to raise a new variety of excellence by this simple mode, is to gather his seeds (before they
are fully ripe,) from a *seedling* sort of promising quality, though
not yet arrived at perfection. The seedling must be quite
young—must be on its own root (not grafted ;) and it must be a
healthy tree, in order to secure a healthy generation of seedlings. Our own experience leads us to believe that he will
scarcely have to go beyond one or two generations to obtain fine
fruit. These remarks apply to most of our table fruits commonly cultivated. On the other hand, our native grapes, the Isabella,
Catawba, &c., which are scarcely removed from the wild state,
must by this ameliorating process be carried through several
successive generations before we arrive at varieties equalling
the finest foreign grapes ; a result, which, judging from what
we see in progress, we have every reason speedily to hope for.

In order to be most successful in raising new varieties by successive reproduction, let us bear in mind that we must avoid—
1st, the seeds of old fruit trees ; 2d, those of grafted fruit trees ;
and 3d, that we have the best grounds for good results when we
gather our seeds from a young seedling tree, which is itself rather a *perfecting* than a *perfect* fruit.

It is not to be denied that, in the face of Dr. Van Mon's theory,
in this country, new varieties of rare excellence are sometimes
obtained at once by planting the seeds of old grafted varieties ;
thus the Lawrence's Favourite, and the Columbia plums, were
raised from seeds of the Green Gage, one of the oldest European
varieties.

Such are the means of originating new fruits by the Belgian
mode. Let us now examine another more direct, more interesting, and more scientific process—cross-breeding ; a mode almost

universally pursued now by skilful cultivators, in producing new and finer varieties of plants ; and which Mr. Knight, the most distinguished horticulturist of the age, so successfully prac- tised on fruit trees.

Cross-breeding.

In the blossoms of fruit-trees, and of most other plants, the seed is the offspring of the *stamens* and *pistil*, which may be considered the male and female parents, growing in the same flower. Cross-breeding is, then, nothing more than removing out of the blossom of a fruit tree the stamens, or male parents, and bringing those of another, and different variety of fruit, and dusting the pistil or female parent with them,—a process suffi- ciently simple, but which has the most marked effect on the seeds produced. It is only within about fifty years that cross-breeding has been practised ; but Lord Bacon, whose great mind seems to have had glimpses into every dark corner of human know- ledge, finely foreshadowed it. " The compounding or mixture of plants is not found out, which, if it were, is more at command than that of living creatures ; wherefore, it were one of the most notable discoveries touching plants to find it out, for so you may have great varieties of fruits and flowers yet unknown."

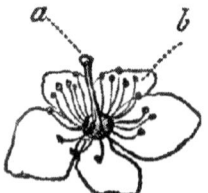

In figure 1, is shown the blossom of the Cherry. The central portion, *a*, connected directly with the young fruit, is the *pistil*. The numerous surrounding threads *b*, are the *stamens*. The summit of the stamen is called the *anther*, and secretes the powdery substance called *pollen*. The *pistil*, has at its base, the embryo fruit, and at its summit, the *stigma*.

Fig. 1.

The use of the stamens is to fertilize the young seed contained at the base of the pistil ; and if we fertilize the pistil of one variety of fruit by the pollen of another, we shall obtain a new variety partaking intermediately of the qualities of both parents. Thus, among fruits owing their origin directly to cross-breeding, Coe's Golden Drop Plum, was raised from the Green Gage, impreg- nated by the Magnum Bonum, or Egg plum ; and the Elton cherry, from the Bigarrieu, impregnated by the White Heart.* Mr. Knight was of opinion that the habits of the new variety would always be found to partake most strongly of the constitu- tion, and habits of the female parent. Subsequent experience does not fully confirm this, and it would appear that the parent

* The seedlings sometimes most resemble one parent sometimes the other ; but more frequently share the qualities of both. Mr. Coxe describes an Apple, a cross between a Newtown Pippin and a Russet, the fruit of which resembled ex- ternally at one end the Russet and at the other the Pippin, and the flavour at either end corresponded exactly with the character of the exterior.

whose character is most *permanent,* impresses its form most for
cibly on the offspring.

The process of obtaining cross-bred seeds of fruit trees is very
easily performed. It is only necessary when the tree blooms
which we intend to be the mother of the improved race, to select
a blossom or blossoms growing upon it not yet fully expanded.
With a pair of scissors, we cut out and remove all the anthers The
next day, or as soon as the blossom is quite expanded, we collect,
with a camel's hair brush, the pollen from a fully blown flower
of the variety we intend for the male parent, applying the pollen
and leaving it upon the stigma or point of the pistil. If your
trees are much exposed to those busy little meddlers. the bees,
it is well to cover the blossoms with a loose bag of thin gauze, or
they will perhaps get beforehand with you in your experiments
in cross-breeding. Watch the blossoms closely as they open,
and bear in mind that the two essential points in the operation are;
1st, to extract the anthers carefully, before they have matured
sufficiently to fertilize the pistil; and, 2d, to apply the pollen
when it is in perfection, (dry and powdery,) and while the stigma
is moist. A very little practice will enable the amateur to judge
of these points.

There are certain limits to the power of crossing plants.
What is strictly called a *cross-bred* plant or fruit is a sub-variety
raised between two varieties of the same species. There are,
however, certain species, *nearly allied,* which are capable of fertilizing each other. The offspring in this case is called a *hybrid,*
or mule, and does not always produce perfect seeds. "This
power of hybridising," says Dr Lindley, "appears to be much
more common in plants than in animals. It is, however, in general only between nearly allied species that this intercourse
can take place; those which are widely different in structure
and constitution not being capable of any artificial union Thus
the different species of Strawberry, of the gourd or melon family,
intermix with the greatest facility, there being a great accordance between them in general structure, and constitution. But
no one has ever succeeded in compelling the pear to fertilize the
apple, nor the gooseberry the currant. And as species that are
very dissimilar appear to have some natural impediment which
prevents their reciprocal fertilization, so does this obstacle, of
whatever nature it may be, present an insuperable bar to the intercourse of the different genera. All the stories that are current as to the intermixture of oranges and pomegranates, of
roses and black currants, and the like, may therefore be set
down to pure invention."

In practice, this power of improving varieties by crossing is
very largely resorted to by gardeners at the present day. Not
only in fruit trees, but in ornamental trees, shrubs, and plants,
and especially in florists' flowers, it has been carried to a great

extent. The great number of new and beautiful Roses, Azaleas Camellias, Fuchsias, Dahlias, and other flowering plants so splendid in colour, and perfect in form, owe their origin to careful cross-breeding.

In the amelioration of fruits it is by far the most certain, and satisfactory process yet discovered. Its results are more speedily obtained, and correspond much more closely to our aim, than those procured by successive reproduction.

In order to obtain a new variety of a certain character, it is only necessary to select two parents of well known habits, and which are both varieties of the same, or nearly allied species, and cross them for a new and intermediate variety. Thus, if we have a very early, but insipid, and worthless sort of pear, and desire to raise from it a variety both early and of fine flavour, we should fertilize some of its pistils, with the pollen of the best flavoured variety of a little later maturity. Among the seedlings produced, we should look for early pears of good quality, and at least for one or two varieties nearly, or quite as early as the female parent, and as delicious as the male. If we have a very small, but highly flavoured pear, and wish for a larger pear with a somewhat similar flavour, we must fertilize the first with the pollen of a large and handsome sort. If we desire to impart the quality of lateness to a very choice plum, we must look out for a late variety, whether of good or bad quality, as the mother, and cross it with our best flavoured sort. If we desire to impart hardiness to a tender fruit, we must undertake a cross between it and a much hardier sort; if we seek greater beauty of colour, or vigour of growth, we must insure these qualities by selecting one parent having such quality strongly marked.

As the seeds produced by cross fertilization are not found to produce precisely the same varieties, though they will nearly all partake of the mixed character of the parents, it follows that we shall be most successful in obtaining precisely all we hope for in the new race, in proportion to the number of our cross-bred seedlings; some of which may be inferiour, as well as some superiour to the parents. It is always well, therefore, to cross several flowers at once on the same plant, when a single blossom does not produce a number of seeds.

We should observe here, that those who devote their time to raising new varieties, must bear in mind that it is not always by the first fruits of a seedling that it should be judged. Some of the finest varieties require a considerable age before their best qualities develop themselves, as it is only when the tree has arrived at some degree of maturity that its secretions, either for flower, or fruit, are perfectly elaborated. The first fruit of the Black Eagle cherry, a fine cross-bred raised by Mr. Knight, was pronounced worthless when first exhibited to the London Horticultural Society; its quality now proves that the tree was not then of sufficient age to produce its fruit in perfection.

CHAPTER II.

PROPAGATION OF VARIETIES. GRAFTING. BUDDING. CUTTINGS LAYERS AND SUCKERS

AFTER having obtained a new and choice kind of fruit, which in our hands is perhaps only a single tree, and which, as we have already shown, seldom produces the same from seed, the next inquiry is how to continue this variety in existence, and how to increase and extend it, so that other gardens and countries may possess it as well as ourselves. This leads us to the subject of the propagation of fruit trees, or the continuation of varieties by grafting and budding

Grafting and budding are the means in most common use for propagating fruit trees. They are, in fact, nothing more than inserting upon one tree, the shoot or bud of another, in such a manner that the two may unite and form a new compound. No person having any interest in a garden should be unable to perform these operations, as they are capable of effecting transformations and improvements in all trees and shrubs, no less valuable, than they are beautiful and interesting.

Grafting is a very ancient invention, having been well known and practised by the Greeks and Romans. The latter, indeed, describe a great variety of modes, quite as ingenious as any of the fanciful variations now used by gardeners. The French who are most expert in grafting, practice occasionally more than fifty modes, and within a few years have succeeded perfectly in grafting annual plants, such as the tomato, the dahlia, and the like.

The uses of grafting, and budding, as applied to fruit trees, may be briefly stated as follows:

1. The rapid increase or propagation of valuable sorts of fruit not easily raised by seeds, or cuttings, as is the case with nearly all varieties.

2. To renew or alter the heads of trees, partially or fully grown, producing in two or three years, by heading-in and grafting, a new head, bearing the finest fruit, on a formerly worthless tree.

3. To render certain foreign and delicate sorts of fruit more hardy by grafting them on robust stocks of the same species native to the country, as the foreign grape on the native. And to produce fine fruit in climates or situations not naturally favourable by grafting on another species more hardy; as in a cool

climate and damp strong soil, by working the Peach on the Plum.

4. To render *dwarf* certain kinds of fruit, by grafting them on suitable stocks of slower growth, as in the case of the Pear on the Quince, the Apple on the paradise stock, &c.

5. By grafting several kinds on the same tree, to be able to have a succession of fruit, from early to late, in a small garden.

6. To hasten the bearing of seedling varieties of fruit, or of such as are a long time in producing fruit, by grafting them on the branches of full grown, or mature bearing trees. Thus a seedling pear, which would not produce fruit on its own root in a dozen years, will generally begin to bear the third or fourth year, if grafted on the extremity of the bearing branches of a mature tree.

The proper time for grafting fruit trees is in the spring, as soon as the sap is in motion, which commences earliest with the Cherry and Plum, and ends with the Pear and Apple. The precise time of course varies with the season and the climate, but is generally comprised from February to the middle of April. The grape vine, however, which suffers by bleeding, is not usu. ally grafted until it is in leaf. The most favourable weather for grafting is a mild atmosphere with occasional showers.

The scions are generally selected previously ; as it is found in nearly all kinds of grafting by scions, that success is more complete when the stock upon which they are placed is a little more advanced—the sap in a more active state than in the scion. To secure this, we usually cut the scions very early in the spring, during winter, or even in the autumn, burying their lower ends in the ground in a shaded place, or keeping them in fine soil in the cellar till wanted for use. In cutting scions, we choose straight thrifty shoots of the last year's growth, which may remain entire until we commence grafting, when they may be cut into scions of three or four buds each. In selecting scions from old trees it is always advisable to choose the most vigorous of the last year's shoots growing near the centre or top of the tree. Scions from sickly and unhealthy branches should be rejected, as they are apt to carry with them this feeble and sickly state. Scions taken from the lower bearing branches will produce fruit soonest, but they will not afford trees of so handsome a shape, or so vigorous a growth, as those taken from the thrifty upright shoots near the centre or top of the tree. Nurserymen generally take their scions from young grafted trees in the nursery-rows, these being usually in better condition than those taken from old trees not always in a healthy state.

The stock for grafting upon, is generally a tree which has been standing, at least for a year previously, on the spot where it is grafted, as success is much less certain on newly moved trees.

2

In the case, however, of very small trees or stocks, which are grafted below the surface of the ground, as is frequently the practice with the Apple in American nurseries, the stocks are grafted in the house in winter, or early spring, put away carefully in a damp cellar, and planted out in the spring; but this method is only successful when the root is small, and when the top of the stock is taken off, and the whole root is devoted to supplying the graft with nourishment.

The theory of grafting is based on the power of union between the young tissues, or organizable matter of growing wood. When the parts are placed nicely in contact, the ascending sap of the stock passes into and sustains life in the scion; the buds of the latter, excited by this supply of sap and the warmth of the season, begin to elaborate and send down woody matter, which, passing through the newly granulated substance of the parts in contact, unites the graft firmly with the stock. "If," says De Candolle, " the descending sap has only an incomplete analogy with the wants of the stock, the latter does not thrive, though the organic union may have taken place; and if the analogy between the albumum of stock and scion is wanting, the organic union does not operate; the scion cannot absorb the sap of the stock and the graft fails."

Grafting therefore is confined within certain limits. A scion from one tree will not, from the want of affinity, succeed on every other tree, but only upon those to which it is allied. We are, in short, only successful in budding or grafting where there is a close relationship and similarity of structure between the stock and the scion. This is the case with *varieties* of the same species, which take most freely, as the different sorts of Apple; next with the different *species* of a genus as the Apple and the Pear, which grow, but in which the union is less complete and permanent; and lastly with the *genera* of the same natural family, as the Cherry on the Plum—which die after a season or two. The ancients boasted of Vines and Apples grafted on Poplars and Elms; but repeated experiments, by the most skilful cultivators of modern times, have clearly proved that although we may, once in a thousand trials, succeed in effecting these ill assorted unions, yet the graft invariably dies after a few months growth.[*]

The range in grafting or budding, for fruit trees in ordinary

'The classical horticulturist will not fail to recall to mind Pliny's account of the tree in the garden of Lucullus, grafted in such a manner as to bear Olives, Almonds, Apples, Pears, Plums, Figs, and Grapes. There is little doubt, however, that this was some ingenious deception—as to this day the Italian gardeners pretend to sell Jasmines, Honeysuckles, &c., growing together and grafted on Oranges and Pomegranates. This is ingeniously managed, for a short lived effect, by introducing the stems of these smaller plants through a hole bored up the centre of the stock of the trees—their roots being in the same soil, and their stems, which after a little growth fill up these holes, appearing as if really grafted.

culture is as the following ; Apples, on apple or crab seedlings for orchards (standards,) or on Paradise apple stocks, for dwarfs ; Pears, on pear seedlings for common culture, or Quince stocks for dwarfs, and sometimes on the thorn for clayey soils ; Peaches, on their own seedlings for standards or for orchards ; on Almonds, for hot and dry climates ; on Plums in cold or moist soils, or to secure them against the worm ; Apricots, on Plum stocks, to render them hardy and productive, or on their own seedlings to render them long-lived.   Nectarines are usually worked on the Peach or Plum ; and Cherries on mazzard seedlings ; or sometimes on the Perfumed Cherry for dwarfs.

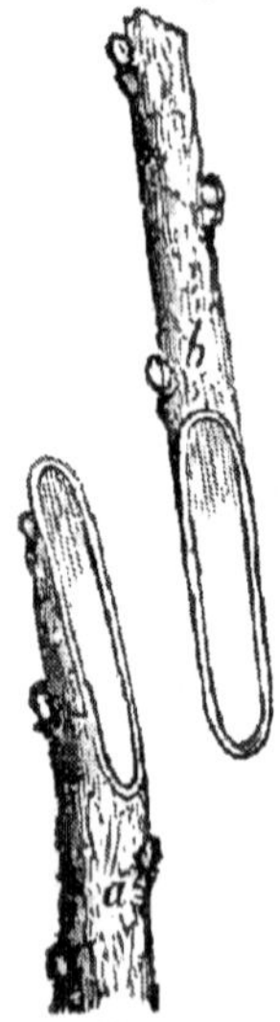

The manual operation of grafting is performed in a very easy and complete manner when the size of the stock, or branch to be grafted, corresponds precisely with that of the scion.   In this case, which is called *splice grafting*, it is only necessary with a smooth sloping cut, upwards on the stock *a*, and downwards on the scion *b*, Fig. 2, to make the two fit precisely, so that the inner bark of one corresponds exactly with that of the other, to bind them firmly together with a strand of matting, and to cover the wound entirely with grafting clay or wax, and the whole is finished.   In this, which is one of the neatest modes, the whole forms a complete union nearly at once ; leaving scarcely any wounded part to heal over.   But, as it is only rarely that the stock is of so small a size as to fit thus perfectly to the scion, the operation must be varied somewhat, and requires more skill.   The method in most common use to cover all difficulties, is called tongue grafting.

Fig. 2.
Splice grafting.

We may remark here that grafting the shoots of Peaches, Nectarines and Apricots, owing to their large pith is more difficult than that of other fruit trees.   A variation of splice-grafting, Fig. 3, has been invented to obviate this.   This consists in selecting the scion *a*, so as to leave at its lower end about a fourth of an inch of two years old wood which is much firmer.   The bottom of the slope on the stock is cut with a dove-tail notch *b*, into which the scion is fitted.

Tongue grafting, (or whip-grafting,) Fig. 4, resembles very nearly splice-grafting, except, instead of the simple splice, a tongue is made to hold the two together more firmly.   In order to understand this method let us explain it a little in detail.

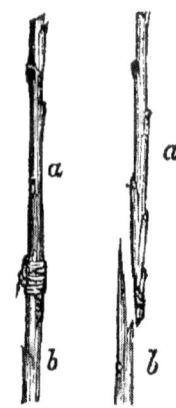

Fig. 3. *Splice grafting the peach.*

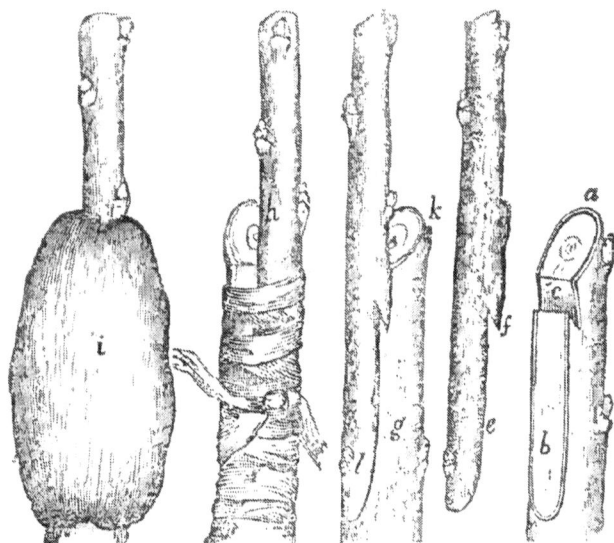

Fig. 3. *Tongue-grafting, progressive stages.*

Having chosen your stock of the proper size, cut it off at the
point where, *a*, it appears best to fix the graft. If the stock is
quite small, it may be within three or four inches of the ground.
Then, with a *very sharp knife*, make a smooth cut upwards *b*, about
two inches in length. Next make a slit, from the top of this
cut about one fourth of the way downwards, *c*, taking out a thin
tongue of wood. Cut the scion four or five inches long, or so as to
have three buds ; then shape the lower end with a single smooth
sloping cut, *e*, about the same length as that on the stock, and make
the tongue upward *f*, to fit in the downward slit of the stock.
Now apply the scion accurately to the stock making the *inner
bark of the scion fit exactly the inner bark of the stock, at least on
one side, g.* Without changing their position, tie them together
carefully with a piece of bass-matting, or tape *h*. And finally
cover the wound with well prepared grafting-clay or wax, *i*.
This ball of clay should more than cover the union, by an inch
above and below, and should be about an inch thick. If grafting-wax is used, the covering need not be above half an inch
thick.

In a month's time, if the graft has taken, it will be expanding
its leaves and sending out shoots. It will then be necessary to
rub or cut off all shoots between the ball and the ground, if it is
a small stock, or all those which would rob it of a principal share
of nourishment, if upon a large tree. If the scion or stock is
very weak, it is usual to leave one or two other buds for a time, to
assist in drawing up the sap. About the middle of July, after a
rainy day, you may remove the ball of clay, and, if the graft is

securely united, also the bandage; and the angle left at the top of the stock, *a*, should now be cut off smoothly, in order to allow the bark of the stock and the scion to heal neatly over the whole wound.

Though it is little attended to in common practice, the amateur will be glad to know that the success of a graft is always greatly insured by choosing the parts so that a bud is left near the top of the stock, *k*, and another near the bottom of the scion, *l*. These buds attract the rising sap to the portions where they are placed, form woody matter, and greatly facilitate the union of the parts near them; the upper part of the stock, and the lower part of the scion, being the portions soonest liable to perish from a want of nourishment.*

Cleft grafting is a very easy though rather clumsy mode, and is in more common use than any other in the United States. It is chiefly practised on large stocks, or trees the branches of which have been headed back, and are too large for tongue-grafting.

Fig. 4.

The head of the stock is first cut over horizontally with the saw, and smoothed with a knife. A cleft about two inches deep is then made in the stock with a hammer and splitting-knife. The scion is now prepared, by sloping its lower end in the form of a wedge about an inch and half long, leaving it a little thicker on the outer edge. Opening the cleft with the splitting knife, or a small chisel for that purpose, push the scion carefully down to its place, fitting its inner bark on one side to that of one side of the stock. When the stock is large, it is usual to insert two scions, Fig. 4. On withdrawing the chisel, the cleft closes firmly on the scions, when the graft is tied and clayed in the usual manner.

Apple stocks in many American nurseries, are grafted in great quantities in this mode—the stocks being previously taken out of the ground, headed down very near the root, cleft grafted with a single scion, sloping off with an oblique cut the side of the stock opposite that where the graft is placed, and then planted at once in the rows so as to allow only a couple of buds of the scion to appear above ground. It is not usual with many, either to tie, or clay the grafts in this case, as the wound is placed below the surface; but when this plan is adopted, the grafts must be set

---

* In grafting large quantities of young trees when stocks are scarce, it is not an unusual practice in some nurseries to tongue or whip-graft upon small *pieces of roots* of the proper sort of tree, planting the same in the earth as soon as grafted. Indeed, Dr. Van Mons considers this the most complete of all modes, with regard to the perfect condition of the grafted sort; 1st, because the smallest quantity of the stock is used; and 2d, because the lower part of the scion being thus placed in the ground, after a time it throws out fibres from that portion, and so at last is actually growing on its own roots.

and the trees planted at once, drawing the well pulverized soil with great care around the graft. Another way of grafting apple stocks, common in some western nurseries, consists in tongue-grafting on seedling stocks of very small size, cut back almost to the root. This is performed in winter, by the fire-side—the grafts carefully tied, and the roots placed in the cellar, in sand, till spring, when they are planted, the top of the graft just above ground.

Grafting the Vine is attended with great success in the cleft manner if treated as follows. Cut your scions during the winter or early spring, keeping them partially buried in a cool damp cellar till wanted. As soon as the leaves of the old vine or stock are fully expanded, and all danger of bleeding is past—say about the 10th of June, cut it off smoothly below the surface of the ground, and split the stock and insert one or two scions in the usual manner, binding the cleft well together if it does not close firmly. Draw the soil carefully over the whole, leaving two or three buds of the scion above the surface. If the root of the stock is a strong native grape, the graft will frequently grow ten or fifteen feet during the first season, and yield a fair crop the second year.

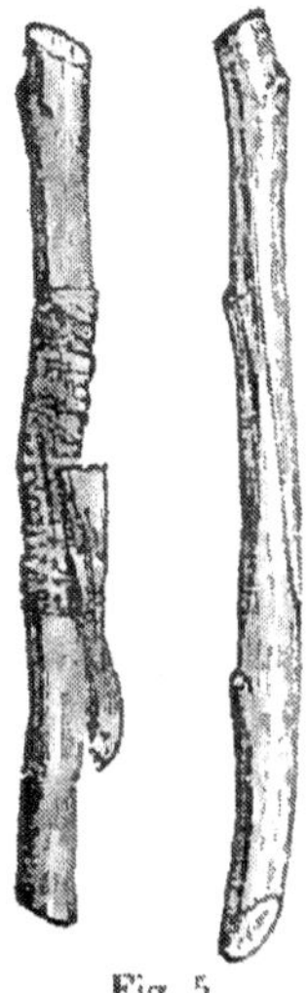

Fig. 5.
Saddle grafting.

The Vine may also be grafted with good success at the usual season if grafted below the ground, but above ground, it should not be attempted, on account of bleeding, until the leaves are nearly expanded.

Saddle grafting, Fig. 5, consists in cutting the top of the stock in the form of a wedge, splitting the scion and thinning away each half to a tongue shape, placing it astride the stock, and fitting the two, at least on one side, as in tongue-grafting. This mode offers the largest surface for the junction of the scion and stock, and the union is very perfect. Mr. Knight, who practised it chiefly upon Cherry trees, states that he has rarely ever seen a graft fail, even when the wood has been so succulent and immature as to preclude every hope of success by any other mode.

A variety of this mode, for stocks larger than the scions, is practised with much success in England after the usual season is past, and when the bark of the stock separates readily. "The scion, which must be smaller than the stock, is split up between two or three inches from its lower end, so as to have one side stronger than the other. This strong side is then properly prepared and introduced between the bark and the wood; while the thinner division is fitted to the opposite side of the stock." The graft, thus placed, receives a large supply of the sustaining fluid from the stock, and the union is rapid; while the wound on the stock is speedily covered by a new layer of bark from that part of the scion which stands astride it.

Grafting clay is prepared by mixing one third horse-dung free from straw, and two thirds clay, or clayey loam, with a little hair, like that used in plaster, to prevent its cracking. Beat and temper it for two or three days, until it is thoroughly incorporated. When used, it should be of such a consistency as to be easily put on and shaped with the hands.

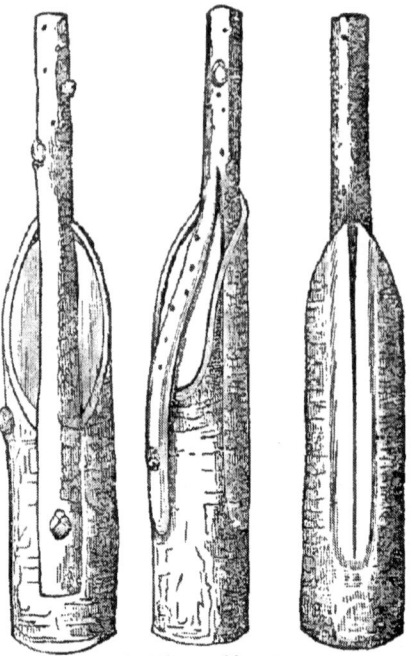

Fig. 6.   *Saddle grafting large stocks.*

Grafting wax of excellent quality we have made by melting together three parts of bees-wax, three parts of rosin and two parts tallow. While yet warm it may be worked with the aid of a little water, like shoemaker's wax, by the hand. The common grafting wax of the French gardeners is of two kinds. The first, is melted and laid on with a brush in a fluid state, and is made of half a pound of pitch, half a pound of bees-wax, and a pound of cow-dung boiled together. The second, which is spread while warm on strips of coarse cotton, or strong paper, and wrapped directly about the graft, answering at once to tie and to protect it, is composed of equal parts of bees-wax, turpentine, and resin. The grafting wax most commonly used here is made of tallow, bees-wax, and resin, in equal parts, or, as many prefer, with a little more tallow to render it pliable.

Grafting wax is a much neater and more perfect protection than grafting clay, but the trifling cost of the latter, where a great deal of work is to be done, accounts for its greater use by nurserymen, and gardeners generally.

Budding.

Budding (*inoculating*, of the old authors) differs from common grafting not the least in its nature or effects. Every bud is a distinct individual, capable of becoming a tree under favourable

circumstances. In grafting, we use a branch, composed of seve.
ral buds with a considerable quantity of bark and wood ; while
in budding, we employ but a single bud, with a very small quan
tity of the adjoining bark and wood.

The advantages of budding fruit trees, compared with grafting,
are so considerable, that in this country it is ten times as much
practised. These are, first, the great rapidity with which it is
performed ; a skilful budder, with a clever boy following him to
tie the buds, being able to work from a thousand to twelve hundred
young nursery stocks in a day. 2*d*. The more convenient season at which it is performed, in all countries where a short spring
crowds garden labours within a small space. 3d. Being able to
perform the operation without injuring the stock in case of failure,
which is always more or less the case in stocks headed down for
grafting. 4th. The opportunity which it affords, when performed
in good season, of repeating the trial on the same stock. To
these we may add that budding is universally preferred here
for all stone fruits, such as Peaches, Apricots, and the like, as
these require extra skill in grafting, but are budded with great
ease.

The proper season for budding fruit trees in this country is
from the first of July to the middle of September ; the different
trees coming into season as follows ; Plums, Cherries, Apricots on Plums, Apricots, Pears, Apples, Quinces, Nectarines
and Peaches. Trees of considerable size will require budding
earlier than young seedling stocks. But the operation is always, and only, performed *when the bark of
the stock parts or separates freely from the wood*,
and when the buds of the current year's growth are
somewhat plump, and the young wood is growing
firm. Young stocks in the nursery, if thrifty, are
usually planted out in the rows in the spring, and
budded the same summer or autumn.

Before commencing you should provide yourself
with a budding knife, Fig. 7, (about four and a half
inches long,) having a rounded blade at one end, and
an ivory handle terminating in a thin rounded edge
called the *haft, a,* at the other.

In choosing your buds, select thrifty shoots that
have nearly done growing, and prepare what is
called a *stick of buds*, Fig. 8, by cutting off a few of
the imperfect buds at the lower, and such as may be
yet too soft at the upper ends, leaving only smooth
well developed single buds ; double buds being fruit-
buds. Cut off the leaves, allowing about half an
inch of the *foot-stalks* to remain for conveniently
inserting the buds. Some strands of bass-matting

Fig. 7. *Bud-
ding knife.* about twelve or fourteen inches long, previously

soaked in water to render them soft and pliable, (or in the absence of these some soft woollen yarn,) must also be at hand for tying the buds.

Shield or T budding is the most approved mode in all countries. A new variety of this method now generally practised in this country we shall describe first as being the simplest and best mode for fruit trees.

American shield budding. Having your stick of buds ready, choose a smooth portion of the stock. When the latter is small, let it be near the ground, and, if equally convenient, select also the north side of the stock, as less exposed to the sun. Make an upright incision in the bark from an inch to an inch and a half long, and at the top of this make a cross cut, so that the whole shall form a T. From the stick of buds, your knife being very sharp, cut a thin, smooth slice of wood and bark containing a bud, Fig. 9, *a.* With the ivory haft of your budding knife, now raise the bark on each side of the incision just wide enough to admit easily the prepared bud. Taking hold of the footstalk of the leaf, insert the bud under the bark, pushing it gently down to the bottom of the incision. If the upper

Fig. 8. *A stick of buds.*

portion of the bud projects above the horizontal part of the T, cut it smoothly off now, so that it may completely fit, *b.* A bandage of the soft matting is now tied pretty firmly over the whole wound, Fig. 10, commencing at the bottom, and leaving the bud, and the footstalk of the leaf only exposed to the light and air.

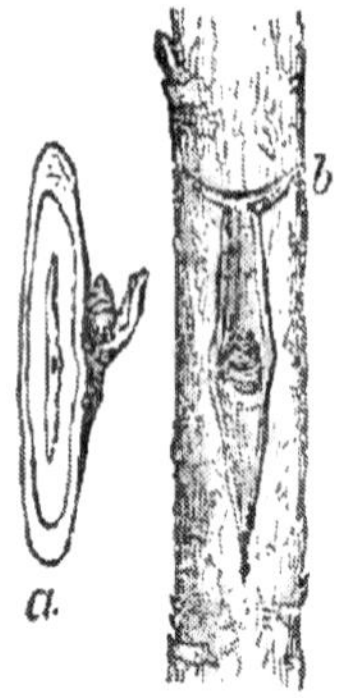

Common shield-budding, Fig. 11, practised in all gardens in Europe, differs from the foregoing only in one respect—the removal of the slice of wood contained in the bud. This is taken out with the point of the knife, holding the bud or shield by the leaf stalk, with one hand, inserting the knife under the wood at the lower extremity,

Fig. 9. *American shield budding.*

and then raising and drawing out the wood by bending it upwards and downwards, with a slight jerk, until it is loosened from the bark; always taking care that a small portion of the wood remains behind to fill up the hollow at the base or heart of the bud. The bud thus prepared is inserted precisely as before described.

The American variety of shield budding is found greatly peferable to the European mode, at least for this climate. Many sorts of fruit trees, especially Plums and Cherries, nearly mature

Fig. 10.

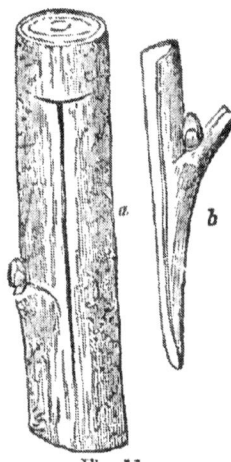

Fig. 11.

their growth, and require to be budded in the hottest part of our summer. In the old method, the bud having only a shield of bark with but a particle of wood in the heart of the bud, is much more liable to be destroyed by heat, or dryness, than when the slice of wood is left behind in the American way. Taking out this wood is always an operation requiring some dexterity and practice, as few buds grow when their eye, or heart wood is damaged. The American method, therefore, requires less skill, can be done earlier in the season with younger wood, is performed in much less time, and is uniformly more successful. It has been very fairly tested upon hundreds of thousand fruit trees, in our gardens, for the last twenty years, and, although practised English budders coming here, at first are greatly prejudiced against it, as being in direct opposition to one of the most essential features in the old mode, yet a fair trial has never failed to convince them of the superiority of the new.

After treatment. In two weeks after the operation you will be able to see whether the bud has taken, by its plumpness and freshness. If it has failed, you may, if the bark still parts readily, make another trial; a clever budder will not lose more than 6 or 8 per cent. If it has succeeded, after a fortnight more has elapsed, the bandage must be loosened, or if the stock has swelled much, it should be removed altogether. When budding has been performed very late, we have occasionally found it an advantage to leave the bandage on during the winter.

As soon as the buds commence swelling in the ensuing spring, head down the stock, with a sloping back cut, within two or three inches of the bud. The bud will then start vigorously, and all " robbers," as the shoots of the stock near to and below the bud are termed, must be taken off from time to time. To secure the upright growth of the bud, and to prevent its being broken by the winds, it is tied when a few inches long to that portion of the stock left for the purpose, Fig. 12, *a.* About midsummer, if the shoot is strong, this support may be removed, and the superfluous portion of the stock smoothly cut away in the dotted line, *b,* when it will be rapidly covered with young bark.

We have found a great advantage, when budding trees which do not take readily, in adopting Mr. Knight's excellent mode of tying with two distinct bandages; one covering that part below the bud,

Fig. 12.
Treatment of the growing bud.

and the other the portion above it. In this case the lower band-age is removed as soon as the bud has taken, and the upper left for two or three weeks longer. This, by arresting the upward sap, completes the union of the upper portion of bud, (which in plums frequently dies, while the lower part is united,) and se-cures success.

Reversed shield budding, which is nothing more than making the cross cut at the bottom, instead of the top of the upright in-cision in the bark, and inserting the bud from below, is a good deal practised in the south of Europe, but we have not found that it possesses any superiour merit for fruit trees.

An ingenious application of budding, worthy the attention of amateur cultivators, consists in using a blossom-bud instead of a wood-bud ; when, if the operation is carefully done, blossoms and fruit will be produced at once. This is most successful with the Pear, though we have often succeeded also with the Peach. Blossom-buds are readily distinguished, as soon as well formed, by their roundness, and in some trees by their growing in pairs ; while wood-buds grow singly, and are more or less pointed. We have seen a curious fruit grower borrow in this way, in September, from a neighbor ten miles distant, a single blossom-bud of a rare new pear, and produce from it a fair and beautiful fruit the next summer. The bud, in such cases, should be inserted on a favourable limb of a bearing tree.

Annular budding, Fig. 12, we have found a valuable mode for trees with hard wood, and thick bark, or those which, like the walnut, have buds so large as to render it difficult to bud them in the common way. A ring of bark, when the sap is flowing freely, is taken from the stock, *a*, and a ring of corresponding size containing a bud, *b*, from the scion. If the latter should be too large, a piece must be taken from it to make

Fig. 12.
Annular budding. it fit ; or should all the scions be too small, the ring upon the stock may extend only three fourths the way round, to suit the ring of the bud.

An application of this mode of great value occasionally occurs in this country. In snowy winters, fruit trees in orchards are sometimes girdled at the ground by field mice, and a growth of twenty years is thus destroyed in a single day, should the girdle extend quite round the tree. To save such a tree, it is only necessary, as soon as the sap rises vigorously in the spring, to apply a new ring of bark in the annular mode taken from a branch of proper size ; tying it firmly, covering it with grafting clay to exclude the air, and finally drawing up the earth so as to cover the wound completely. When the tree is too large to apply an entire ring, separate pieces, carefully fitted, will an-swer ; and it is well to reduce the top somewhat by pruning, that it may not make too large a demand on the root for a supply of food.

Budding may be done in the spring as well as at the latter end of summer, and is frequently so performed upon roses, and other ornamental shrubs, by French gardeners, but is only occasional use upon fruit trees

Influence of the stock and graft.

The well known fact that we may have a hundred different varieties of pear upon the same tree, each of which produces its fruit of the proper form, colour, and quality; and that we may have, at least for a time, several distinct, though nearly related species upon one stock, as the Peach, Apricot, Nectarine, and Plum, prove very conclusively the power of every grafted or budded branch, however small, in preserving its identity. To explain this, it is only necessary to recall to mind that the ascending sap, which is furnished by the root or stock, is nearly a simple fluid; that the leaves digest and modify this sap, forming a proper juice, which re-descends in the inner bark, and that thus every bud and leaf upon a branch maintains its individuality by preparing its own proper nourishment, or organizing matter, out of that general aliment, the sap. Indeed, according to De Candolle,* each separate cellule of the inner bark has this power of preparing its food according to its nature; in proof of which, a striking experiment has been tried by grafting rings of bark, of different allied species, one above another on the same tree without allowing any buds to grow upon them. On cutting down and examining this tree, it was found that under each ring of bark was deposited the proper wood of its species, thus clearly proving the power of the bark in preserving its identity, even without leaves.

On the other hand, though the stock increases in size by the woody matter received in the descending sap from the graft, yet as this descends through the inner bark of the stock, it is elaborated by, and receives its character from the latter; so that, after a tree has been grafted fifty years, a shoot which springs out from its trunk below the place of union, will always be found to bear the original wild fruit, and not to have been in the least affected by the graft.

But, whilst grafting never effects any alteration in the identity of the variety or species of fruit, still it is not to be denied that the stock does exert certain influences over the habits of the graft. The most important of these are dwarfing, inducing fruitfulness, and adapting the graft to the soil or climate.

Thus every one knows that the slower habit of growth in the

* *Physiologie Végétable.*

Quince stock, is shared by the Pear grafted upon it, which becomes a dwarf; as does also the Apple when worked on the
Paradise stock, and, in some degree, the Peach on the Plum.
The want of entire similarity of structure between the stock and
graft, confines the growth of the latter, and changes it, in the
case of the Pear, from a lofty tree to a shrub of eight or ten feet
in height. The effect of this difference of structure is very apparent, when the Peach is grafted on the Plum, in the greater
size of the trunk above, as compared with that below the graft;
a fact which seems to arise from the obstruction which the descending sap of the graft finds in its course through the bark of
the stock.

To account for the earlier and greater fruitfulness caused by
grafting on a stock of slower growth, Mr. Knight, in one of his
able papers, offers the following excellent remarks.

"The disposition in young trees to produce and nourish blossom buds and fruit, is increased by this apparent obstruction of
the descending sap; and the fruit, I think, ripens somewhat earlier than upon other young trees of the same age which grow
upon stocks of their own species. But the growth and vigor of
the tree, and its power to nourish a succession of heavy crops,
are diminished, apparently, by the stagnation in the branches
and stock of a portion of that sap which, in a tree growing on
its own stem, or upon a stock of its own species, would descend
to nourish and promote the extension of its own roots. The
practice, therefore, of grafting the Pear on the Quince, and the
Peach on the Plum, when extensive growth and durability are
wanted is wrong; but it is eligible wherever it is wished to
diminish the vigour and growth of the tree, and its durability is
not so important."

In adapting the graft to the soil the stock has a marked influence. Thus in dry chalky soils where the Peach on its own
roots will scarcely grow, it is found to thrive admirably budded on the Almond. We have already mentioned that in clay
soils too heavy and moist for the Peach, it succeeds very well
if worked on the Plum. M. Floss, a Prussian gardener, succeeded in growing fine pears in very sandy soils, where it was
nearly impossible to raise them before, by grafting them on the
Mountain Ash, a nearly related tree, which thrives on the dryest
and lightest soil.

A variety of fruit which is found rather tender for a certain
climate, or a particular neighborhood, is frequently acclima-
tised by grafting it on a native stock of very hardy habits. Thus
near the sea-coast where the finer plums thrive badly, we have
seen them greatly improved by being worked on the beech-
plum, a native stock adapted to the spot; and the foreign grape
is more luxuriant when grafted on our native stocks.

A slight effect is sometimes produced by the stock on the

3

quality of the fruit. A few sorts of pear are superiour in flavour, but many are also inferiour, when grafted on the Quince,
while they are more gritty on the thorn. The Green Gage, a
Plum of great delicacy of flavour, varies considerably upon different stocks; and Apples raised on the crab, and Pears on
the Mountain Ash, are said to keep longer than when grown on
their own roots.

In addition to the foregoing, a diseased stock should always
be avoided, as it will communicate disease slowly to the graft,
unless the latter is a variety of sufficient vigour to renew the
health of the stock, which is but seldom the case

The cultivator will gather from these remarks that, in a favourable climate and soil, if we desire the greatest growth, duration, and development in any fruit, (and this applies to orchards generally,) we should choose a stock of a closely similar
nature to the graft—an apple seedling for an apple; a pear
seedling for a pear. If we desire dwarf trees, that come into
bearing very young, and take little space in a garden, we employ for a stock an allied species of slower growth. If our soil
or climate is unfavourable, we use a stock, which is adapted
to the soil, or which will, by its hardier roots, endure the cold.

The influence of the graft on the stock seems scarcely to extend beyond the power of communicating disease. A graft taken
from a tree enfeebled by disease, will recover with difficulty,
even if grafted on healthy stocks for a dozen times in repeated
succession. And when the disease is an inherent or hereditary
one, it will certainly communicate it to the stock. We have
seen the *yellows*, from a diseased peach tree, propagated through
hundreds of individuals by budding, and the stock and graft
both perish together from its effects. Hence the importance, to
nurserymen especially of securing healthy grafts, and working
only upon healthy stocks.

Propagation by cuttings.

Propagating by cuttings, as applied to fruit trees, consists in
causing a shoot of the previous seasons' wood to grow, by detach-
ing it from the parent tree at a suitable season, and planting it
in the ground under favourable circumstances.

In this case, instead of uniting itself by woody matter to another
tree, as does the scion in grafting, the descending woody matter
becomes roots at the lower end, and the cutting of which, is then a
new and entire plant. Every bud being a distinct individual, capable of forming a new plant, has indeed theoretically the power, if
separated from the parent stem, of throwing out roots and main-
taining a separate existence; and some plants as the grape vine
are frequently propagated by single buds planted in the soil
But in practice, it is found necessary, with almost all trees an.

plants, to retain a considerable portion of the *stem* with the bud, to supply it with food until it has formed roots to draw nourishment from the soil.

All fruit trees may be propagated by cuttings with proper care and attention, but only a few grow with sufficient facility in this way to render their propagation by cuttings a common mode. These are the Gooseberry, the Currant, the Vine, the Quince, the Fig, and the Mulberry.

Cuttings of the Currant, Gooseberry, and the hardy sorts of Vine, will root readily, in a soil not too dry, in the open garden. Currants and Gooseberries are generally taken off in the fall or winter, prepared for planting, and two thirds of their lower ends buried in the ground till the commencement of spring, when they are planted out, either where they are to remain, or in nursery rows. If planted in autumn, they are liable to be thrown out by winter frosts. They will succeed nearly as well if taken off in the spring, but, owing to the period at which they commence growing, this must be attended to *very early*, if deferred till that season.

In order to raise plants of the Gooseberry and Currant, with straight, clean stems, which shall not throw up suckers, it is only necessary, before planting the cutting, to cut out every eye or bud to be placed below the surface of the ground, Fig. 14. The cutting should be about a foot long, eight inches of which may be inserted in the ground. To insure greater success in raising the finer sorts of gooseberry, or other shrubs, it is customary to plant the cuttings on the shaded side of a wall or fence, in deep rich loam, rather damp than dry. Cuttings of the vine are generally prepared when trimming the old plants in autumn, or winter; they may then be buried with their lower ends in the ground, or kept in earth in the cellar till spring.

Fig. 14. *A gooseberry cutting, prepared and planted.*

Scarce sorts of foreign grapes, which it is desirable to multiply extensively, are frequently propagated by joints; that is, by buds having about two inches of wood attached to each—every bud in this way forming a plant. When this mode is adopted, it is usual to plant the joints about half an inch deep, in light soil, in a common hot bed prepared for the purpose, or each joint is planted in a pot by itself. In the first way a great number of plants may be grown in a small space. Success is more certain in propagating the vine by joints, where the joint is halved before planting, Fig. 15.

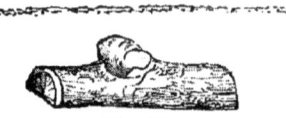

Fig. 15.
A vine joint, prepared and planted.

The large English black mulberry is propagated by cuttings

as follows : about the last of October, take cuttings from the
thrifty shoots of a bearing tree, cut out all the buds except two
or three at the top, and pare off the bottom of the cutting just
below a bud.   Lay-in the cuttings in a sheltered border, bury
ing them so that only the two buds at the top are exposed, ar
covering them with some loose straw or litter.   In the spring,
make a small hot-bed with very sandy soil in which to plant the
cuttings on taking them out of the ground, or place each one in
a small pot in any hot-bed ready at hand, and in a few weeks
they will be found to have made roots freely.

As a general rule, cuttings succeed best when they are taken
off just between the young and the previous year's wood ; or,
in the case of young side shoots, when they are cut off close to
the branch preserving the *collar* of the shoot.   The lower end
should be cut smoothly across just below a bud, the soil should
in all cases be pressed firmly about the lower end of the cutting,
and it should always be planted before the buds commence
swelling, that the wound may in some measure heal before
growth and the absorption of fluid commences.

Propagation by Layers and Suckers.

A layer may be considered as a cutting not entirely separated
from the plant.

Layering is a mode of propagation resorted to in increasing
some fruit tree stocks, as the Paradise stock, the Muscle Plum,
and some kinds which do not grow so well from the seed.
Certain varieties of native grape, as the Bland's Virginia, which
do not root readily by cuttings are also raised in this way, and
it may be applied to any sort of fruit tree which it is desirable
to continue on its own root without grafting.

Fruit trees are generally layered in the spring, and the layers
may be taken off well rooted plants in the autumn.   But they
may also be layered with success early in uly.

In making layers the ground around the mother plant should
be made light and mellow by digging.   Being provided with
some hooked pegs to fast-
en down the layers, bend
down a branch so that
the end may recline upon
the ground.   Open a little
trench three or four inches
deep to receive the young
wood   to   be   layered ;
make a cut or tongue, Fig.
3 *a*, half way through the
under side of the shoot,
pegging down the branch
with the hooked peg *b*, to

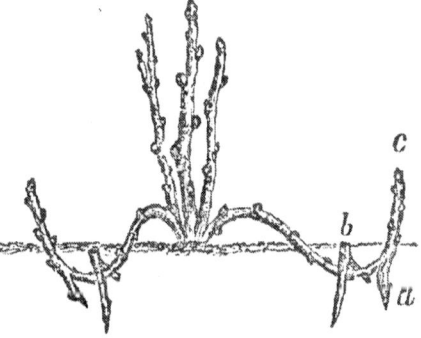

Fig. 16.   *Layering.*

keep it in its place ; press the earth slightly round the tongue, and, in filling in the soil, raise nearly upright the end of the layer *c*, which remains above the surface of the ground.

The descending sap, filled with organizable matter, is arrested by this tongue, accumulates there, and the emission of roots speedily takes place. Ringing, wounding, or twisting the limb, answers the same purpose less perfectly, and indeed many trees root readily from the mere position of the branches as layers, and the moisture of the soil.

A tree or plant which is kept for raising layers is called a *stool*, and is headed down, both to facilitate the rooting of the layers, and to afford an abundance of shoots near the earth. Shoots of some of the fruit tree stocks in the English nurseries are pegged down to the surface before growth commences in the spring, covered about an inch deep with soil, and at the end of autumn afford hundreds of plants ; almost every bud making a separate root.

Suckers are shoots sent up from the root, or from portions of the stem below the surface of the soil, which are easily separated from the parent plant.

Suckers of fruit trees are frequently used as stocks for budding or grafting upon, but they are greatly inferiour to seedlings for this purpose, as they are always more liable to produce suckers, and they have not the thrifty vigorous habit, or the same power of forming as good roots as seedlings. Beside this, should the tree from which they are taken be diseased, they will be likely to carry the malady with them.

Propagating by suckers, is an easy and desirable way when we wish to continue a seedling fruit of value on its own root, and some of our common fruits appear to be more healthy and permanent when growing in that way. It is also the only mode in use for increasing the Raspberry ; as is also that of runners, which is a kind of sucker above ground, for the Strawberry.

CHAPTER III.

PRUNING.

1. *Pruning to promote growth or modify the form of fruit trees.*

In this country almost all fruit trees are grown as *standards*. In this way they develop their natural forms, attain the largest size, and produce the greatest quantity of fruit, with the least possible care. Our bright and powerful sun, reaching every part of the tree, renders the minute systems of pruning and training, which occupy so large a portion of the English works on this subject, of little or no moment to the cultivator here. Pruning is, therefore, commonly resorted to only for the purpose of increasing the vigour of feeble trees, or to regulate and improve the form of healthy and luxuriant trees.

Pruning has the power of increasing the vigour of a tree in two ways. If we assume that a certain amount of nourishment is supplied by the roots to all the branches and buds of a tree, by cutting off one half of the branches, at the proper season, we direct the whole supply of nourishment to the remaining portion, which will, consequently, grow with nearly double their former luxuriance. Again, when a tree becomes stunted or enfeebled in its growth, the thinness of its inner bark, with its consequent small sap-vessels, (which it must be remembered are the principal channel for the passage of the ascending supply of food) renders the upward and downward circulation tardy, and the growth is small. By heading back or pruning judiciously, all the force of the nourishing fluid is thrown into a smaller number of buds, which make new and luxuriant shoots, larger sap-vessels, and which afford a ready passage to the fluids, and the tree with these renewed energies will continue in vigour for a long time.

This treatment is especially valuable in the case of small trees of feeble or stunted growth, which are frequently cut back to a single bud, and a new shoot or shoots, full of vigour, gives a healthy habit to the tree. In the nurseries, this practice of heading down unthrifty trees is frequently pursued, and small orchard trees which have become enfeebled may be treated in the same manner; cutting back the head as far as the place where it is wished that new shoots should spring out. Older trees should be headed back more sparingly, unless they are greatly enfeebled; and their roots should at the same time be assisted by manure.

A judicious pruning to modify the form of our standard trees is nearly all that is required in ordinary practice. *Every fruit tree, grown in the open orchard or garden as a common standard should be allowed to take its natural form, the whole efforts of the pruner going no further than to take out all weak and crowded branches;* those which are filling uselessly the interior of the tree, where their leaves cannot be duly exposed to the light and sun, or those which interfere with the growth of others. All pruning of large branches in healthy trees should be avoided by examining them every season and taking out superfluous shoots while small. Mr. Coxe, the best American author on fruit trees, remarks very truly " when orchard trees are much pruned, they are apt to throw out numerous (superfluous) suckers from the boughs in the following summer; these should be rubbed off when they first appear, or they may easily be broken off while young and brittle—cutting is apt to increase their number."

Where pruning is not required to renovate the vigour of an enfeebled tree, or to regulate its shape—in other words, in the case of a healthy tree which we wish to retain in a state of the greatest luxuriance, health, and vigour, it may be considered worse than useless. Bearing in mind that growth is always corresponding to the action of the leaves and branches, if these are in due proportion, and in perfect health, the knife will always be found rather detrimental to luxuriance and constitutional vigour than beneficial.*

The best season for pruning to promote growth, theoretically, is in autumn soon after the fall of the leaf. Next to this, winter pruning, performed in mild weather, is best, and in orchards this is the season usually most convenient. In all parts of the country where the winters are not very severe, (and always in the southern and western states,) the roots are collecting a certain stock of nourishment during the whole autumn and winter. When a tree is pruned in autumn or winter this whole supply goes to the remaining branches, while in the case of spring pruning it is partly lost. North of the 43° of latitude, however, the winters are so severe that winter pruning should be deferred till the last of February.

We should especially avoid pruning at that period in spring when the buds are swelling, and the sap is in full flow, as the loss of sap by bleeding is very injurious to most trees, and, in some, brings on a serious and incurable canker in the limbs.

There are advantages and disadvantages attending all seasons of pruning, but our own experience has led us to believe that, practically, *a fortnight before midsummer is by far the best season, on the whole, for pruning in the northern and middle states.* Wounds made at this season heal over freely and rapidly; it is the most favourable time to judge of the shape and balance of the head, and to see at a glance which branches require removal; and all the stock of organizable matter in the tree is directed to the branches that remain.

In pruning large limbs, some composition should always be at hand to cover the wound. This will not only prevent its cracking by the cold in winter pruning, but will keep out the air, and maintain the exposed wood in a sound state, until it is covered

---

* Ignorant cultivators frequently weaken the energies of young trees, and cause them to grow up with lean and slender stems, by injudiciously trimming off the young side shoots and leaves, in the growing season. By taking off these shoots, the stem is deprived of all the leaves which would attract and elaborate the sap, thus preparing nourishment for the growth of the stem; and the trunk of the tree does not increase in size half so fast as when the side branches are allowed to remain for a time, pruning them away gradually. It is better, in the case of these young trees, to *stop* the side branches when of moderate length by pinching out the terminal bud.

with a new layer of bark. Many compositions have been in fashion, abroad, for this purpose, which, under our summer sun and wintry frosts, are nearly worthless, as they generally crack and fall off in a single year. The following is a cheap and admirable application, which we recommend to all cultivators of fruit trees.

Composition for wounds made in pruning. Take a quart of alcohol and dissolve in it as much gum shellac as will make a liquid of the consistence of paint. Apply this to the wound with a common painter's brush, always paring the wound smoothly first with the knife. The liquid becomes perfectly hard, adheres closely, excludes the air perfectly, and is affected by no changes of weather; while at the same time its thinness offers no resistance to the lip of new bark that gradually closes over the wound If the composition is kept in a well corked bottle, sufficiently wide mouthed to admit the brush, it will always be ready for use and suited to the want of the moment.

2. *Pruning to induce fruitfulness.*

When a young fruit tree is too luxuriant, employing all its energies in making vigorous shoots, but forming few or no blossom buds, and producing no fruit, we have it in our power by different modes of pruning to lessen this over-luxuriance, and force it to expend its energies in fruit-bearing. The most direct and successful mode of doing this is by pruning the roots, a proceeding recently brought into very successful practice by European gardeners.

Root pruning has the effect of at once cutting off a considerable supply of the nourishment formerly afforded by the roots of a tree. The leaves, losing part of their usual food, are neither able to grow as rapidly as before, nor to use all the nutritious matter already in the branches; the branches therefore become more stunted in their growth, the organizable matter accumulates, and fruit buds are directly formed. The energies of the tree are no longer entirely carried off in growth, and the returning sap is employed in producing fruit buds for the next year.

Root pruning should be performed in autumn or winter, and it usually consists in laying bare the roots and cutting off smoothly at a distance of a few feet from the trunk, (in proportion to the size of the tree) the principal roots. Mr. Rivers, an English nurseryman of celebrity, who has practised this mode with great success, digs a trench early in November, eighteen inches deep, round his trees to be root pruned, cutting off the roots with a sharp spade. By following this practice every year, he not only throws his trees into early bearing, but forces Apples, Pears, and the like, grafted on their own roots, to become prolific dwarfs, growing only six feet apart, trained in a conical form, full of fruit branches, and producing abundantly, These dwarf trees, thus annually root pruned, he supplies abundantly with manure at the ends of the roots, thus keeping up their health and vigour. The plan is an admirable one for small gardens, or for amateurs who wish to grow a great many sorts in a small surface. Mr. Rivers, in a pamphlet on this subject enumerates the following among the advantages of *systematic root pruning.*

"1. The facility of thinning, (owing to the small size of the trees,) and, in some varieties, of setting the blossoms of shy-bearing sorts, and of thinning and gathering the fruit.

"2. It will make the gardener independent of the natural soil of his garden, as a few barrowsful of rich mould will support a tree for a lengthened period, thus placing bad soils nearly on a level with those the most favourable.

"3. The capability of removing trees of fifteen or twenty years growth, with as much facility as furniture. To tenants this will indeed be a boon, for perhaps one of the greatest annoyances a tenant is subject to, is that of being obliged to leave behind him trees that he has nurtured with the utmost care."

In conclusion, Mr. Rivers recommends *caution ;* "enough of vigour must be left in the tree to support its crop of fruit, and one, two, or three seasons cessation from root pruning, will often be found necessary."

Root pruning in this country will, we think, be most valuable in its application to common standard trees, which are thrifty, but bear little or no fruit. They will generally be found to require but a single pruning to bring them into a permanently fruitful condition ; and some sorts of Pears and Plums, which do not usually give a fair crop till they are twelve or fourteen years old, may be brought into fruit by this means as soon as they are of proper size. Several nearly full grown peach, pear, and plum trees, on a very rich soil on the Hudson, which were over-luxuriant but bore no fruit, were root pruned by our advice two years ago, and yielded most excellent and abundant crops last season.

In the case of Apple orchards, where the permanent value depends on the size, *longevity,* and continued productiveness of the trees, it is better to wait patiently and not resort to pruning to bring them into bearing ; as it cannot be denied that all excessive pruning shortens somewhat the life of a tree. Mr. Coxe, indeed, recommended that the first fruit should never be allowed to ripen on a young apple orchard, as it lessens very materially the vigour of the trees.

Shortening-in the shoots of Peaches, Nectarines, and Apricots, as we shall hereafter point out, has a strong tendency to increase the fruitfulness of these trees, since by reducing the young wood, the sap accumulates in the remainder of the branch, and many bearing shoots are produced instead of one. And the English practice of *spurring-in*, which consists in annually shortening the lateral shoots of trained Pears, Apples, and the like. in order to make them throw out short fruit branches, or spurs, is founded on the same principle.

Bending down the limbs is an easy and simple means of throwing such branches directly into fruit By this means the circulation is retarded, rapid growth ceases, organizable matter accumulates, and fruit buds, as before stated, surely follow. The limbs are bent, while flexible, in June or July, and tied down below a horizontal line until they retain of themselves their new position. When this can be easily applied, it is a never failing mode of rendering such branches fruitful. It is stated in Loudon's Gardener's Magazine that " a very large crop of Pears was obtained by the Rev. Mr Fisher, in Buckinghamshire, from trees which had not borne at all, by twisting and breaking down the young shoots, late in the autumn, when the wood had become tough ; and the pendent branches afterwards continued perfectly healthy."

Disbarking and *Ringing* are two modes that have been recommended by some authors, but of which, except as curious experiments, we entirely disapprove Disbarking, that is, removing the outer bark of the trunk in February, May, or March, is and may be practised with good results on trees in very sheltered positions, and under glass, but must always be a somewhat dangerous practice in open orchards, and in a variable climate like ours , while its good effects may in a great measure be attained by keeping the bark in a healthy state by a wash of soft soap. *Ringing*, which is nothing more than stopping the descending sap in a branch and forcing it to organize blossom buds, by taking off a ring of bark, say a fourth or half an inch, near midsummer, is a mode always more or less injurious to the health of the branch, and if carried to any extent, finally destroys the tree. It is gradually falling into disuse, since root pruning, and other and better modes, are becoming known. A ligature or bandage tightly applied to the limb, will have temporarily the same effect as ringing, without so much injury to the branch.

Inducing fruitfulness by other means.

The influence of certain soils on the productiveness of fruit trees is a subject of every day observation, but the particular ingredients of the soil, which insure this abundant bearing, is not so well known. Limestone soils are almost invariably productive of all sorts of fruit ; and certain strong loams in this coun try seem to be equally well adapted to this end.

In a curious work called the "Rejuvenescence of Plants," etc. by Dr. Schultz, of Berlin, the author, who has devoted consider able time to the subject, states that common salt and chloride of lime contribute greatly to the flowering of most plants, to which, however, they can only be applied with safety, in small quantities. " Salts of lime," he continues, " appear to produce so nearly the same effect as those of potash and soda, that it is only necessary to place lime within their reach, if there is no deficiency of manure in the shape of general food. Lime will in the main promote, in an astonishing degree, the fruiting and flowering of most plants, because calcareous salts promote evaporation and the concentration of the sap."

Although we cannot coincide with many of Dr. Schultz's views as expressed in this work, yet, the remarks just quoted agree so entirely with facts that have come under our own observation, that we gladly place them before the cultivator of fruit trees. One of the most productive fruit gardens in our knowledge is on a limestone soil, and another more than usually prolific, in a neighbourhood not very fruitful, is every year treated with a top dressing of coarse salt, at the rate of two bushels to the acre. These facts are surely worth the attention of growers, and should be the subject of more extended and careful experiments.

Rendering trees more fruitful by *dwarfing*, and by adapting them to soils naturally unfruitful by growing them upon other and better stocks, we have already placed before the reader under the head of *Grafting*.

CHAPTER IV.

TRAINING.

TRAINING fruit trees is, thanks to our favourable climate, a proceeding entirely unnecessary in the greater part of the United States. Our fine dry summers, with the great abundance of strong light and sun, are sufficient to ripen fully the fruits of temperate climates, so that the whole art of training, at once the trial and triumph of skill with English fruit gardeners, is quite dispensed with : and in the place of long lines of brick wall and espalier rails, surrounding and dividing the fruit garden, all covered with carefully trained trees, we are proud to show the open orchard, and the borders in the fruit garden filled with thrifty and productive standards. Nothing surprises a British gardener more, knowing the cold of our winter, than the first sight of peaches, and other fine fruits, arriving at full perfection in the middle states, with so little care ; and he sees at once that three fourths of the great expense of a fruit garden here is rendered entirely needless.

Training fruit trees, in this country, is therefore confined to the colder districts north of the 43° of latitude, and to the gardens of amateurs. There can, however, scarcely be a more beautiful display of the art of the horticulturist, than a fine row of trained trees, their branches arranged with the utmost symmetry and regularity, and covered, in the fruit season, with large and richly coloured fruit.

North of the 43° latitude, (or north of the Mohawk,) the peach does not ripen well, and this, as well as some other rather tender trees, will, in such situations, generally yield abundant crops when trained on a common upright trellis, or espalier rail, seven or eight feet high.* Still farther north, as in Maine, or Canada a wall must be resorted to . but our own observation leads us to believe that, generally, the espalier rail will be found not only cheaper, and more easily managed in training, but really preferable to a wall, as full exposure to light is sufficient without much additional heat With regard to walls themselves, in the middle portions of the Union, a southern aspect is almost always the worst, being too hot in midsummer ; a wall running north and south, and affording east and west aspects, is much the best. The western aspect is indeed preferable for all tender fruits, as the blossoms are not there liable to injury from early frosts A north wall is useful for producing a later crop.

The objects of training are, by a more complete exposure of the leaves and branches to the light and sun, to ripen fruits in a naturally unfavourable climate ; to render them more fruitful,—lessening vigour and excessive growth by the lateral or horizontal arrangement of the branches ; and lastly economy of space, as trees when trained on a flat surface occupy much less space in the fruit garden than standards, and leave the borders more open for cropping with vegetables.

Training conical standards. A very easy and simple mode of training fruit trees, which has lately come into great favour with amateurs, is the conical standard, or *Quenouille*, (pronounced *kenool*) of the French. It is applied chiefly to pears, which, when treated in this way, may be planted about eight feet apart, and thus a great variety of sorts may be grown in a small garden. The best example of this kind of training in this country, at present, is in the garden of Mr. Johnson of Lynn, Mass. A great number of the specimen trees in the London Horticultural Society's garden are trained in this manner ; and Loudon remarks, that in 1840 the Royal Kitchen garden of Versailles

* Cedar or locust posts, set four or eight feet apart, with horizontal bars let in, and crossed by light perpendicular strips of pine from six to twelve inches apart, will form an excellent and durable trellis for espaliers See Fig. 21. Indeed many gardeners here prefer having a light trellis a few inches from the wall, upon which to train, instead of nailing directly on the wall.

contained two hundred trees trained in the conical manner, with the current year's shoots tied down *en quenouille*. "They had attained the height of from six to twelve feet before the branches were bent down ; but the effect of this was to cover the shoots with blossom buds, and to produce the most extraordinary crops."

Fig. 16. *Quenouille or conical training, progressive stages.*

To produce Quenouille standards, plant a young tree, three or four feet high, and, after the first summer's growth, head back the top, and cut-in the side branches, as represented by the dotted lines, on *a*, Fig. 16. The next season the tree will shoot out three or four tiers of side branches, according to its strength. The lowest should be left about eighteen inches from the ground, and, by pinching off superfluous shoots, others may be made to grow pretty regularly, so as not to crowd the head. At the end of this season head back the leader as in *b*, to strengthen the side shoots. Next season a fresh series of lateral shoots will be produced, four or five of which may be kept every year ; and, the third or fourth year, the lower branches may be bent down in midsummer, *c*, and kept in a pendulous position for a year or two, by tying them to stakes driven in the ground, or to the main stem. This successive growth at the top, and arrangement of the limbs below, must be continued till the requisite height— say ten feet—is attained, when all the branches assuming their final form, the tree will resemble Fig. 17. A moderate pruning to produce new wood, and the occasional tying in of a rambling shoot, will be all that is required. The French quenouille training is performed with dwarf stocks, but the trees are more thrifty and durable when grafted

Fig. 17. *Conical or Quenouille training, complete.*

on their own stocks, and kept within proper bounds by root pruning, after Mr. Rivers' method, explained in a previous page.

The two best modes of training for this country, on walls or espaliers, are fan-training, and horizontal training. The first is the simplest and easiest mode of training the Peach, the Apricot, Nectarine, and Cherry; and the latter is best adapted to the Pear. In training to a wall, the branches are fastened in their places by shreds of leather and nails; and, as espaliers, by tying them with slips of bass-matting to the rails of the trellis. The following account of these two modes of training is so concisely abridged from the practice of the best English gardens, in the Suburban Horticulturist, that we cannot do better than to place it before the reader.

Fan-training in the common English manner. A maiden plant (a tree but one year from the graft,) being planted " is to be

headed down to four buds or eyes, placed in such a manner as to throw out two shoots on each side, as shown in Fig. 18. The following season the two uppermost shoots are to be headed down to three eyes, placed in such a

Fig. 18. *Fan-training, first stage.*

manner as to throw out one leading shoot, and one shoot on each side; the two lowermost shoots are to be headed down to two eyes, so as to throw out one leading shoot, and one shoot on the uppermost side, as shown in Fig. 19. We have now five leading shoots on each side, well placed, to form our future tree. Each of these shoots must be placed in the exact position in which it is to remain; and as it is these

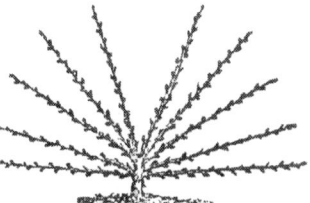

Fig. 19. *Fan training, second stage.*

shoots which are to form the future tree, none of them are to be shortened. The tree should by no means be suffered to bear any fruit this year. Each shoot must now be allowed to produce, besides the leading shoot at its extremity, two other shoots on the uppermost side, one near to the bottom and one about

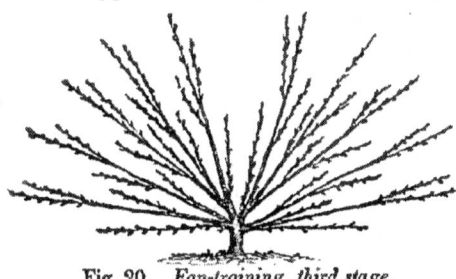

Fig. 20. *Fan-training, third stage.*

midway up the stem; there must also be one shoot on the undermost side, placed about midway between the other two. All the other shoots must be pinched off in their infant state. The tree will then assume, at the end of the third year, the appearance shown in Fig. 20. From this time it may be allowed to bear what crop of fruit the gardener thinks it able to carry; in determining which, he ought never to overrate the vigour of the tree. All of these shoots, except the leading ones, must at the proper season be shortened, but to what length must be left entirely to the judgment of the gardener, it of course depending upon the vigour of the tree. In shortening the shoot, care should be taken to cut back to a wood bud that will produce a shoot for the following year. Cut close to the bud, so that the wound may heal the following season. The following year each shoot at the extremities of the leading branches should produce, besides the leading shoot, one on the upper and two on the under part, more or less, according to the vigour of the tree; whilst each of the secondary branches should produce besides the leading shoot, one other placed near to the bottom; for the grand art of pruning, in all systems to which this class of trees is subjected, consists in preserving a sufficient quantity of young wood at the bottom of the tree; and on no account must the gardener cut away clean any shoots so placed, without well considering if they will be wanted, not only for the present but for the future good appearance of the tree. The quantity of young wood annually laid in must depend upon

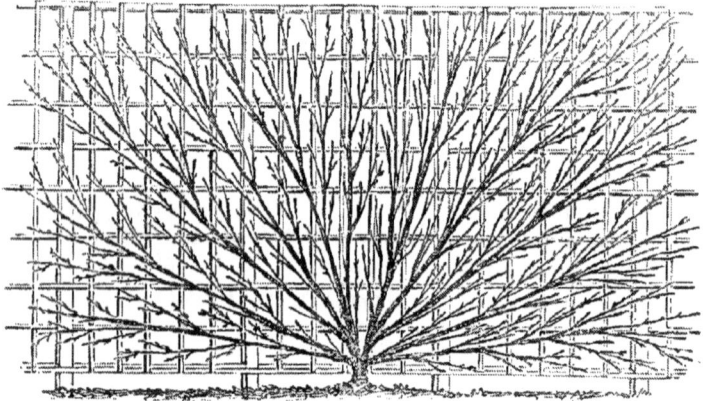

Fig. 21.   *Fan-training complete.*

the vigour of the tree. It would be ridiculous to lay the same quantity into a weakly tree as into a tree in full vigour. The gardener here must use his own judgment. But if any of the leading shoots manifest a disposition to outstrip the others, a portion of young shoots must be laid in, and a greater quantity of fruit suffered to ripen on the over-vigorous branch. At the same time a smaller quantity of fruit than usual must be left to ripen on the weaker branch. This will tend to restore the equilibrium better than any other method. Fig. 21, presents us with the figure of a tree in a more advanced state well balanced, and well calculated for an equal distribution of the sap all over its surface. [We have varied this figure by representing it trained on a trellis, instead of a wall.] Whenever any of the lower shoots have advanced so far as to incommode the others, they

should be cut back to a yearling shoot; this will give them
room, and keep the lower part of the tree in order. In nailing
to a wall, care must be taken not to bruise any part of the
shoot; the wounds made by the knife heal quickly, but a bruise
often proves incurable. Never let a nail gall any part of the
tree; it will endanger the life of the branch. In nailing-in the
young shoots, dispose them as straight and regular as possible
it will look workman-like. Whatever system of training is
pursued, the leading branches should be laid-in in the exact
position they are to remain; for wherever a large branch is
brought down to fill the lower part of the wall, the free ascent
of the sap is obstructed by the extension of the upper, and con-
traction of the lower parts of the branch. It is thus robbed of
part of its former vigour, while it seldom fails to throw out, immediately behind the parts most bent, one or more vigorous shoots."

Horizontal training consists in preserving an upright leader,
with lateral shoots trained at regular intervals. These intervals
may be from a foot to eighteen inches for pears and apples, and
about nine inches for cherries and plums. "A maiden plant
with three shoots having been procured, the
two side shoots are laid in horizontally, and
the centre one upright, as in Fig. 22; all the
buds being rubbed off the latter but three,
viz., one next the top for a vertical leader,
and one on each side near the top, for horizontal branches. In the course of the first

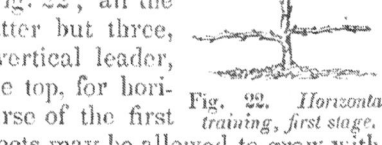

Fig. 22. *Horizontal
training, first stage.*

summer after planting, the shoots may be allowed to grow without being stopped. In the autumn of the first year the two lat-

Fig. 23. *Horizontal training, second stage.*

erals produced are nailed or tied in,
and also the shoots produced from
the extremities of the lower laterals;
the centre shoot being headed down
as before, as shown in Fig. 23. But
in the second summer, when the
main shoot has attained the length
of ten or twelve inches, it may be

stopped; which, if the
plant is in proper
vigour, will cause it
to throw out two ho-
rizontal branches,
in addition to those
which were thrown
out from those of
the preceding year.
The tree will now
be in its second
summer, and will

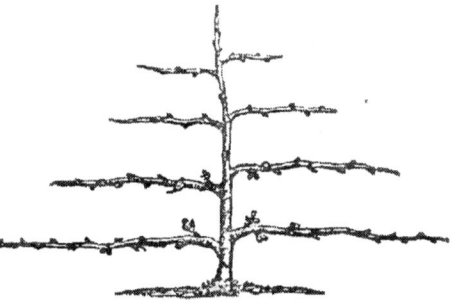

Fig. 24. *Horizontal training, third stage.*

have four horizontal branches on each side of the upright stem, as in Fig. 24; and by persevering in this system four horizontal branches will be produced in each year till the tree reaches the top of the wall (or espalier,) when the upright stem must terminate in two horizontal branches. In the following autumn the

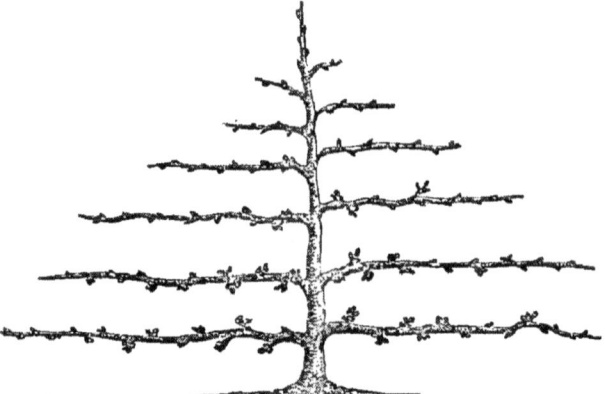

Fig. 25. *Horizontal training, fourth year.*

tree will have the appearance of Fig. 25."—*Suburban Horticulturist*, pp. 363 : 372.

Training fruit trees is nowhere in the United States practised to much extent except in the neighborhood of Boston; and some of the best specimens of the foregoing methods in that neighborhood are in the gardens of J. P. Cushing, Esq., Col. Perkins, and S. G. Perkins, Esq.

CHAPTER V.

TRANSPLANTING.

As nearly all fruit trees are raised first in nurseries, and then removed to their final position in the orchard or fruit garden; as upon the manner of this removal depends not only their slow or rapid growth, their feebleness or vigour afterwards, and in many cases even their life, it is evident that it is in the highest degree important, to understand and practise well this *transplanting*.

The season best adapted for transplanting fruit trees is a matter open to much difference of opinion among horticulturists; a difference founded mainly on experience, but without taking into account variation of climate and soils, two very important circumstances in all operations of this kind.

All physiologists, however, agree that the best season for transplanting deciduous trees is in autumn, directly after the

fall of the leaf. The tree is then in a completely dormant state.
Transplanted at this early season, whatever wounds may have
been made in the roots commence healing at once, as a deposit directly takes place of granulous matter from the wound, and when
the spring arrives the tree is already somewhat established, and
ready to commence its growth. Autumn planting is for this
reason greatly to be preferred in all mild climates, and dry soils;
and even for very hardy trees as the apple, in colder latitudes;
as the fixed position in the ground, which trees planted then get
by the autumnal and early spring rains, gives them an advantage, at the next season of growth, over newly moved trees.

On the other hand, in northern portions of the Union, where
the winters commence early, and are severe, spring planting is
greatly preferred. There, autumn and winter are not mild
enough to allow this gradual process of healing and establishing
the roots to go on; for when the ground is frozen to the depth of
the roots of a tree, all that slow growth and collection of nutriment by the roots is necessarily at an end And the more
tender sorts of fruit trees, the Peach and Apricot, which are less
hardy when newly planted than when their roots are entire, and
well fixed in the soil, are liable to injury in their branches by
the cold The proper time, in such a climate, is as early as the
ground is in a fit condition in the spring.

Early in autumn, and in spring before the buds expand, may
as a general rule be considered the best seasons for transplanting. It is true that there are instances of excellent success in
planting at all seasons, except midsummer; and there are many
who, from having been once or twice successful in transplanting
when trees were nearly in leaf, avow that to be the best season;
not taking into account, that their success was probably entirely
owing to a fortunately damp state of the atmosphere at the time, and
abundant rains after the experiment was performed. In the middle
states, we are frequently liable to a dry period in early summer,
directly following the season of removal, and if transplanting is
deferred to a late period in spring, many of the trees will perish
from drought, before their roots become established in the soil.
Spring planting should, therefore, always be performed as soon
as possible, that the roots may have the great benefit of the early
and abundant rains of that season, and get well started before
the heat of summer commences. For the neighborhood of New-
York, therefore, the best periods are, from the fall of the leaf,
to the middle of November, in autumn; and, from the close of
winter, to the middle of April, in the spring; though commonly,
the seasons of removal are frequently extended a month beyond
these limits.

Taking up the trees is an important part of the operation. A
transplanter should never forget that it is by the delicate and
tender points or extremities of the root that trees take up their

food ; and that the chance of complete success is lessened, by every one of these points that is bruised or destroyed. If we could remove trees with every fibre entire, as we do a plant in a pot, they would scarcely show any sign of their change of position. In most cases, especially in that of trees taken from nurseries, this is, by the operation of removal, nearly impossible. But although we may not hope to get every root entire, we may, with proper care, preserve by far the larger portion of them, and more particularly the small and delicate fibres. After being taken up, they should be planted directly; or, if this cannot be done, they should be kept from drying by a covering of mats, and when sent to a distance by being packed in damp moss.*

Preparing the places. Here is the fatal stumbling block of all novices and ignorant persons in transplanting. An English gardener, when he is about to plant fruit trees, talks about *preparing his borders,* an American says he will *dig his holes ;* and we cannot give a more forcible illustration of the ideas of two persons as to the wants of a fruit tree, or a better notion of the comparative provision made to supply these wants, than by contrasting the two phrases themselves. The one looks upon a tree as a living being, whose life is to be rendered long, vigorous, and fruitful by a good supply of food, and a soil mellow and easily penetrated by the smallest fibre ; the other considers it very much in the light of a truncheon or a post, which he thrusts into the smallest possible hole, and supplies with the least portion of manure, trusting to what he seems to believe the inextinguishable powers of nature to make roots and branches under any circumstances. It is true that the terms differ somewhat from the nature of the culture and the greater preparation necessary in planting fruit trees in England, but this is not by any means sufficient to justify the different modes of performing the same operation there and here.

In truth, in this country, where the sun and climate are so favourable, where pruning and training are comparatively so little necessary, the great requisite to success in the ordinary culture of fruit trees is the *proper preparation of the soil* before a tree is planted. Whether a transplanted tree shall struggle several years to recover, or grow moderately after a short time, or at once start into a very luxuriant and vigorous growth, depends entirely upon the amount of care and labor the planter is willing to bestow on the soil for his trees. We have seen several instances where, side by side, one man planted his trees in large spaces of deeply moved and rich soil, and another in

---

* We should notice an important exception to this in the case of trees packed for shipping across the Atlantic. In this case they should be packed only in *dry* moss; the moisture of the sea air being sufficient to keep the roots in good condition, while if packed in damp moss they will be injured by rotting or excessive growth.

small holes in the common mode, which uniformly showed the
trees of the first, larger after five years, than those of the last,
after twelve.

No fruit tree should be planted in a hole of less size than
three feet square, and eighteen inches to two feet deep. To this
size and depth the soil should be removed and well pulverized,
and it should if necessary be properly enriched by the application of manure, which must be thorough mixed with the whole
mass of prepared soil by repeated turnings with the spade.
This preparation will answer, but the most skilful cultivators
among us make their spaces four or five feet in diameter, or
three times the size of the roots, and it is incredible how much
the luxuriance and vigour of growth, even in a poor soil, is pro
moted by this.   No after mending of the soil, or top dressings
applied to the surface, can, in a climate of dry summers like ours,
equal the effects of this early and deep loosening and enriching
the soil.   Its effects on the growth and health of the tree are
permanent, and the little expense and care necessary in this
preparation is a source of early and constant pleasure to the
planter.   This preparation may be made just before the tree is
planted, but, in heavy soils, it is much better to do it several
months previously ; and no shallow ploughing of the soil can
obviate the necessity and advantages of the practice, where
healthy, vigorous orchards or fruit gardens are desired.

The whole art of transplanting, after this, consists in placing
the roots as they were before, or in the most favourable position
for growth.   Begin by filling the hole with the prepared soil,
within as many inches of the top as will allow the tree to stand
exactly as deep as it previously stood.   With the spade, shape
this soil for the roots in the form of a little hillock on which to
place the roots—and not, as is commonly done, in the form of a
hollow ; the roots will then extend in their natural position, not
being forced to turn up at the ends.   Next examine the roots,
and cut off all wounded parts, paring the wound smooth   Hold
the tree upright on its little mound in the hole of prepared soil ;
extend the roots and cover them carefully with the remaining pulverized soil.   As much of the success of transplanting depends
on bringing the soil in contact with every fibre, so as to leave
no hollows to cause the decay of the roots, not only must this be
secured by patiently filling-in all cavities among the roots, but
when the trees are not quite small, it is customary to pour in a
pail of water when the roots are nearly all covered with soil.
This carries the liquid mould to every hidden part.   After the
water has settled away, fill up the hole, pressing the earth gently
about the tree with the foot, but avoiding the common practice
of shaking it up and down by the stem.   In windy situations it
will be necessary to place a stake by the side of each tree to
hold it upright, until it shall have taken firm root in the soil, but
it is not needful in ordinary cases.

Avoid deep planting. More than half the losses in orchard planting in America arises from this cause, and the equally common one of crowding the earth too tightly about the roots. No tree should be planted deeper than it formerly grew, as its roots are stifled from the want of air, or starved by the poverty of the soil at the depth where they are placed. It is much the better and more natural process in fact to plant the tree so that it shall, when the whole is complete, appear just as deep as before, but standing on a little mound two or three inches higher than the level of the ground about. This, when the mound settles, will leave it nearly on the level with the previous surface.

Mulching is an excellent practice with transplanted trees, and more especially for those which are removed late in the spring. Mulching is nothing more than covering the ground about the stems with coarse straw, or litter from the barn-yard, which by preventing evaporation keeps the soil from becoming dry, and maintains it in that moist and equable condition of temperature most favourable to the growth of young roots. Very many trees, in a dry season, fail at midsummer, after having made a fine start, from the parched and variable condition of the earth about the roots. Watering, frequently fails to save such trees, but mulching when they are planted will entirely obviate the necessity of watering in dry seasons, and promote growth under any circumstances. Indeed watering upon the surface, as commonly performed, is a most injurious practice, as the roots stimulated at one period of the day by water, are only rendered more susceptible to the action of the hot sun at another, and the surface of the ground becomes so hard, by repeated watering, that the beneficial access of the air is almost cut off. If trees are well watered in the holes, while transplanting is going on, they will rarely need it again, and we may say *never*, if they are well mulched directly after planting.

The best manure to be used in preparing the soil for transplanting trees is a compost formed of two thirds muck or black peat earth, reduced by fermenting it several months in a heap with one third fresh barn-yard manure. Almost every farm will supply this, and it is more permanent in its effects, and less drying in its nature, than the common manure of the stable. An admirable manure, recently applied with great success, is charcoal—the small broken bits and refuse of the charcoal pits—mixed intimately with the soil. Air-slaked lime is an excellent manure for fruit trees in soils that are not naturally calcareous. Two or three handsful may be mixed with the soil when preparing each space for planting, and a top dressing may be applied with advantage occasionally afterwards, to increase their productiveness. But wherever large orchards or fruit gardens are to be planted, the muck compost heap should be made ready beforehand, as it is the cheapest, most valuable, and durable of all manures for fruit trees.

Pruning the heads of transplanted trees, at the season of re moval, we think generally an injurious practice. It is certainly needless and hurtful in the case of small trees, or those of such a size as will allow the roots to be taken up nearly entire ; for, as the action of the branches and the roots is precisely reciprocal, and as new roots are rapidly formed just in proportion to the healthy action of the leaves, it follows that by needlessly cutting off branches we lessen the vital action of the whole tree. At the same time, where trees are transplanted of so large a size that some of the roots are lost in removing them, it is necessary to cut back or shorten a few of the branches—as many as will restore the balance of the system—otherwise the perspiration of the leaves may be so great, as to exhaust the supply of sap faster than the roots can collect it. A little judgment only is necessary, to see at a glance, how much of the top must be pruned away before planting the tree, to equalize the loss between the branches and the roots.

When it is necessary to transplant fruit trees of large size, the best practice is to prepare them previously by digging a trench round the whole mass of roots, undermining them, and cut ing off all roots projecting beyond this line. The trench should be dug at such a distance from the tree as will include all the large and sufficient ball of roots, and it should be done in the spring, or before midsummer, when it is desirable to remove the tree the next year. After all the roots that extend to this circular trench are cut off, the earth is replaced, and by the season following an abundance of small fibres is sent out by the amputated roots, which, when the whole is now removed, will insure the success and speedy growth of the tree. This is more completely the case when the tree is prepared two years before transplanting. A variation of this mode, which has been found quite as successful and less laborious, consists in leaving the trench open, and covering it with boards only, or boards with a top layer of turf. The tree then is somewhat checked in its growth, it throws out an abundance of small fibres into the ball of earth containing the roots, and is the next season transplanted with great ease and safety.

The proper size for transplanting varies somewhat with the sort of tree, and the kind of culture intended. It is, however, a maxim equally well settled, both among theorists and the best practical men, that health, immediate vigour, and duration, are all greatly promoted by transplanting fruit trees of small size— from three to six or seven feet We are fully aware with what impatience the beginner, or a person who knows little of the culture of trees, looks upon trees of this size—one who is eager to plant an orchard, and stock a garden with large trees, thinking to *gather a crop the next year*. The latter may indeed be done, but the transplanting so affects the tree, that its first scanty crop is followed by a long season of rest, and feeble growth, while the plantation of young trees is making wood rapidly, and soon comes into a healthy and long-continued state of productiveness—often long indeed before the large trees have fairly arrived at that condition. The small tree, transplanted with its system of roots and branches entire, suffers little or no check; the older and larger tree, losing part of its roots, requires several years to resume its former vigour. The constitution of the small tree is healthy and unimpaired; that of the large is frequently much enfeebled. A stout and vigorous habit—what the nurserymen call a *good stocky plant*—is the true criterion of merit in selecting fruit trees for transplanting.

Trees intended for orchards, being often more exposed than those in gardens, should be somewhat larger—not less than six, or more than eight feet is the best size. For gardens, all experienced cultivators agree that a smaller size is preferable; we prefer plants two years old from the graft. Most gardeners abroad, when they select trees with more than usual care, take what are called maiden plants—those one year old from the graft, and there can be no doubt that, taking into account health, duration, and the ease with which such a tree can be made to grow into any form, this is truly the preferable size for removal into a fruit garden. But we are an impatient people, and it is not till after another century of trial and experience in the culture of fruit trees, that cultivators generally in this country will become aware of the truth of this fact.

The facility with which the different fruit trees may be transplanted differs considerably. Plums are generally removed with most success and after them nearly in the order as follows: Quinces, Apples, Pears, Peaches, Nectarines, Apricots, and Cherries; the latter succeeding with some difficulty when of large size.

Laying-in by the heels is a practice adopted as a temporary kind of planting, when a larger quantity of trees is at hand than can be set out immediately. A trench is opened, and the roots are laid in and covered with soil, the tops being previously placed in a sloping position, inclining to within a few feet of the surface. In this way they are kept fresh and in good order, until it is convenient to plant them finally. In northern districts, where the autumn is often too severe for planting, and the spring is frequently too late to receive trees in time from nurseries farther south, it is a common and successful mode to procure trees in autumn and lay them in by the heels until spring, covering over the tops of the more tender sorts if necessary with coarse litter.

In planting an orchard, always avoid placing the trees in the same spot or near where an old tree stood before. Experience has taught us that the growth of a young tree, in such a position, is weak and feeble; the nourishment suitable to that kind of tree having already been exhausted by a previous growth, and the soil being half filled with old and decayed roots which are detrimental to the health of the young tree.

——————— —— — ——

CHAPTER VI.

THE POSITION OF FRUIT TREES. SOIL AND ASPECT.

IN our favourable climate many fruit trees will thrive and produce some fruit in almost any soil, except dry sand, or wet swamps. But there is much to be gained in all climates by a judicious selection of soil, when this is in our power, or by that improvement which may generally be effected in inferiour soils where we are necessarily limited to such. As we shall, in treating the culture of each genus of fruit, state more in detail the soils especially adapted to its growth, our remarks here will be confined to the subject of soils generally, for the orchard and fruit garden.

The soils usually selected for making plantations of fruit trees may be divided into light sandy loams, gravelly loams, strong loams, and clayey loams ; the first having a large proportion of sand, and the last a large proportion of clay.

The soil most inviting to the eye is a *light sandy loam,* and, as it is also a very common soil, more than half the fruit gardens in the country are composed of this mould. The easy manner in which it is worked, owing to its loose and very friable nature, and the rapidity with which, from its warmth, crops of all kinds come into bearing, cause it to be looked upon with almost universal favour. Notwithstanding this, a pretty careful observation, for several years, has convinced us that a light sandy soil is, on the whole, the worst soil for fruit trees. Under the bright skies of July and August, a fruit tree requires a soil which will retain and afford a moderate and continued supply of moisture, and here the sandy soil fails. In consequence of this the vigour of the tree is checked, and it becomes feeble in its growth, and is comparatively short-lived, or unproductive As a tree in a feeble state is always most liable to the attacks of insects, those on a sandy soil are the first to fall a prey to numerous maladies.* The open loose texture of a sandy soil, joined to its warmth, affords an easy passage, and an excellent habitation for all insects that pass part of their lives in the ground, preparatory to

* This remark applies to the middle and southern portions of this country. **North** f the **43°** a light sandy soil is perhaps preferable as warmer and earlier.

rising out of it to attack the fruit, foliage, or branches of the tree.

Such are some of the disadvantages of a light sandy soil; and, in thoroughly examining many of the fruit gardens of the middle states the last few seasons, we could not fail to be struck with the fact that in nine cases out of ten, where a variety of fruit was unusually liable to disease, to blight, or to the attacks of certain fruit-destroying insects, as the curculio, the trees themselves were on sandy soils; while on the other hand, and frequently in the same neighbourhood, the same sorts were growing luxuriantly and bearing abundant crops, where the soil was a rather strong loam.* For a few years, the growth and productiveness of the trees upon sandy soil, is all that can be desired; but the trees are shorter lived and sooner fall into decay than where the soil is stronger. If there is any exception to this rule, it is only in the case of the Peach, and judging from the superiour flavour of this fruit on stronger soils, we are inclined to doubt the value of the exception even here.

Gravelly loams are frequently much better adapted for orchards than sandy, especially where the loam is of a strong quality, and the gravel is not in excess; and the hardier fruits usually do well on this kind of soil.

Strong loams, by which we mean a loam with only just a sufficient portion of sand to make it easily worked, are on the whole by far the best for fruit gardens in this country. A strong loam is usually a deep soil, and affords during the whole heat of summer, a proper supply of moisture and nourishment to the roots of trees. Fruit trees do not come into a bearing state so soon in a strong as in a sandy loam, because the growth of wood is more vigorous, and fruit buds are not so soon formed; but they bear larger crops, are much less liable to many diseases, and their longevity is much greater. The largest and most productive orchards of the apple and pear in this country are upon soils of this kind.

Clayey loams are, when well drained, and when the clay is not in excess, good fruit soils—they are usually strong and deep soils though rather heavy and difficult to work. Trees that will flourish on these soils such as the Apple, Pear, Cherry, Plum, and Apricot, usually are very free from disease, or insects, and bear large crops. In a moist climate, like that of England, fruit trees on a clayey loam would die of canker, brought on by the excessive quantity of water contained in the soil, but such is

---

* As an instance in point, the owner of one of the most highly cultivated gardens in the vicinity of Boston was showing us, in despair, some trees of the Seckel pear upon which he could no longer get good crops, or fair fruit, and lamenting the *degeneracy* of the sort. The next day we saw in a neighbouring garden beautiful crops of this pear growing with the least possible care. The garden in the first case was a light sandy loam; in the second, a strong loam.

5

not the case under the high and warm temperature of our summers.   The finest, largest. and most productive Plums and Pears
within our knowledge, grow in sites on the North river, when
the soil is a stiff clayey loam, almost approaching a clay.
Those fruits that on light sandy soils are almost worthless from
their liability to disease, and the attacks of insects, are here
surprisingly luxuriant and fruitful.

It is, however, well to remark, that some varieties of fruit,
perhaps from the circumstances of their origin, succeed better
on sandy soils than any other ; thus the Newtown pippin will
only arrive at perfection in a strong loam, while the Yellow Bellflower is finer when grown on a sandy soil.   But these are exceptions to all rules, and what we have already stated, as to the
relative quality of soils, will apply pretty generally to the whole
of this country south of the Mohawk river ; and it may be added
that calcareous soils, of whatever texture, are better than soils
of the same quality where no limestone is present.

Trenching is the most complete method of improving a soil
too sandy, when the subsoil below is of a loamy or clayey nature.   Deep subsoil ploughing, by bringing up a sufficient quantity of the stratum below, will answer the same purpose.   When
the subsoil of a sandy soil is sand or gravel, the surface can only
be improved by top dressings, or the application of manures.
Top-dressing with clay is the most simple means of changing the
nature of such a soil, and it is surprising how moderate a quantity of clay will give a closer texture to light sandy soils.   In
manuring such soils, we may greatly improve their nature as
well as condition, by using composts of peat or bog earth, swamp
muck, or river mud, instead of common barn-yard or stable
manure.   The former are not only more permanent and better
as manures for fruit trees, but they gradually consolidate and
improve the whole texture of the soil.

Indeed no fruit garden, where the soil is not naturally deep
and rich, is in *perfect* condition for planting trees, unless the
soil has been well trenched two spades in depth.   This creates
a matrix for the roots, so deep and permanent, that they retain
their vigour and luxuriance through the droughts of summer,
and continue for a long time in a state of health and productiveness.

It is difficult to give any precise rules as to *aspect*.   We have
seen fine fruit gardens here in all aspects.   Perhaps the very
best aspect, on the whole, is a gentle slope to the southwest, because in such positions the trees, when in blossom. are somewhat
protected from the bad effects of a morning sun after spring
frosts.   But, to remedy this more perfectly, it is sometimes the
practice to plant on the north sides of hills, and this is an effectual way where early frosts are fatal, and where the season is
long and warm enough to ripen the fruit in any exposure.   A

aue south slope, is, south of New-York, frequently found too warm for many fruit trees, in soils that are light and dry.

Deep vallies, with small streams of water, are the worst situations for fruit trees, as the cold air settles down in these vallies in a calm frosty night, and buds and blossoms are very frequently destroyed. We know a rich and fertile valley of this kind in Connecticut where the Cherry will scarcely grow, and a crop of the Apple, or the Pear, is not obtained once in ten years ; while the adjacent hill tops and high country, a couple or three miles distant, yield abundant crops annually. On the other hand the borders of large rivers, as the Hudson, or of some of our large inland lakes, are the most favourable situations for fruit trees, as the climate is rendered milder by large bodies of water. In the garden where we write, a fourth of a mile from the Hudson, we have frequently seen ice formed during the night, of the thickness of a dollar, when the blossoms of the Apricot were fully expanded, without doing the least harm to that tender fruit. This is owing to the slight fog rising from the river in the morning, which, softening the rays of the sun, and dissolving gradually the frost, prevents the injurious effects of sudden thawing. At the same time, a couple of miles from the shores, this fruit will often be quite destroyed. In short, the season on the lower half of the Hudson, may, from the ameliorating influence of the river, be said to be a month longer—a fortnight earlier in spring, and later in autumn, than in the same latitude a few miles distant ; and crops of the more tender fruits are, therefore, much more certain on the banks of large rivers or lakes, than in inland districts of the same climate.

CHAPTER VII.

GENERAL REMARKS ON INSECTS.

THE insects injurious to fruit trees are numerous, and to combat them successfully requires a minute acquaintance with their character and habits. While considering the culture of each class of fruit in the succeeding pages, we shall point out the habits, and suggest means of destroying the most important of these insects ; but, in the meantime, we wish to call attention to some general practical hints on this subject.

In the first place, we cannot too strongly impress upon the attention of the fruit grower the importance of watching carefully, and making an early attack, upon every species of insect. It is only necessary to look for a moment at the astonishing rapid.

ity with which many kinds of insects increase, if allowed to
get well established in a garden, to become fully aware of this.
The common caterpillars are the young of moths or butterflies,
and that careful observer of the habits of insects, Dr. Harris,
says as each female lays from two to five hundred eggs, a thousand moths or butterflies will, on the average, produce three
hundred thousand caterpillars , if one half this number, when
arrived at maturity, are females, they will give forty-five millions
of caterpillars in the second, and six thousand seven hundred
and fifty millions in the third generation.*   To take another example the *aphides*, or plant lice, which are frequently seen in
great numbers on the tender shoots of fruit trees have an almost
incredibly prolific power of increase,—the investigations of
Réaumur having shown that one individual, in five generations,
may become the progenitor of nearly six thousand millions of
descendants.   With such surprising powers of propagation,
were it not for the havoc caused among insects by various species
preying upon each other, by birds, and other animals, and espe-
pecially by unfavourable seasons, vegetation would soon be entirely destroyed by them   As it is, the orchards and gardens of
careless and slovenly cultivators are often overrun by them, and
many of the finest crops suffer great injury, or total loss from
the want of a little timely care.

In all well managed plantations of fruit, at the first appearance of any injurious insect, it will be immediately seized upon
and destroyed.   A few moments, in the first stage of insect life—
at the first birth of the new colony—will do more to rid us for
the season, of that species, than whole days of toil after the matter has been so long neglected that the enemy has become well
established.   We know how reluctant all, but the experienced
grower, are to set about eradicating what at first seems a thing
of such trifling consequence.   But such persons should consider
that whether it is done at first, or a fortnight after, is frequently
the difference between ten and ten thousand.   A very little time,
regularly devoted to the extirpation of noxious insects, will keep
a large place quite free from them.   We know a very large
garden, filled with trees, and always remarkably free from insect
ravages, which, while those even in its vicinity suffer greatly, is
thus preserved, by half an hour's examination of the whole premises two days in the week during the growing season   This
is made early in the morning, the best time for the purpose, as
the insects are quiet while the dew is yet upon the leaves, and
whole races, yet only partially developed, may be swept off in a
single moment   In default of other more rapid expedients, the
old mode of *hand-picking*, and crushing or burring, is the safest
and surest that can be adopted.

* For much valuable information on the habits of insects injurious to vegetation,
see the Treatise on the Insects of Massachusetts, by Dr. T. W. Harris, Cambridge

For practical purposes, the numerous insects infesting fruit trees may be divided into four classes ; 1st, those which for a time harbour in the ground and may be attacked in the soil ; 2d, winged and other species, which may be attacked among the branches ; 3d, aphides, or plant lice which infest the young shoots ; 4th, moths, and all night-flying insects.

Insects, the larvæ or grubs of which harbour in the ground during a certain season, as the curculio or plum-weevil, are all more or less affected by the application of common salt as a top dressing. On a larger scale—in farm crops—the ravages of the cut-worm are frequently prevented by sowing three bushels of salt to the acre, and we have seen it applied to all kinds of fruit grounds with equal success. Salt seems to be strongly disagreeable to nearly all this class of insects, and the grubs perish, where even a small quantity has for two or three seasons been applied to the soil. In a neighbourhood where the peach worm usually destroys half the peach trees, and where whole crops of the plum are equally a victim to the plum-weevil, we have seen the former preserved in the healthiest condition by an annual application of a small handful of coarse salt about the collar of the tree at the surface of the ground ; and the latter, made to hold abundant crops, by a top dressing applied every spring of packing salt, at the rate of a quart to the surface occupied by the roots of every full grown tree.

Salt, being a powerful agent, must be applied for this purpose with caution and judgment. In small quantities it promotes the verdure and luxuriance of fruit trees, while if applied very frequently, or too plentifully, it will certainly cause the death of any tree. Two or three years top-dressing in moderate quantity will usually be found sufficient to drive away these insects, and then the application need only be repeated once in two or three seasons. Any coarse, refuse salt will answer the purpose ; and packing salt is preferable to that of finer quality, as it dissolves slowly by the action of the atmosphere.

In the winged state, most small insects may either be driven away by powerful odours, or killed by strong decoctions of tobacco, or a wash of diluted whale-oil or other strong soap. Attention has but recently been called to the repugnance of all insects, to strong odours, and there is but little doubt that before a long time, it will lead to the discovery of the means of preventing the attacks of most insects by means of strong smelling liquids or odourous substances. The moths that attack furs, as every one knows, are driven away by pepper-corns or tobacco, and should future experiments prove that at certain seasons, when our trees are most likely to be attacked by insects, we may expel them by hanging bottles or rags filled with strong smelling liquids in our trees, it will certainly be a very simple and easy way of ridding ourselves of them. The brown scale, a trouble-

5*

some enemy of the orange tree, it is stated in the *Gardener's Chronicle* have been destroyed by hanging plants of the common chamomile among its branches. The odour of the coal tar of gas works is exceedingly offensive to some insects injurious to fruits, and it has been found to drive away the wire worm, and other grubs that attack the roots of plants. The vapour of oil of turpentine is fatal to wasps, and that of tobacco smoke to the green fly. Little as yet is certainly known respecting the exact power of the various smells in deterring insects from attacking trees. What we do know, however, gives us reason to believe that much may be hoped from experiments made with a variety of powerful smelling substances.

Tobacco water, and diluted whale oil soap, are the two most efficient remedies for all the small insects which feed upon the young shoots and leaves of plants. Tobacco water is made by boiling tobacco leaves, or the refuse stems and stalks of the tobacco shops. A large pot is crowded full of them, and then filled up with water, which is boiled till a strong decoction is made. This is applied to the young shoots and leaves with a syringe, or, when the trees are growing in nursery rows, with a common white-wash brush ; dipping the latter in the liquid and shaking it sharply over extremities or the infested part of each tree This, or the whale oil soap-suds, or a mixture of both, will kill every species of plant lice, and nearly all other small insects to which young fruit trees are subject.

The wash of whale oil soap is made by mixing two pounds of this soap, which is one of the cheapest and strongest kinds, with fifteen gallons of water. This mixture is applied to the leaves and stems of plants with a syringe, or in any other convenient mode, and there are few of the smaller insects that are not destroyed or driven away by it. The merit of this mixture belongs to Mr. David Haggerston, of Boston, who first applied it with great success to the rose slug, and received the premium of the Massachusetts Horticultural Society for its discovery. When this soap cannot be obtained, a good substitute may be made by turning into soap the lees of common oil casks, by the application of potash and water in the usual way.

Moths and other insects which fly at night are destroyed in large numbers by the following mode, first discovered by Victor Adouin, of France. A flat saucer or vessel is set on the ground in which is placed a light, partially covered with a common bell glass besmeared with oil. All the small moths are directly attracted by the light, fly towards it, and, in their attempts to get at the light, are either caught by the glutinous sides of the bell glass, or fall into the basin of oil beneath, and in either case soon perish. M. Adouin applied this to the destruction of the *pyralis*, a moth that is very troublesome in the French vineyards ; with two hundred of these lights in a vineyard of four acres, and in a single night, 30,000 moths were killed and found dead on or about the vessels. By continuing his process through the season, it was estimated that he had destroyed female moths sufficient to have produced a progeny of over a million of cater-pillars. In our orchards, myriads of insects may be destroyed by lighting small bonfires of shavings, or any refuse brush ; and in districts where the apples are much worm-eaten, if repeated two or three nights at the proper season, this is a very efficient and cheap mode of getting rid of the moth which causes so much mischief. Dr. Harris, knowing how important it is to destroy the caterpillar in the moth state, has recommended flambeaux, made of tow wound round a stake and dipped in tar, to be stuck in the fruit garden at night and lighted. Thousands of moths will find a speedy death, even in the short time which these flambeaux are burning. The melon-bug may be extirpated by myriads, in the same way.

A simple and most effectual mode of ridding the fruit garden of insects of every description, which we recommend as a gene-ral extirpator, suited to all situations, is the following. Take a number of common bottles, the wider mouthed the better, and fill them about half full of a mixture of water, molasses, and vinegar. Suspend these among the branches of trees, and in various parts of the garden. In a fortnight they will be found full of dead insects, of every description not too large to enter the bottles—wasps, flies, beetles, slugs, grubs, and a great variety of others. The bottles must now be emptied, and the liquid re-newed. A zealous amateur of our acquaintance, caught last season in this way, *more than three bushels* of insects of various kinds ; and what is more satisfactory, preserved his garden al-most entirely against their attacks in any shape.

The assistance of birds in destroying insects should be duly estimated by the fruit-grower. The quantity of eggs and in-sects in various states, devoured annually by birds, when they are encouraged in gardens, is truly surprising. It is true that one or two species of these, as the ring-tail, annoy us by prey-ing upon the earlier cherries, but even taking this into account, we are inclined to believe that we can much better spare a rea-sonable share of a few fruits, than dispense with the good ser-vices of birds in ridding us of an excess of insects.

The most serviceable birds are the common sparrows, the wren, the red-breast, and, in short, most of the birds of this class. All these birds should be encouraged to build nests and inhabit the fruit garden, and this may most effectually be done by not allowing a gun to be fired within its boundaries. The introduc-tion of hedges or live fences, greatly promotes the domestication of birds, as they afford an admirable shelter for their nests. Our own gardens are usually much more free from insects than those a mile or two distant, and we attribute this in part to our practice of encouraging birds, and to the thorn and arbor vitæ hedges growing here, and which are greatly resorted to by those of the feathered tribe which are the greatest enemies of the insect race.

Among animals, the *toad* and the *bat* are great insect destroyers. The common bat lives almost entirely upon them, and in its evening sallies devours a great number of moths, beetles, weevils, etc. ; and the toad quietly makes way with numberless smaller insects.

CHAPTER VIII.

THE APPLE.

Pyrus Malus. L. Rosaceæ, of botanists.
Pommier, of the French ; *Apfelbaum*, German ; *Apfel*, Dutch ; *Melo pomo*, Italian ; and *Manzana*, Spanish.

THE Apple is the world-renowned fruit of temperate climates. From the most remote periods it has been the subject of praise among writers and poets, and the old mythologies all endow its fruit with wonderful virtues. The allegorical tree of knowledge bore apples, and the celebrated golden fruit of the orchards of Hesperus, guarded by the sleepless dragon which it was one of the triumphs of Hercules to slay, were also apples, according to the old legends. Among the heathen gods of the north, there were apples fabled to possess the power of conferring immortality, which were carefully watched over by the goddess Iduna, and kept for the especial dessert of the gods who felt themselves growing old ! As the mistletoe grew chiefly on the apple and the oak, the former tree was looked upon with great respect and reverence by the ancient Druids of Britain, and even to this day, in some parts of England, the antique custom of saluting the apple trees in the orchards, in the hope of obtaining a good crop the next year, still lingers among the farmers of portions of Devonshire and Herefordshire. This odd ceremony consists of saluting the tree with a portion of the contents of a wassail bowl of cider, with a toast in it, by pouring a little of the cider about the roots, and even hanging a bit of the toast on the branches of the most barren, the farmer and his men dancing in a circle round the tree, and singing rude songs like the following :

" Here's to thee, old apple tree,
Whence thou mayst bud, and whence thou mayst blow ;
And whence thou mayst bear apples enow,
Hats full ! caps full—
Bushels and sacksfull !
Huzza !"

The species of crab from which all our sorts of Apples have originated, is wild in most parts of Europe. There are indeed two or three kinds of wild crab belonging to this country; as the *Pyrus coronaria*, or sweet scented crab, with fruit about an inch in diameter grows in many parts of the United States; and the wild crab of Oregon, *P. rivularis*, bearing a reddish yellow fruit about the size of a cherry, which the Chenook Indians use as an article of food; yet none of our cultivated varieties of apple have been raised from these native crabs, but from seeds of the species brought here by the colonists from Europe.

The Apple tree is, however, most perfectly naturalized in America, and in the northern and middle portions of the United States succeeds as well, or, as we believe, better than in any part of the world. The most celebrated apples of Germany and the north of Europe, are not superiour to many of the varieties originated here, and the American or Newtown Pippin is now pretty generally admitted to be the finest apple in the world. No better proof of the perfect adaptation of our soil and climate to this tree can be desired, than the seemingly spontaneous production of such varieties as this, the Baldwin, the Spitzenburg or the Swaar—all fruits of delicious flavour and great beauty of appearance.

The Apple is usually a very hardy and rather slow growing fruit tree, with a low spreading, rather irregular head, and bears an abundance of white blossoms tinged with red. In a wild state it is very long-lived, but the finest garden sorts usually live about fifty or eighty years; though by proper care, they may be kept healthy and productive much longer. Although the apple generally forms a tree of medium growth, there are many specimens in this country of enormous size. Among others we recollect two in the grounds of Mr. Hall of Raynham, Rhode Island, which, ten years ago, were 130 years old; the trunk of one of these trees then measured, at one foot from the ground, thirteen feet two inches, and the other twelve feet two inches. The trees bore that season about thirty or forty bushels, but in the year 1780 they together bore one hundred and one bushels of apples. In Duxbury, Plymouth county, Mass., is a tree which in its girth measures twelve feet five inches, and which has yielded in a single season 121½ bushels.

USES OF THE APPLE. No fruit is more universally liked or generally used than the apple. It is exceedingly wholesome, and, medicinally, is considered cooling, and laxative, and useful in all inflammatory diseases. The finest sorts are much esteemed for the dessert, and the little care required in its culture, renders it the most abundant of all fruits in temperate climates. As the earliest sorts ripen about the last of June, and the latest can be preserved until that season, it may be considered as a fruit in perfection the whole year. Besides its merits for the dessert, the value of the apple is still greater for the kitchen, and in sauces, pies, tarts, preserves, and jellies, and roasted and boiled, this fruit is the constant and invaluable resource of the kitchen. *Apple butter*, made by stewing pared and sliced sweet apples in new cider until the whole is soft and pulpy, is a common and excellent article of food in many farmers' families, and is frequently made by the barrel, in Connecticut. In France, nearly the same preparation is formed by simmering apples in new wine, until the whole becomes a sort of marmalade, which is called *Raisiné*. The juice of the apple unfermented, is, in some parts of the country, boiled down till it becomes molasses. When fermented it forms *cider*, and if this is carefully made from the best cider apples, it is nearly equal to wine ; in fact many hundreds of barrels, of the cider of New-Jersey, have been manufactured in a single year, into an imitation Champagne, which is scarcely distinguished by many from that made from the grape.

Dried apples are also a considerable article of commerce. Farmers usually pare and quarter them by hand, and dry them in the sun ; but those who pursue it as a matter of trade pare them by machinery, and dry them slowly in ovens. They are then packed in bags or barrels, and are used either at home, in sea stores, or are exported.

In perfumery, the pulp of this fruit, mixed intimately with lard, forms pomatum. The wood is employed for lasts, and for other purposes by turners ; and being fine grained and compact is sometimes stained black, and used for ebony, by cabinet makers.

The quality of an apple is always judged of by the use to which it is to be applied. A table or dessert apple of the finest quality should be of medium size, regular form and fine colour ; and the flesh should be fine-grained, crisp, or tender, and of a sprightly or rich flavour, and aroma. Very large sized, or coarse apples are only admired by persons who have little knowledge of the true criterion of excellence. Apples for kitchen use should have the property of cooking evenly into a tender pulpy consistence, and are generally acid in flavour ; and, although there are many good cooking apples unfit for the table, many sorts, as the Fall Pippin and the Greening, are excellent for both purposes. To this we may add that for the common applesauce made by farmers a high flavoured sweet apple, which boils somewhat firm, is preferred, as this is generally made with cider. The very common use made of this cheap preserve at the north and west, and the recent practice of fattening hogs, horses, and other animals upon sweet apples, accounts for the much greater number of varieties of sweet apples held in esteem here than in any other country. In fact, so excellent has the saccharine matter of the apple been found for this purpose, that whole orchards of sweet apples are frequently planted here for the purposes of fattening swine and cattle, which are allowed to run at large in them.

Cider apples are varieties frequently useless for any other purpose. The best for this purpose are rather tough, piquant, and astringent; their juice has a high specific quality, and they are usually great bearers; as the Harrison, the Red Streak, and the Virginia Crab.

PROPAGATION. The apple for propagation is usually raised from seeds obtained from the pomace of the cider mills, and a preference is always given to that from thrifty young orchards. These are sown in autumn, in broad drills, in good mellow soil, and they remain in the seed buds, attention being paid to keeping the soil loose and free from weeds, from one to three years, according to the richness of the soil. When the seedlings are a little more than a fourth of an inch in diameter, they should be taken up, in the spring or autumn, their tap roots shortened, and then planted in nursery rows, one foot apart and three to four feet between the rows. If the plants are thrifty, and the soil good, they may be budded the following autumn, within three or four inches of the ground, and this is the most speedy mode of obtaining strong, straight, thrifty plants. Grafting is generally performed when the stocks are about half an inch thick; and for several modes of performing it on the apple, see the remarks on *grafting* in a previous page. When young trees are feeble in the nursery, it is usual to head them back two thirds the length of the graft, when they are three or four feet high, to make them throw up a strong vigorous shoot.

Apple stocks for dwarfs are raised by layers, as pointed out in the article on Layers.

Apple trees for transplanting to orchards should be at least two years budded, and six or seven feet high, and they should have a proper balance of head or side branches.

SOIL AND SITUATION. The apple will grow on a great variety of soils, but it seldom thrives on very dry sands, or soils saturated with moisture. Its favourite soil, in all countries, is a strong loam of a calcareous or limestone nature. A deep, strong gravelly, marly, or clayey loam, or a strong sandy loam on a gravelly subsoil, produces the greatest crops, and the highest flavoured fruit, as well as the utmost longevity of the trees. Such a soil is moist rather than dry, the most favourable condition for this fruit. Too damp soils may often be rendered fit for the apple by thorough draining, and too dry ones by deep subsoil ploughing, or trenching, where the subsoil is of a heavier texture. And many apple orchards in New-England are very flourishing and productive on soils so stony and rock-covered (though naturally fertile) as to be unfit for any other crop.*

* Blowing sands, says Mr. Coxe, when bottomed on a dry substratum, and aids

As regards site, apple orchards flourish best, in southern and middle portions of the country, on north slopes, and often even on the steep north sides of hills, where the climate is hot and dry. Farther north a southern or southeastern aspect is preferable, to ripen the crop and the wood more perfectly.

We may here remark that almost every district of the country has one or more varieties which, having had its origin there, seems also peculiarly adapted to the soil and climate of that locality. Thus the Newtown pippin, and the Spitzenburgh are the great apples of New-York; the Baldwin, and the Roxbury Russett, of Massachusetts; the Bellflower and the Rambo, of Pennsylvania and New-Jersey; and the Peck's Pleasant and the Seek-no-further, of Connecticut; and though these apples are cultivated with greater or less success in other parts of the country, yet nowhere is their flavour and productiveness so perfect as in the best soils of their native districts—excepting in such other districts where a *soil containing the same elements*, and a *corresponding climate* are also to be found.

PLANTING AND CULTIVATION OF ORCHARDS. With the exception of a few early and very choice sorts in the fruit garden, the orchard is the place for this tree, and indeed, when we consider the great value and usefulness of apples to the farmer, it is easy to see that no farm is complete without a large and well selected apple orchard.

The distance at which the trees should be planted in an orchard, depends upon the mode in which they are to be treated. When it is desired finally to cover and devote the whole ground to the trees. thirty feet apart is the proper interval, but where the farmer wishes to keep the land between the trees in grain and grass, fifty feet is not too great a distance in strong soils. Forty feet apart, however, is the usual distance at which the trees are planted in orchards.

Before transplanting, the ground should be well prepared for the trees, as we have insisted in a previous page, and vigorous healthy young trees should be selected from the nurseries. As there is a great difference in the natural growth, shape, and size of the various sorts of apple trees, those of the same kinds should be planted in the rows together, or near each other; this

---

by marl or meadow mud, will be found capable of producing very fine apple trees. Good cultivation. and a system of high manuring, will always remunerate the proprietor of an orchard, except it be planted on a quicksand or a cold clay; in such soils, no management can prevent an early decay One of the most thrifty orchards I possess, was planted on a blowing sand, on which I carted three thousand loads of mud on ten acres, at an expense of about twenty-five dollars per acre, exclusive of much other manure; on this land I have raised good wheat and clover. Of five rows of the Winerap apple planted upon it eight years ago, on the summit of a sandy knoll, not one has died out of near an hundred trees—all abundant bearers of large and fair apples —*View of Fruit Trees*, p 31

will not only facilitate culture and gathering the fruit, but will add to the neatness and orderly appearance of the orchard.

It is an indispensable requisite, in all young orchards, to keep the ground mellow and loose by cultivation; at least for the first few years, until the trees are well established. Indeed, of two adjoining orchards, one planted and kept in grass, and the other ploughed for the first five years, there will be an incredible difference in favour of the latter. Not only will these trees show rich dark luxuriant foliage, and clean smooth stems, while those neglected will have a starved and sickly look, but the size of the trees in the cultivated orchard will be treble that of the others at the end of this time, and a tree in one will be ready to bear an abundant crop, before the other has commenced yielding a peck of good fruit. Fallow crops are the best for orchards,—potatoes, vines, buckwheat, roots, Indian corn, and the like. An occasional crop of grass or grain may be taken; but clover is rather too coarse-rooted and exhausting for a young orchard. When this, or grass, is necessarily grown among young trees for a year or two, a circle of three feet diameter should be kept loose by digging every season about the stem of each tree.

When the least symptom of failure or decay in a bearing orchard is perceived, the ground should have a good top dressing of manure, and of marl, or mild lime, in alternate years. It is folly to suppose that so strong growing a tree as the apple, when planted thickly in an orchard, will not, after a few heavy crops of fruit, exhaust the soil of much of its proper food. If we desire our trees to continue in a healthy bearing state, we should, therefore, manure them as regularly as any other crop, and they will amply repay the expense. There is scarcely a farm where the *waste* of barn-yard manure,—the urine, etc., if properly economized by mixing this animal excrement with the muck-heap—would not be amply sufficient to keep the orchards in the highest condition. And how many moss-covered, barren orchards, formerly very productive, do we not every day see, which only require a plentiful new supply of food in a substantial top-dressing, thorough scraping of the stems, and washing with diluted soft soap, to bring them again into the finest state of vigour and productiveness !

The bearing year of the Apple, in common culture, only takes place every alternate year, owing to the excessive crops which 't usually produces, by which they exhaust most of the organizable matter laid up by the tree, which then requires another season to recover, and collect a sufficient supply again to form fruit buds. When half the fruit is thinned out in a young state, leaving only a moderate crop, the apple, like other fruit trees, will bear every year, as it will also, if the soil is kept in high condition. The bearing year of an apple tree, or a whole orchard may be changed by picking off the fruit when the trees

6

first show good crops, allowing it to remain only on the alternate seasons which we wish to make the bearing year.*

PRUNING. The apple in orchards requires very little pruning
if the trees, while the orchard is young, are carefully in-
spected every year, a little before midsummer, and all crossing
branches taken out while they are small. When the heads are
once properly adjusted and well balanced, the less the pruning
saw and knife are used the better, and the cutting out of dead
limbs, and removal of such as may interfere with others, or too
greatly crowd up the head of the tree, is all that an orchard will
usually require. But wherever a limb is pruned away, the surface of the wound should be neatly smoothed, and if it exceeds
an inch in diameter, it should be covered with the liquid shellac
previously noticed, or brushed over with common white lead,
taking care with the latter, not to paint the bark also.

INSECTS. There are three or four insects that in some parts
of the country, are very destructive or injurious to this tree; a
knowledge of the habits of which, is therefore, very important to

---

* One of the finest orchards in America is that of Pelham farm, at Esopus, on
the Hudson. It is no less remarkable for the beauty and high flavour of its fruit,
than the constant productiveness of trees The proprietor, R. L. Pell, Esq , has
kindly furnished us with some notes of his experiments on fruit trees, and we sub-
join the following highly interesting one on the Apple.

"For several years past I have been experimenting on the apple, having an orchard of 2,000 bearing Newtown Pippin trees I found it very unprofitable to
wait for what is termed the 'bearing year,' and it has been my aim to assist nature, so as to enable the trees to bear every year. I have noticed that from the
excessive productiveness of this tree, it requires the intermediate year to recover
itself—to extract from the earth and the atmosphere the materials to enable it to
produce again This it is not able to do, unassisted by art, while it is loaded with
fruit, and the intervening year is lost ; if however, the tree is supplied with proper
food it will bear every year , at least such has been the result of my experiments
Three years ago, in April, I scraped all the rough bark from the stems of several
thousand trees in my orchards, and washed all the trunks and limbs within reach
with soft soap , trimmed out all the branches that crossed each other, early in June,
and painted the wounded part with white lead, to exclude moisture and prevent
decay I then, in the latter part of the same month, slit the bark by running a sharp
pointed knife from the ground to the first set of limbs, which prevents the tree from
becoming bark bound, and gives the young wood an opportunity of expanding. In
July I placed one peck of oyster shell lime under each tree, and left it piled about
the trunk until November, during which time the drought was excessive In November the lime was dug in thoroughly The following year I collected from these
trees 1700 barrels of fruit, part of which was sold in New-York for four, and others
in London for nine dollars per barrel The cider made from the refuse, delivered
at the mill two days after its manufacture, I sold for three dollars and three quarters per barrel of 32 gallons, exclusive of the barrel In October I manured these
trees with stable manure in which the ammonia had been fixed, and covered this
immediately with earth. The succeeding autumn they were literally bending to
the ground with the finest fruit I ever saw, while the other trees in my orchard not
so treated are quite barren, the last season having been their bearing year I am
now placing round each tree one peck of charcoal dust, and propose in the spring
to cover it from the compost heap.

My soil is a strong, deep, sandy loam on a gravelly subsoil I cultivate my orchard grounds, as if there were no trees on them, and raise grain of every kind except rye, which grain is so very injurious that I believe three successive crops of
it would destroy any orchard younger than twenty years I raised last year in
an orchard containing 20 acres, trees 18 years old, a crop of Indian corn which
averaged 140 bushels of ears to the acre."

the orchardist. These are chiefly the borer, the caterpillar, and the canker worm.

The apple Borer is, as we usually see it in the trunks of the apple, quince, and thorn trees, a fleshy white grub, which enters the tree at the collar, just at the surface of the ground, where the bark is tender, and either girdles the tree or perforates it through every part of the stem, finally causing its death. This grub is the larva, of a brown and white striped beetle, half an inch long, (*Saperda bivittata*,) and it remains in this grub state two or three years, coming out of the tree in a butterfly form early in June—flying in the night only, from tree to tree after its food, and finally depositing its eggs during this and the next month, in the collar of the tree.

The most effectual mode of destroying the borer, is that of killing it by thrusting a flexible wire as far as possible into its hole. Dr. Harris recommends placing a bit of camphor in the mouth of the aperture and plugging the hole with soft wood. But it is always better to prevent the attack of the borer, by placing about the trunk, early in the spring, a small mound of ashes or lime ; and where orchards have already become greatly infested with this insect, the beetles may be destroyed by thousands, in June, by building small bonfires of shavings in various parts of the orchard. The attacks of the borer on nursery trees may, in a great measure, be prevented by washing the stems in May, quite down to the ground with a solution of two pounds of potash in eight quarts of water.

The Caterpillar is a great pestilence in the apple orchard. The species which is most troublesome to our fruit trees (*Clisiocampa americana*,) is bred by a sort of lackey moth, different from that most troublesome in Europe, but its habits as a caterpillar are quite as annoying to the orchardist. The moth of our common caterpillar is a reddish brown insect, whose expanded wings measure about an inch and a half. These moths appear in great abundance in midsummer, flying only at night, and often buzzing about the candles in our houses. In laying their eggs, they choose principally the apple or cherry, and they deposit thousands of small eggs about the forks and extremities of the young branches. The next season, about the middle of May, these eggs begin to hatch, and the young caterpillars in myriads, come forth weaving their nests or tents in the fork of the branches. If they are allowed by the careless cultivator to go on and multiply, as they soon do, incredibly fast, they will in a few seasons,—sometimes in a single year,—increase to such an extent as almost to cover the branches. In this caterpillar state they live six or seven weeks, feeding most voraciously upon the leaves, and often stripping whole trees of their foliage. Their effect upon the tree at this period of the season, when the leaves are most important to the health of the tree and the growth of the fruit, is most deplorable. The crop is stunted, the health of the tree enfeebled, and, if they are allowed to remain unmolested for several seasons, they will often destroy its life or render it exceedingly decrepid and feeble.

To destroy the caterpillar various modes are adopted One of the most effectual is that practised by Mr. Pell in his orchards, which is to touch the nest with a sponge, attached to the end of a pole, and dipped in strong spirits of ammonia ; the sponge should be turned slowly round in the nests, and every insect coming in contact will be instantly killed This should be done early in the season. Or, they may be brought down and destroyed with a round brush fixed to the end of a pole, and worked about in the nests. On small trees they may be stripped off with the hand, and crushed under the foot ; and by this plain and simple mode, begun in time, with the aid of a ladder, they may in a large orchard be most effectually kept under by a few moments daily labour of a single man As they do not leave their nests until nine in the morning, the extirpator of caterpillars should always be abroad and busy before that time, and while they are all lying quietly in the nests. And let him never forget that he may do more in an hour when he commences early in the season, than he will in a whole day at a later period, when they are thoroughly scattered among the trees If they are allowed to remain unmolested, they spin their cocoons about the middle of June, and in a fortnight's time comes forth from them a fresh brood of moths—which, if they are not put an end to by bonfires, will again lay the eggs of an infinite number of caterpillars for the next spring.

The canker worm, (*Anisopteryx pometaria*, of Harris,) is in some parts of the country, one of the worst enemies of the apple, destroying also its foliage with great rapidity It is not yet common here, but in some parts of New-England it has become a serious enemy. The male is a moth with pale, ash-coloured wings with a black dot, a little more than an inch across. The female is wingless, oval, dark ash-coloured above, and gray beneath.

The canker worm usually rises out of the ground very early in the spring, chiefly in March, as soon as the ground is free from frost ; though a few also find their way up in the autumn. The females having no wings, climb slowly up the trunks of the trees, while the winged males hover about to pair with them. Very soon after this if we examine the trees we shall see the eggs of which every female lays some sixty or a hundred, glued over, closely arranged in rows and placed in the forks of branches and among the young twigs. About the twentieth of May, these eggs are hatched, and the canker worms, dusky brown, or ash-coloured with a yellow stripe, make their appearance and commence preying upon the foliage. When they are abundant they make rapid progress, and in places, where the colony is firmly established, they will sometimes strip an orchard in a few days, making it look as if a fire had passed over it. After feeding about four weeks, they descend into the ground three or four inches, where they remain in a chrysalis form, to emerge again the next season. As the female is not provided with wings, they do not spread very rapidly from one place to another.

The attacks upon the canker worm should be chiefly made upon the female, in her way from the ground up the trunk of the tree.

The common mode of protecting apple trees is to surround the trunk with a belt or bandage of canvass, four or five inches wide, which is then thickly smeared with tar. In order to prevent the tar from soon becoming dry and hard, a little coarse train oil must be well mixed with it ; and it should be watched and renewed as often as it appears necessary. This tarred belt catches and detains all the females on their upward journey. and prevents them from ascending the tree to lay their eggs. And if kept in order it will very effectually deter and destroy them. When the canker worm is abundant, it is necessary to apply the tarred bandage in October, and let it remain till the last of May, but usually it will be sufficient to use it in the spring It is probable that a mixture of coal tar and common tar would be the best application ; as it is more offensive and will not so easily dry and become useless, by exposure to the air and sun. Some persons apply the tar directly to the stems of the tree, but this has a very injurious effect upon the trunk. Old India rubber, melted in an iron vessel over a very hot fire, forms a very adhesive fluid which is not affected by exposure to the weather, and is considered, by those who have made use of it, the best substance for smearing the bandages, as being a more effectual barrier, and seldom or never requiring renewal.

Mr. Jonathan Dennis, jr. of Portsmouth, Rhode Island, has invented and patented a circular leaden trough, which surrounds the trunk of the tree, and is filled with oil, and stops effectually the ascent of the canker worm. There appear, however, to be two objections to this trough, as it is frequently used ; one, the escape of the oil if not carefully used, which injures the tree ; and the other, the injurious effect of nailing the troughs to the bark or trunk. They should be supported by wedges of wood driven in between the trough and the trunk, and the spaces completely filled up with liquid clay put on with a brush. The insects must be taken out and the oil renewed, from time to time. For districts where the canker worm greatly abounds, this leaden trough is probably the most permanent and effectual remedy yet employed.

Experiments made by the Hon. John Lowell, and Professor Peck, of Massachusetts, lead to a belief that if the ground, under

trees which suffer from this insect, is dug and well pulverized to
the depth of five inches in October, and a good top dressing of
lime applied as far as the branches extend, the canker worm
will there be almost entirely destroyed.   The elm, and linden
trees in many places, suffer equally with the apple, from the attacks of the canker worm.

The Bark-louse, a dull white oval scale-like insect, about a
tenth of an inch long, (a species of *coccus,*) which sometimes
appears in great numbers on the stems of young apple and pear
trees, and stunts their growth, may be destroyed by a wash of
soft soap and water, or the potash solution.   The best time to
apply these is in the month of June, when the insects are
young.

The Woolly aphis (aphis langinera,) or American blight* is a
dreadful enemy of the apple abroad, but is fortunately, very
rarely seen as yet, in the United States.   It makes its appearance in the form of a minute white down, in the crotches and
crevices of the branches, which is composed of a great number
of very minute woolly lice, that if allowed, will increase with
fearful rapidity, and produce a sickly and diseased state of the
whole tree.   Fortunately, this insect is too easily destroyed.   "This
is effected by washing the parts with diluted sulphuric acid ;
which is formed by mixing ¾ oz. by measure, of the sulphuric
acid of the shops, with 7½ oz. of water.   It should be rubbed
into the parts affected, by means of a piece of rag tied to a stick,
the operator taking care not to let it touch his clothes.   After
the bark of a tree has been washed with this mixture, the first
shower will re-dissolve it, and convey it into the most minute
crevice, so as effectually to destroy all insects that may have
escaped."—(*Loudon's Magazine IX.* p. 336)

The Apple worm (or Codling moth, *Carpocapsa pomonana,* of
European writers,) is the insect, introduced with the apple tree
from Europe, which appears in the early worm-eaten apples
and pears, in the form of a reddish white grub, and causes the
fruit to fall prematurely from the tree.   The perfect insect is a
small moth, the fore-wings gray, with a large round brown spot
on the hinder margin.   These moths appear in the greatest
numbers in the warm evenings of the 1st of June, and lay their
eggs in the eye or blossom-end of the young fruit, especially of
the early kinds of apples and pears.   In a short time, these eggs
hatch, and the grub burrows its way till it reaches the core ;
the fruit then ripens prematurely, and drops to the ground.
Here the worm leaves the fruit and creeps into the crevices of
the bark and hollow of the tree, and spins its cocoon, which

* It is not a little singular that this insect which is not indigenous to this country, and is never seen here except where introduced with imported trees, should
be called in England the *American* blight.   It is the most inveterate enemy of the
apple in the north of France and Germany.

usually remains there till the ensuing spring, when the young moth again emerges from it. The readiest way of destroying them, when it can be done conveniently, is to allow swine and poultry to run at large in the orchards when the premature fruit is falling ; or otherwise, the fruit may be picked up daily and placed where the worms will be killed. It is said that if an old cloth is placed in the crotch of the tree about the time the fruit begins to drop, the apple worm will make it a retiring place, and thousands may be caught and killed from time to time. As the cocoons are deposited chiefly under the old loose bark, the thorough cultivator will take care, by keeping the trunks of his trees smooth, to afford them little harbour ; and by scraping and washing the trunks early in the spring, to destroy such as may have already taken up their quarters there.

When the fruit of orchards is much liable to the attacks of this insect we cannot too much insist on the efficacy of small bonfires lighted in the evening, by which myriads of this and all other moths may be destroyed, before they have time to deposit their eggs and cause worm-eaten fruit.

The Blight which occasionally kills suddenly the ends of the limbs of the apple and the quince, appears to be caused by an insect similar to that which produces the fire blight of the pear, and must be treated in the same way as directed for that tree.

GATHERING AND KEEPING THE FRUIT. In order to secure soundness and preservation, it is indispensably necessary that the fruit should be gathered by hand. For winter fruit the gathering is delayed as long as possible, avoiding severe frosts, and the most successful practice with our extensive orchardists is to place the good fruit directly, in a careful manner, in new, tight flour barrels as soon as gathered from the tree. These barrels should be gently shaken while filling, and the head closely pressed in ; they are then placed in a cool shady expo-sure under a shed open to the air, or on the north side of a building, protected by covering of boards over the top, where they remain for a fortnight, or until the cold becomes too severe, when they are carefully transferred to a cool, dry cellar, in which air can be admitted occasionally in brisk weather.

A cellar, for this purpose, should be dug in dry, gravelly, or sandy soil, with, if possible, a slope to the north ; or, at any rate, with openings on the north side for the admission of air very rarely in weather not excessively cold. Here the barrels should be placed on tiers on *their sides*, and the cellar should be kept as dark as possible. In such a cellar, one of the largest apple growers in Dutchess county is able to keep the Greening apple, which, in the fruit room, usually decays in January, until the 1st of April, in the freshest and finest condition. Some per-sons place a layer of clean rye straw between every layer of apples, when packing them in the barrels.

Apples are frequently kept by farmers in pits or ridges in the ground, covered with straw and a layer of earth, in the same manner as potatoes, but it is an inferior method, and the fruit very speedily decays when opened to the air. The English apple growers lay their fruit in heaps, in cool dry cellars, and cover them with straw.

When apples are exported, each fruit in the barrel should be wrapped in clean coarse paper, and the barrels should be placed in a dry, airy place, between decks.

CIDER. To make the finest cider, apples should be chosen which are especially suited to this purpose. The fruit should be gathered about the first of November, and coarse cloths or straw should be laid under the tree to secure them against bruising when they are shaken from the tree. If the weather is fine the fruit is allowed to lie in heaps in the open air, or in airy sheds or lofts for some time, till it is thoroughly ripened. All immature and rotten fruit should then be rejected, and the remainder ground in the mill as nearly as possible to an uniform mass. This pulp should now remain in the vat from 24 to 48 hours, or even longer if the weather is cool, in order to heighten the colour and increase the saccharine principle. It is then put into the press (without wetting the straw,) from whence the liquor is strained through hair cloth or sieves, into perfectly clean, sweet, sound casks. The casks, with the bung out, are then placed in a cool cellar, or in a sheltered place in the open air. Here the fermentation commences, and as the pomace and froth work out of the bung-hole, the casks must be filled up every day with some of the same pressing, kept in a cask for this purpose. In two or three weeks this rising will cease, when the first fermentation is over, and the bung should, at first, be put in loosely—then, in a day or two, driven in tight—leaving a small vent hole near it, which may also be stopped in a few days after. If the casks are in a cool airy cellar, the fermentation will cease in a day or two, and this state may be known by the liquor becoming clear and bright, by the cessation of the discharge of fixed air, and by the thick crust which has collected on the surface. The clear cider should now be drawn off and placed in a clean cask. If the cider, which must be carefully watched in this state to prevent the fermentation going too far, remains quiet, it may be allowed to stand till spring, and the addition at first of about a gill of finely powdered charcoal to a barrel will secure this end; but if a scum collects on the surface, and the fermentation seems inclined to proceed further, it must be immediately racked again. The vent-spile may now be driven tight but examined occasionally. In the beginning of March a final racking should take place, when, should the cider not be perfectly fine, about three fourths of an ounce of Isinglass should be dissolved in the cider and poured in each barrel, which will render it perfectly clear. It may be bottled now, or any period before the blossoming of the apple or afterwards, late in May. When bottling, fill the bottles within an inch of the bottom of the cork, and allow the bottles to stand an hour before the corks are driven in. They should then be sealed, and kept in a cool cellar, with clean dry sand up to their necks; or laid on their sides in boxes or bins, with the same between each layer.

VARIETIES. The varieties of the apple, at the present time, are very numerous. The garden of the Horticultural Society, of London, which contains the most complete collection of fruit in the world, enumerates now about 900 varieties, and nearly 1500 have been tested there. Of these, the larger proportion are of course inferiour, but it is only by comparison in such an experimental garden that the value of the different varieties, for a certain climate, can be fully ascertained.

The European apples generally, are in this climate, inferiour to our first rate native sorts, though many of them are of high merit also with us. The great natural centre of the apple culture in America, is between Massachusetts bay and the Delaware river, where the Newtown pippin, the Spitzemberg, the Swaar, the Baldwin, and the yellow Belle Fleur, have originated, and are grown in the greatest perfection. The apples raised on the very fertile bottoms of the western states are very large and beautiful, but as yet, owing to the excessive luxuriance of growth, are far inferiour in flavour to those of the same quality, raised on the strong, gravelly or sandy loams of this section of the country. New varieties of apples are constantly springing up in this country from the seed, in favourable soils; and these, when of superiour quality, may, as a general rule, be considered much more valuable for orchard culture than foreign sorts, on account of their greater productiveness and longevity. Indeed, every state has some fine apples, peculiar to it, and it is, therefore, impossible in the present state of pomology in this country, to give any thing like a complete list of the finest apples of the United States. To do this, will require time, and an extended and careful examination of their relative merits collected in one garden. The following descriptions comprise all the finest American and foreign varieties yet known in our gardens.

In the ensuing pages, apples are described as regards *form* as follows; *round*, or *roundish*, when the height and the diameter are nearly equal; *flat*, or *oblate*, when the height is much less; *oblong*, when the height is considerably more than the diameter; *ovate*, (egg-shaped,) when the blossom-end is narrowed and rounded; *conical*, when the fruit is oblong and somewhat conical on its sides. *Pearmain-shaped* is a short or flattened cone; and *Calville-shaped* signifies a ribbed or furrowed surface.

APPLES.*

Class 1. *Summer Apples.*

1. AMERICAN SUMMER PEARMAIN. § Thomp.

Early Summer Pearmain. *Coxe.*

A rich, high-flavoured fruit, much esteemed in New-Jersey, where it is most known It appears to be quite different from the Summer Pearmain, (of the English,) and is probably a seed-ling raised from it It ripens gradually from the tenth of August to the last of September.

Fruit of medium size, oblong, widest at the crown, and taper-ing slightly to the eye. Skin, red spotted with yellow in the shade, but streaked with livelier red and yellow on the sunny side. Stalk three fourths of an inch long, and pretty deeply in-serted. Eye deeply sunk. Flesh yellow, remarkably tender, with a rich and pleasant flavour, and often bursts in falling from the tree. This is a valuable apple for all purposes, and it thrives admirably on sandy soils. In the nursery the tree grows slowly.

2. BOROVITSKY. Thomp. Lind.

A good early Russian apple of the middle size, which ripens here the last of July. Form roundish, a little angular. Stalk, an inch long, planted rather deeply. Skin, pale green, with a semi-transparent appearance, faintly striped on the sunny side with light and dark red. · Calyx in a large basin. Flesh, white, pretty firm, and juicy, with an agreeable sub-acid flavour.

3. BENONI. Man. Ken.

This excellent early apple is a native of Dedham, Mass. The fruit is of medium size, nearly round. Skin, deep red. Flesh, yellow, tender, and of an agreeable rich, sub-acid flavour. Ripens during the whole month of August, and is a good and regular bearer.

* In describing apples, we shall designate the size by comparison, as follows: small, as the English Golden pippin; medium size, as the Newtown pippin, large, as the Yellow Bellflower and Fall pippin—as we consider this reference to a stan-dard, generally known, better than an exact description by measure owing to the variation in different soils and seasons

The blossom-end, apex or crown of the fruit, is called the *eye*; but we shall, for the sake of precision, call the remains of the blossom still found there the *calyx* and the hollow in which it is placed the *basin*.

§ This mark denotes varieties particularly recommended by the author.

4. Cole. Thomp. Lind. Ron.

Scarlet Perfume.

A variety from England of second quality, but admired for its beauty of appearance.

Fruit large, roundish, somewhat flattened and slightly angular. Skin nearly covered with deep crimson on a yellowish ground, or sometimes entirely red, with a little russet. Stalk long, woolly, planted in a cavity which is sometimes nearly closed up. Calyx large, in a broad basin. Flesh white, rather firm, juicy, with a somewhat rich and agreeable flavour. August.

5. Devonshire Quarrenden. Thom. P. Mag. Fors.

Red Quarrenden. *Lind.*
Sack Apple.

A handsome English dessert fruit. The editor of the Pomological Magazine says, "there is no better autumn dessert apple;" but after giving it a trial for several years by the side of the *Williams' Favourite*, we consider the latter greatly superiour in flavour, and equally beautiful. Fruit scarcely of medium size, roundish, flattened, and slightly narrowed at the eye. Stalk short, deeply planted. Calyx with long segments, scarcely sunk in a very shallow plaited basin. Skin rich deep crimson, with lighter crimson, and occasionally a spot of green on the shaded side, sprinkled with numerous green dots. Flesh nearly white, crisp, juicy, with a pleasant sub-acid flavour. Ripe during all August and September.

6. Drap d'Or. § Coxe. Thomp. Ron.

Vrai Drap d'Or. *O. Duh.*
Early Summer pippin, *of some New-York gardens.*
Bay Apple } *ac. to*
Bonne de Mai } *Thomp.*

This large, handsome, and excellent summer apple is highly deserving general cultivation. It is better (though incorrectly known on the Hudson as the Summer Pippin, but it is very distinct from the apple known by that name in New-Jersey, which is the Holland pippin. It is also a very different fruit from the Drap d'Or of Lindley, and of Noisette, and most French authors, which is quite a small apple; but it is the *Vrai Drap d'Or* of the old Duhamel, pl. xii. Fig. 4.

Fruit large, roundish, sometimes a little oblong, narrowing slightly to the eye. Skin smooth, yellow or dead gold colour, with distinct small brown dots, or specks. Stalk short, moderately sunk. Calyx set in a shallowish basin, which is rather plaited or irregular. Flesh crisp, juicy, and of a pleasant, sprightly, mild flavour, agreeable for the dessert or for cooking. [This is the Summer Pippin of the previous catalogues of the nurseries here.] August to October. The tree grows vigorously, and bears well, and the wood is smooth and dark brown.

7. EARLY HARVEST. § Thomp. Man

Prince's Harvest, or Early French Reinette, *of Coxe.*
July Pippin. *Floy.*
Yellow Harvest.
Large White Juneating.
Tart Bough.
Early French Reinnette.

An American apple; and taking into account its beauty, its excellent qualities for the dessert and for cooking, and its productiveness, we think it the finest early apple yet known. It begins to ripen about the first of July, and continues in use all that month. The smallest collection of apples should comprise

Fig. 26. *Early Harvest.*

this and the Red Astrachan. Form round, above medium size, rarely a little flattened. Skin very smooth, with a few faint white dots, bright straw colour when fully ripe. *Stalk* half to three fourths of an inch long, rather slender, inserted in a hollow of moderate depth. *Calyx* set in a shallow basin. *Flesh* very white, tender and juicy, crisp, with a rich, sprightly, sub-acid flavour. The young trees of moderate vigour, with scarcely diverging shoots. Manning errs by following Coxe in calling this a flat apple.

8. EARLY RED MARGARET. § Thomp. Lind.

Red Juneating.
Margaret, or Striped Juneating. *Ronalds.*
Early Red Juneating.
Eve Apple of *the Irish.*
Striped Juneating.
Margaretha Apfel, of *the Germans.*

An excellent early apple, ripening about the middle of July, or directly after the Early Harvest. The tree while young is rather slender with upright woolly shoots. It is a moderate bearer.

Fruit below medium size, roundish-ovate, tapering towards the eye. Skin greenish yellow, pretty well covered by stripes of dark red. Stalk short and thick. Calyx closed, and placed in a very shallow plaited basin. Flesh white, sub-acid, and when freshly gathered from the tree, of a rich agreeable flavour.

Fig. 27. *Early Red Margaret.*

This is distinct from the Margaret Apple, of Miller, the Red Juneating of some of our gardens, which resembles it, but is round, with a short slender stalk, and dull yellow skin striped with orange red on one side, the fruit fragrant and the leaves very downy.

9. EARLY STRAWBERRY APPLE. (§)

American Red Juneating?
Red Juneating, *erroneously, of some American gardens.*

A beautiful variety which is said to have originated in the neighbourhood of New-York, and appears in the markets there from July till September. Its sprightly flavour, agreeable perfume, and fine appearance, place it among the very finest sum-

7

mer apples. It is quite distinct from the Early Red Margaret, which has no fragrance, and a short stem.

Fruit roundish, narrowing towards the eye. Skin smooth and fair, finely striped and stained with bright and dark red, on a yellowish white ground. Stalk an inch and a half long, rather slender and uneven, inserted in a deep cavity. Calyx rather small, in a shallow, narrow basin. Flesh white, slightly tinged with red next the skin, tender, sub-acid, and very sprightly and brisk in flavour, with an agreeable aroma.

Fig. 28. *Early Strawberry.*

10. Irish Peach Apple. Thomp. Lind. P. Mag.

Early Crofton. *Ronalds.*

Fruit of medium size, round or a little flattened, and obtusely angular. Calyx pretty large and spreading, in a rather narrow basin. Stalk short, in a cavity of moderate depth. Skin yellowish green, with small dots in the shade, washed and streaked with brownish red in the sun. Flesh white, tender, juicy, and pretty well flavoured. A pleasing fruit, but does not rank so high here as in England.

11. Large Yellow Bough. § Thomp.

Early Sweet Bough. *Kenrick.*
Sweet Harvest.
Bough. *Coxe. Floy.*

A native apple, ripening in harvest time, and one of the first quality, only second as a dessert fruit to the Early Harvest. It is not so much esteemed for the kitchen as the latter, as it is too sweet for pies and sauce, but it is generally much admired for the table, and is worthy of a place in every collection.

Fruit above the middle size, an oblong-ovate in form. Skin smooth, pale, greenish yellow. Stalk rather long, and the eye narrow and deep. Flesh white, very tender and crisp when fully ripe, and with a rich sweet sprightly flavour. Ripens from the middle of July to the tenth of August. Tree moderately vigorous, bears abundantly, and forms a round head.

12. LYMAN'S LARGE SUMMER.

Large Yellow Summer. *Ken.*

A large and handsome American fruit, introduced to notice by Mr. S. Lyman, of Manchester, Conn. The bearing trees are easily recognized by their long and drooping branches, which are almost wholly without fruit spurs, but bear in clusters at their extremities. They bear poorly until the tree attains considerable size, when it yields excellent crops. Fruit quite large, roundish, flattened at the ends: skin smooth, pale yellow. Flesh yellow, tender, sub-acid, rich, and high flavoured, and excellent either for the table or for cooking. Last of August.

13. OSLIN. Thomp. Lind.

Arbroath Pippin. *Forsyth.*

An excellent Scotch apple, ripening early in August. Form roundish, below medium size, a little flattened. Skin rather tough, clear lemon yellow when quite ripe, mingled with a little bright green, and sprinkled with a few grayish green dots. Stalk short and thick, set in a rather shallow depression. Calyx in a shallow basin, a little plaited, with prominent segments. Flesh yellowish, firm, crisp, juicy, with a spicy aromatic flavour. The wood is strong, and grows pretty freely from cuttings.

14. RED ASTRACHAN. § Thomp. Lind.

A fruit of extraordinary beauty, first imported into England with the White Astrachan, from Sweden, in 1816. It bears abundantly with us, and its singular richness of colour is heightened by an exquisite bloom on the surface of the fruit, like that of a plum. It is one of the handsomest dessert fruits, and its quality is good, but if not taken from the tree as soon as ripe, it is liable to become mealy. Ripens from the last of July to the middle of August.

Fruit pretty large, rather above the middle size, and very smooth and fair, roundish, a little narrowed towards the eye. Skin almost entirely covered with deep crimson, with sometimes a little greenish yellow in the shade, and occasionally a little russet near the stalk, and covered with a pale white bloom. Stalk rather short and deeply inserted. Calyx set in a slight

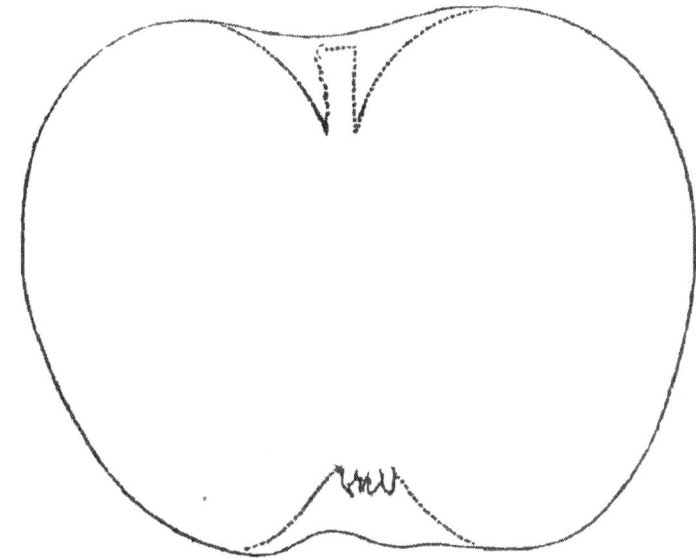

Fig. 29.   *Red Astrachan.*

basin, which is sometimes a little irregular.   Flesh quite white, crisp, moderately juicy, with an agreeable, rich, acid flavour.

15. Sine-qua-non.

A native of Long Island, named by the late Wm. Prince. Fruit roundish - ovate, about medium size. Skin smooth, pale greenish yellow. Stalk slender. Flesh white, very tender, juicy, and of a delicate and very sprightly flavour. The young trees are rather slow and crooked in growth. August.

16. Sugar Loaf Pippin.   Thomp. Lind. P. Mag.

Hutching's Seedling.

A foreign sort, which is ranked among first rate sorts by Thompson, but from specimens of two seasons produced here, it does not seem likely to take this rank with us.   Fruit of medium size, oblong or conical, smooth, clear pale yellow, becoming nearly white on one side when fully ripe. Stalk nearly an inch long, deeply set in a regular cavity. Calyx sunk in a pretty deep basin. Flesh white, firm, very slightly acid, and moderately juicy. According to Lindley it has in England " a most agreeable lively flavour."   Ripens here the latter part of July, and is very showy on the tree.

17. SUMMER ROSE. Thomp. Coxe.

Woolman's Harvest.

A very pretty and very excellent apple, highly esteemed as a dessert fruit.

Fruit scarcely of medium size, roundish. Skin smooth, r ch waxen yellow, streaked and blotched with a little red on the sunny side. Stalk rather short, and slender. Calyx closed, set in an even basin. Flesh tender, abounding with sprightly juice. Ripens early in August.

18. SUMMER QUEEN. Coxe.

A popular midsummer apple for the dessert and kitchen. The fruit is large and broad at the crown, tapering towards the eye. The stalk is rather long, and is planted in a pretty deep cavity, sometimes partially closed. Calyx but little sunk in a narrow plaited basin. Skin fine deep yellow in its ground, though well striped and clouded with red. Flesh aromatic, yellow, rich and of good flavour. This variety forms a large tree with somewhat pendant boughs, and the fruit is in perfection by the tenth of August.

19. SUMMER GOLDEN PIPPIN. Thomp. Lind. P. Mag.

A nice little English dessert apple, but inferiour to many of our own. Fruit small, ovate, flattened at the eye. Stalk short and calyx set in a wide shallow basin. Skin shining bright yellow, with a little orange next the sun. Flesh yellow, firm, crisp and rich. Ripens in August.

20. SOPS OF WINE. § Lind. Ron.

Sops in Wine. *Ray.* (1688.)
Rode Wyn Appel. *Knoop.*
Sapson. *Kenrick.*

A charming little apple for the dessert, which the amateur's garden should always contain. Its flavour is spr'..dy, though not first rate, and its colour is very handsome. Its name probably comes from the red stain in its flesh. Its branches have a spreading habit, and bear plentifully; and the fruit, in our garden, ripens gradually from the first of August to October. Fruit small, from an inch and a half to two and a half in diameter, globular, narrowing to the eye. Skin smooth, crimson in the shade, stained and striped with purplish crimson in the sun, and covered with a delicate white bloom. Stalk slender, three fourths of an inch long. Calyx spreading, in a shallow basin. Flesh white, with stains of a pinkish hue, firm, crisp, juicy, and of a pleasant sub-acid flavour.

21. TETOFSKY. Thomp.

The Tetofsky is a Russian summer apple newly introduced, which promises well. Fruit of medium size, roundish oblong, sometimes nearly round. Skin smooth, with a yellow ground handsomely striped with red, and, like most apples of that country, covered with a whitish bloom, under which is a shining skin. The flesh is white and juicy with a sprightly and agreeable flavour. August.

22. WHITE JUNEATING. Ray. Thomp. Lind.

Owen's Golden Beauty, *ac. Thomp.*
Juneating. *Coxe.*

This is an old variety mentioned by Evelyn in 1660, and described by Ray in 1688, and is a very tolerable little apple, ripening among the very earliest, during the last of June and the first of July, and deserves a place in a large collection chiefly on that account and its excellent bearing quality. It is very distinct from the Early Harvest, sometimes called by this name. Fruit small, round, a little flattened. Calyx closed in a wrinkled basin, moderately sunk. Stalk rather long and slender, three fourths to an inch in length, slightly inserted in a shallow

Fig. 30. *White Juneating.*

depression. Skin smooth, pale green, at first light yellow, with sometimes a faint blush on the sunny side. Flesh crisp, and of pleasant flavour, but soon becomes dry. Tree straight and forms an upright head.

23. WHITE ASTRACHAN. Thomp. Lind. P. Mag.

Pyrus Astracanica. *De Candolle,* ⎫
Transparent de Moscovie, ⎬ *of the French gardens.*
Glace de Zélande, ⎭

A nearly white, semi-transparent, Russian apple, which bears freely and ripens about the tenth of August; but in this country is of little or no value, as it nearly always grows mealy and water cored as soon as ripe. Fruit of medium size, roundish, inclining to conical, and a little ribbed at the eye. Skin very smooth, nearly white, with a few faint streaks of red on one side, and covered with a white bloom. Stalk thick and short; calyx set in a small basin. Flesh quite white, partially transparent, tender and of delicate flavour, but rather dry.

24. WILLIAMS'S FAVOURITE. § Man. Ken.

A large and handsome dessert apple, worthy of a place in every garden. It originated at Roxbury, near Boston, bears abundantly, and ripens from the last of July to the first of September.

Fruit of medium size, oblong, and a little one-sided. Stalk an inch long, slender, slightly sunk. Calyx closed, in a narrow angular basin. Skin very smooth of a light red ground, but nearly covered with a fine dark red. Flesh yellowish-white, and of a very mild and agreeable flavour.

Class II. Autumn Apples.

25. ALEXANDER. § Thomp.

Emperor Alexander. *Lind. Ron.*
Russian Emperor.
Aporta.

This is a very magnificent Russian sort, which thrives well in our gardens. The tree is no less striking in the spring when covered with its very large blossoms, than in autumn when loaded with its superb fruit. It is, properly, a cooking apple.

Fruit very large, frequently measuring five inches in diameter, and weighing nearly a pound, regularly formed, generally conical or cordate, tapering from the base to the eye. Skin greenish yellow, faintly streaked with red on the shaded side, but orange, brilliantly streaked and marked with bright red in the sun. Calyx large, set in a deep basin. Stalk rather slender, three fourths of an inch long, planted in a deep cavity. Flesh yellowish white, crisp, tender and juicy, with a rather pleasant flavour. A moderate bearer. October to December.

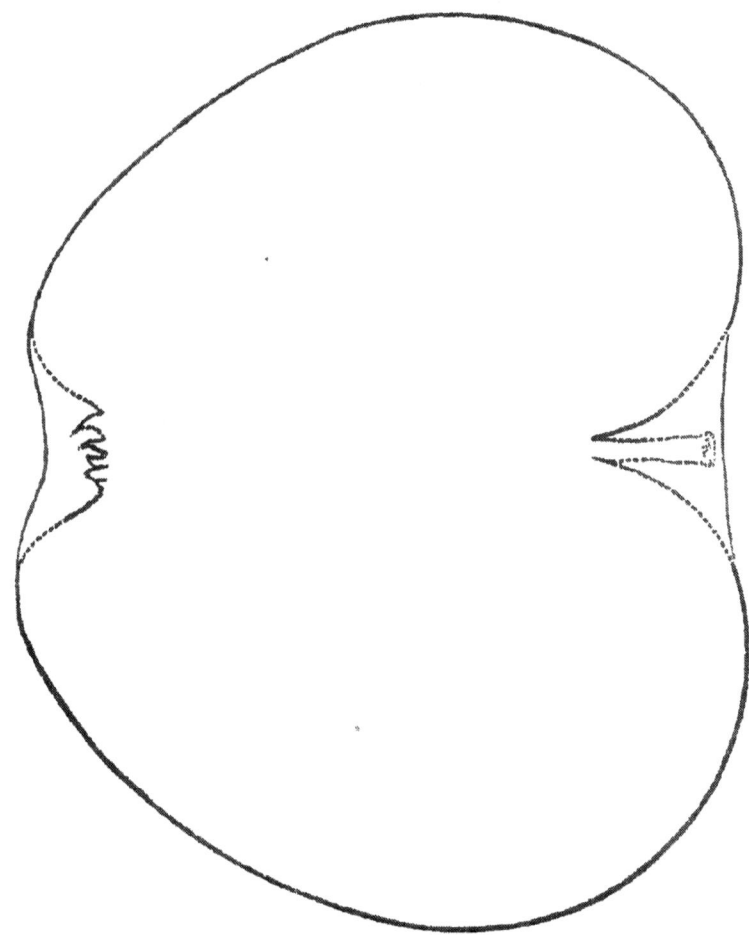

Fig. 31. *Alexander.*

26. Autumn Pearmain. Thomp.

Summer Pearmain. *Lind. Miller, P. Mag.*
Winter Pearmain, *of the Middle States.*
Parmain d'Eté. *Knoop.*

A slow growing tree, but producing a good, high-flavoured
dessert fruit. Fruit of medium size, oblong, narrowing gradually towards the eye. Skin brownish yellow, mixed with green
on the shaded side, but next the sun, reddish, blended with yellow, streaked with deeper red, and sprinkled with numerous
small brown specks. Stalk short, obliquely planted under a
fleshy lip. Calyx set in a broad shallow basin, which is sometimes scarcely at all sunk, and obscurely plaited. Flesh pale
yellow, crisp, firm, a little dry, but rich and high flavoured.

Branches slender. This most excellent old dessert fruit is the "Winter Pearmain" of most old American orchards, and is a great favourite with many amateurs. October and November. and keeps till March.

27. BLENHEIM PIPPIN. Thomp. Lind.

Blenheim Orange.
Woodstock Pippin.

A large and showy English apple, admirable for baking, but which is not so highly esteemed for the table here, as abroad. The trees make strong and vigorous shoots.

Fruit very large, roundish, three inches in diameter at the base. Skin yellowish, becoming deep orange, stained on the sunny side with dull and dark red stripes. Calyx set in a large hollow basin. Flesh yellow, breaking, very sweet, and of tolerable flavour. October to December.

28. BEAUTY OF KENT. Thomp. Lind. Ron.

The Beauty of Kent is, in this climate, one of the most magnificent of all apples, frequently measuring sixteen or eighteen inches in circumference. The flavour is of second quality, but as a kitchen fruit, it is among the finest. The tree grows very strong and upright.

Fruit very large, roundish, but flat at the base, and narrowing distinctly to the eye, where it is slightly ribbed. Skin smooth, greenish-yellow, marked with large, broken stripes of purplish red. Stalk short, slender, deeply planted in a round, shallow cavity. Calyx small, set in a narrow basin. Flesh juicy, crisp, tender, with a simple sub-acid flavour. October and November.

29. BEAUTY OF THE WEST. Ken.

A large, showy, sweet apple, of fair flavour.

Fruit large, round and regularly shaped. Skin smooth, light greenish-yellow, marked with small stripes of red. Stalk short, set in a round cavity. Flesh tender, juicy, sweet, and pleasant. A fall fruit, but may be kept for some time.

30. CORNISH AROMATIC. Thomp. Lind.

A rich flavoured English apple. The quality is excellent, but the fruit not very fair with us.

Fruit of medium size, roundish and angular. Skin rich red, much marked with russet yellow dots, on a pale russet ground. Stalk short, set in a deep, narrow cavity. Calyx small, in a narrow basin. Flesh yellow, with a rich aromatic sub-acid flavour. October to December.

31. CATLINE.   Coxe. Thomp.

Gregson Apple.

We have not been able to procure this variety; which we believe is a native of Maryland, and we therefore insert here Mr.
Coxe's description.   The Catline is an apple rather below the
middling size.   It is a great bearer—the form is flat, the stalk
short and thick, the skin smooth, and of a beautiful yellow, with
a clear and brilliant red towards the sun, with numerous streaks
and many dark spots scattered on the surface.   The flesh is a
pale yellow, tender, rich, juicy and sweet; as an eating apple
in October, November and December, it is particularly fine.
The tree is small, the form regular, and round in the head; the
shoots straight and delicate; the foliage of a lively green—it is
very productive, and in six or seven years after transplanting, it
bears abundantly, when well cultivated.

32. DUTCHESS OF OLDENBURGH.   Thomp. Ron.

A handsome Russian fruit of good quality.   Fruit medium
size, regularly formed, roundish.   Skin smooth, finely washed
and streaked with red on a golden or yellow ground.   Calyx
pretty large and nearly closed, set in a wide even hollow.   There
is a faint blue bloom on this fruit.   The flesh is rich and juicy,
with an excellent flavour.   Ripens early in September.

33. DOWNTON PIPPIN.   Thomp. Lind.

Elton Pippin,   ⎱ of some English gardens
Knight's Golden Pippin,   ⎰
Downton Golden Pippin.   Ken.

A rather early variety of the English Golden Pippin, raised
by Mr. Knight of Downton Castle.   It is a beautiful, small dessert fruit, and will please those who like the rich, sharp, acid
flavour of the Golden Pippin.

Fruit a little larger than the Golden Pippin, about two and a
quarter inches in diameter, roundish, flat at the ends.   Calyx
set in a wide, but very shallow basin.   Stalk short, not deeply
inserted.   Skin smooth, yellow, dotted with small obscure specks.

Flesh yellowish, crisp, with a brisk, rich, tart flavour.   The
tree grows more vigorously and bears more abundantly than its
parent, the old Golden Pippin.   It is also considered a fine cider
apple.   October and November.

34. DYER, OR POMME ROYALE. Ken.

Smithfield Spice.

A popular New-England dessert apple, very sprightly, tender, and excellent. It is supposed to be of French origin, and to have been brought to Rhode Island more than a hundred years ago. It was re-named Dyer by the Mass. Hort. Society, who supposed it to be a seedling of Mr. Dyer, of R. I., but the old and familiar name of *Pomme Royale* should be preferred.

Fruit of medium size, roundish, pretty regularly formed. Skin smooth, pale greenish yellow, with a faint blush and a few dark specks on one side. Stalk about half an inch long, set in a smooth, round cavity. Calyx closed, basin plaited, moderately deep. Core round, hollow. Flesh white, very tender and juicy; flavour very mild and agreeable—slightly sub-acid. Sept., Oct.

35. DUTCH CODLIN. Thomp. Lind. Ron.

Chalmer's Large.

A very large kitchen apple, valued only for cooking, from August to September. Fruit of the largest size, irregularly roundish, or rather oblong, strongly marked by ribs extending from the base to the eye. Calyx set in a narrow, deep-furrowed basin. Stalk short and thick. Skin pale yellow, becoming orange yellow on the sunny side. Flesh white, sub-acid, and moderately juicy. Inferiour to the Holland Pippin or the Drap d'Or. The tree makes very strong shoots.

36. FLOWER OF KENT. Thomp. Lind. Ron.

A large and handsome English apple, chiefly valued for baking and kitchen use. Fruit quite large, roundish, a little ribbed on its sides, often considerably flattened, and rather broadest at the base. Skin tawny yellow, washed with dull red, with occasionally, a few stripes of brighter red. Calyx rather small, but set in a large basin, rather furrowed or irregular. Stalk nearly an inch long, not very deeply inserted. Flesh greenish yellow, abounding with a lively sub-acid juice. October to January.

37. FRANKLIN'S GOLDEN PIPPIN. Thomp. Lind. Man.

Sudlow's Fall Pippin.

This should be an American variety, named after Dr. Franklin, as it appears, by the Horticultural Transactions, to have been taken from the United States to England, in 1806; but it is, we believe, only known to nurserymen here, by importation back again. It is an excellent dessert fruit, larger than the common English Golden Pippin, ripening in October. Fruit of medium size, oval, very regular in shape, rather broadest at the base. Eye sunk in an even hollow. Stalk short, slender, deeply planted. Skin deep yellow, freck.ed with numerous dark spots Flesh pale yellow, crisp, tender, with a fine rich aromatic flavour. The tree grows freely, and forms an upright head.

38. FALL HARVEY. § Man. Ken.

A fine large Fall fruit from Essex co., Mass., very highly esteemed in that neighbourhood. We do not think it comparable to the Fall pippin, which it a little resembles.

Fruit large, a little flattened, obscurely ribbed or irregular about the stalk, which is rather slender, an inch long, set in a wide, deep cavity. Calyx closed, small, in a rather shallow basin. Skin pale straw yellow, with a few scattered dots. Flesh white, juicy, crisp, with a rich, good flavour. October and November.

39. FALL PIPPIN. § Coxe. Floy.

The Fall Pippin is, we think, decidedly an American variety, Thompson and Lindley to the contrary, notwithstanding. It is, very probably, a seedling raised in this country, from the *White Spanish Reinette*, or the Holland pippin, both of which it so much resembles, and from which it, in fact, differs most strongly in the season of maturity. The Fall Pippin is a noble fruit, and is considered the first of Autumn apples in the middle states, where its beauty, large size, and its delicious flavour for the table or for cooking, render it very popular.

Fruit very large, roundish, generally a little flattened, pretty regular, sometimes with obscure ribs at the eye. Stalk rather long, three-fourths of an inch, projecting considerably beyond the fruit, (which distinguishes it from the Holland Pippin,) set in a rather small, shallow, round cavity. Calyx not very large, rather deeply sunk in a round, narrow cavity. Skin smooth, yellowish-green, becoming a fine yellow, with often a tinge of brownish blush, on one side, and with a few scattered dots. Flesh white, very tender and mellow with a rich, aromatic flavour. October to December.

There are several spurious sorts—the true one is always rather flattened, with a projecting stalk. (See Holland Pippin.)

40. GOLDEN SWEET.

Orange Sweeting, or ⎱ *Kenrick.*
Golden Sweet. ⎰

A celebrated Connecticut fruit sent us by Mr. Lyman, of that state. Fruit above the medium size, roundish, scarcely flattened, fair, and well formed. Skin, when fully ripe, pale yellow or straw colour. Stalk about an inch long, slender at its junction with the fruit. Calyx closed, and set in a basin of moderate depth. Flesh tender, sweet, rich and excellent. The tree is a pretty free grower, and bears large crops. This we think will prove a valuable sort. Ripe in August and September.

41. GRAVENSTEIN. § Thomp. Lind.

Grave Slije.

A superb looking German apple, which originated at Graven-stein, in Holstein, and is thought one of the finest apples of the north of Europe. It fully sustains its reputation here, and is, unquestionably, a fruit of first rate quality. Fruit large, rather flattened, and a little one sided or angular, broadest at the base.

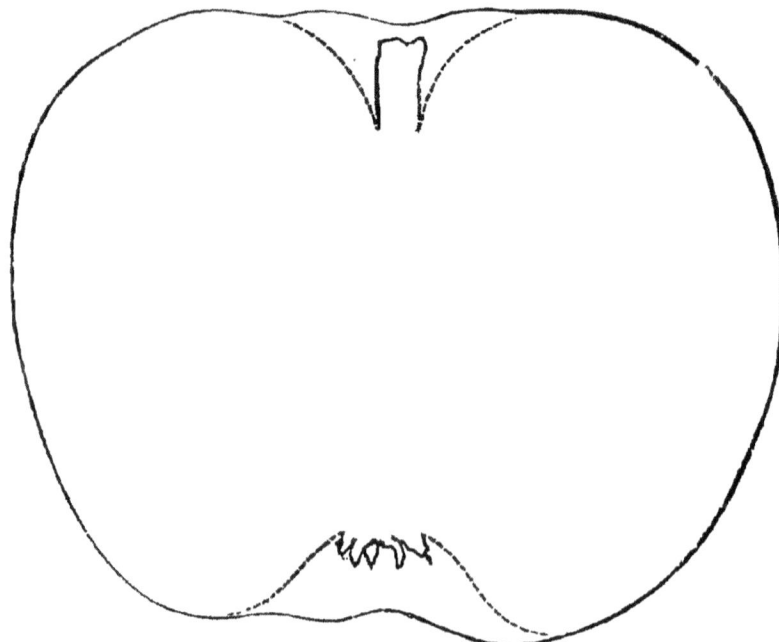

Fig. 32. *Gravenstein.*

Stalk quite short and strong, deeply set. Calyx large, in a wide deep, rather irregular basin. Skin greenish yellow at first, but becoming bright yellow, and beautifully dashed and pencilled and marbled with light and deep red and orange. Flesh tender and crisp, with a high flavoured, somewhat aromatic taste. Ripens with us in September and October, but will keep a month longer. The trees are very thrifty strong growers, and bear young.

42. Grand Sachem.

A showy, large, dark, blood-red fruit, but rather coarse, and scarcely worth cultivation. Fruit very large, roundish, distinctly ribbed, and irregular in its outline. Stalk short and strong, and calyx set in a well marked basin. Skin smooth, deep, dingy red, over the whole surface. Flesh white, rather dry, and without much flavour. September.

43. Holland Pippin. Thomp. Lind. Miller.

Reinnette d'Hollande. *Noisette ?*
Summer Pippin } *of New-Jersey.*
Pie Apple.

This and the Fall Pippin are frequently confounded together. They are indeed of the same origin, and the leaves, wood, and strong growth of both are very closely similar. One of the strongest points of difference, however, lies in their time of ripening. This being with us a late summer, the Fall Pippin a late autumn, and the White Spanish Reinnette an early winter fruit.

The Holland Pippin, in the gardens here, begins to fall from the tree, and is fit for pies about the middle of August, and from that time to the first of November, is one of the very best kitchen apples, making the finest tarts and pies. It is not equal to the Fall Pippin for eating.

Fruit very large, roundish, a little more square in outline than the Fall Pippin, and not so much flattened, though a good deal like it; a little narrowed next the eye. Stalk half an inch long, thick, deeply sunk. Calyx small, closed, moderately sunk in a slightly plaited basin. Skin greenish yellow or pale green, becoming pale yellow when fully ripe, washed on one side with a little dull red or pale brown, with a few scattered, large, greenish dots. Deserves a place in every garden

44. Hawthornden. Thomp. Lind. Ron.

White Hawthorden *Nicoll.*

A celebrated Scotch apple, which originated at Hawthornden, the birth-place of the poet Drummond. It resembles, somewhat, our Maiden's Blush, but is inferiour to that fruit in flavour. Fruit rather above the medium size, (occasionally ribbed, according to Lindley,) with us, pretty regularly formed, roundish, rather flattened. Skin very smooth, pale, light yellow, nearly white in the shade, with a fine blush where exposed to the sun. Calyx nearly closed, set in a rather shallow basin, with a few obscure plaits. Stalk half an inch long, slender. Flesh white, juicy, of a simple, pleasant flavour. An excellent bearer, a handsome fruit, and good for cooking or drying. The ends of the bearing branches become pendulous.

45. JERSEY SWEETING.

A very popular apple in the middle states, where it is not only highly valued for the dessert, but, owing to its saccharine quality, it is also planted largely for the fattening of swine, which are allowed to run under the trees and gather the fruit as it falls. It is a highly valuable sort, and deserves extensive culture.

Fruit medium size, roundish-ovate, tapering to the eye. The calyx is small, closed, very slightly sunk, in a small plaited basin. Stalk half an inch long, in a rather narrow cavity. Skin thin, greenish yellow, washed and streaked, and often entirely covered with stripes of pale and dull red. Flesh white, fine grained, and exceedingly juicy, tender, sweet and sprightly. Young wood stout, and short jointed. This apple commences maturing about the last of August, and continues ripening till frost.

46. KESWICK CODLIN.   Thom. Lind.

A noted English cooking apple, which may be gathered for tarts, as early as the month of June, and continues in use till November. It is a great bearer and a vigorous tree.

Fruit a little above the middle size, rather conical, with a few obscure ribs. Stalk short and deeply set. Calyx rather large. Skin greenish yellow, washed with a faint blush on one side. Flesh yellowish white, juicy, with a pleasant acid flavour.

47. KILHAM HILL.   Man.

A native of Essex co., Mass., raised by Daniel Kilham. Fruit pretty large, roundish, ribbed, narrowing to the eye. Skin pale yellow, slightly splashed with red in the shade, deep red in the sun. Stalk rather long and slender, set in a wide deep hollow. Calyx in a narrow basin. Flesh of sprightly, rather high flavour, but is apt to become dry and mealy. Bears well. September.

48. KENRICK'S AUTUMN.   Ken.

A handsome apple of second quality. Fruit large, roundish, much flattened at the base. Stalk long, projecting beyond the fruit a good deal, set in a close cavity. Skin pale yellowish-green, striped and stained with bright red. Flesh white, a little stained with red, tender, juicy, and of a sprightly acid flavour. September.

49. KING OF THE PIPPINS. Thomp. Lind. Ron.

Hampshire Yellow.

An apple highly rated in England, whence it comes, but which scarcely proves first rate here. Fruit of medium size, of a conical or pearmain shape. Skin smooth, pale yellow, delicately streaked and washed with red next the sun. Stalk slender, an inch long. Calyx large, set in a deep even basin. Flesh white, very firm and of fair quality. The tree is an upright grower, and bears abundantly. October and November.

50. KERRY PIPPIN. Thomp. Lind. Ron.

Edmonton's Aromatic Pippin. ac *Thomp.*

An Irish dessert apple, from the county of Kerry, as its name implies. Fruit middle size, oval, a little flattened at the eye. Skin pale yellow, mingled with a deeper yellow, with a glossy surface, and stained and streaked with red. Stalk of medium length, sometimes short, set in a narrow cavity, with a projection of the fruit on one side, and occasionally, a line or ridge, running from the eye to the stalk. Calyx set in a plaited basin. Flesh yellow, tender, crisp, with a sugary flavour. Ripens in September and October.

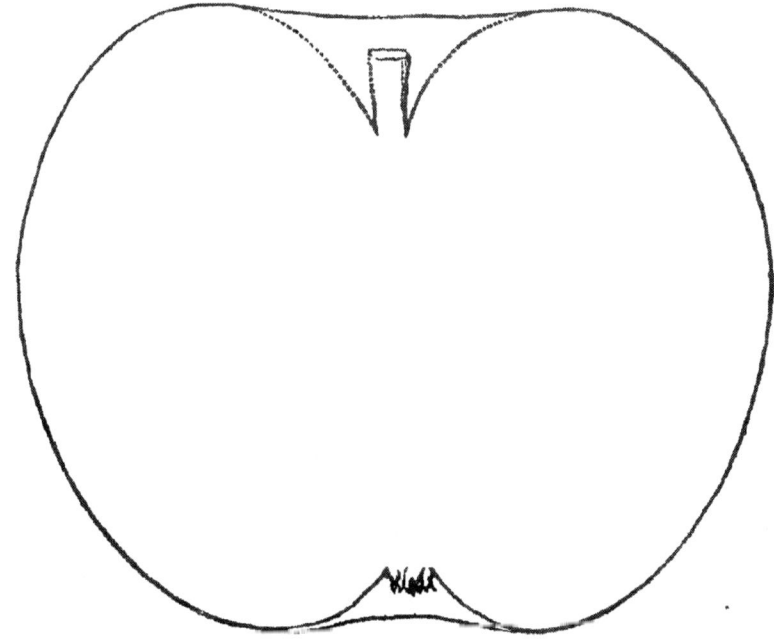

Fig. 33. *Lyscom.*

51. LYSCOM. Man. Ken.

Osgood's Favourite.

Another Massachusetts variety of merit. Fruit large, round, skin greenish yellow, with a few broken stripes or splashes of red. Stalk short, planted in a deep, round, even cavity. Calyx small, in a very narrow, plaited basin. Flesh fine grained, and exceedingly mild and agreeable in flavour. A large, fine fruit, which is worthy of general cultivation. In use from September to November.

52. LYMAN's PUMPKIN SWEET. Ken.

A very large fair sweet apple which we received from Mr. S Lyman, of Manchester, Conn. It is, perhaps, inferiour to the Jersey Sweet or the Summer Sweet Paradise for the table, but it is a very valuable apple for baking, and deserves a place on this account in every orchard. The original tree of this sort, is growing in Mr. Lyman's orchard.

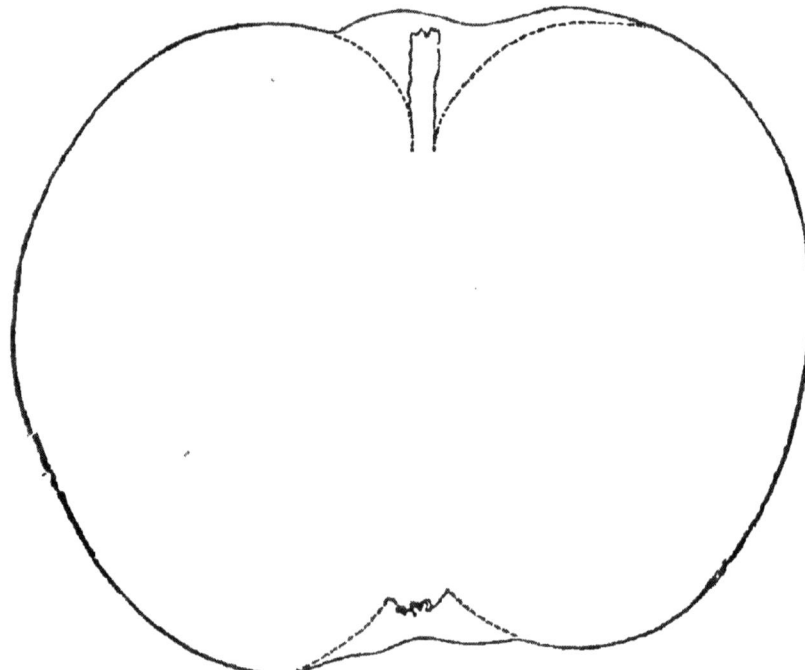

Fig. 34. *Lyman's Pumpkin Sweet.*

Fruit very large, roundish, more or less furrowed or ribbed, especially near the stalk. Skin smooth, pale green, with obscure whitish streaks near the stalk, and numerous white dots near the eye, sometimes becoming a little yellow next the sun.

8*

Stalk short, deeply sunk in a narrow cavity. Calyx rather small, set in an abruptly sunk, rather irregular basin. Flesh white, very sweet, rich and tender, but not very juicy. September to December.

There is another Pumpkin Sweeting known in this state, which is an oblong or permain-shaped fruit, striped with yellow and red, and ripens in August and September; a second rate apple.

53. LONGVILLE'S KERNEL. Thomp. Lind. P. Mag.

Sam's Crab.

An apple introduced into our orchards from the garden of the London Horticultural Society, but which does not compare favourably with many native sorts of this season.

Fruit rather below medium size, oval, rather flattened. Stalk short, deeply inserted. Eye small, with a short erect calyx. Skin greenish yellow, streaked with pale brownish red, with a few streaks of bright red. Flesh firm, yellow, slightly perfumed, sub-acid. The tree is a great bearer. August and September.

57. MAIDEN'S BLUSH. Coxe. Thomp.

A remarkably beautiful apple, a native of New-Jersey, and first described by Coxe. It begins to ripen about the 20th of August, and continues until the last of October. It has all the beauty of colour of the pretty little Lady Apple, and is much cultivated and admired, both for the table and for cooking. It is also very highly esteemed for drying.

Fruit medium sized, flat, and quite smooth and fair. Skir.

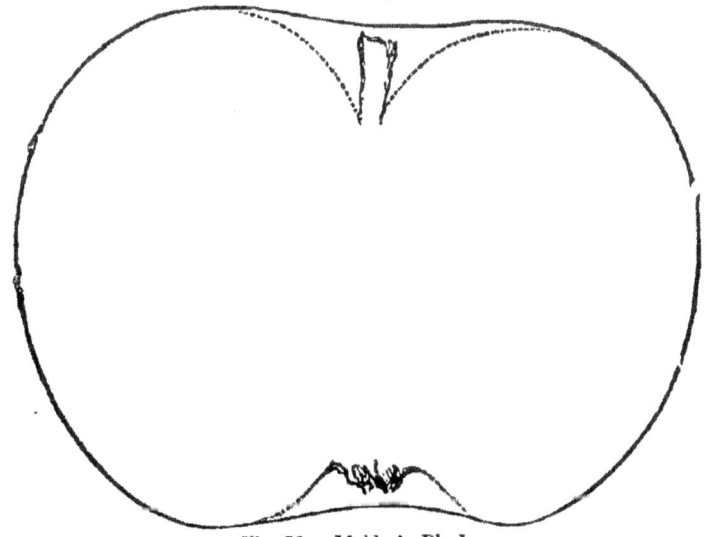

Fig. 35. *Maiden's Blush.*

thin, clear lemon yellow, with a coloured cheek, sometimes deli
cately tinted like a blush, and in others with a brilliant red.
Stalk short, planted in a rather wide, deep hollow. Basin moderately depressed, calyx closed. Flesh white, tender, sprightly
with a pleasant sub-acid flavour. The fruit is very light. This
variety forms a handsome, rapid growing tree, with a fine
spreading head, and bears large crops.

55. Nonsuch. Thomp. Lind.

Nonsuch. *Ron. Forsyth.*

An old English sort, chiefly valued for the beautiful transparent jelly which it makes.

Fruit of medium size, regular form, flat. Skin greenish yellow, striped and spotted with dull brick red. Calyx set in a
wide, regular, shallow basin. Stalk short and slender. Flesh
white, soft, with a plentiful sub-acid juice. A great bearer.

56. Old English Codlin. Thomp.

English Codlin. *Coxe. Lind. Ray.*

A large and fair cooking apple, in use from July to November.
Fruit generally above medium size, oblong or conical, and a
little irregular. Skin clear lemon yellow, with a faint blush
next the sun. Stalk stout and short. Flesh white, tender, and
of a rather pleasant, sub-acid flavour. Much esteemed for cooking, ripens gradually upon the tree, and is free from liability to
rot. In New-Jersey this fine old fruit is largely cultivated for
market, as it produces handsome and abundant crops. The
leaves are large, and the trees are very vigorous and fruitful.

57. Peach-Pond Sweet.

This is a most excellent autumn variety, from a small village
of this name, in Dutchess county, N. Y., which we received
from Mr. J. R. Comstock, an extensive orchardist near Pough-
keepsie. It appears well worthy of a more general dissemination.

Fruit of medium size, rather flat, and a little one-sided or angular in its form. Skin striped light red. Stalk long and
slender. Flesh tender or very mellow, moderately juicy, with a
very rich, sweet, and agreeable flavour. September to November.

58. Pomme de Neige. Thomp. Lind.

Fameuse. *Forsyth.*
Sanguineus.

A very celebrated Canada fruit, which has its name from the

snow-white colour of its flesh, or, as some say, from the village whence it was first taken to England. It is an excellent, productive, autumn apple, and is especially valuable in northern latitudes.

Fruit of medium size, roundish, somewhat flattened. Skin with a ground of pale greenish yellow, mixed with faint streaks of pale red on the shady side, but marked with blotches and short stripes of darker red, and becoming a fine deep red in the sun. Stalk quite slender, half an inch long, planted in a narrow funnel shaped cavity. Calyx small and set in a shallow rather narrow basin. Flesh remarkably white, very tender, juicy and good, with a slight perfume. Ripe in October and November. A regular bearer, and a handsome dessert fruit.

59. PORTER. § Man. Thomp.

A first rate New-England fruit, raised by the Rev. S. Porter, of Sherburne, Mass., and deservedly a great favourite in the Boston market. The fruit is remarkably fair, and the tree is very productive.

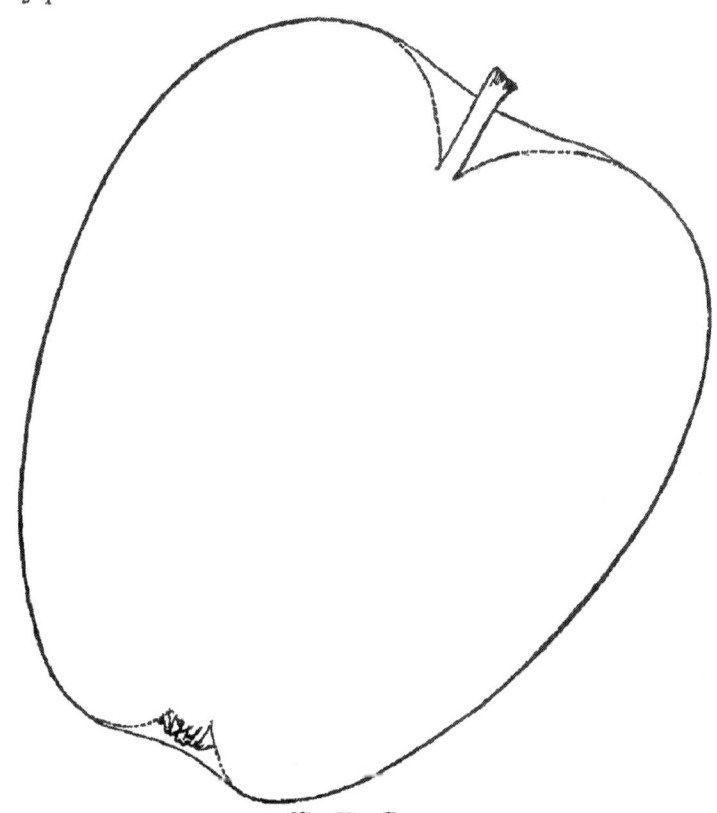

Fig. 37. *Porter.*

Fruit rather large, regular, oblong, narrowing to the eye. Skin clear, glossy, bright yellow, and when exposed, with a dull blush next the sun. Calyx set in a narrow and deep basin. Stalk rather slender, not three fourths of an inch long. Flesh fine grained, and abounding with juice of a sprightly agreeable flavour. Ripens in September, and deserves general cultivation.

60. Pine Apple Russet. Lindley.

We have at last been able to procure this variety, and we insert Lindley's description, in order to draw attention to a sort which appears to be highly deserving of trial in this country.

" Fruit above the middle size, roundish, ovate, with broad obtuse angles on its sides, about two inches and three quarters in diameter, and two inches and a half deep. Eye small, with a very short, connivent calyx, placed in a shallow depression, surrounded by ten rather unequal plaits. Stalk an inch long, inserted in an uneven cavity, one half of which protrudes beyond the base. Skin pale greenish yellow, almost covered with white specks on one part, and a thick scabrous, yellowish russet on the other, which extends round the stock. Flesh very pale yellow, crisp, very short, and tender. Juice more abundant than in any apple I have ever met with, as it generally runs very copiously as soon as cut open, saccharine, with that just proportion of acid which characterizes our most valuable fruits, and of a spicy aromatic flavour, with a high perfume.

A dessert apple from the end of September to the middle of October."

61. Pumpkin Russet.

Sweet Russet. *Kenrick.*
Pumpkin Sweet, }
Flint Russet,   } *of some.*

This is another of the large sweet apples so popular in New England, and is considered valuable by many. It is, however much inclined to rot.

Fruit large, round ; flesh, pale yellowish green, slightly covered with russet. Stalk long, set in a wide shallow cavity. Eye narrow, slightly sunk. Flesh exceedingly rich and sweet. September to January. Trees large and spreading.

62. Rambo. § Coxe. Thomp.

Romanite,   }
Seek-no-further,   } *of New-Jersey.*
Bread and Cheese Apple, }

The Rambo is one of the most popular autumn fruits to be

found in the Philadelphia markets. It is a highly valuable apple for the table or kitchen, and the tree thrives well on light sandy soils, being a native of the banks of the Delaware.

Fig. 37. *Rambo.*

Fruit of medium size, flat. Skin smooth, yellowish white in the shade, streaked and marbled with pale yellow and red in the sun, and speckled with large rough dots. Stalk long, rather slender, curved to one side, and deeply planted in a smooth, funnel-like cavity. Calyx closed, set in a broad basin, which is slightly plaited around it. Flesh greenish white, very tender, with a rich, sprightly, sub-acid flavour. October to December. This apple resembles externally the American Domine, which, however, is a very late-keeping winter fruit.

63. RAMBOUR FRANC. Duh. Thomp.

> Frank Rambour. *Lindley.*
> Rambour d'Ete, or
> Summer Rambour. *Coxe.*
> Rambour d'Ete. *Poiteau.*

This is a French fruit, common in many parts of this country, and according to Coxe, was introduced from the garden of St. Cloud. It is of pretty good quality, though most esteemed for cooking.

Fruit a little above medium size, (sometimes quite large,) flat, generally evenly formed, but occasionally a little irregular. Skin pale, greenish yellow, slightly stained and streaked with red on the sunny side. Stalk short, rather fleshy and deeply inserted. Eye large, the nearly closed calyx set in a deep, slightly furrowed basin. Flesh rather soft, of a sprightly, sub-acid flavour, a little bitter before maturity. Ripens early in September.

64. Ross Nonpareil. § Thomp. Lind. Ron.

Fig. 38. *Ross Nonpareil.*

This is an Irish fruit, and, to our taste, one of the highest flavoured and most delicious of all apples, for the dessert, approaching in flavour some kinds of pear. In England this is a winter fruit, but with us, owing to the greater warmth of our autumn, it is in perfection the last of October, and will keep a month.

Fruit rather below medium size, roundish, narrowing a little to the eye. Skin covered with a thin mellow russet, and faintly stained with red on the sunny side. Stalk an inch or more long, slender, and rather deeply inserted. Calyx set in a shallow basin. Flesh greenish white, tender, with a rich aromatic flavour,—what is called a Fennel flavour by the English. A profuse bearer, and worthy of a place in every amateur's garden.

65. Red Ingestrie. Thomp. Lind.

This, and the Yellow Ingestrie, are cross-bred seedlings, raised by Mr. Knight, from the English Golden Pippin. They are greatly admired as dessert apples in England.

Fruit small, about two and a half inches in diameter, oblong or ovate, with a wide basin at the eye, and a short and slender stalk. Skin bright yellow, tinged and mottled with red on the sunny side, and speckled with obscure dots. Flesh very firm, juicy and high flavoured. Ripens in September and October.

The Yellow Ingestrie differs from the above as follows: fruit of smaller size, of a clear, bright gold colour, without red. Eye small and shallow. Flesh tender and delicate, with a plentiful juice when freshly gathered from the tree. October.

66. SUMMER SWEET PARADISE. ◊.

A Pennsylvania fruit, sent to us by J. B. Garber, Esq., a zealous fruit-grower of Columbia, in that state. It is a large, fair, sweet apple, and is certainly one of the finest of its class, for the dessert. The tree is an abundant bearer, begins to bear while young, and is highly deserving general cultivation. It has no affinity to the Paradise Apple used for stocks.

Fruit quite large, round and regular in its form, a little flattened at both ends. Skin rather thick, pale green, sometimes faintly tinged with yellow in the sun, and very distinctly marked with numerous, large, dark, gray dots. Stalk strong, and set in an even, moderately deep hollow. Flesh tender, crisp, very juicy, with a sweet, rich, aromatic flavour. Ripe in August and September.

67. SCARLET PEARMAIN. Thomp. Lind.

Bell's Scarlet Pearmain. *Ronalds.*
Oxford Peach *of some English gardens.*

A showy dessert apple, raised, according to Ronalds, by Mr. Bell, land stewart at Sion House, the seat of the Duke of Northumberland, about the year 1800.

Fruit medium sized, pearmain or conical shaped. Skin light crimson, or yellow, in the shade, rich crimson on the sunny side; stalk nearly an inch long, deeply set. Calyx full and spreading, in a deeply sunk basin, surrounded by a few plaits. Flesh white, stained with a tinge of pink, crisp, juicy, and of good flavour. In eating from the last of August to the tenth of October. A plentiful bearer.

68. SEEK-NO-FURTHER. Coxe.

Autumn Seek-no-further. *Ken.*

This seems to be a favourite name in this country, and it is difficult to say to what variety it should be exclusively applied. The Seek-no-further of New-Jersey and Pennsylvania is the Rambo, (see Rambo;) that of some parts of New-York is the American Domine, (see the latter.) The Seek-no-further of Coxe is a large, roundish fruit, narrower at the eye. Skin smooth, pale yellowish green, or nearly white; the flesh yellow, juicy, rich and tender. The trunk straight and tall, supporting a regular well-formed head. Ripe in October, and will keep a couple of months.

The *Westfield Seek-no-further* is the Seek-no-further of Connecticut, and is an old and highly esteemed variety of that district. It has a Pearmain flavour, and is much superior to the

Green Seek-no-further just described. Fruit large, pretty regu larly round. Skin pale, or dull red over a pale clouded green ground—the red sprinkled with obscure russety yellow dots. Stalk very slender, three-fourths of an inch long, inserted in an even cavity. Calyx closed, or with a few reflexed segments, and set in an even basin of moderate depth. Flesh white, fine grained, tender, with a rich, pearmain flavour. A first rate fruit. October to February.

69. STROAT. Floy. Ken.

Straat. *Thomp.*

An apple in high esteem among the descendants of the Dutch settlers on the North River, the original tree of which is said to have grown in a street (*stroat*, Dutch) of Albany. It is well known at Kingston, N. Y.

Fruit above the middle size, regularly formed, roundish, oblong, and tapering a little to the eye. Skin smooth, yellowish green. Stem short, pretty stout, and planted in a rather shallow cavity. Flesh yellow, very tender, with an excellent, rich, brisk flavour. In eating from September to December.

70. WORMSLEY PIPPIN. § Thomp. Lind. P. Mag.

Knight's Codlin.

A well-flavoured autumnal fruit, from the English Gardens, ripening the last of August and beginning of September.

Fruit middle-sized, roundish, tapering a little towards the eye, which is deeply sunk, and the basin slightly plaited. Skin pale green, or straw colour, darker next the sun, and sprinkled with dark specks. Stalk deeply planted, nearly an inch long. Flesh white, crisp, firm, with a rich high flavoured juice. This is considered, abroad, one of the richest flavoured apples, but it appears to us to have been over-praised, being rather too firm and too acid.

Class III. Winter Apples.

---

71. ALFRISTON. Thomp. Lind. Ron.

Oldaker's New.
Lord Gwydr's Newtown Pippin. } *ac. to Thomp.*

A third rate apple, valued in England as excellent for cook. ing. Fruit large, roundish, a little ribbed, and rather broadest at the base. Skin pale greenish-yellow, faint.y marked with

9

streaks or network of russet. Stalk short, planted in a deep cavity. Calyx with open, long segments set in a deep, rather uneven basin. Flesh yellowish white, crisp, tender, with a tolerable, somewhat acid flavour. The English trace some resemblance between this and the Newtown pippin, but we perceive no similarity. October to January.

72. American Pippin. Coxe. Thomp.

Grindstone

Valuable only for its late keeping and for cider, the American pippin has never been much cultivated out of New-Jersey. The Newtown pippin which is frequently called by this name abroad, is very different, and infinitely superiour to this

Fruit of medium size, and regular form, roundish, somewhat flattened. Skin dull red in patches and stripes, on a dull green ground, marked by pretty large star-like, yellowish russet specks, which make the surface rather rough. Stalk short, somewhat fleshy and set in an irregular shallow cavity. Calyx small, set almost even with the surface of the fruit. Flesh white, firm, juicy, with a somewhat brisk, acid flavour. Keeps till June. Trees with crooked shoots.

73. Baldwin. § Ken. Thomp. Man.

Woodpecker.
Pecker.

The Baldwin stands at the head of all New-England apples, and is unquestionably a first rate fruit in all respects. It is a native of Massachusetts, and is more largely cultivated for the Boston market than any other sort. It bears most abundantly with us, and we have had the satisfaction of raising larger, more beautiful, and highly flavoured specimens here, than we ever saw in its native region. The Baldwin, in flavour and general characteristics, evidently belongs to the same family as our Esopus Spitzenburgh, and deserves its extensive popularity.

Fruit large, roundish, and narrowing a little to the eye. Skin yellow in the shade, but nearly covered and striped with crimson, red, and orange, in the sun; dotted with a few large russet dots, and with radiating streaks of russet about the stalk. Calyx closed, set in a rather narrow, plaited basin. Stalk half to three fourths of an inch long, rather slender for so large a fruit, planted in an even, moderately deep cavity. Flesh yellowish white, crisp, with that agreeable mingling of the saccharine and acid which constitutes a rich, high flavour. The tree is a vigorous, upright grower, and bears most abundantly. Ripe from November to March, but with us, is in perfection in January.

Fig. 39. *Baldwin.*

74. BLACK APPLE. Coxe.

Black American. *Thomp. ?*

A native fruit, of a very dark red colour, and of a mild, rather agreeable flavour.

Fruit rather below medium size, round or very slightly flattened. Skin dark red, almost black, with a mealy, whitish bloom on the surface. The stalk half to three fourths of an inch long, pretty deeply inserted. Calyx in a rather shallow basin. Flesh yellowish red, crisp, juicy, and of medium quality. The tree when fully grown has a rather drooping head. Ripe from November to February.

75. BORSDORFFER. Thomp. Knoop.

Borsdorff. *Lind.*
King George the Third. *Ron.*
Queen's,
Reinnette Bâtarde,
Edler Winter Borsdorffer,   } *of various*
Reinnette de Misnie,   *gardens,*
Ganet Pippin,   *ac. to*
King,   *Thomp.*
Le Grand Bohemian Borsdorffer,

A small, celebrated German apple introduced into England by Queen Charlotte. It is much admired as a dessert fruit.

Fruit about two inches in diameter, roundish-oval, narrowing at the eye. Skin pale yellow, with a full red cheek, sprinkled with a little russet. Calyx set in a small, even basin but little sunk. Stalk half an inch long, slender. Flesh yellowish-white, very firm and crisp, with a rich, brisk, perfumed flavour. The tree grows rather loosely, and the blossoms appear late. November to February.

76. BELLE-FLEUR, YELLOW. § Thomp.

Bell-Flower. *Coxe. Floy. Ken.*
Yellow Bellflower, *of most nurseries.*

The Yellow Belle-Fleur is a large, handsome, and excellent winter apple, every where highly esteemed in the United States. It is most abundantly seen in the markets of Philadelphia, as it thrives well in the sandy soils of New-Jersey. Coxe first described this fruit; the original tree of which, grew in Burling-

Fig. 40. *Yellow Belle-Fleur.*

ton, New-Jersey. We follow Thompson, in calling it *Belle.
Fleur*, from the beauty of the blossoms, with the class of French
apples, to which it belongs.

Fruit very large, oblong, a little irregular, tapering to the eye.
Skin smooth, pale lemon yellow, often with a blush next the sun.
Stalk long and slender, in a deep cavity. Calyx closed and set
in a rather narrow, plaited basin. Seeds in a large hollow cap-
sule or core. Flesh tender, juicy, crisp, with a sprightly, sub-
acid flavour ; before fully ripe, it is considerably acid. Wood
yellowish, and tree vigorous, with spreading, drooping branches.
A regular and excellent bearer, and worthy of a place in every
orchard. November to March,

77. BELLE-FLEUR, WHITE. §

White Bellflower. } *of Indiana, and the*	White Pippin.	
Green Bellflower. } *North, and West.*	Crane's Pippin.	
Detroit. } *of Cincin-*	Ohio Favourite.	
White Detroit. } *nati.*	Hollow Cored Pippin, (*of some.*	

The White Belle-Fleur is one of the most widely disseminated and popular apples in the Western states. It is a native,
and was originally carried to the west by Mr. Brunson, a nurseryman, who emigrated from New-York first to Huron co.,
Ohio, and afterwards to Wayne co., Indiana—disseminating it
largely.
It grows
pretty
strongly,
bears ve-
ry abun-
dantly,
and its
brittle
bearing
shootsare
inclined
to break.
Head
spread-
ing, but
notdroop-
ing.
This is
a very
fair and
hands'me
fruit, less
acid than

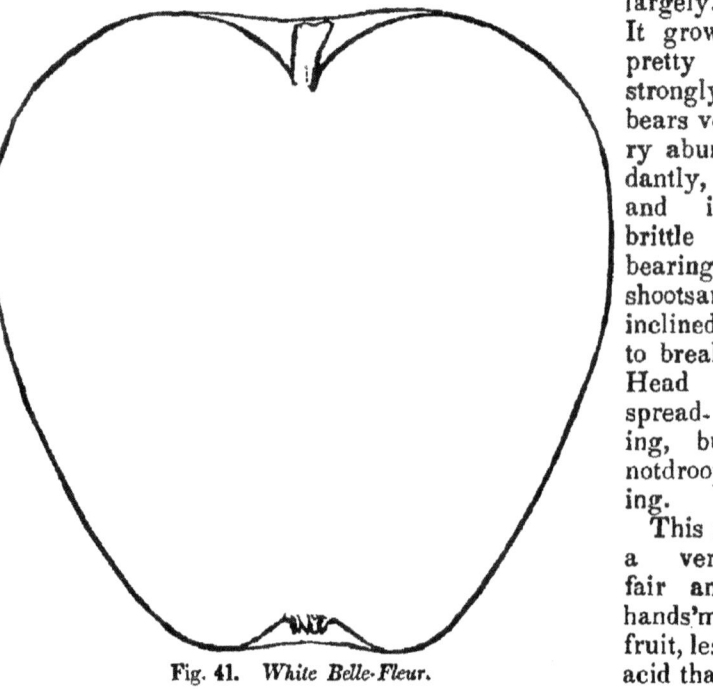

Fig. 41. *White Belle-Fleur.*

the Yellow Belle-Fleur. The *Cumberland Spice*, of Coxe, well known here, and given in previous editions as a synonym, is, we find on farther acquaintance with the white Belle-Fleur, an entirely distinct variety.

Fruit medium to large. Skin smooth, pale yellowish-white, marked with small brown dots, and rarely with a faint blush. Stalk long, slender, planted in a deep cavity. Calyx small, set in a small, narrow basin. Flesh white, tender and juicy, with a delicate, sprightly flavour. Core large and hollow. October to March.

78. Belle-Fleur, Red.

Belle-Fleur. *Poiteau.*   Belle-Fleur Rouge ? *Thomp.*

A third rate, well *known*, French variety, scarcely worth cultivation.

Fruit large, regular, oblong-conical   Skin pale greenish-yellow, but nearly covered with red, striped with dark red, and dotted with yellow. Stalk pretty long, planted in a deep, narrow cavity. Calyx closed, sunk in a deep, narrow basin. Flesh white, tender, of tolerable, and mild flavour, apt to become mealy. November to January.

79. Belle-Fleur, Brabant.   Thomp. Ron.

The Brabant Belle-Fleur is a new variety from Holland. The fruit is large and heavy, and bids fair to prove a very excellent winter apple. The habit of the tree is spreading, and it requires to be grafted high to make a good head.

Fruit large, roundish-oblong, slightly ribbed. Skin pale yellow, slightly striped with red. Calyx large, set in a pretty wide, irregular basin. Flesh firm, juicy, with a rich, pleasant, sub-acid flavour. December to April.

82. Cornish Gilliflower.   Thomp. Lind. Ron.

Cornish July-flower.
Pomme Regelans.

This is considered one of the highest flavoured apples in England, whence it comes; it is rather a shy bearer there, but we think it promises better here, in this respect.

Fruit medium size, ovate, narrowing much to the eye where it is ribbed. Skin dull green, or dark yellowish green, with a sunny side of brownish red, intermixed with a few streaks of richer red. Calyx large, set in a very narrow, furrowed or knobby basin. Stalk three fourths of an inch long. Flesh yellowish, firm, with a rich, high flavour, and a slight perfume, resembling that of the Gilliflower. November to April.

83. CATSHEAD. Coxe. Lind.

Round Catshead. *Thomp. ?*
Cathead Greening.

A very large apple, cultivated for drying in some parts of the country, but of little other value except as a cooking apple.

Fruit of the largest size round. Stalk half an inch long, and very deeply sunk. Calyx set in a deep, open basin. Skin quite smooth, pale green. Flesh tender, with a sub-acid juice. October and November.

84. CALVILLE, WHITE WINTER. Lind.

Calville Blanche d'Hiver. *Thomp. O. Duh. Noisette.*
White Calville. *Coxe.*

The White Winter Calville is a celebrated old French sauce and cooking apple; but like most others of its class, is not worthy of cultivation here.

Fruit large, rather flat, with the broad uneven ribs on its sides which characterize Calville apples. Skin smooth, pale greenish yellow, becoming when fully ripe, yellow, with a faint blush on one side. Calyx small, deeply set in an angular irregular basin. Stalk three fourths of an inch long, slender, deeply planted. Flesh white, large grained, tender and light, with a pleasant, third rate flavour; juice scarcely acid. A strong growing tree, and a good bearer. November to February.

85. CALVILLE, RED WINTER. Lind.

Calville Rouge d'Hiver. *Thomp. Noisette.*
Calville Rouge. *O. Duh.*
Red Calville. *Coxe.*

The Red Winter Calville is another old French variety of the same general character as the foregoing—good for culinary use, but of very indifferent flavour.

Fruit pretty large, roundish-oblong, a little flattened at the stem, and narrowing to the eye. Stalk stout, of medium length, deeply planted. Calyx in a large deep basin. Skin on the shaded side pale red, on the sunny side dark red, covered with bloom. Flesh tender, and flavour a mild sub-acid. November to March.

86. COS, OR CAAS. Ken. Buel.

A native of Kingston, N. Y., where it is productive, and very highly esteemed.

Fruit large, one sided or angular, roundish, broad and flattened at the stalk, narrowing a good deal to the eye. Skin smooth, pale greenish yellow in the shade, but red in the sun, with splashes and specks of bright red, and a few yellow dots. Stalk very short, and rather strong, downy, deeply inserted in a wide one sided cavity. Calyx small, in a narrow, shallow basin. Flesh white, tender, with a mild, agreeable flavour. December to March.

87. Chandler. §

We received this fine variety, which is a great favourite in Connecticut, from the Rev. H. S. Ramsdell, of Thompson, in that state. He informs us that it originated in the town of Pomfret, Conn., (celebrated as the place of Gen. Putnam's adventure with the wolf.)

Fruit large, roundish, slightly flattened, and one-sided or angular in its form; obscurely ribbed on its sides. Skin thickly streaked and overspread with dull red, (with a few streaks of brighter red) on a greenish yellow ground; the red sprinkled with light gray dots. Stalk short, deeply sunk in a wide cavity. Calyx small and closed, set in a plaited, wide basin. Core and seeds small. Flesh greenish white, tender, juicy, with a moderately rich, sub-acid flavour. The tree is one of moderate vigour, and is a great bearer. November to February.

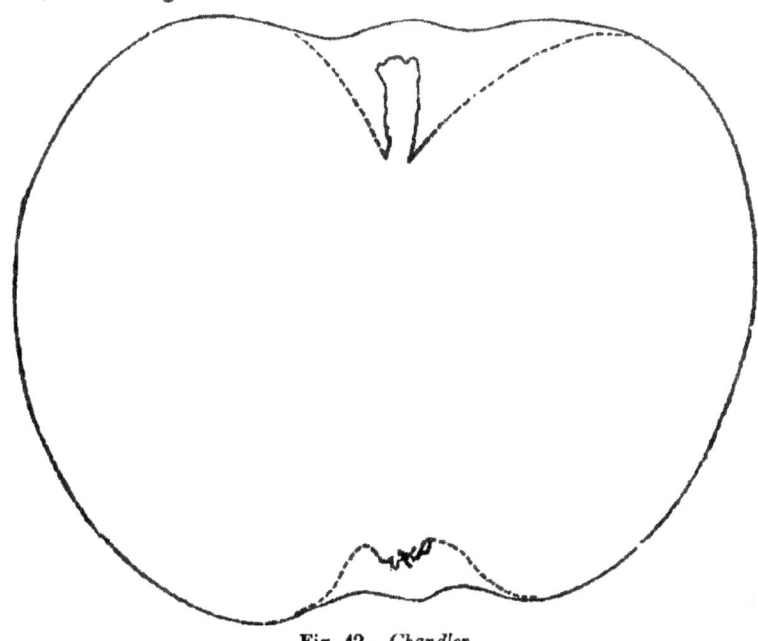

Fig 42. *Chandler*

88. COURT-PENDU PLAT. § Thomp.

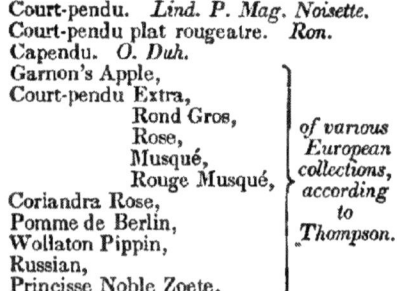

Court-pendu. *Lind. P. Mag. Noisette.*
Court-pendu plat rougeatre. *Ron.*
Capendu. *O. Duh.*
Garnon's Apple,
Court-pendu Extra,
   Rond Gros,
   Rose,
   Musqué,
   Rouge Musqué,
Coriandra Rose,
Pomme de Berlin,
Wollaton Pippin,
Russian,
Princisse Noble Zoete,
    of various European collections, according to Thompson.

This handsome French apple is very popular abroad, as may readily be seen by the great variety of names under which it is known in various nurseries in England, and on the continent. It thrives equally well here, and proves a beautiful acquisition to the dessert.

Fruit of medium size, regularly formed and quite flat. Skin rich, deep crimson on the sunny side, with a little pale greenish yellow in the shade. Stalk short, inserted in a very deep cavity. Calyx large, set in a wide shallow basin. Flesh yellow-crisp, with a rich, brisk, acid flavour. The tree bears young and plentifully. November to February.

This sort in England is frequently grafted on the French Paradise stock, when it forms a neat little bush, not much larger than a Gooseberry, and bears an abuudance of handsome and good fruit.

89. COURT OF WICK. § Thomp. Ron.

Court of Wick Pippin. *Lind. P. Mag.*
Court de Wick. *Hooker.*
Rival Golden Pippin,
Fry's Pippin,
Golden Drop,
Wood's Huntingdon,
Transparent Pippin,
Phillip's Reinette,
Knightwick Pippin,
Week's Pippin,
Yellow,
    of various English nurseries.

A high flavoured English dessert apple, of the Golden pippin class, which succeeds well with us.

Fruit below the middle size, regularly formed, about two and a half inches in diameter, roundish-ovate, somewhat flattened. Skin greenish yellow in the shade, but becoming a warm orange, with a little red, and dotted with small russet brown specks in the sun. Calyx with wide spread segments, and set in a wide even shallow basin. Stalk short, rather slender. Flesh yellow, crisp, and juicy, with a high, poignant flavour. October to February.

The Court of Wyck is an exceedingly hardy tree, and is therefore, well adapted for Canada or Maine.

90. CRANBERRY PIPPIN.

This strikingly beautiful apple we found growing on a farm near Hudson, N. Y. It is only second rate in point of flavour—about equal to the Hawthornden—but it is an excellent cooking apple, and its beautiful appearance and great productiveness, will, we think, render it a popular variety. It is not unlike in appearance a very handsome specimen of the Maiden's Blush, and it comes into use just as that sort goes out.

Fruit above medium size, very regularly formed, a little flattened. Skin very smooth, of a fine clear yellow in the shade, with a bright scarlet cheek. Stalk nearly three fourths of an inch long, slender, planted in a very even and moderately deep cavity. Calyx rather small, set in a deep, regular basin. Flesh white, moderately juicy, with a mild, sub-acid flavour. November to February.

91. DETROIT.

Red Detroit.
Black Detroit
Black Apple.   ⎫
Large Black.   ⎬ of some.
Crimson Pippin.   ⎭

This fruit, commonly known in Western New-York and Michigan as the Detroit, is supposed to have been brought to the neighbourhood of Detroit by early French settlers, and thence disseminated. There is little doubt that, like many other varieties grown at the west, and supposed to be indigenous there, this will yet prove to be some old variety. It is a very good fruit, of striking appearance.

There is another apple incorrectly called Detroit, or White Detroit, at Cincinnati, which is synonymous with the White Belle-Fleur. [See the latter.]

Fruit of medium or rather large size, roundish, somewhat flattened, and pretty regular. Stalk three-fourths of an inch long, planted in a deep cavity. Skin pretty thick, smooth and glossy, bright crimson at first, but becoming dark blackish purple at maturity, somewhat dotted and marbled with specks of fawn colour on the sunny side. Calyx closed, set in a rather deep, plaited basin. Flesh white, (sometimes stained with red to the core in exposed specimens,) crisp, juicy, of agreeable sprightly, sub-acid flavour. October to February.

92. BEDFORDSHIRE FOUNDLING. Thomp. Lind.

A large green English apple, excellent for kitchen use. Fruit large, roundish, obscurely ribbed. Skin deep green, paler at maturity. Stalk short, deeply planted. Calyx open, rather deeply set. Flesh yellowish, tender, juicy, with a pleasant acid flavour. October to February.

92. DUTCH MIGNONNE. § Thomp. Lind. P. Mag.

Reinette Dorée, (*of the Germans.*)	Paternoster Apfel.
Pomme de Laak.	Settin Pippin.
Grosser Casselar Reinette.	Copmanthorpe Crab.

This magnificent and delicious apple from Holland, proves one of the greatest acquisitions that we have received from abroad. We believe, indeed, that the Dutch Mignonne is larger and finer here than at home. At any rate we know none superior to it in superb appearance and rich flavour as an early winter fruit. The tree makes very strong upright shoots, and bears fine crops. (Hawthornden, incorrectly, of some gardens here.)

Fruit large, often very large, roundish, very regularly formed. Skin dull orange, half covered or more with rich, dull red, dotted and mottled with large yellow russet specks. Calyx open, set in a deep, round, regular basin. Stalk nearly an inch long, slender, bent, and planted in a narrow, deep cavity. Flesh at first firm, but becoming tender, with a rich, very aromatic flavour. November to February.

93. DOCTOR. Coxe. Thomp.

Red Doctor.
De Witt.

A Pennsylvania apple, named in honour of a physician of Germantown, who first brought it into notice. It is not so much esteemed here at the north, as the tree is rather an indifferent grower and bearer.

Fruit medium sized, regularly formed and flat. Skin smooth, yellow, striped and washed with two or three shades of red, with a few darker spots. Calyx set in a deep basin. Stalk very short, deeply inserted. Flesh tender, juicy, and breaking in its texture, with an excellent, slightly aromatic flavour. October to January.

94. DOMINE.

This apple, extensively planted in the orchards on the Hudson, so much resembles the Rambo externally, that the two are often confounded together, and the outline of the latter fruit (see

Rambo,) may be taken as nearly a fac-simile of this. The Domine is, however, of a livelier colour, and the flavour and season of the two fruits are very distinct,—the Rambo being rather a high flavoured early winter or autumn apple, while the Domine is a sprightly, juicy, long keeping winter fruit.

Fruit of medium size, flat. Skin lively greenish-yellow in the shade, with stripes and splashes of bright red in the sun, and pretty large russet specks. Stalk long and slender, planted in a wide cavity and inclining to one side. Calyx small, in a broad basin moderately sunk. Flesh white, exceedingly tender and juicy, with a sprightly pleasant, though not high flavour. Young wood of a smooth, lively, light brown, and the trees are the most rapid growers and prodigious bearers that we know— the branches being literally weighed down by the rope-like clusters of fruit.

The Domine does not appear to be described by any foreign author. Coxe says that he received it from England, but the apple he describes and figures does not appear to be ours, and we have never met with it in any collection here. It is highly probable that this is a native fruit. It is excellent from December till April.

95. Danver's Winter Sweet.   Man. Ken.

Epse's Sweet.

In Massachusetts, from a town in which this variety takes its name, it has been for a long time one of the best market apples— but we think it inferiour to the Ladies' Sweeting. It is an abundant bearer, and a very rapid tree in its growth.

Fruit of medium size, roundish-oblong. Skin smooth, dull yellow, with an orange blush. Stalk slender, inclining to one side. Calyx set in a smooth, narrow basin. Flesh yellow, firm, sweet, and rich. It bakes well, and is fit for use the whole winter, and often till April.

96. De Saint Julien.   Thomp.

Seigneur d'Orsay.
Saint Julian   *P. Mag.*

This French apple of considerable reputation has not yet borne with us, and we therefore copy Mr. Thompson's description in the Pomological Magazine, vol. iii. p. 165.

" Fruit large, roundish, slightly and obtusely angular on the sides. Eye in a moderate sized cavity, surrounded with slight plaits. Stalk slender, about an inch in length, inserted very shallow. Skin a little rough, with scars of gray russet, beneath which it is remarkably, though somewhat obscurely, striped with yellow and grayish green. Flesh firm, yellowish-white, rich, sweet and excellent. Shoots strong, dark chestnut, moderately downy, with numerous distinct whitish spots. A good bearer, in perfection in December, January, and February."

97. EASTER PIPPIN. Thomp. Lind.

Young's Long Keeping.
Claremont Pippin
Ironstone Pippin.
French Crab. *Forsyth, (not of Coxe.)*

Remarkable for keeping sound and firm two years. It is an English variety, rare with us. Fruit of medium size, skin deep green, with a pale brown blush. Stalk short, slender, deeply inserted. Calyx small, in a plaited basin. Flesh very firm. and though not juicy, of a good, sub-acid flavour.

98. FALLAWATER. Thomp.

This is a native of Pennsylvania, and was first brought into notice by Mr. Garber, of Columbia, Pa. It is a very good and productive apple, with a rich flavour. Fruit rather large, regularly formed, ovate or slightly conical. Skin smooth, green, with a brown blush, dotted with large, gray spots. Stalk slender, set in a narrow, round cavity. Calyx small, closed, and placed in a smooth, narrow basin. Flesh greenish, juicy, with a rich, agreeable, sub-acid flavour. November to February.

99. FENNOUILLET JAUNE. Thomp. Poit. Coxe.

Embroidered Pippin. *Lind.*
Drap d'Or. *O. Duh. No.* 12. *Knoop.*
Pomme de Caractère.

A beautiful, little, French dessert fruit, of that class of highly aromatic apples, which are called Fenouillets—(fennel flavour,) in France.

Fruit small, about two and a half inches in diameter, regularly formed, a little broadest at the base. Skin fine bright yellow, marked with a gray russet network, slightly resembling letters or characters. Stalk short, deeply inserted. Calyx quite small, set in a rather small basin. Flesh white, quite firm, with a high, and peculiarly aromatic flavour. The tree rather low October to March.

100. FENOUILLET ROUGE. Thomp. Poit. Lind. O. Duh.

Bardin.
Court-pendu Gris.

Fruit under medium size, between two and three inches in
10

diameter, regularly formed, roundish, a little flattened. Skin grayish in the ground, but nearly overspread with dark brownish-red and rather rough. Stalk quite short, and sunk in a small cavity. Eye rather narrow and shallow. Flesh firm, withering a little when fully ripe, with a sugary and somewhat musk-like, perfumed flavour. October to January.

101. FENOUILLET GRIS. Thomp. Poit. Nois.

Pomme d'Anis.

A neat little Anise flavoured apple, but the tree is of too weakly and feeble a growth to be worth cultivation. Its leaves are very small and narrow, and the branches slender. The fruit is small, roundish, slightly flattened. Skin fawn-coloured russet on a yellowish ground, and rather rough. Eye quite small, in a small basin. Stalk three fourths of an inch long. Flesh firm, with a saccharine, perfumed flavour. December to February.

102. GLORIA MUNDI. Thomp.

Monstrous Pippin. *Coxe. Floy Ken.*
Baltimore.
Glazenwood Gloria Mundi.
New-York Gloria Mundi.
American Mammoth
Ox Apple.

This magnificently large apple is a native fruit, and we have frequently seen it weighing nearly a pound and a half, and measuring 14 inches in circumference. It is an excellent cooking apple, and, when in perfection, of a fair quality for eating; but, owing to its great weight, it blows from the tree, and is rather unproductive.

Fruit very large, roundish, rather angular, and slightly flattened at the ends. Skin smooth, greenish-white before fully ripe, when it is pale lemon yellow, becoming a little darker on one side, with very rarely a faint blush, and sprinkled with dull whitish spots imbedded under the surface. Stalk strong, deeply inserted in a large cavity. Calyx large, set in a very deep, wide basin, a little irregular, or obscurely furrowed. Core small. Flesh white, tender, with a pleasant, acid flavour. October to January.

After a careful comparison of the fruit and wood, we do not hesitate to pronounce this synonymous with the Baltimore apple. (The Alfriston is sometimes erroneously called Baltimore.)

It is not a little curious that the origin of this apple, is claimed for Red Hook (on the Hudson,) for Long Island, and Baltimore

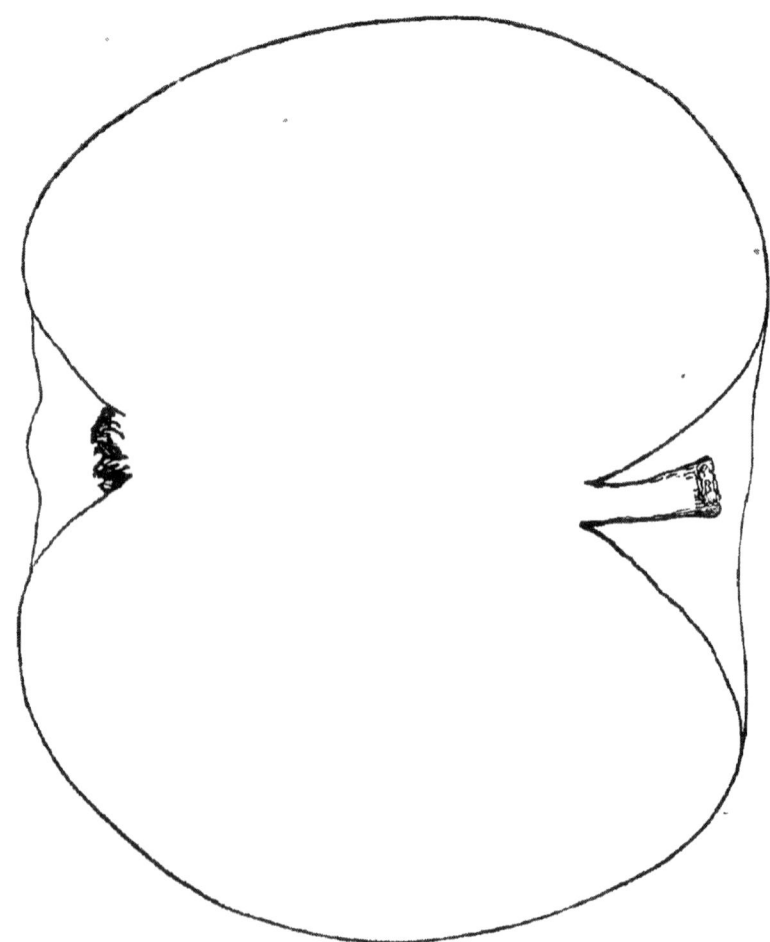

Fig. 43. *Gloria Mundi.*

103. GOLDEN BALL.   Ken.

This is a favourite apple in the state of Maine, and a vigorous, hardy variety. Fruit large, roundish, narrowing a little to the eye, about three inches deep—and a good deal ribbed at the sides and towards the crown. Skin smooth, golden yellow, with a few dots. Stalk set in a broad, shallow cavity. Eye rather narrow. Flesh crisp, tender, with a rich, aromatic flavour. Dec. to March. A native of Connecticut. Moderate bearer.

104. GOLDEN HARVEY.   Thomp. Lind. Ron.

Brandy Apple. *Forsyth.*

An excellent, high flavoured little dessert apple from Eng

land, which bears well, and retains its character with us. It is rather adapted for the fruit garden than the orchard—as the tree is of slender growth, and it would not be a popular market fruit here.

Fruit small, irregularly round, and about two inches in diameter. Skin rather rough, dull russet over a yellow ground, with a russety red cheek. Calyx small, open, with stiff segments, and set in a very shallow basin. Stalk half an inch long, and rather slender. Flesh yellow, of remarkably fine texture, with a spicy, rich, sub-acid flavour. The fruit should be kept in a cellar, or it is apt to shrivel. December to April.

105. GOLDEN PIPPIN. Ray. Thomp. Lind.

English Golden Pippin,	
Old Golden Pippin,	*ac. to Thomp.*
Balgone Pippin,	
Milton Golden Pippin,	
Russet Golden Pippin,	
Herefordshire Golden Pippin,	
London Golden Pippin,	
Warter's Golden Pippin,	
Bayfordbury Golden Pippin,	
Pepin d'Or. *Knoop*,	
Pomme d'Or. *Noisette o. Duh.*	
Koening's Pippelin.	
Reinette d'Angleterre.	

The Golden Pippin of the English, is the queen of all dessert apples, in the estimation of the English connoisseurs, as it unites the qualities of small size, fine form, and colour, with high flavour and durability. It is a very old variety, being mentioned by Evelyn, in 1660, but it thrives well in many parts of England still. The Golden Pippin has never become popular in this country, either because the taste here, does not run in favour of small apples, with the high, sub-acid flavour of the Golden

Fig. 44. *Golden Pippin.*

Pippin, and other favourite English sorts, or because our Newtown pippins, Swaars, and Spitzenburghs, etc., are still higher flavoured, and of a size more admired in this country. The Golden Pippin is not a very strong grower, and is rather suited to the garden than the orchard, with us.

Fruit small, round, and regularly formed. Skin gold colour, dotted with gray, russety dots, with also obscure white specks im bedded under the skin. Stalk nearly an inch long, slender. Calyx small, and set in a regular, shallow basin. Flesh yellowish, crisp, rather acid, but with a rich, brisk, high flavour. A great bearer, but requires a strong, deep, sandy loam. November to March.

There are many varieties of the English Golden Pippin, differing but little in general appearance and size, and very little in flavour, from the old sort, but of rather more thrifty growth; the best of these are Hughes', and Kirke's new Cluster, Golden Pippins.

There are half a dozen sorts of apples which are improperly called AMERICAN GOLDEN PIPPIN, but we have never yet been able to find a distinct and new variety of this name. What are so termed are, usually, the Fall, or the Yellow Newtown Pippin.

106. HOARY MORNING. Thomp. Lind. Ron.

Dainty Apple.
Downy.
Sam Rawlings.

A large and handsome English fruit, of good flavour, and esteemed for culinary purposes.

Fruit large, roundish, a little flattened. Skin broadly and irregularly striped with red, on a yellowish ground, and covered with a downy bloom, which gives it a somewhat hoary appearance. Calyx quite small, in a narrow, and shallow, plaited basin. Stalk of medium length, inserted in a wide depression. Flesh firm, sometimes a little pinkish next the skin, with a brisk, subacid flavour. October to December.

107. HUBBARDSTON NONSUCH. § Man. Ken.

A fine, large, early winter fruit, which originated in the town of Hubbardston, Mass., and is of first rate quality. The tree is a vigorous grower, forming a handsome branching head, and bears very large crops. It is worthy of extensive orchard culture.

Fruit large, roundish-oblong, much narrower near the eye. Skin smooth, striped with splashes, and irregular broken stripes of pale and bright red, which nearly cover a yellowish ground. The calyx open, and the stalk short, in a russetted hollow. Flesh yellow, juicy, and tender, with an agreeable mingling of sweetness and acidity in its flavour. October to January.

108. JONATHAN. § Buel. Ken.

Philip Rick.
King Philip.

The Jonathan is a very beautiful dessert apple, and its
10*

great .beauty, good flavour, and productiveness in all soils, unite to recommend it to orchard planters. The original tree of this new sort is growing on the farm of Mr. Philip Rick, of Kingston, New-York, a neighbourhood unsurpassed in the world for its great natural congeniality to the apple. It was first described by the late Judge Buel, and named by him, in compliment to Jonathan Hasbrouck, Esq., of the same place, who made known the fruit to him. The colour of the young wood is a lively light brown, and the buds at the ends of the shoots are large. Growth rather slender, slightly pendulous.

Fruit of medium size, regularly formed, roundish-ovate, or tapering to the eye. Skin thin and smooth, the ground clear light yellow, nearly covered by lively red stripes, and deepening into brilliant or dark red in the sun. Stalk three fourths of an inch long, rather slender, inserted in a deep, regular cavity. Calyx set in a deep, rather broad basin. Flesh white, rarely a little pinkish, very tender and juicy, with a mild sprightly flavour. This fruit, evidently, belongs to the Spitzenburgh class November to March.

109. Kirke's Lord Nelson.   Thomp. Lind. Ron.

A large and beautiful English, early winter sort; of good quality. Fruit, about three and a half inches in diameter, roundish, and regularly formed. Skin straw colour, nearly covered with red, and washed and stained with very bright red in the sun. Calyx open, set in a pretty large and regular basin, with a few small plaits at the bottom. Stalk rather slender and short. Flesh yellowish, juicy, firm, with an agreeable, though not very high flavour.

110. Kentish Fill-Basket.   Thomp. Lind. Ron.

Potter's Large Seedling   *Ron.*
Lady de Grey's

An immense English fruit, properly named, and much admired by those who like great size, and beauty of appearance. The flavour is tolerable, and it is an excellent cooking apple. The tree grows strongly, and bears well.

Fruit very large—frequently four and a half inches in diameter, roundish, slightly ribbed or irregular. Skin smooth, yellowish green, in the shade, but pale yellow in the sun, with a brownish red blush on the sunny side; slightly streaked or spotted with darker red. Calyx large, set in a pretty large, slightly irregular basin. Flesh tender, juicy, with a sub-acid, sprightly flavour. October to January.

111. LADY APPLE. § Coxe

Api. *O. Duh.*
Api Petit. *Thomp. Ron.*
Pomme Rose.
Pomme d'Api Rouge. *Poit.*
Petit Api Rouge, } *Nois.*
Gros Api Rouge, }

An exquisite little dessert fruit, the pretty size and beautiful colour of which, render it an universal favourite; as it is a great bearer it is also a profitable sort for the orchardist, bringing the highest price of any fancy apple in market. It is an old French variety, and is nearly always known abroad by the name of *Api ;* but the name of Lady Apple has become too universal here, to change it now. No amateur's collection should be without it.

Fruit quite small, but regularly formed and flat. Skin smooth and glossy, with a brilliant deep red cheek, contrasting with a lively lemon yellow ground. Stalk of medium length, and deeply inserted. Calyx small, sunk in a basin with small plaits. Flesh white, crisp, tender and juicy, with a pleasant flavour. The tree has

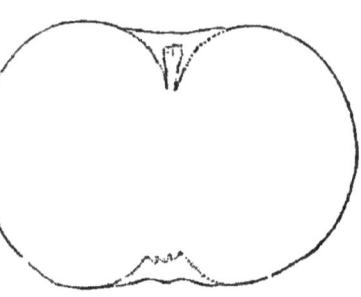

Fig. 45. Lady Apple.

straight, almost black shoots, with small leaves ; forms a very upright, small head, and bears its fruit in bunches. The latter is very hardy, and may be left on the tree till severe frosts. The Lady Apple is in use from December to May.

The API NOIR, or *Black Lady Apple*, differs from the foregoing sort only in the colour, which is nearly black. In shape, size, season, and flavour, it is nearly the same. It is, from its unusually dark hue, a singular, and interesting fruit.

The true API ÉTOILÉ, or *Star Lady Apple*, figured and described by Poiteau, in the Pomologie Française, is another very distinct variety; the fruit, which is of the same general character, but having five prominent angles, which give it the form of a star. This variety is rather scarce, the common Lady Apple being frequently sent out for it, by French nurserymen. It keeps until quite late in the spring, when its flavour becomes excellent, though in winter it is rather dry. The growth of the tree resembles that of the other Apis.

112. LEMON PIPPIN. Thomp. Forsyth.

Kirke's Lemon Pippin.

This is an old variety, which has been for a long time in high estimation.   It is, properly, an autumn sort, though it will keep till January.

Fruit of medium size, and of a regular oval shape. Calyx short and slender, set in a small, evenly formed basin.   The stalk is short, fleshy, and curled round, and it grows from a small fleshy protuberance, giving the apple the form of a lemon.   Skin pale green, becoming nearly lemon yellow when ripe.   Flesh firm, with a brisk, and pleasant, sub-acid flavour.   The tree grows erect, and produces good crops.   October to January.

113. MINISTER.   Man. Ken.

A very excellent New-England variety, introduced to notice by the late R. Manning.   It originated on the farm of Mr. Saunders, Rowley, Mass.; but was first exhibited to Mr. M by a minister—the Rev. Dr. Spring, of Newburyport, whence its name.   Mr. Manning recommended it very strongly for orchard culture.

Fruit large, oblong, tapering to the eye, around which, are a few furrows—and resembling the Yellow Belle-Fleur in outline. Skin striped and splashed near the stalk, with bright red on a greenish yellow ground.   Stalk an inch long, slender, curved to one side, and pretty deeply inserted.   Calyx small, closed, in a very narrow, plaited or furrowed basin.   Flesh yellowish white, very tender, with a somewhat acid, but very agreeable flavour. October to January.

114. MALE CARLE.   Thomp. Lind.

Mela di Carlo.
Mela Carla
Pomme de Charles.
Pomme Finale.
Charles Apple.

The Male Carle is the most celebrated of all apples in Italy and the south of Europe, whence it comes.   It is raised in great quantities about Genoa, and its great beauty, and delicacy of flavour, render it quite an article of commerce in the Italian and Spanish seaports.   Here or in New-England, it does not always attain perfection, but south of New-York it becomes beautiful and fine, as it needs a warm and dry soil.

Fruit of medium size, very regularly shaped, and a little narrower towards the eye. Skin smooth, with a delicate, waxen appearance, pale lemon yellow in the shade, with a brilliant crimson cheek next the sun, the two colours often joining in strong contrast.   Stalk an inch long, slender, planted in a narrow, regular cavity.   Calyx set in an even, rather narrow and deep basin.   Flesh white, not very juicy, but tender, and with a delicate, slightly rose-perfumed flavour.   September to January.

115. Maclean's Favourite. Thomp.

This is a new variety, lately received from England, which has not yet borne fruit. Mr. Thompson describes it as follows: " Middle size, roundish, yellow, crisp, rich, with the flavour of the Newtown pippin. November to February. Tree moderately vigorous, a good bearer, of the highest excellence."

116. Mouse Apple. §

Moose Apple.

This is an excellent, native fruit, which originated in Ulster county, on the west bank of the Hudson. It is there, one of the most popular winter fruits, being considered, by some, superiour to the Rhode Island Greening, and it deserves extensive trial elsewhere.

Fruit in weight, light; in size, large, roundish-oblong, or slightly conical. Skin, when first gathered, dull green, but when ripe, it becomes pale greenish yellow, with a brownish blush on one side, and a few scattered, russety gray dots. Stalk three fourths of an inch long, rather slender, not deeply inserted. Calyx closed, and set in a narrow basin, slightly plaited at the bottom. Flesh very white and fine grained, and moderately juicy, with a sprightly, delicate, and faintly perfumed flavour

117. Margil. Thomp. Lind. Ron.

Neverfail.
Munche's Pippin.

A well flavoured, old English dessert apple, but rather a slow grower. It is of too small size to be popular here, without greater beauty of appearance. Fruit small, a little angular, ovate, about an inch and a half in diameter. Skin orange in the sun, dull yellow in the shade, streaked and mottled with red. Calyx set in a small irregular basin. Stalk short. Flesh yellow, firm, with a high flavoured, aromatic juice. November to January.

118. Menagère. Thomp. Man.

We received this fruit from Mr. Manning, who, we believe, had it from Germany. It is an immense, flat, turnip-shaped apple, but, so far as we have yet tested it, with but little flavour, and only fit for cooking. Fruit very large, regularly formed, but very much flattened. Stalk short. Skin pale yellow, with sometimes a little red in the sun. Flesh tolerably juicy. September to January.

119. MURPHY.   Man. Ken.

This is an agreeable, Pearmain flavoured apple, strongly re.
sembling, indeed, the Blue Pearmain.   It is a seedling, raised by
Mr. D. Murphy, of Salem, Mass.   Fruit pretty large, roundish,
oblong.   Skin pale red, streaked with darker red, and marked
with blotches of the same colour.   Calyx set in a narrow basin.
Flesh white, tender, with an agreeable, rather rich flavour.
November to February.

120. MICHAEL HENRY PIPPIN.   Coxe. Thomp.

A New-Jersey fruit, a native of Monmouth county, first
described by Coxe, and highly esteemed in many parts of the
Middle States.   Fruit of medium size, roundish, oblong or
ovate, narrowing to the eye, smooth, and when first picked, of
a dull green, resembling slightly the Newtown Pippin.   Skin
when ripe, of a lively yellowish green.   Stalk short and rather
thick.   Calyx set in a narrow basin.   Flesh yellow, very tender,
juicy, and high flavoured.   The tree forms a very upright head,
with pretty strong shoots.   November to March.

121. NEWTOWN PIPPIN. § Coxe. Thomp.

> Green Newtown Pippin.
> Green Winter Pippin
> American Newtown Pippin.
> Petersburgh Pippin.

The Newtown Pippin stands at the head of all apples, and is,
when in perfection, acknowledged to be unrivalled in all the
qualities which constitute a high flavoured dessert apple, to
which it combines the quality of long keeping without the
least shrivelling, retaining its high flavour to the last.   It is
very largely raised in New-York and New-Jersey for expor-
tation, and commands the highest price in Covent Garden
Market, London.   This variety is a native of Newtown, Long
Island, and it requires a pretty strong, deep, warm soil, to
attain its full perfection, and in the orchard it should be well
manured every two or three years.   For this reason, while it
is planted by acres in orchards in New-York and the Middle
States, it is rarely raised in large quantities or with much success in New-England.   On the Hudson, thousands of barrels
of the fairest and richest Newtown pippins are constantly produced.   The tree is of rather slender and slow growth, and even
while young, is always remarkable for its rough bark.
Fruit of medium size, roundish, a little irregular in its outline, caused by two or three obscure ribs on the sides—and

broadest at the base, next the stalk; about three inches in diameter, and two and a half deep. Skin dull green, becoming olive green when ripe, with a faint, dull brownish blush on one side, dotted with small gray specks, and with delicate russet rays around the stalk. Calyx quite small and closed, set in a narrow and shallow basin. Stalk half an inch long, rather slender, deeply sunk in a wide, funnel-shaped cavity. Flesh greenish-white, very juicy, crisp, with a fine aroma, and an exceedingly high and delicious flavour. When the fruit is not grown on healthy trees, it is liable to be spotted with black spots. This is one of the finest keeping apples, and is in eating from December to May—but is in the finest perfection in March.

122. NEWTOWN PIPPIN, YELLOW. § Coxe. Thomp.

The Yellow Newtown Pippin strongly resembles the forego ing, and it is difficult to say which is the superiour fruit. The Yellow is handsomer, and has a higher perfume than the Green, and its flesh is rather firmer, and equally high flavoured; while the Green is more juicy, crisp, and tender. The Yellow Newtown Pippin is rather flatter, measuring only about two inches

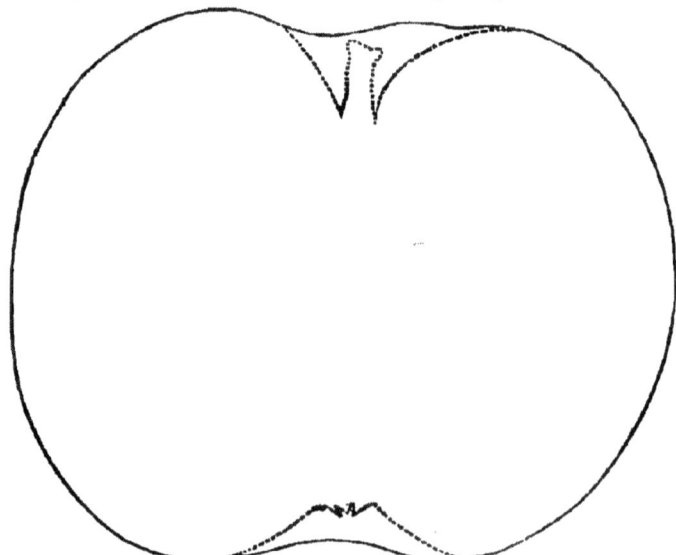

Fig. 46. Yellow Newtown Pippin.

deep, and it is always quite angular—projecting more on one side of the stalk than the other. When fully ripe, it is yellow, with a rather lively red cheek, and a smooth skin, few or none of the spots on the Green variety, but with the same russet marks at the stalk. It is also more highly fragrant before, and after, it is cut than the Green. The flesh is firm, crisp, juicy, and with a very rich and high flavour. Both the Newtown pippins grow alike, and they are both excellent bearers. This variety is rather hardier and succeeds best in the eastern states. We have kept the fruit until the 4th of July.

123. NORTHERN SPY.

This beautiful new American fruit is one of the most delicious, fragrant, and sprightly of all late dessert apples. It ripens in January, keeps till June, and always commands the highest market price. The tree is of rapid, upright growth, and bears moderate crops. It originated on the farm of Oliver Chapin, of Bloomfield, near Rochester, N. Y.

Fruit large, conical-flattened. Skin thin, smooth, in the shade greenish or pale yellow, in the sun covered with light and dark stripes of purplish-red, marked with a few pale dots, and a thin, white bloom. Stalk three-fourths of an inch long, rather slender, planted in a very wide, deep cavity, marked with russet. Calyx small, closed; basin narrow, abrupt, furrowed. Flesh white, fine-grained, tender, slightly sub-acid, with a peculiarly fresh and delicious flavor.

123. NONPAREIL, OLD.   Lang. Lind. Thomp.

English Nonpareil.   Non Pareille.   O. Duh.

The Old Nonpareil is a favourite apple in England, but it is little esteemed in this country. November to January.

Fruit below medium size, roundish, a little ovate, and flattened. Skin greenish-yellow, thinly coated with pale russet. Stalk slender, an inch long. Calyx small, set in a narrow, round basin. Flesh firm, crisp, with a rich, acid, poignant flavour.

124. NONPAREIL, SCARLET.   Thomp. Lind. Ron.

New Scarlet Nonpareil.

A handsomer and larger variety of the foregoing. Fruit of medium size, roundish, two and a half inches in diameter, and half an inch less in depth—regularly formed. Skin, in the sun deep red, sprinkled with brownish gray dots on a ground of yellowish green, slightly streaked. Calyx set in a regularly formed, shallow basin, with a few small plaits. Stalk nearly an inch long, and rather stout. Flesh firm, yellowish-white, with a rich, acid juice. The tree is a much stronger grower than the old sort. November to February.

125. NORFOLK BEAUFIN.   Thomp. Lind.

Read's Baker
Catshead Beaufin.

Chiefly valued for drying. In Norfolk, England, quite a

trade is carried on in the dried fruit of this apple—which is also in high esteem for preserves, and all kitchen uses.

Fruit large, flat, a little irregular in outline. Skin dark dingy red, or copper colour, on a greenish ground. Stalk half an inch long, fleshy, deeply sunk. Calyx set in an irregular, plaited basin. Flesh firm, of poor flavour, with a sub-acid juice. November to May. A great bearer.

126. NEWARK KING. Coxe. Thomp.

Hinckman.

A new-Jersey fruit, of medium size, conical or Pearmain-shaped, and of handsome appearance. Skin smooth, red, with a few yellow streaks and dots, on a greenish yellow ground. Calyx set in a narrow basin. Flesh tender, with a rather rich, pleasant flavour. The tree is spreading, and bears well. November to February.

127. NEWARK PIPPIN. Coxe.

French Pippin. }
Yellow Pippin. } *of some American gardens.*

A handsome and very excellent early winter variety, easily known by the crooked, irregular growth of the tree, and the drooping habit of the branches.

Fruit rather large, roundish-oblong, regularly formed. Skin greenish yellow, becoming a fine yellow when fully ripe, with clusters of small black dots, and rarely a very faint blush. Calyx in a regular and rather deep basin. Stalk moderately long, and deeply inserted. Flesh yellow, tender, very rich, juicy, and high flavoured. A very desirable fruit for the amateur's garden. November to February.

128. PEARMAIN, HEREFORDSHIRE. § Thomp.

Winter Pearmain. *Coxe.*
Royal Pearmain. *Lind. Ron.*
Parmin Royal. *Knoop.*
Old Pearmain.
Royale d'Angleterre.

This delicious old variety, generally known here as the English or Royal Pearmain, is one of the finest of all winter dessert fruits, and its mild and agreeable flavour renders it here, as abroad, an universal favourite, both as a dessert apple, and for cooking.

Fruit of medium size, oblong, and of a pretty regular Pearmain-shape. Skin stained, and mottled with soft, brownish red on a dull, russety green ground, dotted with grayish specks. The red thickly mottled near the eye, with yellowish russet spots.

11

Stalk slender, half an inch long. Calyx with wide-spread, reflexed segments, and set in a shallow, narrow, slightly plaited
basin. Flesh pale yellow, very mellow and tender, with a
pleasant, aromatic flavour. A moderate bearer, but often pro-

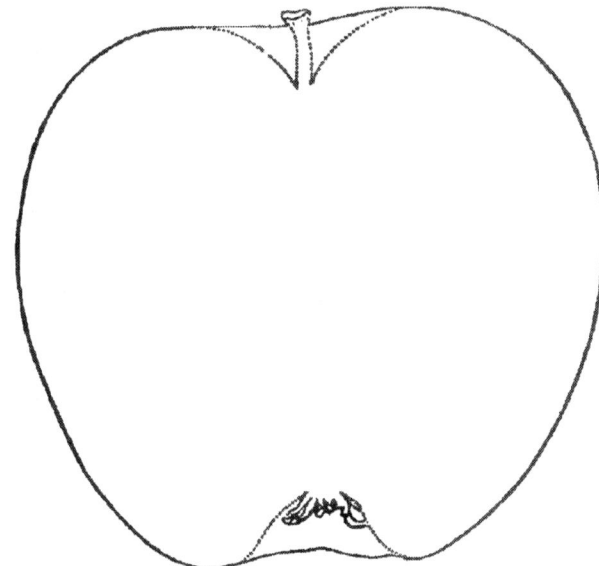

Fig. 47. *Herefordshire Pearmain.*

duces large crops on light soils, which are well adapted to this
sort. November to February. A strong grower.

The Winter Pearmain of most American orchards, is the Autumn Pearmain of this, and most English works.

129. PEARMAIN, BLUE. § Man. Ken. Thomp.

The Blue Pearmain is a large and very showy fruit, and is
therefore popular in the New-England markets. The numerous large russetty yellow dots which are sprinkled over the
skin, and the bloom which overspreads it, mark this apple.

Fruit of the largest size, roundish, regularly formed, very
slightly conical. Skin covered with stripes and blotches of
dark purplish-red, over a dull ground—and appearing bluish
from the white bloom. Stalk short, slender, sunk in a deep
hollow, rather uneven. Calyx small, pretty deeply sunk in an
even basin. Flesh yellowish, mild, rather rich and good. The
tree grows strongly, and bears moderate crops. October to
February.

130. PEARMAIN, CLAYGATE. Thomp. Lind.

This is a new kind of Pearmain, lately received from England, which has not yet fruited with us, but bears the highest
character abroad.

Fruit of medium size, and Pearmain shape. Skin greenish-
yellow, nearly covered with brownish red. Flesh yellow, tender, with a very rich, aromatic " Ribston pippin flavour." The
tree is very hardy. November to March.

131. PEARMAIN, ADAMS. Thomp. Lind.

Norfolk Pippin.

The Adams' Pearmain is a handsome variety, which stands
high in England, but, as yet, does not hold its character with us.
Fruit above medium size, of a roundish, Pearmain-shape.
Skin pale yellow, with a few stripes and patches of salmon red
and yellow, on the sunny side, and dotted with white specks
near the stalk—and slightly touched with russet. Stalk three
fourths of an inch long, rather slender. Calyx closed, and set
in a narrow basin, slightly plaited. Flesh yellowish, quite firm
and crisp, with a brisk, sub-acid, and rather rich flavour. November to February.

132. PEARMAIN, SWEET. §

A handsome, dark red, sweet apple, of the Pearmain class, of
very saccharine flavour, and much esteemed in some parts of

Fig. 48. *Sweet Pearmain.*

the eastern states for baking and eating. It has long been cultivated near Hartford, and also in Rhode Island, and was introduced from England before the revolution.

Fruit of medium size, and roundish Pearmain shape. Skin fine dark red, with rough russet dots, and covered with a bluish bloom—near the eye a lighter red. Stalk rather long and slender, deeply sunk in a wide funnel-shaped cavity. Calyx woolly, set in a very shallow and narrow basin. Flesh tender, moderately juicy, and very sweet and rich. December.

132. PARADISE, WINTER SWEET.

The Winter Sweet Paradise is a very productive and excellent orchard fruit, always fair, and of fine appearance. We received it some years ago, along with the Summer Sweet Paradise, from Mr. Garber, of Columbia, Pa., and consider it a native fruit.

Fruit rather large, regularly formed, roundish. Skin fair and smooth, dull green when picked, with a brownish blush, becoming a little paler at maturity. Stalk short, set in a round cavity. Calyx small, basin shallow and narrow. Flesh white, fine grained, juicy, sweet, sprightly, and very good. November to March.

133. POMME GRISE.

Grise   *Thomp.*
Gray Apple.

A small gray apple, from Canada, and undoubtedly one of the finest dessert apples for a northern climate. It is not a strong grower, but is a good bearer, and has an excellent flavour.

Fruit below medium size, roundish, somewhat flattened. Skin greenish gray or russet, with a little red towards the eye. Calyx small, set in a round basin. Flesh tender, rich, and high flavoured.

134. POUND ROYAL §

A charming winter apple, as yet only known in Connecticut, but deserving extensive cultivation. We have this sort from the Rev. Mr. Ransdell, of that state, who informs us that the oldest known trees are growing on the Putnam estate, in Pomfret, Conn. It is not unlikely from the name by which it is generally known, that it may be of French origin,—either introduced as a young tree, or raised from seeds given Gen. Putnam by the French officers of his acquaintance, during the war. The trees are vigorous growers, and abundant bearers.

Fruit large, roundish-oblong, with a slightly uneven surface—and sometimes an obscure furrow on one side. Skin pale yellowish-white, rarely with a faint blush, and marked when ripe with a few large ruddy or dark specks. Stalk an inch and a quarter long, slender, rather deeply inserted. Calyx set in a furrowed, irregular basin. Flesh very tender, breaking, fine grained, with a mild, agreeable, sprightly flavour. Seeds enclosed in a hollow chamber. In use from December to April. This is distinct from the Pomme Royale (p. 83).

Fig. 49. *Pound Royal.*

135. Pennock's Red Winter. Thomp.

Pennock. *Coxe.*

This is a Pennsylvania fruit, of good quality for the table, and an excellent baking apple. Unfortunately it is, of late, so liable to the bitter-rot, that it is scarcely worth cultivation.

Fruit quite large, angular or one-sided, generally flat, but occasionally roundish-oblong. Skin fine deep red, with faint, indistinct streaks of yellow, and a few black specks. Stalk short. Flesh yellow, tender and juicy, with a pleasant, sweet flavour. The tree is large, makes a firm, spreading head, and is a regular bearer. November to March.

11*

136. Priestly. Coxe. Thomp.

Priestley's American.

Another native of the same state as the foregoing variety, and named, like it, after the cultivator who first brought it into notice. This sort has a pleasant, spicy flavour, and is much esteemed for eating and cooking.

Fruit large, roundish-oblong. Skin smooth, dull red, with small streaks of yellowish green, dotted with greenish specks. Stalk of medium length, and inserted in a round, pretty deep cavity. Flesh white, moderately juicy, with a spicy, agreeable flavour. The foliage is large, and the tree, which is a handsome upright grower, bears well on light sandy soils. December to March.

137. Pearson's Plate. Thomp.

A new variety, lately received from England, and not yet well tested here, but which has a very high reputation. Fruit small, about two and a half inches in diameter, regularly formed, flat. Skin greenish-yellow, becoming yellow, with a little red in the sun. Flavour first rate in all respects. Mr. Thomson says this is a good bearer, and a remarkably handsome dessert fruit.

138. Peck's Pleasant.

A first rate fruit in all respects, belonging to the Newtown pippin class. It has long been cultivated in Rhode Island, where we think it originated, and in the northern part of Connecticut, but as yet is little known out of that district of country, but deserves extensive dissemination. It considerably resembles the Yellow Newtown pippin, though a larger fruit, with more tender flesh, and is scarcely inferiour to it in flavour.

Fruit above medium size, roundish, a little angular, and slightly flattened, with an indistinct furrow on one side. Skin smooth, and when first gathered, green, with a little dark red ; but when ripe, a beautiful clear yellow, with bright blush on the sunny side and near the stalk, marked with scattered gray dots. The stalk is peculiarly fleshy and flattened, short, and sunk in a wide, rather wavy cavity. Calyx woolly, sunk in a narrow, abruptly, and pretty deeply sunk basin. Flesh yellowish, fine grained, juicy, crisp and tender, with a delicious, high aromatic flavour. The tree is only a moderate grower, but bears regularly and well, and the fruit commands a high price in market. Mr. S. Lyman, who raises this fruit in great perfection, informs us that with him the apples on the lower branches of old trees are flat, while those on the upper branches are nearly conical. November to March.

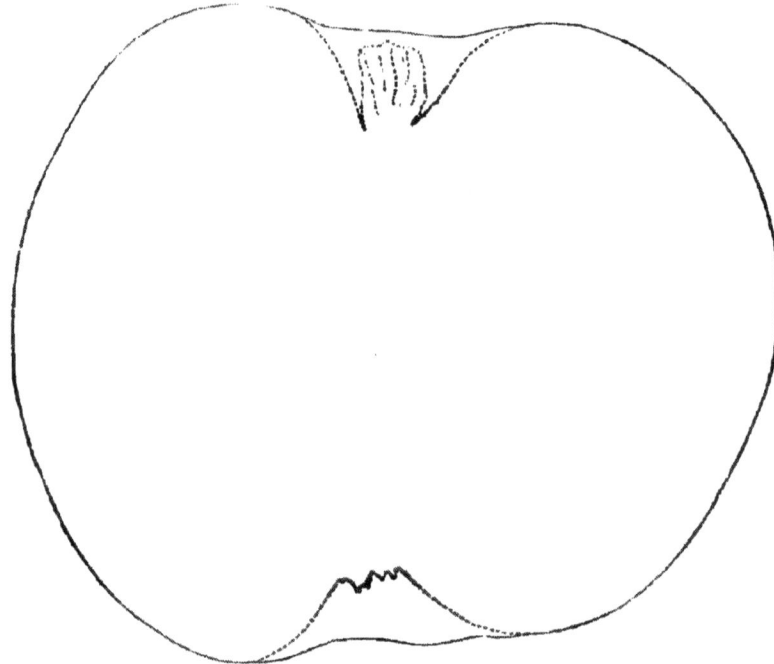

Fig. 50. *Peck's Pleasant.*

139. PENNINGTON'S SEEDLING. Thomp. Lii d.

This is a new russet variety from England, which, we think, will prove a valuable one.

Fruit of medium size, nearly flat, a little angular, and broadest at the base. Skin mostly covered with rough yellow russet, with a little pale brown in the sun. Stalk three fourths of an inch long, pretty stout, planted in a wide, irregular cavity. Calyx with long segments, set in a rather shallow, wavy basin. Flesh yellowish, firm, crisp, with a brisk, high flavoured, acid juice. November to March.

140. POUND. Coxe. Thomp.

A very large and showy fruit, but of very indifferent quality, and not worth cultivation where better sorts are to be had. The fruit is roundish-oblong, striped with red, on a dull greenish yellow ground. The stalk short, and deeply inserted. The flesh yellowish green, and without much flavour. October to January.

141. RHODE ISLAND GREENING.   Coxe. Thomp. Man.

Burlington Greening.
Jersey Greening ! *Coxe.*

The Rhode Island Greening is such an universal favourite, and is so generally known, that it seems almost superfluous to give a description of it.   It succeeds well in almost all parts of the country, and on a great variety of soils, and is, perhaps, more generally esteemed than any other early winter fruit.   In the eastern states where the Newtown pippin does not attain full perfection, this apple takes its place—and in England, it is frequently sold for that fruit, which, however, it does not equal. [The *Green* Newtown Pippin described by Lindley is this fruit.]

Fig. 51. *Rhode Island Greening.*

Fruit large, roundish, a little flattened, pretty regular, but often obscurely ribbed.   Skin oily smooth, dark green, becoming pale green when ripe, when it sometimes shows a dull blush near the stalk.   Calyx small, woolly, closed, in a slightly sunk, scarcely plaited basin.   Stalk three fourths of an inch long, curved, thickest at the bottom.   Flesh yellow, fine grained, tender, crisp, with an abundance of rich, slightly aromatic, lively, acid juice.   The tree grows very strongly, and resembles the Fall pippin in its wood and leaves, and bears most abundant crops.   The fruit is as excellent for cooking, as for the dessert. November to February—or, in the north, to March.

142. REINETTE, CANADA. Thomp. Nois.

Canadian Reinette. *Lind.*
Grosse Reinette d'Angleterre. *O. Duh.*
Pomme du Caen. ⎫
Reinette du Canada Blanche. ⎬ *of various*
Reinette Grosse du Canada. ⎪ *European*
Reinette du Canada à Cortes. ⎭ *collections*
De Bretagne.
Portugal.
Januarea.
Wahr Reinette.

It is easy to see that the Canada Reinette is a popular and highly esteemed variety in Europe, by the great number of synonyms under which it is known. It is doubtful, notwithstanding its name, whether it is truly of Canadian origin, as Merlet, a French writer, describes the same fruit in the 17th century; and some authors think it was first brought to this continent from Normandy, and carried back under its new name. At any rate, it is a very large and handsome fruit, a good bearer, and of excellent quality in all respects. It is yet little known in the United States, but deserves extensive orchard culture.

Fruit of the largest size, conical, flattened; rather irregular, with projecting ribs; broad at the base, narrowing towards the eye, four inches in diameter, and three deep. Skin greenish-yellow, slightly washed with brown on the sunny side. Stalk short, inserted in a wide hollow. Calyx short and large, set in a rather deep, irregular basin. Flesh nearly white, rather firm, juicy, with a rich, lively, sub-acid flavour. Ripe in December, and, if picked early in autumn, it will keep till April.

143. REINETTE, GOLDEN. Thomp. Ron. Lind.

Aurore. ⎫
Kirke's Golden Reinette. ⎪
Yellow German Reinette. ⎪
Reinette d'Aix. ⎪ *of various*
English Pippin. ⎪ *European*
Court-pendu Doré. ⎬ *collections,*
Wyker Pippin. ⎪ *ac. to*
Elizabet. ⎪ *Thomp.*
Wygers. ⎪
Megginch Favourite. ⎪
Dundee. ⎭

The Golden Reinette is a very popular dessert fruit in England and on the continent, combining beauty and high flavour It is yet but little known here.

Fruit below medium size, very regularly formed, roundish, a little flattened. Skin smooth, greenish,—becoming golden yellow in the shade, washed and striped with fine soft red, on the

sunny side, mingled with scattered, russet dots. Stalk long,
and inserted moderately deep. Calyx large, set in a broad, but
shallow basin. Flesh yel'ow, crisp, with a rich, sugary, or
scarcely acid juice. October to January.

This is different and superiour to the *Reinette Doreé,* or *Jaune
Hâtive* of the French, which is more yellow, and somewhat resembles it.

144. REINETTE BLANCHE D'ESPAGNE. Thomp. Nois.

White Spanish Reinette. *Pom Mag Lind.*
D'Espagne   ⎫ *of some*
Fall Pippin   ⎬ *English*
Large Fall Pippin. ⎬ *gardens.*
Cobbett s Fall Pippin. ⎭

A very celebrated old Spanish variety, which is said to be the
national apple of Spain, where it is called *Cameusar.* Notwithstanding that Thompson and other English authorities consider
this apple the same as our Fall Pippin, we are yet strongly of
opinion that it is different. The true Fall Pippin is only an
autumn variety, while this is a winter sort, keeping till mid-
winter here, and in England till March. It is quite probable
that the White Spanish Reinette is the parent of both the Fall
and Holland Pippins. The fruit of the present variety is rather
more oblong than that of the Fall Pippin.

Fruit very large, roundish-*oblong,* somewhat angular, with
broad ribs on its sides, terminating in an uneven crown, where
it is nearly as broad as at the base. Calyx large, open, very
deeply sunk in a broad-angled, oblique, irregular basin. Stalk
half an inch long, set in a rather small, even cavity. Skin
smooth, yellowish-green on the shaded side, orange, tinged with
brownish-red next the sun, and sprinkled with blackish dots.
Flesh yellowish-white, crisp, tender, with a sugary juice.
Noisette, (*Jardin Fruitier*) adds, " the skin is covered with a
bloom, like that on a plum, which distinguishes this variety from
all those most resembling it." The tree has the same wood,
foliage, and vigorous habit, as our Fall Pippin, and the fruit
keeps from November to February, or March.

145. REINETTE TRIOMPHANTE. M. Christ.

Victorious Reinette.

A German early winter apple, which we have recently received, and which has only borne once in this country.

Fruit large, oblong, regularly formed. Skin pale yellow,
thickly dotted with white specks, and rough, projecting warts.
Flesh yellow, firm, juicy, with a pleasant aromatic flavour.
The tree is of thrifty growth, and is said to bear well.

146. RIBSTON PIPPIN. Thomp. Lind. Ron.

Glory of York.
Travers'.
Formosa Pippin.

The Ribston Pippin, a Yorkshire apple, stands as high in Great Britain as the Bank of England, and to say that an apple has a Ribston flavour is, there, the highest praise that can be bestowed. But it is scarcely so much esteemed here, and must be content to give place, with us, to the Newtown Pippin, the Swaar, the Spitzemberg, or the Baldwin. In Maine, and parts of Canada, it is very fine and productive.

Fruit of medium size, roundish. Skin greenish-yellow, mixed with a little russet near the stalk, and clouded with dull red on the sunny side. Stalk short, slender, planted in a rather wide cavity. Calyx small, closed, and set in an angular basin. Flesh deep yellow, firm, crisp, with a sharp, rich, aromatic flavour. The tree forms a spreading top. November to February.

147. ROMAN STEM. Coxe.

The Roman Stem is not generally known out of New-Jersey. It originated at Burlington, in that state, and is much esteemed in that neighbourhood. In flavour, it belongs to the class of sprightly, pleasant apples, and somewhat resembles the Yellow Belle Fleur. Tree very productive.

Fruit scarcely of medium size, roundish-oblong—or often ovate. Skin whitish-yellow, with a faint brownish blush, sprinkled with patches of small black dots, and, when ripe, having a few reddish specks, unless the fruit is very fair. Stalk three-fourths of an inch long, inserted in a shallow cavity, under a fleshy protuberance, which the farmers have likened to a Roman nose, whence the name. Calyx set in a rather narrow basin, with a few plaits. Core hollow. Flesh tender, juicy, with a sprightly, agreeable flavour—not first rate. November to March.

148. RUSSET, AMERICAN GOLDEN. §

Golden Russet. *Man. Ken.*
Sheep Nose.
Bullock's Pippin. } *Coxe.*

The American Golden Russet is one of the most delicious and tender apples, its flesh resembling more in texture that of a buttery pear, than that of an ordinary apple. It is widely cultivated at the west, and in New-England as the Golden Russet, and though neither handsome, nor large, is still an universal favourite from its great productiveness and admirable flavour. The uncouth name of Coxe, *Sheep-nose*, is nearly obsolete, except in New-Jersey, and we therefore adopt the present one, to which it is well entitled. The tree is thrifty, with upright *drab* coloured shoots.

Fruit below medium size, roundish-ovate. Skin dull yellow, sprinkled with a very thin russet. Stalk rather long and slender. Calyx closed, and set in a rather narrow basin. Flesh yellowish, very tender, (almost melting,) juicy, with a mild, rich, spicy flavour. October to January.

The ENGLISH GOLDEN RUSSET is a sub-acid sort, much inferiour to the above. Fruit middle sized, ovate. Skin rough and thick, of a dingy, yellow russet, rarely with a red blush. Stalk very short, deeply planted in a narrow cavity. Flesh pale yellow, very firm and crisp, with a brisk, rather aromatic flavour. Trees with many slender, weeping branches. November to March.

148. RUSSET, PUTNAM. §

For a knowledge of this celebrated western apple, we are indebted to that zealous pomologist, our friend, Professor Kirtland, of Cleveland. It is considered decidedly the most valuable late keeping apple in the West, not inferiour to the Newtown Pippin, and the growth of the tree very luxuriant. It originated at Marietta, Ohio, and is largely grown for the New-Orleans and West India markets. Fruit medium, or large, form rather flat. Skin yellow, blotched with russet, and at times tinged with a dull red cheek. Flesh firm, yet tender, deep yellow, juicy, sub-acid, rich, and very high flavoured March and April.*

149. RUSSET, ENGLISH.

The English Russet is a valuable, long keeping variety, extensively cultivated, and well known by this name on the Hudson, but which we have not been able to identify with any English sort. It is not fit for use until February, and may be kept till July, which, together with its great productiveness and good flavour, renders it a very valuable market fruit. It is acknowledged one of the most profitable orchard apples.

Fruit of medium size, ovate, or sometimes conical, and very regularly formed. Skin pale greenish yellow, about two-thirds covered with russet, which is thickest near the stalk. Calyx small, closed, and set in an even, round basin, of moderate depth. Stalk rather small, projecting even with the base, and pretty deeply inserted, in a narrow, smooth cavity. Flesh yellowish-white, firm, crisp, with a pleasant, mild, slightly sub-acid flavour.

---

* This is since ascertained to be identical with the ROXBURY RUSSET. [7th Ed.]

The trees grow very straight, and form upright heads, and the wood is smooth and of a lively brown.

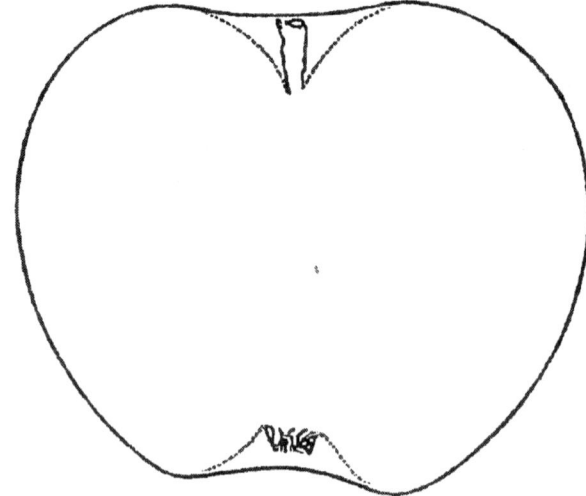

Fig. 53. *English Russet.*

150. RUSSET, BOSTON OR ROXBURY. Man. Thomp.

Roxbury Russeting. *Ken.*

This Russet, a native of Massachusetts, is one of the most popular market fruits in the country, as it is excellent, a pro-

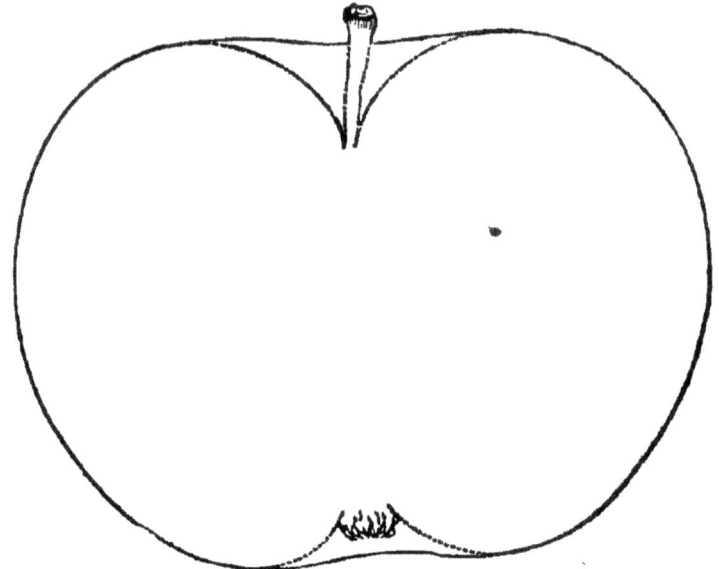

Fig. 54. *Boston Russet.*

digious bearer, and keeps till late in the spring. It is in every
way, highly deserving extensive cultivation.

Fruit of medium size, often large roundish, a little flattened,
and slightly angular. Skin at first dull green, covered with
brownish-yellow russet when ripe, with, rarely, a faint blush
on one side. Stalk nearly three fourths of an inch long, rather
slender, not deeply inserted. Calyx closed, set in a round basin,
of moderate depth. Flesh greenish-white, moderately juicy,
with a rather rich, sub-acid flavour. Ripens in January, and
may be brought to market in June.

There are several native varieties of Russet or " Leather
Coats," of larger size than the foregoing, but they are much
inferior, being apt to shrivel and become tasteless.

151. Red Gilliflower.

This appears to be a native variety, and, although second
rate, is esteemed in some parts of the country. Fruit of
medium size, oblong, narrowing rapidly to the eye, where it is
somewhat ribbed. The skin is smooth, and of a fine dark red.
The calyx is set in a narrow, rather shallow, furrowed basin.
Flesh white, of a mild flavour. November to January.

152. Sam Young. Thomp. Lind. P. Mag.

Irish Russet.

An exceedingly high flavoured, little dessert Russet from
Kilkenny, in Ireland, and fit for use in early winter.

Fruit small, slightly flattened, and regularly formed. Skin
bright yellow, a good deal covered with gray russet, and dotted
on the yellow portion with small brown specks. Stalk short.
Calyx large and expanded, placed in a broad basin. Flesh
greenish, quite juicy and tender, with a rich and excellent flavour. November to January.

153. Surprise. Thomp.

A small, round, whitish-yellow apple, of little or no value, but
admired by some, for its singularity,—the flesh being stained
with red. November to January.

154. Swaar. Coxe. Floy. Thomp.

This is a truly noble American fruit, produced by the Dutch
settlers on the Hudson, near Esopus, and so termed, from its
unusual weight, this word, in the Low Dutch, meaning *heavy*,
It requires a deep, rich, sandy loam, to bring it to perfection

and, in its native soils, we have seen it twelve inches in circumference, and of a deep golden yellow colour.   It is one of the
finest flavoured apples in America, and deserves extensive cultivation, in all favourable positions, though it does not succeed
well in damp or cold soils.

Fig. 55. *Swaar.*

Fruit large, regularly formed, roundish.   Skin greenish-yellow when first gathered, but when entirely ripe, of a fine, dead
gold colour, dotted with numerous distinct brown specks, and
sometimes faintly marbled with gray russet on the side, and
round the stalk.   Stalk slender, three fourths of an inch long,
inserted in a very round cavity.   [Sometimes this cavity is partially closed.]   Calyx small, greenish, set in a shallow basin—
scarcely plaited.   Flesh yellowish, fine grained, tender, with
an exceedingly rich, aromatic flavour, and a spicy smell.   Core
small.   The trees bear fair crops, and the fruit is in season
from December to March.

155. STURMER PIPPIN.   Thomp.

This is a new English variety, of the very highest reputation.
We have just received trees, but we have, for the following description, the high authority of Mr. Thompson.   Fruit of middle
size, short, conical.   Skin yellowish-green, and brownish red ;
flesh firm, with a brisk, rich flavour.   The tree is healthy, and
a good bearer, and the fruit retains its flavour and briskness till
midsummer.

156. Sweeting, Hartford.

Spencer Sweeting.

A very excellent winter sweet apple, introduced to notice by
Dr. E. W. Bull, a zealous amateur of Hartford. It may be kept
till June, and this, added to its great productiveness, renders it
a most profitable market fruit. The original tree of the Hartford Sweeting is growing on the farm of Mr. Spencer, a few
miles from Hartford, and has borne over forty bushels in a
season. The wood is rather strong, but of slow growth, and is
very hardy; (branches not pendulous, as stated by Kenrick.)
Fruit rather large, roundish, slightly flattened. Skin smooth,
and fair, almost covered and striped with fine red over a yellowish-green ground,—and sprinkled with small gray dots. Stalk
nearly three quarters of an inch long, slender, inserted in a
rather shallow, round cavity. Calyx broad, closed, with few
segments, set in a slightly uneven basin which is but little sunk.
Flesh very juicy, tender, with a rich, agreeable flavour. December to May or June.

157. Sweeting, Ladies'. §

The Ladies' Sweeting we consider the finest winter sweet
apple, for the dessert, yet known or cultivated in this country.

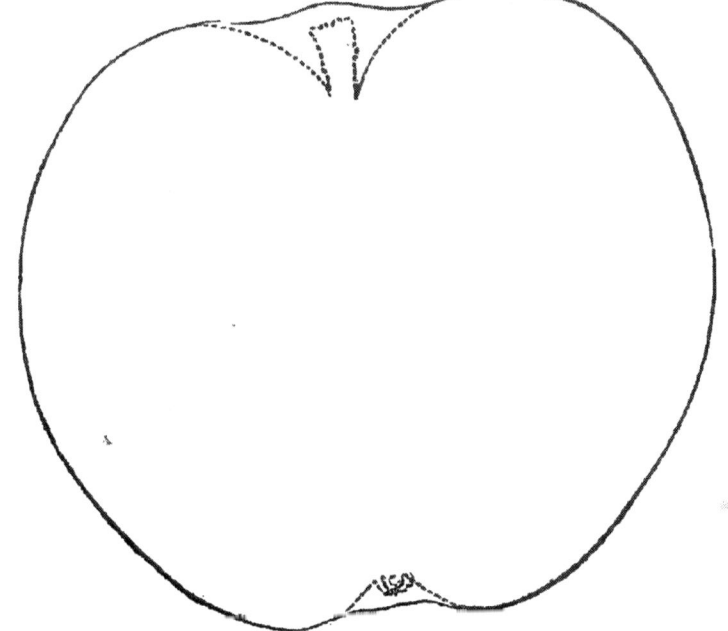

Fig. 56. *Ladies' Sweeting.*

ιts handsome appearance, delightful perfume, sprightly flavour, and the long time which it remains in perfection, render it universally admired wherever it is known, and no garden should be without it. It is a native of this neighbourhood, and thousands of trees of this variety, have been sent from this garden, to various parts of the union. The wood is not very strong, but it grows thriftily, and bears very abundantly.

Fruit large, roundish-ovate, narrowing pretty rapidly to the eye. Skin very smooth, nearly covered with red in the sun, but pale yellowish-green in the shade, with broken stripes of pale red. The red is sprinkled with well marked, yellowish-gray dots and covered, when first gathered, with a thin white bloom. There is also generally a faint marbling of cloudy white over the red, on the shady side of the fruit, and rays of the same around the stalk. Calyx quite small, set in a narrow, shallow, plaited basin. Stalk half an inch long, in a shallow cavity. Flesh greenish-white, exceedingly tender, juicy and crisp, with a delicious, sprightly, agreeably perfumed flavour. Keeps without shrivelling, or losing its flavour, till May.

158. Sweeting, Tolman's.

The Tolman's Sweeting is scarcely second rate as a table fruit, but it is one of the most popular orchard sorts, from its great productiveness, its value as food for swine and cattle, as well as for baking. Form nearly globular. Skin, when fully ripe, whitish-yellow, with a soft blush on one side. Stalk rather long and slender, inclining to one side, and inserted in a rather wide, shallow, but regular cavity. Calyx set in a small basin, slightly depressed. Flesh quite white, rather firm, fine grained, with a rich, sweet flavour. November to April. This fruit, a native of Rhode Island, considerably resembles the Danver's Winter Sweet, of Massachusetts.

159. Sweeting, Ramsdell's. ◊

Ramsdel's Red Pumpkin Sweet. *Ken.*
Ramsdell's Sweet.
Red Pumpkin Sweet.

Ramsdell's Sweeting we have lately received from Connecticut, where it is greatly esteemed for the very large crops it bears, as well as for its remarkably rich saccharine flavour. We believe it is a native of Connecticut; and it derives its name from the Rev. H. S. Ramsdell, of Thompson, in that

state, who has introduced it to public attention.   The tree is
very vigorous, grows remarkably straight, and upright, comes
early into bearing, and yields every year enormously.

Fruit rather above medium size, oblong, regularly shaped,
and tapering slightly towards the eye.   Skin rich, dark red
dotted with fawn-coloured specks, and covered with a blue
bloom.   Stalk quite short, deeply sunk in a rather narrow cavity.   Calyx set in a pretty deep even basin.   Flesh yellowish,
very tender and mellow, unusually sweet and rich.   In weight
the apple is light.   October to February.

161. Spitzenburgh, Esopus.   Coxe.

Æsopus Spitzemberg.   *Thomp. Lind.*
Æsopus Spitzenburg.   *Ken.*
True Spitzenburgh.

The Esopus Spitzenburgh is a handsome, truly delicious apple,
and is generally considered, by all good judges, equal to the

Fig. 57.   *Esopus Spitzenburgh.*

Newtown Pippin, and unsurpassed as a dessert fruit, by any other variety. It originated at Esopus, a famous apple district, originally settled by the Low Dutch, on the Hudson, where it is still raised in its highest perfection. But throughout the whole of New-York, it is considered the first of apples, and its beauty and productiveness render it highly profitable for orchard culture. The fruit of this variety brought from Western New-York, seems deficient in flavour, which is, perhaps, owing to the excessive richness of the soil there. The tree has rather slender shoots, and when in bearing, has long and hanging limbs.

Fruit large, oblong, tapering roundly to the eye. Skin smooth, nearly covered with rich, lively red, dotted with distinct yellowish russet dots. On the shaded side, is a yellowish ground, with streaks and broken stripes of red. Stalk rather long,—three fourths of an inch—and slender, projecting beyond the base, and inserted in a wide cavity. Calyx small, and closed, set in a shallow basin, which is slightly furrowed. Flesh yellow, rather firm, crisp, juicy, with a delicious rich, brisk flavour. Seeds in a hollow core. December to February

162. SPITZENBURGH, FLUSHING.

This variety has been confounded by Coxe, and more recently by Thompson, with the foregoing, but is really quite distinct. The tree makes strong, brown shoots, different from the slender yellowish ones of the Esopus Spitzenburgh.

The fruit is roundish-conical, stalk set in a narrow cavity, projecting beyond the fruit. Skin nearly covered with red, on a greenish yellow ground, dotted with large fawn spots, and coated with a slight bloom. Calyx small, in an even basin. Flesh white, juicy, crisp, nearly sweet, and of pleasant flavour, but without the brisk richness, or yellow colour of the Esopus Spitzenburgh. October to February.

KAIGHN'S SPITZENBERGH is an inferior variety, of a conical form, and pale red colour. It originated in New-Jersey and is only of third rate quality. The tree is also an ugly, rambling grower. The fruit keeps till April.

163. SPITZENBERG, NEWTOWN. Coxe. Thomp. Lind.

Matchless.
Burlington Spitzenberg.

The Newtown Spitzenberg comes from Newtown, on Long Island. It is a roundish, handsome fruit, of good flavour, but inferiour to the Esopus variety.

Fruit of medium size and regular form, roundish, slightly flattened. Skin smooth, beautiful yellow, with a fine red cheek, a little streaked with brighter red, and marked with numerous dots. Calyx set in a rather wide, even basin. Stalk short, deeply inserted. Flesh rather yellowish, firm, with a mild and agreeable flavour. November to February.

164 SWEETING, WELLS'. §

Wells' Sweeting is one of the most sprightly and agreeable, for the dessert, of all the early winter sweet apples. The only old tree in our knowledge, grows in the orchard of Mr John Wells, near Newburgh, N. Y. We have not been able to trace it farther than this neighbourhood, though it may not have originated here. It makes stout, stiff, upright shoots, and bears well.

Fruit of medium size, roundish, broadest in the middle, and lessening each way. Skin smooth, pale, dull green, (like a Rhode Island Greening in colour, but paler,) with a dull red, or brownish cheek. Stalk rather slender and short. Calyx short, set in quite a shallow basin. Flesh very white, and very tender, abounding with a rich, agreeable, sprightly juice. November to January.

165. TWENTY OUNCE. H. Mag.

Twenty Ounce Apple. } of Cayuga
Eighteen Ounce Apple. } co., *N. Y.*   Cayuga Red Streak ?

A very large and showy apple, well known in Cayuga co., N. Y., and probably a native there. It is a good, sprightly fruit, though not very high flavoured, but its remarkably handsome appearance, and large size, render it one of the most popular fruits in market. The tree is thrifty and makes a compact, neat head, bears regular crops, and the fruit is always fair and handsome.

Fruit very large, roundish. Skin slightly uneven, greenish-yellow, boldly splashed and marbled with stripes of purplish-red. Stalk short, set in a wide deep cavity. Calyx small, basin moderately deep. Flesh coarse-grained, with a sprightly, brisk sub-acid flavor. Oct. to Jan. This is quite distinct from the TWENTY OUNCE PIPPIN, a large, smooth, dull-coloured cooking apple.

166. TEWKSBURY WINTER BLUSH. Coxe.

Mr. Coxe says, this apple was brought from Tewksbury, Hunterdon county, N. J. It is a handsome, fair fruit, with more flavour and juiciness than is usual in long-keeping apples. They may be kept till August, without particular care, quite plump and sound. The size is small, rather flat. The skin smooth, yellow, with a red cheek. Flesh yellow, with more juice and flavour than any other long-keeping variety. The tree grows rapidly and straight—and the fruit hangs till late in the autumn. January to July.

167. VICTUALS AND DRINK.

Big Sweet.
Pompey

This is a large and delicious sweet apple, highly esteemed in the neighbourhood of Newark, New-Jersey, where it originated, about 1750. It was first introduced to notice by Mr. J. W. Hayes, of Newark, from whom we first received trees and specimens of the fruit. The fruit is very light.

Fruit large, oblong, rather irregular, and varies a good deal in size. Skin thin, but rough, dull yellow, marbled with russet, with a faint russet blush on the sunny side. Stalk moderately long and slender, deeply inserted in an irregular cavity. Calyx small, set in a rather shallow basin. Flesh yellowish, tender, breaking, with a rich, sprightly, sweet flavour. In perfection from October to January, but will keep till April. The tree is a moderate bearer.

168. VANDERVERE. Coxe. Thomp. Floy.

Stalcubs.

The Vandervere, when in perfection, is one of the most beautiful and finest apples. But it requires a rich, light, sandy soil, as in a damp heavy soil, it is almost always liable to be spotted, unfair, and destitute of flavour. It is a native of Wilmington, Delaware, and took its name from a family there. It is a fine old variety, and is highly worthy of extensive cultivation, where

Fig. 53. *Vandervere*

the soil is favourable. We have before us some apples of this sort, which are exceedingly beautiful and excellent.

Fruit of medium size, flat. Skin, in its ground colour, yellow, streaked and stained with clouded red, but on the sunny side, deepening into rich red, dotted with light gray specks. Stalk short, inserted in a smooth, rather wide, cavity. Calyx small, closed, set in a regular, well-formed basin, of moderate depth. Flesh yellow, crisp and tender, with a rich and sprightly juice. October to January.

169. WAXEN APPLE. Coxe.

Gate Apple   } *of various parts*
White Apple. } *of Ohio.*
Belmont. *Ken.*

The Waxen Apple, for whose correct history we are indebted to that careful pomologist, Professor Kirtland, of Cleveland, is esteemed in Ohio, where it is now most largely cultivated, one of the very finest of all early winter varieties. It was carried from eastern to western Virginia, by Neisley, a nurseryman on the banks of the Ohio, about the commencement of the present century. Thence it was introduced into Belmont co., and other parts of Ohio. From Rockport it was carried by C. Olmstead, Esq., to Boston in 1834, incorrectly under the name of Belmont.

Fruit of middle size, globular, a little flattened and narrower towards the eye—sometimes oblong ; when of the latter form, the eye is knobby. Stalk short. Skin pale yellow, rarely tinged with a bright vermillion blush, waxy, or oily smooth. Flesh white, crisp, tender, sometimes almost melting, and of a mild, agreeable flavour. November to February.

170. WATSON'S DUMPLING.

A very large, English kitchen apple, of fair quality. Fruit about four inches in diameter, of regular form, nearly round. Skin smooth, yellowish-green, faintly striped with dull red. Stalk short. Flesh juicy, rather tender, with a pleasant, sub-acid flavour, and stews well. October to January.

171. WOOLMAN'S LONG.

Ortley Apple. *Lind.*
Ortley Pippin. *Man.*
Van Dyne, (*of some.*)

This high flavoured and excellent fruit, was sent to England by Mr. Floy, in 1825, who named it after Michael Ortley, Esq., from whose orchard, in South Jersey, it was obtained. But we observe that Thompson, in the last edition, makes it synonymous with Woolman's Long, which is, perhaps, an English variety.

The Ortley has, hitherto, always been thought an American variety, and we regret that it is so little cultivated here.

Fruit of medium size, oblong or oval, otherwise somewhat resembles the Yellow Newtown Pippin. Skin lively yellow, in the shade, with a scarlet blush, sprinkled with white specks and gray russet patches in the sun. Stalk slender, inserted in an even, smooth depression. Calyx large, set in a plaited, rather shallow basin. Flesh nearly white, crisp, and rather firm, breaking, with an excellent, sprightly, perfumed flavour. An abundant bearer, and will, no doubt, prove a most valuable sort. November to April.

172. WINE APPLE. § Coxe.

Hay's Winter.

The Wine Apple is a very handsome, and an admirable winter fruit, a most abundant bearer, and a hardy tree ; all of which qualities render it a very popular orchard and market fruit. It is a native of Delaware, but is now very largely cultivated, also in Western New-York. The tree has small leaves, grows thriftily, and makes a fine, spreading head.

Fruit rather above medium size—in rich soils large ; form regular, nearly round, a little flattened at the ends. Skin smooth, of a lively deep red, over a yellow ground, or, more frequently, with a few indistinct stripes of yellow. Stalk short, inserted in a round, smooth cavity, with a little russet around it. Flesh yellowish-white, juicy and crisp, with a rather vinous, rich, and pleasant flavour. This apple is not only fine for the table, but is also excellent for cooking and cider. October to March.

173. WINESAP. § Coxe.

Wine Sop ! *Thomp.*

This is not only a good apple for the table, but it is also one of the very finest cider fruits, and its fruitfulness renders it a great favourite with orchardists. The tree grows rather irregularly, and does not form a handsome head, but it bears early, and the apples have the good quality of hanging late upon the trees, without injury, while the tree thrives well on sandy light soils.

Fruit of medium size, rather oblong. Skin smooth, of a fine dark red, with a few streaks, and a little yellow ground, appearing on the shady side. Stalk nearly an inch long, slender. set in an irregular cavity. Calyx small, placed in a regular basin. with fine plaits. Flesh yellow, firm, crisp, with a rich, high flavour. November to May.

174. Winter Queen. Coxe.

Winter Queening *Thomp*

A fruit of medium quality, much cultivated in the lower part of New-Jersey. Fruit conical, considerably broadest at the base. Skin fine deep crimson in the sun, dotted with yellow; of a paler and livelier red, in the shade. Stalk slender, three fourths of an inch long, planted in a wide cavity. Calyx small, moderately sunk. Flesh yellowish, of a mild and rather pleasant, sub-acid flavour. The tree is an abundant bearer. November to February.

Class IV. Cider Apples.

175. Cooper's Russeting. Coxe.

This native apple is especially suited to light sandy soils, where some other sorts fail. It makes an exceedingly strong cider, of delicious flavour.

Fruit small, oblong or ovate, pale yellow, partially covered with russet. Stalk slender, and very long. Flesh dry, rich and sweet. The fruit is fit for cider in November, keeps well through the winter, and is esteemed by many for cooking. Tree small, with numerous little branches.

176. Campfield. Coxe.

Newark Sweeting.

Another capital New-Jersey, cider apple, ranking next to the Harrison. It forms a fine large tree, with straight, spreading limbs, and is very productive.

Fruit of medium size, roundish, rather flattened. Skin smooth, washed and striped with red, over a greenish-yellow ground. Flesh white, rather dry, firm, rich and sweet.

177. Gilpin. Coxe. Thomp.

Carthouse

A handsome cider fruit, from Virginia, which is also a very good table fruit from February to May. A very hardy, vigorous and fruitful tree.

Fruit of medium size, roundish-oblong. Skin very smooth and handsome, richly streaked with deep red and yellow. Stalk

short, deeply inserted. Calyx in a round, rather deep basin.
Flesh yellow, firm, juicy and rich, becoming tender and
sprightly in the spring.

178. HARRISON. Coxe.

New-Jersey is the most celebrated cider making district in
America, and this apple, which originated in Essex county, of
that state, has long enjoyed the highest reputation as a cider
fruit. Ten bushels of the apples make a barrel of cider. The
tree grows thriftily, and bears very large crops.

Fruit medium size, ovate or roundish-oblong. Skin yellow,
with roughish, distinct black specks. Stem one inch, or more,
long. Flesh yellow, rather dry and tough, but with a rich flavour, producing a high coloured cider, of great body. The
fruit is very free from rot, falls easily from the tree about the
first of November, and keeps well. The best cider of this variety, is worth from six to ten dollars a barrel, in New-York.

179. HEWE'S VIRGINIA CRAB. Coxe.

The Virginia Crab makes a very high flavoured dry cider,
which, by connoisseurs, is thought unsurpassed in flavour by
any other, and retains its soundness a long time. It is a prodigious bearer, and the tree is very hardy, though of small size.

Fruit quite small, about an inch and a half in diameter, nearly
round. Skin dull red, dotted with white specks, and obscurely
streaked with greenish-yellow. Stalk long and slender. Flesh
fibrous, with an acid, rough, and astringent flavour, and when
ground, runs clear and limpid from the press, and ferments
very slowly. The Virginia Crab is often mixed with rich pulpy
apples, to which it imparts a good deal of its fine quality.

The ROANE'S WHITE CRAB is a sub-variety of the foregoing,
about the same size, with a yellow skin. It makes a rich,
strong, bright liquor, and keeps throughout the summer, in a
well-bunged cask, perfectly sweet.

180. HAGLOE CRAB. Lind.

This is a celebrated old English cider fruit, scarcely known in
this country. Lindley says, when planted on a dry soil, with a
calcareous bottom, it produces a most excellent cider. The
specific gravity of its juice is 1081.

" Fruit small, ill-shaped, something between an apple and a
crab, more long than broad, wide at the base and narrow at the
crown, which is a little sunk, and the eye flat. Skin pale yellow,
a little marbled in different directions with a russet-gray, and
having a few red specks or streaks on the sunny side. Eye flat,
with a spreading calyx. Stalk short."

13

This is totally distinct from the SUMMER HAGLOE of American nurseries [*Hagloe Crab*, of Coxe], a large, handsome, round an, purplish-red apple, covered with bloom and ripe in August—flesh soft and woolly, of pleasant sub-acid flavor—the tree a slow grower, with thick, blunt shoots.

181. RED STREAK. Coxe.

Herefordshire Red Streak, } *of English gardens.*
Scudamore's Crab,

A capital English cider apple, which thrives admirably in this country, and is very highly esteemed, as it makes a rich, high flavoured, strong liquor. It is a handsome grower, and a great bearer.

Fruit of medium size, roundish. Calyx small, set in a rather deep basin. Stalk rather slender and short. Skin richly streaked with red, with a few yellow streaks and spots. Flesh yellow, rich, firm and dry.

182. STYRE. Thomp.

Forest Styre. *Lind.*
Styre. *Coxe.*

The Stire is a famous old English cider fruit, and Lindley remarks that Styre cider may be found in the neighbourhood of Chepstow, thirty or forty years old. Fruit middle sized, round, pale yellow, with a orange cheek. Stalk short. Flesh firm, of high flavour and makes a high coloured liquor. The tree thrives well here, and forms a very upright, broom-like head. October to January.

In addition to the foregoing, several of the table apples already described are esteemed for cider, as the Newtown Pippin, Wine Apple, Winesap, etc., and some of the high flavoured English varieties in the preceding pages are very highly valued for cider in Britain,—the Golden Pippin, Golden Harvey, Downton, &c. The Fox WHELP is a very celebrated apple of this class, used to flavour and give strength to nearly all the choice cider of Herefordshire, which is not yet introduced here, to our knowledge. It is middle sized, ovate, dark red, with a rich, heavy juice, of the specific gravity 1078. The SIBERIAN BITTER SWEET is a variety of crab raised by Mr. Knight, and about twice the size of the Siberian Crab, small roundish, ovate, yellow; an immense bearer, and held in very high esteem in England, for mixing with other cider apples, to impart richness.

Class V. *Apples for Ornament or Preserving.*

---

183. SIBERIAN CRAB. Arb. Brit.

Malus baccata. *Lind.*
Pyrus baccata. *Arb. Brit.*

The common Siberian Crab is a beautiful little fruit, which is produced in rich clusters on the branches, and, at a distance, resembles large and handsome cherries. It is highly esteemed for preserving, and almost every large garden in the middle states, contains a tree of this variety. It forms a vigorous, neat tree, of rather small size, and its blossoms, which are white, are produced in beautiful profusion in spring, and a large crop of fruit regularly follows.

Fruit about three fourths of an inch in diameter, very regularly formed, and rather flat. Skin smooth, of a lively scarlet, over a clear yellow ground, and when the bloom is rubbed off, is highly polished. Stalk nearly two inches long, and very slender. Calyx small, slightly sunk. Fit for preserving in September and October.

184. LARGE RED SIBERIAN CRAB.

Pyrus Pruifolia. *Arb. Brit.*

This variety is about twice the size of the foregoing, roundish-ovate, with a large and prominent calyx, and a pale red and yellow skin. It forms a larger tree, with rather coarser foliage than the common variety, and is esteemed for the same purposes. September and October.

185. YELLOW SIBERIAN CRAB.

Amber Crab.

This scarcely differs from the common Siberian Crab, except in its fruit, which is rather larger, and of a fine amber or golden yellow. Both this and the red are beautiful ornaments to the fruit garden in summer and autumn, and are equally esteemed for preserves and jellies. September.

Quite a number of seedlings have been raised from the Siberian Crab in this country, mostly of larger size—some by Mr. Manning, of Salem, and several by Mr. Thompson, of Catskill, but scarcely deserving of especial notice here.

186. Double Flowering Chinese Crab.

Pyrus Spectabilis. *Arb. Brit.*
Malus Spectabilis. *N. Duh.*
Double flowering Apple

This very beautiful crab tree from China, which produces a small green fruit, of no value, is highly admired for its showy blossoms. These are large, tipped with deep red in the bud, but when open, are of a pale rose colour, semi-double, large, and produced in fine clusters. It is an exceedingly ornamental, small tree, growing from ten to twenty feet in height.

Select list of apples for a small garden, to ripen in succession.

Summer	
Early Harvest.	Rambo
Red Astrachan	*Winter*
Early Strawberry	Newtown Pippin.
Drap d'Or	Dutch Mignonne.
Early Red Margaret.	Esopus Spitzenburgh.
William's Favourite	Baldwin
Autumn.	Ladies' Sweeting
Porter.	Northern Spy.
Fall Pippin	Swaar
Ross Nonpareil	Boston Russet.
Maiden's Blush.	Rhode Island Greening.
Jersey Sweet	Yellow Belle-Fleur.
Fall Harvey	American Golden Russet.
Gravenstein	Lady Apple.
Summer Sweet Paradise.	Peck's Pleasant
Golden Sweet	Herefordshire Pearmain

Apples of fine quality, suited to a cold northern climate Fameuse, Canada Reinette, Pomme de Neige, Rhode Island Greening, Boston Russet, Porter, Baldwin, Swaar, Red Astrachan, Ladies' Sweeting, Northern Spy, Golden Ball.

Apples of fine quality, suited to a southern climate. Early Red Margaret, Large Yellow Bough, English Golden Pippin, Sheep-Nose, Lady Apple, Maiden's Blush, Gravenstein, Golden Reinette, Green Newtown Pippin. English Russet, Mal Carle, Yellow Belle-Fleur, Wine Apple, Roman Stem.

A number of native varieties, which have originated at the extreme south, are found to succeed better there than most of our northern apples. Among these are the Horse Apple, Mountain Pippin, Father Abram, etc. These are not fine at the north, but are well adapted to the climate of Georgia, Alabama, &c.

CHAPTER IX.

THE ALMOND.

Amygdalus communis, Dec. *Rosaceæ,* of botanists.
Amandier, of the French; *Mandelbaum,* German; *Mandorlo,* Italian; *Almendra,*
Spanish.

THE Almond tree, which is a native of the north of Africa,
and the mountains of Asia, has long been cultivated, and is
mentioned in scripture as one of the charms of the fertile land
of Canaan. It so strongly resembles the peach tree that it is
difficult to distinguish it by the leaves and wood only; indeed,
several botanists are of opinion, from experiments made in
raising the almond from seed, that this tree and the peach are
originally the same species, and that the rich and luscious
peach is the effect of accidental variation, produced by culture
on the almond. The chief distinction between the two in our
gardens lies in the fruit, which, in the almond, consists of little
more than a stone covered with a thick, dry, woolly skin, while
the Peach has in addition a rich and luscious flesh. The blossoms of the almond resemble those of the peach, but are larger;
they are produced in great profusion, early in the season, before
the leaves, and are very ornamental.

Uses. The kernel of the sweet almond is highly esteemed as
an article of food, and is largely used as an ingredient in
confectionary, cookery, and perfumery. It is raised in great
quantities in the south of Europe, especially in Portugal, and is
an important article of commerce. The bitter almond is used
in cookery and confectionary, and in medicine, it furnishes the
prussic acid of the shops, one of the most powerful of poisons.
From both species an oil is also obtained.

In France the almond is preferred as a stock on which to
bud and graft the peach, which, in a very dry climate or chalky
soil, it is found, renders the latter more healthy and fruitful
than its own bottom. The sweet hard-shelled variety (*Douce à
coque dure,*) is preferred for stocks by French nurserymen.

Cultivation. The almond thrives best in a warm dry soil,
and its general cultivation in this country is precisely like that
of the Peach. The sweet almond is the only variety considered
of value here, and it is usually propagated by budding it on
Plum stock, or on the bitter almond seedlings. It is rather
more hardy at the north when budded on the former, and as the
buds of the sweet almond are rather slender and small, the
plum stocks to be budded should be thrifty seedlings not more

13*

than a fourth of an inch in diameter at the place where the bud
is inserted.

The Common Almond, the Hard-Shell Sweet Almond, and the
bitter Almond, are hardy in the latitude of New-York, and
will bear tolerable crops without care.   The Soft-Shell Sweet
Almond, or Ladies' Almond, will not thrive well in the open
garden as a standard, north of Philadelphia ; but they succeed
well trained to a wall or on espalier rails in a warm situation ;
the branches being slightly protected in winter.

There is no apparent reason why the culture of the Almond
should not be pursued to a profitable extent in the warm and
favourable climate of some of the southern states   Especially
in the valley of the Ohio and Tennessee it would be likely to
succeed admirably.

1. COMMON ALMOND. § Thomp. Lind.

A c dulcis *Dec.*
Amandier à Petit Fruit, ⎰
——— commun,   ⎰ *O. Duh.*
Amande commune.
Common Sweet.

This is the common Sweet Almond of France and the south
of Europe, and is one of the most hardy and productive sorts
here.   Nuts hard, smooth, about an inch and a quarter long,
compressed and pointed, of an agreeable flavour, but inferior to
the following.   Flowers expand before the leaves.   Ripens last
of September.

2. THE LONG HARD-SHELL ALMOND. §

Amandier à gros fruit *O. Duh.*
——— ——— dur. *Nois.*

A variety with handsome large, pale rose coloured flowers,
opening before the leaves, and large and long fruit a third longer
than other varieties.   The stone is about as large as the soft-
shell variety, but the kernel is larger and plumper.   This is a
good hardy sort and it is very ornamental when in blossom,
Ripens about the last of September.

3. SOFT-SHELL SWEET ALMOND. § Lind.

Doux à coque tendre, ⎰ *Thomp.*
Sultan à coque tendre, ⎰
Amandier à coque tendre. *O. Duh*
——— des Dames. *N. Duh. Poit.*
Amandier des Dames, ⎰ *Noisette.*
Ou Amande Princesse ⎰
Ladies' thin Shell.

The Soft-Shell or Ladies' Almond, is the finest of all the Al-

monds. It is the variety very common in the shops of the confectioners, with a shell so thin as to be easily crushed between
the fingers, and the kernel of which is so highly esteemed at the
dessert. It ripens early in the season, and is also highly esteemed in a young or fresh state, being served on the table for this
purpose about the middle of July in Paris. The blossoms of
this variety expand at the same time with the leaves, and are
more deeply tinged with red than the foregoing. Several varieties are made of this in France, but they are (as quoted above)
all essentially the same.

Fruit two inches long, oval, compressed. The nut is more
than an inch long, oval pointed, one-sided, with a light coloured,
porous, very tender shell. The kernel sweet and rich.

On the plum stock, in a favourable aspect, this almond succeeds, with a little care, in the middle states.

4. SULTANA SWEET ALMOND. Lind.

Amande Sultane   *O. Duh. Nois.*
Amandier Sultane.
Sultan. *Thomp.**

A tender shelled almond of excellent quality, with smaller
fruit and narrower kernel than the Soft-Shell Almond, but of
equally excellent flavour, and which is preferred by many.
It is thought, by Poiteau, to be scarcely different from the Soft-
Shell or Ladies' Almond.

5. PISTACHIA SWEET ALMOND. Lind.

Amande Pistache.   *O. Duh. Nois.*
Amandier Pistache.

A variety of almond with a very small pointed fruit, about
the size and shape of that of a Pistachia, enclosing a kernel of
a delicate sweet flavour. The shell not quite so soft as the Soft-
Shell Almond. This is scarcely known yet in this country, but
is worth further trial at the south.

6. PEACH ALMOND.

Pêcher,
Peach Almond, } *Thomp.*
Amandier-Pêcher. *N. Duh. Nois. Poit.*

A rather indifferent variety, nearly sweet, but often slightly
bitter. It is a true cross between the peach and the almond, and

---

* We cannot follow Mr. Thompson in his nomenclature of Almonds, as he (or
his printer) mistakes the meaning of the French terms; Amande Sultane of all the
French authors should be translated Sultana, not Sultan.

in its leaves, flowers, and stone strongly resembles the peach , the fruit is also pulpy and of tolerable flavour, like an indifferent peach. The nut scarcely ever ripens well as far north as this.

7. Bitter Almond. Thomp. Lind.

The Bitter Almond has large pale blossoms, differing little from the common almond, except in the kernel, which is bitter. There are two varieties one with a hard, and the other with a brittle shell. The fruit, which is produced abundantly, ripens in September. The leaves are longer and of a darker green than those of most of the sweet fruited varieties.

Ornamental Varieties. The *Dwarf Double Flowering Almond*, (*Amygdalus pumila*, Lin. *Prunus sinensis*, of some,) is a beautiful, well known, low shrub, extremely ornamental in spring, being covered with a profusion of small pink blossoms, very double.

The Large Double Flowering Almond (*A. à grand fleur, N. Duh.*) (*A communis pleno*,) is a beautiful French variety, with large, nearly white flowers, two inches in diameter. It also bears a good, small, hard-shell Almond.

CHAPTER X.

THE APRICOT.

Armeniaca vulgaris, Dec   *Rosaceæ*, of botanists.
Abricotier, of the French , *Avrikosenbaum*, German , *Albercoco*, Italian; *Albaricoque*, Spanish

The Apricot is one of the most beautiful of stone fruit trees, easily known by its glossy *heart-shaped* foliage, large white blossoms, and smooth-skinned, golden or ruddy fruit. In the fruit garden it is a highly attractive object in early spring, as its charming flowers are the first to expand. It forms a fine spreading tree of about twenty feet in height, and is hardy enough to bear as an open standard south of the 42° of latitude in this country.

The native countries of this tree are Armenia, Arabia, and the higher regions of central Asia. It is largely cultivated in China and Japan ; and, indeed, according to the accounts of Grosier the mountains west of Pekin are covered with a natural growth of apricots. The names by which it is known in various European countries all seem to be corruptions of the original Arabic term *Berkoche.*

USES. A very handsome and delicious dessert fruit, only inferior to the peach, ripening about midsummer, after cherries, and before plums, at a season when it is peculiarly acceptable. For preserving in sugar or brandy, for jellies, or pastries, it is highly esteemed, and, where it is abundant, an admirable liqueur is made from the fruit ; and it is also dried for winter use. In some parts of Germany, the free bearing sorts—the Turkey, Orange, and Breda—are largely cultivated for this purpose.

CULTIVATION. This tree is almost always budded on the plum stock (on which in July it takes readily,) as it is found more hardy and durable than upon its own root. Many American nurserymen bud the apricot on the peach, but the trees, so produced, are of a very inferior quality—short lived, more liable to diseases, and the fruit of a second rate flavour. Budded on the plum they are well adapted to strong soils, in which they always hold their fruit better than in light sandy soils.

Apricots generally grow very thriftily, and soon make fine heads, and produce an abundance of blossoms and young fruit ; but the crop of the latter frequently falls of when half grown, from being stung by the Plum-weevil or curculio, to which the smooth skin of this fruit seems highly attractive. To remedy this, the same course must be pursued as is directed for the plum. Seedling apricots are usually more hardy and productive here, than the finer grafted sorts.

This is a favourite tree for training on walls or espaliers, and, in town gardens especially, we often see it trained against the sides of brick houses, and yielding most abundantly. As it bears its fruit in the same way as the peach, and requires the same management, we must refer our readers to the latter head for direction as to pruning and training. As the apricot, however, expands its blossoms very early, it should not be placed on an east wall, or in a situation where it is too much exposed to the full morning sun.

DISEASES. When budded on the Plum, this tree is but little liable to diseases, and may be considered a hardy fruit tree. In order to render it fruitful, and keep it for a long time in a productive state, we cannot too strongly urge the advantages of the *shortening-in* system of pruning recommended for the peach.

1. ALBERGIER. Thomp. N. Duh. Nois.

Alberge. *O. Duh. Bon. Jard.*

This is a variety very common in the interiour of France, where it is constantly reproduced with but little variation from the seed—*Alberge* being the name of the apricot in some of the provinces. It is a free grower, and bears well, but is neither so large nor fine as many other varieties. The leaves are small, and often have little wing-like ears at the base. The Albergiers are much used for stocks in France.

Fruit small, roundish, deep yellow. Flesh reddish, firm, with a brisk, vinous flavour. Stone compressed; kernel bitter. Esteemed for preserving. There are several varieties of this not yet introduced into the United States, the finest of which are the *Albergier de Tours,* and *A. de Montgamet.* Ripe middle of August.

2. Breda. § Thomp. Lind. P. Mag.

De Hollande,
Amande Aveline,
Ananas,
Persique,
Hasselnussmandel,
} *ac. to Thomp*

This is a very excellent small Apricot, said to be originally from Africa, which bears well with common culture, and deserves a place in all gardens, as it is not only a high flavoured dessert sort, but it makes one of the richest preserves. The blossom buds are tinged with deep red before they expand.

Fruit rather small, about an inch and a half in diameter, roundish, sometimes rather four sided. Suture well marked. Skin orange, becoming dark orange in the sun. Flesh deep orange, rich, high flavoured and rather juicy—separating freely from the stone. The kernel, which is sweet, is eaten in France, whence the name *Amande Aveline.* First of August.

3. Black. Thomp. Fors.

Amygdalus dasycarpa   *Dec.*
Purple Apricot.   *Lind.*
Angoumois? *O. Duh.?*
Noir.
Violet
Du Pape.

This remarkable little Apricot so strongly resembles a dark round Plum, that, at a little distance, it might easily be mistaken for one. (It was indeed called Prunus dasycarpa by the old botanists.) It is pretty good, and very hardy, and its unique appearance renders it sought after by amateurs. The tree has a rough, somewhat crooked trunk, and small, *oval* foliage.

Fruit about an inch and a half in diameter, round. Skin pale red in the shade, but dull reddish purple in the sun, covered with a slight down. Flesh pale red next the skin, yellow near the stone, adhering somewhat to the stone, juicy, with a pleasant, slightly astringent flavour. Kernel sweet. August.

4. BRUSSELS. Thomp. Lind. Miller.

The Brussels Apricot is not a fine fruit in this country, but it is a good bearer in light soils. Fruit of medium size, rather oval, and flattened on its sides. Skin pale yellow, dotted with white in the shade, but often marked with a little russety brown in the sun. Suture deep next the stalk. Flesh yellow, rather firm, with a lively but not rich flavour. Kernel bitter. Middle of August. The Brussels of some collections is the *Breda.*

5. HEMSKIRKE. § Thomp. Lind. P. Mag.

A large and beautiful English variety, of the finest quality, yet little disseminated in the United States, but which highly deserves extensive planting. It strongly resembles the Moorpark, from which it is known by its stone not being perforated like that variety. It also ripens a little earlier.

Fruit large, roundish, but considerably compressed or flattened on its sides. Skin orange, with a red cheek. Flesh bright orange, tender, rather more juicy and sprightly than the Moorpark, with a rich and luscious plum-like flavour. Stone rather small, and kernel bitter. End of July.

6. LARGE EARLY. § Thomp. Lind. P. Mag.

Gros Precoce,
De St. Jean,
De St. Jean Rouge, } *ac. to Thomp.*
Gros d'Alexandrie,
Gros Fruhe,

This variety which we have just received from abroad, has the reputation of being the finest large early Apricot known. It ripens in France on midsummer day (the *fête de St. Jean,*) which will be about its season here.

Fruit of medium size, rather oblong, and compressed. Suture deep. Skin slightly downy, pale orange in the shade, fine bright orange with a few ruddy spots in the sun. Flesh separating readily from the stone, orange coloured, rich and juicy. Kernel bitter.

7. MOORPARK. § Thomp. Lind.

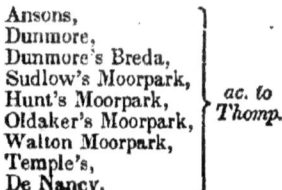

Ansons,
Dunmore,
Dunmore's Breda,
Sudlow's Moorpark,
Hunt's Moorpark, } *ac. to Thomp.*
Oldaker's Moorpark,
Walton Moorpark,
Temple's,
De Nancy,

This fine old variety is the most popular and widely dissem.

inated in this country, except the Red Masculine. It has its name from Moorpark, the seat of Sir William Temple, in England, where it was cultivated more than one hundred and forty years ago. It is only a moderate bearer here, and especially requires the shortening-in mode of pruning as recommended for the Peach.

Fruit large, roundish, about two inches and a quarter in diameter each way, on a standard tree ; rather larger on one side of the suture than the other. Skin orange in the shade, but deep orange or brownish red in the sun, marked with numerous dark specks and dots. Flesh quite firm, bright orange, parting free from the stone, quite juicy, with a rich and luscious flavour. Stone peculiarly *perforated* along the back, where a pin may be pushed through, nearly from one end to the other. Kernel bitter. Ripe early in August.

8. Musch-Musch. Thomp. Nois.

D'Alexandrie.

This delicious little Apricot takes its name from the city of Musch on the frontiers of Turkey, in Asia ; but it is also common about Alexandria, and in northern Egypt it is said to be raised in such abundance that the dried fruit is an article of commerce. The tree is rather delicate, and requires a sheltered position.

Fruit rather small, about an inch and a half in diameter, round. Skin deep yellow, with a little orange red on the sunny side. Flesh yellow, with a *transparent pulp*, tender, melting, and very sweet. Kernel sweet.

9. Orange. Thomp. Lind Mill.

Early Orange.
Royal Orange
Royal George.
Persian.
Royal Persian.

An Apricot of only tolerable quality for the dessert, but it is much esteemed by many for preserving , and it makes delicious tarts, even before the fruit begins to acquire colour.

Fruit of medium size, roundish, with a well marked suture, deeply hollowed near the stalk. Skin firm, orange, sometimes tinged with a ruddy tint in the sun. Flesh dark orange, moderately juicy, but often rather dry and insipid, (unless ripened in the house,) not separating entirely from the flesh. Stone small, roundish. Kernel sweet. Middle of July.

10. PEACH. § Thomp. Fors. Lind.

Anson's Imperial.
Royal Peach.
Pêche.
Abricot Pêche. *N. Duh. Poit.*
De Nancy. *O. Duh.*
Du Luxembourg.
Pêche Grosse.
Wurtemburg.
Pfirsiche.

The Peach Apricot, originally from Piedmont, has long been considered the finest variety; and it is with us the largest and most excellent sort cultivated—being often as large as a Peach of medium size, handsome, and of delicious flavour. It very strongly resembles the Moorpark, but the two are readily distinguished by the eye when standing near each other, and the fruit of the Peach is rather larger and finer, and a few days earlier.

Fruit of the largest size, about two and a half inches in diameter, roundish, rather flattened, and somewhat compressed on its sides, with a well marked suture. Skin yellow in the shade, but deep orange, mottled with dark brown, on the sunny side. Flesh of a fine yellow saffron colour, juicy, rich, and high flavoured. Stone with the same pervious passage as the Moorpark, and with a bitter kernel.

11. ROMAN. Thomp. Lind.

Abricot Commun. *O. Duh.*
Germine.
Grosse Germine.
Transparent.

This is with us one of the largest growing and hardiest Apricot trees, and produces good crops every year in cold or unfavourable situations, where none of the other sorts, except the Masculine, succeed. It is, therefore, though inferior in flavour, a valuable sort for northern situations. The blossoms will bear quite a severe frost without injury.

Fruit middle sized, oblong, with the sides slightly compressed, with but little or no suture. Skin entirely pale yellow; or very rarely dotted with a few red spots on one side. Flesh dull yellow, soft, rather dry. When ripened by keeping a few days in the house, the flavour is tolerably good. Stone oblong, with a bitter kernel. Ripe the last of July and first of August.

There is a BLOTCHED LEAVED ROMAN, (*commun à feuilles panachés*, of the French,) precisely like the foregoing in all respects, except the white or yellow stain in the leaf—but it is quite distinct from the Blotched leaved Turkey, cultivated here.

14

12. ROYAL. § Thomp. Nois. P. Mag.

A fine large French variety, raised a few years since at the Royal Luxembourg gardens. It is nearly as large as the Moorpark, but with larger leaves borne on long footstalks, and without the pervious stone of that sort. It is quite as high flavoured and ripens a week or ten days earlier

Fruit roundish, large, oval, slightly compressed. Skin dull yellow, with an orange cheek, very faintly tinged with red, and a shallow suture. Flesh pale orange, firm and juicy, with a rich vinous flavour. Ripe the latter end of July.

13. RED MASCULINE. Thomp. Lind.

Early Masculine
Brown Masculine
Abricot precoce,   ⎰ O. Duh.
Abricot hâuf musquee.   ⎱
Abricotier hauf. N Duh.
Abricotier
Fruhne Muscateller.

The Red Masculine is a good deal cultivated with us. It is very hardy, ripens the earliest, and bears very regularly and well. On the other hand the fruit is quite small, and only of second rate flavour. It is likely, therefore, to give place to the Large Early, which ripens only a few days later, and is much superiour.

Fruit small and nearly round, scarcely an inch and a half in diameter, with a well marked suture on one side. Skin bright yellow, tinged with deep orange and spotted with dark red on the sunny side. Flesh yellow, juicy, with a slightly musky, pleasant flavour. Stone thick, obtuse at the ends. Flowers smaller than in most other sorts. Kernel bitter. Ripe about the 12th of July.

14. SHIPLEYS. Thomp.

Blenheim.
Shipley's Large.

This is a new variety which we have lately received from England, and which is not yet fully proved in this country. It has the reputation of being nearly equal to the Moorpark, and more productive, while it is next in point of earliness to the Large Early.

Fruit large, oval, orange, with a deep yellow, juicy, and tolerably rich flesh. Stone roundish, impervious, with a bitter kernel. Ripens here about the 25th of July.

15. Turkey. § Thomp. P. Mag. Lind.

Large Turkey.
De Nancy, (*of some.*)

The Turkey Apricot is a fine old variety, which is seldom seen in our gardens, the sort generally sold under this name being the Roman. It is quite a late sort, ripening after the Moorpark, from which it is easily known by its impervious stone, and sweet kernel.

Fruit of middle size, nearly round, not compressed. Skin fine deep yellow in the shade, mottled with brownish orange in the sun. Flesh pale yellow, firm, quite juicy, with a flavour in which there is an excellent mingling of sweet and acid. Kernel nearly as sweet as that of an almond, which, as well as the form and colour, distinguishes this sort from the Roman. Ripe the middle of August.

The Blotched leaved Turkey, or Gold Blotched, (*Abricot maculé*,) is a sub-variety, very well known here, resembling the common Turkey in all respects, except that it has in the centre of each leaf a large yellowish spot. It is a thrifty tree and bears delicious fruit. Ours is not identical with the Turkey, as the last edition of the L. H. S.'s Catalogue arranges it, but is a globular fruit, and a true variation of the Turkey.

16. White Masculine. Thomp. Lind. Fors.

White Apricot.
Abricot Blanc. *O. Duh. Nois.*
Abricotier Blanc. *N. Duh.*
Early White Masculine.
Blanc. } *ac. to*
White Algeirs? } *Thomp.*

This scarcely differs from the Red Masculine before described, except in colour. It is four or five days later.

Fruit small and roundish. Skin nearly white, rarely with a little reddish brown on one side. Flesh white, delicate, a little fibrous, adheres a little to the stone, and has a delicate, pleasant juice. Kernel bitter.

Curious, or ornamental varieties. The Briancon Apricot, (*A. brigantiaca*, Dec.) a very distinct species so much resembling a plum as to be called the Briancon Plum by many authors, (*Prune de Briançon*, Poit.) is a small, irregular tree or shrub, ten or twelve feet high, a native of the Alps. It bears a great abundance of small round yellow plum-like fruit in clusters, which are scarcely eatable; but in France and Piedmont the kernels of this variety make the "huile de marmotte," which is worth double the price of the olive oil.

The DOUBLE FLOWERING APRICOT is a pretty ornamental tree, yet rare with us.

Selection of Apricots for a small garden. Large Early, Breda, Peach, Moorpark.

Selection for a cold, or northern climate. Red Masculine, Roman, Breda.

----- --

CHAPTER XI.

THE BERBERRY.

Berberis vulgaris * L *Berberaceæ*, of botanists
Epine-vinette, of the French , *Berberitzen*, German ; *Berbero*, Italian ; *Berberis*, Spanish

The Berberry (or barberry) is a common prickly shrub, from eight to ten feet high, which grows wild in both hemispheres, and is particularly abundant in many parts of New-England. The flowers, the roots, and the inner wood are of the brightest yellow colour, and the small crimson fruit is borne in clusters. It is a popular but fallacious notion, entertained both here and in England, that the vicinity of this plant, in any quantity, to grain fields, causes the rust.

The barberry is too acid to eat, but it makes an agreeable preserve and jelly, and an ornamental pickle for garnishing some dishes. From the seedless sort is made in Rouen a celebrated sweetmeat, *confiture d'épine-vinette.* The inner bark is used in France for drying silk and cotton bright yellow.

CULTURE. The culture is of the easiest description. A rich light soil, gives the largest fruit. It is easily propagated by seed, layers, or suckers. When fine fruit of the barberry is desired it should be kept trained to a single stem—as the suckers which it is liable to produce, frequently render it barren or make the fruit small.

1. COMMON RED.

This is too well known to need description. In good soils it grows twelve or fifteen feet high, and its numerous clusters of bright, oval berries, are very ornamental in autumn. There is a Large Red variety of this, which is only a variation produced

* Or B. Canadensis—they are scarcely distinct ours has rather the most fleshy berry.

by cultivation in rich soil. There are also varieties of this in
Europe with pale yellow, white, and purple fruit, which are not
yet introduced into this country, and which scarcely differ in
any other respect than the colour. Finally, there is a so-called
sweet variety of the common Berberry from Austria, (*B. v.
dulcis,*) but it is scarcely less acid than the common.

2. STONELESS.

B. v. Asperma.
Seedless.
Vinetier sans noyeau.

The fruit of this, which is only a variety of our common barberry, is without seeds. But it does not appear to be a permanent variety, as the plants frequently do produce berries with
seeds ; and it is stated in the New Duhamel that in order to
guard against this, the sort must be propagated by layers or
cuttings, as the suckers always give the common sort. It is
considered the best for preserving.

3. BLACK SWEET MAGELLAN. Loudon.

Berberis dulcis. *D. Don.*
B. ratundifolia.

A new evergreen sort from the Straits of Magellan, South
America. It is very rare, and has not yet fruited in this country, but it is likely to prove hardy. Loudon, in the Suburban
Gardener, says it bears round black berries, about the size of
those of the black currant, which are used in its native country
for pies and tarts, both green and ripe. It has ripened fruit in
Edinburgh, in the nursery of Mr. Cunningham, who describes
it as large and excellent.

4. NEPAL.

Berberis aristata.

This is a new variety from Nepal, India. We have cultivated it three or four years, and find it tolerably hardy, but,
though it has produced flowers, it has yet given no fruit. It is
said to yield " purple fruit, covered with a fine bloom, which in
India are dried in the sun like raisins, and used like them at
the dessert."

The MAHONIAS, or *Holly leaved Berberries*, from Oregon are
handsome low evergreen ornamental shrubs, with large deep
green prickly leaves, and yellow flowers, but the fruit is of no
value.

14*

CHAPTER XII.

THE CHERRY.

Cerasus sylvestris and *C. vulgaris*. Arb Brit *Rosaceæ*, of botanists.
Cerisier, of the French, *Kirschenbaum*, German, *Ciriego*, Italian , *Cerezo*, Spanish.

THE cherry is a fine. luxuriant fruit tree, with smooth, light
coloured bark, and, generally of rapid growth.   The varieties
of the black and heart-shaped cherries are always vigorous, and
form fine large spreading heads, forty or fifty feet in height;
but those of the acid or red cherry are of lower, more bushy
and tardy growth.   In the spring the cherry tree is profusely
covered with clusters of snow white blossoms, and earlier in
summer than upon any other tree, these are followed by abundant crops of juicy, sweet, or acid fruit hanging upon long
stalks, and enclosing a smooth stone.

The cherry comes originally from Asia, and the Roman general, Lucullus, after a victorious expedition into Pontus, has the
reputation of having brought it to Italy, from *Cerasus*. a town
in that province. in the year 69 B C   According to Pliny, the
Romans. 100 years after this, had eight varieties in cultivation,
and they were soon afterwards carried to all parts of Europe.
The seeds of the cultivated cherry were brought to this country
very early after its settlement, both from England and Holland.

USES.   As a pleasant and refreshing dessert fruit, the cherry
is every where highly esteemed   The early season at which it
ripens, its juiciness, delicacy, and richness. render it always
acceptable.   While the large and fleshy varieties are exceedingly sweet and luscious others which are more tender, and
more or less acid, are very valuable for pies, tarts. and various
kinds of cookery.   The fruit of the Kentish or Early Richmond
is excellent when stoned and dried, and the Mazzard, and our
wild Virginia cherries, are used to give a flavour to brandy.

The celebrated German *Kirschwasser* is made by distilling
the liquor of the common black mazzard or gean, (in which the
stones are ground and broken. and fermented with the pulp,)
and the delicious *Ratifia* cordial of Grenoble, is also made from
this fruit. *Maraschino*, the most celebrated liqueur of Italy, is
distilled from a small gean or mazzard, with which, in fermenting, honey, and the leaves and kernels of the fruit are mixed

The gum of the cherry is nearly identical with gum arabic,
and there are some marvellous stories told of its nutritive properties. The wood of the cherry is hard and durable, and is,
therefore, valuable for many purposes, but the best wood is

afforded by our common wild or Virginia cherry, which is a very good substitute for mahogany, taking a fine polish.

The larger growing sorts of black cherry are the finest of all fruit trees for shade, and are, therefore, generally chosen by farmers, who are always desirous of combining the useful and the ornamental. Indeed, the cherry, from its symmetrical form, its rapid growth, its fine shade, and beautiful blossoms, is exceedingly well suited for a road side tree in agricultural districts. We wish we could induce the planting of avenues of this and other fine growing fruit trees in our country neighbourhoods, as is the beautiful custom in Germany, affording ornament and a grateful shade and refreshment to the traveller, at the same moment. Mr. Loudon in his Arboretum, gives the following account of the cherry avenues in Germany, which we gladly lay before our readers.

"On the continent, and more especially in Germany and Switzerland, the cherry is much used as a road side tree : particularly in the northern parts of Germany, where the apple and the pear will not thrive. In some countries the road passes for many miles together through an avenue of cherry trees. In Moravia, the road from Brunn to Olmutz, passes through such an avenue, extending upwards of sixty miles in length ; and, in the autumn of 1828, we travelled for several days through almost one continuous avenue of cherry trees, from Strasburg by a circuitous route to Munich. These avenues, in Germany, are planted by the desire of the respective governments, not only for shading the traveller, but in order that the poor pedestrian may obtain refreshment on his journey. All persons are allowed to partake of the cherries, on condition of not injuring the trees ; but the main crop of the cherries when ripe, is gathered by the respective proprietors of the land on which it grows ; and when these are anxious to preserve the fruit of any particular tree, it is, as it were, tabooed ; that is, a wisp of straw is tied in a conspicuous part to one of the branches, as vines by the road sides in France, when the grapes are ripe, are protected by sprinkling a plant, here and there, with a mixture of lime and water, which marks the leaves with conspicuous white blotches. Every one who has travelled on the Continent in the fruit season, must have observed the respect that is paid to these appropriating marks ; and there is something highly gratifying in this, and in the humane feeling displayed by the princes of the different countries, in causing the trees to be planted. It would indeed be lamentable if kind treatment did not produce a corresponding return."

SOIL AND SITUATION. A *dry* soil for the cherry is the universal maxim, and although it is so hardy a tree that it will thrive in a great variety of soils, yet a good, sandy, or gravelly loam is its favourite place. It will indeed grow in much thinner and dryer soils than most other fruit trees, but to obtain the finest fruit a deep and mellow soil, of good quality, is desirable. When it is forced to grow in wet places, or where the roots are constantly damp, it soon decays, and is very short lived. And we have seen this tree when forced into too luxuriant a growth in our over-rich western soils, become so gross in its wood as to bear little or no fruit, and split open in its trunk, and soon perish. It is a very hardy tree, and will bear a great variety of exposures without injury. In deep warm valleys, liable to spring frosts, it is, however, well to plant it on the north sides of hills, in order to retard it in the spring.

PROPAGATION. The finer sorts are nearly always propagated by budding on seedlings of the common black mazzard, which is a very common kind, producing a great abundance of fruit, and very healthy, free growing stocks To raise these stocks, the cherries should be gathered when fully ripe, and allowed to lie two or three days together, so that they may be partially or wholly freed from the pulp by washing them in water. They should then be planted immediately in drills in the seed plot, covering them about an inch deep. They will then vegetate in the following spring, and in good soil will be fit for planting out in the nursery rows in the autumn or following spring, at a distance of ten or twelve inches apart in the rows. Many persons preserve their cherry stones in sand, either in the cellar or in the open air until spring, but we have found this a more precarious mode; the cherry being one of the most delicate of seeds when it commences to vegetate, and its vitality is frequently destroyed by leaving it in the sand twenty-four hours too long, or after it has commenced sprouting

After planting in the nursery rows, the seedlings are generally fit for budding in the month of August following And in order not to have weak stocks overpowered by vigorous ones, they should always be assorted before they are planted, placing those of the same size in rows together. Nearly all the cherries are grown with us as standards. The English nurserymen usually bud their standard cherries as high as they wish them to form heads, but we always prefer to bud them on quite young stocks, as near the ground as possible, as they then shoot up clean, straight, smooth stems, showing no clumsy joint when the bud and the stock are united. In good soils, the buds will frequently make shoots, six or eight feet high, the first season after the stock is headed back.

When dwarf trees are required, the *Morello* seedlings are used as stocks; or when very dwarf trees are wished the Perfumed Cherry, (Cerasus Mahaleb,) is employed; but as standards are almost universally preferred, these are seldom seen here. Dwarfs in the nursery must be headed back the second year, in order to form lateral shoots near the ground.

CULTIVATION. The cherry, as a standard tree, may be said
.o require little or no cultivation in the middle states, further
than occasionally supplying old trees with a little manure to
keep up their vigour, pruning out a dead or crossing branch,
and washing the stem with soft soap should it become hard and
bark bound. Pruning, the cherry very little needs, and as it is
always likely to produce gum (and this decay,) it should be
avoided, except when really required. It should then be done
in *midsummer*, as that is the only season when the gum is not
more or less exuded. The cherry is not a very long lived tree,
but in favourable soil the finest varieties generally endure about
thirty or forty years. Twenty feet apart for the strong, and
eighteen feet for the slow growing kinds is the proper distance
for this tree.

Training the Cherry is very little practised in the United
States. The Heart and Bigarreau cherries are usually trained
in the horizontal manner, explained in page 40. When the
wall or espalier is once filled, as there directed, with lateral
branches, it is only necessary to cut off, twice every season—in
the month of May and July—all additional shoots to within an
inch or so of the branch from which they grew. As the trees
grow older, these fruit spurs will advance in length, but by cutting them out whenever they exceed four or five inches, new
ones will be produced, and the tree will continue to keep its
proper shape and yield excellent fruit. The Morello cherries,
being weaker growing sorts, are trained in the fan-manner,
(page 38.)

Gathering the fruit. This tender and juicy fruit is best
when freshly gathered from the tree, and it should always be
picked with the stalks attached. For the dessert, the flavour of
many sorts in our climate, is rendered more delicious by placing
the fruit, for an hour or two previous, in an ice-house or refrig-
erator, and bringing them upon the table cool, with dew drops
standing upon them.

VARIETIES. For the sake of enabling the amateur the more
readily to identify varieties, we shall divide cherries into four
classes, viz.

I. *Heart cherries.* The Common Mazzard and the Black
Heart may be taken as types of this division. The trees are
rapid growing, with ample and lofty heads, and broad, light
green, waved leaves. The fruit is more or less heart-shaped,
with rich, *tender*, sweet flesh. (This includes the *Merisiers*
and *Guiniers* of the French, which seem to us, practically, not
distinct.) This section comprises excellent cherries, universally admired. Colour mostly black.

II. *Bigarreau cherries.* This term comes originally from the
French *bigarrée*—speckled or variegated skin—but it is now in
general use by all pomologists, to signify hard, or firm-fleshed,

sweet cherries—those which are firm and *crackling*, as compared with the melting, tender flesh of section I.   The Common Bigarreau or Graffion, may be taken as the type of this class, which is mainly composed of the largest and most beautiful of cherries, admirable for the dessert, and whose firmness renders them well suited for carriage to market.   The trees like the Heart cherries, are lofty and spreading, with similar foliage. (*B'garreaux*, and *Bigarreautiers*, of the French.)

III. *Duke cherries.*   This class is characterised by the roundish form of its fruit, thin skin, and juicy, melting flesh; the flavour being generally sub-acid before fully ripe, when it is rich, and nearly or quite sweet.   The Mayduke is the type of this class.   The trees are upright in their growth while young, and finally form lower heads than those of the two previous sections, with narrower leaves, which are flat and darker coloured.   The young wood is also darker, and a little less strong than that of the Heart and Biggarreau classes.   These are excellent varieties, succeeding well in almost all soils and climates, and invaluable both for the dessert and for cooking.   (*Cerisiers*, of the French)

IV. *Morello cherries.*   The common Kentish or pie cherry, and the Morello, are well known types of this class.   The fruit is mostly round, with thin skin, juicy, tender, and quite *acid*, being chiefly valued for cooking, preserving, and various culinary purposes.   The trees are of rather low and spreading growth, with small wiry branches, and narrow dark green foliage   (*Griottiers*, and *Cerisiers*, of the French.)

In describing cherries we shall designate their size by comparison, as follows: *large*, as the Tartarian, and Bigarreau; *middle sized*, as the Mayduke and Black Heart; *small*, as the Transparent Guigne and Honey, (see the outlines of these sorts.) As regards form, *heart-shaped*, as the Black Heart; *obtuse heart-shaped*, as the Bigarreau; and *round*, as the Kentish. As regards texture, *tender*, as the Mayduke; *half tender*, as the Tartarian, and *firm*, as the Bigarreau.

Class I.   Heart Cherries.

Fruit sweet, with tender or half tender flesh, heart-shaped, or oval ; trees with broad, somewhat pendant foliage.)

1. AMERICAN AMBER.

Bloodgood's Amber.
Bloodgood's Honey.
Bloodgood's New Honey.

This exceedingly bright and pretty cherry, was raised some years ago by Mr. Daniel Bloodgood, of Flushing, Long Island.   It is a most abundant bearer, the fruit hanging in the richest bunches from the branches, giving the tree a fine appearance when in fruit, but it is only second rate in point of flavour.   At a little distance it resembles the American Heart, from which, however, it differs in being a tender fleshed fruit, of very regular outline, while the latter is partially firm, (belonging to the Bigarreau class,) and of an irregular figure.

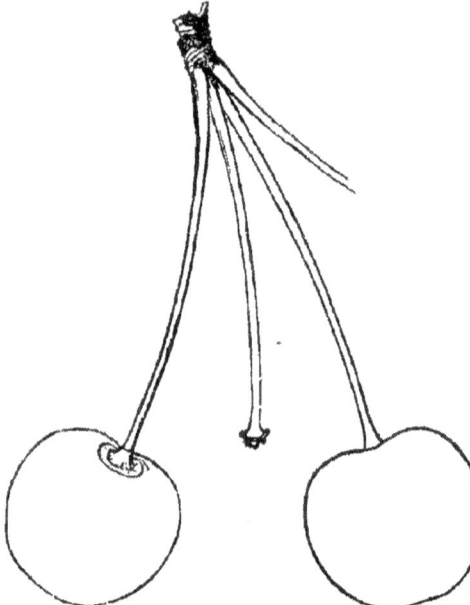

Fruit of medium size, (borne three or four in a cluster,) and very regular form, roundish heart-shaped, often nearly round, with a slightly indented point at the apex, (like a Mayduke.) Skin very thin, smooth, even, and glossy, clear light amber at first, but,

Fig. 59.   *American Amber.*

when ripe, delicately mottled and overspread with clear bright red.   Stalk long, slender, and inserted in a very slight and narrow cavity.   Flesh amber colour, tender, abounding with a sprightly, though not high flavoured juice.   Ripe about the 25th of June.   This is nearly related, but is inferior in quality, to Downer's Late, and Sparhawk's Honey, which ripen at the same time.

2. Amber Gean. Thomp.

Gean Amber.

A pretty little Gean (or Mazzard,) with a very thin and transparent skin, and sweet flavour. It is exceedingly productive, ripens late, and hangs till the middle of July.

Fruit small, oval or obtuse heart-shape, quite regular in form, generally borne in threes. Skin very thin and pellucid, showing the texture of the flesh beneath, colour pale yellow, partially overspread with a very faint red. Stalk long and slender, very slightly inserted. Flesh white, juicy, melting, of a sweet and pleasant flavour.

This considerably resembles the Transparent Guigne, but it is rather smaller and less handsome. It is also more pellucid, more yellow, less distinctly *spotted* with red, and is borne in clusters, which the latter is not.

3. Baumann's May.

Bigarreau de Mai. *Ken.*
Wilder's Bigarreau de Mai.
Bigarreau de Mai. *Thomp.?*

This cherry, which, under the name of Bigarreau de Mai, has already obtained quite a reputation as the *earliest cherry*, was received several years ago by our friend M. P. Wilder, Esq., President of the Massachusetts Horticultural Society, from the Messrs. Baumann, of Boll-wyller, in France. The label was lost on the passage, and the "Bigarreau de Mai," being in the invoice it was supposed that such might be the name of this variety. As, however, it is not a Bigarreau, but a tender fleshed cherry, we think it best for the present to call it Baumann's May. The young branches are literally covered with the abundance of the fruit, it being a most prolific bearer. Branches strong, leaves large.

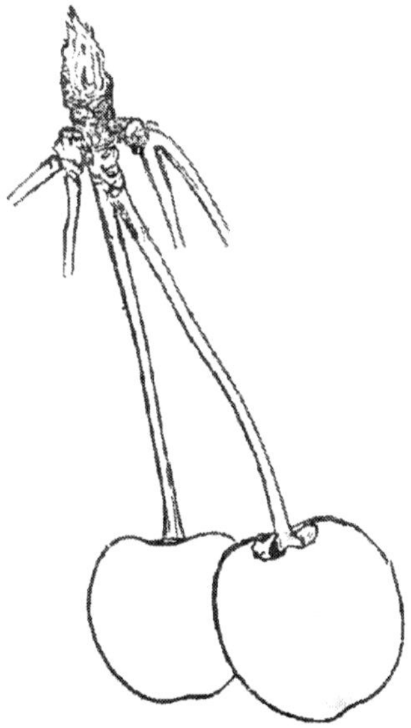

Fruit rather small, oval heart-shaped, and rather angular in outline. Skin deep rich red, becoming rather dark when fully ripe. Stalk an inch and three fourths

Fig. 60. *Baumann's May.*

long, pretty stout at either end, and set in a very narrow, and rather irregular cavity. Flesh purplish, tender, juicy, and when fully ripe, tolerably sweet and good. Ripens here the 20th of May.

4. BLACK HEART. § Thomp. Mill. Lind.

Early Black.
Ansell's Fine Black.
Spanish Black Heart.
Black Russian, (*of American gardens.*)
Black Caroon, (*erroneously, of some.*)
Guinier à fruit noir. *O. Duh.*
Guigne grosse noir.
Grosse Schwarze Hertz Kirsche.

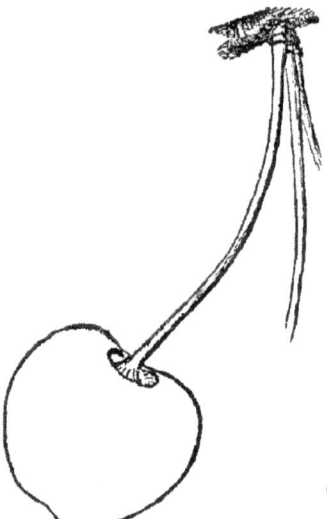

The Black Heart, an old variety, is better known than almost **any** other cherry in this country, and its great fruitfulness and good flavour, together with the hardiness and the large size to which the tree grows, render it every where esteemed.

Fruit above medium size, heart-shaped, a little irregular. Skin glossy, dark purple, becoming deep black when fully ripe. Stalk **an** inch and a half long, slender, set in a monerate hollow. Flesh, before fully ripe, half tender, but finally becoming tender and juicy, with a rich, sweet flavour. Ripens the last of June, about ten days after the Mayduke.

Fig. 61. *Black Heart.*

5. BLACK HEART, MANNING'S EARLY. Man.

This is a seedling raised by the late Robert Manning, of Salem, Mass., from the common Black Heart. In size, form and colour, it scarcely differs from the original variety, but it has the merit of ripening ten days earlier—about the same time, or even a little before the Mayduke.

6. BLACK HEART, WERDER'S EARLY. Thomp.

Werder's Early Black.
Werdersche Frühe Schwarze Herz Kirsche.

A new variety, recently introduced from England, and which promises to be very valuable on account of its ripening among the very earliest cherries. Fruit of medium size, heart-shaped; skin black; flesh purplish, tender, sweet and excellent. **Ripens the last of May, or very early in June.**

15

7. BLACK EAGLE. § Thomp. Lind.

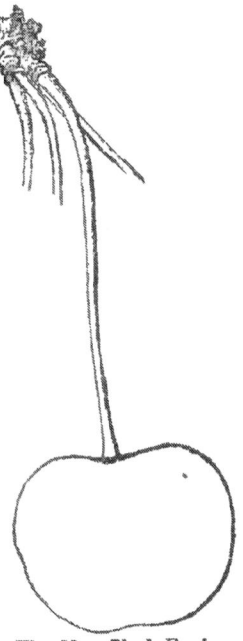

A very excellent English variety,
raised by the daughter of Mr. Knight, at
Downton Castle, in 1806, from the seed
of the Bigarreau fertilized by the Mayduke. It ripens at the beginning of
July or a few days later than the Black
Tartarian.

Fruit rather above medium size, borne
in pairs and threes; obtuse heart-shaped.
Skin deep purple, or nearly black. Stalk
of medium length, and rather slender.
Flesh deep purple, tender, with a rich,
high flavoured juice, superiour to the
Black Heart. Branches strong, with
large leaves.

Fig. 62. Black Eagle.

8. BLACK TARTARIAN. § Thomp. Lind. P. Mag.

Tartarian.
Fraser's Black Tartarian,   ⎫ *Fors.*
Ronald's Large Black Heart, ⎬
Black Circassian. *Hooker.* ⎭
Superb Circassian,   ⎫
Ronald's large Black Heart, ⎪
Ronald's Heart,   ⎪ *ac. to*
Fraser's Black Heart,   ⎬ *Thomp.*
Fraser's Black,   ⎪
Fraser's Tartarische,   ⎪
Schwarze Herz Kirsche, ⎭
Black Russian, *of the English, but
    not of American gardens.*

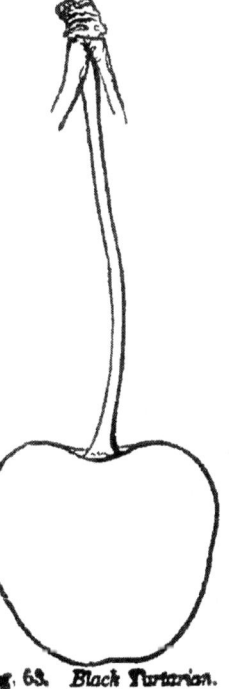

This superb fruit has already become
a general favourite in all our gardens;
and in size, flavour, and productiveness,
it has no superiour among black cherries. It is a Russian, and West Asian
variety, introduced into England about
1796, and brought thence to this country
about twenty years ago. It is remarkable for its rapid, vigorous growth, large
leaves, and the erect habit of its head.
The fruit ripens about the middle of
June, a few days after the Mayduke.

Fruit of the largest size, heart-shaped,

Fig. 63. Black Tartarian.

(sometimes rather obtuse,) irregular and uneven on the surface. Skin glossy, bright purplish black. Flesh purplish, thick, (the stone being quite small,) half-tender, and juicy. Flesh very rich and delicious.

9. BOWYER'S EARLY HEART. Thomp.

A new English variety, as yet little known with us. It is one of the earliest of light coloured cherries, and a good bearer, being in eating very early in June.

Fruit rather below medium size, obtuse heart-shaped. Skin amber, mottled with red. Flesh white, soft, or very tender, juicy, with a pleasant, sweet flavour.

10. BLACK MAZZARD. Thomp. Lind.

Mazzard,
Common English,
Wild English Cherry, } *of American*
Black Honey,   *gardens.*
Bristol Cherry.
Cerasus avium. *Dec.*
Wild Black Fruited,
Small Wild Black, } *of English*
Whixley Black,   *gardens.*
Merry Cherry.
Merisier à petit fruit. *O. Duh.*
Merisier à petit fruit noir.

This is the wild species of Europe, being common in the forests of France and some parts of England; and it has now become naturalized, and grows spontaneously on the borders of woods in many parts of the Atlantic states. It is the original species from which nearly all the fine Heart and other sweet cherries, have sprung. It is small, and of little value for eating, retaining, unless very ripe, a certain bitterness; but it ripens and hangs on the tree until the middle or last of July, so that it then becomes somewhat acceptable. It is, however, chiefly valued for the manufacture of cherry brandy, and in districts where this is carried on, from the large size and great fruitfulness of the trees it is quite a profitable sort. It affords the most valuable seedling stocks on which to bud and graft finer varieties.

Fruit small, roundish or oval heart-shaped, flattened a little on both sides. Stalk long and very slender, inserted in a small depression. Skin thin, and when fully ripe, jet black. Flesh soft and melting, purple, with an abundant, somewhat bitter juice.

The WHITE MAZZARD, of Mr. Manning, is a seedling raised by that pomologist, which differs little except in its colour.

11. Corone.   Thomp. Fors.

Couronne. *Lind.*
Coroun. *Lang.*
Herefordshire Black.
Black Orleans.
Large Wild Black.

The Corone is a natural cherry in many parts of England, reproducing itself from seed, growing with great vigour, and bearing most abundantly. It is only of second quality being merely an improved Mazzard, and does not deserve a place in a small collection, but as it is very hardy and ripens late, it is of some value at the north on that account.

Fruit below middle size, roundish heart-shaped. Skin dingy black when fully ripe. Stalk two inches long, slender, and inserted in a deep and narrow cavity. Flesh when ripe, tender, abounding in a deep purple juice, of tolerably good flavour. Middle of July. The Black Heart is often incorrectly called by this name in the middle states.

12. Downton. § Thomp. Lind.

A very beautiful and excellent large variety raised by T. A. Knight, Esq., of Downton Castle, from the seed, it is believed, of the Elton. It ripens a little later than the majority of sorts, and is a very desirable cherry.

Fruit large, very blunt heart-shaped, nearly roundish. Stalk one and a half to two inches long, slender, set in a pretty deep, broad hollow. Skin pale cream colour, semi-transparent, delicately stained on one side with red, and marbled with red dots. Flesh yellowish, without any red, tender, adhering slightly to the stone, with a delicious, rich flavour. Early in July.

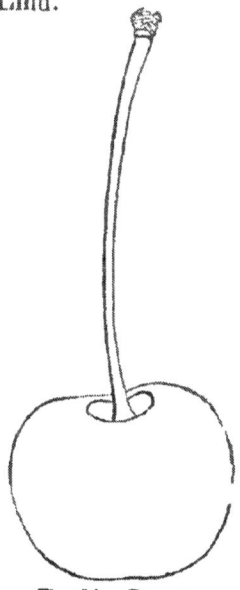

Fig. 64. *Downton.*

13. Davenport's Early.

Davenport.
Davenport's Early Black. *Ken.*

Scarcely different from the Black Heart—indeed, we find it

impossible to distinguish any difference in the fruit—except that it ripens a few days earlier. The leaves, however, are larger and of a lighter green skin, and waved on the margin, and the tree comes early into bearing. The thin, light brown bark, on the young trees, resembles that of the Birch. This native variety has been called *New Mayduke* by some, but it has no resemblance to a Duke Cherry.

14. DOWNER'S LATE. §

Downer. *Man.*
Downer's late Red.

This valuable late cherry was raised by Samuel Downer, Esq., an ardent cultivator of Dorchester, near Boston. It is a very regular and great bearer, ripens about a week after the cherry season, and hangs for a considerable time on the tree. It is a delicious, melting fruit, and deserves a place in every garden.

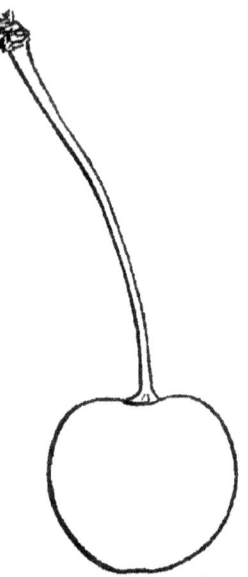

Fruit of medium size, roundish, heart-shaped, inclining to oval. Skin very smooth, of a soft but lively red. mottled with a little amber in the shade. Stalk inserted with a very slight depression. Fruit borne thickly, in clusters. Flesh tender, melting, with a sweet and luscious flavour. Ripens from the 4th to the 10th of July.

Fig. 65. *Downer's Late.*

15. EARLY WHITE HEART.

Arden's Early White Heart.
White Heart. *Coxe. Prince's Pom. Man.*
White Heart,
Dredge's Early White Heart, } *Thomp. ?*
White Transparent,
Amber Heart.

An old variety, long cultivated in this country, and one of the earliest, ripening before the Mayduke. At Ardenia, the seat of R. Arden, Esq., opposite West Point, on the Hudson, there are many large trees of this variety, received by him originally from France, which are most abundant and regular bearers—and we do not perceive that in this part of the country this cherry is open to Coxe's accusation of being a bad

15*

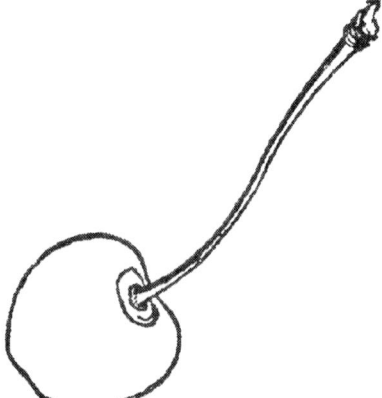

Fig. 66.   *Early White Heart.*

bearer.   Though a very good early fruit, this will no doubt be supplanted by Bowyer's Early Heart, and other newer and finer sorts.

The White Heart of Thompson and Lindley, may perhaps prove the same variety as this, though they describe it as a late ripening sort.

Fruit below medium size, rather oblong heart-shaped— often a little one-sided.   Suture quite distinct.   Stalk an inch and three fourths long, rather slender, inserted in a wide shallow cavity.   Skin dull whitish yellow, tinged and speckled with pale red in the sun.   Flesh half tender, unless fully ripe, when it is melting, with a sweet and pleasant flavour.   Tree grows rather erect, with a distaff-like head when young.   In the nursery the young trees are easily known by their long and slender shoots, with few branches First of June.

16. EARLY PURPLE GUIGNE. § Thomp.

Early Purple Griotte.

An exceedingly early variety ripening the last of May, newly introduced from England, and which promises to be a most valuable acquisition.

Fruit of medium size, and very handsome appearance.   Skin smooth, dark red, becoming purple.   Flesh purple, tender, juicy, with a rich and sweet flavour.   The leaves have longer petioles than those of most other sorts.

17. GASCOIGNE'S HEART.   Thomp.

Bleeding Heart.   *Lind.*
Red Heart, (*of some,*) }   *ac. to*
Herefordshire Heart,   }   *Thomp.*
Guigne Rouge Hative,   }

An old English variety, very seldom seen in our gardens. Fruit of medium size, long heart-shaped, and remarkable for the small drop or tear, with which the end is terminated.   Skin dark red.   Flesh reddish, half tender, with only a tolerable flavour.   Ripe the last of June.   Unfortunately, this variety **has the reputation of being a bad bearer.**

18. Honey. Thomp.

Large Honey.
Yellow Honey.
Late Honey.
Merisier à fruit blanc. *N. Duh.*

The Honey cherry is a variety of the Mazzard but little larger than the common black variety, and its chief merits are great productiveness and lateness of ripening. It is exceedingly sweet when fully ripe, and will hang for a long time upon the tree, which is one of the hardiest and thriftiest in its growth; but Downer's Late, which ripens at the same time is, every way, so much superior, that when that variety can be had, the Honey cherry will scarcely find a place in the garden.

Fruit small, roundish or oval. Skin smooth, yellowish, marbled with red at first, but becoming deep amber-red. Stalk long and slender, very slightly inserted. Flesh tender, melting, with a honied sweetness. Middle of July.

19. Hyde's Red Heart. Man.

A new variety which we received from Mr. Manning, not yet proved here. The fruit is said to be heart-shaped, medium size; skin, at first, pale, but becoming a rather lively red. Flesh tender, with a pleasant, sprightly flavour. The young trees make strong shoots, the bark of which is light gray, dotted with clusters of small white specks.

20. Knight's Early Black. § Thomp. Lind. P. Mag.

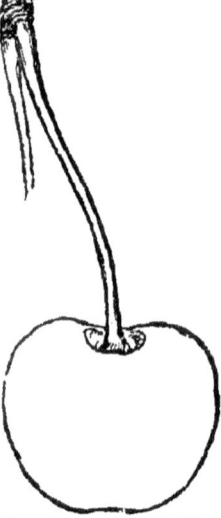

A most admirable early cherry, resembling the Black Tartarian, though much more obtuse in form, but ripening nearly a week earlier, or about the tenth of June. It is one of Mr. Knight's seedlings, a cross-breed between the Bigarreau or Graffion and the Mayduke, originated about 1810, and is universally admired.

Fruit large, a little irregular in outline, obtuse heart-shaped. Stalk of moderate length, rather stout, (much more so than in the Black Eagle,) and inserted in a deep, open cavity. Skin dark purple, becoming black. Flesh purple, tender, juicy, with a rich and sweet juice of high flavour. Tree spreading.

Fig. 67. *Knight's Early Black.*

21. MANNING'S MOTTLED. §

Mottled Bigarreau.   *Man.*

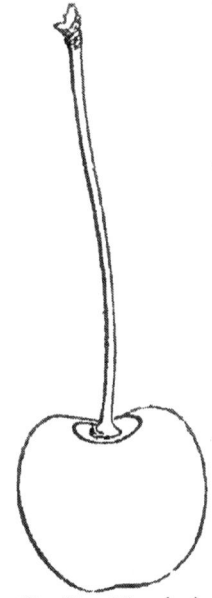

A beautiful cherry, raised by Mr. Manning, from the seed of the Bigarreau. It is a very tender fleshed, heart cherry, and, therefore, should not be called a Bigarreau. It is a most abundant bearer, and will soon become a favourite variety. Bark on the young tree, dark, with a few large, scattered dots.

Fruit rather large, roundish heart-shaped, flattened on one side, with distinct suture lines. Skin amber colour, finely mottled and overspread with red, with a semi-transparent, glossy appearance. Stalk slender, inserted in a shallow hollow. Flesh when fully ripe, yellow, tender, with a sweet and delicious juice. Stone pretty large. Ripens the last of June.

Fig. 68. *Manning's Mottled.*

22. OX HEART.   Thomp.

Lion's Heart.
Bullock's Heart.
Very Large Heart.
Ochsen Herz Kirsche.

This has been made synonymous, by Manning, with Gascoigne's Heart ; but it is a larger and later fruit, obtuse, instead of pointed in its form. It is very scarce in collections here. the White Bigarreau being generally known by the name of Ox Heart in New-York. Fruit large, obtuse heart-shaped. Skin dark red. Flesh red, half tender, with a pleasant juice, of second quality in point of flavour. Ripens about the eighth of July.

23. ROBERTS' RED HEART.   Man.

A new variety, which originated in the garden of David Roberts, Esq., of Salem, Mass. Fruit large, obtuse heart-shaped. Skin a bright, lively red. Stalk set in a rather wide hollow. Flesh red, juicy, tender, with an excellent, sweet flavour. Shoots on young trees strong, dotted with **large white dots.** Rather late, ripening the last of June.

24. RIVERS' EARLY HEART.

A variety, raised by Mr. Rivers, a noted English nursery-man, which has not yet borne fruit with us. It is described as a medium sized heart-shaped cherry, ripening about the middle of June, and a very hardy and productive tree.

25. RIVERS' EARLY AMBER. §

Another seedling from the same source. A large and beautiful amber coloured cherry, tinged with a soft red on the sunny side, heart-shaped, a hardy and very prolific tree. It is also one of the earliest in maturing its fruit, which will be in perfection here about the tenth of June.

26. SPARHAWK'S HONEY. § Man. Ken.

Sparrowhawk's Honey. *Thomp.*

A delicious, melting, sweet cherry, introduced to the notice of fruit growers by Edward Sparhawk, Esq., of Brighton, near Boston. It ripens a little later than most varieties, is a profuse bearer, and a truly valuable sort.

Fruit of medium size, roundish heart-shaped—very regular in form. Stalk of moderate length, rather slender, set in a round, even depression. Skin thin, of a beautiful glossy pale amber-red, becoming a lively red when fully ripe, partially transparent. Flesh melting, juicy, with a very sweet and deicate flavour. Ripe the last of June.

27. TRANSPARENT GUIGNE. § Forsyth. Prince. Pom. Man.

Transparent Gean. *Forsyth.*
Transparent.

A nice little fruit, ripening with the common Honey cherry, about ten days after the cherry season. The skin is thin and pellucid, so that the stone is nearly visible on holding the fruit up to the light. Some writers have stated this to be a bad bearer ; this is incorrect. We have uniformly found it a most productive variety, the tree growing large with spreading branches. It is a valuable and pretty variety for the dessert, hanging late on the tree, and is admired by all amateurs.

Fruit small, borne in pairs, regular, oval heart-shaped. Skin glossy, thin, and nearly transparent, showing the network texture of the flesh beneath, yelllowish-white, delicately blotched with fine red ; distinct suture line on both sides. Stalk

Fig. 69. *Transparent Guigne.*

long and slender set in a slight hollow.   Flesh tender and melting, and when fully ripe very sweet, mingled with a very slight
portion of the piquant bitter of the Mazzard class of cherries.
First of July.

28. WATERLOO § Thomp. Lind. P. Mag.

A capital variety, cross-bred by Mr. Knight, by fertilizing
the Bigarreau with the pollen of the Mayduke.   It retains, ir
part, the habits of both parents, the flowers and the tender flesh
resembling considerably those of the Mayduke, and the strong
wood and leaves those of the Bigarreau.   It was named from
the circumstance of its having first shown fruit about the time
of the Battle of Waterloo.   The tree is rather irregular and
spreading in its head, and is, with us, only a moderate bearer.
    Fruit large, obtuse heart-shaped.   Skin dark purplish,
becoming black at maturity.   Stalk long and slender.   Flesh
purplish-red, juicy, tender when fully ripe, with a rich and
sweet flavour.   Beginning of July.   A thrifty, spreading tree.

29. WHITE TARTARIAN.   Thomp.

Fraser's White Tartarian,   ⎫   *ac. to*
Fraser's White Transparent, ⎬   *Thomp.*
Ambér à petit fruit.   ⎭

The White Tartarian is a pretty cream coloured fruit of medium size and delicate flavour, ripening the last of June.   The
skin is somewhat pellucid, but not so much so as in the Transparent Gean.
    Fruit of medium size, obtuse heart-shaped.   Skin pale yel-
low or cream colour.   Stalk of moderate length, slender.   Flesh
whitish yellow, half tender and of very sweet and excellent
flavour.   The tree is a moderate bearer.

Class II.   Bigarreau Cherries.

(Fruit sweet, heart-shaped, with flesh more or less firm, and crisp or *crackling;*
trees with tall and spreading heads, and large leaves.)

30. AMERICAN HEART.

American Heart.   *Thomp.*

This productive and good cherry, which we have cultivated
for the last eighteen years, and widely disseminated under this
name, came to us from Long Island, as a native, and is really

one of the Bigarreau class. Its origin is uncertain, and there are other sorts often incorrectly called by this name. The fruit is remarkable for its pink colour, and rather *square* form, often being nearly as broad at the apex as at the base near the stalk. The tree is quite luxuriant, with wide-spreading branches, a very horizontal head, and large, rather waved leaves.

Fruit pretty large, heart-shaped, often nearly four sided, and irregular, in its outline—borne in clusters. Skin, at first, pale, but becoming covered with light red or pink, mixed with very little amber. Stalk rather long and slender, inserted in a small and shallow cavity. Flesh half tender and crackling, adhering to the skin, which is rather tough; juice abundant, and, in dry seasons, sweet and excellent, but rather wanting in sweetness in cool or wet seasons. Ripens a week before the following—or early in June.

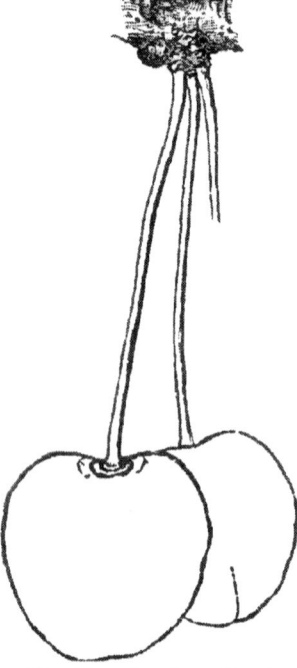

Fig. 70. *American Heart.*

Mr. Manning, who confounds this with the Early White Heart, had evidently never seen it correct.

31. BIGARREAU. § Thomp. Lind.

Graffion.
Yellow Spanish, (*of most American gardens.*)
White Bigarreau, (*of Manning and Kenrick.*)
Amber, or Imperial. *Coxe.*
Turkey Bigarreau? ⎫
Bigarreau Royal, ⎪
Italian Heart, ⎪
Bigarreau Gros? ⎪
West's White Heart, ⎬ *ac. to*
Bigarreau Tardif, ⎪ *Thomp.*
Groote Princess, ⎪
Hollandische Grosse, ⎪
Prinzessin Kirsche, ⎪
Cerise Ambrée. *N. Duh* ⎭

This noble fruit is the Bigarreau *par excellence*, and is unquestionably one of the largest, most beautiful and delicious of cherries. It was introduced into this country about the year 1800, by the late William

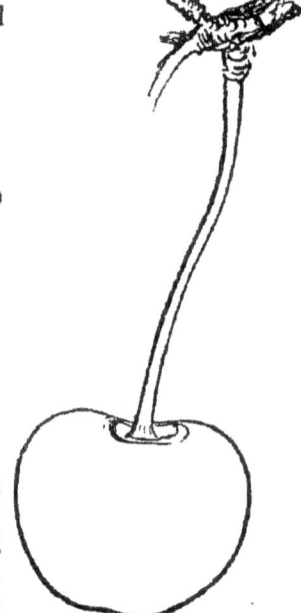

Fig. 71. *Bigarreau.*

Prince, of Flushing, and has been very extensively disseminated under the names of Yellow Spanish, Graffion, and Bigarreau. The tree is short but thrifty in growth, making strong lateral shoots, and forming a large and handsome head with spreading branches—and it commences bearing abundantly and regularly even while young. Its very large size and beautiful appearance, together with the firmness of its flesh renders it a very valuable variety to cultivate for market.

Fruit very large, and of a beautiful waxen appearance, regularly formed, obtuse heart-shaped, the base a good deal flattened. Stalk stout, nearly two inches long, inserted in a wide hollow. Skin pale whitish yellow on the shaded side, bordered with minute carmine dots and deepening into bright red finely marbled on the sunny side. Flesh pale yellow, quite firm, juicy, with a rich, sweet, and delicious flavour if allowed fully to ripen. In perfection the last of June.

This is often confounded with the following sort, from which it is easily known by its long and *broad* leaves. It is most commonly known in the middle states as the Yellow Spanish, an incorrect name, which has been applied to two or three sorts, and the cherry so-called by the older pomologists does not now appear to be known.

32. BIGARREAU, WHITE.   Prince's Pom. Man.

White Ox Heart, (*of the middle states.*)
White Bigarreau.   *Thomp. ?*
Large White Bigarreau.
Tradescant, } *Coxe.*
Ox Heart. }
Harrison Heart ?
Turkey Bigarreau ?
Bigarreau blanc ?

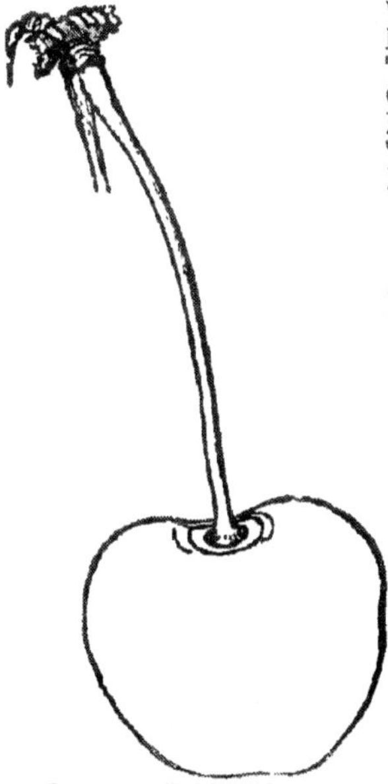

The White Bigarreau, which is more common in the neighbourhood of New-York and Philadelphia, than any other part of the country, is frequently confounded with the foregoing, from which it is materially distinct. The first trees of this cherry were, we believe, introduced from France, by Chancellor Livingston. It does not appear, at this time, to be known in England, though it is probably identical with the Harrison Heart of Forsyth, and the Bigarreau of Hooker. It is inferior to the Bigarreau or Graffion in hardiness, and in

Fig. 72. *White Bigarreau.* the circumstance that it is a very poor bearer while the tree is young, though it bears fine crops when it has arrived at from twelve to fifteen years' growth. The fruit strongly resembles that of the Bigarreau, but is not so *obtuse* heart-shaped, and is more irregular in its outline. But the trees may be readily distinguished even when very small, as the Bigarreau has broad flat foliage, while the White Bigarreau has *narrow waved leaves.* Growth upright.

Fruit of the largest size, heart-shaped, with a rather irregular outline, and a pretty distinct suture line on one side. Skin yellowish white at first, but becoming quite overspread with marbling of red. Flesh firm, but scarcely so much so as that of the Bigarreau, and when fully ripe, half tender, and more luscious than the latter cherry. It is very liable to crack after rain. Middle and last of June.

Mr. Kenrick, in his description of the White Bigarreau, has confused the characteristics of this and the former variety.

On the whole, this variety is likely to be supplanted by the Bigarreau, which joins to most of its good qualities those of greater hardiness, vigour and productiveness.

33. Bigarreau Rouge. Thomp.

This variety, which we have cultivated for several years, scarcely differs from the foregoing, except in the colour of the fruit, which is a little darker red.

34. Bigarreau, Holland. §

Bigarreau d'Hollande. *Noisette.*
Spotted Bigarreau.
Armstrong's Bigarreau.

The Holland Bigarreau is certainly one of the most beautiful of all cherries. The tree first imported into this country from France, is now growing at Dans Kamer, on the Hudson, the seat of the late Edward Armstrong, Esq.; and it appears to us identical with the Bigarreau de Hollande, of which a coloured figure and description are given by Noisette, in the second edition of his *Jardin Fruitier.* It is there stated to have been received from Holland in 1828.*

Fig. 73. *Holland Bigarreau.*

* The B. d'Hollande is made synonymous with the Bigarreau by Thompson in the 3d edition of the London Horticultural Society's Catalogue. This is undoubtedly an error.

A cherry so large, fine and beautiful, and so productive even when young, and which is of rapid and hardy growth, cannot fail soon to become a general favourite in our fruit gardens. It ripens about a week earlier than the Bigarreau, and the branches, which are spreading, or even drooping, are literally loaded with heavy bunches of fruit.

Fruit very large, of a regular heart-shape, rather pointed. Skin white or very pale yellow in the shade, beautifully mottled and spotted on the sunny side, with bright carmine red. Stem rather slender, set in a deep hollow, and the fruit borne in thick clusters. Flesh firm, but not so much so as that of the Bigarreau; a little more juicy; sweet and excellent, perhaps scarcely so high flavoured, but this depends somewhat on the dryness of the season. Leaves very large and broad with rather light footstalks. Ripens 20th of June.

35. BIGARREAU, COULEUR DE CHAIR. § Thomp.

Flesh-coloured Bigarreau.
Gros Bigarreau, Couleur de Chair, ⎫
Gros Bigarreau Blanc.   ⎬ *Noisette.*
Bigarreau à Gros Fruit Blanc.   ⎭
Large Heart-shaped Bigarreau, *of Manning.*
Bigarreau de Rocmont.
Cœur de Pigeon.
Belle de Rocmont?

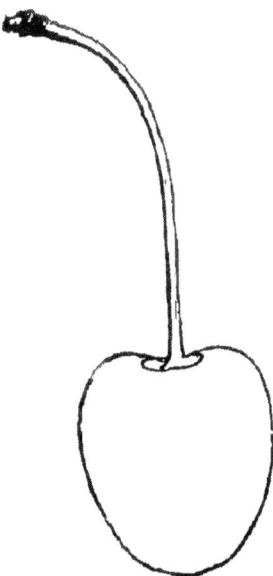

The Flesh-coloured Bigarreau is a beautiful and excellent variety, much more tender in its flesh than most of its class, and which attains, under our warm skies, a higher flavour than it does in England. The leaves are not large, dark green, flat, with purplish footstalks. Tree moderately vigorous.

Fruit very large, of a very *oblong* heart-shape, pointed at the end. Skin shining, of the palest yellow or flesh colour, with a bright red marbled cheek. Stalk moderately long and slender, set in a rather deep and narrow hollow. Flesh half tender, or becoming nearly tender when fully ripe, quite juicy and sweet, and in this climate high flavoured and luscious. Ripe the middle and last of June. On fruiting several of the synonymes above, we find them identical with this variety, which is truly first rate.

Fig. 74. *Flesh-coloured Big-arreau.*

36. BIGARREAU, NAPOLEON. § Thomp.

Bigarreau Lauermann,
Lauermann's Kirsche,
Lauermann's Grosse Kirsche, } *ac. to*
Lauermann's Herz Kirsche. } *Thomp.*

The Napoleon Bigarreau is one of the finest of the firm fleshed cherries—large, well flavoured, handsome, and productive. It was introduced into this country from Holland, by the late Andrew Parmentier, of Brooklyn. (The fruit cultivated and described by Mr. Manning and Kenrick under this name is, we think, not the true sort.)

Fruit of the largest size, very regularly heart-shaped, a little inclining to oblong. Skin pale yellow, becoming amber in the shade, richly dotted and spotted with very deep red, and with a fine marbled dark crimson cheek. Flesh very firm, (almost too much so,) juicy, with an excellent flavour. Stalk very stout, short and set in a narrow cavity. Ripens a few days after the Bigarreau, about the first of July, and is a good and constant bearer. The fruit is not so obtuse as the Bigarreau, and is much more firm than the Holland, or the Flesh coloured varieties.

37. BIGARREAU GROS CŒURET. Thomp. Poiteau.

Large Heart-shaped Bigarreau.
Bigarreau Gros Monstrueux.
Gros Cœuret. *Bon. Jard.*

This, the true Large Heart-shaped Bigarreau, is a French variety only rarely seen in the fruit gardens of this country.

Fruit large, roundish heart-shaped, with a suture line frequently raised, instead of being depressed. Skin at first yellowish red, marked with deeper red streaks, but becoming, when fully ripe, a dark shining red, almost black. Stalk inserted in a shallow hollow. Stone oval and rather large. Flesh firm, purplish, a little bitter at first, but of an excellent rich flavour when fully matured. Ripe from the 10th to the middle of July.

38. BIGARREAU, LARGE RED.

Gros Bigarreau Rouge. *Poiteau.*
Bigarreau à Gros Fruit Rouge. *Bon. Jard.*
Bigarreau à Gros Fruit Rouge. *Thomp. ?*
Belle de Rocmont, (*of some.*)

The Large Red Bigarreau is another handsome French variety, very rare in the United States, and which we hope to see more extensively known.

Fruit very large, of an oblong heart-shape, rather irregular in its outline, a good deal swollen on one side, the shoulders

projecting and marked with a distinct suture line often on both
sides. Stalk rather large, and planted in a very deep and large
hollow. Skin shining, yellowish, dotted and streaked with red
in the shade, but dark red in the sun. Flesh yellowish, or
stained with red next the stone, firm, and of a rich and very excellent flavour. Matures early in July. Tree of very strong
growth.

39. BIGARREAU, CHINA.   Prince's Pom. Man.

Chinese Heart.   *Thomp. ?*

A very striking and peculiar variety, having
the skin beautifully mottled and of a shining
waxen colour. It was raised by the late Wm.
Prince, of Flushing, from the seed of the Bigarreau, and is worthy of a place in the amateur's
garden.

Mr. Thompson incorrectly calls this, "Chinese Heart." It is a true Bigarreau, and we
prefer to continue its proper name. The tree
grows large, and the lateral branches are
somewhat drooping, leaves broad, light green.

Fruit of medium size, roundish or oval
heart-shaped, with a distinct suture line. Skin
shining, at first light amber colour, mottled
with red spots, but becoming red, speckled with numerous lighter spots when fully
ripe. Stalk long and slender, set in a shallow
hollow. Flesh firm, or half tender when fully
ripe, with a sweet, rich and peculiar flavour.
This variety is the more valuable as it ripens
a few days later than the cherry season.

Fig. 75. *China Big-
arreau.*

40. BIGARREAU TARDIF DE HILDESHEIM.   Thomp. Sickler.

Bigarreau marbré de Hildesheim.   *Dict. D'Agri.*
Bigarreau Blanc Tardif de Hildesheim.
Hildesheimer ganz Späte Knorpel Kirsche.
Hildesheimer Späte Herz Kirsche.
Späte Hildesheimer Marmor Kirsche.
Hildesheim Bigarreau.   *Prince.*

The Hildesheim Bigarreau is a rare German variety, which
ripens here in August, and according to Thompson, is the latest
sweet cherry known ; a quality that renders it peculiarly valuable.

Fruit of medium size, heart-shaped. Skin yellow, mottled
and marbled with red. Flesh pale yellow, firm, with a sweet
and agreeable flavour. The tree is hardy, and will doubtless
prove a valuable variety in this country.

41. Bigarreau, Black.

Bigarreau Noir.

The Black Bigarreau is a second rate sort, and an indifferent bearer. Fruit middle sized, heart-shaped, looking much like a Black Heart. Skin at first dotted with red, but finally becoming quite black. Flesh firm and rather dry. First of July. Scarcely worth cultivation.

42. Black Bigarreau of Savoy.   Ken.

A very firm, large, black cherry, very recently imported from Savoy, by George Brown, Esq., of Beverly, near Boston. It has been rather more highly rated by the cultivators of Boston, than it deserves, as, though a handsome and rich fruit, it is rather too firm and dry in its flesh to rank as first rate. Its chief merit is that of hanging late upon the tree—till the middle of July.

Fruit large, regularly heart-shaped, very slightly obtuse. Skin smooth and even on the surface, not very glossy, quite black at maturity. Stalk an inch and three fourths long, rather stout, set in a narrow even hollow. Flesh purple, quite firm and solid, with a rich but not abundant juice. Stone rather large.

43. Bigarreau, New Large Black.   Ken.

The new large black Bigarreau, a variety recently obtained from France, appears likely to prove one of the finest. The fruit is very large quite as handsome as that of the Black Tartarian, and ripens among the late varieties.

Fruit very large, obtuse heart-shaped. Skin quite black and glossy at maturity. Flesh purple, pretty firm, but with a very rich and luscious flavour, more juicy than the other Black Bigarreaus. The tree is very thrifty in its growth, with large broad leaves. [This proves to be only the Black Tartarian. 8th ed.]

44. Buttner's Yellow.   Thomp.

Büttner's Wachs-Knorpel Kirsche.
Büttner's Gelbe-Knorpel Kirsche.

Raised by Büttner, of Halle, in Germany, and one of the few cherries *entirely yellow*. We have just received this variety from abroad. It is said to be a good bearer, and will no doubt, be a very interesting addition to the dessert. Mr. Thompson describes it as follows:

Fruit of medium size, roundish, a little compressed on its sides. Skin pale yellow. Flesh firm, yellowish, sweet, and good. It ripens at the usual cherry season.

45. DOWNING'S RED CHEEK.

A very handsome and excellent seedling cherry, just raised
at this establishment, and which
promises to be a charming addition to the dessert. It somewhat
resembles the Bigarreau, but is
more tender and sweet, and
rather more highly coloured.

Fruit rather large, regularly
obtuse heart-shaped, with a pretty
distinct suture. Skin thin,
(slightly pellucid when fully
ripe,) white, with a rich dark
crimson cheek (somewhat mottled,) covering more than half the
fruit. Stalk an inch and a half
long, set in an even hollow of
moderate depth. Flesh yellowish, half tender, and of a very

Fig. 76. *Downing's Red Cheek.*

delicately sweet and luscious flavour. Leaves coarsely serrated, with dark footstalks. Ripens a few days before the Bigarreau, or about the 14th of June.

46. ELTON. § Thomp. Lind. P. Mag.

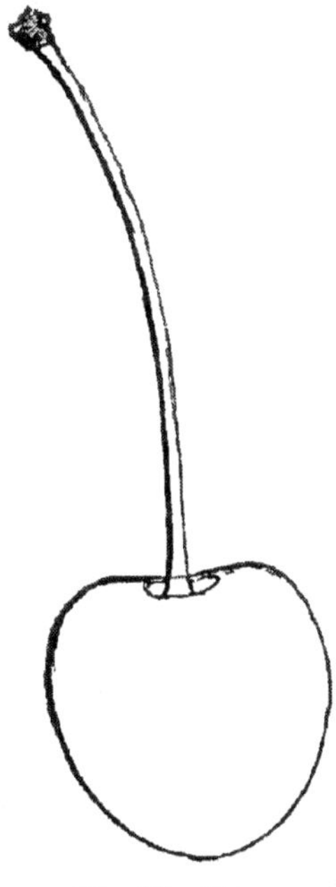

The Elton, a seedling raised in 1806,
by the late President of the London Horticultural Society, is certainly one of the
first of cherries in all respects. Its large
size, early maturity, beautiful appearance, luscious flavour, and productiveness,
render it universally esteemed. It is a
cross-bred variety raised from the Bigarreau or Graffion with the White Heart for
its male parent. The trees grow very
vigorously, and are readily known, when
in foliage, by the unusually dark red colour of the footstalks of the leaves.

Fruit large, rather pointed, heart
shaped. Skin thin, shining pale yellow
on the shaded side, but with a cheek nex.
the sun delicately mottled and streaked
with bright red. Stalk long and slender.
Flesh somewhat firm at first, but becoming nearly tender, juicy, with a very rich
and luscious flavour, not surpassed by any
large cherry known. Ripens about the
middle of June, or directly after the Mayduke.

Fig. 77. *Elton.*

47. FLORENCE. § Thomp. Lind.

Knevett's Late Bigarreau.

A most excellent cherry, originally brought from Florence, in Italy, which considerably resembles the Bigarreau, but ripens a little later, and has the additional good quality of hanging a long time on the tree.

Fruit large, heart-shaped, and regularly formed. Skin amber yellow, delicately marbled with red, with a bright red cheek, and when fully exposed, the whole fruit becomes of a fine lively red. Stalk over two inches long, slender, set in a deep hollow. Flesh yellowish, firm, very juicy, and sweet. In perfection from the last of June till the 10th or 15th of July.

48. GRIDLEY. Man. Ken.

Apple Cherry.
Maccarty.

A native of Roxbury, Mass., which sprung up on the farm of Mr. Samuel Gridley, of that town. An excessive bearer, and from its firmness, bears carriage well, and is a good sort to cultivate for market.

Fruit of medium size, about that of the Black Heart, roundish. Stalk rather short, and inserted in a shallow cavity. Skin black. Flesh quite firm, purplish, moderately juicy and of quite a rich flavour. Stone small. Ripens after the Black Heart, about the 4th of July.

49. LADY SOUTHAMPTON'S YELLOW. Thomp.

Lady Southampton's Duke,
——— Golden Drop, } ac. to
Yellow or Golden, . } Thomp.
Spanish Yellow.

A yellow cherry, very rare yet in our collections and scarcely meriting general cultivation, being more admired for its colour. The best flavoured yellow cherry is Büttner's Yellow.

Fruit of medium size, heart-shaped. Skin yellow. Flesh firm, not very juicy. Ripens about the middle of July.

50. MADISON BIGARREAU. Man.

The Madison Bigarreau was recently raised, and named, by Mr. Manning, from the common Bigarreau. It is a pretty fruit, and of good flavour, but only of medium size, and not, therefore, equal to many of this class.

Fruit of medium size, half as large as the Bigarreau, very regularly heart-shaped. Skin much dotted and marbled with rich red on an amber yellow ground. Stalk rather short and slender. Flesh yellowish, half tender, with a sweet and pleasant flavour. Ripe middle to the last of June. Young trees thrifty, with spreading, rather drooping branches—slender at the ends, and light gray bark. A good bearer.

51. Manning's Late Black.   Man.

Manning's Late Black Heart.

A seedling, raised by Mr. Manning, of Salem, its parent the Black Heart. Fruit large, roundish. Skin deep purple, or nearly black when fully ripe. Flesh purplish, pretty firm, moderately juicy and sweet. Ripens about the second week in July.

52. Remington.

Remington White Heart.   *Prince.*
Remington Heart.

A small, firm fleshed, yellow cherry, a native of Rhode Island, which ripens very late, but is of too indifferent flavour to be worthy of cultivation.

Fruit small, heart-shaped. Skin yellow, rarely with a faint tinge of red on one side. Flesh yellowish, dry, and somewhat bitter. Middle and last of August.

53. Tradescant's Black Heart. § Thomp.

Elkhorn,	} *Prince.*
Elkhorn of Maryland.	
Large Black Bigarreau.	*Man.*
Tradescant's,	
Bigarreau Gros Noir,	
Guigne Noire Tardive,	*ac. to Thomp.*
Grosse Schwarze Knoorpel,	
Kirsche mit Säftigem Fleisch.	

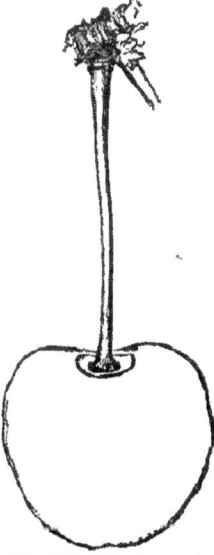

Fig. 78. *Tradescant's Black Heart.*

A very remarkable, and a very good fruit. It is remarkable for the exceedingly solid "liver like" consistence of its flesh, and the irregular surface of its skin. Its good qualities are, handsome appearance, late ripening, rich flavour, and moderate and uniform productiveness. When the trees are young and thrifty, the fruit is often of the largest size, fully as large as that of the Black Tartarian. It is an European variety, but a tree growing about 40 years since in the garden of an inn in

Maryland, attracted the notice of the late Wm. Prince, who propagated it under the name of Elkhorn, by which it was there known. The leaves are broad, the bark of a peculiarly gray colour, and the growth quite vigorous.

Fruit large, heart-shaped, with a very irregular or uneven surface. Skin deep black, glossy, (before fully ripe, deep purple, mottled with black.) Stalk rather short, set in a pretty deep hollow. Flesh very solid and firm, dark purple, moderately juicy, with an excellent flavour. Ripe first and second week in July.

54. TOBACCO LEAVED. Thomp. Lind.

Four to the Pound.
Cerisier de 4 à Livre.
Bigarreautier à Feuilles de Tabac.
Bigarreautier à Grandes Fenilles.
Guignier à Feuilles de Tabac.
Vier auf ein Pfund.

The tobacco leaved cherry is an example of one of the impositions sometimes practised upon the public by dishonest nurserymen. It has been extensively sold, both in Europe and this country, under the high sounding title of " Four (cherries) to the Pound," while in fact it only bears a very small hard fleshed yellowish cherry tinged with a little red, with a long stalk, and a large stone, and of inferior flavour. The leaves are very large and coarse.

Class III. Duke Cherries.

Fruit roundish, sub-acid at first, becoming nearly sweet; skin thin; flesh very juicy and melting. Trees of upright or horizontal growth, with flat, dark coloured leaves.)

55. ARCH DUKE. Thomp. Lind. Fors.

Griotte de Portugal. *O. Duh. Nois.*
Portugal Duke.
Late Arch Duke.
Late Duke, (*of some.*)

This is a variety of the Mayduke, with considerably larger fruit; ripening a fortnight later, but we think inferior to it in flavour. It is very scarce in this country, and even abroad more than half the cherries sold under this name are either the Mayduke or the Late Duke. The trees of the true sort are good bearers, rather more vigorous than those of the Mayduke, with longer *diverging* branches, which become slightly pendulous in bearing specimens.

Fruit large, about a fourth larger than that of the **Mayduke,** nearly round or a little flattened. Skin, at first, red, but becoming a very dark red, almost black. Stalk an inch and a half long, rather stout at its point of insertion in the fruit. Flesh dark red, melting, juicy, slightly bitter until fully ripe, when it is of an excellent, rich, sub-acid flavour. Ripe about the first of July.

56. Belle de Choisy. § Thomp. Nois. P. Mag.

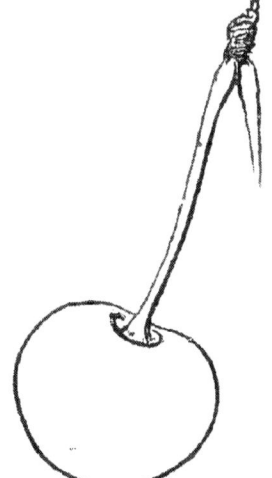

Ambreé de Choisey,
Ambreé à Gros Fruit,
Cerise Doucette,   *of French*
Cerise de la Palembre,   *gardens*
Cerise à Noyau Tendre,
Schöne von Choisy.

In our estimation, there is no cherry for the dessert, more delicate or delicious than the Belle de Choisy. It comes from the village of Choisy near Paris, where it was raised in 1760. The habit of the tree is nearly that of the Mayduke, the leaves dark, and the head upright. But the fruit is rounder, of a beautiful *cornelian* colour, and the flavour is very sweet and delicious. It thrives well, appears very hardy, is a regular, moderate bearer,

Fig. 79.   *Belle de Choisy.*

and deserves a widely extended planting in this country.

Fruit round or slightly depressed. Skin very thin and translucent, showing a net-like texture of flesh beneath; in colour, pale amber in the shade, but in the sun finely mottled with yellowish-red—the fruit fully exposed becoming a bright cornelian red. Flesh amber coloured, very tender and melting, of a delicate, sweet flavour. Stalk rather short, swollen at the upper end. Middle of June, or directly after the Mayduke.

57. Jeffrey's Duke.   Thomp.

Jeffrey's Royal. *Lind.*
Jeffrey's Royal Caroon.
Royale,   *O. Duh.*
Cherry Duke,
Royale Ordinaire. *Poiteav.*

Jeffrey's Duke, or the *Cerise Royale* of the French gardens, is a fine sort considerably resembling the Mayduke, and is yet very rare in this country. It is much rounder than the Mayduke, and seldom or ever becomes of that *dark* hue which the latter fruit always assumes when fully ripe.

Fruit of medium size, round, or a little flattened at the apex and base. Skin of a fine lively red. Stalk moderately long. Flesh yellowish amber, scarcely red. Juice abundant, and of a rich flavour. The trees are of a distinct habit of growth, being very compact, and growing quite slowly. The buds are very closely set, and the fruit is borne in thick clusters. Middle and last of June.

58. LATE DUKE. § Thomp. Lind. P. Mag.

Anglaise Tardive.

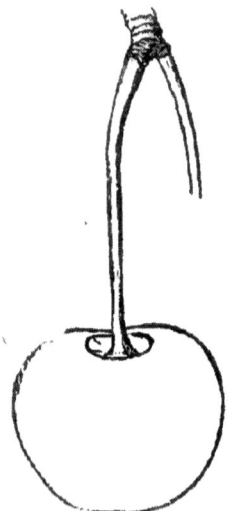

A very large and fine Duke cherry, ripening a month later than the Mayduke, and therefore a very valuable sort for the dessert or for cooking. The tree is of vigorous growth, but when of bearing size, the whole branches spread almost *horizontally*. Leaves larger than those of the Mayduke.

Fruit large, flattened or obtuse heart-shaped, much more depressed in its figure than the Mayduke. Colour, when fully ripe, rich dark red; (but at first white, mottled with bright red.) Stalk rather slender, inserted in a shallow hollow. Flesh yellowish, tender, juicy, with a sprightly sub-acid flavour, not quite so sweet and rich as the Mayduke. Ripens gradually, and hangs on the tree from the middle of July till the 10th of August.

Fig. 80. *Late Duke.*

The branches of this tree are slender in their growth, and the whole habit of the tree seems to incline more to the Morella than the Duke class.

59. MAYDUKE. § Mill. Thomp. Lind.

Royale Hâtive,		Early Duke,		
Cherry Duke, (*of some*,)		Large Mayduke,		
Cerise Guigne,		Morris Duke,		*of various*
Coularde,	*of various*	Morris' Early Duke,		*English*
De Hollande,	*French*	Benham's Fine Early Duke,		*gardens.*
D'Espagne,	*gardens.*	Thompson's Duke,		*ac. to*
Griotte Grosse Noire,		Portugal Duke,		*Thomp.*
Griotte D'Espagne, (*of some*,)		Buchanan's Early Duke,		
Griotte Précoce, (*of some*,)		Millett's Late Heart Duke.		

This invaluable early cherry is one of the most popular sorts in all countries, thriving almost equally well in cold or warm climates. This, the Black Heart, and the Bigarreau, are the most extensively diffused of all the finer varieties in the United States. And among all the new varieties none has been found

to supplant the Mayduke. Before it is
fit for table use, it is admirably adapted
for cooking ; and when fully ripe, it is,
perhaps, the richest of the sub-acid cherries. In the gardens here, we have noticed a peculiar habit of this tree of producing very frequently some branches
which ripen much later than the others,
thus protracting for a long time the period in which its fruit is in use. The
Mayduke is remarkable for its upright,
or, as it is called, *fastigiate* head, especially while the tree is young, in distinction to other sorts, which produce many
lateral branches.

Fruit roundish or obtuse heart-shaped,
growing in clusters. Skin at first of a
lively red, but when fully ripe of a rich
dark red. Flesh reddish, tender and
melting, very juicy, and, at maturity,

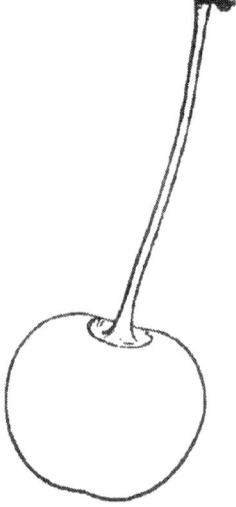

Fig. 81. *Mayduke.*

rich and excellent in flavour. This fruit is most frequently
picked while it is yet red, and partially acid, and before it attains
its proper colour or flavour. It begins to colour, about New-
York, in favourable seasons, the last of May, and ripens during
the first half of June.

Mayduke is said to be a corruption of *Médoc*, the province in
France, where this variety (the type of all the class now called
Dukes) is believed to have originated.

HOLMAN'S DUKE, appears to be only an accidental variety of
the Mayduke, ripening from a week to two weeks later. The
Late Mayduke, of some gardens, is of similar character, and
was obtained by grafting from the late ripening branches of
the common Mayduke

60. ROYAL DUKE. Thomp.

Royale Anglaise Tardive.

Fruit large, roundish, and distinctly oblate or flattened. Skin
dark red. Flesh reddish, tender, juicy and rich. A good bearer. Ripens in the last of June.

The true Royal Duke is very rare in this country. The
fruit is a good deal larger than the May Duke, and more flattened at the top and bottom. It is readily known from the Late
Duke and Archduke, by its *upright* growth, which is similar to
that of the Mayduke.

61. Sweet Montmorency. § Man.

Allen's Sweet Montmorency.

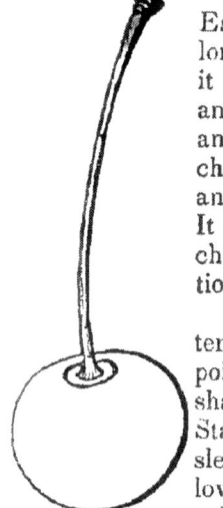

Fig. 82. *Sweet Mont-morency.*

This cherry, a seedling raised by J. F. Allen, Esq., of Salem, Mass., does not properly belong here, as, though in external appearance it resembles a Montmorency, it is of very sweet and delicate flavour, and the whole growth and habit of the tree is rather that of a Heart cherry than a Duke, or Morello. It is no doubt an accidental hybrid between these two classes. It is a good bearer, ripens long after sweet cherries are gone, and is a valuable acquisition to all collections of this fruit.

Fruit of medium size, round, slightly flattened at the base, with a distinctly depressed point at the apex. Skin pale amber in the shade, light red, slightly mottled, in the sun. Stalk an inch and three fourths long, rather slender, inserted in a small, shallow, even hollow. Flesh yellowish, tender, sweet and excellent. Ripens here the last week in July; in Boston during the early part of August.

Class IV. *Morello, or Acid Cherries.*

(Fruit round, or flattened, acid, skin thin, flesh juicy and melting. Trees of low and spreading growth, with slender branches, which are often drooping and wiry, and small dark green foliage.)

62. Belle Magnifique. Man.

Belle et Magnifique. *Ken.*

A sort recently imported into the neighbourhood of Boston, from France, and first introduced to notice here by Gen. Dearborn. The tree is of stronger growth than most of its class, and bears moderate crops.

Fruit large, round. Skin light red, mottled with darker spots. Stalk pretty long and inserted in a hollow of moderate depth. Flesh juicy, but quite acid. Good for preserving. Ripens about the middle or last of July.

63. Buttner's October Morello. Thomp.

Büttner's October Zucker Weichsel.

A new, Dutch, acid cherry, said to be the latest variety known

in Europe, and chiefly valued for ripening long after all others have disappeared. We have received trees, but they have not yet borne fruit. It is described as a dark red fruit of medium size, round, flesh juicy and tender, and quite acid, being only fit for culinary uses. Ripens in September and hangs on the tree till October.

64. CARNATION. § Thomp. Lind.

Wax Cherry.
Crown.
Cerise Nouvelle d'Angleterre,
Cerise de Portugal,
Grosse Cerise Rouge Pâle,
Griottier Rouge Pâle,
Griotte de Villennes.
} *(of French gardens, ac. to Thomp.*

A very handsome, light red, large cherry, highly esteemed here for brandying and preserving.

Fruit large, round. Skin at first yellowish white, mottled with red, but becoming a lively red slightly marbled. Stalk about an inch and a half long, stout. Flesh tender, a little more firm than most of this division, but juicy, and when fully ripe, of a sprightly and good sub-acid flavour. The foliage is pretty large, and the wood strong, but the tree has a spreading, rather low habit. It is a moderate but regular bearer, and the fruit hangs a long while on the branches, without decaying. Ripe the middle and last of July.

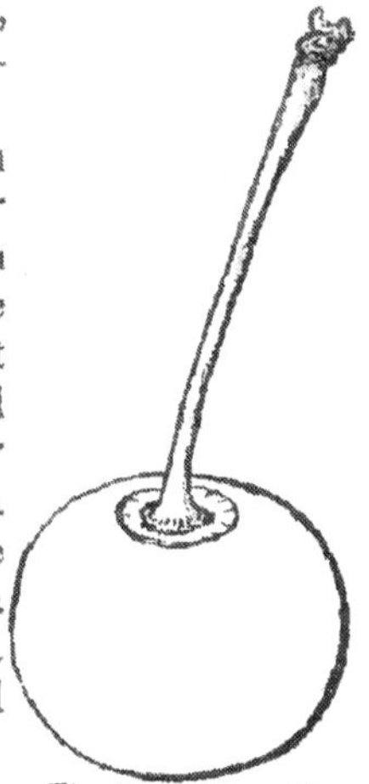

Fig. 83. *Carnation.*

PRINCE'S DUKE is a very large variety of this cherry, raised from a seed of it, by Mr. Prince, of Long Island. Its shy habit of bearing renders it of little value.

65. CLUSTER. Thomp.

Cerise à Bouquet. *Poiteau, Duh.*
Cerisier à Trochet,
Chevreuse,
Commune à Trochet,
Tres Fertile,
Griottier à Bouquet.
} *of French gardens.*

Bouquet Amarelle,
Trauben Amarelle,
Busch Weichsel,
Flandrische Weichsel,
Büschel Kirsche.
} *of the Germans.*

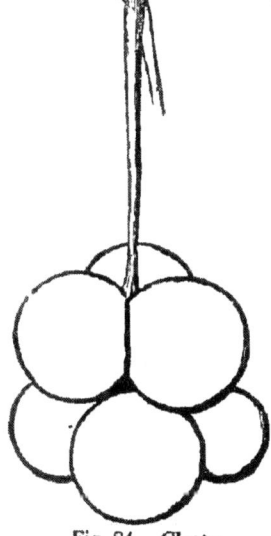

Fig. 81. *Cluster.*

A very curious fruit, growing closely clustered around a common stalk. Each flower varies from the normal state, by having several pistils or styles, several of which, frequently five or six, become perfect fruits forming a bouquet or cluster. The fruit is too acid to be of any value except for preserving.

Fruit of small size, borne in clusters of from two to six; round, of a lively red. Ripens the last of June. The tree is small in all its parts.

66. EARLY MAY. Thomp. Lind.

May Cherry. *Lang.*
Small May.
Cerisier Nain à Fruit Roud.
———— Précoce. *O. Duh.*
Griottier Nain Précoce.
Hative.
Précoce.
Nain Précoce.
Petite Cerise Rouge Précoce.
Königliche Amarelle.
Frühe Kleine Runde.
Zwerg Weichsel.

One of the smallest, as well as the earliest of cherries. The tree very small and dwarfish, scarcely growing more than eight feet high. It is not worth cultivation now that we have the Early Purple Guigne, Baumann's May, and the like.

Fruit small, round, slightly flattened. Stalk an inch long, rather slender, pretty deeply set. Skin pale red; or, at maturity, a rather lively light red. Flesh soft, juicy, and quite acid

67. FLEMISH. Thomp.

Montmorency, (*of Lindley.*)
Kentish, (*of some.*)
Cerise a Courte Quene. *Poit.*
Montmorency à Gros Fruit, }
Gros Gobet, } *O. Duh.*
Gobet a Courte Queue. }
A Courte Queue de Provence.
English Weichsel. ?
Weichsel mit gauzkurzen stiel, } *of the*
Double Volgers. } *Dutch.*

Fig. 85. *Flemish.*

This is a very odd looking fruit, being much flattened, and having a very short stalk. The only bearing tree we have seen, in this country, is one in the garden of Madame Parmentier, Brooklyn, N. Y. The Flemish is not a good bearer, and has not, therefore, ever become a popular fruit even in France or Flanders, where it originated. It is well suited to the grounds of the curious amateur.

Fruit rather large, very much flattened both at the top and base, and generally growing in pairs. Stalk stout, scarcely ever an inch long, deeply inserted in a hollow which has often a *furrow* or hollowed slope on one side. Skin shining, of a bright lively red. Flesh yellowish white, juicy, and sub-acid. Good for preserving—but, unless very ripe, scarcely rich enough for table use. Last of July.

68. KENTISH. § Thomp

Virginian May,   } of American
Early Richmond, } gardens.
Kentish, or } Lind.
Flemish.   }
Common Red, }
Sussex,   }
Pie Cherry, } of the English.
Kentish Red. }
Montmorency. O. Duh. }
Montmorency à longue queue, } of the
Commune,   } French.
Muscat de Prague. }

The true Kentish cherry, an old European sort, better known here as the Early Richmond is one of the most valuable of the acid cherries. It begins to colour about the 20th of May, and may then be used for tarts, while it will hang upon the tree, gradually growing larger, and losing its acidity, until the last of June, or, in dry seasons, even till July, when it becomes of a rich, sprightly, and excellent acid flavour. The tree grows about 18 feet high, with a roundish spreading head, is exceedingly productive, and is from its early maturity a very profitable market fruit, being largely planted for this purpose in New-Jersey. This kind is remarkable for the tenacity with which the stone adheres to the stalk. Advantage is taken of this to draw out the stones. The fruit is then exposed to the sun, and becomes one of the most excellent of all dried fruits.

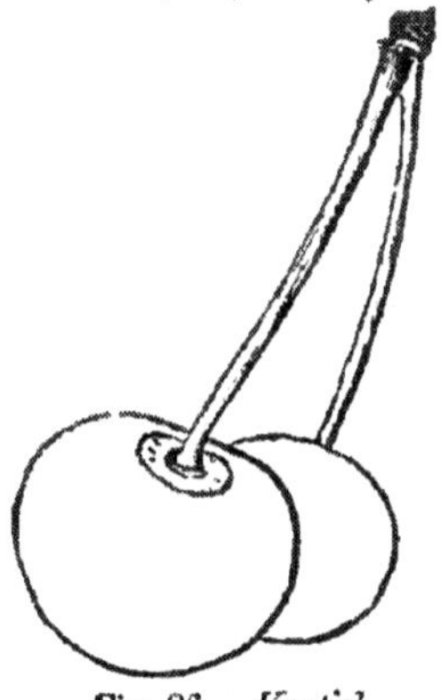

Fruit when it first reddens rather small, but, when fully ripe, of medium size,

Fig. 86.   *Kentish.*

round, or a little flattened; borne in pairs, (our *fig.* should be one half larger.) Skin of a fine bright red, growing somewhat dark when fully ripe. Stalk an inch and a quarter long, rather stout, set in a pretty deep hollow. Flesh melting, juicy, and, at maturity, of a sprightly rather rich acid flavour.

We follow Thompson in making the true MONTMORENCY of the French synonymous with this. But we confess that we are inclined to believe that it may prove distinct. The true *Mont. morency,* which is now very scarce in France, (and is rather a shy bearer,) is carefully described and figured by Poiteau and others, as a larger growing tree, producing much richer fruit, with a longer and thicker stalk, and quite as sweet and high flavoured as that of the finest Duke cherry.

69. LATE KENTISH.

Common Red.	
Pie Cherry.	
Common Sour Cherry.	*of American gardens.*
Kentish Red.	
Kentish.	

This cherry, a variety of the Kentish, is better known among us than any other acid cherry, and is especially abundant on the Hudson, and in the neighbourhood of New-York, where it is most extensively disseminated along the fences and road sides, propagating itself readily by seeds and suckers. It does not seem to be exactly identical with any one of this class known abroad, and is perhaps a seedling sort belonging to America. It is emphatically the *Pie Cherry* of this country, being more generally grown than any other sort, the poorest and most neg-lected garden affording so hardy a fruit in abundance. It is quite acid even when fully ripe, and the stone does not adhere to the stalk, like that of the foregoing. It ripens two or three weeks after the cherry season, or about the middle or last of July. It is two weeks later than the preceding sort, and is much more acid.

Fruit of medium size, round, slightly flattened. Stalk an inch, to one and a half long, strong, and straight. Skin deep lively red, when fully ripe. Flesh very tender and abounding with a highly acid juice.

70. MORELLO. Thomp. Lind. Lang.

English Morello.
Large Morello.
Dutch Morello.
Late Morello.
Ronald's Large Morello.
Milan. *Lang.*
Cerise du Nord. *Nois.*
Griotte Ordinaire du Nord.
September Weichsel Grosse.

The Morello is a fine fruit. Its name is said to be derived from the dark purple colour of its juice, which resembles that of the *Morus* or Mulberry.* When grown in a shaded situation,

* Or, as others say, from the French *morelle,* (a negress,) from the dark and shining skin.

17*

the fruit will hang on the tree, here, til. August, and in England where it is trained on north walls especially to retard its season, it frequently hangs till near frost, when it becomes a rich and agreeable table fruit.   This sort, the Large or true Morello, is yet very scarce in this country, but we hope wi'l not long continue so, as it is highly valuable for all kinds of preserves, and is an agreeable addition to a dessert.

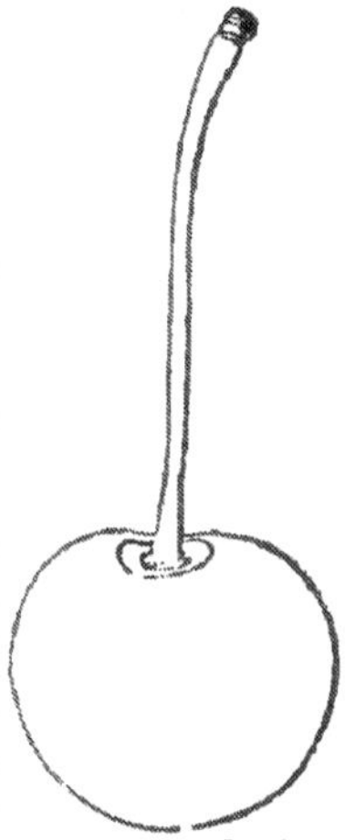

Fruit of pretty large size, round—or slightly obtuse heart-shaped.   Skin dark red, becoming nearly black when fully ripe.   Flesh dark purplish red, tender, juicy, and of a pleasant subacid flavour when quite mature.   Ripe 20th of July.

The COMMON MORELLO of this country, largely cultivated in some districts, is a smaller variety of the foregoing, its fruit being about two thirds the size, and a little darker in colour. It is of equally fine flavour, and is highly esteemed for drying, for preserving in sugar or brandy, or for bottling ; keeping, in the latter

Fig. 86.   *Morello.*

mode, like green gooseberries without sugar or brandy, for several months.   The branches are smaller and more slender than those of the true Morello, and unfortunately are more liable to the attacks of the *weevil*, which causes the *knots* on the Plum, than those of any other cherry ; for which cutting off and burning, early in the spring, is the only remedy.

71. PLUMSTONE MORELLO. § Thomp. Prince.

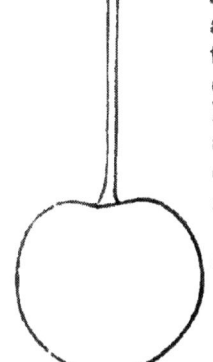

This is undoubtedly one of the best of the acid cherries.   Its late maturity, handsome appearance, and good flavour, as well as its thrifty and productive habit, render it highly esteemed wherever it is known.   It is, perhaps, the largest of this division of cherries, and it receives its name from the rather longer and more pointed stone, than is commonly seen in acid cherries.

Fruit large, roundish, inclining to a heart-shape.   Skin deep red.   Stalk an inch and a half long, rather slender and straight, set in a hollow of moderate depth.   Flesh reddish, tender, juicy, and when fully matured, of a sprightly and agreeable acid flavour.   **Last of** July.

Fig 87.   *Plumstone Morello.*

72. Rumsey's Late Morello. §

A new variety, of remarkable habit, of which the original tree now ten or twelve years old, was raised by our friend, Dr. J. S. Rumsey, of Fishkill Landing, on the Hudson. It is just coming into bearing, and gives promise, from its extraordinary lateness, large size, and handsome appearance, of becoming a very favourite acid cherry for preserving and cooking. The tree has the Morello habit, with, however, unusually *light* coloured wood and leaves.

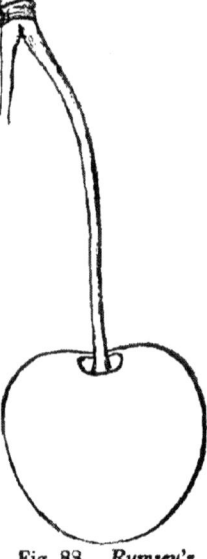

Fig. 83. *Rumsey's Late Morello.*

A few of the fruit commence ripening about the first of August, while many on the tree are yet small and green, and they continue ripening gradually until the first frosts.

Fruit frequently borne in pairs, large, roundish heart-shaped. Skin very smooth and polished; before fully ripe, of a light yellowish red or cornelian colour—becoming at maturity, a rich lively red, with a distinct suture line on one side. Stalk long (for a Morello,) inserted in a narrow and rather deep hollow. Flesh very juicy and melting, with too much acid for the table. Stone long, resembling that of the Plumstone Morello.

Ornamental Varieties.

73. Large Double Flowering.

Double French Cherry.
Merisier à Fleurs Doubles. *Thomp. Duh.*
Prunus cerasus pleno.
Cerasis sylvestris, flore pleno. *Arb. Brit.*

The double blossomed cherry bears no fruit, but whoever admires a beautiful flowering tree, cannot refuse a place in his garden to this one, so highly ornamental. Its blossoms, which appear at the usual season, are produced in the most showy profusion; they are about an inch and a half in diameter, and resemble clusters of the most lovely, full double, white roses. The tree has the habit and foliage of the Mazzard Cherries, and soon forms a large and lofty head.

74. Dwarf Double Flowering.

Double Flowering Kentish.
Small Double Flowering.
Cerisier a Fleurs Doubles.   *Thomp N. Duh*

This is a double floweting variety of the sour, or Kentish
cherry, and has the more dwarfish habit and smaller leaves
and branches of that tree—scaicely forming more than a large
shrub, on which account it is perhaps more suitable for small
gardens.   The flowers are much like those of the large double
flowering, but they are not so regular and beautiful in their
form.

75. Chinese Double Flowering.

Yung To
Cerasus serrulata.   { *Arb. Brit*
Serrulated leaved Cherry. {

This is a very rare variety, recently imported from China,
with the leaves cut on the edges in that manner known as serrulate by botanists.   Its flowers which are borne in fascicles
are white, slightly tinged with pink, and nearly as double as
those of the large double flowering.   The tree considerably resembles the sour cherry tree, and appears rather dwarfish in its
growth.

76. Weeping, or Allsaints.   Thomp.

Ever flowering Cherry.   } *Arb. Brit.*
C. vulgaris, semperplorens }
Cerise de la Toussainte. *N Duh. Nois.*
Guignier à rameaux pendans, }
Cerise Tardive,   } *of the*
Cerisier Pleurant,   } *French.*
Cerise de St. Martin.   }
St Martin's Amarelle,   }
Martin's Weichsel,   } *of the*
Monats Amarelle,   } *Dutch.*
Allerheiligen Kirsche.   }

This charming little tree, with slender, weeping branches,
clothed with small, almost myitle-like foliage, is a very pleasing
ornament, when introduced on a lawn.   Its fruit is a small, deep
red Morello, which is acid, and in moist seasons, is produced
for a considerable period successively.   When grafted, as it
generally is, about the height of one's head, on a straight stem
of the common Mazzard, it forms a beautiful parasol-like top,
the ends of the branches weeping half way down to the ground,

77. VIRGINIAN WILD CHERRY.

Wild Cherry, *of the United States.*
Cerasus Virginiana. *Arb. Brit. Dec.*
Cerasier de Virginie. *French.*
Virginisch Kirsche. *German.*

Our native wild cherry is too well known to need minute description. It forms a large and lofty forest tree, with glossy, dark green leaves, and bears currant-like bunches of small fruit, which are palatable, sweet, and slightly bitter when fully ripe, at midsummer. They are, however, most esteemed for preparing *cherry bounce,* a favourite *liqueur* in many parts of the country, made by putting the fruit along with sugar in a demijohn or cask of the best old rum.

The *black* wild cherry, (*C. serotina,* Torrey and Gray,) which ripens the first of September, is the best kind. The other species, (*C. Virginiana,*) which is commonly known as the *Choke Cherry,* bears *reddish* coloured fruit, which is more astringent, and ripens a month earlier.

Selection of cherries for a small garden. Early Purple Guigne, Baumann's Early, Knight's Early Black, Mayduke, Bigarreau, Tartarian, Downer's Late, Elton, Tradescant's Black, Belle de Choisy, Sweet Montmorency, Kentish, Morello.

The hardiest cherries are the Kentish, (or Virginian May,) the Morello, and the Mayduke. These succeed well at the farthest limits, both north and south, in which the cherry can be raised, and when all other varieties fail, they may be depended on for regular crops. Next to these, in this respect, are the Black Heart, Downer's Late, Downton, and Elton.

CHAPTER XIII.

THE CURRANT.

Ribes rubrum, Lin. *Grossulaceæ,* of botanists.
Grossilier commun, of the French; *Die Johannisbeere,* German; *Aalbesseboom,* Dutch; *Ribes rosso,* Italian; and *Grossella,* Spanish.

THE name currant is said to be derived from the resemblance in the fruit to the little *Corinth* grapes or raisins, which, under the name of *currants,* are sold in a dried state in such quantities by grocers; the latter word being only a corruption of *Corinth,* and, the fruit of this little grape, being familiarly known as such long before the common currants were cultivated.

The currant is a native of Britain, and the north of Europe, and is, therefore, an exceedingly hardy fruit bearing shrub, seldom growing more than three or four feet high. The fruit of the original wild species is small and very sour, but the large garden sorts produced by cultivation, and for which we are chiefly indebted to the Dutch gardeners, are large and of a more agreeable, sub-acid flavour.

The Black Currant, (*Ribes nigrum,*) is a distinct species, with larger leaves, and coarser growth, and which, in the whole plant, has a strong odour, disagreeable, at first, to many persons.

Uses. The cooling acid flavour of the currant is relished by most people, in moderate quantities, and the larger varieties make also a pretty appearance on the table. Before fully ripe, currants are stewed for tarts, like green gooseberries, and are frequently employed along with cherries or other fruits in the same way; but the chief value of this fruit is for making *currant jelly*, an indispensable accompaniment to many dishes. *Currant shrub*, made from the fruit in the same manner as lemonade, is a popular summer drink in many parts of the country, and corresponds to the well known Paris beverage, *eau de grosseilles*. A sweet wine, of very pleasant taste, is made from their expressed juice, which is very popular among farmers, but which we hope to see displaced by that afforded by the Isabella and Catawba grapes,—which every one may make with less cost and trouble, and which is infinitely more wholesome, because it requires less additions, of any kind, to the pure juice.

The fruit of the black currant is liked by some persons in tarts, but it is chiefly used for making a jam, or jelly, much valued as a domestic remedy for sore throats. The young leaves dried, very strongly resemble green tea in flavour, and have been used as a substitute for it.

The season when currants are in perfection is midsummer, but it may be prolonged until October by covering the bushes with mats, or sheltering them otherwise from the sun.

Propagation and culture. Nothing is easier of culture than the currant, as it grows and bears well in any tolerable garden soil. Never plant out a currant sucker. To propagate it, it is only necessary to plant, in the autumn, or early in the spring, slips or cuttings, a foot long, in the open garden, where they will root with the greatest facility. The currant should never be allowed to produce suckers, and, in order to ensure against this, the superfluous eyes or buds should be taken out before planting it, as has been directed under the head of Cuttings. When the plants are placed where they are finally to remain, they should always be kept in the form of trees—that is to say, with single stems, and heads branching out at from one foot, to three feet from the ground. The after treatment is of the simplest kind, thinning out the superfluous wood every winter, is all that is required here. Those who desire berries of an extra large size *stop*, or pinch out, the ends of all the strong growing shoots, about the middle of June, when the fruit is two-thirds grown. This forces the plant to expend all its strength in enlarging and maturing the fruit. And, we may add to this, that it is better not to continue the cultivation of currant trees after they have borne more than six or eight years, as finer fruit will be obtained, with less trouble, from young plants, which are so easily raised.

There are, nominally, many sorts of currants, but the following sorts comprise all at present known, worthy of cultivation. The common Red, and the common White, are totally undeserving a place in the garden, when those very superior sorts, the White, and Red Dutch, can be obtained.

I. Red and White Currants, (R. rubrum.)

1. Red Dutch. § Thomp. Lind.

> Large Red Dutch.
> New Red Dutch.
> Morgan's Red.
> Red Grape.
> Large Bunched Red.
> Long Bunched Red.
> Grosillier Rouge à Gros-Fruit.

Fruit twice the size of the common currant, red, and a little less acid. Clusters two to three inches long.

2. White Dutch. § Thomp. Lind.

> New White Dutch.
> Reeve's White.
> White Crystal.
> Morgan's White.
> White Leghorn.

This is precisely similar to the foregoing in size and habit, and the fruit is equally large and of a fine yellowish white colour with a very transparent skin. It is considerably less acid than the Red Currants, and is therefore much preferred for the table.

Fig. 9t. *White Dutch.*

3. CHAMPAGNE. § Thomp. Lind.

Pleasant's Eye.
Groselier à Fruit Couleur de Chair.

A large and handsome currant, of a pale pink, or flesh co-lour, exactly intermediate, in this respect, between the red and white Dutch. It is quite an acid sort, but is admired by many for its pretty appearance.

4. KNIGHT'S LARGE RED. Thomp.

This seedling of Mr. Knight's is one of the largest of currants, being a third larger than the Red Dutch.

5. KNIGHT'S EARLY RED. Thomp.

The merit of this variety is its ripening ten days earlier than other sorts.

6. KNIGHT'S SWEET RED. § Thomp.

This is not a sweet currant, in a literal sense, but it is considerably less acid than the White Dutch, and much less so than all other varieties.

7. STRIPED FRUITED. Thomp.

Grosse Weiss und Rothgestreifte Johannisberre

A very pretty new currant from Germany, the fruit of which is distinctly striped with white and red. It is yet very rare.

3. MAY'S VICTORIA. §

A new variety recently received from England. It is said to bear very large bright red fruit, in bunches 5 or 6 inches in length. The fruit is bright red and hangs on the tree a month longer than any other sort.

II. *Black Currants*, (*R. nigrum*.)

9. COMMON BLACK. Thomp.

Black English.
Cassis, (*of the French*)

The common Black English Currant is well known. The

berries are quite black, less than half an inch in diameter, and borne in clusters of four or five berries. It is much inferior to the following.

10. BLACK NAPLES. § Thomp. P. Mag. Lind.

The Black Naples is a beautiful fruit, the finest and largest of all black currants, its berries often measuring nearly three fourths of an inch in diameter. Its leaves and blossoms appear earlier than those of the common black, but the fruit is later, and the clusters, as well as the berries, are larger and more numerous.

ORNAMENTAL VARIETIES. There are several very ornamental species of currant, among which we may here allude to the MISSOURI CURRANT (*Ribes Aureum,*) brought by Lewis and Clark from the Rocky Mountains, which is now very common in our gardens, and generally admired for its very fragrant yellow blossoms. Its oval blue berries, which are produced in great abundance, are relished by some persons. But there is a *Large Fruited* Missouri Currant, a variety of this, which bears berries of the size of the Black Naples, and of more agreeable flavour.

The RED FLOWERING CURRANT (*R. sanguineum,*) is a very beautiful shrub from the western coast of America, with foliage somewhat like that of the common black, but which bears very charming clusters of large light crimson blossoms, in April. It is not quite hardy enough to stand the winters to the *north* of this. There are several varieties with white and pale pink flowers.

CHAPTER XIV.

THE CRANBERRY.

Oxycoccus, Arb. Brit. *Ericaceæ,* of botanists.
Airelle, of the French ; *Die Moosebeere,* German ; *Veen bessen,* Dutch ; *Ossicocci ,* Italian.

THE cranberry is a familiar trailing shrub growing wild in swampy, sandy meadows, and mossy bogs, in the northern portions of both hemispheres, and produces a round, red, acid fruit. Our native species, (*O. macrocarpus,*) so common in the swamps of New-England, and on the borders of our inland lakes, as to form quite an article of commerce, is much the largest and finest species ; the European cranberry, (*O. palustris,*) being

18

much smaller in its growth, and producing fruit inferior in size and quality.

The value of the common cranberry for tarts, preserves and other culinary uses, is well known, and in portions of the country where it does not naturally grow, or is not abundantly produced, it is quite worth while to attempt its culture. Although naturally, it grows mostly in mossy, wet land, yet it may be easily cultivated in beds of peat soil, made in any rather moist situation, and if a third of old thoroughly decayed manure is added to the peat, the berries will be much larger, and of more agreeable flavour than the wild ones. A square of the size of twenty feet, planted in this way, will yield three or four bushels annually—quite sufficient for a family. The plants are easily procured, and are generally taken up like squares of sod or turf, and planted two or three feet apart, when they quickly cover the whole beds.

In some parts of New-England, low and coarse meadows, of no value, have been drained and turned to very profitable account, by planting them with this fruit. The average product is from eighty to 100 bushels of cranberries, worth at least one dollar a bushel, and the care they require after the land is once prepared and planted is scarcely any at all, except in gathering. Some of the farms in Massachusetts, yield large crops, partly from natural growth, and partly from cultivated plantations. The " New-England Farmer" states that Mr. Hayden, of Lincoln, Mass., gathered 400 bushels from his farm in 1830. The cranberry grows wild in the greatest abundance, on the sandy low necks near Barnstable, and an annual cranberry festival is made of the gathering of the fruit, which is done by the mass of the population, who turn out on the day appointed by the authorities, and make a general gathering with their cranberry rakes, a certain portion of the crop belonging, and being delivered, to the town.

Capt. Hall, one of the most successful cranberry cultivators of that neighbourhood, thus turns his sandy bogs and rush-covered land to productive beds of cranberry. After draining the land well, and removing all brush, he ploughs the soil where it is possible to do so; but he usually finds it sufficient to cover the surface with a heavy top-dressing of beach sand, digging holes four feet apart into which he plants sods, or square bunches, of the cranberry roots. These soon spread on every side, overpowering the rushes, and forming a thick coating to the surface. A laborer will gather about thirty bushels of the fruit in a day, with a cranberry rake.

Cranberry culture would be a profitable business in this neighbourhood, where this fruit is scarce, and, of late years, sells for two or three dollars a bushel.

CHAPTER XV.

THE FIG.

Ficus Carica, L. Arb. Brit. *Urticaceæ*, of botanists.
Figuier, of the French; *Feigenbaum*, German; *Fico*, Italian; *Higuera*, Spanish

THIS celebrated fruit tree, whose history is as ancient as that of the world, belongs properly to a warm climate, though it may be raised in the open air, in the middle states, with proper care.

In its native countries, Asia and Africa, near the sea-coast it forms a low tree, twenty feet in height, with spreading branches, and large, deeply lobed, rough leaves. It is completely naturalized in the south of Europe, where its cultivation is one of the most important occupations of the fruit grower.

The fruit of the Fig tree is remarkable for making its appearance, growing, and ripening, without being preceded by any apparent blossom. The latter, however, is concealed in the *interior* of a fleshy receptacle which is called, and finally becomes, the fruit. The flavour of the fig is exceedingly sweet and luscious, so much so as not to be agreeable to many persons, when tasted for the first time; but, like most fruits of this kind, it becomes a great favourite with all after a short trial, and is really one of the most agreeable, wholesome, and nutritious kinds of food. It has always, indeed, been the favourite fruit of warm countries, and the ideal of earthly happiness and content, as typified in the Bible, consists in sitting under one's own fig tree.

Its cultivation was carried to great perfection among the Ancient Romans, who had more than twenty varieties in their gardens. But the Athenians seem to have prided themselves most on their figs, and even made a law forbidding any to be exported from Attica. Smuggling, however, seems to have been carried on in those days, and a curious little piece of etymological history is connected with the fig. The informers against those who broke this law were called *sukophantai*, from two words in the Greek, meaning the "discoverers of figs." And as their power appears also to have been used for malicious purposes, thence arose our word *sycophant*. The fig was first introduced from Italy about 1548, by Cardinal Poole, and to this country about 1790, by Wm. Hamilton, Esq.*

---

* Dr. Pocock, the oriental traveller, first brought the fig to Oxford, and planted a tree in 1648, in Oxford College Garden, of which tree the following anecdote is told. Dr. Kennicott, the celebrated Hebrew scholar, and compiler of the Polyglott Bible, was passionately fond of this fruit, and, seeing a very fine fig on this tree that he wished to preserve, wrote on a label "Dr. Kennicott's fig," which he tied to the fruit. An Oxonian wag, who had observed the transaction, watched the fruit daily, and, when ripe, gathered it, and exchanged the label for one thus worded—"a fig for Dr. Kennicott."—*McIntosh.*

PROPAGATION. This tree is very readily increased by cuttings taken off in the month of March, and planted in light soil
in a hot bed, when they will make very strong plants the same
season. Or, they may be planted in a shady border in the open
air, quite early in April, with tolerable success. In either case
the cuttings should be made eight or ten inches long, of the last
year's shoots, with about half an inch of the old, or previous
year's wood left at the base of each.

SOIL AND CULTURE. The best soil for the fig is one moderately deep, and neither too moist nor dry, as, in the former
case, the plant is but too apt to run to coarse wood, and, in the
latter, to drop its fruit before it is fully ripe. A mellow, calcareous loam, is the best soil in this climate—and marl, or mild
lime in compost, the most suitable manure.

As in the middle states this tree is not hardy enough to be allowed to grow as a standard, it is the policy of the cultivator to
keep it in a low and shrub-like form, near the ground, that it
may be easily covered in winter. The great difficulty of this
mode of training, with us, has been that the coarse and over-
luxuriant growth of the branches, when kept down, is so great
as to render the tree unfruitful, or to rob the fruit of its due
share of nourishment. Happily the system of *root-pruning*,
recently found so beneficial with some other trees, is in this climate, most perfectly adapted to the fig. Short jointed wood,
and only moderate vigour of growth, are well known accom-
paniments of fruitfulness in this tree; and there is no means by
which firm, well ripened, short-jointed wood is so easily obtained as by an annual pruning of the roots—cutting off all that
project more than half the length of the branches. In this way
the fig tree may be kept in that rich and somewhat strong soil
necessary to enable it to hold its fruit, and ripen it of the largest
size, without that coarseness of growth which usually happens
in such soil, and but too frequently renders the tree barren.
The mode of performing root-pruning we have already described,
but we may add here that the operation should be performed on
the fig early in November. When this mode is adopted but
little pruning will be necessary, beyond that of keeping the
plant in a somewhat low, and regular shape, shortening-in the
branches occasionally, and taking out old and decaying wood.

In winter, the branches of the fig must be bent down to the
ground, and fastened with hooked pegs, and covered with three
or four inches of soil, as in protecting the foreign grape. This
covering should be removed as soon as the spring is well settled. Below Philadelphia, a covering of straw, or branches of
evergreens, is sufficient—and south of Virginia the fig is easy
of culture as a hardy standard tree.

Two crops are usually produced in a year by this tree; the
first which ripens here in midsummer, and is borne on the pre-

vious season's shoots ; and the second which is yielded by the young shoots of this summer, and which rarely ripens well in the middle states. It is, therefore, a highly advantageous practice to rub off all the young figs of this second crop after midsummer, as soon as they are formed. The consequence of this is to retain all the organizable matter in the tree ; and to form new embryo figs where these are rubbed off, which then ripen the next season as the first crop.

RIPENING THE FRUIT. In an unfavourable soil or climate, the ripening of the fig is undoubtedly rendered more certain and speedy by touching the eye of the fruit with a little oil. This is very commonly practised in many districts of France. "At Argenteuil," says Loudon, " the maturity of the latest figs is hastened by putting a single drop of oil into the eye of each fruit. This is done by a woman who has a phial of oil suspended from her waist, and a piece of hollow rye straw in her hand. This she dips into the oil, and afterwards into the eye of the fig."

We have ourselves frequently tried the experiment of touching the end of the fig with the finger dipped in oil, and have always found the fruits so treated to ripen much more certainly and speedily, and swell to a larger size than those left untouched.

There are forty-two varieties enumerated in the last edition of the London Horticultural Society's Catalogue. Few of these have, however, been introduced into this country, and a very few sorts will comprise all that is most desirable and excellent in this fruit. The following selection includes those most suitable for our soil and climate. Fruit nearly all ripen in August.

Class I.   Red, Brown, or Purple.

1. BRUNSWICK. Thomp. Lind. P. Mag.

Madonna.
Hanover.
Brown Hamburgh.
Black Naples.   } *ac. to Thomp.*
Clementine.
Bayswater.
Red.

One of the largest and finest purple figs, well adapted to hardy culture. Fruit of the largest size, pyriform in shape, with an oblique apex. Eye considerably sunk. Stalk short, and thick, of a fine violet brown in the sun, dotted with small pale brown specks, and, on the shaded side, pale greenish yellow. Flesh reddish brown, slightly pink near the centre, and

18*

somewhat transparent. Flavour rich and excellent. The only fault of this variety for open air culture is, that it is rather too strong in its growth, not being so easily protected in winter as more dwarfish sorts.

2. BROWN TURKEY. § Thomp.

Brown Italian *Forsyth.*
Large Blue, *of Lind.*
Italian
Brown Naples.
Murrey *Lind*
Lee's Perpetual.

This is undoubtedly one of the very best for this country, and for open air culture, as it is perhaps the very hardiest, and one of the most regular and abundant bearers. Fruit large, oblong, or pyriform. Skin dark brown, covered with a thick blue bloom. Flesh red, and of very delicious flavour.

3. BLACK ISCHIA. Thomp. Lind.

Early Forcing.
Blue Ischia

One of the most fruitful sorts, and pretty hardy. Fruit of medium size, roundish, a little flattened at the apex. Skin dark violet, becoming almost black when fully ripe. Flesh deep red, and of very sweet, luscious flavour.

4. BROWN ISCHIA § Thomp.

Chestnut. *Lind Mill.*
Chestnut-coloured Ischia.

A good variety, with, however, a rather thin skin, rendering it liable to crack or burst open when fully ripe. It is hardy, of good habit, and a very excellent bearer.
Fruit of medium size, roundish-obovate. Skin light or chestnut-brown ; pulp purple, very sweet and excellent.

5. BLACK GENOA. Lind.

The fruit of this fig is long-obovate, that portion next the stalk being very slender. Skin dark purple, becoming nearly black, and covered with a purple bloom. Pulp bright red, flavour excellent. Habit of the tree moderately strong.

6. MALTA. § Lind.

Small Brown.

A small, but very rich fig, which will often hang on the tree until it begins to shrivel, and becomes "a fine sweetmeat." Fruit much compressed at the apex, and very much narrowed in towards the stalk. Skin light brown. Pulp pale brown, and of a sweet, rich flavour. Ripens later than the foregoing, about the last of August.

7. SMALL BROWN ISCHIA. § Lind.

A very hardy sort, which, in tolerably warm places south of Philadelphia, will make a small standard tree in the open air, bearing pretty good crops, that ripen about the first of September. Fruit small, pyriform, with a very short footstalk. Skin light brown. Pulp pale purple, of high flavour. Leaves more entire than those of the common fig.

8. VIOLETTE. Lind. Duh.

A very good sort from the neighbourhood of Paris, where it produces two crops annually. Fruit small, roundish-obovate, flattened at the apex. Skin dark violet. Pulp nearly white, or a little tinged with red on the inside, and of pleasant flavour.

9. VIOLETTE DE BORDEAUX. Thomp.

Bordeaux. *Lind. Duh.*

A fig which is much cultivated in France, being quite productive, though of inferior flavour to many of the foregoing sorts. Fruit large, pyriform, about three inches long, and two in diameter. Skin deep violet when fully ripe, but at first of a brownish red. Pulp reddish purple, sweet and good.

Class II. Fruit, White, Green, or Yellow.

---

10. ANGELIQUE. § Thomp. Lind. Duh.

Concourelle Blanche
Mélitte.

This little fig is a very abundant bearer, and a pretty hardy sort. Fruit small, obovate. Skin pale greenish yellow, dotted with lighter coloured specks. Pulp white, but only tolerably sweet. It will usually bear two crops.

11. LARGE WHITE GENOA. Thomp. Lind. Fors.

Fruit large, roundish-obovate. Skin thin, pale yellow. Pulp red, and well flavoured.

12. MARSEILLES. Thomp. Lind.

White Marseilles.
White Naples.
Pocock
Ford's Seedling.
White Standard.
Figue Blanche   *Duh*

A very favourite sort for forcing and raising under glass, but which does not succeed so well as the Brown Turkey, and the Ischias, for open culture. Fruit small, roundish-obovate, slightly ribbed. Skin nearly white, with a little yellowish green remaining. Flesh white, rather dry, but sweet and rich.

13. NERII. § Thomp. Lind.

A fruit rather smaller and longer than the Marseilles, and which, from a mingling of slight acid, is one of the most exquisite in its flavour. Fruit small, roundish-obovate. Skin pale greenish yellow. Pulp red. Flavour at once delicate and rich. This is a very favourite variety, according to Loudon, "the richest fig known in Britain."

14. PREGUSSATA. § Thomp.

A sort lately introduced from the Ionian Isles into England. It is tolerably hardy, quite productive, and succeeds admirably under glass. Fruit of medium size, roundish, a good deal flattened. Skin purplish brown in the shade, dark brown in the sun. Pulp deep red, with a luscious, high flavour. Seeds unusually small. Ripens gradually, in succession.

15. WHITE ISCHIA. Thomp.

Green Ischia. *Lind. Fors.*

A very small fig, but one of the hardiest of the light coloured ones. Fruit about an inch in diameter, roundish-obovate. Skin pale yellowish green, very thin, and, when fully ripe, the darker coloured pulp appears through it. Pulp purplish, and high flavoured. A moderate grower, and good bearer.

CHAPTER XVI.

THE GOOSEBERRY.

Ribes Grossularia, Arb. Brit. *Grossulaceæ*, of botanists.
Grossciller, of the French; *Stachelbeerstrauch*, German; *Uva Spino*, Italian;
Grossella, Spanish.

THE gooseberry of our gardens is a native of the north of Europe, our native species never having been improved by garden culture. This low prickly shrub, which, in its wild state bears small round or oval fruit, about half an inch in diameter, and weighing one fourth of an ounce, has been so greatly improved by the system of successive reproduction from the seed, and high culture by British gardeners, that it now bears fruit nearly, or quite two inches in diameter, and weighing an ounce and a half. Lancashire, in England, is the meridian of the gooseberry, and to the Lancashire weavers, who seem to have taken it as a hobby, we are indebted for nearly all the surprisingly large sorts of modern date. Their annual shows exhibit this fruit in its greatest perfection, and a GOOSEBERRY BOOK is published at Manchester every year giving a list of all the prize sorts, etc. Indeed the climate of England seems, from its moistness and coolness, more perfectly fitted than any other to the growth of this fruit. On the continent it is considered of little account, and with us, south of Philadelphia, it succeeds but indifferently. In the northern, and especially in the eastern states, however, the gooseberry, on strong soils, where the best sorts are chosen, thrives admirably, and produces very fine crops.

USES. This fruit is in the first place a very important one in its green state, being in high estimation for pies, tarts, and puddings, coming into use earlier than any other. The earliest use made of it appears to have been as a sauce with green goose, whence the name, goose-berry. In its ripe state, it is a very agreeable table fruit, and in this country, following the season of cherries, it is always most acceptable. Unripe gooseberries are bottled in water for winter use, (placing the bottles nearly filled, a few moments in boiling water, afterwards corking and sealing them, and burying them in a cool cellar, with the necks downward.) As a luxury for the poor, Mr. London considers this the most valuable of all fruits " since it can be grown in less space, in more unfavourable circumstances, and brought sooner into bearing than any other." In the United States the gooseberry, in humble gardens, is frequently seen in a very wretched state—the fruit poor and small, and covered with mildew   This arises partly from ignorance of a proper mode of cultivation, but chiefly from the sorts grown being very inferior ones. always much liable to this disease

PROPAGATION   Gooseberry plants should only be raised from cuttings.   New varieties are of course raised from seed, but no one here will attempt to do what, under more favourable circumstances, the Lancashire growers can do so much better.   In preparing cuttings select the strongest and straightest young shoots of the current year, at the end of October (or very early in the ensuing spring ;) cut out all the buds that you intend to go below the ground (to prevent future suckers,) and plant the cuttings in a deep rich soil, on the north side of a fence, or in some shaded border.   The cuttings should be inserted six inches deep, and from three to six or eight inches should remain above ground.   The soil should be pressed very firmly about the cuttings, and, in the case of autumn planting, it should be examined in the spring, to render it firm again should the cutting have been raised by severe frost.   After they have become well rooted—generally in a year's time—they may be transplanted to the borders, where they are finally to remain.

CULTIVATION.   The gooseberry in our climate is very impatient of drought, and we have uniformly found that the best soil for it is a deep strong loam, or at least whatever may be the soil, and it will grow in a great variety, it should always be *deep*—if not naturally so, it should be made deep by trenching and manuring.   It is the most common error to plant this fruit shrub under the branches of other trees for the sake of their shade—as it always renders the fruit inferior in size and flavour, and more likely to become mouldy.   On the contrary, we would always advise planting in an open border, as if the soil is sufficiently deep, the plants will not suffer from dryness, and should it unfortunately be of a dry nature, it may be rendered less injurious by covering the ground under the plants with straw or litter.   In any case a *rich* soil is necessary, and as the gooseberry is fond of manure a pretty heavy top-dressing should be dug in every year, around bearing plants.   For a later crop a few bushes may be set on the north side of a fence or wall.

For the gooseberry, regular and pretty liberal pruning is absolutely necessary.   Of course no suckers should be allowed to grow.   In November the winter pruning should be performed.   The leaves now being off it is easy to see what proportion of the new as well as old wood may be taken away ; and we will here remark that it is quite impossible to obtain fine gooseberries here, or any where, without a very thorough thinning out of the branches.   As a general rule, it may safely be said that **one** half of the head, including old and young branches (more especially the former, as the best fruit is borne on the young wood,) should now be taken out, leaving a proper distribution of shoots throughout the bush, the head being sufficiently thinned to admit freely the light and air. An additional pruning is, in England, performed in June, which consists in stopping the growth of long shoots by pinching out the extremities, and thinning out superfluous branches; but if the annual pruning is properly performed, this will not be found necessary, except to obtain fruit of extraordinary size.

The crop should always be well thinned when the berries are about a quarter grown. The gooseberry is scarcely subject to any disease or insect in this country. The *mildew*, which attacks the half grown fruit, is the great pest of those who are unacquainted with its culture. In order to prevent this, it is only necessary—1st, to root up and destroy all inferior kinds subject to mildew; 2d, to procure from any of the nurseries some of the best and hardiest Lancashire varieties; 3d, to keep them well manured, and very thoroughly pruned every year.

We do not think this fruit shrub can be said to bear well for more than a half dozen years successively. After that the fruit becomes inferior and requires more care in cultivation. A succession of young plants should, therefore, be kept up by striking some cuttings every season.

VARIETIES. The number of these is almost endless, new ones being produced by the prize growers every year. The last edition of the London Horticultural Society's Catalogue enumerates 149 sorts considered worthy of notice, and Lindley's Guide to the Orchard, gives a list of more than seven hundred prize sorts. It is almost needless to say that many of these very closely resemble each other, and that a small number of them will comprise all the most valuable.

The sorts bearing fruit of medium size are generally more highly flavoured than the very large ones. We have selected a sufficient number of the most valuable for all practical purposes.

I. Red Gooseberries.

1. BOARDMAN'S BRITISH CROWN. Fruit very large, roundish, hairy, handsome and good. Branches spreading.

2. CHAMPAGNE. A fine old variety, of very rich flavour. Fruit small, roundish-oblong, surface hairy, pulp clear; branches of very upright growth.

3. CAPPER'S TOP SAWYER. Fruit large, roundish, pale red, hairy; rather late, flavour very good. Branches drooping.

4. FARROW'S ROARING LION. An immense berry, and hangs late. Fruit oblong, smooth; flavour excellent; branches drooping.

5. HARTSHORN's LANCASHIRE LAD. Fruit large, roundish dark red, hairy ; flavour very good ; branches erect.

6. KEEN's SEEDLING. Fruit of medium size, oblong, hairy, flavour first rate ; branches drooping. Early and productive.

7. LEIGH's RIFLEMAN. Fruit large, roundish, hairy ; flavour first rate ; branches erect.

8. MELLING's CROWN BOB. Fruit large, oblong, hairy ; flavour first rate ; branches spreading.

9. MISS BOLD. Fruit of medium size, roundish, surface downy ; flavour excellent ; branches spreading.

10. RED WARRINGTON. Fruit large, roundish-oblong, hairy ; flavour first rate ; branches drooping.

II. Yellow Gooseberries.

11. BUERDSILL's DUCKWING. Fruit large and late, obovate, smooth ; flavour good ; branches erect.

12. CAPPER's BUNKER HILL. Fruit large, roundish, smooth ; flavour good ; branches spreading.

13. EARLY SULPHUR. Fruit middle size, and very early, roundish, hairy ; flavour first rate ; branches erect.

14. GORTON's VIPER. Fruit large, obovate, smooth ; flavour good ; branches drooping.

15. HILL's GOLDEN GOURD. Fruit large, oblong, hairy ; flavour good ; branches drooping.

16. PART's GOLDEN FLEECE. Fruit large, oval, hairy ; flavour first rate ; branches spreading.

17. PROPHET's ROCKWOOD. Fruit large and early, roundish, hairy ; flavour good ; branches erect.

18. YELLOW CHAMPAGNE. Fruit small, roundish, hairy ; flavour first rate ; branches erect.

19. YELLOW BALL. Fruit of middle size, roundish, smooth ; flavour first rate ; branches erect.

III. Green Gooseberries.

20. COLLIERS' JOLLY ANGLER. Fruit large and late, oblong, downy ; flavour first rate ; branches erect.

21. BERRY's GREENWOOD. Fruit large, oblong, smooth ; flavour good ; branches drooping.

22. EARLY GREEN HAIRY, (or *Green Gascoigne*.) Fruit small and early, round, hairy ; flavour excellent ; branches spreading.

23. EDWARD's JOLLY TAR. Fruit large, obovate, smooth ; flavour first rate : branches drooping.

24. GLENTON GREEN. Fruit of middle size, oblong, hairy ; flavour excellent ; branches drooping.

25. GREEN WALNUT. Fruit middle sized, obovate, smooth; flavour first rate; branches spreading.

26. HEPBURN GREEN PROLIFIC. Fruit of middle size, round-ish, hairy; flavour first rate; branches erect.

27. MASSEY'S HEART OF OAK. Fruit large, oblong, smooth; flavour first rate; branches drooping.

28. PARKINSON'S LAUREL. Fruit large, obovate, downy; flavour first rate; branches erect.

29. PITMASTON GREEN GAGE. Fruit small, and hangs long, obovate, smooth; flavour rich and excellent; branches erect.

30. WAINMAN'S GREEN OCEAN. Fruit very large, oblong, smooth; flavour tolerably good; branches drooping.

IV. White Gooseberries.

31. CLEWORTH'S WHITE LION. Fruit large and hangs late, obovate, downy, flavour first rate; branches drooping.

32. CROMPTON SHEBA QUEEN. Fruit large, obovate, downy, flavour first rate; branches erect.

33. COOK'S WHITE EAGLE. Fruit large, obovate, smooth; flavour first rate; branches erect.

34. CAPPER'S BONNY LASS. Fruit large, oblong, hairy; flavour good; branches spreading.

35. HAPLEY'S LADY OF THE MANOR. Fruit large, roundish-oblong, hairy; flavour good; branches erect.

36. SAUNDER'S CHESHIRE LASS. Fruit large and very early, oblong, downy; flavour excellent; branches erect.

37. WOODWARD'S WHITESMITH. Fruit large, roundish-ob-long, downy; flavour first rate; branches erect.

38. WELLINGTON'S GLORY. Fruit large, rather oval; very dowy; skin quite thin; flavour excellent; branches erect.

39. WHITE HONEY. Fruit of middle size, roundish-oblong, smooth; flavour excellent; branches erect.

40. TAYLOR'S BRIGHT VENUS. Fruit of middle size, hangs a long time, obovate, hairy; flavour first rate; branches erect.

Selection of sorts for a very small garden. RED; Red War-rington, Keen's Seedling, Crown Bob. YELLOW; Early Sulphur, Yellow Ball. WHITE; Woodward's Whitesmith, Early White, Taylor's Bright Venus, White Honey. GREEN; Pitmaston Green Gage, Green Walnut, Parkinson's Laurel.

CHAPTER XVII.

THE GRAPE.

Vitis vinifera, L. *Vitaceæ*, of botanists.
Vigne, of the French; *Weintrauben*, German; *Vigna*, Italian; *Vid*, or *Vina*, Spanish.

THE history of the grape is almost as old as that of man. Growing in its highest perfection in Syria and Persia, its luscious fruit and the unrivalled beverage which its fermented juice affords, recommended it to the especial care of the patriarchal tillers of the soil, and vineyards were extensively planted, long before orchards or collections of other fruit trees were at all common.

The grapes of the old world are all varieties of the wine grape, (*Vitis vinifera*,) which, though so long and so universally cultivated and naturalized in all the middle and southern portions of Europe, is not a native of that continent, but came originally from Persia.   From the latter country, as civilization advanced westward, this plant accompanied it—first to Egypt, then to Greece and Sicily, and gradually to Italy, Spain, France and Britain, to which latter country the Romans carried it about two hundred years after Christ.   To America the seeds and plants of the European varieties were brought by numerous emigrants and colonists within the first fifty years after its settlement.

The wild grapes of our own country are quite distinct species from the wine grape of Europe—are usually stronger in their growth, with larger and more entire foliage, and, in their native state, with a peculiar foxy odour or flavour, and more or less hardness of pulp.   These traits, however, disappear in process of cultivation, and we have reason to hope that we shall soon obtain, from the wild type, new varieties of high quality, and of superiour hardiness and productiveness in this climate.

The grape vine is in all cases a trailing or climbing deciduous shrub, living to a great age,* and, in its native forests, clambering over the tops of the tallest trees.   In the deep rich alluvial soils of western America, it is often seen attaining a truly prodigious size, and several have been measured on the banks of the Ohio, the stems of which, were three feet in circumference, and the branches two hundred feet long, enwreathing and fes-

---

* Pliny gives an account of a vine six hundred years old, and there are said to be vines in Burgundy more than four hundred years old.

tooning the tops of huge poplars and sycamores. In a cultivated state, however, it is found that fine flavour, and uniform productiveness, require the plants to be kept pruned within a small compass.

USES. The grape in its finest varieties, as the Hamburgh and the Muscat, is in flavour hardly surpassed by any other fruit in delicacy and richness, and few or none are more beautiful in the dessert. Dried, it forms the raisin of commerce, the most excellent of all dried fruits, every where esteemed, And wine, the fermented juice, has always been the first of all exhilarating liquors. Some idea of the past consumption of this product may be formed from the fact that more than 500,000,000 imperial gallons have been made in France, in a single year; and as a data to judge of its value, we may add, that, while a great proportion of the *vin ordinaire*, or common wine, is sold at 10 or 12 cents a bottle; on the other hand, particular old and rare vintages of Madeiras or Sherries will not unfrequently command twenty or thirty dollars a gallon.

SOIL. The universal experience in all countries has established the fact that a dry and warm soil is the very best for the vine. Where vineyards are cultivated, a limestone soil, or one composed of decaying calcareous rocks, is by far the best; but where, as in most gardens, the vine is raised solely for its fruit, the soil should be highly enriched. The foreign grape will scarcely thrive well here on a heavy soil, though our native varieties grow and bear well on any strong land, but the essence of all that can be said in grape culture respecting soil is that it be dry and light, deep and rich. Frequent top-dressings of well rotted manure should be applied to vines in open borders, and this should every third or fourth year be alternated with a dressing of slacked lime.

PROPAGATION. The grape vine makes roots very freely, and is, therefore, easy of propagation. Branches of the previous or current year's wood bent down any time before midsummer, and covered with earth, as layers, root very freely, and make bearing plants in a couple of years, or very frequently indeed bear the next season.

But the finer varieties of the vine are almost universally propagated by cuttings, as that is a very simple mode, and an abundance of the cuttings being afforded by the annual trimming of the vines.

When cuttings are to be planted in the open border, a somewhat moist and shaded place should be chosen for this purpose. The cuttings should then be made of the young wood of the previous years' growth, cut into lengths about a foot or eighteen inches long, and having three buds—one near the top, one at the bottom, and the third in the middle. Before planting the cutting pare off its lower end smoothly, close below the buds, and, finally, plant it in mellow soil, in a slit made by the spade, pressing the earth firmly about it with the foot.*

The rarer kinds of foreign grapes are usually grown by cuttings of shorter length, consisting only of two buds ; and the most successful mode is to plant each cutting in a small pot, and plunge the pots in a slight hotbed, or place the cuttings at once in the mould of the bed itself. In either case they will make strong plants in the same season.

But the most approved way of raising vine plants in pots is that of propagation by *eyes*, which we have fully explained in the first part of this work. This, as it retains the least portion of the old wood, is manifestly the nearest approach to raising a plant from the seed, that most perfect of all modes with respect to the constitution of a plant. In the case of new or rare sorts it offers to us the means of multiplying them with the greatest possible rapidity. As the grape usually receives its annual pruning in autumn or winter, the cuttings may be reduced to nearly their proper length, and kept in earth, in the cellar, until the ensuing spring. The hardier sorts may be buried in the open ground.

The foreign and the native grapes are very different in their habits, in this climate, and, therefore, must be treated differently. The native sorts, as the Isabella and Catawba, are cultivated with scarcely any further care than training up the branches to poles or a trellis, and are, on this account, highly valuable to the farmer, while the European varieties are of little value in this climate except with especial care, and are, therefore, confined to the garden.

1. *Culture of the Foreign Grape.*

The climate of the temperate portion of this country, so favourable to all other fruits, is unfortunately not so for the foreign grape. This results, perhaps, from its *variability*, the great obstacle being the *mildew*, which, seizing upon the young fruit, prevents its further growth, causes it to crack, and renders it worthless. Unwilling to believe that this was not the fault of bad culture, many intelligent cultivators, and among them men of capital, and much practical skill, have attempted vineyard culture, with the foreign sorts, in various sections of the country, under the most favourable circumstances, and have uniformly failed. On the other hand, the very finest grapes are produced under glass, in great quantities, in our first rate gardens, especially in the neighbourhood of Boston ;† in the small yards or

* In sandy or dry soils the cuttings may be left longer
† The vineries at the seats of J. P. Cushing and Col. Perkins, near Boston, produce annually many tons of these grapes, grown in the highest perfection.

gardens of our cities, owing to the more uniform state of the atmosphere, the foreign grape thrives pretty well ; and, finally, in
all gardens of the middle states, the hardier kinds may, under
certain modes of culture, be made to bear good fruit.

Without entering into any inquiries respecting the particular
way in which the mildew (which is undoubtedly a parasitical
plant,) is caused, we will endeavour to state concisely some
practical truths, to which our own observation and experience
have led us, respecting the hardy culture of the foreign grape.

In the first place, it is well known, to gardeners here, that
young and thrifty vines generally bear one or two fair crops of
fruit ; second, that as the vine becomes older if it is pruned in
the common mode, (that is to say the *spurring-in* mode of shortening the side branches, and getting fresh bearing shoots from
main branches every year,) it soon bears only mildewed and
imperfect fruit ; and, finally, that the older and larger the vine,
the less likely is it to produce a good crop.

This being the case, it is not difficult to see that, as the vine
like all other trees is able to resist the attacks of disease or
unfavourable climate just in proportion as it is kept in a young
and highly vigorous state, it follows if we allow a plant to retain
only young and vigorous wood, it must necessarily preserve
much of the necessary vigour of constitution. And this is only
to be done, so far as regards training, by what is called the *renewal* system.

The renewal system of training consists
in annually providing a fresh supply of
young branches from which the bearing
shoots are produced, cutting out all the
branches that have borne the previous
year. Fig. 61 represents a bearing vine
treated in this manner, as it would appear
in the spring of the year, after having been
pruned. In this figure, *a*, represents the
two branches of last year's growth trained
up for bearing the present year ; *b*, the

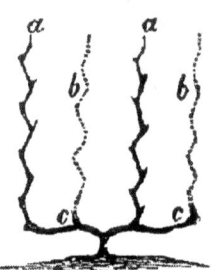

Fig. 91.   *Renewal Training.*

places occupied by the last year's wood, which, having borne,
has been cut down to within an inch of the main arm, *c*.   The
present year, therefore, the two branches *a*, will throw out side
shoots, and bear a good crop, while the young branches will be
trained up in the places of *b*, to bear the next year when *a*, are
in like manner cut down.

This renewal training will usually produce fair fruit, chiefly
as it appears to us, because the ascent and circulation of the sap
being mainly carried on through young wood, is vigorous, and
the plant is healthful and able to resist the mildew, while, on the
contrary, the circulation of the sap is more feeble and tardy,

19*

through the more compact and rigid sap vessels of a vine full oi old wood *

The above mode of training is very easily understood, but we may add here for the benefit of the novice; 1st, that vines, in order that they may bear regularly and well, should always be kept within small bounds; 2d, that they should always be trained to a wall, building, or *upright trellis* ;† and, 3d, that the leaves should never be pulled off to promote the ripening of the fruit. The ends of the bearing shoots may be *stopped*, (pinched off,) when the fruit is nearly half grown, and this is usually all the summer pruning, that under our bright sun the grape vine properly treated requires.

Following out this hint, that here, the vine only bears well when it is young, or composed mainly of young wood, an intelligent cultivator near us secures every year abundant crops of the Chasselas, by a system of renewal by *layers*. Every year, from his bearing vines, he lays down two or more long and clean shoots of the previous year's growth These root freely, are allowed to make another season's growth, and then are made to take the place of the old plants which are taken out; and by this continual system of providing young plants by layers, he always succeeds in obtaining from the same piece of ground fair and excellent grapes

CULTURE UNDER GLASS WITHOUT ARTIFICIAL HEAT. The great superiority of this fruit when raised under glass, renders a vinery an indispensable feature in every extensive garden. Even without fire-heat grapes may, under our bright sun, be grown admirably; the sudden changes of the weather being guarded against, and the warmth and uniformity of the atmosphere surrounding the vines being secured. In the neighbourhood of Boston, cheap structures of this kind are now very common, and on the North River, even the Muscat of Alexandria and other sorts which are usually thought to require fire-heat, ripen regularly and well, with moderate attention.

A vinery of this kind may be erected so as to cost very little, nearly after the following manner. Its length may be thirty feet; its width sixteen feet; height at the front, two feet; at the back twelve feet. This part of the structure may all be built of wood, taking, for the frame, cedar or locust posts, setting them three and a half feet in the ground, the portion rising above the ground being squared to four or five inches. On these posts, (which are placed six feet apart,) nail, on both sides, matched and grooved planks, one and a quarter inches thick. The space between these planks not occupied by the

* See *Hoare on the Grape Vine*
† And never on an arbour, except for the purposes of shade.

post, fill in with dry tan, which should be well rammed down. The rafters should be fixed, and from three to four feet apart. The sashes forming the roof, (which are all the glass that will be necessary,) must be in two lengths, lapping in the middle, and arranged with a double groove in the rafters, so that the top and bottom ones may run free of each other. The building will, of course, front the south, and the door may be at either end.

The border for the grapes should be made partly on the inside and partly on the outside of the front wall, so that the roots of the vines may extend through to the open border. A trellis of wire should be fixed to the rafters, about sixteen inches from the glass, on which the vines are to be trained. Early in the spring, the vines, which should be two year old roots, may be planted in the inside border, about a foot from the front wall— one vine below each rafter.

SOIL. The border should be thoroughly prepared and pulverized before planting the grapes. Two thirds of mellow sandy loam mixed with one third of a compost formed of well fermented manure, bits of broken charcoal, and a little lime rubbish, forms an excellent soil for the grape in this climate. If the soil of the garden is old, or is not of a proper quality for the basis of the border, it is best to prepare some for this purpose by rotting and reducing beforehand, a quantity of loamy turf from the road sides for this purpose. The depth of the border need not exceed two feet, but if the subsoil is not dry at all seasons, it should be well drained, and filled up half a foot below the border with small stones or brick bats.

PRUNING. Decidedly the best mode of pruning for a cold house, or vinery without fire-heat, is what is called the long or renewal mode, which we have already partially explained. Supposing the house to be planted with good young plants, something like the following mode of training and pruning may be adopted. The first season one shoot only is allowed to proceed from each plant, and this, at the end of the first season, is cut down to the second or third eye or bud. The year following two leading shoots are encouraged, the strongest of which is headed or stopped when it has extended a few joints beyond the middle of the house or rafter, and the weaker about half that length. In November these shoots are reduced, the strong one having four or five joints cut from its extremity, and the weaker one to the third eye from its lower end or place of origin. In the third season one leading shoot is laid in from each of these, the stronger one throwing out side shoots on which the fruit is produced, which side shoots are allowed to mature one bunch of grapes each, and are topped at one or two joints above the fruit. No side shoots are allowed to proceed from the weaker shoot, but it is laid in, to produce fruit the ensuing season, so that by the third season after planting, the lower part of the house or rafters is furnished with a crop of fruit proceeding from wood of the preceding year. At nex autumn pruning, the longest of these main shoots is shortened about eighteen inches from the top of the rafter, and the next in strength to about the middle of the rafter, and all the spurs which had borne fruit are removed. Each vine is now furnished with two shoots of bearing wood, a part of old barren wood which has already produced fruit, and a spur near the bottom for producing a young shoot for the following year. In the fourth summer a full crop is produced, both in the upper and lower part of the house, the longer or oldest shoot producing fruit on the upper part of its length, and the shorter on its whole length; from this last, a leading shoot is laid in, and another to succeed it is produced from the spur near the bottom. At the next autumn pruning, the oldest or longest shoot, which has now reached the top of the house, is entirely cut out and removed, and replaced by that which was next in succession to it, and this in its turn is also cut out and replaced by that immediately behind it, a succession of a yearly shoot being obtained from the lower part of the old stem. (*McIntosh.*) This is decidedly the most successful mode for a vinery without heat, producing abundant and fair crops of fruit. Hoare, who is one of the most experienced and ingenious writers on the Grape, strongly recommends it, and suggests that " the old wood of a vine, or that which has previously produced fruit, is not only of no further use, but is a positive injury to the fertility of the plant. The truth of this remark depends on the fact that every branch of a vine which produces little or no foliage, appropriates for its own support a portion of the juices of the plant that is generated by those branches that do produce foliage."

ROUTINE OF CULTURE. In a vinery without heat this is comparatively simple. As soon as the vines commence swelling their buds in the spring, they should be carefully washed with mild soap suds, to free them from any insects, soften the wood, and assist the buds to swell regularly. At least three or four times every week, they should be well syringed with water, which, when the weather is cool, should always be done in the morning. And every day the vine border should be duly supplied with water. During the time when the vines are in blossom, and while the fruit is setting, all sprinkling or syringing over the leaves must be suspended, and the house should be kept a little more closed and warm, than usual, and should any indications of mildew appear on any of the branches it may at once be checked by dusting them with flower of sulphur. Air must be given liberally every day when the temperature rises in the house, beginning by sliding down the top sashes a little in the morning, more at mid-day, and then gradually closing them in the same manner. To guard against the sudden changes of temperature out of doors, and at the same time to keep up as moist and warm a state of the atmosphere within the vinery as is consistent with pretty free admission of the air during sun shine, is the great object of culture in a vinery of this kind.

Thinning the fruit is a very necessary practice in all vineries—and on it depends greatly the flavour, as well as the fine appearance and size of the berries and bunches. The first thinning usually consists in taking off all superfluous blossom buds, leaving only one bunch in the large sorts or two in the small ones to each bearing shoot. The next thinning takes place when the berries are set and well formed, and is performed with a pair of scissors, taking care not to touch the berries that are left to grow. All this time, one third of the berries should be taken off with the point of the scissors, especially those in the centre of the cluster. This allows the remainder to swell to double the size, and also to form larger bunches than would otherwise be produced. Where the bunches are large, the shoulders should be suspended from the trellis by threads, in order to take off part of the weight from the stem of the vine. The last thinning, which is done chiefly to regulate the form of the bunch, is done by many gardeners, just before the fruit begins to colour—but it is scarcely needed if the previous thinning of the berries has been thoroughly done.

The regular autumnal pruning is best performed about the middle of November. The vines should then be taken down, laid down on the border, and covered for the winter with a thick layer of straw, or a slight covering of earth.

CULTURE UNDER GLASS, WITH FIRE-HEAT. As the foreign grape is almost the only fruit of temperate climates, which cannot be raised in perfection in the open air in this climate, we shall give some concise directions for its culture in vineries with artificial heat. Those who only know this fruit as the Chasselas or Sweetwater appears, when grown in the open air, have little idea of the exceeding lusciousness, high flavour, size and beauty of such varieties as the Black Hamburgh or Muscat of Alexandria, when well grown in a first rate vinery. By the aid of artificial heat, which, in this climate, is, after all, chiefly required in the spring and autumn, and to counteract any sudden cold changes of atmosphere, this most admirable fruit may easily be produced for the dessert, from May till December. Indeed by vineries constructed in divisions, in some of which vines are forced and in others retarded, some gentlemen near Boston, have grapes nearly every month in the year.

Construction of the vinery. The vinery with fire-heat may be built of wood, and in the same simple manner as just described, with the addition of a flue above the surface of the ground, running close along the end, two feet from the front wall, and about a foot from the back wall, and returning into a chimney in the back wall over the furnace.

For the sake of permanence, however, a vinery of this kind is usually built of brick; the ends and front wall eight inches thick; the back wall a foot thick—or eight inches with occasional abutments to increase its strength. In fig. 92 (I) is shown a simple plan of a vinery of this kind. In this the surface of the ground is shown at *a*, below which, the foundation walls are sunk three feet. Above the surface the front wall *b*, rises two feet, the back wall *c*, twelve feet, and the width of the house is fourteen feet. On these walls are placed the rafters, from three to four feet distant, with the sashes in two lengths.

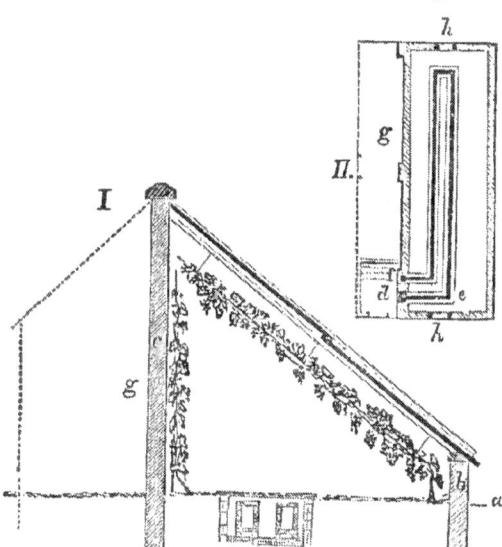

Fig. 92. *Plan and section of a vinery, with fire-heat.*

In the present example the flues are kept out of the way, and the space clear, by placing them in a square walled space, directly under the walk; the walk itself being formed by an open grating or lattice, through which the heat rises freely. The arrangement of the flue will be better understood by referring to the ground plan (II.) In this the furnace is indicated at *d*, in the back wall;* from this the flue rises gradually to *e*, whence it continues nearly the length of the house, and returning enters the chimney at *f*. For the convenience of shelter, firing, etc., it is usual to have a *back shed*, *g*, behind the back wall. In this shed may be a bin for wood or coals, and a sunk area (shown in the dotted lines around *d, f*,) with steps to descend to the furnace and ash-pit.† There are two doors *h*, in the vinery at either end of the walk.

* This furnace should be placed two feet below the level of the flue at *e*, in order to secure a draught, after which it may be carried quite level till it enters the chimney. An air chamber may be formed round it, with a register to admit heated air to the house when necessary. A furnace fourteen inches square and deep, with an ash-pit below, in which anthracite coal is burned, will be found a very easy and perfect mode of heating a house of this width, and thirty feet long.

† The most perfect vinery that we have seen in this country is one of two hundred feet long at the country residence of Horace Gray, Esq., Newtown, near Boston. It is built of wood, with a curved span roof, after a plan of Mr. Gray's which seems to us to combine fitness and beauty in an unusual degree.

The border should be thoroughly prepared previously to planting the vines, by excavating it two feet deep and filling it up with suitable compost. This is best formed of one half loamy turf, well rotted by having been previously laid up in heaps, (or fresh and pure loamy soil from an old pasture or common;) one third thoroughly fermented horse or cow manure, which has laid in a turf-covered heap for three months; and one third broken pieces of charcoal and old lime rubbish. The whole to be thoroughly mixed together before planting the vines.

The vines themselves should always be planted in a border prepared inside the house, and in order to give the vines that extent of soil which is necessary for them, the best cultivators make an additional border twelve or fourteen feet wide outside, in front of the vinery. By building the foundation of the front wall on piers within a couple of inches of the surface, and supporting the wall above the surface on slabs of stone reaching from pier to pier, the roots of the vines easily penetrate to the border on the outside.

The vines should be planted early in the spring. Two year old plants are preferable, and they may be set eighteen inches from the front wall—one below each rafter, or, if the latter are over three feet apart, one also in the intermediate space.

The pruning and training of the vines we have already described. The *renewal* system of pruning we consider the best in all cases. The *spur* system is, however, practised by many gardeners, with more or less success. This, as most of our readers are aware, consists in allowing a single shoot to extend from each root to the length of the rafters; from the sides of this stem are produced the bearing shoots every year; and every autumn these spurs are shortened back, leaving only one bud at the bottom of each, which in its turn becomes the bearing shoot, and is again cut back the next season. The fruit is abundantly produced, and of good flavour, but the bunches are neither so large nor fair, nor do the vines continue so long in a productive and healthy state as when the wood is annually renewed.

" The essential points in pruning and training the vine, whatever mode be adopted, according to Loudon, " are to shorten the wood to such an extent that no more leaves shall be produced than can be fully exposed to the light; to stop all shoots produced in the summer that are not likely to be required in the winter pruning, at two or three joints, or at the first large healthy leaf from the stem where they originate; and to stop all shoots bearing bunches at one joint, or at most two, beyond the bunch. As shoots which are stopped, generally push a second time from the terminal bud, the secondary shoots thus produced should be stopped at one joint. And if at that joint they push also, then a third stopping must take place at one joint, and so on as long as the last terminal bud continues to break. Bearing these points in mind, nothing can be more simple than the pruning and training of the vine."

When early forcing of the vines is commenced, the heat should be applied very gently, for the first few days, and afterwards very gradually increased. Sixty degrees of Fahrenheit's thermometer may be the maximum, till the buds are all nearly expanded. When the leaves are expanded sixty-five may be the maximum and fifty-five the minimum temperature. When the vines are in blossom, seventy-five or eighty, in midday, with the solar heat should be allowed, with an abundance of air, and somewhat about this should be the average of midday temperature. But, as by far the best way of imparting information as to the routine of vine culture under glass is to present a precise account of a successful practice, we give here the diary of O. Johnson, Esq., of Lynn, Mass., as reported by him in Hovey's Magazine. Mr. Johnson is a very successful amateur cultivator, and we prefer to give his diary rather than that of a professional gardener, because we consider it as likely to be more instructive to the beginner in those little points which most professional men are likely to take for granted as being commonly known. We may premise here that "the vines were planted out in the border in May, 1835; they were then one year old, in pots. In 1836 and 1837, they were headed down. In 1838 they bore a few bunches of grapes, and made fine wood for the following year, when the date of the diary commences.

FEBRUARY.	Feb. 1839. Temperature.			DIARY OF THE VINERY.
	Morn.	Noon.	Night.	
13				Commenced fire heat in the vinery. [The thermometrical observations are taken at 6 o'clock in the morning, at noon, and 10 o'clock at night.]
14	50	80	60	Placed horse manure in the house to warm the border. Washed the house. Took up the vines, (which had been covered to protect them from the frost,) and washed them with warm soap suds: raised as much moisture as possible. Weather moderate and cloudy.
15	50	70	58	Weather quite moderate and thawy. Sleet.
16	48	60	55	Covered inside border with sand for sprinkling. Thaw. Whitewashed the vinery.

17	50	55	58	Earthen pans on the flues kept filled with water, but syringing suspended on account of the moisture in the atmosphere, it having been damp for three days. Cloudy.
18	51	67	60	Washed vines with soap suds. Weather moderate: a slight snow last night.
19	40	75	60	Pans kept full of water for the sake of steam, and vines syringed *twice* a day in sunny weather. Weather changed suddenly last night; cold, and temperature fell 10° below minimum point.
20	57	70	61	A Sweetwater vine in a pot, taken from the cellar on the 18th, and pruned at that time, is now bleeding profusely. At this season of the year, in order to economize with fuel, the furnace should be managed carefully. We found it a good plan about 10 o'clock at night to close the door of the ash-pit and furnace, and push the damper in the chimney as far in as possible. No air is then admitted, except through the crevices of the iron work. The thermometer fell only 4° during the night. Watered vines with soap suds.
21	57	75	61	The last seven days have been very mild for the season: to-day appears like an April day.
22	57	64	63	Weather became cold during the night.
24	60	63	64	Weather cloudy and thawy for the last three days. The floor of the vinery kept constantly damp, and the flues watered twice at night.
25	57	64	64	Rainy and thaw.
26	59	70	65	Muscat of Alexandria vine bleeding at the buds. Weather clear and rather cool.
27	59	64	64	Muscat vine continuing to bleed excessively, and finding all attempts to stop it unsuccessful, we hastily concluded to prune it down beyond the bleeding bud, and cover the wound with bladder of triple thickness (two very fast:) this, it was supposed, would stop it; but in a few moments the sap re-appeared, forcing its way through other buds, and even through the smooth bark in many places. The buds on the Sweetwater vines in pots began to swell. Rain last night: dull weather during the day: snow nearly gone.

28	58	75	65	Morning fine ; afternoon cloudy. When the fire is at a red heat, the damper and furnace door are closed to keep up the heat.
1	56	80	71	Bright morning ; weather cool.
2	64	70	68	Quite warm and pleasant for the season.
3	58	64	64	Weather changed last evening suddenly ; a cold snow storm set in to-day. Afternoon clear.
4	62	80	63	Buds of some black Hamburg vines beginning to swell. Dug up the inside border, and, notwithstanding all precautions, destroyed a few of the grape roots, which were within three inches of the surface. From this circumstance, we have determined not to disturb the border outside, but merely to loosen two inches below the surface : we are satisfied that the vines have been injured by deep digging the borders. Cold severe : last night temperature 2° below 0.
5	51	70	68	The cold very severe. The sudden changes render it almost impossible to keep a regular temperature in the house, which should not stand (at this stage of forcing) below 60°. The house having originally been intended for a grapery without fire heat, it is not well adapted to forcing.
6	60	73	68	Weather cool and pleasant.
7	62	75	68	Buds of the vine in pot breaking.
8	59	74	64	
9	60	75	63	Buds of Hamburgs breaking. Snow last night.
10	60	73	63	
11	50	75	60	Quite cold last night. Windy.
12	54	76	62	Buds of Hamburgs mostly breaking. Owing to the changeable weather, there is some fear that there has been too much heat, as a few of the shoots appear weak. Plenty of air has been given daily.
13	60	75	64	Buds of Muscat of Alexandria breaking. Fruit buds appear on the Hamburgs.
14	60	74	60	
15	54	70	64	
16	60	75	61	
17	60	80	61	The buds have broken remarkably fine : almost every bud throughout the house is opening. Longest shoot on Hamburg was four inches at noon. The Muscat, which broke first last year, is now the most back-

(MARCH)

ward. Quere—Is it not owing to excessive bleeding ?

18	63	63	64	
19	62	60	63	
20	62	65	64	
21	62	62	66	
22	60	60	66	
23	62		66	After this period, the thermometer was observed only at morning and at night.
24	60		69	The temperature ranging from 62° to 80° during the remainder of the day, with an abundance of air in good weather.
25	60	65		
26	62	63		
27	63	64		
28	61	67		
29	64	67		
30	66	68		
31	62	70		The last six days cloudy ; wind east ; quite cold last night for the season.

APRIL.

1	60	72		
2	62	71		
3	66	70		
4	64	74		
5	65	73		
6	66	76		Topped the fruit-bearing shoots one joint above the fruit, and when the lower shoots appear weak, top the leading shoot of the vine.
7	74	66		
8	62	72		Discontinued syringing the vines.
9	66	74		
10	64	73		
11	70	73		A few clusters of flowers began to open on two vines.
12	73	78		
13	66	80		
14	68	76		The last three days wind north-east, with much rain ; to-day sleet and rain. Grapes blooming beautifully : keep up a high temperature with moisture, when the weather is cloudy during the day.
15	67	77		
16	72	77		Floor sprinkled to create a fine steam.
17	77	74		
18	66	78		A few clusters of flowers open on the Muscat of Alexandria.

19	73	77	
20	70	76	
21	64	78	Temperature kept up. The thermometer should not be allowed, at this stage of the growth of the vines, to fall below 75°; but owing to the faulty construction of the house, it has been almost impossible to keep up a regular heat.
22	71	78	The grapes on the black Hamburg vines are mostly set; those at the top of the house as large as small peas, while those below are just out of bloom. Many of the bunches show great promise, and the vines look remarkably vigorous and strong, with the exception of one vine, next the partition glass, which made the largest wood last season, apparently fully ripe and little pith; notwithstanding these favourable promises, it showed little fruit, and the shoots are small and weak.
23	69	81	Cut out about fifty bunches in thinning.
24	77	75	
25	74	78	
26	77	63	
27	71	80	
28	73	75	
29	70	70	
30	70	70	Commenced syringing again, twice a day, in fine weather. Moisture is also plentifully supplied by keeping the pans well filled with water.
May. 1	70	70	
2	68	66	
3	66	68	Much rain during the last week: have kept a brisk fire in the day, and admitted air. The vines look finely. Continue thinning and shouldering the bunches, after cutting out about one half their number. [By shouldering is understood tying up the shoulders on the large clusters to the trellis, so that they may not press upon the lower part of the bunch.]
4	68	70	
5	60	77	
6	61	62	
7	59	66	
8	57	73	Plenty of air admitted.
9	70	68	
10	58	62	
11	56	54	Grapes now swelling off finely.
12	56	71	Abundance of moisture kept up.
13	65	66	

14	63	73	A fine rain to-day. The month has been rather cool; several nights the past week the earth has frozen slightly. The grapes are now swelling finely. Continue to thin the fruit daily.
15	65	68	The process of thinning the berries continued, taking out some almost every day, and always the smallest.
16	69	70	
17	68	61	
18	58	71	
19	68	74	Abundance of air given in fine weather.
20	68	69	
21	62	69	
22	70	76	
23	66	72	
24	69	72	Next year's bearing wood carefully laid in.
25	70	72	
26	68	72	
27	72	74	
28	74	72	
29	73	72	
30	70	70	
31	62	68	The month of May has been, as a whole, unfavourable for the grape. Much rainy and dull weather: we have been obliged to light fires every night, and occasionally in the day. The grapes have been often looked over and thinned, yet there is no doubt the scissors have been used too sparingly.

JUNE.

1	69	68	
2	66	66	
3	66	64	
4	66	68	All lateral branches cut clean out.
5	61	68	
6	64	76	
7	60	70	Bunches supported by tying to the trellis.
8	61	70	
9	62	70	
10	64	69	The grapes have now completed their stoning process, and a few near the furnace swelling off. No mildew, or disease of any kind, has yet been discovered, and the vines generally have the most healthy and vigorous appearance. The weather has been dull and disagreeable, which has rendered fires necessary.
11	64	64	
12	55	69	
13	66	66	A few of the black Hamburgs and Zinfindals,

			near the flue, perceived to be changing colour. Weather quite unfavourable ; fires at night.
14	65	71	
15	71	62	Syringing now discontinued.
16	61	68	
17	58	66	
18	50	66	The month, thus far, has been remarkable for high
19	61	60	winds, which have injured many plants.
20	56	68	
21	66	65	
22	60	67	
23	64	62	The grapes are now swelling finely. Those at the western flue mostly coloured ; also the Zinfindal next. The second vine from the partition, having to sustain the heaviest crop, is rather backward, and we fear some of the berries may shrink : having left different quantities on vines of the same apparent strength, we shall be able to ascertain their powers of maturation. After this period the thermometrical observations were discontinued ; as the crop was now beginning to colour, and the weather generally warm, abundance of air is admitted in all fine weather.
26	—	—	Bunches of the Zinfindal near the furnace, and at the top of the house, are now perfectly coloured, and apparently ripe. Ceased making fires.
29	—	—	A little air is admitted at night. Weather delightful.

July 4.—Cut six bunches of Zinfindal grapes ; the largest a pound and a half; weight of the whole, five pounds and a quarter.

6*th.*—Exhibited Zinfindal grapes at the Massachusetts Horticultural Society.

13*th.*—Exhibited black Hamburg grapes at the Massachusetts Horticultural Society's room.

15*th.*—A few bunches of the Muscat of Alexandria are now ripe ; the flavour exceedingly fine.

20*th.*—Continued to cut Zinfindal grapes.

22*d.*—The ripening of all the grapes being now completed, we have not deemed it necessary to continue the diary. In the vinery we shall cut about two hundred and thirty pounds of grapes from nine vines, [being about twenty-five pounds to each.] The Hamburgs average nearly one pound and a quarter to the bunch throughout.

In the cold house, separated from the vinery by the partition, a little mildew was perceived. By dusting sulphur on the infected bushes, the mischief is instantly checked. Most of the cultivators with whom we have conversed complain grievously of mildew this season, and some have lost part of their crops by inattention on its first appearance.

Aug. 10th.—Again exhibited some of the Hamburg grapes at the Massachusetts Horticultural Society's room. One fine bunch weighed two and a half pounds, and a beautiful cluster of Muscat of Alexandria one pound. Some of the berries of the former measured three inches in circumference, and the latter three and a quarter by three and three quarter inches.

Another season we intend to use a larger quantity of soap suds on the grape border. Have not paid sufficient attention to the watering of the border, and the inside, especially, must have suffered. Another fault to be removed next year is, to tie up all the projecting grapilons as well as the shoulders, which would allow the grapes to swell without crowding.

The grapes in the cold house are swelling finely. The bunches were thinned much more severely than in the vinery, but, notwithstanding this, they are all filled up, and many are too crowded. The berries are also larger than the grapes in the vinery, though none of the clusters have attained the same size.

Much has been written upon the subject of the *shrivelling* or shrinking of grapes : none of the clusters in the vinery were affected ; but in the cold house, some shrivelling was perceived on a few bunches. We are inclined to believe that the moisture given after the grapes begin to colour, and want of sufficient air, are the causes.

To insure a good crop of grapes, we are satisfied that they must have—*plenty of heat—plenty of air—plenty of moisture—severe thinning of bunches—*and *severe thinning of berries.* The vines, also, must be pruned often, and kept free : the wood *never* crowded. Great attention must be paid to the airing of the house, which must be done gradually, that there may be at no time a *sudden* change in the temperature.

With such attention, and the prerequisite of a rich border, on a dry subsoil, good crops of fine grapes are always to be obtained. The vines require much moisture until they have completed their last swell, when the moisture should be withdrawn."

INSECTS AND DISEASES. When properly grown under glass, the grape is a very vigorous plant, liable to few diseases. The bleeding which often happens at the commencement of growth, usually ceases without doing harm, when the foliage begins to expand. If excessive, it may be stopped by a mixture of three parts cheese parings and one part lime, applied to the wound. The red-spider which sometimes infests vineries kept at a high temperature, is usually destroyed by coating over the flues with a wash of quick lime and sulphur, after which, the house must be kept closed for half a day. The smaller insects which occasionally prey on the young shoots, are easily kept down by syringing the parts affected, with a solution of whale oil soap.

VARIETIES. There are in the catalogues a vast number of names of grapes, many of which belong to the same fruit. But there are really only twenty or thirty varieties which are at all worthy of cultivation in gardens. Indeed, the most experienced gardeners are satisfied with half a dozen of the best sorts for their vineries, and the sorts universally admired are the Black Hamburgh, Black Prince, White Muscadine, and Muscat of Alexandria. We will describe all the finest foreign grapes that have been introduced, and for the sake of simplifying their arrangement, shall divide them into three classes, 1st, those with dark red, purple or black berries; 2d, those with white or yellow berries; 3d, those with light red, rose-coloured, gray, or striped berries.

Class I.   Grapes with dark red, purple, or black berries.

1. BLACK CLUSTER.   Thomp.

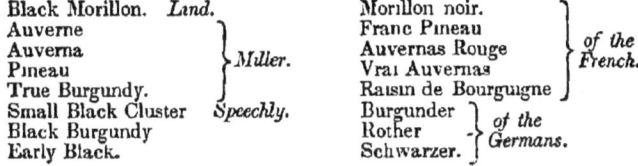

This excellent hardy grape is the true Burgundy grape so highly valued for wine in France. It is readily distinguished from Miller's Burgundy, by the absence of the down on its leaves, which peculiarly distinguishes that sort. The fruit is very sweet and excellent, and the hardiness of the vine renders it one of the best varieties for the open air in this climate.

Bunches small, compact, (i. e berries closely set.) Berries middle sized, roundish-oval. Skin deep black. Juice sweet and good. Ripens in the open air about the 20th of September. Thompson gives more than 40 synonymes to this grape.

2. BLACK FRONTIGNAN. § Thomp.

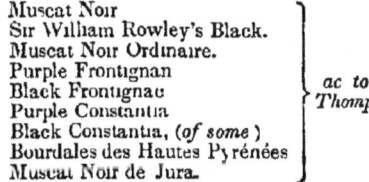

An excellent grape for the vinery, originally from the town

of Frontignan, in France, where it and other similar sorts are largely cultivated for making the Muscadine or Frontignac wine.

Bunches rather long. Berries of medium size, round, quite black. Skin thin, flavour musky and rich. Ripens in October. A good bearer.

The BLUE FRONTIGNAN, (*Violet Frontignan* and *Black Contantion*, of some,) is rather inferiour to the above, having only a slightly musky flavour; the bunches are more compact, the berries not quite round, purplish, with a thick skin.

3. BLACK HAMBURGH. § Thomp. Lind. Speechly.

Warner's Black Hamburgh.	Frankenthaler.	
Purple Hamburgh.	Frankenthaler Gros Noir.	
Red Hamburgh.	Trollinger.	
Brown Hamburgh.	Blue Trollinger.	*of various*
Dutch Hamburgh.	Troller.	*European*
Victoria.	Welscher.	*gardens.*
Salisbury Violet.	Fleish Traube.	*ac. to*
Hampton, Court Vine.	Hudler.	*Thomp.*
Valentine's.	Languedoc.	
Gibaralter.	Mohrendutte.	
Frankendale.	Weissholziger Trollinger.	

The Black Hamburgh has long been considered the first of black grapes for the vinery, but it will very rarely perfect its fruit out of doors. Its very large size and most luscious flavour render it universally esteemed.

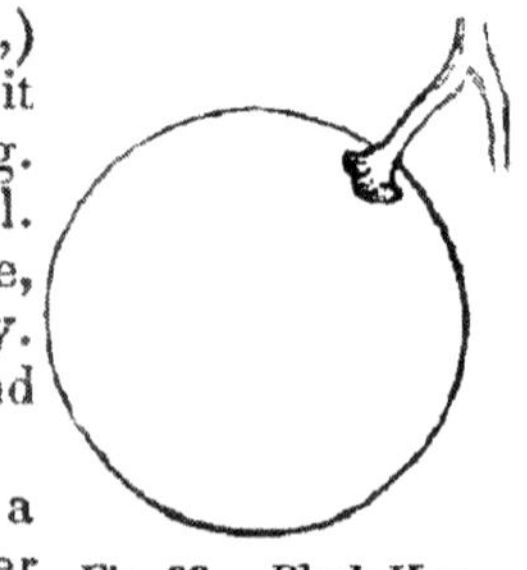

Bunches large, (about nine inches deep,) and mostly with two shoulders, making it broad at the top. Berries very large (fig. 93,) roundish, slightly inclining to oval. Skin rather thick, deep brownish purple, becoming nearly black at full maturity. Flavour very sugary and rich. A good and regular bearer.

WILMOT'S NEW BLACK HAMBURGH is a recent variety which is said to bear larger and handsomer fruit.

Fig. 93. *Black Hamburgh.*

4. BLACK PRINCE. § Lind. Thomp.

Alicant.	Sir A. Pytches' Black.	
Black Spanish.	Pocock's Damascus.	*ac. to*
Black Valentia.	Cambridge Botanic Garden.	*Thomp.*
Black Portugal.	Steward's Black Prince.	
Boston.	Black Lisbon.	

The Black Prince is very highly esteemed. It is hardier than the Black Hamburgh, ripening very well here in good situations in the open air, and bearing profusely, with the easiest culture, in the vinery.

Bunches long and not generally shouldered, berries large, rather thinly set, oval. Skin thick, black, covered with a thick blue bloom. Flavour first rate—sweet and excellent.

5. BLACK LOMBARDY. § Lind. Thomp.

> Wests' St. Peters.
> Poonah
> Money's.
> Raisin des Carmes
> Raisin de Cuba.

Bunches large and long, with shoulders. Berries large, roundish-oval. Skin thin, very black at maturity. Flavour very rich and sugary. The leaves are rather small, and turn purple as the fruit ripens. Thompson considers this synonymous with the Poonah grape introduced by Sir Joseph Banks, from Bombay. It requires a pretty high temperature, and is then a great bearer.

6. BLACK MOROCCO. Thomp.

> Le Cœur. *Lind.*
> Ansell's Large Oval Black.
> Black Muscadel
> Raisin d'Espagne.

A large and showy grape, ripening late, but requiring a good deal of heat. The blossoms are a little imperfect, and require to be fertilized with those of the Black Hamburgh, or some other hardy sort
Bunches large; berries very large, oval; skin thick, dark red, flavour tolerably sweet and rich.

7. BLACK SAINT PETER'S. § Thomp.

> Saint Peter's. *Lind Speechly*
> Black Palestine.
> Oldaker's West's St Peter's.

A capital variety, ripening quite late and which may be kept on the vines if it is allowed to ripen in a cool house until winter. This is one of the best sorts for a vinery without fire-heat.
Bunches of pretty good size, rather loose. Berries rather large, round. Skin thin and black. Flavour delicate, sweet, and excellent.

8. BLACK MUSCAT OF ALEXANDRIA. Thomp.

> Red Muscat of Alexandria. *Lind.*
> Red Frontinac of Jerusalem

Bunches large, and shouldered. Berries large, oval, skin

thick, of a reddish colour, becoming black at maturity. Flesh quite firm, with a rich musky flavour. Requires a vinery with fire-heat.

9. BLACK TRIPOLI. Thomp.

Black Grape from Tripoli. *Lind. Speech.*

This grape, which we have not yet seen in fruit, is said to be a large and very excellent one, ripening late, and well worthy of a place in the vinery. It requires some fire-heat.

Bunches of medium size, shouldered, rather loose. Berries large, round, often slightly flattened. Stones quite small. Skin thin, purplish black, slightly covered with bloom. Flesh tender and sweet, with a very high flavoured, rich juice.

10. BLACK MUSCADINE. Lind. Thomp.

Black Chasselas
Chasselas noir ?

A pretty good black grape, scarcely succeeding well, however, in the open air, and inferior to other sorts for the vinery.

Bunches of medium size, compact. Berries roundish-oval. Skin thick, black, overspread with a blue bloom. Juice sweet, and of pretty good flavour.

11. BLACK SWEETWATER. Thomp. Lind.

Water Zoet Noir.

Bunches small, compact. Berries small, round. Skin thin, with a sweet and pleasant juice. A second rate, but rather hardy sort.

12. EARLY BLACK JULY. § Thomp. Lind.

July Grape.
Madeleine.
Madeleine Noir.
Raisin précoce. *Poiteau.*
Morillon Hâtif. *O. Duh.*
De St. Jean.
Schwarzer Frühzeitiger ⎫
Burgunder. ⎬ *of the*
August Traube. ⎭ *Germans.*
Jacobs straube.

The earliest of grapes, and chiefly valued for the dessert on that account. In the open air it ripens, here, the last of July, or early in August. The leaves are rather small, and light green above and beneath.

Bunches small and compact. Berries small, quite round.

Skin thick, black, covered with a blue bloom.   Flavour mode-rately sweet, but not rich or perfumed.

13. ESPERIONE. Thomp. Lind.

Turner's Black.
Hardy Blue Windsor.
Cumberland Lodge

The Esperione is a hardy, luxuriant, and prolific grape, growing as well in the open air as the Muscadine, and even better in many situations.   It is yet very rare with us, but merits more general cultivation.

Bunches large, shouldered, like the Black Hamburgh in size. Berries round, or occasionally flattened, and often indented with a groove.   Skin thick, dark purple, powdered with a thick blue bloom.   Flesh adheres to the skin, of a pleasant, sprightly fla vour, not very rich.

14. MILLER'S BURGUNDY. Lind. Thomp. Speechly.

Miller Grape.	Muller	
Le Meunier.	Mullevrebe	
Morillon Taconné.	Morone Farinaccio.	*of European*
Fromenté.	Pulverulenta	*gardens*
Aleatica du Po.	Farineux noir.	
Sauvignien noir.	Noirin.	

A favourite variety, long known and cultivated in all parts of the world as a hardy grape for wine and table use.   It ripens pretty well in the open air, and is readily known by the dense covering of *cottony down* which lines both sides of the leaves, whence the name *miller's* grape.

Bunches short, thick, and compact.   Berries roundish-oval, very closely set together.   Skin thin, black, with a blue bloom. Flesh tender, abounding with a sweet high flavoured juice. Each berry contains two small seeds.

Class II.   Grapes with White or Yellow berries.

15. CIOTAT. Thomp. Lind. Duh.

Parsley-leaved.
White Parsley-leaved.
Parsley-leaved Muscadine.
Malmsey Muscadine
Raisin d'Autriche.

The Parsley-leaved grape, as its name denotes, is remarkable for its very deeply divided leaves, quite unlike those of any other sort. It succeeds very well with us in the open air, and may therefore be considered a valuable sort, but it is greatly superior in flavour when grown under glass.

Bunches of middle size, long, rather loose. Berries round. Skin thin, white, with a sweet and pleasant, but not rich flavoured juice.

There is a variety of this grape with red fruit.

16. CHASSELAS MUSQUÉ. § Thomp. Duh.

Musk Chasselas.
Le Cour.

A very delicious grape, the highest flavoured Chasselas, having much of the flavour of the Muscat of Alexandria.

Bunches of medium size, long and rather loose. Berries middle size, round. Skin thin, yellowish white. Flesh tender with an abundant juice, of a rich musky flavour. Leaves smaller and deeper green than those of the Sweetwater or Muscadine.

17. CHARLSWORTH TOKAY. Thomp.

A new variety very recently received from England, reputed to be of superior quality.

Bunches long, compact. Berries large, oval; skin thick, white. Flavour rich and excellent, with a Muscat perfume.

18. EARLY WHITE MALVASIA. Thomp

Morna Chasselas.	Mornair blanc.	
Early Chasselas.	Le Melier.	of the
Grove End Sweet Water.	Melier blanc.	French.
White Melier.	Blanc de Bonneuil.	

A nice early grape, and a good bearer, which is in fact only an earlier variety of the Chasselas. It bears very well in the open air.

Bunches in size and form, much like those of the white Chasselas or Royal Muscadine. Berries round, yellowish white. Skin thin. Flesh sweet, juicy and agreeable in flavour. Ripens in August. The leaves are pale green on the upper side, slightly downy below, out into five, rather deep lobes.

19. PITMASTON WHITE CLUSTER. §

A pretty hardy grape, raised in Pitmaston, England, from the Black Cluster, ripening rather earlier than the Sweetwater, of good quality and well deserving a place where the foreign grapes are cultivated in the open air.

Bunches of medium size, compact and shouldered. Berries middle sized, round. Skin thin, amber colour, occasionally tinged with a little russet when fully ripe. Flesh tender, juicy, sweet and excellent.

20. ROYAL MUSCADINE. § Thomp. Lind. Mill.

Amber Muscadine.	Chasselas blanc.	
Early White Teneriffe.	Chasselas de Fontainebleau.	
Golden Chasselas.	D'Arbois.	*ac. to Thomp.*
White Chasselas.	Raisin de Champagne.	
Chasselas doré.	Amiens.	

A truly excellent grape in all respects—one of the very best for hardy culture in this climate, or for the vinery. It is every where highly esteemed, and is the Chasselas *par excellence* of the French.

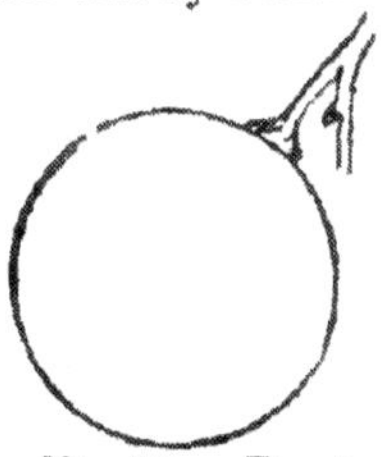

Fig. 94. *Royal Muscadine.*

Bunches large, and shouldered. Berries, (fig. 94,) larger than those of the Sweetwater, round. Skin thin, at first greenish white, but turning to an amber colour when fully ripe. Flesh tender, with e rich and delicious flavour. Ripens here about the 20th of September. Wood and foliage stronger than those of the Sweetwater.

21. SCOTCH WHITE CLUSTER. § Thomp.

Blacksmith's White Cluster.

This is a new grape, not yet fairly tested in this country, but which is likely to prove a valuable one for garden culture, as it has the reputation in England of being very hardy, very early, and a great bearer. It was raised from the seed by a blacksmith of Edinburgh in 1812.

Bunches of middle size, compact. Berries medium sized, roundish-oval. Skin white, thin. Flesh tender, juicy, sweet, and excellent.

22. SYRIAN. Thomp. Lind. Speech.

Jews.

This is believed to be the grape mentioned in the scriptures as found by the Israelites on the brook of Eschol, the bunches of which were so large as to be borne on a staff by two men. It is a very superb looking fruit, and has been grown in this country to very large size. In England, bunches of it have been produced weighing $19\frac{1}{2}$ lbs. It is much inferiour in flavour to No. 24, and is, perhaps, therefore scarcely desirable in a small collection.

Bunches enormously large, and regularly formed, with broad shoulders. Berries large, oval. Skin thick, white at first, but becoming a tawny yellow, or amber when at full maturity. Flesh firm and solid, moderately juicy and sweet, though not rich. Will hang till Christmas in a vinery. The wood and foliage are very large.

23. VERDELHO. Thomp. Lind.

Verdal.
Verdilhio.
Madeira Wine Grape.

A vigorous growing grape, of good quality, from Madeira, which is largely used in that island for making the best wines.

Bunches rather small, loose. Berries small, rather unequal in size, and often without seeds. Skin thin, semi-transparent, yellowish-green, a little tinged with russet when very ripe. Juice a little acid at first, but rich and excellent at maturity.

24. WHITE MUSCAT OF ALEXANDRIA. § Thomp. Lind.

Frontniac of Alexandria. ⎫ *Miller.*
Jerusalem Muscat. ⎬
Malaga. ⎭
White Muscat.
Tottenham Park Muscat.
White Muscat of Lunel.
Lunel.
Muscat d'Alexandria.
Passe-longue Musqué. *Duh.*
Passe Musqué.
Zebibo, (*of Sicily.*)

The most delicious of all grapes, but requires to be grown under glass in this climate. In favourable seasons it reaches maturity well in a vinery without fire-heat, but it can scarcely be said to attain its highest flavour except with the aid of artificial heat.

Bunches very large, often 9 to 12 inches long, rather loose and irregular. Berries, (fig. 95,) very large, an inch or more long, oval. Skin thick, white or pale amber when fully ripe. Flesh quite firm and crisp, with a peculiarly musky, rich, perfumed flavour, very delicious. Seeds small, and occasionally absent from the larger berries. This variety is a very strong grower, and is raised in great perfection about Boston. It will hang a long time on the vines.

Fig. 95. *White Muscat of Alexandria.*

Mr. Thompson considers the MALAGA grape (brought to this country in jars,) as synonymous. It is picked so early for importation as to have little flavour.

The CANNON-HALL MUSCAT, an English seedling, closely resembles this grape, but the flesh is firmer, the skin yellower, and
it is not quite so rich in flavour.   It also sets rather badly, requiring to be fertilized by hand with the pollen of some other sort.

25. WHITE FRONTIGNAN. § Lind. Thomp.

White Constantia.	Moschata Bianca.
White Frontniac.	Moscado Bianco.
Nepean's Constantia.	Moscatel Commun
Muscat Blanc.	Muscateller.
Raisin de Frontignan.	Wiesser Muscateller.
Muscat Blanc de Jura.	Weisse Muscaten Traube.

The White Frontignan is a very favourite grape, as the
many names, quoted above, by which it is known in various
parts of Europe sufficiently prove.   Its hardy habit, uniform
productiveness in the vinery, and most luscious flavour, make
it every where esteemed.

Bunches of medium size, or pretty long, and without shoulders.   Berries middle sized, round, rather thickly set.   Skin
thin, dull white or yellow, covered with a thin bloom.   Flesh
tender, with a rich, perfumed, musky flavour.

26. WHITE SWEETWATER.   Thomp.

Early White Muscadine.
White Muscadine, (of *Lind.*)
Early Sweetwater.
Stillward's Sweetwater.
Dutch Sweetwater.
Chasselas Precoce.
Chasselas Royal.
Water Zoete Blanc.

This grape is better known, and more commonly cultivated
than any other in this country, although it is inferior to the
Royal Muscadine.   It differs from the latter in having weaker
wood, and open, loose, bunches of a paler colour.

Bunches middle sized, loose or open, usually with many
small imperfect berries, shouldered.   Berries of the middle size,
round.   Skin thin, clear watery green, rarely becoming amber
except very fully exposed to the sun.   Flesh crisp, watery,
sweet, but not high flavoured.   Ripens in the open air from the
20th to the last of August—a fortnight earlier than the Royal
Muscadine.

27. WHITE TOKAY.   Thomp.

Genuine Tokay.   *Lind. Speech.*
Gray Tokay !
Tokai blanc.

This is the fruit from which the delicious Tokay wine **of**

Hungary is made. We have ripened it very well in the open air. Its flavour is good and its aroma peculiarly agreeable.

Bunches of medium size, compact. Berries rounded oval, closely set. Skin thin, of a dull white. Flesh very delicate, sweet and perfumed. Leaves deeply 5-lobed, and covered with a satiny down on the lower surface.

28. White Hamburgh. Thomp

White Lisbon.
White Portugal.
White Raisin.

This is the Portugal grape of commerce which is so largely exported to different parts of the world in jars. It is not a high flavoured though a very showy grape, and will hang a long time on the vines after maturity. It requires a vinery.

Bunches very large and loose. Berries large, oval. Skin thick, greenish-white. Flesh solid, sweet, and sometimes with a slight Muscat flavour. Bunches of this variety weighing over three pounds have been grown near Boston.

29. White Nice. Thomp. M'Intosh.

A very large and showy fruit, and, in a vinery with fire-heat, a very excellent sort. M'Intosh, an English gardener of reputation, has grown bunches of this the White Nice to the enormous weight of eighteen pounds, and considers it " one of the noblest of grapes."

Bunches very large, with loose shoulders. Berries roundish, medium size, thinly distributed over the shoulders and sides of the bunch. Skin thin, rather tough, greenish-white, becoming, finally, a little yellowish. Flesh crisp, sweet, and of very good flavour. Leaves and wood very strong, the latter remarkably downy beneath.

30. White Rissling. Thomp.

Schloss Johannisberg.
Rudesheimerberg.
Reissling.
Petit Riessling.
Grosser Riessling.
Rössling.
Kleier Rissling.

The most celebrated grape of the Rhine, producing the celebrated hock wines. It is yet little known in this country, but from its very great hardiness and productiveness, in the cold districts of its native soil, we hope to find in it a valuable acquisition for our gardens—if not for our vineyards.

21*

Bunches of medium size, compact. Berries rather small, round. Skin thin. Flesh tender and juicy, with sweet and sprightly pleasant flavour.

Class III. Grapes with light red, rose-coloured, or striped berries.

31. ALEPPO. Thomp. Lind.

Switzerland Grape.
Striped Muscadine.
Variegated Chasselas.
Raisin Suisse.
Raisin d'Aless.
Chasselas panaché
Maurillan panaché.
Maurillan noir panaché

A very singular grape, the berries being mostly striped with white and black in distinct lines ; or sometimes half the bunch will be black, and half white. It bears very well, and is deserving a place in the vinery of the amateur. The foliage is also prettily striped in autumn.

Bunches rather below medium size. Berries medium size, roundish. Skin thin, striped with white and dark red, or black Flesh juicy, and of a rich and excellent flavour.

32. GRIZZLY FRONTIGNAN. § Thomp. Lind.

Red Frontignan, (*of some.*
Grizzly Frontignac.
Red Constantia.
Muscat Rouge.
Muscat Gris.
Muscado Rosso.
Kummel Traube.
Grauer Muscateller.

This delicious grape requires to be grown in a vinery when it is, to our taste, scarcely surpassed.

Bunches rather long, with narrow shoulders. Berries round, of medium size, and growing closer upon the bunches than those of the White Frontignan. Skin thick, pale brown, blended with red and yellow. Flesh very juicy, rich, musky and high flavoured.

The RED FRONTIGNAN Thompson considers the same as the foregoing only being more deeply coloured in some situations. But Lindley, with whom we are inclined to agree in this case, keeps it distinct. The latter describes the Red Frontignan as having bunches without shoulders, berries perfectly round, and deep red, flavour excellent. These two sorts require more careful comparison.

33. KNIGHT'S VARIEGATED CHASSELAS. Thomp.

Variegated Chasselas. *Lind*

A hybrid seedling, raised by Mr. Knight from the White Chasselas, impregnated by the Aleppo. A curious and pretty fruit, but not first rate in flavour.

Bunches rather long, unshouldered. Berries below the middle size, round, loosely set. Skin quite thin, white, shaded with bluish violet, sometimes becoming purplish in the sun. Flesh tender, sweet, and pleasant. The leaves die off in autumn of fine red yellow and green colours.

34. LOMBARDY. Thomp. Lind.

Flame Coloured Tokay.
Rhenish Red.
Wantage.
Red Grape of Taurida.

The Lombardy is remarkable for the very large size of the bunches, which are frequently twelve to eighteen inches long. It is a handsome fruit, the berries thickly set, (so much so as to need a good deal of thinning,) and it requires fire-heat to bring it to full perfection.

Bunches very large, handsomely formed, with large shoulders. Berries large roundish. Skin thick, pale red or flame colour. Flesh firm, sweet, with a sprightly, very good flavour.

35. RED CHASSELAS. Thomp. Lind. Fors.

Red Muscadine. *Mill.*
Chasselas Rouge. *Duh.*

This grape a good deal resembles the White Chasselas, except that the berries are slightly coloured with red. Very rarely, when over ripe, they become a dark red.

Bunches loose, not large ; berries medium size, round. Skin thin, at first pale green, but when exposed to the sun they become red. Flesh tender, sweet, and very good. Not very hardy.

II. *Cultivation of the Native Grapes.*

The better varieties of the native grapes, as the Isabella, Catawba, etc., are among the most valuable of fruits in the middle

states. Hardy, vigorous, and productive, with very trifling
care they yield the farmer, and the common gardener, to whom
the finer foreign sorts requiring much attention and considerable
expense in culture, are denied, the enjoyment of an abundance
of very good fruit. In the neighbourhood of New-York and
Philadelphia their culture is carried to a large extent for supplying the markets, a single grower on the Hudson, (Dr. Un-
derhill,) sending thousands of baskets to New-York annually.
In this part of the country no fruit is more common than the
Isabella grape, and many families preserve large quantities for
use during the winter months, by packing them away, as soon as
ripe, in jars, boxes, or barrels, between layers of cotton batting—
in which way they may be kept plump and fresh till March.

North of the 42° of latitude, and east of the Hudson river,
these varieties, except in favourable situations, do not always
succeed perfectly—the summers being frequently too short to
mature their fruit, and the winter injuring the vines ; but this
may be guarded against by planting them against the south side
of walls and buildings. In nearly all the middle and western
states they thrive perfectly. But in many localities at the
south, especially in Georgia, the fruit is very liable to rot before ripening, and this is most successfully remedied by allowing the vines to run very high—in the tops of trees, or upon a
very tall trellis.

The varieties of native grapes at present grown are chiefly
either the finer sorts of wild species, or, which is most generally
the case, they are accidentally improved varieties, that have
sprung up in woods and fields from wild vines. They are,
therefore, but one remove from a wild state, and, as extensive
trials are now being made by various cultivators to produce
new varieties from these, there is little doubt that in a few
years we shall have many new native sorts, combining the good
qualities of the best foreign grapes, with the hardiness of the
indigenous ones, and with also the necessary adaptation to the
various soils and climates of the United States.

GARDEN CULTURE. The garden culture of these grapes is
very easy. They grow with vigour in any soil not absolutely
poor, and bear abundant crops in sandy or heavy soils, though
being of grosser habit than many of the foreign grapes, they
prefer a rather strong and rich soil. One of the first points to
be attended to in planting them is to secure a perfectly *sunny,
open exposure,* as it may always be assumed that, with us, no atmosphere can be too bright or sunny for the grape ; for although
it will make the most luxuriant and vigorous shoots in the shade
of trees or buildings, yet the crops will be small and uncertain,
and the berries will be likely to fall a prey to mildew.

In the second place the vines should be *kept within moderate
bounds,* and trained to an *upright trellis.* The Isabella and Ca-

tawba are so rampant in their growth, when young, that the in-
dulgent and gratified cultivator is but too apt to allow them to
cover a large space. Experience, however, has convinced us
that this is an error. For two or three seasons, vines of great
size will produce enormous crops,* but they soon exhaust the
supply of nourishment at hand, (which, indeed, it is difficult to
supply again,) the vine becomes filled with useless, old wood,
and speedily becomes unfruitful and worthless. About **6** or **8**
feet apart we have found to be the best distance at which to plant
the native grapes. Assuming the trellis to be 8 feet high, then
each vine will extend either way 3 or 4 feet, covering a space 8
feet square. In this form, the roots and branches extending but
a short distance, they may be kept in high vigour, and a state
of constant productiveness, for a great length of time.

The system of pruning and training these grapes generally
pursued is the upright mode, with the spur mode of training.
The first seasons' growth of a newly planted vine is cut back
to two buds the ensuing fall or spring. These two buds are
allowed to form two upright shoots the next summer, which, at
the end of the season, are brought down to a horizontal position,
and fastened each way to the lower horizontal rail of the trellis,
being shortened at the distance of three or four feet from the
root—or as far each side as the plant is wished to extend. The
next season, upright shoots are allowed to grow one foot apart,
and these, as soon as they reach the top of the trellis, are also
stopped. The next year, the trellis being filled with the vines,
a set of lateral shoots will be produced from the upright leaders
with from one to three bunches upon each, which will be the
first crop. The vine is now perfect, and, in the spur mode of
pruning, it is only necessary at the close of every season, that
is, at the autumnal or winter pruning, to cut back these lateral
shoots, or fruit spurs, to within an inch of the upright shoot from
which they sprung, and a new lateral producing fruit will annually supply its place, to be again cut out at the winter pruning.

After several years bearing, if it is found that the grapes fail
in size or flavour, the vines should be cut down to the main
horizontal shoots at the bottom of the trellis. They will then
speedily make a new set of upright shoots which will produce
very abundantly, as at first.

It cannot be denied that the *renewal* system of training, (see
page 221,) is certain of yielding always the largest and finest
fruit, though not so large a crop—as half the surface of the vine
is every year occupied with young wood, to take the place of
that annually cut out.

What we have already stated, in page 222, respecting pruning
will apply equally well here. If the vine is *fully exposed to the*

* An old vine of the Isabella, still standing in these gardens, has produced 3,000 clusters of grapes in a year.

sun it will require very little summer pruning; in fact, none, except stopping the young shoots three joints beyond the farthest bunch of grapes, at midsummer—for the leaves being intended by nature to elaborate the sap, the more we can retain of them (without robbing the fruit unduly of fluids expended in making new growth,) the larger and higher flavoured will be the fruit ; careful experiments having proved that there is no more successful mode of impoverishing the crop of fruit than that of pulling off the leaves.

The annual pruning of the hardy grapes is usually performed during mild days in February or March—at least a month before vegetation is likely to commence. Many cultivators prefer to prune their vines in November, and, except for cold latitudes or exposures, this is undoubtedly the better season.

Every third year, at least, the borders where the vines are growing should have a heavy top-dressing of manure. The vine soon exhausts the soil within its reach, and ceases bearing well when that is the case. We have frequently seen old and impoverished vines entirely resuscitated by digging in about the roots, as far as they extend, a very heavy top-dressing of slightly fermented stable manure.

VINEYARD CULTURE. While many persons who have either made or witnessed the failures in raising the foreign grapes in vineyards in this country, believe it is folly for us to attempt to compete with France and Germany in wine-making, some of our western citizens, aided by skilful Swiss and German vine-dressers—emigrants to this country, have placed the fact of profitable vineyard culture beyond a doubt, in the valley of the Ohio. The vineyards on the Ohio, now covering many acres, produce regular, and very large crops, and their wine of the different characters of Madeira, Hock, and Champagne, brings very readily from 75 cents to one dollar a gallon in Cincinnati. The Swiss, at Vevay, first commenced wine-making in the West, but to the zeal and fostering care of N. Longworth, Esq., of Cincinnati, one of the most energetic of western horticulturists, that district of country owes the firm basis on which the vine culture is now placed.* The native grapes—chiefly the Catawba—are entirely used there, and as many parts of the middle

---

* From an interesting letter on this subject which Mr. Longworth has kindly favoured us with, we gladly extract the following, knowing how much it will interest the practical reader.

"I can scarcely now state the present extent of the culture of the grape for wine in this country. We have a large German population who are yearly planting new vineyards, and I believe the Ohio river will be, in the course of the next century, as celebrated for its wine as the Rhine. After 30 years of experience, with vines from Madeira in the south, and the mountains of Jura in the north, and most of the intermediate latitudes, I am satisfied that the foreign vine can never succeed with us. Nor do I believe in its acclimation. I have cultivated the Chasselas for the table for 30 years, and it does not now succeed so well as it did the first few seasons that I had it. I have found two or three foreign varie-

states are quite as favourable as the banks of the Ohio for these varieties, the much greater yield of these grapes leads us to believe that we may even here pursue wine-making profitably.

The vineyard culture of the native grape is very simple

ties that may be worthy of cultivation, and one that may make a wine equal to Madeira, but it produces small wood and will not bear a large crop. It was received from Prince under the name of the Missouri, but it is clearly a foreign grape, and I believe of the *Pineau* family. We must rely on our native grapes, and new varieties raised from their seed. Our best success, with present materials, will be with the Catawba grape, as we can make from it a wine equal to the best Hock, and with a finer aroma. I sent recently a sample of some Catawba wine to New-Orleans, and was offered the highest price of Hock wine if I would forward a quantity for sale.

The Isabella rots with us more than other grapes, and is only fit to make a sweet wine by adding sugar. I have made a fine, white, sweet wine from it, and have samples now 12 years of age. The Ohio grape is, with us, quite as hardy as the Catawba and Isabella. It does not bear to be crowded, but requires the full benefit of the sun and air. I deem it better for the table than for wine, as it is free from the hard pulp common to most of our native grapes.

The cultivation of the grape at Vevay is on the wane, as they cultivate only one variety—the Cape grape—a native sort, otherwise known as the Alexander's, or Schuylkill Muscadell. From it they may make a rough, red, acid wine. This same grape makes a wine resembling, and equal to, the Tenereiffe, when made without being fermented on the skins, and with the addition of brandy as is usual with the Tenereiffe.

I have now 14 vineyards, under the management of Germans and Swiss, and containing about 70 acres. The wine meets a ready sale with our German population, at prices varying from 75 cents to one and a half dollars per gallon, by the quantity.

The grape requires a good soil, and is benefitted by well rotted manure. For aspect I prefer the sides of our hills, but our native grapes would not succeed well in a *dry* sandy soil, particularly the Catawba, which is a cousin german to the old *fox-grape*, that prefers a spot near a stream of water. The north sides of *our* hills are the richest, and I believe they will, as our summers are warm, in the majority of seasons produce the best crops. In my first attempts at vineyard culture, to gratify my Germans, I went to unnecessary expense in deep trenching. In a loose soil, like mine, it can do no good; in a clay soil it is injurious to put the rich soil below and have from one to two feet of clay on the top. The root seldom gets to the rich soil, and grows too near the surface, which should be guarded against, as the fruit then suffers from the drought. Deep ploughing is better, and is not a twentieth part of the expense. Where a hill is steep, trenching and walling—or sod terracing, is necessary.

I believe our best wine will be made in latitudes similar to ours. A location farther north may answer well if the ground be covered with snow all the winter, to protect the vine. It is to this cause that they are indebted for their success in the cultivation of the grape on the Jura mountains, in France. There is little doubt that the grape will bear better with us, and (judging from samples I have had from the first grower at the south,) will make a better wine here than in Carolina.

There was lately published an absurd statement respecting the product of a vineyard at the south—that the product was at the rate of 3,400 gallons of wine to the acre. This arose from a false calculation, made by measuring the yield of a single vine, which grew over the top of a tree, and calculating the product of the vineyard by the space occupied by the root of this vine! One favourable year I selected, from the best part of one of my vineyards, the fourteenth part of an acre, the product of which was 105 gallons—at the rate of 1,470 gallons per acre. The best *crop* I have ever seen, was here, at the vineyard of Mr. Hackinger, a German—about 900 gallons to the acre, from the Catawba grape. It was a truly gratifying sight to see, in the midst of the vintage, his aged father sitting in his arm chair, under the shade of a tree, in the centre of the vineyard, with his bottle and glass "just as he did in Germany."

We generally leave six feet between the rows, and use the plough, setting the plants 3 to 4 feet apart, and training them to stakes about 6 feet high. The Ger-

Strong loamy or gravelly soils are preferable—limestone soils being usually the best—and a *warm, open, sunny exposure* being indispensable. The vines are planted in rows, about six feet apart, and trained to upright stakes or posts as in Europe. The ordinary culture is as simple as that of a field of Indian corn—one man and horse with the plough, and the horse-cultivator, being able to keep a pretty large surface in good order. The annual pruning is performed in winter, top-dressing the vines when it is necessary in the spring; and the summer work, stopping side shoots, thinning, tying, and gathering, being chiefly done by women and children. In the fermentation of the newly made wine lies the chief secret of the *vigneron*, and, much as has been said of this in books, we have satisfied ourselves that careful experiments, or, which is better, a resort to the experience of others, is the only way in which to secure success in the quality of the wine itself.

DISEASES. The mildew, which is troublesome in some districts, is easily prevented by keeping the vine of small size, and by the renewal system of pruning, or, never allowing the vine to bear more than two years on spurs from the same old wood.

The beetles which sometimes infest the grape vines in summer, especially the large brownish yellow vine beetle, (*Pelidnota punctata*,) and the grape-vine flea-beetle (*Haltica chalybea*,) are very destructive to the foliage and buds, and the most effectual remedy is hand-picking when taken in time. But we would also very strongly recommend again the use of open mouthed bottles, half filled, (and kept renewed,) with a mixture of sweetened water and vinegar, and hung here and there among the vines. Indeed, we have seen *bushels* of beetles, and other insects, destroyed in a season, and all injury prevented, simply by the use of such bottles.

VARIETIES. There are yet but few varieties of our native grapes that are really worthy of cultivation. Adlum and Prince, in their treatises, describe quite a large number, but many of these are really quite worthless. In the following list will be found described all that we have yet been able to find of any value. Most of these as the Isabella, Catawba, Alexander's, &c., are no doubt accidental seedlings from the wild Fox-

---

man women and children do most of the labor, in tying the vines, trimming the lateral shoots, topping the fruit branches, etc.

In our first experiments we generally used to add sugar to the juice, but our Germans, and indeed all foreigners, give the wine made without sugar the preference. I have now Catawba wine made without sugar 20 years old, sound and still improving. The Catawba will convert from 8 to 10 oz. to the gallon, but when sugar is added it does not so readily fine itself. When I add sugar I mix it with the must as it comes from the press. The wines our climate will best produce are the dry Hock wines; though, from our dry Catawba wine, a skilful *wine-cooper* can make all the varieties of sparkling Hock, etc., equal to the imported. The best Champagne I have ever drunk was made by one of my German tenants, from the Catawba grape."

grape of the northern states. (*Vitis Labrusca*, L.) While others of a different habit in leaf, and berry, as the Elsingburgh, Ohio, &c., are, perhaps, the offspring of the Frost Grape, (*V. cordifolia*,) or the Summer Grape, (*V. estivalis*.) The most popular American Grapes, as yet, are the Isabella and Catawba. More delicate sorts for the dessert, being free from pulp, are the Ohio, Elsingburgh and Bland. All these grapes require a warm summer to enable them to attain their flavour, which is the reason why, in the cool climate of England, they have been pronounced so " harsh and disagreeable."

Native Grapes.

1. ALEXANDER'S. Thomp. Prin.

Schuylkill Muscadell. *Adlum.*
———— Muscadine.
Cape Grape. }
Spring Mill Constantia. } *of Vevay, Ill.*
Clifton's Constantia. }
Madeira, *of York, Pa.*
Tasker's Grape.
Winne.

This grape, a natural seedling, was first discovered by Mr. Alexander, gardener to Gov. Penn, before the war of the revolution. It is not unfrequently found, as a seedling, from the wild Foxgrape, on the borders of our woods. It is quite sweet when ripe, and makes a very fair wine, but is quite too pulpy and coarse for table use. The bunches are more compact, and the leaves much more *downy*, than those of the Isabella.

Bunches rather compact, not shouldered. Berries of medium size, oval. Skin thick, quite black. Flesh with a very firm pulp, but juicy, and quite sweet and musky, when fully ripe, which it is not till the last of October.

2. BLAND.

Bland's Virginia.
Bland's Madeira.
Bland's Pale Red.
Powell.
Red Suppernong, (*of some.*)

The Bland is one of the best of our native grapes, approaching, in flavour and appearance, the Chasselas grapes of Europe, with very little pulp, and only a slight astringency. It does not ripen well to the north of this, except in favourable situations, and should always be planted in a warm exposure. It is a genuine native sort, (doubtless a natural seedling,) and is said to have been found on the eastern shore of Virginia, by Col. Bland of that state, who presented scions to Mr. Bartram, the botanist, by whom it was first cultivated. The Bland is not a great bearer, but it merits a place in every good garden in this country. The fruit keeps admirably, in jars, for winter use.

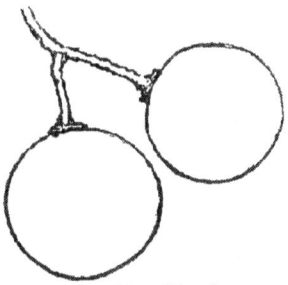

Bunches rather long, loose, and often with small, imperfect berries. Berries, (fig. 96,) round, on long stalks—hanging rather thinly. Skin thin, at first, pale green, but pale red when ripe. Flesh slightly pulpy, of a pleasant, sprightly, delicate flavour, and with little or no musky scent, but a slight astringency. Ripens pretty late. Foliage lighter green than that of the Catawba, smoother, and more delicate.

Fig. 96.   *Bland.*

This vine is quite difficult of propagation by cuttings.

3. CATAWBA.   Adlum. Ken.

Red Muncy.
Catawba Tokay.

This excellent native grape was first introduced to notice by Major Adlum, of Georgetown, D. C., and was found by him in Maryland. It probably has its name from the Catawba river, but it has been found growing at various points from that river to Pennsylvania. It is one of the hardiest, most productive, and excellent of our native sorts, either for wine or table use, and succeeds well in all situations not too cold for grape culture. In habit of growth, it so closely resembles the Isabella that it is difficult to distinguish the two, except in the colour and shape of the fruit. Unless it be very ripe, it is, perhaps, a little more musky in flavour, than the Isabella.

Bunches of medium size, somewhat loose, shouldered. Berries, (fig. 97,) round, (or sometimes slightly oval,) pretty large. Skin rather thick, pale red in the shade, but pretty deep red in the sun, covered with a lilac bloom. Flesh slightly pulpy, juicy, very sweet, with an aromatic, rich, musky flavour. Ripe from the 1st to the

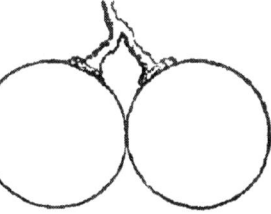

Fig. 97.   *Catawba.*

middle of October, and should be allowed to hang till fully ripe.

The To KALON, is a seedling of this grape raised by the late Dr. Spofford, of Lansingburgh, N. Y. It has no pulp, but it **proves,** with us, too shy a bearer to be worth cultivation.

POND'S SEEDLING is a sub-variety from the neighbourhood of Boston, which ripens earlier than the Catawba, but is also a shy bearer.

4. DIANA.

A seedling of the Catawba, raised by Mrs. Diana Crehore, of Boston, and named by the Massachusetts Horticultural Society. It is said to be of superiour quality, and to ripen a fortnight earlier, which will make it valuable at the north.

Fruit much resembling the Catawba, but paler in colour, being a pale grayish red. Bunches loose. Berry round, almost without pulp, juicy, with a sweet, rich flavour.

5. ELSINBURGH. Ken. Prin. Adlum.

Smart's Elingburg.
Elsenborough.

A very nice little grape for the dessert, perfectly sweet and melting, without pulp, originally brought from a village of this name in Salem co., New-Jersey. It is not a great deal larger than the common Frost grape, in the size of the berry. A moderate, but regular bearer, ripens well, and much esteemed by many for the table.

Bunches pretty large, loose, and shouldered. Berries, (fig. 98,) small, round. Skin thin, black, covered with a blue bloom. Flesh entirely without pulp, melting, sweet, and excellent. The leaves are deeply 5-lobed, pretty dark green, and the wood rather slender, with long joints.

Fig. 98. *Elsing-burgh.*

6. ISABELLA. Prin. Ken. Adlum.

This very popular grape, a native of South Carolina, was brought to the north and introduced to the notice of cultivators. about the year 1818, by Mrs. Isabella Gibbs, the wife of George Gibbs, Esq., in honor of whom it was named. Its great vigour, hardiness, and productiveness, with the least possible care, have caused it to be most widely disseminated. A vine growing here has borne 12 bushels of grape in a single year. It is, perhaps, a little more hardy, and ripens earlier than the Catawba, which renders it valuable at the northern part of this state, or the colder portions of New-England. No farmer's garden, however small, should be without this and the Catawba.

Bunches of good size—five to seven inches long, rather loose, shouldered. Berries, (fig. 99,) oval, pretty large. Skin thick,

dark purple, becoming at last nearly
black, covered with a blue bloom.
Flesh tender, with some pulp, which
nearly dissolves when fully mature ;
juicy, sweet, and rich, with slight
musky aroma.

This grape is frequently picked as
soon as it is well coloured, and long
before it is ripe.

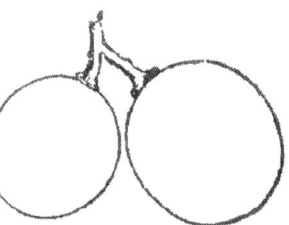

Fig. 99.   *Isabella.*

7. Lenoir.

Sumpter ?
Clarence ?

A very excellent table grape, perhaps superior in flavour for
the dessert to any of the foregoing. It comes, originally, from
Mr. Lenoir, of the Santee River, Carolina, and is believed to be
a seedling raised by him from a seed of one of the Burgundy
grapes. It has very much the habit of a foreign vine, but appears to bear well, and ripen admirably here. The wood is
grayish brown, strong, and long jointed, and, like the Elsingburgh and Ohio grapes should be left rather long in pruning.

Bunches very handsome, large, compact, not much shouldered.
Berries small, round. Skin thin, purple, with a slight bloom.
Flesh tender, melting, (without pulpiness,) sweet, and excellent.

8. Norton's Virginia.   Prin. Ken.

Norton's Seedling.

A native seedling, produced by a cross between the Bland
and Miller's Burgundy, by Dr. N. Norton, of Richmond, Virginia. It is a most productive grape in garden or vineyard,
bearing very large crops (especially at the south, where many
kinds rot,) in all seasons. It has been confounded by some
with Ohio grape, from which it is quite distinct, more pulpy,
and less agreeable for the dessert, though, probably a much
better wine grape.

Bunches long, sometimes eight or nine inches, occasionally
shouldered, somewhat compact. Berries small, round. Skin
thin, dark purple. Flesh pulpy, with a brisk, rather rough flavour. The foliage is light coloured, shaped like the Elsingburgh.
Shoots strong and hardy.

9. Missouri.

Missouri Seedling.

This grape we received from Cincinnati, where it is con

siderably cultivated, and much esteemed in the vineyards, making a wine much resembling Madeira. It was received there from the east, under this name, and we think, may very probably be a seedling from one of the Pineau or Burgundy grapes. It is not very productive, and makes little wood. The latter is grayish, spotted with dark brown specks, short jointed, buds in clusters, double and triple. Leaves deeply cut, trilobed.

Bunches loose, and of moderate size. Berries small, round. Skin thin, almost black, with very little bloom. Flesh tender, with little pulp, sweet, and pleasant, but inferiour to the Ohio for the table.

10. Ohio.

Segar Box Grape.
Longworth's Ohio.

This grape, which has recently attracted a good deal of attention, has a rather singular history. The cuttings, from which all the present stock has originated, were left in a segar box, at the residence of N. Longworth, Esq., Cincinnati, Ohio, during his absence from home, by some person who was not known, and who left no account of them. It is still commonly known as the Segar Box in that vicinity. Subsequent efforts to trace its origin have not been successful, but there is no doubt, from its strong general resemblance to the Elsingburgh, that it is a native. It is a capital dessert fruit, free from pulp, and of excellent flavour, in Cincinnati, but does not maintain that reputation here; it requires a very warm and dry climate to develop its flavour. It ripens early, but we fear it will prove a little tender to the north of this. The wood is strong, long jointed, lighter red than that of the Norton's Virginia, and smooth, with peculiarly pointed buds. Leaves large, trilobed.

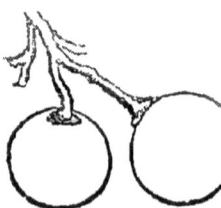

Fig. 100. *Ohio.*

Bunches large and long, from six to ten inches, and often fifteen inches in length, rather loose, tapering, shouldered. Berries, (fig. 100,) small, round. Skin thin, purple, with a blue bloom. Flesh tender, and melting, without any pulp, sweet, and very excellent.

This grape is a good bearer, requires to be well pruned, and the wood laid-in thin and long.

11. Shurtleff's Seedling.

A new variety raised by Dr. S. A. Shurtleff, of Pemberton Hill, near Boston. It is a seedling from the foreign grape, but appears to have a hardier habit than most foreign varieties. But little, however, is yet known of it, as it has not yet been placed in the hands of cultivators generally for trial, but we hope soon to see it disseminated.

Bunches large, often weighing a pound, shouldered. Berries nearly as large as Black Hamburgh, oval, pretty thickly set. Skin thick, light purple, or lilac, (obscurely spotted,) with a grayish bloom. Flesh firm, with a rich, sweet, and very excellent flavour. This fruit ripens early in September, or, in favourable situations the last of August.

12. SCUPPERNONG.   Prin. Adlum.

Fox Grape.
Bull or Bullet.
American Muscadine.   } *of the south.*
Roanoake.
Vitis vulpina.   *Lind.*
—— rotundifolia.   *Michx.*

The Scuppernong grape is a very distinct southern species, found growing wild, from Virginia to Florida, and climbing the tops of the tallest trees. It is easily known from every other grape by the small size of its leaves, which are seldom over two or three inches in diameter, and by their being glossy and smooth on both the under and upper surfaces. These leaves are roundish, and coarsely serrated, and the young shoots are slender; the old wood is smooth, and not shaggy, like that of most vines. This species is diœcious.

We have made several trials with the Scuppernong grape, but find it quite too tender for a northern climate, being killed to the ground by our winters. At the south it is a very hardy, productive, and excellent wine grape. The White and Black Scuppernong scarcely differ, except in the colour of the fruit. The *tendrils* of each correspond in hue with the fruit.

Bunches small, loose, seldom composed of more than six berries. Berries round, large. Skin thick, light green in the white, dark red in the black variety. Flesh quite pulpy, except when very thoroughly ripe, juicy and sweet, but with a strong, musky scent and flavour.

12. WARREN.

A variety recently brought into notice by Mr. Prince, of Flushing, which may prove synonymous with Nos. 7 or 9. We made the following memoranda from an examination of the fruit last season.

Bunches long, loose, slightly shouldered. Berries round, small, of the same size, and form of those of the Elsingburgh, but rather more closely set. Skin thin, dark purple, with but little bloom. Flesh tender, melting, with no pulp, and a very sweet, pleasant flavou-

OTHER WILD VARIETIES. There are many other wild varieties recently introduced into gardens, but which are of little or
no value for the table. Among these, the Cunningham and
Woodson Prince Edward, from Virginia, are pretty good wine
grapes, though the former is a shy bearer. *Gimbrede's Hudson*
and *Ladies'* grapes, as well as the *Hyde's Black*, *Red River*,
Perfumed Red, and several others, are Foxgrapes, with a strong
scent, and harsh flavour, of no value for the dessert, and unworthy of cultivation. The *Troy Grape*, *Hyde's Eliza*, and
some others, are varieties of the Isabella, in no way remarkable.
Worthington and Luffborough are recommended by Adlum for
wine ; we have found them harsh and worthless for the dessert.

*Selection of foreign grapes for hardy culture. Royal Musca-
dine, Early Black July, Early White Malvasie, Black Prince.*

*Selection of foreign grapes for a vinery. Black Hamburgh,
White Muscat of Alexandria, White Frontignan, Royal Muscadine, West's St. Peters, Red Frontignan.*

*Selection of native grapes for a small garden. Catawba,
Bland, Ohio, Lenoir, Isabella.*

CHAPTER XVIII.

THE MULBERRY.

Morus, Tourn. *Urticaceæ*, of botanists.
Murier, of the French; *Maulbeerbaum*, German; *Moro*, Italian; *Morel*, Spanish.

THE Mulberry is a hardy, deciduous fruit tree, but little cultivated in this country, though it is really a very considerable
acquisition to our list of summer fruits, and every garden of
considerable size, ought to contain one or two trees. The fruit
ripens in July, very soon after the season of cherries. It is
rarely picked from the trees, as it falls as soon as ripe, and it is
therefore the custom to keep the surface below it in short turf,
and the fruit is picked from the clean grass. Or, if the surface
is dug ground, it may be sown thickly with cress seed, six weeks
previously to the ripening of the fruit, which will form a temporary carpet of soft verdure.

The RED MULBERRY (*Morus rubra*, L.) is a native species,
more or less common in our woods, with large, rough, heart-
shaped or lobed leaves. The fruit is about an inch long, and
very pleasant and palatable—though much inferiour to the following sort. It bears transplanting well, or is easiy raised

from seed, and may, undoubtedly, be greatly impr ved by repeated reproduction in this way. As it forms a large ornamental tree with a fine spreading head, 40 feet high, it is wel'
deserving a place on the lawn, or near the house, in ornamental
plantations.

JOHNSON MULBERRY. We have lately received from Professor Kirtland, of Cleveland, one of the most intelligent horticulturists in the country, this new variety of our native Mulberry,
the fruit of which is said to be of extra large size and superior
flavour.

Fruit very large, oblong, cylindric ; blackish colour, sub-
acid, and of mild, agreeable flavour. Growth of the wood
strong and irregular. Leaves uncommonly large.

The BLACK MULBERRY, or English Mulberry, (*Morus nigra*,
L.) is a very celebrated old fruit tree, originally from Asia,
more or less commonly cultivated in all parts of Europe, but
yet quite rare in this country. Its growth is slow, and it seldom
attains a height of more than 12 or 15 feet, forming a low,
branching tree, with lobed leaves, but it is very long lived, and
there is a specimen in England, at the seat of the duke of Northumberland, 300 years old. In this country it is scarcely
hardy enough for the eastern states ; but it thrives pretty well
here, and we have seen very fine crops on a tree in a sheltered
position, at Hyde Park, on the Hudson, 80 miles above New-
York. The fruit is incomparably larger and finer than that of
the Red Mulberry, being an inch and a half long, and nearly
an inch across—black, and of delicious flavour.

There are many varieties of the White Mulberry, commonly
cultivated for silk, but which produce fruit of no value.

The best soil for the Mulberry, is a rich, deep, sandy loam.
The tree requires little or no pruning, and is of very easy culture. It is usually propagated by cuttings, three feet long,
planted in the spring, half their depth in the ground ; cuttings
made of pieces of the roots will also send up shoots and become
plants.

CHAPTER XIX.

NUTS.

The EUROPEAN WALNUT, (*Juglans regia*, L.; *Noyer*, **of the**
French ; *Walnaussbaum*, German ; *Nocil*, Italian ; and *Nogal*,
Spanish ;) better known here as the *Madeira Nut*, is a fine lofty

growing tree, with a handsome spreading head, and bearing crops of large and excellent nuts, enclosed like those of our native black walnut in a simple husk. It stands the winter very well here, and to the south of this it would undoubtedly be a profitable fruit to plant for the market. The fruit in a green state is very highly esteemed for pickling, and the great quantities of the ripe nuts annually imported and sold here, prove the estimation in which they are held for the table. There are several varieties reputed to be of rather finer quality, which, however, have not displaced the original species, even in the gardens of Europe, and have not yet borne fruit here.

This tree is usually propagated by the seed, and transplanted from the nurseries when from three to six feet high. But it may also be grafted, with due care, on the common hickory nut.

The HICKORY NUT (*Carya alba*,) or shell-bark. The Black Walnut (*Juglans nigra*,) and the Butternut, (*J. cineria*,) are native nut-bearing trees, common in our forests, and too well known to need description here. There are occasionally found in the woods, accidental varieties of the *shell-bark hickory*, of much larger size and finer flavour than the common species, which are highly worthy of cultivation, as we confess, to our own taste, this nut is much superiour to the European walnut. There is indeed no doubt, that with a little care in reproduction by seed, the shell-bark may be trebled in size, and greatly improved in flavour.

The FILBERT, (*Noisette*, of the French; *Nassbaum*, German; *Avellano*, Spanish;) is an improved variety of the common hazel-nut of the woods of Europe, *Corylus avellana*, L.) The fruit is three or four times as large as that of our common hazel-nut, and from its size and excellent flavour is admired for the dessert. The old Spanish filbert common in many of our gardens, is a worthless, nearly barren variety, but we have found the better English sorts productive and excellent in this climate, and at least a few plants of them, should have a place in all our gardens. They are generally raised from layers, made in the spring, but they may also be grafted readily on the common hazel-nut, or the Spanish nut. When planted out they should not be permitted to sucker, and should be kept in the form of bushes with low heads, branching out about two feet from the ground, and they should be annually pruned somewhat like the gooseberry, so as to preserve a rather thin, open head—shortening back the extremities of the young shoots one half, every spring.

The following are the best filberts known.

1. COSFORD. (Thomp. P. Mag.) Nut large, oblong; husk hairy; shell remarkably thin, and kernel of excellent flavour. A good bearer.

2. FRIZZLED. (Thomp. P. Mag.) Easily known by its hand-

some, deeply cut husk. Nut of medium size, oval, compressed; husk hairy; shell thick; kernel sweet and good.

3. NORTHAMPTONSHIRE PROLIFIC. (Thomp.) Ripens early. Nut of medium size, oblong, husk hairy; shell thick.

4. RED FILBERT. Easily known from other sorts, by the crimson skin of the kernel. Fruit of medium size, ovate. Shell thick. Kernel with a peculiar, excellent flavour.

5. WHITE FILBERT. (Thomp. Lind.) Resembles the last, but with a light yellow or white skin. The tree is also quite bushy. Nuts ovate. Husk long and tubular.

The English generally call those varieties with long husks, *filberts*, (*full-beards*,) and those with short husks, simply *nuts*.

The CHESTNUT, (*Castanea vesca*, W.; *Chatagnier*, of the French; *Castainenbaum*, German; *Castagno*, Italian;) is one of our loftiest forest trees, common in most parts of the United States and Europe, and bearing excellent nuts. The foreign variety best known in this country, is the Spanish Chestnut, with fruit nearly as large as that of the Horse-Chestnut, and which is excellent when boiled or roasted. It thrives very well here, but is not quite hardy to the north or east of this. One or two English varieties have been produced, of considerable excellence, among which, the Downton is considered the best. The French cultivate a dozen or more varieties of greater or less excellence, but though some of them have been introduced, we have not yet fairly tested them in this country.

The CHINQUAPIN, or Dwarf Chestnut, common in some parts of the middle and southern states, is a dwarf species of the chestnut, usually growing not more than six to ten feet high, and bearing fruit of half the size as the common chestnut, with the same flavour. It is worth a place in a small fruit garden, as a curiosity.

All the chestnuts are very easily cultivated in any good, light soil, and may be propagated by grafting, and by sowing the seeds.

CHAPTER XX.

THE PLUM.

Prunus domestica, L. *Rosaceæ*, of botanists.
Prunier, of the French; *Pflaumenbaum*, German; *Prugno*, Italian; *Ciruelo*, Spanish.

THE original parent of most of the cultivated plums of our gardens is a native of Asia and the southern parts of Europe, but it has become naturalized in this country, and in many parts of it is produced in the greatest abundance.* That the soil and climate of the middle states are admirably suited to this fruit is sufficiently proved by the almost spontaneous production of such varieties as the Washington, Jefferson, Lawrence's Favourite, etc. ; sorts which equal or surpass in beauty or flavour the most celebrated plums of France or England.

Uses. The finer kinds of plums are beautiful dessert fruits, of rich and luscious flavour. They are not, perhaps, so entirely wholesome as the peach or the pear, as, from their somewhat cloying and flatulent nature, unless when very perfectly ripe, they are more likely to disagree with weak stomachs.

For the kitchen the plum is also very highly esteemed, being prized for tarts, pies, sweetmeats, etc. In the south of France an excellent spirit is made from this fruit fermented with honey. In the western part of this state, where they are very abundant, they are halved, stoned, and dried in the sun or ovens, in large quantities, and are then excellent for winter use. For eating, the plum should be allowed to hang on the tree till perfectly ripe, and the fruit will always be finer in proportion as the tree has a more sunny exposure. The size and quality of the fruit is always greatly improved by thinning the fruit when it is half grown. Indeed to prevent rotting and to have this fruit in its highest perfection, no two plums should be allowed to touch each other while growing, and those who are willing to take this pains, are amply repaid by the superior quality of the fruit.

One of the most important forms of the plum in commerce is that of *prunes*, as they are exported from France to every part of the world. We quote the following interesting account of the best mode of preparing prunes from the *Arboretum Britanicum*.

The best *prunes* are made near Tours, of the St. Catherine

---

* There are three species of wild plum indigenous to this country—of tolerable flavour, but seldom cultivated in our gardens. They are the following.

I. The CHICKASAW PLUM. (*Prunus Chicasa*, Michaux.) Fruit about three fourths of an inch in diameter, round, and red or yellowish red, of a pleasant, sub-acid flavour, ripens pretty early. Skin thin. The branches are thorny, the head rather bushy, with narrow lanceolate, serrulate leaves, looking at a little distance, somewhat like those of a peach tree. It usually grows about 12 or 14 feet high, but on the Prairies of Arkansas it is only 3 or 4 feet high, and in this form it is also common in Texas. The DWARF TEXAS PLUM described by Kenrick is only this species. It is quite ornamental.

II. WILD RED OR YELLOW PLUM. (*P. americana*, Marshall.) Fruit roundish-oval, skin thick, reddish orange, with a juicy, yellow, sub-acid pulp. The leaves are ovate, coarsely serrate, and the old branches rough and somewhat thorny. Grows in hedges, and by the banks of streams, from Canada to the Gulf of Mexico. Tree from 10 to 15 feet high. Fruit ripens in July and August.

III. The BEACH PLUM, or Sand Plum. (*P. maratima*, Wang.) A low shrub, with stout straggling branches, found mostly on the sandy sea-coast, from Massachusetts to Virginia, and seldom ripening well elsewhere. Fruit roundish, scarcely an inch in diameter, red or purple, covered with a bloom ; pleasant, but somewhat astringent. Leaves oval, finely serrate.

plum and the prune d'Agen ; and the best *French plums* (so-called in England,) are made in Provence, of the Perdrigon blanc, the Brignole, and the prune d'Ast ; the Provence plums being most fleshy, and having always most bloom. Both kinds are, however, made of these and other kinds of plums, in various parts of France. The plums are gathered when just ripe enough to fall from the trees on their being slightly shaken. They are then laid, separately, on frames, or sieves, made of wicker-work or laths, and exposed for several days to the sun, till they become as soft as ripe medlars. When this is the case, they are put into a spent oven, shut quite close, and left there for twenty-four hours ; they are then taken out, and the oven being slightly reheated, they are put in again when it is rather warmer than it was before. The next day they are again taken out, and turned by slightly shaking the sieves. The oven is heated again, and they are put in a third time, when the oven is one-fourth degree hotter than it was the second time. After remaining twenty-four hours, they are taken out, and left to get quite cold. They are then rounded, an operation which is performed by turning the stone in the plum without breaking the skin, and pressing the two ends together between the thumb and finger. They are then again put upon the sieves, which are placed in an oven, from which the bread has been just drawn. The door of the oven is closed, and the crevices are stopped round it with clay or dry grass. An hour afterwards, the plums are taken out, and the oven is again shut with a cup of water in it, for about two hours. When the water is so warm as just to be able to bear the finger in it, the prunes are again placed in the oven, and left there for twenty-four hours, when the operation is finished, and they are put loosely into small, long, and rather deep boxes, for sale. The common sorts are gathered by shaking the trees ; but the finer kinds, for making French plums, must be gathered in the morning, before the rising of the sun, by taking hold of the stalk, between the thumb and finger, without touching the fruit, and laid gently on a bed of vine-leaves in a basket. When the baskets are filled, without the plums touching each other, they are removed to the fruit room, where they are left for two or three days exposed to the sun and air ; after which, the same process is employed as for the others ; and in this way the delicate bloom is retained on the fruit, even when quite dry.

PROPAGATION AND CULTURE. The plum is usually propagated in this country by sowing the seeds of any common free growing variety, (avoiding the damsons which are not readily worked,) and budding them when two years old, with the finer sorts. The stones should be planted as soon as gathered, in broad drills, (as in planting peas,) but about an inch and a half deep. In good soil the seedlings will reach eighteen inches or two feet

ieight, the next season, and in the autumn or the ensuing
spring, they may be taken from the seed beds, their tap roots
reduced, and all that are of suitable size, planted at once in the
nursery rows, the smaller ones being thickly bedded until after
another season's growth.

The stocks planted out in the nursery will, ordinarily, be ready
for working about the ensuing midsummer, and, as the plum is
quite difficult to bud in this dry climate, if the exact season is
not chosen, the budder must watch the condition of the trees,
and insert his buds as early as they are sufficiently firm,—say,
in this neighbourhood, about the 10th of July.   Insert the buds,
if possible, on the north side of the stock, that being more protected from the sun, and tie the bandage rather more tightly
than for other trees.

The English propagate very largely by layers three varieties
of the common plum—the *Muscle*, the *Brussels* and the *Pear*
Plum, which are almost exclusively employed for stocks with
them.   But we have not found these stocks superiour to the
seedlings raised from our common plums, (the Blue Gage,
Horse-plum, &c.,) so abundant in all our gardens.   For dwarfing, the seedlings of the Mirabelle are chiefly employed.

Open standard culture, is the universal mode in America, as
the plum is one of the hardiest of fruit trees.   It requires little or no pruning, beyond that of thinning out a crowded head,
or taking away decayed or broken branches, and this should be
done before midsummer, to prevent the flow of gum.   Old trees
that have become barren, may be renovated by heading them
in pretty severely, covering the wounds with our solution of
gum shellac, and giving them a good top dressing at the roots.

SOIL.   The plum will grow vigorously in almost every part
of this country, but it only bears its finest and most abundant
crops in heavy loams, or in soils in which there is a considerable mixture of clay.   In sandy soils, the tree blossoms and
sets plentiful crops, but they are rarely perfected, falling a prey
to the curculio, an insect that harbors in the soil, and seems to
find it difficult to penetrate or live in one of a heavy texture,
while a warm, light, sandy soil, is exceedingly favorable to its
propagation.   It is also, undoubtedly true, that a heavy soil is
naturally the most favourable one.   The surprising facility with
which superior new varieties are raised merely by ordinary reproduction from seed, in certain parts of the valley of the Hudson, as at Hudson, or near Albany, where the soil is quite
clayey, and also the delicious flavour and great productiveness and health of the plum tree there almost without any care,
while in adjacent districts of rich sandy land it is a very uncertain bearer, are very convincing proofs of the great importance
of clayey soil for this fruit.

Where the whole soil of a place is light and sandy, we would

23

recommend the employment of pure yellow loam or yellow clay, in the place of manure, when preparing the border or spaces for planting the plum. Very heavy clay, burned slowly by mixing it in large heaps with brush or faggots, is at once an admirable manure and alterative for such soils. Swamp muck is also one of the best substances, and especially that from salt water marshes.

Common salt we have found one of the best fertilizers for the plum tree. It not only greatly promotes its health and luxuriance, but from the dislike which most insects have to this substance, it drives away or destroys most of those to which the plum is liable. The most successful plum grower in our neighbourhood, applies, with the best results, half a peck of coarse salt to the surface of the ground under each bearing tree, annually, about the first of April.

INSECTS AND DISEASES. There are but two drawbacks to the cultivation of the plum in the United States, but they are in some districts so great as almost to destroy the value of this tree. These are the *curculio*, and the *knots*.

The curculio, or plum-weevil, (*Rhynchænus Nenuphar,*) is the uncompromising foe of all smooth stone fruits. The cultivator of the Plum, the Nectarine, and the Apricot, in many parts of the country, after a flattering profusion of snowy blossoms and an abundant promise in the thickly set young crops of fruit, has the frequent mortification of seeing nearly all, or indeed, often the whole crop, fall from the trees when half or two-thirds grown.

If he examines these falling fruits, he will perceive on the surface of each, not far from the stalk, a small semi-circular scar. This star is the crescent-shaped insignia of that little Turk, the curculio; an insect so small, as perhaps, to have escaped his observation for years, unless particularly drawn to it but which nevertheless appropriates to himself the whole product of a tree, or an orchard of a thousand trees.

The habits of this curculio, or plum-weevil, are not yet fully and entirely ascertained. But careful observation has resulted in establishing the following points in its history.

Fig. 101. *The curculio, and its mark.*

The plum-weevil is a small, dark brown beetle, with spots of white, yellow, and black. Its length is scarcely one-fifth of an inch. On its back are two black humps, and it is furnished with a pretty long, curved throat and snout, which, when it is at rest, is bent between the forelegs. It is also provided with two wings with which it flies through the air. How far this insect flies is yet a disputed point, some cultivators affirming that it scarcely goes farther than a single tree, and others believing that it flies over a whole neighbourhood. Our own observation inclines us to the belief that this insect emigrates just in proportion as it finds in more or less abundance the tender fruit for depositing its eggs. Very rarely do we see more than one puncture in a plum, and, if the insects are abundant, the trees of a single spot will not afford a sufficient number for the purpose ; then there is little doubt (as we have seen them flying through the air,) that the insect flies farther in search of a larger supply. But usually, we think it remains nearly in the same neighbourhood, or migrates but slowly.

About a week or two after the blossoms have fallen from the trees, if we examine the fruit of the plum in a district where this insect abounds, we shall find the small, newly formed fruit, beginning to be punctured by the proboscis of the plum-weevil. The insect is so small and shy, that unless we watch closely it is very likely to escape our notice. But if we strike or shake the tree suddenly, it will fall in considerable numbers on the ground, drawn up as if dead, and resembling a small raisin, or, perhaps more nearly, a ripe hemp seed. From the first of April until August, this insect may be found, though we think its depredations on fruit, and indeed its appearance in any quantity, is confined to the month of May in this climate. In places where it is very abundant, it also attacks to some extent the cherry, the peach, and even the apple.

Early in July the punctured plums begin to fall rapidly from the tree. The egg deposited in each, at first invisible, has become a white grub or larva, which slowly eats its way towards the stone or pit. As soon as it reaches this point, the fruit falls to the ground. Here, if left undisturbed, the grub soon finds its way into the soil.

There, according to most cultivators of fruit, and to our own observations, the grubs or larvæ remain till the ensuing spring, when in their perfect form they again emerge as beetles and renew their ravages on the fruit. It is true that Harris, and some other naturalists, have proved that the insect does sometimes undergo its final transformation and emerge from the ground in twenty days, but we are inclined to the opinion that this only takes place with a small portion of the brood, which, perhaps, have penetrated but a very short distance below the surface of the soil. These making their appearance in midsummer, and finding no young fruit, deposit their eggs in the young branches of trees, etc. But it is undeniable that the season of the plum-weevil is early spring, and that most of the larvæ which produce this annual swarm, remain in the soil during the whole period intervening since the fall of the previous year's fruit.

There are several modes of destroying this troublesome insect. Before detailing them, we will again allude to the fact, that we have never known an instance of its being troublesome

in a heavy soil. Almost always the complaint comes from portions of country where the soil is light and sandy. The explanation of this would seem to be that the compact nature of a clayey
soil is not favourable to the passage or life of this insect, while
the warm and easily permeable surface of sandy land nurses
every insect through its tender larvæ state. Plum trees growing in hard trodden court-yards, usually bear plentiful crops,
Following these hints some persons have deterred the plum-
weevil by paving beneath the trees ; and we have lately seen a
most successful experiment which consisted in spreading beneath the tree as far as the branches extended a mortar made
of stiff clay about the thickness of two or three inches—which
completely prevented the descent of the insect into the earth.
This is quickly and easily applied, and may therefore be renewed every season until it is no longer found necessary.

The other modes of destroying the plum-weevil are the following :—

1. *Shaking the tree and killing the beetles.* Watch the young
fruit, and you will perceive when the insect makes its appearance, by its punctures upon them. Spread some sheets under
the tree, and strike the trunk pretty sharply several times with
a *wooden mallet.* The insects will quickly fall, and should be
killed immediately. This should be repeated daily for a week,
or so long as the insects continue to make their appearance.
Repeated trials have proved, beyond question, that this rather
tedious mode, is a very effectual one if persisted in.* Coops of
chickens placed about under the trees at this season will assist
in destroying the insects.

2. *Gathering the fruit and destroying the larvæ.* As the insect, in its larvæ or grub form, is yet within the plums when
they fall prematurely from the tree, it is a very obvious mode of
exterminating the next year's brood to gather these fallen fruits,
daily, and feed them to swine, boil, or otherwise destroy them.
In our own garden, where several years ago we suffered by the
plum-weevil, we have found that this practice, pursued for a
couple of seasons, has been pretty effectual. Others have reported less favourably of it ; but this, we think, arose from their
trying it too short a time, in a soil and neighbourhood where the
insect is very abundant, and where it consequently had sought
extensively other kinds of fruit besides the plum.

* Merely *shaking* the tree is not sufficient. The following memorandum, as additional proof, we quote from the Genesee Farmer. "Under a tree in a remote
part of the fruit garden, having spread the sheets, I made the following experiment. On *shaking* the tree well I caught five curculios ; on jarring it with the
hand I caught twelve more ; and on striking the tree with a stone, eight more
dropped on the sheets. I was now convinced that I had been in error ; and calling
in assistance, and using a hammer to jar the tree violently, we caught in less
than an hour, more than two hundred and sixty of these insects." We will add to
this, that to prevent injury to the tree a large wooden mallet should be substituted
for a hammer, and it is better if a thick layer of cloth is bound over its head.

A more simple and easy way of covering the difficulty, where there is a plum orchard or enclosure, is that of turning in swine and fowls during the whole season, when the stung plums are dropping to the ground. The fruit, and the insects contained in it, will thus be devoured together. This is an excellent expedient for the farmer, who bestows his time grudgingly on the cares of the garden.

3. *The use of salt.* A good deal of attention has lately been drawn to the use of common salt, as a remedy for the curculio. Trials have been made with this substance in various parts of the country, where scarcely a ripe plum was formerly obtained, with the most complete success. On the other hand, some persons after testing it, have pronounced it of no value. Our own experience is greatly in favour of its use. We believe that, properly applied, it is an effectual remedy against the curculio, while it also promotes the growth of the tree, and keeps the soil in that state most congenial to its productiveness. The failures that have arisen in its use, have, doubtless, grown out of an imperfect application, either in regard to the quantity or the time of applying it.

In the directions usually given, it seems only considered necessary to apply salt, pretty plentifully, at any season. If the soil be thoroughly saturated with salt, it is probable that it would destroy insects therein, in any stage of their growth. But, though the plum tree seems fond of saline matter, (and one of the most successful experimenters applied strong fish brine, at the rate of three or four pails full to a tree of moderate size,) it must be confessed this is a somewhat dangerous mode, as the roots are forced to receive a large supply of so powerful an agent at once.

The best method of applying salt against the plum-weevil is that of strewing it pretty thickly over the surface, *when the punctured plums commence dropping.* The surface of the ground should be made smooth and hard, and fine packing salt may then be evenly spread over it, as far as the branches extend, and about a fourth of an inch in depth. Should the weather be fine, this coat will last until the fruit infected has all fallen; should it be dissolved or carried off by showers, it must be replaced directly. The larvæ or grubs of the weevil, in this most tender state, emerging from the plum to enter the ground, will fall a prey to the effect of the salt before they are able to reach the soil. If this is carefully and generally practised, we have little doubt of its finally ridding the cultivator of this troublesome enemy, even in the worst districts and soils.

The knots, or black gum. In some parts of the country this is a most troublesome disease, and it has, in neighbourhoods where it has been suffered to take its course, even destroyed the whole race of plum trees.

23*

The knots is a disease attacking the bark and wood. The former at first becomes swollen, afterwards bursts, and, finally, assumes the appearance of large, irregular, black lumps, with a hard, cracked, uneven surface, quite dry within. The passage of the sap upwards, becomes stopped by the compression of the branch by the tumor, and, finally, the poison seems to dissemi nate itself by the downward flow of the sap through the whole trunk, breaking out in various parts of it.

The sorts of plum most attacked by this disease, are those with purple fruit, and we have never known the green or yellow fruited varieties infected, until the other sorts had first become filled with the knots. The common horse plum, and damson, appear to be the first to fall a prey to it, and it is more difficult to eradicate it from them, than from most other sorts. The common Morella cherry is, also, very often injured by the same disease in Pennsylvania.

There is yet some doubt respecting the precise cause of these knotty excrescences, though there is every reason to think it is the work of an insect. Professor Peck and Dr. Harris believe that they are caused by the same curculio or plum-weevil that stings the fruit ; the second brood of which, finding no fruit ready, choose the branches of this tree and the cherry. This observation would seem to be confirmed by the fact that the grubs or larvæ of the plum-weevil are frequently found in these warts, and that the beetles have been seen stinging the branches.

On the other hand, the following facts are worthy of attention. First, in some parts of the country, where the curculio has been troublesome for many years, the knots have never been known. Secondly, in many cases, the knots have been abun- dant on plum trees, when the fruit was entirely fair and unin- jured by the curculio, even upon the same branches.

These facts seem so irreconcilable with the opinion that the curculio produces both these effects, that we rather incline at present to the belief, that though the curculio deposits its eggs in the tumors on the branches while they are yet soft and tender, yet it is not to the curculio, but to some other insect or cause, that we owe this unsightly disease.

Practically, however, this is of little account. The experi- ence of many persons, besides ourselves, has proved, most satis- factorily, that it is easy to extirpate this malady, if it is taken in season, and unremittingly pursued. As early as possible in the spring, the whole of the infected trees should be examined, and every branch and twig that shows a tumor, should be cut off, and immediately burned. Whatever may be the insect, we thus destroy it, and, as experience has taught us that the malady spreads rapidly, we will thus effectually prevent its increase. If the trees are considerably attacked by it, it will probably be necessary to go over them again, about the middle of May, but, usually, once a year will be sufficient. If any of the trees are very much covered with these knots, it is better to head back the shoots severely, or dig them up and burn them outright, and it will be necessary to prevail on your neighbours, if they are near ones, to enter into the plan, or your own labors will be of little value. Pursue this simple and straightforward practice, for two or three seasons, (covering any large wounds made, with the solution of gum shellac,) and the knots will be found to disappear, the curculio to the contrary notwithstanding.

VARIETIES. There are now a pretty large number of fine plums, and some most important additions have been made by the seedlings raised in this country. The Green Gage still stands at the head of the list for high flavour, though several other sorts are nearly or quite equal to it. The Washington, the Jefferson and the Columbia, are among the largest and most beautiful ; and Coe's Golden Drop and Roe's Autumn Gage, are very desirable for their late maturity.

In describing plums, the surface of the young wood, when just ripened, is an important character; as it is *smooth*, in some varieties. and *downy*, or covered with soft hairs, in others. In some varieties, the flesh *parts* from the stone, while in others, it *ad-heres*. And, finally, the depressed line or channel which runs down one side of the exterior surface of the plum, is called the *suture*, and the prominence or absence of this feature enables us to distinguish many kinds at first sight.

Class I.   Green, White, or Yellow Plums.

---

1. AUTUMN GAGE.

Roe's Autumn Gage.

A new plum, raised by Wm. Roe, Esq., of Newburgh, of good quality, a very abundant bearer, and so late in its maturity, as to be valuable. The tree forms a spreading head, with regular, pointed, ovate leaves ; the branches drooping with the weight of the fruit, which is in perfection about the middle of September.

Branches smooth. Fruit medium size, oval, rather broadest towards the stalk. Stalk three-fourths of an inch long, inserted without any de-

Fig. 102   *Autumn Gage.*

pression. Skin pale yellow, covered with thin whitish bloom. Flesh greenish yellow, separating from the stone ; juicy, sweet, and of delicate, pleasant flavour. Stone long, compressed, pointed at both ends.

2. APRICOT.   Lind   Miller.

Apricot Plum of Tours.
Abricoteé de Tours. ⎱
Abricotee.   ⎰ *Duh.*
Yellow Apricot.

Branches quite downy, nearly white. Fruit above medium size, roundish, with a deep suture or furrow. Stalk very short, seldom half an inch long. Skin yellow, dotted and tinged with red on the sunny side, covered with a white bloom Flesh yellow, rather firm, separates from the stone ; slightly bitter, until fully ripe, when it is melting, juicy, and high flavoured. Ripe the middle of August.

This is the true old Apricot plum of Duhamel. The Apricot plum of Thomson is an inferiour, clingstone, oval fruit. (with *smooth* branches,) fit only for cooking.

3. BYFIELD   Man.

This plum, not having yet borne fruit with us, we can only give its character from the MSS. of Mr. Manning.

Branches smooth Fruit small, round ; suture a mere line. Stalk half an inch long, set in an even basin. Skin light yellow, with red spots around the stem. Flesh yellow, of good flavour, adheres to the stone, which is thick. Middle to last of August.

4. BUEL'S FAVOURITE.

An excellent new plum, raised by that successful grower Isaac Denniston, of Albany, and named after his friend, the distinguished agriculturist, Judge Buel.

Branches smooth, reddish. Fruit pretty large, ovate, broadest towards the stalk. Suture quite distinct for half the circumference. Stalk nearly three quarters of an inch long, rather stout, slightly inserted. Skin pale green, thickly sprinkled with lighter dots, and speckled with a little red next the stalk. Flesh greenish-yellow, rather firm, juicy, and quite rich and high flavoured, adheres to the stone, which is long and pointed. Last of August.

5. BINGHAM. §Man. Ken. Thomp.

A native fruit, originally from Pennsylvania, and named after the Bingham family, but better known now near Boston, where it is very popular.

Fruit large, handsome, productive, and excellent. Branches downy. Fruit an inch and three fourths long, oval, rather widest towards the stalk. Skin deep yellow, somewhat spotted with rich red on the sunny side. Stalk slightly inserted. Flesh yellow, adhering to the stone, juicy, and of rich and delicious flavour. Last of August and first of September.

6. BLEECKER'S GAGE. § Man.

German Gage.

A fruit of the first quality, and the most popular plum in the northern and western portion of this state, being not only excellent, but remarkably hardy, and a good and regular bearer. It was raised by the late Mrs. Bleecker, of Albany, about 30 years ago, from a prune pit given her by the Rev. Mr. Dull, of

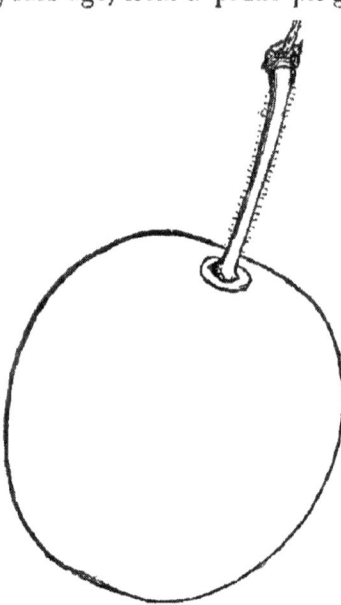

Kingston, N. Y., which he received from Germany. The original tree still stands in her garden.

It ripens the last of August, from a week to two weeks later than our Yellow Gage. Branches downy. Fruit of medium size, roundish-oval, very regular. Suture scarcely perceptible. Stalk quite long, an inch or more, straight and pretty stout, downy, slightly inserted. Skin yellow, with numerous imbedded white specks, and a thin white bloom. Flesh yellow, rich, sweet, and luscious in flavour. Separates almost entirely from the stone, which is pointed at both ends. Leaves dark green. Easily distinguished from Yellow Gage by its longer and stouter stalk.

Fig. 103. *Bleecker's Gage.*

7. COE'S GOLDEN DROP. Thomp. Lind. P. Mag.

Bury Seedling.
Coe's Imperial.
New Golden Drop.
Fair's Golden Drop.
Golden Gage.

Coe's Golden Drop is worthy of its name, being the largest, most beautiful, and delicious of late plums. It succeeds admirably in the middle states, ripening from the middle to the last of September. It bears abundantly, keeps well, and frequently grows larger than the Magnum Bonum. No garden is complete without it. It is an English variety, raised by a market gardener, in Suffolk, whose name it bears.

Branches smooth. Fruit of the largest size, oval, with a well marked suture, on one side of which it is a little more swollen than the other, the outline narrowing towards the stalk. Skin light yellow, with a number of rich, dark red spots on the sunny side. Stalk nearly an inch long, rather stiff, set on the end of the fruits. Flesh yellow, rather firm, adhering closely to the stone, which is quite

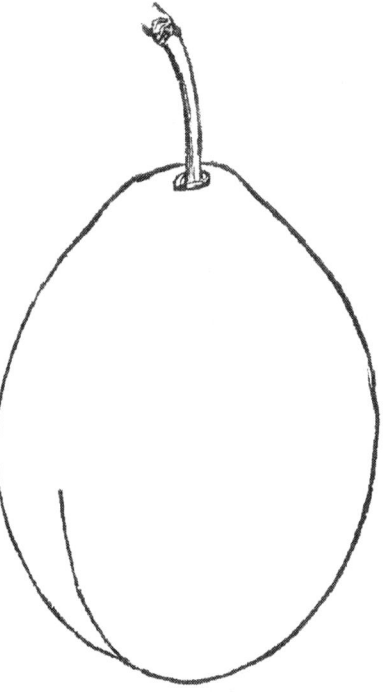

Fig. 104. *Coe's Golden Drop.*

pointed. Flavour rich, sweet, and delicious.

8. Drap d'Or. Thomp. Lind. Lang.

Mirabelle Double. *Duh.*
Mirabelle Grosse.
Yellow Perdrigon.

The Drap d'Or, or Cloth of Gold, Plum is about the size and figure of the Green Gage, but of a fine golden yellow and ripens a week earlier.

Branches slightly downy. Fruit below medium size, round, with an indistinct suture and a dimpled or pitted apex. Stalk slender, half an inch long. Skin rich bright yellow, with a few crimson specks when fully exposed. Flesh yellow, sugary and rich, but sometimes a little dry ; separates freely from the stone. Early in August.

9. Downton Imperatrice. Thomp. Lind.

A hybrid, raised by Mr. Knight, from the White Magnum Bonum, fertilized by the Blue Imperatrice. A strong, upright growing tree, and a brisk, sprightly flavoured fruit. Ripens late, and is valuable for preserving.

Branches long, smooth. Fruit of medium size, oval, narrow. Ing a little to the stalk. Skin pale yellow, quite thin. Flesh yellow, melting and sweet when fully ripe, with a little acidity before; adhering to the stone. Ripens last of September, and hangs some time on the tree.

10. DENNISTON'S ALBANY BEAUTY.

A good variety. Branches slightly downy. Fruit rather below medium size, roundish-oval, with an obscure suture. Skin pale whitish-green, marked with numerous small purplish dots, and covered with a thin bloom. Stalk an inch or more long, slender, very slightly inserted. Flesh yellow, moderately juicy, rich, and sweet, separates from the stone, which is small and pointed. Ripe 24th of August.

11. DENNISTON'S SUPERB. §

An excellent seedling, from Mr. Denniston's famous plum orchard, near Albany, N. Y., of the Green Gage family, a third larger than the latter variety, and nearly as rich in flavour.

Branches downy. Fruit round, a little flattened, and having a distinct suture, often extending quite round the fruit. Skin pale yellowish-green, marked with a few large purple blotches and dots, and overspread with a thin bloom. Stalk rough, three fourths of an inch long, set in a cavity of moderate size. Flesh very thick, (the stone being small,) moderately juicy, with a rich vinous flavour. Stone parts readily, and is roundish and thick. Middle and last of August.

12. DANA'S YELLOW GAGE. Man.

A New-England variety, raised by the Rev. Mr. Dana, of Ipswich, Mass. It is a very hardy and healthy tree, and bears abundantly. The flavour good, and rather more sprightly than our common Yellow Gage, though not so luscious.

Fruit of medium size, oval, pale yellow, with a very thin bloom, the skin clouded like that of the Imperial Gage. Flesh adheres to the stone, juicy, sweet, with a lively, peculiar flavour. Last of August and first of September.

13. EMERALD DROP.

A variety produced in our own gardens, from a stone of the Washington. It is a rich juicy plum, nearly first rate, and a most abundant bearer.

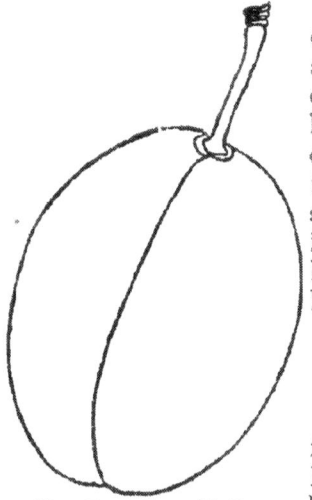

Branches long and smooth. Fruit of medium size, long-oval. Suture strongly marked, and the fruit larger on one of its sides. Skin pale yellowish-green, sometimes dull green only, in the shade. Stalk three-fourths of an inch long, inserted with scarcely any depression. Flesh greenish-yellow, very juicy and rich, adheres somewhat to the stone, which is long and pointed. Last of August.

14. Ghiston's Early.

A large and handsome (native?) fruit, resembling, a good deal, the Magnum Bonum or Yellow Egg Plum, but a freestone. Branches smooth,

Fig. 105. *Emerald Drop.*

short-jointed. Fruit large, oval, skin clear yellow, with a light bloom. Flesh yellow, separates from the stone, of pleasant flavour. Middle of August.

15. Green Gage. § Lang. Lind. Thomp.

Bruyn Gage.		Reine Claude.	
Bradford Gage,		Grosse Reine Claude.	
Schuyler's Gage !		Grosse Reine.	
Wilmot's Green Gage.		Damas Vert.	*of various*
———— New Green Gage.	*of some*	Sucrin Vert.	*French*
———— late Green Gage.	*English*	Vert Bonne.	*gardens.*
Isleworth Green Gage.	*gardens.*	Abricot Vert.	
Burgnon Gage.		Dauphine.	

The Green Gage is universally admitted to hold the first rank in flavour among all plums, and is every where highly esteemed. In France, this variety is generally known as the Reine Claude, having, it is said, been introduced into that country by Queen Claude, wife of Francis I. During the last century, an English family by the name of *Gage*, obtained a number of fruit trees from the monks of Charteuse, near Paris. Among them was a tree of this plum, which, having lost its name, was called by the gardener the Green Gage. It is pronounced, by Lindley, the best plum in England, and we must admit that we have no superiour to it here.

Fig. 106. *Green Gage.*

The Green Gage is a very short-jointed, slow growing tree, of spreading and rather dwarfish habit. It is an abundant and pretty regular bearer, though the fruit is a little liable to crack upon the tree in wet seasons.

Branches smooth. Buds with large shoulders. Fruit round, rather small, seldom of medium size. Suture faintly marked, but extending from the stalk to the apex. Skin green, or yellowish-green at full maturity, when it is often a little dotted or marbled with red. Stalk half to three-fourths of an inch long, slender, very slightly inserted. Flesh pale green, exceedingly melting and juicy, and usually separates freely from the stone. Flavour, at once, sprightly and very luscious. Ripe about the middle of August.

There are several seedling varieties of this plum in various parts of this country—but none superiour or scarcely equal to the old. That known as the Bruyn Gage, which has been disseminated from the garden of A. Bruyn, Esq., of Kingston, N. Y., is only the true Reine Claude, brought by Chancellor Livingston from France.

16. HUDSON GAGE.

A new early plum, which promises to rank among the first, of the season at which it ripens. It is one of the seedlings which Mr. Lawrence, of the city of Hudson, (see Lawrence's Favourite,) has had the good fortune to give to the public within a few years. It has some affinity to the Imperial Gage, but ripens three weeks earlier.

Branches slightly downy. Fruit of medium size, oval, a little enlarged on one side of the obscure suture. Skin yellow, clouded with green streaks under the skin, and covered with a thin white bloom. Stalk short, little more than half an inch long, inserted in a moderate hollow. Flesh greenish, very juicy and melting, with a rich, sprightly, excellent flavour. It separates from the stone, (adhering very slightly,) which is quite small. First week in August, two weeks before the Washington.

17. HULINGS' SUPERB. § Pom. Man.

Keyser's Plum.

A noble plum, of the largest size, raised from seed by Mr. Keyser, of Pennsylvania, but first made known to cultivators by Dr. Wm. G. Hulings, of the same state. It is as large as the Washington, frequently measuring six inches in circumference, or two and a fourth in diameter, the longest way. In flavour, it is more sprightly than that plum, having its sweetness relieved by a little acidity, and is scarcely inferiour to the Green Gage. It is productive, and in every way, a fruit of great merit.

24

The tree is remarkable for its vigorous growth, its stout, *blunt* shoots with large shouldered buds, and its fine luxuriant foliage It is a good bearer, especially in strong soils.

Branches downy. Fruit very large, globular, a little inclining to ovate, with a distinct suture. Stalk three fourths of an inch long, set in a shallow depression. Skin dull, greenish-yellow. Flesh pale greenish-yellow, rather firm, with a rich, brisk, excellent flavour; partly clinging to the stone. Ripens middle of August.

18. IMPERIAL OTTOMAN. Thomp.

A very neat, early plum, of good flavour, and a prolific bearer. It has the reputation of having been brought from Turkey, but it is uncertain whether this is correct.

Branches slightly downy. Fruit scarcely below medium size, roundish, between Green Gage and the American Yellow Gage in appearance, and having a suture on one side, from the stalk half way down. Stalk downy, slender, curved, three-fourths of an inch long, inserted in a very slight cavity. Skin dull yellow, clouded with darker streaks, and covered with a thin bloom. It adheres considerably to the stone, which is pointed at both ends. The flesh is juicy, sweet, melting, and of very good flavour. It ripens the last of July, or four or five days before the American Yellow Gage.

19. IMPERIAL GAGE. § Pom. Man. Ken.

Flushing Gage.   *Thomp. Floy.*
Prince's Imperial Gage.
White Gage, *of Boston.*
Superiour Green Gage.

The Imperial Gage has long enjoyed the reputation of one of the most excellent and productive of plums. It was raised at Prince's Nursery, Flushing, N. Y., from the seed of the Green Gage, and the fact of the fruit of a single tree near Boston having produced fruit to the value of near fifty dollars, annually, has often been repeated as a proof of the profit of its cultivation for market. It should be remarked, however, as an exception to the general rule, that it is peculiarly fitted for *dry, light* soils, where many sorts drop their fruit, and

Fig. 107. *Imperial Gage.*

that in rich heavy soils, like those of Albany, the fruit is often insipid.

The tree grows freely and rises rapidly, and has long dark shoots and leaves, slightly downy. Fruit rather above medium size, oval, with a distinct suture. Stalk nearly an inch long, slightly hairy, and pretty stout, inserted in an even hollow. Skin pale green, until fully ripe, when it is tinged with yellow, showing a *peculiar marbling of dull green stripes*, and covered with copious white bloom. Flesh greenish, very juicy, melting, and rich, with a very sprightly, agreeable flavour. In some situations it adheres to the stone, but it generally separates pretty freely. The latter is oval, and pointed at both ends. It is a great and regular bearer, and the fruit is therefore improved by thinning, when half grown. Ripens about the 1st of September, or a week later than the Washington.

20. Jaune Hative. Thomp. Lind. O. Duh.

Early Yellow.
Catalonian.
White Primordian.
Amber Primordian.

Jaune de Catalogne.
Prune de St. Barnabe.
D'Avoine.

The earliest of plums, which is its chief recommendation. It is a very old variety from Catalonia, and the south of France, and has been in cultivation more than two hundred years. It is a pretty little fruit, and is worthy of a place in the garden of the amateur. The tree has long, slender, downy branches.

Fruit small, oval, or obovate, with a shallow suture on one side. Stalk slender, half an inch long. Skin pale yellow, thinly coated with bloom. Flesh yellow, tolerably juicy, and melting, of sweet and pleasant flavour; separates from the stone. Ripens from the 10th to the middle of July.

21. Jefferson. §

If we were asked which we think the most desirable and beautiful of all dessert plums, we should undoubtedly give the name of this new variety. When fully ripe, it is nearly, shall we not say *quite*—equal in flavour to the Green Gage, that unsurpassable standard of flavour. But when we contrast the small and rather insignificant appearance of the Green Gage, with the unusual size and beauty of the Jefferson, we must admit that it takes the very first rank. As large as the Washington, it is more richly and deeply coloured, being dark yellow, uniformly and handsomely marked with a fine ruddy cheek. It is about ten days or a fortnight later than the Washington, ripening the last of August, when it has the rare quality of hanging long on the tree, gradually improving in flavour. It does not, like many sorts, appear liable to the attacks of wasps, which destroy so many of the light coloured plums as soon as they arrive at maturity.

We received the Jefferson Plum a few years ago, from the late Judge Buel, by whom it was raised and named. The original tree is still, we believe, growing in his garden near Albany. It is a good and regular bearer, and the crop is very handsome upon the tree.

Branches slightly downy, leaves oval, flat. Fruit large, oval, slightly narrowed on one side, towards the stalk. Skin golden yellow, with a beautiful purplish-red cheek, and covered with a thin white bloom. Stalk an inch long, pretty stout, very slightly inserted.

Fig. 108. *Jefferson.*

Suture indistinct. Flesh deep orange, (like that of an Apricot,) parts freely, and almost entirely from the stone, which is long and pointed ; very rich, juicy, luscious and high flavoured. Hangs a fortnight on the tree.

22. LAWRENCE'S FAVOURITE. §

Lawrence's Gage.

Fig. 109. *Lawrence's Favourite.*

Lawrence's Favourite is a fruit of high merit, raised by Mr. L. U. Lawrence, of Hudson, N. Y., from a seed of the Green Gage. The exceeding congeniality to the plum of the soil of Hudson, which is almost a stiff clay, is fully attested by the seemingly spontaneous production of such varieties as this, the Columbia and several others.

The general appearance of the fruit is like that of its parent, except that it is two or three times as large. It hangs well on the tree, and its remarkable size, flavour and productiveness,

will soon give it a place in every garden, and we think it deserving our highest commendation.   Specimen trees only 8 feet
high, have borne abundantly with us this season.

Lawrence's Favourite forms an upright tree of thrifty growth,
with dark green leaves, (which are rather below the medium
size,) and upright growing short-jointed shoots.   Young branches, downy.

Fruit large, heavy, roundish, a little flattened at either end.
Skin dull yellowish-green, clouded with streaks of a darker
shade beneath, and covered with a light bluish-green bloom.
The upper part of the fruit, when fully ripe, is covered with a
peculiar brownish net-work, and a few reddish dots.   Stalk short,
only half an inch long, slender, inserted in a narrow cavity.
Flesh greenish, resembling that of the Green Gage, remarkably
juicy, and melting, perhaps scarcely so rich as the latter, but
with a very rich, sprightly, vinous flavour, and one of the most
delicious of plums.   Stone five eighths of an inch long, flattened ; the flesh sometimes adheres a little, when not fully
ripe, but then separates freely.   Ripens at the middle of August.

23. Lucombe's Nonesuch.   Thomp. Lind. P. Mag.

An English plum raised by Lucombe, of the Exeter Nursery.
It is a large, yellowish-green clingstone fruit, of good quality,
but, unless fully ripe, not very rich in flavour.   Branches
smooth.

Fruit above medium size, roundish, shaped and coloured
much like the Green Gage, but much more distinctly streaked
with yellow and orange, and covered with a whitish bloom.
Suture broad.   Stalk straight, three fourths of an inch long, set
in a wide hollow.   Flesh pretty firm, greenish, rich, sweet
mingled with acid, adheres to the stone.   Bears well, and ripens
about the middle of August.

24. Large Green Drying. § Thomp.

Knight's Large Drying. *Ken.*

A new late variety, raised, we believe, by Mr. Knight, and
introduced here from the garden of the Horticultural Society,
of London.   It has produced fruit for the first time this season,
scarcely giving us an opportunity of judging, but Mr. Thompson, the head of the fruit department, in that garden, describes it
as of the first quality, bearing " fruit as large as that of the
Washington, which when perfectly ripened, is exceedingly rich."
The tree is vigorous, and the branches are smooth ; the fruit
large, round, greenish-yellow, the flesh yellowish, moderately

24*

juicy, rich and excellent, adheres to the stone.   Ripens about
the middle of September, and is a moderate bearer.

25. MULBERRY.

Raised by Isaac Denniston, of Albany, and is likely to prove
a desirable sort.   The leaves are remarkably luxuriant, broad
and crumpled.   Fruit large, oval, somewhat narrowest towards
the stalk.   Skin pale, whitish-yellow, sprinkled with white dots,
and dusted with a pale bloom.   Stalk an inch long, rather
slender, very slightly inserted.   Flesh greenish-yellow, juicy,
sweet and good ; adheres slightly to the stone.   The latter is
long and pointed.   First of September.

26. MIRABELLE.   Thomp. Lind. O. Duh.

Mirabelle Petite.
Mirabelle Jaune.

A very pretty little fruit, exceedingly ornamental on the tree, the branches of which are
thickly sprinkled with its abundant crops.   The
tree is small in all its parts, and although the
fruit has a tolerable flavour, yet from its size
and high perfume, it is chiefly valued for preserving.

Branches downy.   Fruit quite small, obovate, with a well marked suture.   Stalk half
an inch long, slightly inserted.   Skin of a
beautiful yellow, a little spotted with red at
maturity, and covered with a white bloom.
Flesh orange, sweet, and sprightly, becoming Fig. 110.   *Mirabelle*
dry when over-ripe, and separates from the stone.   Ripens with
the Green Gage.

27. ORANGE.

Orange Gage, (*of some.*) *

The Orange Plum is a new variety, which we have recently introduced, from the garden of Mr. Teller, of Rhinebeck,
Dutchess co., N. Y.   It is considerably disseminated about
that locality, and undoubtedly originated there.   It is only of
second quality in flavour, but its extraordinary size, and showy
appearance, as well as the abundance of its crops, will recommend it to all large planters of the plum.   It is, perhaps, the
largest of all plums, and has a peculiar bronze gold colour.

* There is a great propensity for calling every plum of merit a Gage, in this
part of the country.   As this has no resemblance whatever to the original type
of this class, we drop that part of its name.

Branches stout and smooth. Fruit very large, oval, flattened at both ends. Skin bronze yellow, marked with roughish white dots, and clouded with purplish red near the stalk. The latter is three-fourths of an inch long, rather rough, inserted in a narrow round cavity. Flesh deep yellow, a little coarse grained, but with acid flavour when fully ripe. It adheres a little to the stone, which is much compressed and furrowed. Ripens the last of August.

Fig. 111. *Orange Plum.*

28. SAINT MARTIN'S QUETSCHE. Thomp.

A very late variety of Prune, recently introduced from Germany, and likely to take its place among the select sorts. Hardy and a good bearer. Branches smooth. Fruit of medium size, ovate, or considerably broadest towards the stalk. Skin pale yellow, covered with a white bloom. Flesh yellowish, with a rich and excellent flavour, and separates readily from the stone. The tree is a good bearer, and the fruit hangs a long while on the tree, but we fear that to the northward of this it may not come to full maturity every season. Ripens the first of October, and will hang a month.

29. SAINT CATHERINE. § Thomp. Lind. O. Duh.

Among the fine old varieties of late plums, the St. Catherine is one of the most celebrated. In France it is raised in large quantities, in some districts making the most de-

Fig. 112. *St. Catherine.*

licate kind of prunes. It is also much esteemed for preserving, and is of excellent quality for the dessert. It bears regularly, and abundantly in this part of the country, and deserves a place in every *good garden*.

Branches smooth, upright, rather slender. Fruit of medium size, obovate, narrowing considerably towards the stalk, and having a strongly marked suture on one side. Stalk three-fourths to an inch or more long, very slender, inserted in a slight cavity. Skin very pale yellow, overspread with thin white bloom, and occasionally becoming a little reddish on the sunny side. Flesh yellow, juicy, rather firm, and adheres to the stone ; in flavour it is sprightly, rich and perfumed. Ripens the middle and last of September.

30. SIAMESE.

A curious growing variety, as its name indicates, in pairs, attached on one side, and hanging by a common stalk. Nearly all the fruit on the tree exhibits this peculiarity, and grafts taken from it continue its habit. The original seedling tree stands in the garden of Wm. Roe, Esq., of this place.

Branches long, slender, and smooth. Fruit mostly in pairs, distinct, but closely joined on one side, medium sized, obovate. Skin pale yellow, with a white bloom. Stalk rather long and slender, slightly inserted. Flesh yellow, juicy and sprightly, of second rate flavour, and adheres to the stone. Bears abundantly, and ripens about the 10th of September.

31. WASHINGTON. § P. Man. Thomp. Lind.

Fig. 113. *Washington*

Bolmar.
Bolmor's Washington.
New Washington.
Franklin.

The Washington undoubtedly stands higher in general estimation in this country, than any other plum. Although not equal to the Green Gage and two or three others, in high flavour, yet its great size, its beauty, and the vigour and hardiness of the tree, are qualities which have brought this noble fruit into notice every where. The parent tree grew originally on Delancey's farm, on the east side of the Bowery, New-York, but being grafted with another sort, escaped notice, until a *sucker* from it, planted by Mr. Bolmar,* a merchant in Chatham-street, came into bearing about the year 1818, and attracted universal attention by the remarkable beauty and size of the fruit. In 1821, this sort was first sent to the Horticultural Society of London, by the late Dr. Hosack, and it now ranks as first in nearly all the European collections.

The Washington has remarkably large, broad, crumpled and glossy foliage, is a strong grower, and forms a handsome round head. Like several other varieties of plum, the fruit of this, especially in sandy soils, does not attain its full perfection until the tree has borne for several years. We have measured them very often six inches in circumference, and once from Mr. Bolmar's original tree, seven and a quarter inches.

Wood light brown, downy. Fruit of the largest size, roundish-oval, with an obscure suture, except near the stalk. Skin dull yellow, with faint marblings of green, but when well ripened, deep yellow, with a pale crimson blush or dots. Stalk scarcely three-fourths of an inch long, a little downy, set in a shallow, wide hollow. Flesh yellow, firm, very sweet and luscious, separating freely from the stone. Stone pointed at each end. Ripens from about the middle to the last of August.

32. WHITE IMPERATRICE. Thomp. Lind. P. Mag.

White Empress.
Imperatrice Blanche. *O. Duh.*

The White Imperatrice is but little known in this country. In the habit of the tree, appearance and flavour of the fruit, and season of maturity, it strongly resembles the St. Catherine, but is a freestone. It is not equal to the latter in flavour, though esteemed by some persons, neither does it hang well after ripening.

Branches smooth. Fruit of medium size, obovate, a little flattened at the ends, suture rather obscure. Skin bright yellow, covered partially with a thin white bloom, and spotted with a little red. Stalk a little more than half an inch long, set in a narrow cavity. Flesh yellow, very juicy, crisp, sweet, and quite transparent in texture ; separates freely from the stone, which is small and oblong. Ripe early in September.

* Which he purchased of a market woman.

93. WHITE MAGNUM BONUM.   Thomp. Lind.

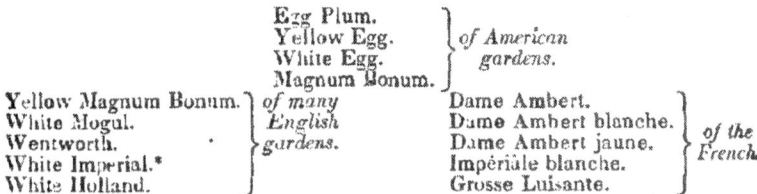

	Egg Plum.			
	Yellow Egg.		*of American*	
	White Egg.		*gardens.*	
	Magnum Bonum.			
Yellow Magnum Bonum.	*of many*		Dame Ambert.	
White Mogul.	*English*		Dame Ambert blanche.	*of the*
Wentworth.	*gardens.*		Dame Ambert jaune.	*French.*
White Imperial.*			Impériale blanche.	
White Holland.			Grosse Luisante.	

The White Magnum Bonum, or *Egg Plum,* as it is almost universally known here, is a very popular fruit, chiefly on account of its large and splendid appearance, and a slight acidity, which renders it admirably fitted for making showy sweetmeats or preserves. When it is raised in a fine warm situation, and is fully matured, it is pretty well flavoured, but ordinarily, it is considered coarse, and as belonging to the kitchen, and not to the dessert.

Branches smooth, long. Fruit of the largest size, measuring six inches in its longest circumference, oval, narrowing a good deal to both ends. Suture well marked. Stalk about an inch long, stout, inserted, without cavity, in a folded border. Skin yellow, with numerous white dots, covered with thin white bloom—when fully ripe, of a deep gold colour. Flesh yellow, adhering closely to the stone, rather acid until very ripe, when it becomes sweet, though of only second rate flavour. Stem long, and pointed at both ends. A pretty good bearer, though apt, in light soils, to drop from the tree before matured. Middle of August.

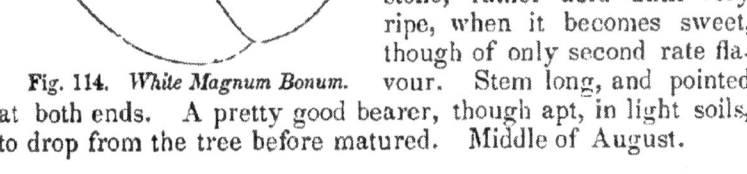

Fig. 114. *White Magnum Bonum.*

* There is really no practical difference between the White, and the Yellow Magnum Bonum. The fruit is precisely similar in appearance and quality though the growth of the two trees may not fully agree.

34. WHITE DAMSON. Thomp. Lind.

Late Yellow Damson.	Shailer's White Damson.
White Prune Damson.	White Damascene.

A very pretty and pleasant little plum of the damson class. In England it is thought of very little value, except for preserving, but here, where it matures more perfectly, it becomes a very pleasant table fruit, and from its lateness, may be considered a very desirable variety. The long slender branches are loaded, so as to be pendant, with the weight of the abundant rich clusters of fruit.

Branches smooth, and of thrifty growth. Fruit small, about an inch long, oval. Skin pale yellow, with a white bloom, and sprinkled with reddish brown spots at maturity. Stalk rather more than half an inch long, downy, inserted without depression. Flesh adheres closely to the stone, yellow, and when fully ripe, of a rich, sprightly, sub-acid, agreeable flavour. Ripens about the last of September, and will hang, shrivelling somewhat, until severe frosts.

35. WHITE PERDRIGON. Thomp. Nois.

Perdrigon blanc. *O. Duh.*
Maitre Claude.
Brignole ?

A very sugary plum, which is largely cultivated in Provence, along with the Brignole, for drying, to form the celebrated Brignole prunes—so called from the little town of that name. Thompson, indeed, makes this and the Brignole synonymous, but the French consider them distinct, the Brignole being larger, rather yellower, and dryer. It is probable that the difference is very slight.

Branches downy. Fruit middle sized, oval, narrowing towards the stalk. Skin pale greenish-yellow, with numerous small white dots, and a few red spots on the sunny side—thinly coated with bloom. Stalk three-fourths of an inch long, slender. Flesh pale yellow, very sweet with a slight perfume, and adheres to the stone. Ripens last of August.

36. YELLOW GAGE, PRINCE'S. § P. Man.

American Yellow Gage, (*of some.*)
White Gage, (*of some.*)

The Yellow Gage was raised, so long ago as the year **1783**, by the elder Mr. Prince, of Flushing, L. I. It is very common on the Hudson river, but we do not find any description of it in Manning or Kenrick. We have noticed that it is sometimes confounded, at Boston, with the Imperial Gage, which is really quite distinct. Its great hardiness and productiveness, joined to its rich sugary flavour, make it a favourite sort. There is a tree in the gardens here, thirty years old, which still bears most excellent crops annually.

Branches smooth, short-jointed, with glossy leaves, and forming a large spreading head. Fruit a little above medium size, oval, rather broadest towards the stalk. Suture a mere line. Skin golden yellow, a little clouded, and covered with a copious white bloom. Stalk an inch long, inserted in a small round cavity. Flesh deep yellow, rich, sugary and melting, though sometimes rather dry; parts freely from the stone. Ripens rather early, about the first week in August.

The growth of this plum is not only very different from the Imperial Gage, but the fruit of the latter is readily distinguished by its abundant *juiciness*, its greenish colour, and the superiour sprightliness of its flavour.

Fig. 115. *Prince's Yellow Gage.*

37. YELLOW GAGE, [of the English.] Thomp.

Little Queen Claude.   *Mill. Lind.*
Petite Reine Claude.   *O. Duh.*
Reine Claude blanche.
———— petite espéce.
Small Green Gage.   ) *of some*
Gonne's Green Gage.   } *English*
White Gage.   ) *gardens.*

This plum, formerly known, we believe, as the Little Queen Claude, but which has now received the *soubriquet* of Yellow Gage, we suppose for good reasons, from the head of the fruit department, in the London Horticultural Society's garden, is an old French variety, described by Duhamel. It is of smaller size than the true Green Gage, much inferior in flavour, and does not appear to us much worthy of cultivation, when that plum, the Jefferson, and Lawrence's Favourite can be had.

Branches smooth and rather long. Fruit below medium size, round, with a distinct suture on one side. Stalk half an inch long, rather slender, inserted in a slight hollow. Skin pale yellowish-green, speckled with a few reddish dots, and overspread with a good deal of bloom. Flesh pale yellow, sweet, and pleasant, separates freely from the stone. Ripens about the middle of August.

Class II. Red, Blue, or Purple Plums.

38. ABRICOTÉE ROUGE. Thomp. O. Duh. Nois

The Abricotée Rouge, or Red Apricot plum, is a French variety, of rather pretty colour, but indifferent in flavour, and not
comparable to several of our native sorts.

Branches smooth. Fruit of medium size, oval, considerably
flattened at each end. Stalk nearly an inch long, set in a slight
cavity. Skin of a fine clear red in the shade, violet in the sun,
covered with an abundant blue bloom. Flesh orange colour,
sweet, but rather dry, and without much flavour ; separates
freely from the stone. Ripens the last of August.

39. AMERICAN WHEAT.

A singular little plum, of second quality, received by us from
the late Robert Manning. Branches slender, smooth, leaves
quite small and light coloured. Fruit quite small, of the shape
of a small bullet, dropping from the tree when ripe. Skin pale
blue, covered with a white bloom. Stalk slender, half an inch
long. Flesh greenish, melting, juicy, and sweet, adheres to
the stone. Last of August. Bears abundantly.

40. BLUE GAGE. Lind. Mill.

Azure Hâtive. *Thomp.*
Black Perdrigon.
Little Blue Gage.

An ordinary little round blue plum, the *Azure Hâtive* of the
French, of sweet and pleasant flavour, and very hardy, but the
most indifferent of all the Gages. It bears most abundant crops
every season, and we have found the seedlings to make good
stocks.

Branches slender and downy. Fruit quite small and round,
about three quarters of an inch in diameter. Skin dark blue,
covered with light blue bloom. Stalk three fourths of an inch
long. Flesh greenish, juicy, a little acid, somewhat rich, and
separates from the stone. Ripe the middle of August.

41. BREVOORT'S PURPLE. Floy. Ken.

New-York Purple. *Floy.*
Brevoort's Purple Bolmar.
Brevoort's Purple Washington.

Originated by Henry Brevoort, Esq., of New-York, from a

25

stone of the Washington planted in 1819. It is a handsome and most productive plum, but appears to us to have been over praised as regards its flavour, which is of second quality.

Branches long, smooth. Fruit large, oval, suture distinct at the base. Skin reddish purple, or reddish, covered with a violet bloom. Stalk three fourths of an inch long, set in a deep but narrow cavity. Flesh yellowish, soft, juicy, not very sweet, but with considerable vinous flavour, adheres closely to the stone. Ripe the first of September.

42. BLUE PERDRIGON.

Violet Perdrigon. } Lind.
Blue Perdrigon. }
Perdrigon Violette.   O. Duh.
Brignole Violette.

The Blue Perdrigon is a very old variety, having been introduced into England from Italy, as long ago as 1582. It is a sweet and pleasant plum, and is largely employed with the White Perdrigon in making the Brignole prunes.

Branches downy. Fruit of medium size, oval, narrowing a little towards the stalk. Skin at first reddish, but becoming purple, sprinkled with many brown dots, and covered with a very thick whitish bloom. Stalk three fourths of an inch long, set in a small cavity. Flesh greenish-yellow, rather firm, sugary, rich and excellent, adhering to the stone. Last of August.

43. BLUE IMPERATRICE. § Thomp. P. Mag.

Impératrice.   Lind. Mill.
Véritable Impératrice.
Violette.
Impératrice Violette.   O. Duh.

Fig. 116.   *Blue Imperatrice.*

The true Blue Imperatrice is an admirable plum, one of the finest of the late plums, hanging for a long time on the tree, and may be kept in the fruit room a considerable period after being gathered. It is rich, sugary and excellent. The branches are long, smooth, and slender, and the smaller twigs start out at nearly right angles with the main branches.

Fruit of medium size, obovate, tapering most towards the stalk. Stalk nearly an inch long, set in a slight hollow. Skin deep purple, covered with a thick blue bloom. Flesh greenish-yellow, pretty firm, rather dry, but quite rich and sugary, adhering closely to the stone. Ripens in October, and will hang, in sheltered situations, till the middle of November.

The so-called SEMIANA, or Blue Imperatrice of Boston, has been considered, until lately, as identical with this plum. It is an acid, rather harsh fruit, only, fit for preserving, and should not, therefore, be confounded with the true Blue Imperatrice, which is sweet and excellent.

The growth of this spurious tree resembles that of the true Imperatrice, the fruit is oval, narrowing to the stalk, which, however, is *scarcely more than half an inch long*, very slender, and set without depression. Skin dark blue, with little bloom, flesh rather acid, and adheres to the stone. An abundant bearer, and hangs till late frosts.

This fruit, so well known about Boston, seems to agree with the figure and description of the Imperatrice Violette of the old Duhamel, and we doubt, therefore, the identity of the English and French Plums of this name. Duhamel, even in the dryer and finer climate of France, only says, " assez douce pour une Prune tardive." This will apply to the Imperatrice or Semiana of Boston, but not to the Blue Imperatrice of the English.

44. COOPER'S LARGE. Coxe. Thomp.

Cooper's Large Red.
Cooper's Large American.
La Délicieuse ! *Lind.*

Coxe who first described this plum, says it was raised by Mr. Joseph Cooper, of New-Jersey, from a stone of the Orleans. He considers it as a fine large plum, but exceedingly liable to rot upon the tree, and we learn from Mr. Ives, of Salem, that the same complaint was made by former cultivators of this sort in his neighbourhood, where it is now nearly abandoned. It seems to be scarcely known now in this country—that is to say, in gardens*—as we have made diligent search for it, the last two years, without being able to obtain the fruit of the true sort.

Lindley describes a plum, La Déliceuse, as having been brought from New-Jersey about 1815, and which was sold by Mr. Kirke, for a guinea a plant. And Mr. Thompson gives this fruit as identical with Cooper's Large. We hope another season to be able to compare the two.

Thompson's description of the Cooper's Large is as follows.

* Some nurserymen here, we regret to say, do not scruple to fill large catalogues with the names of varieties which have no corresponding existence in their grounds.

THE PLUM.

292

Branches smooth. Fruit purple, oval, of medium size, separates from the stone, of second quality, ripens at the end of September, and a great bearer.

Coxe describes it as ripening in August, and of the largest size.

The following is Lindley's description of La Déliceuse, which we give in order to assist in identifying the two, if they prove really distinct. Branches long and smooth. Fruit oval, about two inches long, and one and three quarters in diameter. Suture rather broad, shallow, swelled a little more on one side than on the other. Stalk an inch long, slender, slightly inserted. Skin pale yellow on the shaded side, but in the sun deep purple full of brown specks. Flesh yellow, and separates from the stone. Juice peculiarly rich and abundant. Ripe in October, with the Imperatrice.

45. Columbia. §

Columbian Gage.

A noble plum, a contemporary of the Lawrence's Favourite, already described, and like that, raised by Mr. Lawrence, of Hudson, from a pit of the Green Gage. It is a superb looking, and a rich flavoured variety—undoubtedly one of the finest of the large dark coloured plums. The tree is remarkable for its very stout blunt shoots, large roundish leaves, and the spreading horizontal form of its head. It is also highly productive. Branches and upper side of the leaves downy. Fruit of the largest size, six or seven inches in circumference, nearly globular, one half rather larger than the other. Skin brownish purple, dotted with numerous fawn-coloured specks, and covered with much blue bloom, through which appears a reddish brown tint on the shaded side.

Fig. 117. *Columbia.*

Stalk about an inch long, rather stout, inserted in a narrow, small cavity. Flesh orange, not very juicy, but when at full maturity, very rich, sugary and excellent; it separates freely from the stone, except a little on the edge. The stone is quite small and compressed. Last of August.

46. Corse's Admiral.

A rather large, light purple plum, which, like the two or three following ones, was raised by Henry Corse, Esq., an intelligent cultivator, of the neighbourhood of Montreal, Canada. They are all well adapted to a northern climate.

Branches quite downy. Fruit above medium size, oval, or a little obovate, considerably enlarged on one side of the suture. Skin light purple, covered with a pale lilac bloom, and dotted with yellow specks. Stalk nearly an inch long, hairy, slightly inserted. Flesh greenish-yellow, juicy and sprightly, but second rate in flavour, and adhering closely to the stone. A prolific tree. September.

47. Corse's Field Marshal.

Handsome in appearance. Skin lively purplish red. Fruit rather large, oval. Stalk rather slender, three-fourths of an inch long, slightly inserted. Flesh greenish-yellow, juicy, but a little tart, adheres closely to the stone, which is long, and pointed at both ends. Ripe middle and last of August.

48. Corse's Nota Bene. Ken.

This is the best of Mr. Corse's varieties that have been proved in the United States.

Branches smooth. Fruit of rather large size, round. Skin pale lilac or pale brown, often dull green on the shaded side, with much light blue bloom. Stalk half an inch long, set in a round hollow. Flesh greenish, rather firm, juicy, sweet and rich, and separates from the stone. The tree is a very great bearer, and is very hardy. First of September.

49. Cruger's Scarlet. §

Cruger's.
Cruger's Seedling.
Cruger's Scarlet Gage.

An exceeding delicate and beautiful dessert fruit, raised from seed, by Henry Cruger, Esq., of New-York, and first disseminated from the gardens here. Its mild and agreeable flavour is preferred by many who do not like the more luscious plums, and its sure and abundant crops render it a favourite on light soils, where the curculio destroys many less hardy. Mr. Ives in-

25*

Fig. 118. *Cruger's Scarlet.*

forms us, that with him, it is less liable to drop from the tree than any other sort.

Branches downy. Fruit rather larger than a Green Gage, roundish-oval, with an obscure suture. Skin, when fully exposed, a lively red, but usually a bright lilac, covered with a thin bluish bloom; and speckled with numerous golden dots; in the shade it is pale fawn-coloured on one side. Stalk half an inch long, set in a shallow depression. Flesh deep orange, not very juicy nor rich, but with a very agreeable, mild, sprightly flavour. It hangs well after ripening. Last of August.

50. CHERRY. Thomp. Coxe.

Early Scarlet.
Myrobolan.
Virginian Cherry. } *of European*
De Virginie. *gardens.*
D'Amérique Rouge. }
Prunus Myrobolana. *O. Duh. Lind.*
Prunus Cerasifera. *Pursh.*
Miser Plum, *of Hoffy.*

The Cherry Plum, or Early Scarlet, is a very distinct species. It has been considered a native of this country, but we doubt this, and think, with Pursh, that it is only found here in the neighbourhood of houses. The tree grows pretty rapidly, forms a small, bushy head, and is easily recognized by the slenderness of its branches, and the smallness of its leaves. It bears the greatest profusion of snowy blossoms in the spring, which from the early date at which they appear, are rather liable to be cut off by frost.

There are several varieties produced from seed, but that most common here, is round, about an inch in diameter, of a lively red, with very little bloom, and a very slender, short stem, set in a narrow cavity. On the trees they resemble cherries, rather than plums. The flesh is greenish, melting, soft, very juicy, with a pleasant, lively, sub-acid flavour—neither rich nor high flavoured, and adheres closely to the stone. The stone is oval, and pointed. It ripens about the middle of July, before most other plums, and this, and its pretty appearance at the dessert, are its chief merits. Branches smooth.

The common cherry plum, or MYROBOLAN, of Europe, is

rather larger, and shaped like a heart. In all other respects the same.

GOLDEN CHERRY PLUM. Mr. Samuel Reeve, of Salem, New-Jersey, has produced a seedling of the cherry plum, which is worthy of notice.* It is heart-shaped, yellow, speckled with scarlet in the sun, but of a glossy waxen yellow in the shade. The habit of the tree is exactly that of the common cherry plum, but as it is a very abundant bearer, and ripens early in July, Mr. R. has found it one of the most profitable plums for the market. It is worthy of more extensive trial.

51. COE'S LATE RED. § Thomp. Lind.

Saint Martin.   } *of the*
Saint Martin Rouge. } *French.*
Prune de la St. Martin. *Nois.*

This plum (which should properly be called the St. Martin's, though as it was also claimed to have been raised by an English nurseryman, it seems difficult to rid it of that title,) proves, with us, to be an exceedingly valuable, late variety. Indeed, it is so late, that we fear, to the north of this, it would not come to maturity. It grows vigorously, bears regularly and heavily, and would prove a valuable market fruit. The flavour is excellent.

Branches downy. Fruit of medium size, nearly round, with a well marked suture running along one side. Skin light purplish-red, with a thin blue bloom. Stalk pretty stout, three-fourths of an inch long, set nearly even with the surface. Flesh yellowish, rather firm and crisp, juicy, with a rich vinous flavour, separating almost entirely from the stone. October and November.

Fig. 119. *Coe's Late Red.*

52. CHESTON. Thomp. Lind.

Matchless. *Lang.*
Diapreé Violette. } *ac. to*
Violet Diaper. } *Thomp.*

A pleasant, early plum, but superseded now by better ones. Branches downy. Fruit rather small, oval. Skin dark purple,

* Described in Hoffy's Orchardist's Companion, (Philadelphia,) as the MARKET PLUM.

with a blue bloom. Stalk quite short, set without depression. Flesh yellow, firm, sweet, and rather sprightly, separating from the stone. Last of July, and first of August.

53. DENNISTON'S RED.

A strikingly handsome, new seedling, which has newly come into bearing, in the celebrated plum orchard of the gentleman whose name it bears, at Albany.

Branches smooth, dark coloured. Fruit rather large, round-ish-oval, narrowed towards the stalk. Suture running half round. Skin of a beautiful light red, sprinkled with many small, fawn coloured dots, and dusted with a very light bloom. Stalk very long and slender, slightly inserted. Flesh amber colour, juicy, rich, and sprightly, with an excellent flavour. It separates from the stone, which is small, oval, and compressed. Last of August.

54. DOMINE DULL. § Floy. Thomp.

German Prune. ⎱ *Man. and of some*
Dutch Prune. ⎰ *American gardens.*
Dutch Quetzen.

This good American prune was raised from a seed brought from Holland, by the Rev. Mr. Dull, a Dutch minister, who afterwards resided at Kingston, N. Y. The parent tree was the common Dutch prune, which this strongly resembles. The same gentleman's little parcel of plum stones from "*fader-land,*" it will be remembered, gave origin to Bleecker's Gage, one of the finest of our yellow varieties.

Branches long and smooth. Fruit of medium size, long-oval, with little or no suture. Skin very dark purple, nearly black, dusted with some blue bloom. Stalk nearly an inch long, inserted with very little cavity. Flesh yellow, quite juicy at first, but if allowed to hang on the tree becomes dry, rich and sweet ; it adheres closely to the stone. A pro digious bearer, and a really good fruit. September.

Fig. 120. *Domine Dull.*

55. DAMSON. Thomp.

Common Damson.
Purple Damson.
Black Damson. ·
Early Damson, (*of many.*)

The common, oval, blue Damson is almost too well known to need description, as every cottage garden in the country contains this tree, and thousands of bushels are annually sold in the market for preserves. The tree is enormously productive, but in the hands of careless cultivators is liable to be rendered worthless by the *knots*, caused by an insect easily extirpated, if the diseased branches are regularly burned every winter or spring.

Branches slender, a little thorny and downy. Fruit small, oval, about an inch long. Skin purple, covered with thick blue bloom ; flesh melting and juicy, rather tart, separates partially from the stone. September.

As the Damson is frequently produced from seed, it varies somewhat in character.

The SHROPSHIRE or PRUNE DAMSON is an English purple variety, rather obovate in figure, but little superiour to our common sort. The SWEET DAMSON resembles the common Damson, and is but slightly acid.

The WINTER DAMSON is a valuable market sort, from its extreme lateness. It is small, round, purple, covered with a very thick light blue bloom ; flesh greenish, acid, with a slight astringency, but makes good preserves. It bears enormous crops, and will hang on the tree till the middle of November, six weeks after the common Damson, uninjured by the early frosts

56. DUANE'S PURPLE. § P. Man. Ken.

A superb looking purple fruit of the largest size, and of very fair quality,—occasionally, in warm dry seasons, first rate. It was originally grown by James Duane, Esq., of Duanesburgh, N. Y., and probably sprung from a seed of the Purple Magnum Bonum. We have seen this fruit, about Albany, confounded with the variety just named. The tree is easily known by the *gray* appearance of the wood, and large leaves, which are unusually *woolly* on the under surface. It is a highly attractive dessert fruit, ripening rather before the plum season, and bearing well.

Branches very downy. Fruit very large, oval or oblong, considerably swollen on one side of the suture. Skin reddish-purple in the sun, but a very pale red in the shade, sparingly dotted with yellow specks, and covered with lilac bloom. Stalk three-fourths of an inch long, slender, set in a narrow cavity. Flesh amber coloured, juicy, sprightly, moderately sweet, adheres partially to the stone. Ripens with the Washington, (or a little before,) about the 10th of August.

Fig. 121. *Duane's Purple.*

57. DIAMOND. Thomp. Man.

A very large plum, but exceedingly coarse in flavour, and of no value, except for cooking. It grows thriftily and bears regularly and abundantly with us, and is very showy on the tree, but it is, otherwise, scarcely third rate. It was raised from seed, by an Englishman, in Kent, named Diamond.

Branches long, downy. Fruit of the largest size, oval, shaped like an Egg Plum or Magnum Bonum. Skin black, covered with a blue bloom. Stalk three-fourths of an inch long, set in a narrow cavity. Flesh deep yellow, coarse-grained, and rather dry—a little acid, and without flavour ; separates from the long pointed stone. [The author of the American Orchardist says, " flavour superior !"]

58. DIAPRÉE ROUGE. § Thomp. Poit. O. Duh.

Roche Corbon.
Mimms.   } *ac. to*
Imperial Diadem. } *Thomp.*

The Diaprée Rouge, or Red Diaper, is a very large and handsome French plum. Mr. Thompson considers it synonymous with a fine English variety, better known here as the MIMMS, or Imperial Diadem. As the Mimms plum has been fully tested by us, and proves to be a *first rate* fruit in all respects, in this climate, we give the following description and outline drawn from the fruit, as produced by us.

A rather slow grower, branches almost smooth. Fruit large, obovate. Skin of a reddish-purple, with a few golden specks, and a light blue bloom easily rubbed off. Stalk three-fourths of an inch long, slender, hairy, slightly inserted. Flesh pale green, juicy, very melting, rich and delicious; separating from the stone, which is quite small. Last of August.

Fig. 122.   *Red Diaper.*

The Diaprée Rouge is described by Poiteau as having a thick, rather bitter skin, exactly the opposite to that of the fruit we have described. It is probable, however, that our climate, more favourable for the plum, may produce it in greater perfection.

59. ELFREY.   Coxe. Man.

Elfry's Prune.

A native plum, first described by Coxe. It belongs to the class of prune plums, with dry, sweet flesh, and is much esteemed by many persons. The tree is thrifty, with rich glossy leaves, and bears to a fault.

Branches smooth. Fruit rather below medium size, oval. Skin blue. Flesh greenish, very sweet, dry and firm, parting very freely from the stone—indeed, often splitting open when fully ripe.

60. FOTHERINGHAM.   Thomp. Lind. Mill.

Sheen.
Grove House Purple.

An old English plum of good quality. It is not unlikely that it originated at Sir William Temple's seat—Sheen, in Surrey, where, according to Lindley, it was grown before 1700, under the name of the Sheen plum.

Branches smooth. Fruit of medium size, obovate, **with a**

distinct suture. Skin purple, where exposed, but in the shade reddish, sprinkled with small specks, and covered with a pale blue bloom. Stalk an inch long. Flesh pale greenish-yellow, juicy, sprightly, and rich, separating from the stone. Ripens about the middle of August.

61. FROST GAGE. § Pom. Man

Frost Plum.

A most valuable late plum, scarcely yielding to any other late variety in the excellence of its flavour. It appears to have originated in Fishkill, Dutchess co., N. Y., where it has, for many years past, been most extensively cultivated for market. Before fully ripe it abounds with sprightly, sub-acid juice, and is highly esteemed for preserving, and when mature is a sweet and luscious fruit for the dessert. It will hang on the tree till very late frosts. The tree is a tall upright grower, with smooth and rather slender shoots, and bears abundantly. The fruit is in perfection about the first of October, and from its lateness and good quality commands from two to five dollars a bushel, even when hundreds of bushels are sent to New-York market at once.*

Fig. 123. *Frost Gage.*

Branches smooth. Fruit rather below medium size, roundish-oval, with a distinct suture on one side. Skin deep purple, with a few brown specks, and a thin bloom. Stalk half to three-fourths of an inch in length, inserted with little or no depression. Flesh greenish-yellow, juicy, sweet, rich and melting, adhering to the stone.

62. GOLIATH. Thomp. Lind.

> Caledonian, (*of some.*)
> Saint Cloud.
> Steers's Emperor.
> Wilmot's late Orleans.

A large and handsome plum, not quite first rate, but well deserving cultivation. It is easily distinguished from the Necta rine plum, with which it has been confounded by its gray, very *downy* shoots. It bears fine crops.

---

* Eighteen hundred dollars have been received by a single farmer in this vicinity, for a single season's crop of this plum. Having some affinity to the Damson, it is, in some districts, liable to the *knots*, but trifling care will soon banish this enemy.

Fruit large, roundish-oblong, enlarged on one side of the suture. Skin a fine deep red, approaching purple, a little paler in the shade, dusted with a thin blue bloom. Stalk three quarters of an inch long, deeply inserted in a well marked hollow. Flesh yellow, adheres considerably to the stone, rather juicy with a brisk, sprightly flavour. Last of August.

63. GWALSH. Thomp.

A fruit little known out of New-Jersey, where, we believe, it is a native. We received it from Thomas Hancock, of Burlington, N. J. It is large, showy and prolific, and about the quality of the Red Magnum Bonum.

Branches nearly smooth. Fruit large, regularly formed, obovate, with scarcely any suture. Skin rich, dark purple, covered with blue bloom. Stalk rather slender, not quite an inch long, slightly inserted. Flesh yellow, juicy, of sprightly flavour, mixed with a slight acid, and adheres to the stone. Second quality. Middle of August.

64. HOLLAND. Pom. Man. Ken.

Blue Holland.
Holland Prune.

A pleasant, late plum, of second quality, handed down from the old Dutch gardens of New-York, and perhaps, originally brought over by the first settlers of that city.

Branches downy, rather slender. Fruit round, slightly flattened. Skin blue or light reddish-purple, covered with a blue bloom. Stalk set in a small cavity. Flesh juicy, melting, sweet and pleasant, separating freely from the stone. It hangs a long while on the tree, to which the stalk adheres rather closely, ripening from the last of August to the middle of September.

65. HORSE PLUM. Thomp. Floy.

Large Early Damson. } of Prince
Sweet Damson.   } and Ken.

A very common and inferiour fruit, which reproduces itself from seed, and is almost naturalized in the gardens of the middle states. The seedlings make good stocks for the nursery.

Branches downy. Fruit of medium size, oval, with a deep suture on one side. Skin purple in the sun, reddish on the shaded side, with blue bloom. Flesh greenish-yellow, rather dry and acid, separates from the stone. Last of August.

26

66. HOWELL'S EARLY.

This is a very desirable early fruit, ripening about the 20th of July, a few days before the Morocco. It takes its name from Mr. B. Howell, of Newburgh, N. Y., who brought the parent tree when a sucker, from Virginia. It appears to us unlike any other described variety. The fruit is remarkably fragrant.

Wood slender, gray and downy. Leaves small, oval, downy. Fruit rather below medium size, oval, without any suture, a little angular. Stalk slender, three fourths of an inch long, set even with the surface. Skin light brown, often greenish-yellow on the shaded side, covered with a thin blue bloom. Flesh amber coloured, melting, juicy, with a sweet and perfumed flavour, separates from the stone, which is quite small and oval. Very productive.

67. ICKWORTH IMPERATRICE. § Thomp.

Knight's No. 6.

The Ickworth Imperatrice was raised by Mr. Knight, of Downton Castle, and is a hybrid between Blue Imperatrice and Coe's Golden Drop. It is one of the numerous recent and valuable additions to the class of late plums, prolonging this formerly fleeting fruit the whole autumn. It hangs a long while on the tree, and if gathered and wrapped in soft paper, will keep many weeks—much longer than any other variety, and is, perhaps, one of the best late dessert sorts.

Branches smooth. Fruit rather above medium size, obovate. Skin purple, peculiarly traced or embroidered with streaks of golden fawn colour. Stalk moderately long and thick. Flesh greenish-yellow, sweet, juicy and rich, mostly adhering to the stone, which is rather small. Ripens early in October, and may be kept till Christmas, gradually becoming dryer and more sugary. It will, even if laid away in paper in a dry place, become an excellent prune, and it has been found in this state, and with an excellent flavour, the next summer.

68. ITALIAN DAMASK. Lind.

Damas d'Italie. *O. Duh. Thomp.*

Branches smooth. Fruit middle sized, nearly round, a little flattened at the base, and having a well marked suture extending from the stalk to the apex. Stalk half an inch long, slender, inserted in a small round cavity. Skin violet, becoming brown when fully ripe. Flesh yellowish-green, firm, and separates clean from the stone. Juice very sweet and high flavoured. Stone oval, rather thick. End of August. [*Lindley's Guide.*]

To this we will add that the Morocco (with *downy* shoots) is often mistaken for this plum in this country.

69. LOMBARD. Ken.

Bleecker's Scarlet.
Beekman's Scarlet.

The Lombard is an exceedingly pretty plum, of pleasant flavour, and it has qualities that will always make it popular ;— great hardiness and productiveness, and the power of holding its fruit uninjured in those light sandy soils where most other sorts are punctured and fall by the curculio.

It was called the Lombard plum by the Massachusetts Horticultural Society, in compliment to Mr. Lombard, of Springfield, Mass., who first brought it into notice in that state; and it is said to have been received by him from Judge Platt, of Whitesborough, N. Y., who raised it from seed. But it was previously well known here by the name of *Bleecker's Scarlet.* Never having been described under that name, however, we adopt the present title. The tree has strikingly crumpled leaves, thrifty, bright purple, glossy shoots, and grows with much vigour.

Fig. 124. *Lombard.*

Branches smooth. Fruit of medium size, roundish-oval, slightly flattened at either end ; suture obscure. Stalk quite slender, scarcely three-fourths of an inch long, set in a broad, abruptly narrowing cavity. Skin delicate violet red, paler in the shade, dotted with red, and dusted thinly with bloom. Flesh deep yellow, juicy, and pleasant, but not rich ; adhering to the stone. Middle and last of August.

70. LONG SCARLET.

Scarlet Gage.
Red Gage, (*incorrectly, of some.*)

A bright red, oblong fruit, very handsome upon the tree, which usually hangs heavy laden with its fruit. It is a native of this part of the Hudson, and has been disseminated by us. It is a little tart, and of second rate flavour, but it is highly valued for the bright red transparent jelly, that is made from the fruit, surpassing that of any other variety.

Shoots downy. Fruit of medium size, oblong-obovate, swollen on one side of the suture, and tapering to the stalk. Skin bright red in the sun, pale yellowish-red on the shady side, covered with a fine lilac bloom. Stalk three-fourths of an inch long, set in a narrow cavity. Flesh deep yellow, juicy, acid at first, but, if allowed to hang, it becomes rather rich and sweet. It adheres to the stone. Last of August.

71. ORLEANS. Lind. Thomp.

Monsieur.	} of the
Monsieur Ordinaire.	French.
Old Orleans.	
Red Damask.	

The most popular English market plum, being hardy and uniformly productive. It is not generally cultivated here, being considered a second rate fruit, and is supplanted by better American sorts. As a kitchen fruit, it is chiefly esteemed.

Branches gray, and very downy. Fruit middle sized, round, a little enlarged on one side of the distinct suture. Skin dark red, becoming purple in the sun. Stalk little more than half an inch long, set in a wide hollow. Flesh yellowish, sweet, mixed with acid, and separates freely from the stone. Ripens a little after the middle of August.

72. ORLEANS, EARLY. Thomp. Lind.

New Early Orleans.	Monsieur Hâtif.	
New Orleans.	Monsieur Hâtif de	of the
Grimwood's Early Orleans.	Montmorency.	French.
Hampton Court.		

The Early Orleans is very near like the foregoing in all respects, except that it ripens ten days earlier—about the first of August here, with the Morocco—which makes it far more desirable. Branches downy. Fruit of the size and colour of the common Orleans, a little more oval, and with a more shallow suture. Stalk sometimes half an inch long and stout, sometimes longer and more slender, set in a moderate hollow. Skin a little marbled. Flesh yellowish-green, of brisk flavour, rather richer than the old Orleans, and separates from the stone. A good bearer.

WILMOT'S NEW EARLY ORLEANS, (*Wilmot's Large Orleans,* &c.,) so strongly resembles the foregoing in appearance, time of ripening, etc., as to be scarcely worthy of a separate description.

73. ORLEANS, SMITH'S. § Pom. Man.*

| Violet Perdrigon. | } incorrectly, of some |
| Red Magnum Bonum. | American gardens. |

Smith's Orleans, the largest and finest of this class of plums,

---

* Described, by an error in the Pomological Manual, as a *freestone.*

is a native variety raised from the old Orleans about 20 years ago by Mr. Smith, of Gowanus, Long Island. It is one o. the most vigorous of all plum trees, making straight, glossy, reddish-purple shoots, seven or eight feet long in the nursery, with dark green, crimped leaves. It bears regularly and well, in almost any soil, its fruit is large and handsome, and has that blending of sweet and acid in its flavour, which renders it, to our taste, one of the most agreeable of all plums. It is deservedly a favourite in American gardens.

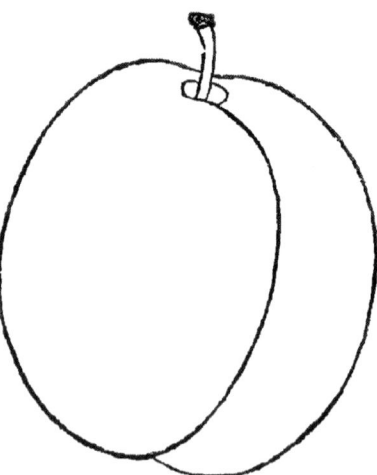

Fig. 125. *Smith's Orleans.*

Bearing branches smooth, or nearly so. Fruit large, often of the largest size, oval, rather widest towards the stalk, a little irregular, with a strongly marked suture on one side. Stalk quite small and slender, little more than half an inch long, inserted in a deep narrow cavity. Skin reddish-purple, covered with a deep blue bloom. Flesh deep yellow, a little firm, very juicy, with a brisk, rich vinous flavour, (not sweet and cloying,) and adheres to the stone. Ripens from the 20th to the last of August, and hangs for some time on the tree, becoming very dark in colour.

By an error, this variety was sent out from the gardens here for several years, as the Violet, or Blue Perdrigon, a smaller, and very different fruit, and bears this name still, in some collections.

74. Isabella. Thomp.

This is an attractive looking English plum, of a fine red colour, and of good flavour, though scarcely so beautiful as the coloured plate in the Pomological Magazine would lead one to suppose ; but well worthy of a place in a large collection.

Branches quite downy and gray, like those of the Orleans. Fruit medium size, oval, rather narrower towards the stalk. Skin dark dull red in the sun, paler in the shade, and thickly sprinkled with darker coloured dots. Stalk three-fourths of an inch long, a little hairy, set in a moderate hollow. Flesh yellow, rich, juicy, with a smart flavour, and adheres to the pointed stone. Last of August.

26*

75. KIRKE'S.   Thomp. Lind.

Kirke's plum is a variety which came to us from England, where it was first brought into notice by Mr. Kirke, the nurseryman at Brompton. Its excellent flavour and productiveness will bring it into favour here. The sort usually known in our nurseries under this name, is incorrect. In general appearance it resembles a good deal the Reine Claude Violette, or Purple Gage.

Branches smooth. Fruit of medium size, round, with very little suture. Skin dark purple, with a few golden dots, and coated with an unusually thick blue bloom, which adheres pretty closely. Stalk three-fourths of an inch long, inserted in a very slight depression. Flesh greenish-yellow, firm, and very rich in flavour. It separates freely from the stone, which is flat and broad. Ripens the last of August and first of September.

76. MOROCCO. § Thomp. Lind.

Early Morocco.
Black Morocco.
Early Black Morocco
Early Damask. *Mill.*
Black Damask. *Fors.*
Italian Damask, (*incorrectly, of some.*)

One of the very best of the early purple plums, ripening at the beginning of August, ten days before the Washington, and therefore worthy of a place, even in small gardens. It is a moderate bearer.

Branches downy. Fruit of medium size, roundish, with a shallow suture on one side. a little flattened at both ends. Skin dark purple, covered with a pale thin bloom. Stalk half an inch long, rather stout. Flesh greenish-yellow, adhering slightly to the stone, juicy, with a smart, rich flavour, becoming quite sweet at maturity.

77. NECTARINE.   Thomp. Lind.

Caledonian.   Peach Plum. } *incorrectly*
Howell's Large.   Prune Pêche. } *of some.*
Jenkins' Imperial.   Louis Philippe.

A fine looking fruit. probably of English origin, and confounded by some with the PEACH PLUM* of the French. Its size, and handsome appearance, will always give it a place in the plum orchard, but it must be confessed that it will hardly rank as a first rate dessert fruit, being decidedly inferiour to the Columbia,

* For the true PEACH PLUM, See Supplement.

a plum of even larger dimensions. The young trees are readily known by their straight, large, blunt purplish shoots, *nearly* smooth, and not gray and downy, like those of the Goliath.

Fruit of the largest size, regularly formed, roundish. Stalk about half an inch long, rather stout, and set in a wide shallow depression. Skin purple, dusted with a blue bloom. Flesh dull greenish-yellow, becoming tinged with red at maturity, a little coarse grained, with a rich, brisk flavour, and adhering partially to the stone. A good and regular bearer. Ripens about the 15th of August.

Mr. Rivers has lately sent to this country trees of the PEACH PLUM, which he says is the *Prune Pêche* of Brittany, superiour to, and quite distinct from the Nectarine.

78. Précoce de Tours. § O. Duh. Thomp. Lind.

Early Tours.
Early Violet.
Violette Hative. } *Lang. Lind.*
Noire Hative.
Violet de Tours.
Perdrigon Violet. } *incorrectly*
Blue Perdrigon. } *of some.*

The Early Tours plum is yet very little known in the United States, but deserves a more general trial, as it is esteemed abroad as an excellent very early plum, ripening the last of July, among the first of the season.

Branches downy. Fruit rather more than an inch in diameter, oval, with a shallow suture. Skin deep purple, covered

with a thick azure bloom. Stalk half an inch long, set in a narrow cavity. Flesh at first greenish, but becoming dull yellow at maturity; a little fibrous, but juicy, sweet, melting, and slightly perfumed; it adheres considerably to the stone.

79. Purple Favourite. §

This delicious fruit received its name from us some years ago. The tree from which the stock now in this country was derived, stood for many years (until it died of old age,) in the centre of the principal garden here, and was planted by the

Fig. 126. *Purple Favourite.*

father of the author. Its origin we were never able to learn,
and we have not been able during all our pomological re-
searches and comparisons, to identify it with any other sort.

The Purple Favourite, when in perfection, is not surpassed
by any other plum in luscious flavour. It is more juicy and
melting than the Purple Gage—and has some affinity to the
Diapreé Rouge, or Mimms. It should have a place in every
garden, as it bears well, and is very hardy. In the nursery
it has the dwarfish habit of the Green Gage, but more slender
shoots.

Branches nearly smooth, short-jointed. Fruit medium size,
often large, roundish-obovate. Suture none. Skin light brown
in the shade, brownish-purple in the sun, dotted with numerous
golden specks, and dusted with thin, light blue bloom. Stalk
three-fourths to one inch long, set in a very slight depression.
Flesh pale, greenish, very juicy, tender, melting, with a luscious sweetness. Parts freely from the stone, which is very
small and roundish. Begins to ripen about the 20th of August,
and will hang for a fortnight on the tree.

This is known, incorrectly, as the Purple Gage, in some parts
of the country.

80. PURPLE GAGE· § Lind. Pom. Mag.

Reine Claude Violette. *Thomp. Nois.*
Die Violette Köning Claudie. *Sickler.*
Violet Queen Claude.

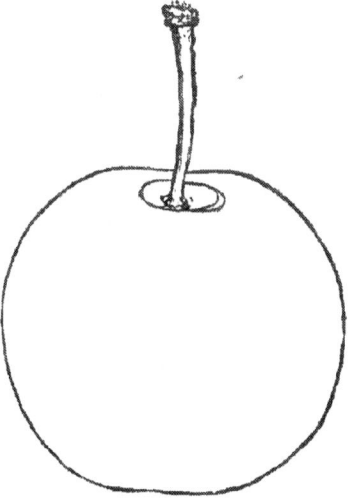

Fig. 127. *Purple Gage.*

The Purple Gage holds the
first place for high flavour
among purple plums abroad.
Athough it is as well known in
France under the title of the
Reine Claude Violette, as in England under that of the Purple
Gage, yet its native country is
not precisely determined.

Branches smooth, much like
those of the Green Gage. Fruit
medium sized, shaped like the
Green Gage, roundish, a little
flattened. Suture shallow, but
distinct. Stalk an inch long,
rather thick, set in a narrow cavity. Skin a little thick, violet,
dotted with pale yellow and covered with light blue bloom.
Flesh greenish-yellow, rather firm, rich, sugary, and very high
flavoured, separates from the stone, which is oval and compressed. Ripens rather late, and will hang on the tree—shrivelling a little, but not cracking—all the month of September.

81. Pond's Seedling.

Pond's Purple. *Ken.*

A productive plum of only second quality. It was brought into notice by Mr. Samuel Pond, a nurseryman near Boston, but the original tree grew in the garden of Henry Hill, Esq., in the city of Boston.

Branches downy. Fruit middle sized, roundish. Skin purple. Stalk short. Flesh yellowish, rather dry, separates from the stone, sweet, mingled with acid, of tolerable flavour. Ripens early in August, and hangs a long time.

82. Peoly's Early Blue.

This is a native fruit, of medium quality, which we received from Mr. Manning. Branches very downy. Fruit middle sized, oblong, suture scarcely visible. Skin very dark blue, covered with light blue bloom. Stalk short, uneven. Flesh yellow, of pleasant flavour, adhering partially to the stone, which is not large, but rather bluntly terminated. Ripens about the 10th of August.

83. Prune D'Agen. Nois.

D'Agen.	} *Thomp.*	Agen Datte.
Prune d'Ast.	}	St. Maurin.
Robe de Sergent.		Prune de Brignole, (*of some.*)

A French prune, of good quality, chiefly used for drying or preserving. Branches smooth, leaves narrow. Fruit of medium size, obovate, flattened on one side. Skin purple, with a blue bloom. Stalk short. Flesh greenish-yellow, sweet. It is a freestone, and makes an excellent prune. It ripens late in September, and bears prodigious crops.

84. Prune, Manning's Long Blue. §

Large Long Blue. *Man.*
Manning's Long Blue.

Manning's Long Blue Prune, we received from the late Mr. Manning, with the account that it was had by him without a name, from Landreth's Nursery, Philadelphia. It is undoubtedly a seedling of the common Quetsche, and is one of the best of this family of plums. Its large size, long keeping, and lateness, added to the fact that it bears most abundant crops, make it a good market fruit.

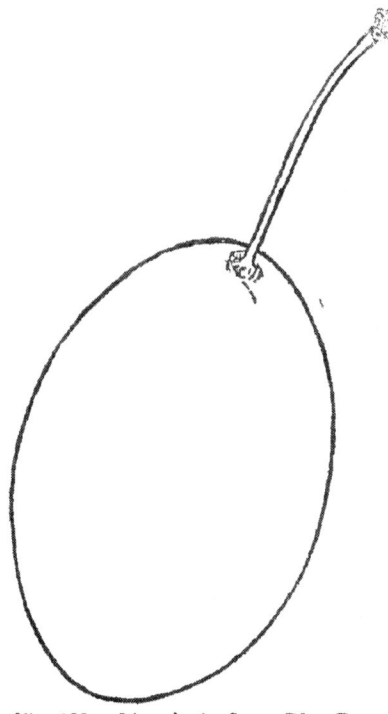

Branches smooth. Fruit quite large, long-oval, a little one-sided, with an obscure suture. Stalk very long, and slender, set in a very trifling depression. Skin dark purple, with a thick blue bloom. Flesh greenish-yellow, firm, rather juicy, with a sweet, sprightly, pleasant flavour. It separates pretty readily from the stone, which is long and pointed. First to last of September. Ripens gradually, and bears carriage well.

85. QUEEN MOTHER. Thomp. Ray. Lind.

Red Queen Mother.
Pigeon's Heart.
Damas Violet.

A neat little reddish plum, long known in European

Fig. 128. *Manning's Long Blue Prune.* gardens. Branches smooth, rather feeble in growth. Fruit rather small, round, about an inch in diameter. Skin dark, purplish-red in the sun, pale reddish amber in the shade, with many reddish dots. Stalk half an inch long. Flesh yellow, sweet and rich, separating freely from the stone, which is quite small. September.

86. QUETSCHE, OR GERMAN PRUNE. Thomp.

Common Quetsche.	Zwetsche.	
True Large German Prune.	Quetsche Grosse.	
Turkish Quetsche.	Prune d'Allemagne.	ac. to
Leipzic.	Quetsche d'Allemagne Grosse.	Thomp.
Sweet Prune.	Damas Gros.	
Damask.	Covetche.	
	Imperatrice Violette.	
	Imperatrice Violette Grosse.	incorrectly, of some.
	Damas Violet Gros.	

So many plums are cultivated under the name of German Prune, that it is difficult to fix this fickle title, a circumstance owing to the fact that the prune frequently comes the same, or nearly the same, from seed, and in prune growing districts this is a popular way of increasing them, while it, of course, gives rise to many shades of character. It is a valuable class of plums, of fair quality for the table, but most esteemed for dry ing and preserving—abundant bearers, and hanging long on the tree. The common German Prune is described as follows.

Branches smooth. Fruit long-oval, near two inches long, peculiarly swollen on one side, and drawn out towards the stalk. Suture distinctly marked. Skin purple, with a thick blue bloom. Stalk three-fourths of an inch long, slender, slightly inserted. Flesh firm, green, sweet and pleasant, separates from the stone, which is flat, very long, and a little curved. Ripens about the 10th of September.

This prune is, perhaps, the most universal and most valuable fruit tree in Germany, Hungary, Saxony, and all central Europe. Preserved, it is used in winter as a substitute for butter, by the laboring peasantry; and dried, it is a source of large profit in commerce. In this country, it is yet but little known, but from the great hardiness and productiveness of the tree, it may be worth trial on a large scale.

The AUSTRIAN QUETSCHE, *Thomp*, (*Quetsche de Brême, Bremen Prune*,) is a sub-variety, much like the foregoing, purple, a freestone, of rather better flavour, and ripening somewhat later.

ST. JAMES' QUETSCHE, is another variety, with smooth branches, and oblong fruit of medium size; flesh purple, *adheres* to the stone, of very good flavour. It yields great crops. September.

87. ROYALE. O. Duh. Thomp. Nois.

La Royale. *Lind. Hooker.*

The Royale, a French variety, is undoubtedly one of the richest plums. It is peculiarly crisp, with a very high flavour, and is remarkable for the exceedingly thick coat of bloom which covers the skin. The tree is a slow grower, forms a bushy, spreading head, and its very downy shoots have a gray or whitish appearance. It bears regularly, but moderately, and, though not fit for the orchard, it is a first rate garden fruit.

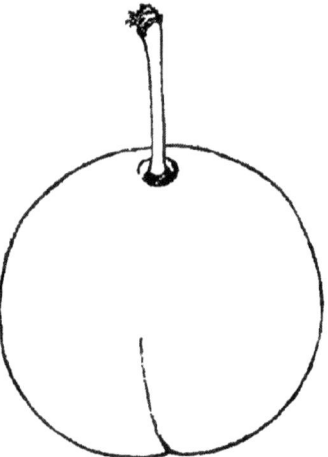

Fig. 129. *Royale.*

Fruit of medium size, often quite large; round, lessening a little towards the stalk. Suture distinct at the apex on one side only. Skin reddish-purple, dotted with light brown specks, and covered with a thick pale bloom, which adheres closely. Stalk three-fourths of an inch long, downy, set in a narrow cavity. Flesh dull yellow, rather firm, but melting, very juicy, with an exceedingly rich, vinous flavour; it separates from the stone, which is small, roundish, pointed at both ends. Ripe the last of August, and will hang, dropping gradually, till the middle of September.

88. RED PERDRIGON. Lind. Fors.

Perdrigon Rouge. *Nois.*

An agreeable late French plum, which hangs a good while on the tree, improving in flavour, till it becomes very sweet and excellent. It appears to be a very hardy grower.

Branches downy. Fruit of medium size, roundish, slightly oval. Skin at first pale, but becoming fine deep red, dotted with fawn-coloured specks, and dusted with much lilac bloom. Stalk an inch long, rather stout, set in a small round cavity. Flesh bright yellow, a little crisp and firm, quite juicy and sweet, and parts freely from the stone. Last of August to the middle of September.

89. RED MAGNUM BONUM. Lind. Thomp. Mill.

Purple Egg.	Impériale Violette.	
Red Imperial.	Impériale Rouge.	
Imperial.	Dame Aubert Violette.	*of the*
Purple Magnum Bonum.	Impériale.	*French.*
Florence.	Prune d'œuf.	
Imperial Violet.		

The Red Magnum Bonum is a large, handsome, egg-shaped fruit, seen in abundance in our markets, and chiefly valued for cooking and preserving, being rather harsh for the dessert. In fine dry seasons, it becomes of tolerable flavour.

Branches smooth. Fruit large, much like the White Magnum Bonum in form, oval, with a strong suture, on one side of which the fruit is more swollen. Skin rather pale in the shade, but deep red in the sun, sprinkled with many gray dots, and dusted with but little pale bloom. Stalk an inch or more long, slender, set in a narrow cavity. Flesh greenish, rather firm and coarse, with a sub-acid flavour, separating from the stone, which is oval and pointed. Last of August and first of September.

It is proper to state here, that this plum has been several times reproduced from seed, on the North River, and with little difference of character, except that some are freestones and others clingstones.

Duane's purple is often confounded with the Red Magnum Bonum. It is a much better plum, and is easily distinguished, even when not in fruit, by its very *gray, downy* shoots.

90. ROYALE DE TOURS. § O. Duh. Poit. Thomp.

Royal Tours.

This capital, early plum, from the neighbourhood of Tours, in France, is yet very scarce in this country, (two or three spurious sorts having been received by this name,) but deserves to become generally known and cultivated. Its flavour is of the finest, and it commences ripening at the last of July, before most of the fine varieties.

Branches always quite downy. Fruit large, roundish, but marked with a large and deep suture extending quite half round, and enlarged on one side. At the apex is a small white depressed point. Skin lively red in the shade, deep violet in the sun, with many minute golden dots, and coated with a thick blue bloom. Stalk half to three-fourths of an inch long, stout, set in a narrow cavity. Flesh greenish, rather firm, with a rich, high flavoured, abundant juice. It adheres closely to the stone, which is large, oval, and flattened.

91. ROYALE HÂTIVE. § Thomp. Nois.

Early Royal.
Mirian.

A new early plum of French origin, and the highest excellence. It is yet very scarce with us, having lately been received from the garden of the London Horticultural Society. It strongly resembles, both in appearance and flavour, the Purple Gage, or Reine Claude Violette, but ripens a month earlier.

Branches *very downy*. Fruit of medium size, roundish, a little wider towards the stalk. Skin light purple, dotted, (and faintly streaked,) with brownish-yellow, and covered with a blue bloom. Stalk half an inch long, stout, inserted with little or no depression. Flesh amber yellow, with an unusually rich, high flavour, and parts from the stone, (adhering slightly, till ripe.) Stone small, flattened, ovate. Begins to ripen about the 20th of July.

92. RED GAGE. § Pom. Man.

An American plum, of delicious flavour, very hardy, and a prodigious bearer. It is a seedling raised from the Green Gage, by the elder Wm. Prince, of the Flushing Nurseries, in 1790. It grows very vigorously, and is distinguished, when young, by its deep green, crimped foliage.

Branches dark reddish, smooth. Fruit about as large as the

27

Fig. 130. *Red Gage.*

Green Gage, but more oval, regularly formed. Skin brownish or brick red, with little bloom. Stalk rather slender, set in a narrow cavity. Flesh greenish-amber, very juicy, melting, sugary, and luscious. It parts freely from the stone, which is small. Middle of August.

[This is quite distinct from the LONG SCARLET, (which see,) sometimes called Red Gage, or Scarlet Gage.]

93. RIVER'S EARLY.

Two new seedlings raised by Mr. Thomas Rivers, an English nurseryman of reputation. Their parent was the Précoce de Tours, but they are said to be earlier, hardier, and more prolific than that variety.

"River's Early, No. 1," has downy shoots; No. 2, has smooth shining shoots. Both bear oval, purple fruit, of medium size; flesh yellow, sweet and excellent. They ripen the last of July.

94. SUISSE. Thomp. Poit.

Simiana.
Monsieur Tardif.
Prune d'Altesse.
Prune Suisse.
Swiss Plum.

A handsome October plum, bearing some affinity to the St. Martin, or Coe's Late Red, and ripening about the same time, or a little earlier. It is very different from the oval plum, incorrectly known as the *Semiana* about Boston.*

Branches smooth. Fruit globular, rather large, with a broad shallow suture on one side, and terminating in a depressed point. Skin pale red in the shade, but lively violet red in the sun, dotted with numerous specks—a little marbled, and coated with a thick blue bloom. Stalk nearly an inch long, pretty stout, set in a wide hollow. Flesh greenish-yellow, crackling and melting, with a brisk, rich flavour, in which there is a slight, but pleasant sharpness. It adheres to the stone, which is thick, with a rough edge. September, to the middle of October

* See Blue Imperatrice.

95. SHARP'S EMPEROR. Thomp.

Denyer's Victoria!
Queen Victoria!

A beautiful new plum from England, which will prove an addition to our collection. It bears abundantly, and has a peculiarly tender stone.

Branches strong, downy, and foliage large. Fruit quite large, roundish-oval. Skin, when exposed, of a fine bright, lively red, paler in the shade, with a delicate bloom. Flesh deep yellow, separates from the stone, of a pleasant, moderately rich flavour. Middle and last of September.

Denyer's Victoria resembles this, but we require another trial before pronouncing them identical.

96. THOMAS.

A new plum, of a lively, deep salmon colour, with a red cheek ; a very attractive contribution to the dessert, though not of first rate flavour. It is a native variety, and the fruit was first exhibited by Mr. Wm. Thomas, of Boston, who has a fine tree in his garden. It was thence named the Thomas Plum, by the Massachusetts Horticultural Society. It has some resemblance to Sharp's Emperor.

Branches slightly downy. Fruit large, roundish-oval, a little irregular, and rather compressed in the direction of the suture. Stalk hairy, half an inch or more, long, stout, set in a small, narrow cavity. Skin salmon colour, with numerous dots, and a soft red cheek. Flesh pale yellow, a little coarse grained, but with a mild, pleasant flavour, separating freely from the stone. The stone is peculiarly light coloured. Ripe the last of August, and bears admirably.

97. VIRGIN. Thomp.

Lately received from England, where it has the reputation of bearing "some resemblance to the Reine Claude Violette, though scarcely so rich." It has not yet been tested here.

Branches smooth. Fruit of medium size, roundish. Skin purple. Flesh yellow, of rich flavour, and separates from the stone. Ripens the last of August and beginning of September.

Ornamental Varieties.

There are few varieties of plums, which are considered

purely ornamental. One, however, is a remarkable exception to this, as it is scarcely exceeded in beauty in the month of May by any other flowery shrub—we mean the DOUBLE FLOW-ERING SLOE. It is a large shrub, only 10 or 12 feet high, with quite slender shoots and leaves, but it is thickly sprinkled, every spring, with the prettiest little double white blossoms about as large as a sixpence, but resembling the Lady Banks' roses. It is one of the greatest favourites of the Chinese and Japanese—those flower-loving people.

The COMMON ENGLISH SLOE, or Blackthorn, (*Prunus spinosa*,) is rather an ornamental tree in shrubbery plantations. The branches are more thorny than those of the common damson, and the fruit is nearly round, quite black, but covered with a thick blue bloom. In the spring, this low tree is a perfect cloud of white blossoms.

The DOUBLE-BLOSSOMED PLUM has large and handsome, double white flowers. Except in strong soils, however, they are apt to degenerate and become single, and are, indeed, always inferiour in effect to the Double Sloe.

The Cherry Plum we have already described. It is one of the fruit bearing sorts.

1. *Selection of choice varieties for a small garden.* Royal Hâtive, Hudson Gage, Green Gage, Jefferson, Lawrence's Favourite, Huling's Superb, Purple Favourite, Purple Gage, Coe's Golden Drop.

2. *Plums that will bear well in light soils, and generally withstand the curculio.* Lombard, Cruger's, Blue Gage, Roe's Autumn Gage, Red Gage, Long Scarlet, Bleecker's Gage, Coe's Golden Drop, and all the Damsons.

3. *Plums suitable for a cold northern climate.* Smith's Orleans, Bleecker's Gage, Denniston's Superb, Corse's Nota Bene, Orleans, Cruger's Scarlet, Washington, Duane's Purple.

4. *Plums suitable for a southern climate.* Bingham, Imperial Gage, Washington, Large Long Blue, Huling's Superb, Coe's Late Red, Coe's Golden Drop.

CHAPTER XXI.

THE PEAR.

Pyrus communis, L. *Rosaceæ*, of botanists.
Poirier, of the French; *Birnbaum*, German; *Peer*, Dutch; *Pero*, Italian; and *Pera*, Spanish.

THE Pear is, undeniably, the favourite fruit of modern times, and modern cultivators. Indeed, we believe the Pear of modern times, thanks to the science and skill of horticulturists, is quite a different morsel for the palate, from the pear of two or three centuries ago. In its wild state it is one of the most austere of all fruits, and a *choke pear* of our fields, really a great improvement on the wild type, seizes ones throat with such an unmerciful gripe, as to leave behind it no soothing remembrances of nectar and ambrosia.

So long ago as the earliest time of the Romans, the pear was considerably cultivated. It was common in Syria, Egypt, and Greece, and from the latter country, was transplanted into Italy. " Theophrastus speaks of the productiveness of old pear trees, and Virgil mentions some pears which he received from Cato. Pliny in his 15th book describes the varieties in cultivation in his time, as exceedingly numerous ; and mentions a number which were named after the countries from which they were received. Of all pears, he says, the Costumine is the most delicate and agreeable. The Falernian pear was esteemed for its juice ; and the Tibernian, because it was preferred by the Emperor Tiberius. There were ' proud pears' which were so-called, because they ripened early and would not keep, and 'winter pears,' pears for baking, as at the present day."* None of these old Roman varieties have been handed down to us, and we might believe some of them approached the buttery lusciousness of our modern pears, did not Pliny pithily add, most unfortunately for their reputation, " all pears whatsoever are but a heavy meat, unless they are well boiled or baked."

In fact the really delicious qualities of this fruit were not developed until about the seventeenth century. And within the last sixty years the pear, subjected to constant reproduction from seed by Van Mons and his followers, and to hybridizing or crossing by Mr. Knight and other English cultivators appears, at length, to have reached almost the summit of perfection, in beauty, duration, and flavour. Of Professor Van Mons and his labours of a whole life, almost *devoted to pears*, we have already spoken in our first chapter. From among the 80,000 seedlings raised by himself, and the many thousands reared by other zealous cultivators abroad, especially in Belgium—the Eden of the pear tree—there have been selected a large number of varieties of high excellence. In this country, we are continually adding to the number, as, in our newer soil, the pear, following the natural laws of successive reproduction, is constantly appearing in new seedling forms. The high flavour of the Seckel pear, an American variety, as yet unsurpassed, in this respect, by any European sort, proves the natural congeniality of the climate of the northern states to this fruit.

The pear tree is not a native of North America, but was in-

* *Arboretum Brittanicum.*

troduced from the other continent. In Europe, Western Asia, and China, it grows wild, in company with the apple, in hedges and woody wastes. In its wild state, it is hardier and longer-lived than the apple, making a taller and more pyramidal head, and becoming thicker in its trunk. There are trees on record abroad, of great size and age for fruit trees. M. Bosc mentions several which are known to be near 400 years old There is a very extraordinary tree in Home Lacy, Herefordshire, England—a perry pear—from which were made more than once, 15 hogsheads of perry in a single year. In 1805 it covered more than half an acre of land, the branches bending down and taking root, and, in turn, producing others in the same way. Loudon, in his recent work on trees, says that it is still in fine health, though reduced in size.

One of the most remarkable pear trees in this country, is growing in Illinois, about ten miles north of Vincennes. It is not believed to be more than forty years old, having been plant-ed by Mrs. Ockletree. The girth of its trunk one foot above the ground, is *ten feet*, and at nine feet from the ground, *six and a half feet ;* and its branches extend over an area sixty-nine feet in diameter. In 1834 it yielded 184 bushels of pears, in 1840 it yielded 140 bushels. It is enormously productive al-ways ; the fruit is pretty large, ripening in early autumn, and is of tolerable flavour.* Another famous specimen, perhaps the oldest in the country, is the *Stuyvesant Pear* tree, originally planted by the old governor of the Dutch colony of New-York, more than two hundred years ago, and still standing, in fine vigour, on what was once his farm, but is now the upper part of the city, quite thickly covered with houses. The fruit is a plea-sant summer pear, somewhat like a Summer Bonchretien.

Uses. The great value of the pear is as a dessert fruit. Next to this, it is highly esteemed for baking, stewing, preserv-ing and marmalades. In France and Belgium the fruit is very generally dried in ovens, or much in the same way as we do the apple, when it is quite an important article of food.

Dessert pears should have a melting, soft texture, and a sugary, aromatic juice. Kitchen pears, for baking or stewing, should be large, with firm and crisp flesh, moderately juicy.

The juice of the pear, fermented, is called *Perry.* This is made precisely in the same way as cider, and it is richer, and more esteemed by many persons. In the midland coun-ties of England, and in various parts of France and Germany, what are called perry pears—very hardy productive sorts, hav ing an austere juice—are largely cultivated for this purpose. In several places in our eastern states, we understand, perry is now annually made in considerable quantities. The fruit

---

* Rev H. W. Beecher, in Hovey's Magazine.

should be ground directly after being gathered, and requires rather more isinglass—(say $1\frac{1}{2}$ oz. to a barrel,) to fine it, on racking, than cider. In suitable soil the yield of perry to the acre is usually about one third more than that of cider.

The wood is heavy and fine grained, and makes, when stain-ed black, an excellent imitation of ebony. It is largely em-ployed by turners for making joiners' tools. The leaves will dye yellow.

GATHERING AND KEEPING THE FRUIT. The pear is a pecu-liar fruit in one respect, which should always be kept in mind; viz. *that most varieties are much finer in flavour if picked from the tree, and ripened in the house,* than if allowed to become fully matured on the tree. There are a few exceptions to this rule, but they are very few. And, on the other hand, we know a great many varieties which are only second or third rate, when ripened on the tree, but possess the highest and richest flavour if gathered at the proper time, and allowed to mature in the house. This proper season is easily known, first, by the ripening of a few full grown, but worm-eaten specimens, which fall soonest from the tree; and, secondly, by the change of colour, and the readiness of the stalk to part from its branch, on gently raising the fruit. The fruit should then be gathered—or so much of the crop as appears sufficiently matured—and spread out on shelves in the fruit room* or upon the floor of the garret. Here it will gradually assume its full colour, and become de-liciously melting and luscious. Many sorts which, ripened in the sun and open air, are rather dry, when ripened within door, most abundantly melting and juicy. They will also last for a considerably longer period, if ripened in this way—maturing gradually, as wanted for use—and being thus beyond the risk of loss or injury by violent storms or high winds.

Winter dessert pears should be allowed to hang on the tree as long as possible, until the nights become frosty. They should then be wrapped separately in paper, packed in *kegs, barrels,* or *small boxes,* and placed in a cool, dry room, free from frost. Some varieties, as the D'Aremberg, will ripen finely with no other care than placing them in barrels in the cellar, like apples. But most kinds of the finer winter dessert pears, should be brought into a warm apartment for a couple of weeks before their usual season of maturity. They should be kept covered, to prevent shrivelling. Many sorts that are com-paratively tough if ripened in a cold apartment, become very melting, buttery and juicy, when allowed to mature in a room kept at the temperature of 60 or 70 degrees.

* So important is the ripening of pears in the house that most amateurs of this fruit, find it to their advantage to have a small room set apart, and fitted up with shelves in tiers, to be used solely as a *fruit room.*

PROPAGATION. The finer sorts of pears are continued or in creased, by grafting and budding, and the stocks, on which to work, are either seedlings or suckers. Sucker stocks have usually such indifferent roots, they are so liable to produce suckers, continually, themselves, and are so much less healthy than seedlings, that they are now seldom used by good cultivators ; though, if quite young and thrifty, they will often make good stocks.

Seedlings, however, are, by far, the best stocks for the pear, in all cases ; and seedlings from strong growing, healthy pears, of common quality—such as grow about most farmer's gardens, are preferable, for stocks, to those raised from the best varieties—being more hardy and vigorous.

As it is, usually, found more difficult to raise a good supply of seedling pear stocks in this country, than of any other fruit tree, we will here remark that, it is absolutely necessary, to ensure success, that two points be observed. The first, is to clean and sow the seed as soon as may be, after the fruit is well matured ; the second, to sow it only in deep rich soil It should be previously trenched—if not naturally deep—at least twenty inches or two feet deep, and enriched with manure or compost mixed with ashes. This will give an abundant supply of nutriment to the young seedlings, the first year—without which, they become starved and parched, after a few inches growth, by our hot and dry summer, when they frequently fall a prey to the aphis and other insects at the root and top. A mellow, rich soil, whose depth ensures a supply of moisture, will give strong seedlings, which are always, at two years growth, fit to go into the nursery rows for budding While a dry, thin soil, will seldom produce good stocks, even in half a dozen years.

The seeds should be sown precisely like those of the apple, in broad drills, and the treatment of the stocks, when planted in the rows for budding, is quite similar. Budding is almost universally preferred by us, for propagating the pear, and this tree takes so readily, that very few failures can happen to an experienced hand. About the first of August, in this latitude, is the proper season for performing this operation

We may add here, that one year old pear seedlings, are often winter-killed, when the autumn has not been such as to ripen the wood thoroughly. A few branches of evergreens, or some slight covering laid along the rows, will prevent this. Or, they may be laid in by the heels, in a sheltered place.

The *thorn* makes very good stocks for the pear, except, that if grafted above ground, the tree is often apt to be broken off at the point of union, by high winds. This is obviated by grafting a little below the surface. Grafting on the thorn is a very useful practice for strong clayey soils, as, on such stocks the pear may be grown with success, when it would not otherwise thrive

It also comes rather earlier into bearing. Grafting on the *mountain ash* is thought to render the pear more hardy, and it retards the blossoming so much as to prevent their being injured by spring frosts. The pear is sometimes budded on the apple, but it is then usually very short-lived.

For rendering the pear *dwarf*, the QUINCE stock is almost universally used, as the pear unites readily with it, becomes quite dwarf in habit, and bears very early. Some large growing pears—as the Duchess of Angouleme—extremely liable to be blown off the tree, bear much better on the Quince stock, and others are considerably improved in flavour by it. The dwarf pear, however, it must be confessed, rather belongs to the small garden of the amateur, than to the orchardist, or him who desires to have regular large crops, and long-lived trees. The dwarf tree is usually short-lived, seldom enduring more than a dozen years in bearing—but it is a pretty, and economical way of growing a good many sorts, and getting fruit speedily, in a small garden.

The pear not being very abundantly supplied with fibrous roots, should never be transplanted, of large size, from the nursery. Small, thrifty plants, five or six feet high, are much to be preferred.

SOIL, SITUATION, AND CULTURE. The best soil for this fruit tree, is a *strong loam* of moderate depth, on a dry subsoil. The pear will, indeed, adapt itself to as great a variety of soils as any fruit tree, but, in unfavourable soils, it is more liable to suffer from disease, than any other. Soils that are damp during any considerable portion of the year, are entirely unfit for the pear tree ; and soils that are over-rich and deep, like some of the western alluvials, force the tree into such over luxuriant growth, that its wood does not ripen well, and is liable to be killed by winter blight. The remedy, in this case, consists in planting the trees on slightly raised hillocks—say eight inches above the level of the surface, and using lime as a manure. Soils that are too light, on the other hand, may be improved by trenching, if the subsoil is heavier, or by top dressing with heavy muck and river mud, if it is not.

In a climate rather cold for the pear, or on a cold soil, it is advantageous to plant on a southern slope, but in the middle states, in warm soils, we do not consider a decidedly southern exposure so good as other, rather cooler ones.

The pear succeeds so well as an open standard, and requires so little care or pruning—less, indeed, in the latter respect, than any other fruit tree, that training is seldom thought of, except in the gardens of the curious or skilful. The system of *quenouille* or *distaff* training, an interesting mode of rendering trees very productive in a small space, we have already fully described in p. 37, as well as root pruning for the same purpose in p. 32.

In orchard culture, the pear is usually planted about **thirty** feet distant each way; in fruit gardens, where the heads are somewhat kept in by pruning, 20 feet is considered sufficient **by** many.

Pear trees in a bearing state, where the growth is no longer luxuriant, should have, *every autumn*, a moderate top dressing of manure, to keep them in good condition. This, as it promotes steady and regular growth, is far preferable to occasional heavy manuring, which, as will presently be shown, has a tendency to induce the worst form of blight to which this tree is subject.

DISEASES. As a drawback to the, otherwise, easy cultivation of this fine fruit, the pear tree is, unfortunately, liable to a very serious disease, called the *pear tree blight*, or *fire blight*, appearing irregularly, and in all parts of the country; sometimes in succeeding seasons, and, again, only after a lapse of several years; attacking, sometimes, only the extremities of the limbs, and, at other times, destroying the whole tree; producing, occasionally, little damage to a few branches, but often, also destroying, in a day or two, an entire large tree; this disease has been, at different times, the terror and despair of pear growers. Some parts of the country have been nearly free from it, while others have suffered so much as almost to deter persons from extending the cultivation of this fine fruit. For nearly an hundred years, its existence has been remarked in this country, and, until very lately, all notions of its character and origin have been so vague, as to lead to little practical assistance in removing or remedying the evil.

Careful observation for several years past, and repeated comparison of facts with accurate observers, in various parts of the country, have led us to the following conclusions:

1st, That what is popularly called the pear blight, is, in fact, two distinct diseases. *2nd,* that one of these is caused by an insect, and the other by sudden freezing and thawing of the sap in unfavourable autumns. The first, we shall therefore call the *insect blight*, and the second, the *frozen-sap blight*.

1. THE INSECT BLIGHT. The symptoms of the *insect blight* are as follows: In the month of June or July, when the tree is in full luxuriance or growth, shoots at the extremities of the branches, and often extending down two seasons' growth, are observed suddenly to turn brown. In two or three days the leaves become quite black and dry, and the wood so shrivelled and hard as to be cut with difficulty with a knife. If the branch is allowed to remain, the disease sometimes extends a short distance further down the stem, but, usually, not much further than the point where the insect had made his lodgment. The insect which causes this blight, was first discovered by the Hon. John Lowell, of Boston, in 1816, and was described by Professor Peck, under the name of *Scolytus pyri*. It is very minute, being

scarcely one-tenth of an inch long ; and it escapes from the branch almost as soon as, by the withering of the leaves, we are aware of its attack ; hence, it is so rarely seen by careless observers. In the perfect state, it is a very small beetle, deep brown, with legs of a paler colour. Its thorax is short, convex, rough in front, and studded with erect bristles. The wing covers are marked with rows of punctured points, between which are also rows of bristles, and they appear cut off very obliquely behind.

This insect deposits its egg some time in July or August, either behind, or below a bud. Whether the egg hatches at once, we are not aware, but the following spring, the small grub or larva grows through the sap wood or tender alburnum, beginning at the root of the bud, and burrows towards the centre of the stem. Around this centre or pith, it forms a circular passage, sometimes devouring it altogether. By thus perforating, sawing off, or girdling, internally, a considerable portion of the vessels which convey the ascending sap, at the very period when the rapid growth of the leaves calls for the largest supply of fluid from the roots, the growth and the vitality of the branch are checked, and finally extinguished. The larva about this time, completes both its transformation, and its passage out, and, in the beetle form, emerges, with wings, into the air, to seek out new positions for laying its eggs and continuing its species. The small passage where it makes its exit, may now more easily be discovered, below or by the side of the bud, resembling a hole bored with a needle or pin.

It is well to remark here, that the attack of this blight insect is not confined to the pear, but in some parts of the country we have observed it preying upon the apple and the quince in the same manner. In the latter tree, the shoots that were girdled, were shorter, and at the extremities of the branches only ; not leading, therefore, to such serious consequences as in the pear.

The ravages of the *insect blight*, we are inclined to think, do not extend much below the point where the insect has deposited its egg, a material point of difference from the *frozen-sap blight* which often poisons the system of the whole tree, if allowed to remain, or if, originally, very extensive.

The remedy for the insect blight is very distinct. It is that originally suggested by Mr. Lowell, which we and many others have pursued with entire success, when the other form of the disease was not also present. This remedy consists, *at the very first indications of the existence of the enemy*, in cutting off and burning the diseased branch, a foot below the lowest mark of discoloration. The insect is usually to be found at the bottom of this blackened point, and it is very important that the branches be removed early, as the *Scolytus* is now about emerging from his burrow, and will speedily escape us, to multiply his mischief elsewhere. If there is much appearance of the insect blight, the tree should be examined every noon, so long as there are any indications of disease, and the amputated branches carried at once to the fire.

II. The frozen sap blight. We give this term to the most formidable phase of this disease that affects the pear tree. Though it is, by ordinary observers, often confounded in its effects, with the insect blight, yet it has strongly characteristic marks, and is far more fatal in its effects.

The symptoms of the *frozen-sap blight* are the following. First; the appearance, at the season of winter or spring pruning, of a *thick, clammy* sap, of a sticky nature, which exudes from the wounds made by the knife; the ordinary cut showing a clean and smooth surface.

Second; the appearance, in the spring, on the bark of the trunk or branches, often a considerable distance from the extremities, of black, shrivelled, dead, patches of bark.

Third; in early summer months, the disease fully manifests itself by the extremities shrivelling, turning black, and decaying, as if suddenly killed. If these diseased parts are cut off, the inner bark and heart-wood will be found dark and discoloured some distance below where it is fresh and green outside. If the tree is slightly affected only, it may pass off with the loss of a few branches, but if it has been seriously tainted, the disease, if not arrested, may, sooner or later, be carried through the whole system of the tree, which will gradually decline, or entirely perish.

To explain the nature of this disease, we must first premise that, in every tree, there are two currents of sap carried on, 1st, the upward current of sap, which rises through the outer wood, (or *alburnum*,) to be digested by the leaves; 2nd, the downward current, which descends through the inner bark, (or *liber*,) forming a deposite of new wood on its passage down.*

Now let us suppose, anterior to a blight season, a very sudden and early winter, succeeding a damp and warm autumn.† The summer having been dry, the growth of trees was completed early, but this excess of dampness in autumn, forces the trees into a vigorous second growth, which continues late. While the sap vessels are still filled with their fluids, a sharp and sudden freezing takes place, or is, perhaps, repeated several times, followed, in the day time, by bright sun. The descending current of sap becomes thick and clammy, so as to descend with difficulty; it chokes up the sap-vessels, freezes and thaws

* Being distributed towards the centre of the stem by the medullary rays which communicate from the inner bark to the pith.

† Which always happens previously to a summer when the blight is very prevalent, and will be remembered, by all, as having been especially the case in the autumn of 1843, which preceded the extensive blight of the past season.

again, loses its vitality, and becomes dark and discoloured, and in some cases, so poisonous, as to destroy the leaves of other plants, when applied to them. Here, along the inner bark, it lodges, and remains in a thick, sticky state, all winter. If it happens to flow down till it meets with any obstruction, and remains in any considerable quantity, it freezes again beneath the bark, ruptures and destroys the sap-vessels, and the bark and some of the wood beneath it shrivels and dies.

In the ensuing spring, the upward current of sap rises through its ordinary channel—the outer wood or alburnum—the leaves expand, and, for some time, nearly all the upward current being taken up to form leaves and new shoots, the tree appears flourishing. Toward the beginning of summer, however, the leaves commence sending the downward current of sap to increase the woody matter of the stem. This current, it will be remembered, has to pass downward, through the inner bark or *liber*, along which, still remain portions of the poisoned sap, arrested in its course the previous autumn. This poison is diluted, and taken up, by the new downward current, distributed toward the pith, and along the new layers of alburnum, thus tainting all the neighbouring parts. Should any of the adjacent sap-vessels have been ruptured by frost, so that the poison thus becomes mixed with the still ascending current of sap, the branch above it immediately turns black and dies, precisely as if poison were introduced under the bark. And very frequently it is accompanied with precisely the odour of decaying frost-bitten vegetation.*

The foregoing is the worst form of the disease, and it takes place when the poisoned sap, stagnated under the bark in spots, remains through the winter in a thick semi-fluid state, so as to be capable of being taken up in the descending current of the next summer. When, on the other hand, it collects in sufficient quantity to freeze again, burst the sap vessels, and afterwards dry out by the influence of the sun and wind, it leaves the patches of dead bark which we have already described. As part of the woody channels which convey the ascending sap probably remain entire and uninjured, the tree or branch will

* We do not know that this form of blight is common in Europe, but the following extract from the celebrated work of Duhamel on fruit trees, published in 1768, would seem to indicate something very similar, a long time ago.
" The sap corrupted by putrid water, or the excess of manure, bursts the cellular membranes in some places, extends itself between the wood and the bark, which it separates, and carries its poisonous acrid influence, to all the neighbouring parts, like a gangrene. When it attacks the small branches, they should be cut off; if it appears in the large branches or body of the tree, all the cankered parts must be cut out down to the sound wood, and the wound covered with composition. If the evil be produced by manure or stagnant water, (and it may be produced by other causes,) the old earth must be removed from the roots, and fresh soil put in its place, and means taken to draw off the water from the roots But if the disease has made much progress on the trunk, the tree is lost " *Traité des Arbres Fruitiers*, vol. 11, p. 109.

28

perhaps continue to grow the whole season and bear fruit, as if nothing had happened to it, drying down to the shrivelled spot of bark the next spring. The effect, in this case, is precisely that of girdling only, and the branch or tree will die after a time, but not suddenly.

From what we have said, it is easy to infer that it would not be difficult on the occurrence of such an autumn—when sudden congelation takes place in unripened wood—to predict a blight season for the following summer. Such has several times been done, and its fulfilment may be looked for, with certainty, in all trees that had not previously ripened their wood.*

So, also, it would and does naturally follow, that trees in a damp, rich soil, are much more liable to the frozen-sap blight, than those upon a dryer soil. In a soil over moist or too rich, the pear is always liable to make late second growths, and its wood will often be caught unripened by an early winter. For this reason, this form of blight is vastly more extensive and destructive in the deep, rich soils of the western states, than in the dryer and poorer soils of the east. And this will always be the case in over rich soils, unless the trees are planted on raised hillocks, or their luxuriance checked by root-pruning.

Again, those varieties of the pear, which have the habit of maturing their wood early, are very rarely affected with the frozen-sap blight. But late growing sorts, are always more or less liable to it, especially when the trees are young, and the excessive growth is not reduced by fruit-bearing. Every nurseryman knows that there are certain late growing sorts which are always more liable to this blight in the nursery. Among these we have particularly noticed the Passe Colmar and the Forelle, though when these sorts become bearing trees, they are

* Since the above was written, we have had the pleasure of seeing a highly interesting article by the Rev. H.W. Beecher, of Indiana, one of the most intelligent observers in the country. Mr. Beecher not only agrees in the main with us, but he fortifies our opinion with a number of additional facts of great value. We shall extract some of this testimony, which is vouched for by Mr B., and for the publication of which the cultivators of pears owe him many thanks.

"Mr R. Reagan of Putnam county, Ind., has for more than twelve years, suspected that this disease originated in the fall previous to the summer on which it declares itself. During the last winter, Mr. Reagan predicted the blight, as will be remembered by some of his acquaintances in Wayne Co., and in his pear orchards he marked the trees that would suffer, and pointed to the spot which would be the seat of the disease, and his prognostications were strictly verified. Out of his orchard of 200 pear trees, during the previous blight of 1832, only four escaped, and those had been transplanted, and had, therefore, made little or no growth.

Mr. White, a nurseryman, near Mooresville, Ind., in an orchard of over 150 trees, had not a single case of blight in the year 1844, though all around him its ravages were felt. What were the facts in this case? His orchard is planted on a mound-like piece of ground, is high, of a sandy, gravelly soil; earlier by a week, than nursery soils in this country; and in the summer of 1843, his trees grew through the summer, ripened and shed their leaves early in the fall, and during the warm spell made no second growth."

not more liable than many others. The Seckel pear is cele
brated for its general freedom from blight, which we attribute
entirely, to its habit of making short jointed shoots, and ripening its wood very early.

To distinguish the blight of the frozen sap from that caused
by the attack of the *Scylutus pyri*, is not difficult. The effects of
the latter cease below the spot where the insect has perforated
and eaten its burrow in the branch. The former spreads
gradually down the branch, which, when dissected, shows
the marks of the poison in the discoloration of the inner
bark and the pith, extending down some distance below the external marks of injury. If the poison becomes largely diffused
in the tree, it will sometimes die outright in a day or two ; but
if it is only slightly present, it will often entirely recover. The
presence of black, dry, shrivelled spots of bark on the branches,
or soft sappy spots, as well as the appearance of thick clammy
sap in winter or spring pruning, are the infallible signs of the
frozen-sap blight.

The most successful remedies for this disastrous blight, it is very
evident, are chiefly preventive ones. It is, of course, impossible for us to avoid the occasional occurrence of rainy, warm
autumns, which have a tendency to urge the trees into late second
growth. The principal means of escaping the danger really lies
in always studiously avoiding a damp soil for the fruit tree. Very
level or hollow surfaces, where heavy early autumnal rains are
apt to lie and saturate the ground, should also be shunned. And
any summer top dressing or enriching, calculated to stimulate
the tree into late growth, is pernicious. A rich, dry soil, is, on
the whole, the best, because there the tree will make a good
growth in time to ripen fully its wood, and will not be likely to
make second growth. A rich, moist soil, will, on the contrary,
serve continually to stimulate the tree to new growth. It is in
accordance with this, that many persons have remarked, that
those pear trees growing in common meadow land, were free
from blight in seasons when those in the rich garden soils were
continually suffering from it.

The first point then should be to secure a rich but dry, well
drained soil. Cold aspects and soils should be avoided, as likely
to retard the growth and ripening of the wood.

The second is to reject, in blighted districts, such varieties as
have the habit of making wood late, and choosing rather, those
of early habit, which ripen the wood fully before autumn.

Severe summer pruning, should it be followed by an early
winter, is likely to induce blight, and should therefore be avoided. Indeed, we think the pear should always be pruned in
winter or early spring.*

* The only severe case of blight in the gardens here, during the summer of
1844, was in the head of a Gilogil pear—a very hardy sort, which had never be

As a remedy for blight actually existing in a tree, we know of no other but that of freely cutting out the diseased branches, at the earliest moment after it appears. The amputation should be continued as far down as the least sign of discoloration, and consequent poisoning is perceptible, and it should not be neglected a single day after it manifests itself. A still better remedy, when we are led to suspect, during the winter, that it is likely to break out in the ensuing summer, is that of carefully looking over the trees before the buds swell, and cutting out all branches that show the discoloured or soft sappy spots of bark that are the first symptoms of the disease.

Finally, as a preventive, when it is evident, from the nature of the season and soil, that a late autumnal growth will take place, we recommend laying bare the roots of the trees for two or three weeks. Root pruning will always check any tendency to over-luxuriance in particular sorts, or in young bearing trees, and is therefore a valuable assistance when the disease is feared. And the use of lime in strong soils, as a fertilizer, instead of manure, is worthy of extensive trial, because lime has a tendency to throw all fruit trees into the production of short-jointed fruit-spurs, instead of the luxuriant woody shoots induced by animal manure.

In gardens, where, from the natural dampness of the soil or locality, it is nearly impossible to escape blight, we recommend that mode of dwarfing the growth of the trees—conical standards, or *quenouilles*, described in the section on pruning. This mode can scarcely fail to secure a good crop in any soil or climate where the pear tree will flourish.

After the blight, the other diseases which affect the pear tree are of little moment. They are chiefly the same as those to which the apple is liable, the same insects occasionally affecting both trees, and we therefore refer our readers to the section on the apple tree.

There is, however, a *slug worm*, which occasionally does great damage on the leaves of the pear tree, which it sometimes entirely destroys. This slug is the *Selandria cerasi* of Harris. It appears on the upper side of the leaves of the pear tree, from the middle of June till the middle of July. It is nearly half an inch long when fully grown, olive coloured, tapering from the head to the tail, not much unlike in shape a miniature tadpole. The best destructive for this insect is Mr. Haggerston's mixture of whale oil soap and water,* thoroughly showered or sprinkled over the leaves. In the absence of this, we have found ashes or quicklime, sifted or sprinkled over the leaves, early in the

fore suffered. The previous midsummer it had been severely pruned, and headed back, which threw it into late growth. The next season nearly the whole remaining part of the tree died with the frozen-sap blight.
* See page 54.

morning, to have an excellent effect in ridding the trees of this vigilant enemy.

VARIETIES. The varieties of pear have so multiplied within the last thirty yea s, that they may almost be considered endless. Of the new varieties, Belgium has produced the greatest number of high quality. England and France many of excellence ; and, lastly, quite a number of valuable sorts have originated in this country, to which some additions are made annually. The latter, as a matter of course, are found even more generally adapted to our climate than any foreign sorts. But we believe the climate of the middle states is so nearly like that of Belgium, that the pear is grown here as a standard to as great perfection as in any other country.

More than 700 kinds of pears, collected from all parts of the world, have been proved in the celebrated experimental garden of the Horticultural Society of London. Only a small proportion of these have been found of first rate quality, and a very large number of them are of little or no value. The great difficulty, even yet, seems to be, to decide which are the really valuable sorts, worth universal cultivation. We shall not, perhaps, arrive at this point, in this country, for several years— not until all the most deserving sorts have had repeated trials— and the difficulty is always increased by the fact of the difference of climate and soil. A variety may be of second quality in New-England, and of the first merit in Pennsylvania or Ohio. This, however, is true only to a very limited extent, as the fact that most sorts of the first character receive nearly the same praise in Belgium, England, and all parts of this country, clearly proves. High flavour, handsome appearance, productiveness, and uniformly good flavour in all seasons—these are the criterions of the first class of pears.*

There is an idea prevalent, which has been greatly extended by Kenrick, in his American Orchardist, that all the finest *old varieties* of pears are worthless and unfit for cultivation, by reason of their degeneration. It is but justice to say that this notion owes its origin to Mr. Knight, but Mr. Kenrick living near the sea-coast, in a climate, naturally rather unfavourable to the pear, has fortified it by what he has observed in his own neighbourhood, forgetting that facts in the country at large, do not bear testimony to the doctrine. We should be glad to show

* The most successful cultivator of pears in this country, whose collection comprises hundreds of varieties, lately assured us, that if he were asked to name all the sorts that he considered of *unvarying and unquestionable excellence* in all respects, he could not count more than 20! It may then be asked, why do all cultivate so large a variety. We answer, because the quality of many is yet not fully decided ; again, there is a great difference in taste, as to the merits of a given sort ; there are also some sorts so productive, or handsome, &c., that they are highly esteemed, though only second rate. In a work like the present, we are also obliged to describe many sorts of second quality, in order to assist in identifying them, as they are already in general cultivation.

him here, in the pear season, a great many varieties, which he
boldly denounces as " rejected outcasts," bearing as handsome
and abundant crops as any kinds originated within the last ten
years.   We shall recur to this subject more at length, hereafter, and will only state now, that by propagation on unhealthy
stocks, in a bad soil or climate, many sorts of pear have become
so enfeebled, as to be nearly worthless, near the sea-coast—
where, indeed, only the hardier sorts will long continue fair and
excellent.   On the other hand, the same sort, (if the tree has
not been brought already diseased from the sea-board,) will
thrive and bear with all its natural vigour in the interiour.
And, finally, we have observed, that some of the newest Flemish
pears, being naturally of feeble habit, already show the same
marks of decay or want of vigour as the oldest sorts.

In describing pears, we shall, as usual, designate the size by
comparison, as follows.   *Large*, as the Beurré Diel or Bartlett ;
medium, as the Doyenné or Virgalieu ; *small*, as the Seckel.
With regard to form, *pyriform*, as the Beurré Bosc ; *obtuse-pyriform*, as the Bartlett ; *obovate*, (egg-shaped reversed,) as the
Doyenné or Virgalieu ; *turbinate*, (*top-shaped*,) as the Dearborn's Seedling ; *roundish*, as the Gansel's Bergamot.

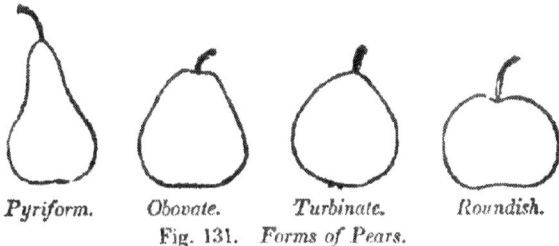

Pyriform.   *Obovate.*   *Turbinate.*   *Roundish.*
          Fig. 131.   *Forms of Pears.*

With regard to the texture of the flesh ; *buttery*, as the Doyenné and Bartlett ; *crisp*, as the Summer Bonchretien ; *juicy*,
as the Napoleon, and St. Germain ; as, in apples, the blossom
end is called the *eye*, the remains of the blossom found there,
the *calyx*, and the hollow in which it is placed, the *basin*.

Class I.   *Summer Pears.*

1. AMIRÉ JOANNET.   Thomp.

Early sugar, *Pom Man.*
Sugar Pear.   Joannette.
Harvest Pear.   St. John s Pear.
St. Jean.   Archduc d'ete ?

This fruit, better known here, as the *Early Sugar* pear, is **one**
of the very earliest, ripening at the beginning of July—**in**

France, whence it originally comes, about St. John's day—whence the name, Joannet. It is a pleasant, juicy fruit, of second quality, and lasts but a few days in perfection. It opens the pear season, with the little Muscat, to which it is superiour. Fruit below the middle size, regularly pyriform, tapering to the stalk, which is an inch and a half long, and thickest at the point of junction. Skin very smooth, at first light green, but becomes bright lemon color at maturity—very rarely with a faint blush. Calyx large, with reflexed segments, even with the surface. Flesh white, sugary, delicate and juicy at first, but soon becomes mealy; seeds very pointed. Head of the tree open, with a few declining branches.

2. AMBROSIA. Lind. Thomp.

Early Beurré.

The Ambrosia is a French pear, which has been about thirty years in cultivation. It is a very sugary and pleasant early fruit, but it keeps only a few days after ripening. It has been very lately introduced into the United States.

It is very distinct from the Julienne, which is sometimes called the Early Beurré in this country.

Fruit nearly of medium size, roundish - obovate, somewhat flattened. Skin

Fig. 131. *Ambrosia.*

smooth, greenish-yellow, thickly dotted with small gray specks, and a little russetted. Stalk about an inch and a half long, slender, and placed in a rather broad cavity. Calyx closed, set in a moderately deep basin. Flesh buttery and melting, with a sweet, rich, perfumed flavour. Last of August and first of September.

3. Bloodgood. § Man.

Early Beurré, of some.

The Bloodgood is the highest flavored of all early pears, and deserves a place even in the smallest garden. It was named from the circumstance of its having been brought into notice about 1835, by the late James Bloodgood, nurseryman, Flushing, L. I. The sort was brought to that nursery as a new variety, without a name however, by some person on Long Island, unknown to Mr. B., who was never able afterward to trace its history further. The tree is rather short jointed, with deep reddish brown wood, grows moderately fast, and bears early and regularly. The fruit, like that of all

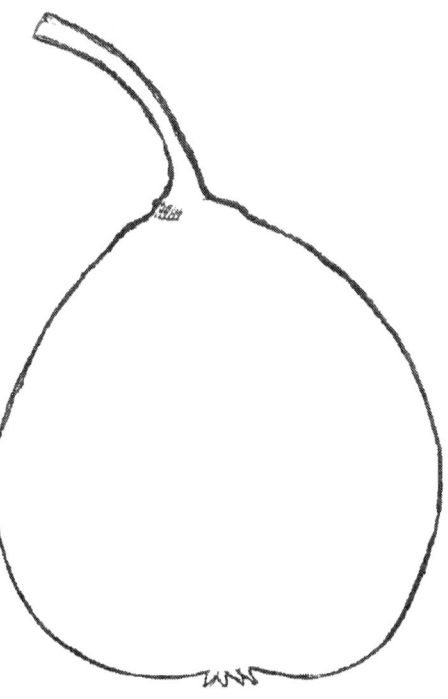

Fig. 132. *Bloodgood.*

early pears, is better if ripened in the house. It surpasses every European variety of the same season, and together with the Dearborn's Seedling, another native sort, will supplant in all our gardens the Jargonelle, and all inferiour early pears.

Fruit of medium size, turbinate, inclining to obovate, thickening very abruptly into the stalk. Skin yellow, sprinkled with russet dots, and net-work markings, giving it a russetty look on one side. Calyx strong, open, set almost without depression. Stalk obliquely inserted, without depression, short, dark brown, fleshy at its base. Flesh yellowish-white, buttery and melting, with a rich, sugary, highly aromatic flavour. The thin skin has a musky perfume. Core small. Ripe from the 25th of July to the 10th of August.

4. Beurré Haggerston. Man.

No. 8 of Van Mons. *Man.*

This is one of Van Mons' Seedlings, sent with others to our American pomologist, the late Mr. Manning, with permission to bestow a name. As it has not fruited here with us, we annex Mr. Manning's description.

" Medium size, oblong, obtuse at the stem, which is one inch long ; colour yellow ; flesh juicy, sharp, agreeable and very abundant." It will ripen here about the middle of August.

5. Bergamot, Early. Thomp. Lind. P. Mag.

A second rate, French sort. Fruit of medium size, roundish, rather flattened, and a little angular towards the eye. Skin pale yellowish-green, with a few streaks of dull red in the sun. Stalk rather thick, a little more than an inch long, set in a shallow cavity. Calyx moderately sunk. Flesh quite juicy, crisp, with a pleasant, sweet flavour. Ripe about the 20th of August.

6. Bergamot, Summer. Thomp. Coxe.

The Summer Bergamot is an old foreign variety, of small size, and second quality, quite supplanted now by such sorts as the Bloodgood, Dearborn's Seedling, &c. The tree is of feeble growth.

Fruit quite small, round. Skin yellowish-green, becoming brownish in the sun, and full of small russet dots. Calyx set in a wide basin. Flesh juicy, and pretty rich in flavour, but quickly becomes mealy and dry. Last of July.

There is a *Large* Summer Bergamot, cultivated in this country, quite distinct from the above. It resembles the Doyenné, but is broader and rounder, dryer and inferiour in flavour. Skin smooth, clear yellow, with very few dots. Stalk 1 1-2 inches long, curved, set in a narrow, deep cavity. Basin narrow, deep, smooth, with a small calyx. Flesh breaking and half buttery, not rich. September. The tree grows and bears finely.

7. Bergamot, Hampden's. Thomp.

Summer Bergamot. *Lind. Mill*
Bergamot d'Eté. *O. Duh.*
Bergamotte d'Angleterre.
Scotch Bergamot. } *ac. to*
Fingal's. } *Thomp.*
Ellanrioch.

Hampden's Bergamot is a strong growing, hardy tree, and a handsome, showy fruit, sometimes as attractive as the Bartlett, but of breaking texture, and not so high flavoured.

Fruit large, roundish, inclining to obovate. Skin at first green, becoming clear yellow at maturity, with small dots, and sometimes with greenish spots in the shade. Stalk scarcely three quarters of an inch long, rather stout, curved, and set in a small round cavity. Calyx small, closed, in a shallow basin. Flesh white, breaking, a little coarse in texture, but, if gathered early and ripened in the house, it becomes half buttery, sweet and agreeable. First of September.

8. Belle de Bruxelles. Nois. Thomp.

Belle d'Août.

A large and handsome fruit, of good quality, little known in this country, as two other sorts, Angleterre, and Flemish Beauty, have been wrongly imported under this name.

Fruit large, about four inches long, pyriform, tapering gradually to the stalk. Skin pale yellow, with a soft red cheek when fully exposed, otherwise entirely yellow. Stalk an inch and a half long, rather stout, obliquely inserted under a slight lip, fleshy at the lower end. Flesh white, juicy and melting, sweet, and slightly perfumed. Middle of August.

9. Bartlett, or Williams' Bonchretien. § Thomp. Man.

Bartlett, *of all American gardens.*
Williams' Bonchretien. *Thomp. Lind.*
Poire Guillaume, *of the French.*

This noble pear is, justly, one of the most popular of all the summer varieties. Its size, beauty and excellence, entitle it to this estimation, apart from the fact that it bears very early, regularly and abundantly. It is an English variety, originated about 1770, in Berkshire, and was afterwards propagated by a London grower by the name of Williams. When first introduced to this country its name was lost, and having been cultivated and disseminated by Enoch Bartlett, Esq., of Dorchester, near Boston, it became so universally known as the *Bartlett* pear, that it is impossible to dispossess it now.* It suits our climate admirably, ripening better here than in England, and has the unusual property of maturing perfectly in the house, even if it is picked before it is full grown. It has no competitor as a summer market fruit. The tree grows upright, with thrifty, yellowish-brown shoots, and narrow, folded leaves.

Fruit of large size, irregularly pyramidal. Skin very thin and smooth, clear yellow, (with a soft blush on the sunny side, in exposed specimens,) rarely marked with faint russet. Stalk one

---

* The first imported tree in Mr. Bartlett's grounds, was sent from England in 1799.

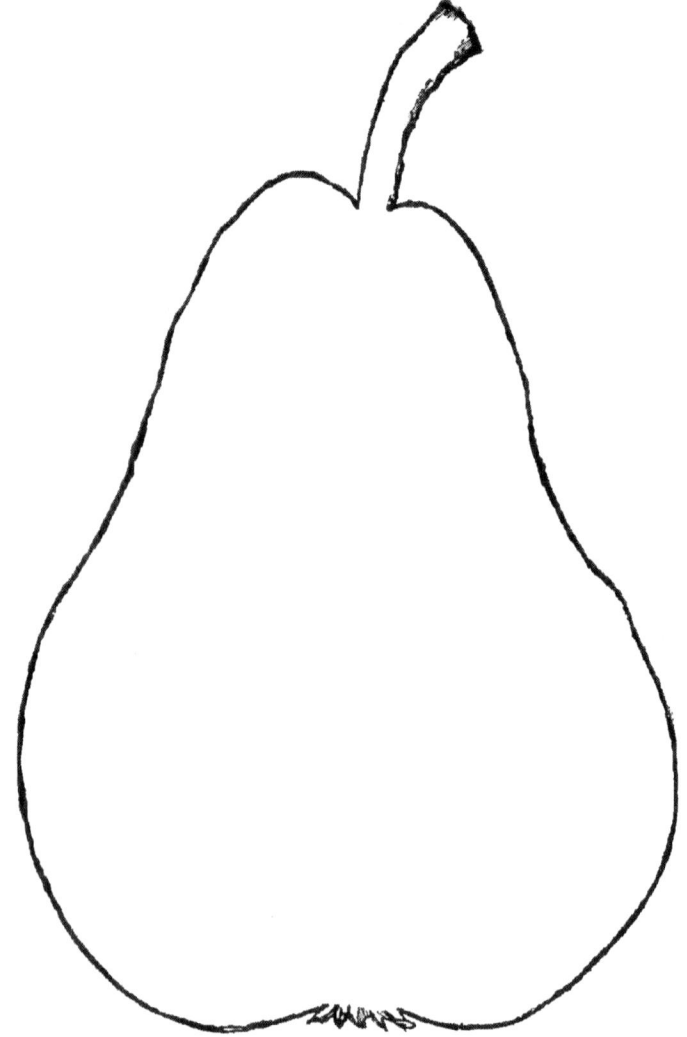

Fig. 134. *Bartlett.*

to one and a half inches long, stout, inserted in a shallow, flat cavity. Calyx open, set in a very shallow, obscurely plaited basin. Flesh white, and exceedingly fine-grained and buttery; it is full of juice, sweet, with a highly perfumed, vinous flavour. (In damp or unfavourable soils, it is sometimes slightly acid.) Ripens from the last of August to the middle and last of September.

10. CRAWFORD. Thomp. Man.

A Scotch fruit, of second quality; the chief merit of which, is its hardiness in a cold climate.

Fruit middle sized, obovate, regularly formed. Skin light yellow, tinged with brown in the sun. Flesh white, buttery, sweet, and of a tolerably pleasant flavour. August.

11. Citron. Wilder. MSS.

One of Gov. Edwards' seedlings, lately originated at New-Haven. The trial of two seasons indicates that it is nearly, if not quite, first rate.

Fruit of medium size, roundish, and shaped somewhat like a Bergamot, to which it has some affinity. Skin dull green, regularly sprinkled with small russetty dots. Flesh greenish-white, a little coarse, melting and juicy, with a rich perfumed flavour. Last of August.

12. Dearborn's Seedling. § Man. Thomp.

A very admirable, early pear, of first quality, raised in 1818, by the Hon. H. A. S. Dearborn, of Boston. It bears most abundant crops in every soil, and is one of the most desirable early varieties, succeeding the Bloodgood, and preceding the Bartlett. Young shoots long, dark brown. Fruit scarcely of medium size, turbinate, and very regularly formed. Skin very smooth, clear light yellow, with a few minute dots. Stalk slender, rather more than an inch long, set with very little depression. Calyx with delicate, spreading segments, set in a very shallow basin. Flesh white, very juicy and melting, sweet and sprightly in favour. Ripens about the middle of August.

No. 135.   *Dearborn's Seedling.*

13. Doyenné d'Eté. Nois. Bon. Jard.

Summer Doyenné.

The Doyénné d'Eté is shaped very much like a small White Doyenné. The skin is smooth, shining, clear yellow, marked with very small dots; and sometimes washed with faint red next the sun. Stalk short, thick, and fleshy. Calyx small, closed, basin very slightly sunk. Flesh white, melting, very juicy, sweet, with a little acid, and of excellent flavour. It ripens at the last of July and beginning of August. The tree bears abun dantly, but is quite different from the Doyenné in its growth. M. Poiteau remarks that this pear has been cultivated for many years at Nantes, though, till lately, little known in Paris.

14. GREEN CHISEL. Thomp. Fors. Lind.

Green Sugar. } of some *English*
, Sugar.   } *gardens.*

A pleasant old English pear, but not at all comparable with the new early sorts already described. The shoots grow quite erect, and the fruit is borne in clusters.

Fruit small, nearly round, tapering a little to the stalk. Skin quite green, with, occasionally, a dull brown cheek at full maturity. Stalk straight, three-fourths of an inch long, set almost without depression. Calyx open, crumpled, rather large. Flesh juicy, a little gritty in texture, with a sweet and pleasant flavour. Ripe the middle of August. This is quite distinct from the *Madeleine*, an *obovate* pear, with which it is sometimes confounded.

15. HESSEL. Thomp.

Hazel.

A Scotch pear, enormously productive, pretty, and of agreeable flavour, though it lasts only a few days in perfection. Tree with weeping branches.

Fruit rather below medium size, obovate. Skin yellowish-green, strongly marked with numerous dots, which give it a brownish, freckled appearance. Stalk an inch long, obliquely inserted. Calyx small, set in a shallow basin. Flesh whitish, juicy, with a pleasant, sugary flavour. First of September.

16. JARGONELLE, (of the English.) Thomp. Lind. P. Mag.

Epargne. *O. Duh. Poit. Pom. Man.*
Grosse Cuisse Madame.
Beau Présent.   } *of various*   Frauenschenkel.
Poire de tables des princes. } *French.*   Real Jargonelle.
Saint Sampson.   } *gardens.*   Sweet Summer.
Saint Lambert.

This fruit, the true Jargonelle pear,* was for a long time considered the finest of Summer pears, and Thompson yet says

* Although called by Thompson the English Jargonelle, to distinguish it from the fruit more common under that name on the continent, there is no doubt that

" the best of its season."   We think, that no man will hesitate, however, to give the most decided preference to our native sorts, the Bloodgood, and Dearborn's Seedling. It is still, however, one of the most common fruits in the New-York market, partly, because it bears abundant crops, and partly, because these superiour new sorts, have scarcely yet, had time to displace it. We consider it only a second rate fruit, and one that quickly decays at the core.

Fruit pretty large, long pyriform, tapering into the stalk. Skin greenish-yellow, smooth, with a little brownish colour on the sunny side. Stalk nearly two inches long, rather slender, curved, obliquely set. Calyx open, with quite long projecting segments, and sunk in a small and furrowed basin. The flesh is yellowish-white, rather coarse grained, juicy, with a sprightly, refreshing flavour. The tree is a strong grower, with a rather straggling, pendant habit. Ripens the last of July and first of August.

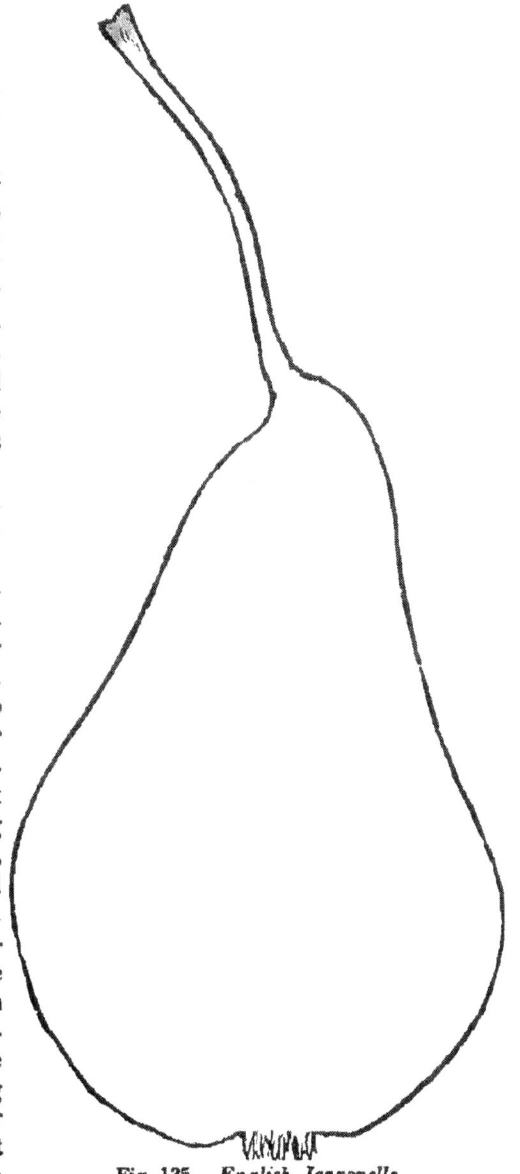

Fig. 135. *English Jargonelle.*

it was introduced originally from France. Antiquarians derive its name from *Gergon*, Italian, a corruption of *Græcum*, whence Merlet supposes it to be the *Numidianum Græcum* of Pliny, and the *Græculum* of Macrobius. This, if correct, would prove it to be a very ancient sort.

The common CUISSE MADAME of the French authors and gardens, is an inferiour and smaller variety of Jargonelle, not worth cultivating. It has long, straight, rather slender, brownish-red branches, while the true Jargonelle has long straggling, dangling branches. The blossoms of the latter are also unusually large. [See also Windsor Pear.]

17. JARGONELLE, (of the French.) Thomp.

Bellisime d'Eté. *O. Duh. Nois.*	Red Muscadel. *Lind. Mill*
Supréme.	Sabine d'Eté.
Bellissime Supréme. } *of French*	Summer Beauty. *Pom. Man.*
Bellisime Jargonelle. } *gardens.*	English Red Cheek. } *of many Ame-*
Vermillion d'Été.	Red Cheek. } *rican gardens*

This, which Mr. Thompson calls, by way of distinction, the *French Jargonelle*, because it is most commonly received under that name from France, is a higher coloured and handsomer fruit than the English Jargonelle, though much inferiour in quality, and, in fact, lasts only a day or two in perfection, and is often mealy and over-ripe, while the exterior is fair and tempting. It has a bright red cheek, and a shorter obovate form, blunt at the stalk.

The tree is of very strong, upright growth. Fruit of medium size, obovate in form. Skin shining, light green, becoming lemon colour, with a very rich, deep red cheek. Stalk about an inch long, rather stiff and stout, and set in a blunt depression. Calyx in a shallow, slightly irregular basin. Flesh white, coarse, breaking, sweet, and soon rots at the core. Ripens the last of July and first of August.

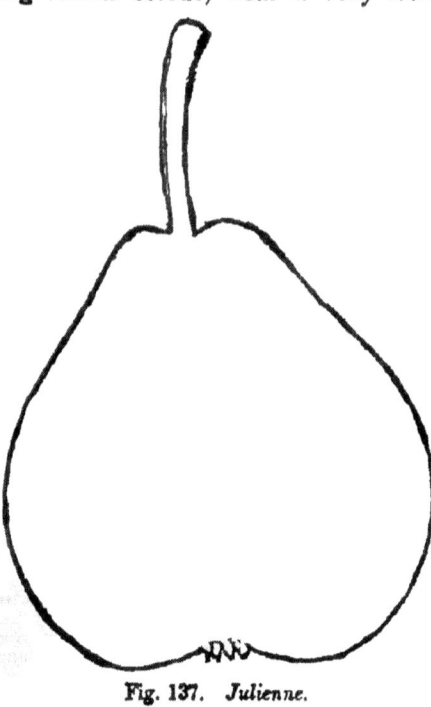

Fig. 137. *Julienne.*

18. JULIENNE. Coxe. Man.

A handsome summer pear, which so much resembles the Doyenné or St. Michael, as to be called, by some, the Summer St. Michael. It is a beautiful and most productive fruit, and comes into bearing very early. It is often of excellent flavour, and of the first quality; but, unfortunately, it is variable in these respects, and some seasons, it is comparatively taste less and insipid. In rich, warm, and dry soils, it is almost al. ways fine. It is a profitable market fruit, and will always command a prominent place in the orchard. The tree is of thrifty upright growth, with light yellowish-brown shoots.

Fruit of medium size, but varying in different soils; obovate, regularly formed. Skin very smooth and fair, clear bright yellow, on all sides. Stalk light brown, speckled with yellow, a little more than an inch long, pretty stout, inserted in a very shallow depression. Calyx small, closed, set in a basin slightly sunk, but often a little plaited. Flesh white, rather firm at first, half buttery, sweet, and moderately juicy. Ripens all the month of August.

Coxe considered this synonymous with Archiduc d'Eté of Duhamel and Lindley—the *Ognonet* pear, a distinct and inferiour fruit, with a brownish cheek, and we therefore follow Mr. Man ning in keeping it distinct. It may yet prove synonymous with the Doyenné d'Ete of the French, which has not yet been fairly proved in this country. (See Doyenné d'Eté.)

19. LIMON.   Van Mons. Man. in H. M.

A fine, sprightly, Belgian pear, originated by Van Mons. The fruit resembles, in outward appearance, the White Doyenné, but it is distinguished from that well known fruit, by its ripening a month earlier. The young shoots are long, slender, reddish brown.

Fruit rather large, obovate. Skin smooth, yellow, with a faint red cheek. Stalk an inch and a half long, rather stout, set in a moderately depressed, round cavity. Calyx set in a rather shallow, round basin. Flesh white, buttery, melting and juicy, with a sprightly, high flavour. Middle of August.

This is evidently quite distinct from the Limon de Louvain, of the *Jardin Frutier*, a winter pear.

20. LITTLE MUSCAT.   Thomp. Lind. Mill.

Little Musk.	} *Coxe.*	Muscat petit. } *O. Duh.*
Primitive.		Sept-en-gueule.
Petit Muscat.		

This very little, French pear, well known in many of our gardens, is allowed a place there, chiefly, because it is the earl iest of all pears, ripening at the beginning of July. The tree is of very handsome, pyramidal growth, and bears the most enormous crops of pears, in *clusters*. The fruit, which is but little more than an inch in diameter, is shaped like a little rounded top, and is just passably good at its season.

Fruit very small, turbinate. Skin yellow, with a dull red cheek. Stalk half, to one and a half inches long, set almost without depression. Calyx open, set nearly level. Flesh breaking, sweet, with a slight musk flavour. Shoots dark brown.

21. MUSCAT ROBERT. Thomp. O. Duh. Lind.

Poire à la Reine.	Musk Robine. *Lind.*
D'Ambre.	Early Queen.
St. Jean Musqueé Gros.	Queen's Pear.

A larger and better kind of Muscat, which might be esteemed first rate, had we not the Bloodgood to compare it with. Shoots yellowish-brown. Middle of July, and lasts only a few days.

Fruit small, about an inch and a half in diameter, turbinate Skin clear greenish-yellow. Stalk nearly an inch long, set with a little unevenness, but no depression. Calyx large, open, scarcely sunk. Flesh white, tender, juicy and pleasant.

22. MADELEINE, OR CITRON DES CARMES. § Lind. P. Mag. Thomp

Madeleine. *Nois.*	Green Chisel. ⎱ *incorrectly, of some*
Citron des Carmes. *O. Duh.*	Early Chaumontelle. ⎰ *American gardens.*
Magdelen.	

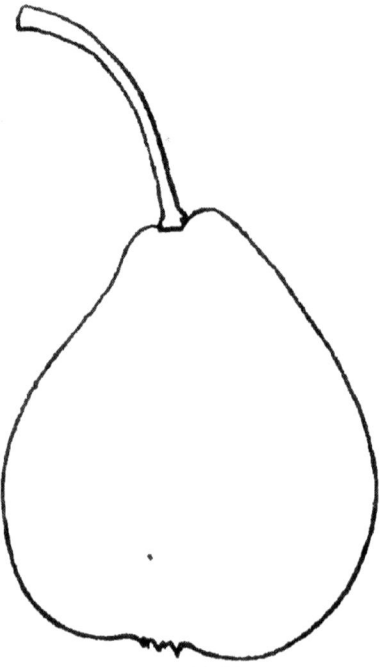

The Madeleine is one of the most refreshing and excellent of the early pears; indeed, as yet, much the best at the time of its ripening—before the Bloodgood. It takes its name from its being in perfection, in France, at the feast of St. Madeleine. Citron des Carmes comes from its being first cultivated by the Carmelite monks. It is much the finest early French variety, and deserves a place in all collections. The tree is fruitful and vigorous, with long erect olive-coloured branches.

Fruit of medium size, obovate, but tapering gradually to the stalk. Stalk long and slender, often nearly two inches, set on the side of a small swelling. Skin smooth, pale yellowish-green, (very

Fig. 133. *Madeleine.*

rarely, with a little brownish blush and russet specks around the stalk.) Calyx small, in a very shallow, furrowed basin. Flesh white, juicy, melting, with a sweet and delicate flavour, slightly perfumed. Middle and last of July.

23. MUSCADINE. §

The Muscadine is a first rate pear, remarkable for its high musky aroma. It was first disseminated by us, the original tree growing on the farm of the late Dr. Fowler, in this county, by whom it was named. Its history is uncertain, and it is believed to be a native. It bears very heavy crops, and if the fruit is picked, and ripened in the house, it is not surpassed in flavour by any pear of its time.

Fruit of medium size, roundish obovate, regularly formed. Skin pale yellowish green, a

Fig. 139. *Muscadine.*

little rough, thickly sprinkled with brown dots. Stalk about an inch long, set in a well formed, small cavity. Calyx with reflexed segments, set in a shallow basin. Flesh white, buttery and melting, with an agreeable, rich, musky flavour. Last of August, and first of September. Shoots stout, dark gray-brown.

24. PASSANS DU PORTUGAL. § Thomp.

Summer Portugal.

A delicate and pleasant pear, which comes early into bearing, and produces very large crops. Shoots upright, reddish-brown.

Fruit below medium size, roundish and much flattened. Skin pale yellow, with a cheek of fairest brown, becoming red in the sun. Stalk nearly an inch long, inserted in a round, regular hollow. Calyx stiff, basin moderately sunk. Flesh white, juicy, breaking, of very delicate; agreeable flavour. Last of August.

25. Rousselet Hâtif. O. Duh. Thomp.

Early Catherine. *Coxe.*	Early Rousselet. *Lind.*
Kattern, *of Boston.*	Perdreau.
Cyprus Pear.	Poire de Chypre. *Poit.*

The Rousselet Hâtif, better known in our markets as the Early Catherine Pear, though not a first rate fruit, has good qualities as an early variety. It bears very heavy crops as soon as the tree is well grown, when its willowy limbs bend with the weight of the fruit. It is, therefore, profitable for the market. The fruit is thought better when ripened on the tree.

Fruit rather small, pyriform, the neck narrowing into the somewhat fleshy stalk, which is one, to one and a half inches long. Skin when fully ripe, yellow, with a brownish red cheek. Calyx small, placed in a shallow basin. Flesh tender, a little coarse grained, sweet, pleasant, and slightly perfumed. Ripens the last of July. Young shoots stout, olive coloured.

26. Rousselet de Rheims. O. Duh. Thomp.

Rousselet.
Petit Rousselet. *Nois.*
Spice or Musk Pear.

This nice French pear, originally from Rheims, is supposed to have been the parent of our Seckel. There is a pretty strong resemblance in the colour, form, and flavour of the two fruits, but the Seckel is much the most delicious. The growth is quite different, and this pear has remarkably long and thrifty dark brown shoots. It is sugary, and with a peculiarly aromatic, spicy flavour, and if it were only *buttery*, would be a first rate fruit.

Fruit below medium size, obovate, inclining to pyriform. Skin yellowish-green on the shady side, but nearly covered with brownish red, with russetty specks. Stalk rather more than an inch long, curved, and inserted without depression. Calyx spreading, set even with the fruit. Flesh

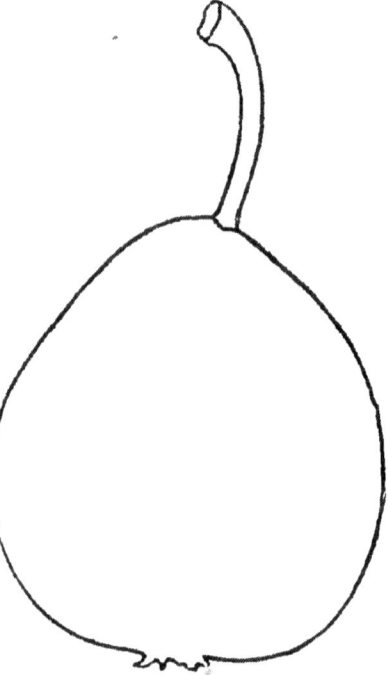

Fig. 140. *Rousselet de Rheims.*

breaking or half buttery, with a sweet, rich, aromatic flavour Ripe at the beginning of September.

27. Sugar Top. Thomp.

July Pear.
Prince's Sugar.
Prince's Sugar Top.

The Sugar Top is one of those indifferent pears, which, from their great productiveness and good appearance, make a figure in our markets, though not worthy of a place in a good garden. Great quantities of the Sugar Top pear may be seen in the New-York markets in July.

Fruit of medium size, very regular, roundish-top-shaped. Skin smooth, and very bright, clear yellow over the whole surface. Stalk stout, obliquely inserted, with a thickening at the point of junction. Calyx in a narrow basin. Flesh white, somewhat juicy and breaking, sweet, but with little flavour. Last of July.

28. Summer Franc Réal. § Thomp. Lind. P. Mag.

Franc Réal d'Eté. *Diel.*
Gros Micet d'Eté.
Fondante. *Knoop.*

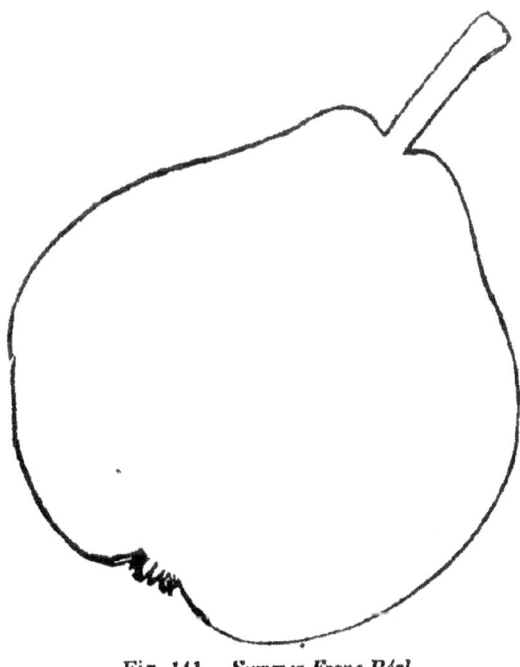

The Summer Franc Réal is one of the best summer pears, always melting and delicious, it fills, along with Dearborn's Seedling, the space, in ripening, between those favourite sorts, the Bloodgood and the Bartlett. *Réal* is a Spanish gold coin, and we presume, this fruit must have been named from its *sterling* merit, as it is not gold *colour*. The tree is thrifty, hardy, and bears well, and is easily known by its rounded, light co-

Fig. 141. *Summer Franc Réal.*

loured leaves. It is hardy, and bears admirably in all kinds of soil.

Fruit of medium size, obovate, but largest in the middle, and tapering each way. Skin green at first, becoming pale yellow-ish-green, dotted with small, brownish-green dots. Stalk short, thick, and rather uneven, inserted in a shallow cavity. Calyx small, closed, with long segments, set in a furrowed basin. Flesh white, fine grained, buttery and melting, with a rich, sugary, excellent flavour. Core large. Ripe early in September.

29. SANSPEAU, OR SKINLESS. Thomp. Lind. Mill.

Poire Sans Peau. *O. Duh.*
Fleur de Guignes.

The Skinless is a very nice little pear, with a remarkably thin, smooth skin, and a delicate, perfumed flavour. It bears in clusters, and very regularly. It is not first rate, but is esteem-ed by many.

Fruit below medium size, long pyriform. Skin very smooth and thin, pale green, becoming light yellow, speckled with light red in the sun. Stalk long, slender, curved, inserted in a very trifling cavity. Calyx closed, set in a small basin. Flesh white, juicy, half melting, with a sweet and slightly perfumed flavour. First of August.

This is quite distinct from the Early Rous-selet.

30. SUMMER ROSE.

Epine Rose. *Duh. Nois.*
Poire de Rose.
Caillot Rosat d'Eté.
Epine d'Eté Couleur Rose.
Thorny Rose. *Mill.*
Rosenbirne, *of the Germans.*
Ognon. } *wrongly, of*
Epine d'Eté. } *some.*

A handsome and peculiar summer pear, very popular, and well known on the other continent. It is quite flat, and remarkably like an apple in ap-pearance.

Fruit of medium size, round, flattened at

Fig. 142. *Summer Rose.*

both ends. Skin faint yellow, blended and speckled with russet in the shade, with a red russet cheek, marked with brown dots. Sta : rather more than an inch long, slender, curved, inserted in a very small hollow. Calyx open, small, set in a very shallow basin. Flesh white, juicy, rich and sugary, hardly first rate. Last of August. Shoots upright, gray-olive.

31. Sucrée de Hoyerswerda. Thomp.

Sugar of Hoyersworda.

A pleasant German pear, of peculiar flavour, excellent when ripened in the house. It bears immense crops. Leaves very narrow.

Fruit of medium size, obovate—sometimes oblong, lengthening into the stalk, which is curved and obliquely inserted. Skin smooth and fair, pale yellowish-green, thickly sprinkled with greenish russet dots. Calyx very small, and placed in a very shallow basin. Flesh white, quite juicy, with a sweet and piquant flavour. It does not keep long. Last of August. Shoots long, olive brown.

32. Epine d'Eté. Thomp. Lind.

Summer Thorn.
Fondante Musquee
Satin Vert.

A second rate, juicy, and pretty good fruit, which may be introduced in a large collection. It looks a little like a small Jargonelle. A good bearer. Shoots yellowish-brown.

Fruit middle sized, pyriform. Skin smooth, greenish-yellow; a little darker on the sunny side. Stalk stout, about an inch long, set without depression. Calyx short, set in a small plaited basin. Flesh tender, melting, with a sweet, musky, peculiar flavour. Last of August and first of September. Set with little or no cavity.

33. Summer Bon Chrétien. Mill. Thomp. Lind. P. Mag.

Bon Chretien d'Eté. *O. Duh.* Summer Good Christian.
                              Musk Summer Bon Chretien. *Coxe.*
Gratioli.   Sommer Apothekerbirne.
Gratioli d'Eté. } *of the*   Sommer Gute Christenbirne. } *of the*
Gratioli di Roma. } *Italians.* Die Sommer Christebirne. } *Germans.*
                Large Sugar, *of some.*

This is one of the oldest pears, having been cultivated for the last two centuries, all over Europe. It is common with us, but the stock is generally somewhat diseased. The tree has drooping shoots, and bears at the extremities of the branches Though a sweet and pleasant pear, it wants the flavour of our finer sorts, and does not deserve a place in a small garden.

Fruit large, irregularly bell-shaped or pyriform, with swollen, *knobby* sides. Skin yellow, with an orange-blush in finely ripened specimens, dotted with many green specks. Stalk long, irregular, curved, obliquely inserted in a knobby depression. Calyx small, in a narrow, uneven, shallow basin. Flesh yellowish, coarse grained, very juicy, and of a pleasant, simply sweet flavour. Very large blossoms and dangling leaves. Last of August, or early in September.

34. SUMMER ST. GERMAIN. Thomp.

Short's Saint Germain.
Saint Germain de Martin.
St. Germain d'Eté. *N. Duh.*

A pleasant, juicy, summer pear, of second rate flavour, bearing large crops, and growing vigorously.

Fruit of medium size, obovate. Skin pale green all over the surface. Stalk an inch and a quarter long, obliquely inserted. Calyx in a basin scarcely sunken. Flesh juicy, tender, sweet, with a very slight acid, and very good.

35. VALLÉE FRANCHE. Thomp. Duh.

De Vallée. *Nois. Poit.*
Bonne de Keinzheim.
De Keinzheim.

A second rate sweet, summer pear, productive, but by no means, in our opinion, of first quality. It ripens with the Bartlett, and is immeasurably inferiour to it in this climate.

Fruit of medium size, obovate, or turbinate, and tapering to the stalk. Skin pale green, becoming pale yellowish-green, regularly sprinkled with numerous small, gray dots. Stalk about an inch long, set with little or no cavity. Calyx in a shallow basin. Flesh white, not fine grained, quite juicy, but not buttery, and of a simply sweet flavour. Last of August.

36. WINDSOR. Lind. Thomp.

Summer Bell.
Cuisse Madame, *of some.*
Konge.

The Windsor is an old European pear, very commonly known in some parts of this country, as the Summer Bell pear. Large quantities are grown for market. It is, however, only a third rate fruit. The tree is remarkable for its stout, perfectly upright dark-brown shoots.

Fruit large, pyriform, or bell-shaped, widest above the middle, narrowing to the eye, and slender in form, tapering into the stalk Skin yellowish-green, dotted with small green specks, and tinged with a little dull orange next the sun. Stalk an inch and a half long, slender. Calyx small, closed, set with little or no depression. Flesh white, tender, or soft, a little coarse-grained at the core, sweet, with a somewhat astringent juice. Last of August.

37. WILLIAMS' EARLY. § Man.

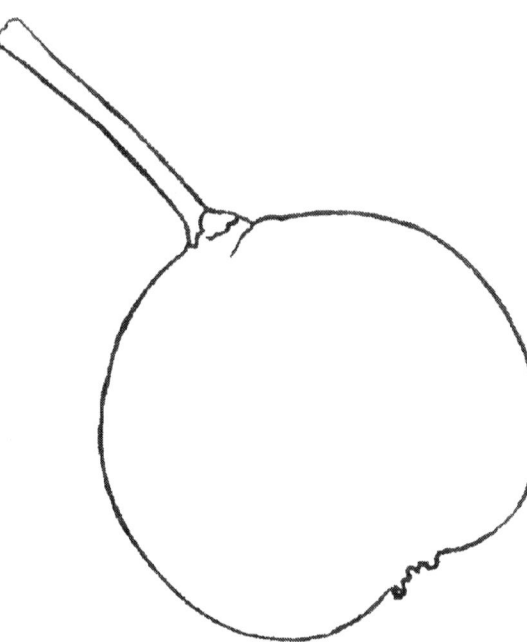

A native fruit, which originated on the farm of Mr. A. D. Williams, of Roxbury, Mass. It is a very handsome, small pear, of excellent quality, and a good bearer.

Fruit below medium size, roundish-turbinate, regularly formed. Skin bright yellow, thickly sprinkled with rich scarlet dots on the sunny side. Stalk an inch and a half long, straight, a little fleshy where it joins the fruit.

Fig. 143. *Williams' Early.*

Calyx very short, open; basin shallow, and slightly plaited. Flesh white, a little coarse-grained at first, but, when ripe, very juicy, half buttery, rich, with a slightly musky flavour. First, to the middle of September. Young wood dark.

Class II. Autumn Pears.

---

38. ALPHA. Thomp.

A Belgian seedling, received from Dr. Van Mons. It is a pleasant pear.

Fruit of medium size, obovate, a little inclining to oblong. Skin smooth, pale yellowish-green, dotted with reddish points, and having a thin, pale brown blush. Stalk little more than an inch long, inserted in a slight depression. Calyx stiff, open, set in a round basin of moderate size. Flesh white, fine grained, buttery and good. Middle of October.

39. ANDREWS. § Man. Ken.

Amory.
Gibson.

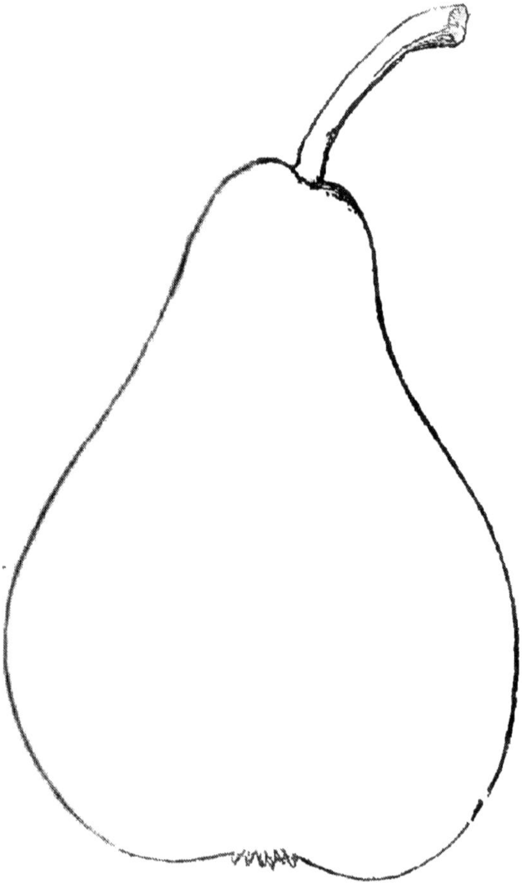

The Andrews is a favorite native seedling, found in the neighbourhood of Dorchester, and first introduced to notice by a gentleman of Boston, whose name it bears. It has, for the last 15 years, been one of the most popular fruits. It is of most excellent flavour, a certain and regular bearer, even while young, and the tree, which is very hardy, never suffers from blight.

Fruit rather large, pyriform, one-sided. Skin smooth, and rather thick, pale yellowish - green, with a dull red cheek, and a few scattered dots. Stalk about an inch and a quarter long, curved, set in a

Fig. 144. *Andrews.*

very shallow, blunt depression, or often without depression. Calyx open, placed in a small basin. Flesh greenish-white, full of juice, melting, with a fine vinous flavour. Early in September. Shoots diverging, light olive.

40. ANANAS. § Bon. Jard.

Poire Ananas. Nois.

This new and delicious pear was introduced very recently from France, by Col. Wilder of Boston. It is a rich flavoured fruit, of the first quality, with an agreeable perfume, not how-

30

ever resembling that of the pine-apple, as its name would lead
one to suppose.

Fruit of medium size, roundish-obovate. Skin greenish-yellow, slightly marked with russet, and occasionally with red on
the sunny side. Stalk rather stout, thicker at the point of insertion. Calyx closed, and set in a shallow basin. Flesh white,
melting, very juicy, with a rich and perfumed flavour. Ripens
the last of September and beginning of October. Young wood
olive.

41. ANANAS D'ETÉ.   Thomp.

Ananas, (*of Manning.*)

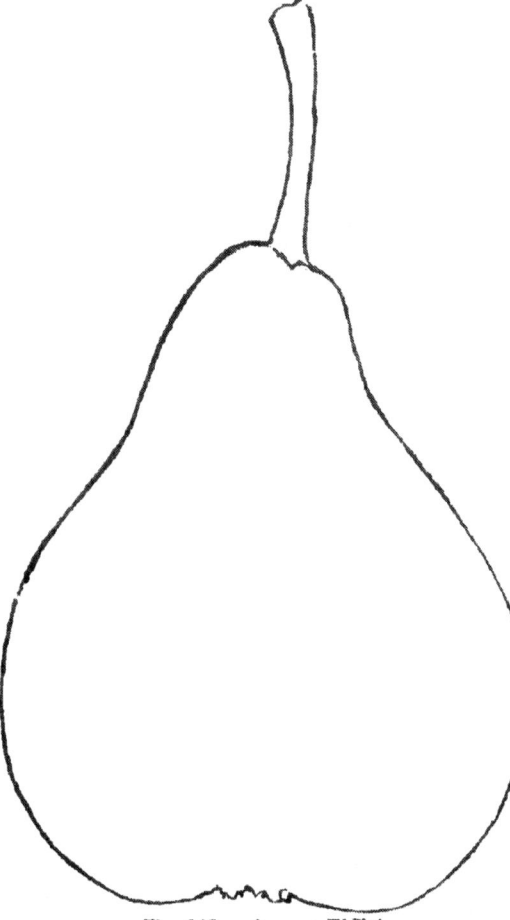

This fruit was first received from the London Horti-cultural Society, by Mr. Manning. It is a very excellent pear, with a rich and somewhat peculiar flavour, but should rather be called an *autumn* pine-apple, than a summer one.

Fruit rather large, pyriform, or occasionally obtuse at the stalk. Skin rough and coarse, dark yellowish-green, with a little brown on one side, and much covered with large rough, brown russet dots. Stalk an inch and a quarter long, inserted sometimes in a blunt cavity, sometimes without depression, by the side of a lip. Calyx open, with

Fig. 145.   *Ananas D'Eté.*

short divisions, basin shallow. Flesh fine grained, buttery and
melting, with a sweet, perfumed and high flavour. September
and October.

42. ANGLETERRE. Thomp.

English Beurré. *Lind.*
Beurré d'Angleterre. *Nois.*

A most productive pear, which has some affinity to Brown Beurré, but is inferiour to it in flavour. It is a good orchard fruit, but is not worthy of a place in a small garden. The tree forms a very erect, pyramidal head. Young wood olive. It is one of the most common fruits in the market of Paris.

Fruit of medium size, pyriform, very evenly shaped, tapering very regularly to its union with the stalk, which is slender, and rather more than an inch long. Skin rather thick and hard, dull light green, thickly speckled with russet dots, and having a thin brownish russet cheek. Calyx set in a very smooth, scarcely sunk basin. Flesh white, buttery and melting, full of juice, and of pleasant, though not high flavour. Middle of September.

43. ASTON TOWN. P. Mag. Thomp. Lind.

A very hardy little pear, from the village of Aston, in Chester, England. It is of tolerable flavour, sometimes excellent, and the tree, when in bearing, is characterized by its long slender branches, which have a half-twisted, dangling appearance. It bears great crops, and is especially worthy of notice in an unfavourable soil, and cold climate.

Fruit rather small, form roundish-turbinate. Skin a little rough, pale brownish-green, becoming yellowish when ripe, and thickly dotted with brown specks. Stalk an inch and a half long, rather straight and slender, inserted with little or no cavity. Calyx nearly closed, in a very

Fig. 146. *Aston Town.*

shallow basin.   Flesh soft, buttery, moderate y sweet, perfumed, and good.   Middle and last of September.

44. ALTHORPE CRASSANE.   Thomp. Lind

This fine English pear is a seedling raised by the late T. A. Knight, Esq., President of the London Horticultural Society.   It was sent by him to the Hon. John Lowell, of Boston, in 1832.   It is very highly rated in England, and is recommended as a very hardy tree.   The specimens as yet raised in this country have proved of excellent quality, but not quite equal to its reputation.

Fruit of medium size, roundish-obovate, but narrowing rather more to the eye than the stalk.   Skin pale green, dotted with small russetty points, and having a little tinge of brown on one side.   Stalk about an inch and a half long, slender, curved, and slightly inserted. Calyx with many divisions, set in a shallow basin, having a few plaits. Flesh white, buttery, and quite juicy,

Fig. 147.   *Althorpe Crassane.*

with a rather rich, slightly perfumed juice.   October and November.

Either there is a spurious sort strongly resembling this, or the Althorpe Crassane is somewhat variable in quality, as we have seen specimens quite indifferent.

45. Amande Double. Van Mons.

Amanda's Double. *Man. in Hov. Mag.*

One of Van Mons' seedlings, received by Mr. Manning, and we suppose named by Van Mons, in allusion to its having double *kernels*. It is a very handsome fruit. By misconception it has been called here *Amanda's Double*. Mr. Manning's description of it is as follows.

"Medium size, pyriform, stem short, fleshy at its junction with the fruit. Skin yellow and bright red. Flesh coarse grained, sweet, tender and excellent. Ripe the middle of September." Shoots stout, upright, dark olive.

A subsequent examination of this pear leads us to think it dry and inferiour in many seasons.

46. Autumn Colmar. Thomp. Lind.

A Flemish pear, of fair quality, and a good bearer.

Fruit of medium size, oblong or obtuse, pyriform, a little uneven. Skin pale green, dotted with numerous russety specks. Stalk about an inch long, straight, planted in a small, uneven cavity. Calyx small, closed, set in a slight basin, a little furrowed. Flesh a little gritty at the core, buttery, with a rich and agreeable flavour. October.

47. Belmont. Thomp.

An English kitchen pear, considerably like the Althorpe Crassane, and of the same origin. It bears abundantly and constantly with us, and is remarkably fine for cooking and preserving, but is scarcely fit for the table.

Fruit roundish-obovate, medium, sometimes of rather large size. Skin fair, yellowish-green, marked with numerous dots, and a little brownish next the sun. Stalk quite long, (two inches or more,) slender and curved. Flesh rather coarse, juicy, and sweet. October.

48. Belle et Bonne. Thomp. Lind. P. Mag.

Schöne und Gute.
Gracieuse.
Belle de Brussels, (*incorrectly.*)

The Belle et Bonne (*beautiful and good,*) pear is a variety from Belgium, of large size, fine appearance, and saccharine flavour. It is a showy and good fruit, but whoever reads Mr. Kenrick's description, and expects to find it "a delicious Ber

30*

Fig. 148. *Belle et Bonne.*

gamot of the best kind," will be disappointed.   It is very far below Gansel's Bergamot in richness.   The tree is a strong
grower.

Fruit large, roundish, a little greater in width than in height.
Skin pale greenish-yellow, with numerous russet green dots,
especially near the eye.   Stalk long, rather slender, deeply inserted in a very narrow cavity.   Calyx with crumpled divisions,
set in a shallow, rather uneven basin.   Flesh white, a little
coarse grained, tender, and when well ripened, buttery, with a
very sweet and agreeable juice.   Middle of September.

49. BROUGHAM.   Thomp.

A new English variety, not yet proved here.   It is said to be
very hardy and very productive.

The fruit is described by Thompson as large, roundish-obovate. Skin yellow, a good deal covered with russet. Flesh buttery, quite melting, and of very excellent flavour. It ripens in November.

50. BLEEKER'S MEADOW. Ken. Pom. Man.

Large Seckel.

A native fruit, said to have been found in a meadow in Pennsylvania. It is a handsome, hardy fruit, and bears large crops, but it has been sadly over-praised as to quality. The truth is, it seems at first to give promise of high flavour, but it rarely becomes mellow, but retains its crisp, hard state. We have raised many fine crops, but cannot recommend it much. In a very dry, warm soil, it is sometimes excellent.

Fruit small, or of medium size, roundish, very regular and smooth. Skin bright clear yellow, occasionally sprinkled with crimson dots on the sunny side. Flesh very white, firm, with a peculiar musky or wasp-like aroma, and spicy taste, but mostly remains crisp and hard. Stalk straight and stiff. Basin shallow. Calyx open and reflexed. October and November.

Fig. 149. *Bleeker's Meadow.*

51. BOUCQUIA. Hov. Mag.

Beurré Boucquia. *Ken.*

A new Flemish pear, raised by Dr. Van Mons, and sent to Mr. Manning in 1836.

Fruit rather large, one-sided, oval-turbinate. Skin pale yellow, with a pale red cheek, thickly sprinkled with reddish, and dark russety dots. Stalk an inch or more long, set a little obliquely, and either fleshy at the point of junction, or set in a very slight depression. Calyx large, basin scarcely sunk. Flesh yellowish-white, abounding with a very sweet, rich juice, of excellent flavour. October. Rather liable to rot at the core.

52. BUFFAM. Man.

Buffam.

The Buffam is a native of Rhode Island, and from its general resemblance to the Doyenné, it is, no doubt, a seedling of that

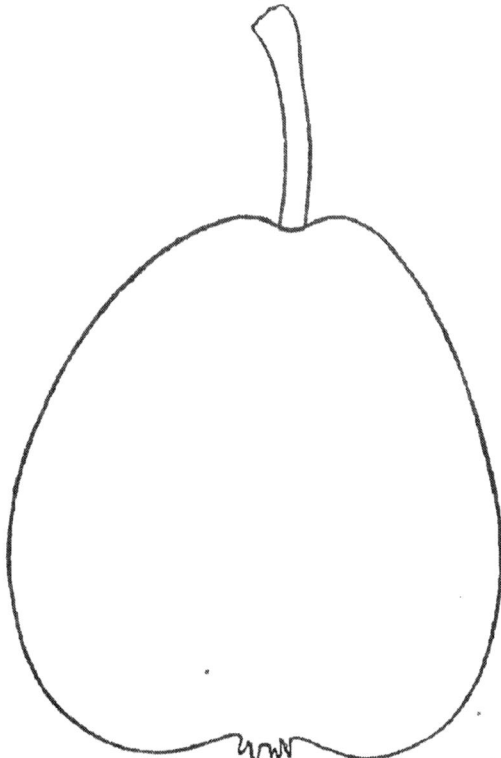

fine sort. It is an *orchard* pear of the first quality, as it is a very strong, upright grower, bears large, regular crops, and is a very handsome and saleable fruit. It is a little variable in quality. We have frequently eaten them so fine, as scarcely to be distinguished from the Doyenné, and again, when rather insipid. It may be considered a beautiful and good, though not first rate variety.

Fruit of medium size, oblong, obovate, a little smaller on one side. Skin fair, deep yellow, (brownish-green at first,) finely suffused over half the fruit, with bright red,

Fig. 150. *Buffam.*

sprinkled with small brown dots, or a little russet. Stalk an inch long, inserted in a very slight cavity. Calyx with small segments, and basin of moderate size. Flesh white, buttery, not so juicy as the Doyenné, but sweet, and of excellent flavour. The strong upright reddish-brown shoots, and peculiar, brownish green appearance of the pear, before ripening, distinguish this fruit. September.

53. Beurré de Capiaumont. Thomp.

Capiumont. *Lind.*

A Flemish pear, very fair, and handsomely formed, and such a capital bearer, and so hardy in all soils and seasons, that it is already a very popular orchard and garden fruit. It is always good, sometimes first rate, but when the tree is heavily laden, it is apt to be slightly astringent. It grows freely; branches a little pendant, grayish-yellow.

Fruit of medium size, long turbinate, very even, and tapering regularly into the stalk. Skin smooth, clear yellow, with a light cinnamon or cinnamon red cheek, and a few small dots and streaks of russet. Calyx large, with spreading segments, prominently placed, and not at all sunk. Stalk from three-fourths to an inch and a half long, curved. Flesh fine grained, buttery, melting, sweet, and when not astringent, of high flavour. September and October.

This is quite distinct from the Frederick of Wurtemburgh, an irregular fruit, sometimes called by this name.

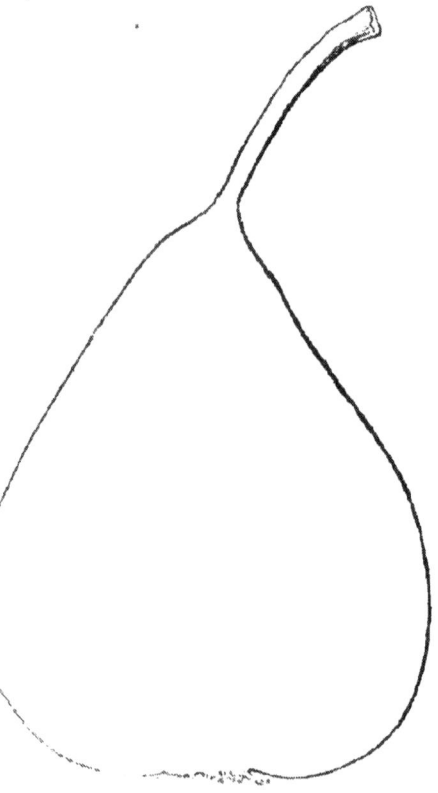

Fig. 151. *Beurré de Capiumont.*

54. Beurré, Brown. Thomp. Lind. Mill.

Beurré Gris. *Nois.*		Beurré. *O. Duh.*
Beurré Rouge.		Golden Beurré.
Beurré d'or.		Red Beurré, (*of some.*)
Beurré Dorée.	*of various French gardens.*	Badham's.
Beurré d'Amboise.		Grey Beurré.
Beurré d'Ambleuse.		Beurré d'Anjou, (*of some.*)
Beurré du Roi.		Beurré Vert.
Poire d'Amboise.		
Isambert.		
Isambert le Bon.		

The Brown Beurré, almost too well known to need description, was for a long time, considered the prince of pears in France, its native country, and for those who are partial to the high vinous flavour—a rich mingling of sweet and acid—it has, still, few competitors. It is, however, quite variable in different soils, and its variety of appearance in different gardens, has given rise to the many names, gray, brown, red and golden, under which it is known. Kenrick calls it " an outcast," but our readers will pardon our dissent from this opinion, while we have the fact in mind, of its general excellence in this region; and especially that of a noble tree, now in view from the library where we write, which is in luxuriant vigour, and gives us, annually, from five to eight bushels of superb fruit. The truth is, this pear is rather tender for New England, and requires a warm climate and strong soil. Shoots diverging, dark brown.

Fruit large, oblong-obovate, tapering convexly quite to the stalk. Skin slightly rough, yellowish-green, but nearly covered with thin russet, often a little reddish brown on one side. Stalk from one to one a half inches long, stout at its junction with the tree, and thickening obliquely into the fruit. Calyx nearly closed in a shallow basin. Flesh greenish white, melting, buttery, extremely juicy, with a rich sub-acid flavour. September.

55. BEURRÉ BOSC.   Thomp.

Calabasse Bosc.	Bosc's Flaschenbirne.
Marianne Nouvelle.	Beurré d'Yelle, (of some.)

The Beurré Bosc is a pear to which we give our unqualified praise. It is large, handsome, a regular bearer, always perfect, and of the highest flavour. It bears singly, and not in clusters, looking as if thinned on the tree, whence it is always of fine size. It was raised in 1807 by Van Mons, and named Calebasse Bosc in honour of M. Bosc, a distinguished Belgian cultivator. Having also been received at the garden of the Horticultural Society of London under the name of Beurré Bosc, Mr. Thompson thought it best to retain this name, as less likely to lead to a confusion with the Calebasse, a distinct fruit. The tree grows vigorously; shoots long, brownish olive.

Fruit large, pyriform, a little uneven, tapering long and gradually into the stalk. Skin pretty smooth, dark yellow, a good deal covered with streaks and dots of cinnamon russet, and slightly touched with red on one side. Stalk one to two inches long, rather slender, curved. Calyx short, set in a very shallow basin. Flesh white, melting, very buttery, with a rich, delicious and slightly perfumed flavour. Ripens gradually, from the last of September to the last of October.

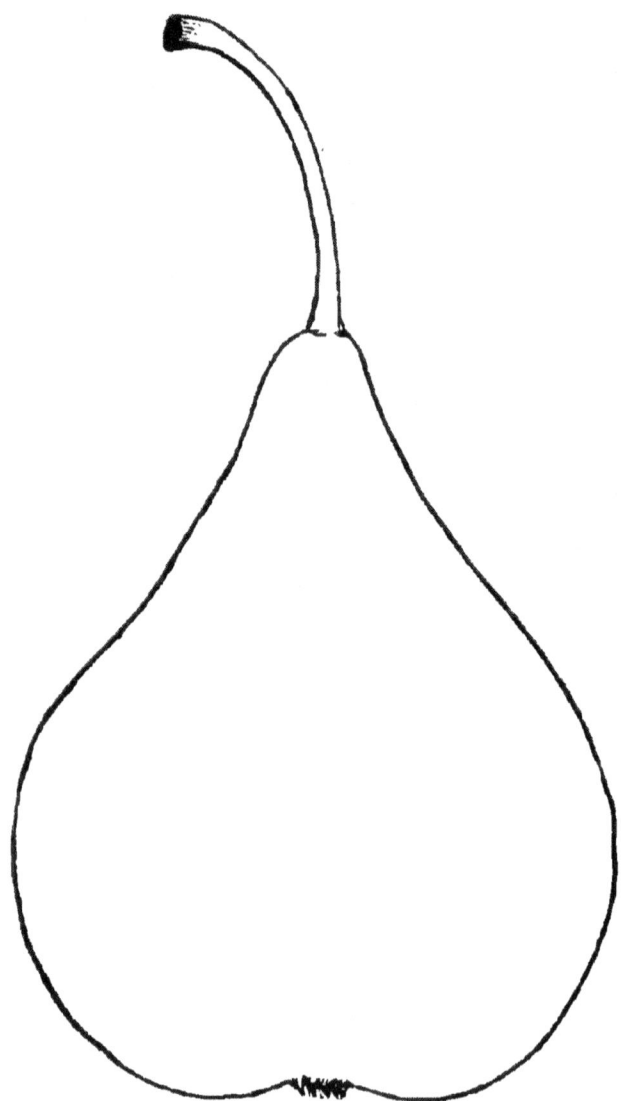

Fig. 152. *Beurré Bosc.*

56. Beurré d'Amalis. Thomp. Nois.

Beurré d'Amanlis.   *Nois Bon. Jard.*
Beurré d'Amaulis.   *Ken Man*

A Belgian pear, of excellent quality, nearly first rate. Very productive.

Fruit large, obovate, not very regular, a little swollen on its sides. Skin rather thick, dull yellowish-green, with a pale reddish brown cheek, overspread with numerous brown dots and russet streaks and patches. Stalk a little more than an inch long, set rather obliquely in a shallow, irregular cavity. Calyx open, with broad divisions, basin shallow. Flesh yellowish, somewhat coarse, but buttery, melting, abundant, rich, with slightly perfumed juice. September.

57. Beurré d'Anjou. Thomp.

This is a first rate pear, recently imported from France by Col. Wilder, of Boston, which appears to us quite distinct from the Brown Beurré.

Fruit rather above medium size, very regular, obovate. Skin greenish-yellow, smooth, a little clouded with russet, especially around the calyx. Calyx small, open, in a round, smooth basin. Stalk rather short, straight, set in a slight cavity. Flesh yellowish-white, very fine grained, buttery, slightly sub-acid, with a rich, sprightly vinous flavour. October.

58. Beurré Diel. § Thomp. Lind. P. Mag.

Diel's Butterbirne.	Beurré Royale.	Beurré d'Yelle.
Diel.	Dorotheé Royale.	De Melon
Dorotheé Royale.	Gros Dillen.	Melin de Kops.
Grosse Dorotheé	Dillen.	Beurré Magnifique.
Sylvanche vert d'hiver	Des Trois Tours	Beurré Incomparable.

A noble Belgian fruit, raised from seed, in 1805, by Dr. Van Mons, and named in honour of his friend Dr. Augustus Frederick Adrien Diel, a distinguished German pomologist. Its vigour, productiveness and beauty, have made it already a general favourite with our planters. It is in every respect, a first rate fruit in favourable situations, but on very young trees and in cold soils, it is apt to be rather coarse and astringent. The tree has long, very stout, twisting branches, and is uncommonly vigorous. Young shoots dark grayish-brown.

Fruit large, varying from obovate to obtuse-pyriform. Skin rather thick, lemon yellow, becoming orange yellow, marked with large brown dots, and marblings of russet. Stalk an inch

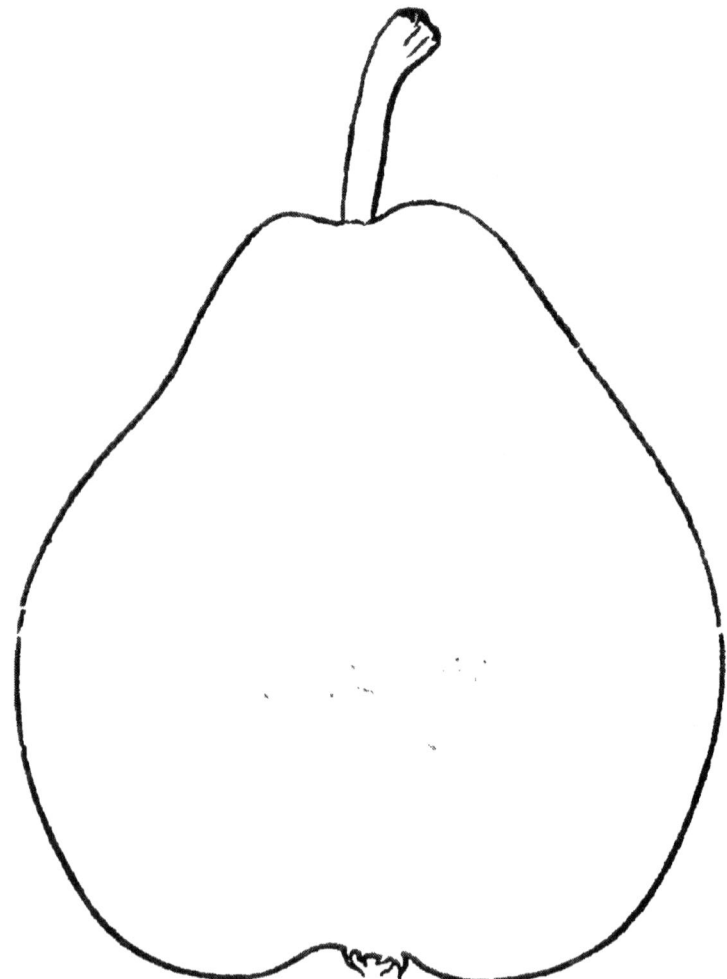

Fig. 153. *Beurré Diel.*

to an inch and three quarters long, stout, curved, set in a rather
uneven cavity. Calyx nearly closed, and placed in a slightly
furrowed basin. Flesh yellowish-white, a little coarse grained,
especially at the core, but rich, sugary, half melting, and in
good specimens, buttery and delicious. In eating, in this country, from September to December, if picked and ripened in the
house.

59. Beurré Knox. Thomp. Lind.

The Beurré Knox is a pleasant, second rate fruit, of large
and handsome appearance, but a little liable to rot at the core.

It is shaped a good deal like the Brown Beurré.   A Flemish variety.

Fruit large, oblong, obovate, tapering to the stalk, which is about an inch long, curved, and set below a fleshy protuberance or lip—and without depression.   Skin pale green, with thin russet on one side.   Calyx open, and set in a small, narrow basin.   Flesh tender and soft, juicy and sweet, but not high flavoured.   Last of September.

This fruit is abundant near Boston.   We received, by some error, a winter fruit, under this name, from the Horticultural Society of London.

60. Beurré Kenrick.   Man. in Hov. Mag.

No. 1599 of Van Mons

A Flemish seedling, sent to this country and named by Manning.

"Medium size, flat at the blossom-end, tapering to the stalk, colour greenish-yellow, with indistinct russet spots ; stem one inch long ; flesh good, juicy, sweet and buttery. Ripe in September." Man.

61. Beurré, Golden of Bilboa.   § Man.

Hooper's Bilboa.

The Golden Beurré of Bilboa was imported from Bilboa, Spain, about eighteen

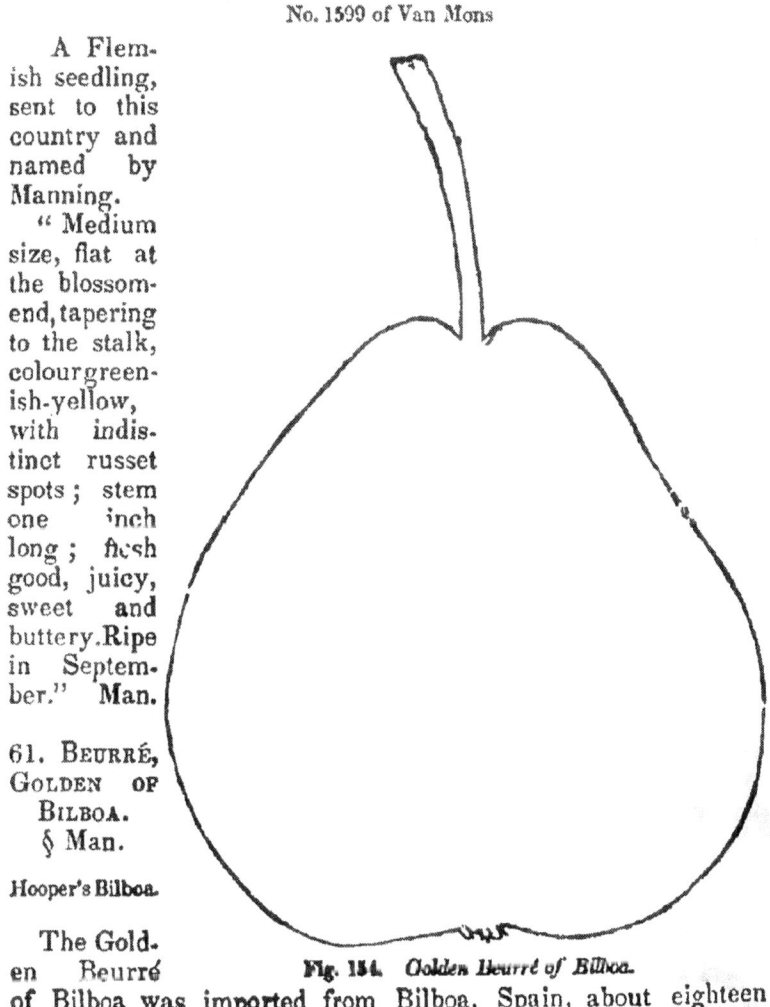

Fig. 154. *Golden Beurré of Bilboa.*

years ago, by Mr. Hooper, of Marblehead, Mass. Its European name is unknown, and it has become a popular fruit here under this title. It is of a fine golden colour, relieved by a little russet, and is certainly a beautiful early autumn pear of the first quality. It bears regularly and most abundantly, and will become a favourite fruit in all parts of the country. In cold soils, it is particularly fine on quince stocks. Shoots stout, upright, light yellowish-brown.

Fruit rather large, regular obovate. Skin very fair, smooth, and thin, golden yellow, evenly dotted with small brown dots, and a little marked with russet, especially around the stalk. Stalk about an inch and a half long, rather slender, set in a moderate depression. Calyx small, closed, placed in a slight basin. Flesh white, very buttery and melting, and fine grained, with a rich vinous flavour. First to the middle of September.

62. Beurré Duval. Thomp.

A new Belgian pear, raised by M. Duval. It is good, and bears abundantly. Fruit of medium size, obtuse pyriform. Skin pale green. Flesh white, buttery, melting and well flavoured. October and November.

63. Beurré Preble. Man. in H. M.

A large and excellent pear, named by Mr. Manning in honour of Commodore Edward Preble, U. S. N., and raised from seed, by Elijah Cooke, of Raymond, Maine.

Fruit large, oblong-obovate. Skin greenish-yellow, mottled with russet and green spots. Stalk about an inch long, very stout, set in a moderate hollow. Flesh white, buttery, and melting, with a rich, high flavour. October and November.

64. Beurré Colmar. Van Mons. Nois.

Beurré Colmar d'Automne

A pleasant, juicy pear, ripening in October. It is one of Dr. Van Mons' seedlings, and is quite distinct from the Autumn Colmar.

Fruit of medium size, almost eliptical, or oval-obovate, regularly formed. Skin smooth, pale green, becoming yellowish at maturity, with a blush next the sun, and thickly sprinkled with dots. Stalk an inch long. Calyx expanded, and set in a very shallow, narrow, irregular basin. Flesh very white, slightly crisp at first, but becoming very juicy and melting, with a slightly perfumed flavour. October.

65. Beurré de Beaumont § Thomp.

A new and highly delicious pear, lately received from France. It appears, to us, to be worthy of extensive dissemination.

Fruit of medium size, roundish-obovate. Skin pale yellow-ish-green, thinly sprinkled with large dark green dots, and thin-ly washed with dull red on the sunny side. Stalk about an inch long, obliquely inserted, under a lip, or in a very slight cavity.

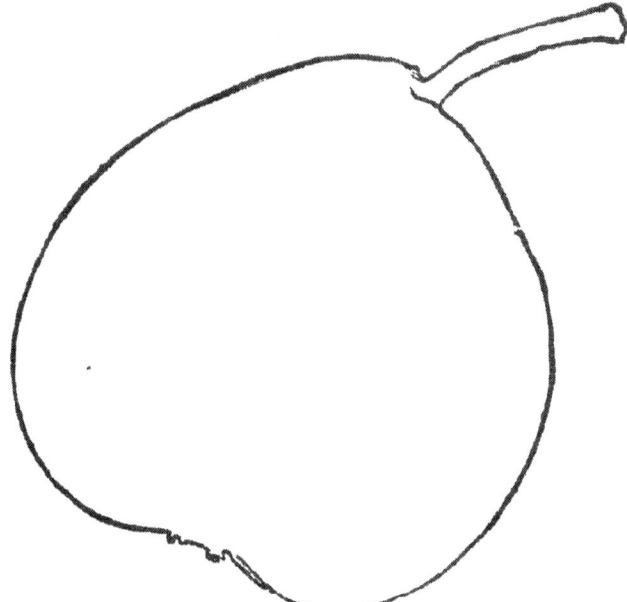

Fig. 155. *Beurré de Beaumont.*

Calyx small, with little or no division, and set in a shallow, smooth basin. Flesh white, buttery, melting, abounding with a rich, sprightly flavoured juice. October.

66. Beurré Van Mons. Thomp.

The Beurré Van Mons is but just received in this country. It bears the reputation of a first rate fruit; it is of medium size, pyriform, skin yellowish, nearly covered with russet. Flesh buttery, melting and excellent. October.

67. Beurré Romain. Thomp. N. Duh.

A melting, juicy pear, of second quality. Fruit of medium size, regularly formed, obovate. Skin pale yellowish-green, dotted with numerous gray specks. Stalk short, inserted without depression. Calyx prominently placed, even with the fruit, flesh white, juicy, melting, sweet and agreeable. September to October. Bears abundantly.

68. Beurré Van Marum. Thomp.

A rather large, and very good, juicy pear, one of the Flemish varieties. It comes early into bearing, and produces well.

Fruit large, oblong-pyriform, not very regular. Skin yellow, rarely with a little red. Stalk rather long and slender, inserted in a flattened cavity. Calyx large, set in an irregular shallow basin. Flesh white, melting, juicy, sweet and agreeable. First of October.

69. Beurré Spence ? Thomp.

It is probable that there *may* be a true Beurré Spence, since Dr. Van Mons claims to have raised one, and once pronounced it the finest of all pears. But it is certain that neither the pomologists of England or America have yet been able to obtain it correct. Beurré Diel, Urbaniste, B. de Capiumont, and one or two others, of very inferiour quality, have been imported into this country for Beurré Spence. We have, however, received a tree from Mr. Rivers, the English nurseryman, which may prove correct. He says " this is the Beurré Spence of the Parisians. I ate it there in October, and thought it, simply, a good pear, scarcely deserving the high encomiums given by Van Mons to Mr. Braddick."*

70. Beurré Crapaud. Thomp.

A new foreign pear, resembling the Doyenné in flavour. Fruit of medium size, obovate. Skin pale greenish-yellow. Flesh buttery, fine-grained and excellent. Ripens in October.

71. Beurré Picquery.

The Beurré Picquery has lately been received from France, where it has the character of a first rate fruit, somewhat resembling the Urbaniste in general appearance; of rather larger size, melting, equally fine in flavour, ripening in October, and keeping a month or more. Shoots dark olive.

* In the mean time we annex Van Mons' original description. "Wood short-jointed, leaves small, branches horizontal or declining. The fruit is of the shape and size of the Brown Beurré ; skin green, handsomely sprinkled and marked with reddish brown and reddish purple. Flesh tender, juicy, sugary and perfumed. It ripens about the last of September."—*Revue des Revues*, 1830, p. 180.

72. Bergamot, Autumn.   Mill. Lind. Thomp.

English Bergamot.
York Bergamot.
Common Bergamot, (of England.)
English Autumn Bergamot.

The Autumn Bergamot is one of the oldest of pears, being supposed by pomologists to have been in England since the time of Julius Cæsar.   It is believed by Manger to be of Turkish origin, and originally to have been called *Begarmoud*,—princely pear—from the Turkish, *beg*, or *bey*, and *armoud*, a pear. Since that time, the standard of excellence has risen much higher, and the title could, with more justice, be applied to the following variety than to this.   The Autumn Bergamot bears well with us, and is of good flavour, but it is going out of cultivation, though the tree is thrifty, and bears well.

Fruit rather small, roundish and flattened.   Skin roughish green, dotted with rough gray specks, and often with a faint or dull brown cheek.   Stalk short, about half an inch long, stout, inserted in a wide, round hollow.   Calyx small, set in a shallow smooth basin.   Flesh greenish-white, coarse-grained at the core, juicy, sugary and rich.   September.

The Bergamotte d'Automne of the French, is a distinct fruit from this, usually more pyramidal; the skin smooth, light yellowish-green, with a brownish red cheek, and speckled with small, grayish dots.   Stalk nearly an inch long, set in a slight cavity.   Calyx very slightly depressed.   Flesh breaking, juicy, and refreshing, but not high flavoured.   A second rate fruit, though of fine appearance.

73. Bergamot, Gansel's. § P. Mag. Thomp. Lind.

Brocas Bergamot.	*Coxe.*	Bonne Rouge.	
Ives' Bergamot.		Gurle's Beurré.	
Staunton.		Diamant.	

Gansel's Bergamot is a well known and delicious pear, raised seventy-seven years ago, from a seed of the Autumn Bergamot, by the English Lieut. General Gansel, of Donneland Hall.   Though a little coarse-grained, it is, in its perfection, scarcely surpassed by any other pear in its peculiarly rich, sugary flavour, combined with great juiciness.   It is stated, by some, to be an unfruitful sort, and it is, in poor, or cold soils, only a thin bearer, but we know a very large tree near us, in a warm, rich soil, which frequently bears a dozen bushels of superb fruit.   The mealy leaves, and spreading, dark gray shoots, distinguish this tree.

Fruit large, roundish-obovate, but much flattened.   Skin roughish brown, becoming yellowish-brown at maturity, tinged sometimes with a russet red cheek, and sprinkled with spots of

Fig. 156. Gansel's Bergamot.

russet. Stalk short, fleshy at both ends. Cavity moderate. Calyx short and small, placed in a smooth, moderate hollow. Flesh white, melting, very juicy, rich, sweet and aromatic. Ripens during all September.

74. BERGAMOTTE SUISSE. O. Duh. Lind.

Swiss Bergamot. *Lind.*

A very pretty, roundish, striped pear, which is a handsome addition to the dessert, and occasionally, when it ripens late, it is juicy, melting and excellent, but it is frequently of indifferent flavour. The tree is, with us, one of the strongest and most vigorous, and bears well. Branches striped.

Fruit of medium size, roundish, a little inclined to turbinate. Skin smooth, pale green, striped with yellow and pale red. Flesh melting, juicy, sweet and pleasant. October.

75. BERGAMOTTE CADETTE. O. Duh. Thomp.

| Beurré Beauchamps. | Poire de Cadet. |
| Beauchamps. | Ognonet, (*incorrectly, of some.*) |

A very good Bergamot from France, not, by any means,

equal, however, to Gansel's, but productive, and ripening for some time, in succession.

Fruit middle sized, roundish obovate. Skin smooth, pale green, rarely with a pale red cheek. Stalk an inch long, thick, set in an angular, shallow cavity. Calyx small, closed, basin nearly flat. Flesh buttery and juicy, sweet, and rather rich. October and November.

76. BEZI* DE MONTIGNY. Thomp. Lind. Poit.

Trouvé de Montigny.
Beurré Romain ? *of some American gardens.*

A pleasant, juicy fruit, with a musky flavour, but not first rate. The skin is remarkably smooth, and the pear is evenly formed. It is a good bearer. Fruit of medium size, very regularly obovate. Skin pale yellowish-green, with numerous gray dots. Stalk stout, thickest at the point of insertion, an inch long, inserted in a small shallow cavity. Calyx small, firm, open, reflexed, in a very smooth basin, scarcely sunk. Flesh white, melting, juicy, half buttery, with a sweet, musky flavour. First of October.

77. BEZI DE LA MOTTE. § O. Duh. Thomp.

Bein Armudi.
Beurré blanc de Jersey.

This admirable old French pear is an especial favourite of ours. Its flesh is solid and heavy, at the same time highly buttery, with a peculiarly pleasant flavour and aroma. The tree is exceedingly vigorous and productive,

Fig. 157. *Bezi de la Motte.*

* *Bezi* signifies *wilding*, i. e. natural seedling found near Montigny, a town in France.

and the grayish-olive shoots, like the fruit, have a peculiarly speckled appearance. Every garden should have a specimen of this fruit. It ripens gradually, and may be kept a good while.

Fruit of medium size, bergamot shaped, roundish, flattened at the eye. Skin pale yellowish-green, thickly sprinkled with conspicuous russet green dots. Stalk about an inch long, green, slightly curved, and inserted in a slight, flattened hollow. Calyx small, open, set in a shallow, rather abruptly sunken basin. Flesh white, very fine-grained, buttery, juicy, with a sweet, delicate, perfumed flavour. October.

78. BISHOP'S THUMB.
Thomp. Lind.

A long, oddly-shaped, English pear, but juicy and excellent in flavour, indeed usually considered first rate. The tree bears abundant crops. Shoots grayish-olive.

Fruit rather large, oblong and narrow, and tapering irregularly, usually a little knobbed. Skin dark yellowish-green, dotted with russet, often nearly covered with russet specks, and having a russet red cheek. Stalk one to two inches long, slender, crooked, and set in a fleshy enlargement. Calyx with spreading divisions, and set in a flat basin. Flesh juicy, melting, with a good, rich vinous flavor. October

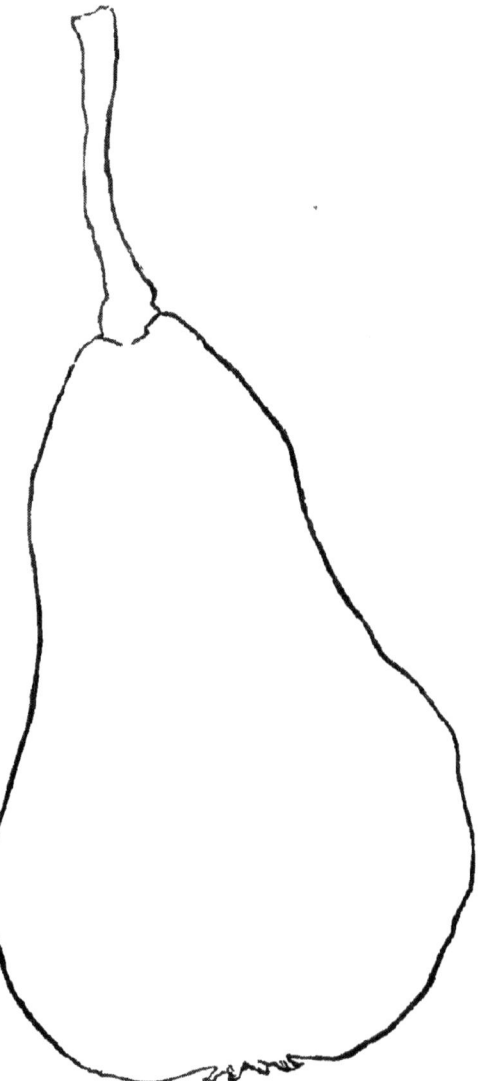

Fig. 158. *Bishop's Thumb*

79. Bon Chretien Fondante. Thomp. Lind.

A recent Flemish pear, abounding with juice, and having a refreshing agreeable flavour. In good seasons, it is first of the quality, and it bears early and abundantly. Young shoots slender, diverging, olive gray.

Fruit pretty large, roundish-oblong, regularly formed. Skin pale green, sprinkled with small russet dots, and considerably covered with russet. Stalk three-fourths of an inch long, curved, inserted in a slight depression. Calyx small, set in a narrow hollow. Flesh yellowish-white, gritty round the core, exceedingly juicy, tender and melting, with a rich and pleasant flavour.

80. Burnett. Ken.

A pleasant, sweet pear, of large size, raised by Dr. Joel Burnett, of Southborough, Mass.

Fruit large, obtuse pyriform. Skin smooth, pale yellow, with numerous greenish-gray dots, and sometimes a little russet. Stalk an inch and a half long, planted in a swollen base, or with a blunt depression. Calyx open, stiff, placed in a shallow basin. Flesh greenish-white, a little coarse grained, but juicy, sweet and good. First of October.

81. Cabot. Man.

Originated from the seed of the Brown Beurré, by J. S. Cabot, Esq., of Salem, Mass. It has a good deal of the flavour of its parent, and is an agreeable, sub-acid fruit. The tree grows upright and very strong, and produces amazing crops, but the fruit, with us, decays very quickly—though, we understand that, in older specimens, this is not the case. It merits a general trial. Col. M. P. Wilder, of Boston, informs us, that with him, it is of the first quality, nearly as good as Fondante d'Automne.

Fruit pretty large, roundish-turbinate, narrowing rather abruptly to the stalk, which is bent obliquely, and inserted on one side, of a tapering summit. Skin roughish, bronze yellow, pretty well covered with cinnamon russet. Calyx small, open, set in a round, smooth basin. Flesh greenish-white, breaking, juicy, with a rich, sub-acid flavour. Middle and last of September.

82. Chelmsford.

A native pear, from the neighbourhood of Boston of large

and showy appearance and of second rate flavour, but much esteemed for stewing. It makes very strong wood, the young shoots yellowish-brown.

Fruit very large, irregular pyriform, with a wide crown. Skin deep yellow, at maturity, with a fine red cheek, sprinkled with distinct brownish-green dots. Stalk an inch and a half long, curved, planted in a crumpled shallow cavity. Calyx large, set in an irregular basin. Flesh white, juicy, rather crisp, with a saccharine flavour. Last of September.

83. COMPTE DE LAMY. § Thomp.

| Beurré Curté. | Marie Louise Nova. | } ac. to |
| Dingler. | Marie Louise the Second. | } Thomp. |

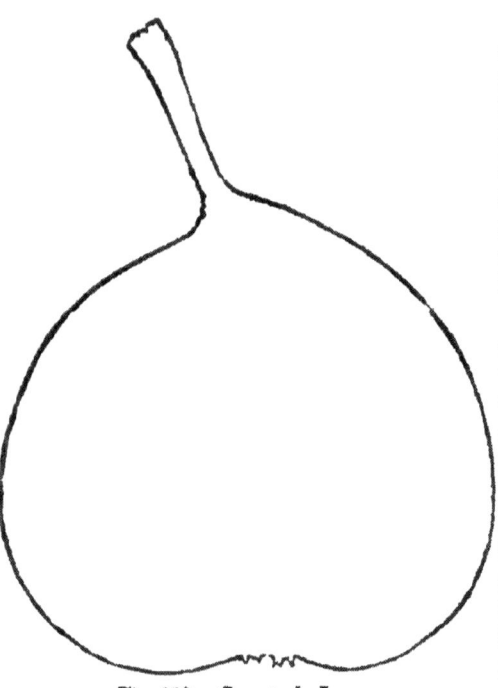

A rich, truly delicious, sugary pear, of the highest quality. It is one of the late new Flemish varieties, and is worthy of unusual attention. Young shoots pretty strong, upright, dark coloured.

Fruit of medium size, roundish-obovate. Skin yellow, with a brownish red cheek, and sprinkled with small russetty dots. Stalk an inch long, straight, obliquely inserted under a lip, or planted in a slight cavity. Calyx small, set in a shallow, smooth basin. Flesh white, fine grained, buttery, melting, saccharine, and high flavoured. Last of September to middle of October.

Fig. 153.   *Compte de Lamy.*

This is quite distinct from the *Marie Louise Nova* of some American gardens, received from Van Mons. [See Marie Louise Nova.]

84. COMPRETTE. Van Mons.

The Comprette is a very fine, new, Flemish seedling, of Dr. Van Mons', which has just begun to bear in this country, and was introduced by Col. Wilder, of Boston. It is, undoubtedly, a fruit of the first quality, and resembles in flavour tne Passe Colmar.

Fruit rather above medium size, obtuse-pyriform ; the short, stout stalk thickening into the termination. Skin yellowish green, thickly sprinkled with brown dots, and, occasionally, marked with a little russet. Calyx pretty large, with few segments, set in a shallow basin. Flesh white, buttery and melting, with a rich, perfumed juice. October to November.

85. COMMODORE. Man. in Hov. Mag.

Van Mons, No. 1218.

A Belgian seedling, named by Mr. Manning, and promising to be of good quality, not quite first rate. Branches slender.

Fruit of medium size, very regular-obovate, tapering to the Stalk. Skin yellow, marked with a little red, some russet in patches, and a very few small dots. Stalk an inch or more long, planted on the slightly flattened summit. Basin scarcely sunk, and having a small calyx. Flesh somewhat like that of the Doyenné—buttery, melting, with a sweet and excellent fla. vour. Last of October, to last of November.

86. CROFT CASTLE. Thomp.

The Croft Castle is a recent English variety, peculiar in its shape, and especially so in its flavour ; the latter being greatly

Fig. 159. Croft Castle.

relished by some persons, and not at all by others. It is very productive.

Fruit of medium size, oval, inclining to flattened ovate—narrowing most towards the eye. Skin pale greenish-yellow, marked with brown dots, and often a little russet. Stalk long and slender, curved, and planted almost even with the flattened summit. Calyx projecting a little beyond the level of the fruit, open, and stiff. Core large. Flesh juicy and a little crisp sweet, with a piquant perfume and flavour. October.

87. COPIA.

A Philadelphia seedling, named in honour of the originator, Jacob Copia, Pine street, Philadelphia. It is a large and pretty good pear, resembling somewhat the Beurré Diel in flavour, but rather inferiour to it. Young shoots very stout, upright, olive brown.

Fruit large, broad-turbinate, tapering into the stalk, which is long, stout, and fleshy at the bottom, obliquely inserted. Skin yellow, with slight traces and specks of russet. Calyx large basin somewhat furrowed. Flesh rather coarse grained, but rich, juicy, and sugary. September and October.

88. CUSHING. § Man.

The Cushing is a native of Massachusetts, having originated on the grounds of Colonel Washington Cushing, of Hingham, about forty years ago. It is a very sprightly, delicious pear, and like many of our native varieties, it produces most abundant crops. Branches rather slender, diverging, grayish-brown.

Fruit medium size, often large, obovate, tapering rather obliquely to the stem. Skin smooth, light green-

Fig. 160. *Cushing.*

ish-yellow, sprinkled with small gray dots, and occasionally a dull red cheek. Stalk an inch long, planted in an abrupt cavity. Calyx rather small, set in a basin of moderate size. Flesh white, fine grained, buttery, melting, and abounding in a sweet, sprightly, perfumed juice, of fine flavour. A hardy and capital variety for all soils. Middle of September.

89. CAPSHEAF. Man. Ken.

This is believed, by the eastern cultivators, to be a native of Rhode Island. It is a very agreeable fruit, not first rate, but from its great hardiness, and steady habit of bearing, is well worthy of the attention of pear growers. Young shoots stout, upright, yellowish-brown.

Fruit of medium size, roundish-obovate. Skin deep yellow, nearly covered with cinnamon russet. Stalk an inch long, stout, inserted in a shallow hollow. Calyx small; basin slightly sunk. Flesh white, juicy, and melting, very sweet and pleasant, but lacking a high flavour. October.

90. CALEBASSE. Thomp. Lind.

Calebasse Double Extra.
Calebasse d'Hollande.
Beurré de Payence.

The Calebasse is a very grotesque-looking Belgian fruit, named from its likeness to a calabash, or gourd. It is a good deal esteemed, especially by curious amateurs, being a crisp, sweet, juicy pear, of second quality, and producing good crops.

Fruit of medium size, oblong, a little crooked, and irregular or knobby in its outline. Skin rough, dull yellow, becoming orange russet on the sunny side. Stalk about an inch and a half long, curved, and planted on the side of a knobby projection. Calyx very short, set in a small basin. Flesh juicy, crisp, a little coarse-grained, but sugary and pleasant. Middle of September.

This is the *Calebasse Bosc* of the *Jardin Fruitier*, but **incor**rectly. [See Beurré Bosc.] The CALEBASSE GROSSE, [Monstrous Calabash, etc.] of Van Mons, is a prodigiously large, pyramidal fruit, 5 or 6 inches long, in the shape of a conical gourd. Skin smooth and shining, yellowish green, with a good deal of reddish gray in the sun. Stalk short and stout, about an inch long. Calyx rather small, but with large divisions. Flesh white, a little coarse, juicy, half melting, sugary and tolerably good. October. (The grafts sent out for this kind, by Van Mons, proved incorrect.)

91. CAPUCIN. Van Mons.
Capuchin.

This promises to be a very good pear. It is one of Var. Mons' Seedlings. Young shoots stout, diverging, dark coloured.

Fruit pretty large, oval, or sometimes obtuse-turbinate. Skin green, becoming pale yellow, a little russeted towards the eye and stalk, and distinctly dotted elsewhere, with also a red cheek. Stalk nearly an inch long, placed in an obtuse hollow. Calyx small, deeply sunk in a narrow, irregular basin. Flesh greenish, juicy, crisp, sugary and rich. October.

92. CLARA. Van Mons.
Claire. *Nois.*

Another seedling, raised by the Belgian pomologist. The young shoots are stout, upright, dark brown. It is of medium size, oval-pyriform. Skin clear yellow, dotted with red, and having a blush on the sunny side. Stalk stout and straight. Calyx small, set in a small, round basin. Flesh white, melting, very juicy and sweet, relieved by a slight acid ; of good quality. In cold seasons it is liable to be too acid. September and October.

93. CUMBERLAND. Man. Ken.

This is a native fruit, and the original tree is still growing in Cumberland, Rhode Island. It is inferiour to the Cushing, and though sometimes very handsome, and always productive, can scarcely be ranked higher than a second rate fruit, and occasionally it is quite indifferent. Branches rather slender.

Fruit rather large, obovate. Skin orange yellow, with a little russet, and a pale red cheek on the sunny side. Stalk about an inch and a half long, stout, rather obliquely planted, in a very slight depression. Calyx with expanded divisions, and placed nearly even with the surface. Flesh white, melting, buttery, and tolerably rich and juicy. September and October.

94 CRASSANE. Thomp. Lind.
Bergamotte Crassane.
Crésane.
Beurré Plat.

A celebrated, old French pear, which is said to take its name from *écrasé*, flattened or crushed, from its depressed, Bergamot-like shape. Its flavour is extolled by all the European writers, but we have never been able to find it to equal its foreign character here, and cannot recommend it. Young shoots stout, diverging, grayish-olive.

Fruit large, roundish, flattened. Skin greenish-yellow, em-broidered thinly with russet. Stalk long, slender, curved, and planted in a slight, shallow cavity. Calyx small, set in a narrow rather deep basin. Flesh whitish, juicy, soft, sweet, and tole-rably pleasant. October, and may be kept for a month longer.

95. CHARLES OF AUSTRIA. Thomp. Lind.

Charles d'Autriche.

A large and handsome Belgian pear, which is likely to be-come a favorite here. Raised by Van Mons. Young shoots stout, upright, yellow-olive.

Fruit large, roundish, a little uneven. Skin greenish-yel-low, a little russeted and thickly dotted with conspicuous brown specks, which give it a brownish appearance. Stalk an inch long, slightly inserted. Calyx set in a rather narrow hollow Flesh white, tender, quite juicy, sweet and agreeable. October

96. COLMAR EPINE. Van Mons. Man. in H. M.

An agreeable, juicy pear. sent to this country by Van Mons, and originated by him Young shoots stout, upright, brown.

"Fruit large, roundish-oblong, tapering, gradually, to an obtuse point at the stem, which is one inch long; colour green ish-yellow; flesh white, sweet, very melting, juicy, high fla voured, and good." Middle of September.

97. CLINTON. Man. in H. M.

Van Mons, No. 1233.

A second rate fruit. Mr. Manning says, "Large size, shaped like the Bezi de Montigny; light yellow skin, flesh soft, buttery and good, but not high flavoured " Middle of November.
The wood is stout, and dark brown.

98. CALHOUN. Wilder Mss.

New, and recently originated by Gov. Edwards, of New-Haven. It promises to be a fruit of the first quality.

Fruit of medium size, obovate, terminating obtusely at the insertion of the stalk. Skin usually smooth and handsome, pale yellow, occasionally with a pale red cheek. Flesh juicy, melting, with a rich, sub-acid, or vinous flavour. October to November.

99. COLMAR NLILL. Thomp.

This is a new variety, lately received from abroad, where it

has a high reputation.   It is a very handsome pear, very productive, and of most excellent flavour.

Fruit large, obovate.   Skin pale yellow.   Flesh white, buttery, melting, of high flavour.   Ripens at the middle of October

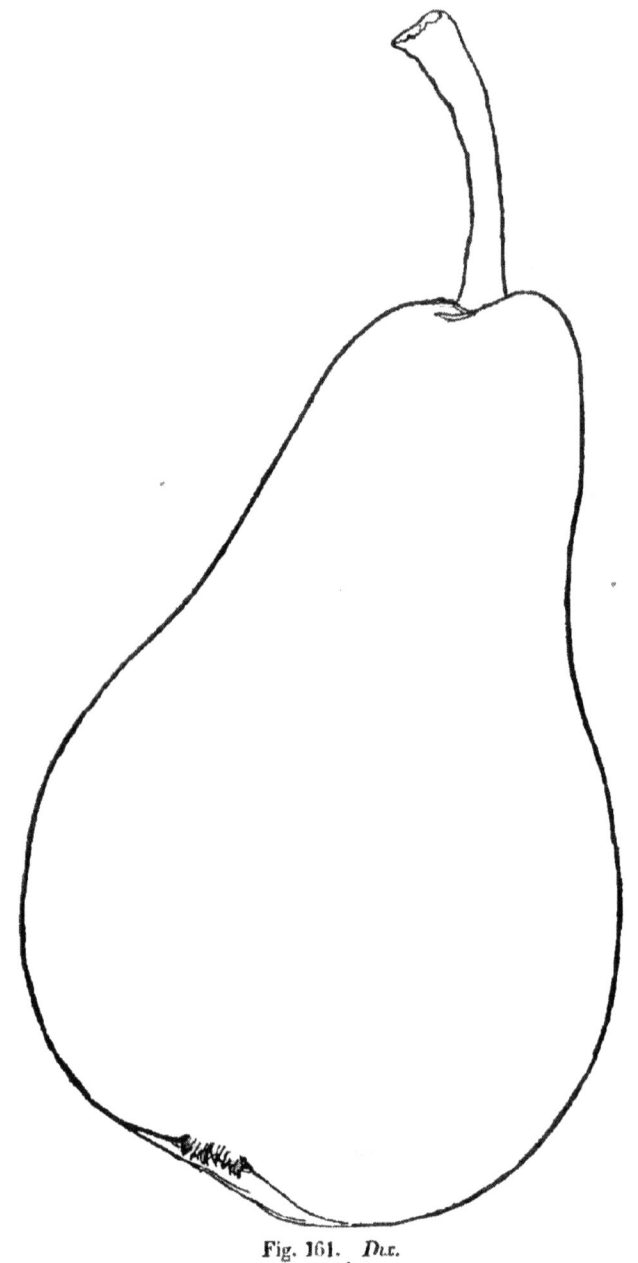

Fig. 161.   *Duc.*
32*

100. DIX. § Man. Ken.

The Dix is, unquestionably, a fruit of the highest excellence, and well deserves the attention of all planters. It is one of the hardiest of pear trees, and although the tree does not come into bearing until it has attained considerable size, yet it produces abundantly, and from its habit, will undoubtedly prove remarkably long-lived, and free from disease. The young branches are pale yellow, upright and slender. The original tree, about thirty-five years old, stands in the garden of Madam Dix, Boston. It bore for the first time in 1826.

Fruit large, oblong, or long-pyriform. Skin roughish, fine deep yellow at maturity, marked with distinct russet dots, and sprinkled with russet around the stalk. Calyx small, for so large a fruit, basin narrow, and scarcely at all sunk. Stalk rather stout, short, thicker at each end, set rather obliquely, but with little or no depression. Flesh not very fine grained, but juicy, rich, sugary, melting and delicious, with a slight perfume. October and November.

101. DUMORTIER. § Thomp. Nois.

A very excellent little Belgian pear, often remarkably high flavoured. Fruit nearly of medium size, obovate. Skin dull yellow marked with russet patches and dots. Stalk nearly two inches long, slender, planted without depression. Calyx open, set in a slight basin. Flesh greenish-white, juicy, melting and sweet. It keeps but a short time. September.

102. DOYENNÉ, WHITE. § Thomp. Lind. P. Mag.

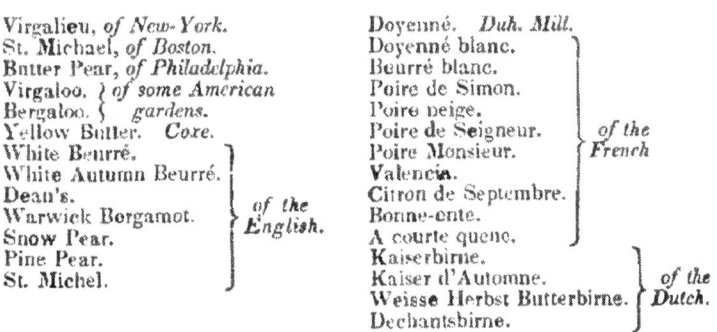

Virgalieu, *of New-York.*	Doyenné. *Duh. Mill.*
St. Michael, *of Boston.*	Doyenné blanc.
Butter Pear, *of Philadelphia.*	Beurré blanc.
Virgaloo. ⎱ *of some American*	Poire de Simon.
Bergaloo. ⎰ *gardens.*	Poire neige.
Yellow Butter. *Coxe.*	Poire de Seigneur. ⎱ *of the*
White Beurré. ⎫	Poire Monsieur. ⎰ *French*
White Autumn Beurré. ⎬	Valencia.
Dean's. ⎪ *of the*	Citron de Septembre.
Warwick Borgamot. ⎬ *English.*	Bonne-ente.
Snow Pear. ⎪	A courte quene.
Pine Pear. ⎪	Kaiserbirne. ⎫
St. Michel. ⎭	Kaiser d'Automne. ⎬ *of the*
	Weisse Herbst Butterbirne. ⎪ *Dutch.*
	Dechantsbirne. ⎭

The White Doyenné is, unquestionably, one of the most perfect of autumn pears. Its universal popularity is attested by the great number of names by which it is known in various parts of the world. As the Virgalieu in New-York, Butter Pear in Philadelphia, and St. Michel's in Boston, it is most commonly known, but all these names, so likely to create confusion, should be laid aside for the true one, White Doyenné.* It is an old French variety, but with us, is in the most perfect health, and bears annually large crops of superb fruit. On the sea-coast, and in various old, or exhausted soils, it has lately become so liable to cracking as to be nearly worthless. In this case it is only necessary to renew the elements wanting—probably potash and lime —and, if the trees are diseased, to plant healthy ones. The branches are strong, up-

Fig. 162. *White Doyenné.*

right, yellowish-gray or light brown.

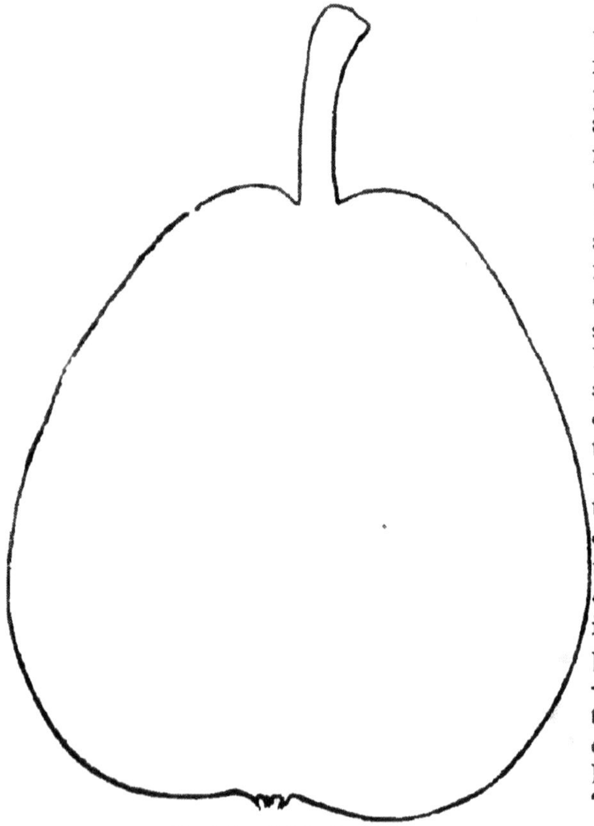

Fruit of medium or large size, regularly formed, obovate. It varies considerably in different soils, and is often shorter or longer on the same tree. Skin smooth, clear, pale yellow, regularly sprinkled with small dots, and often with a fine red check. Stalk brown, from three-fourths to an inch and a fourth long, a little curved, and planted in a small, round cavity. Calyx always very small, closed, set in a shallow basin, smooth or delicately plaited. Flesh white, fine-grained, very buttery, melting, rich, high-flavored, and delicious. September, and, if picked early from the tree, will often ripen gradually till December.

* Virgalieu seems an American name, and is always liable to be confounded with the Virgouleuse, a very different fruit. The Doyenné, (pronounced *dwoy-an-nay*,) literally *deanship*, is probably an allusion to the Dean, by whom it was first brought into notice.

The DOYENNE PANACHE, or *Striped Dean*, is a variety rather more narrowing to the stalk, the skin prettily striped with yellow, green, and red, and dotted with brown. Flesh juicy, melting, but not high flavoured. October.

103. DOYENNE, GRAY. § Thomp. Lind. P. Mag.

Gray Butter Pear.	Doyenné Gris. *Duh.*
Gray Deans.	Doyenné Rouge.
Gray Doyenné.	Doyenné Roux. *Nois. Poit.*
Red Doyenné.	Doyenné d'Automne.
St. Michel Doré.	Red Beurré. } *incorrectly*
Doyenné Galeux.	Beurré Rouge. } *of some.*
Doyenné Boussouck, (*of some.*)	

The Gray Doyenné strongly resembles the White Doyenné in flavour and general appearance, except that its skin is covered all over with a fine, lively cinnamon russet. It is a beautiful pear, usually keeps a little longer, and is considered by many rather the finer of the two, but in the valley of the Hudson where both are remarkably fine, we do not perceive its superiority. It is much less known than the foregoing sort, and richly deserves more general attention. Shoots upright, grayish-brown.

Fruit of medium size, obovate, but usually a little rounder than the White Doyenné. Skin wholly covered with smooth cinnamon russet, (rarely a little ruddy next the sun.) Stalk half, to three-fourths of an inch long, curved, set in a narrow, rather deep and abrupt cavity. Calyx small, closed, and placed in a smooth, shallow basin. Flesh white, fine grained, very buttery, melting, rich, and delicious. Middle of October, and will keep many weeks.

[The tree received in this country for *Doyenné Boussouck*, and *Bossouck Nouvelle*, have proved synonymous with this variety.]

104. DUNMORE. § Thomp.

The Dunmore is a large, and truly admirable pear, raised by Knight, which has been introduced into this country from the garden of the London Horticultural Society. It is a strong growing tree, bears exceedingly well, and is likely to become a very great favourite. Its blossoms resist even severe frosts.

Fruit large, oblong-obovate, rather swollen on one side. Skin greenish, dotted and speckled with smooth, brownish-red russet. Stalk stout, one to two inches long, fleshy at the base, planted obliquely on an obtuse end, or in a very flat depression. Calyx rather small, open, sunk in a narrow basin. Flesh yellowish-white, buttery, exceedingly melting, with a rich, high-flavour. September.

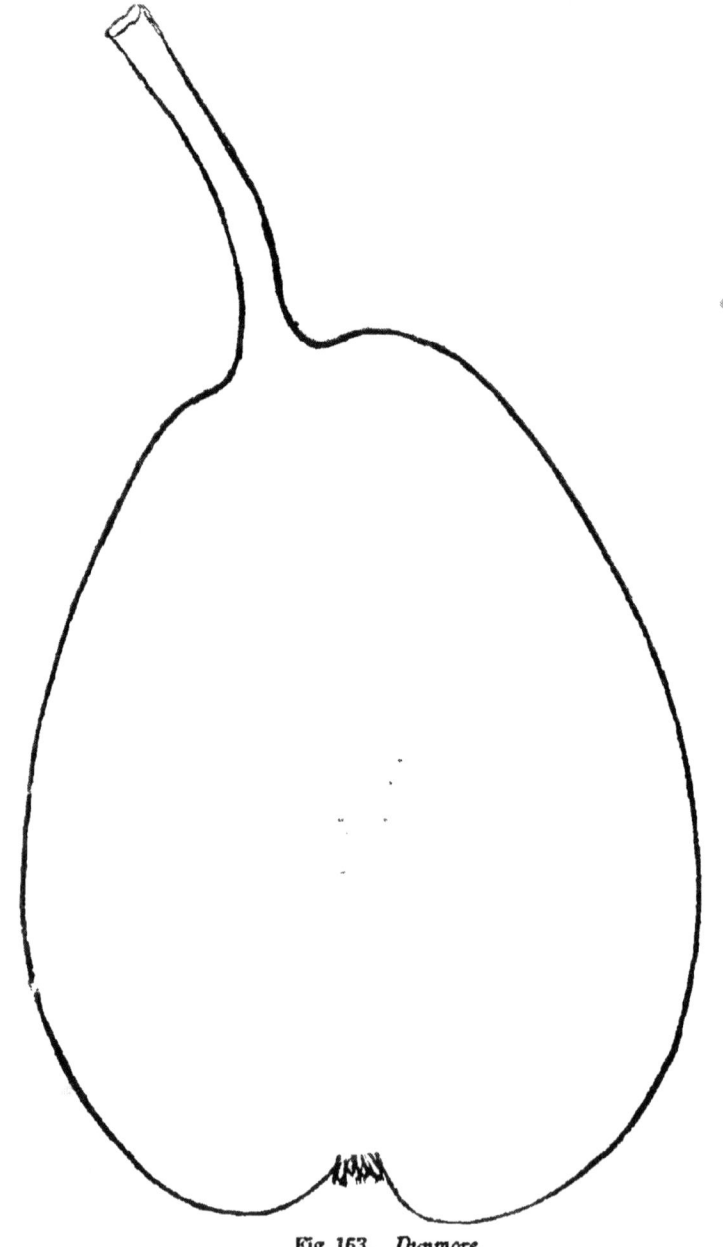

Fig. 163. *Dunmore.*

105. Duchesse d'Angoûleme. § Lind. Thomp.

A magnificent large dessert pear, sometimes weighing a
pound and a quarter, named in honour of the Dutchess of An-

goulême, and said to be a natural seedling, found in a forest hedge, near Angers. When in perfection, it is a most delicious fruit, of the highest quality. We are compelled to add, however, that the quality of the fruit is a little uncertain on young standard trees. On the quince, to which this sort seems well adapted, it is always fine. The tree is a strong grower, the shoots upright, light yellowish-brown, and it is deserving trial in all warm dry soils.

Fruit very large, oblong-obovate, with an uneven, somewhat knobby surface. Skin dull greenish-yellow, a good deal streaked and spotted with russet. Stalk one to two inches long, very stout, bent, deeply planted in an irregular cavity. Calyx set in a somewhat knobby basin. Flesh white, buttery, and very juicy, with a rich and very excellent flavour. October.

The quality of the fruit is often injured by the excessive *luxuriance* of the tree. This should, in such cases, be obviated by root pruning. (See p. 32.)

106. DUCHESSE DE MARS. Thomp.

Duchesse de Mars.

The Dutchess of Mars lately received from France, and first introduced by J. C Lee, Esq., of Salem, Mass., proves to be a rich, melting pear, in this climate, with a peculiar and good flavour.

Fruit nearly of medium size, obovate. Skin dull yellow, considerably covered with brown russet, and becoming ruddy on the sunny side. Stalk an inch long, inserted with little or no depression. Calyx small, stiff, closed and placed in a slight basin. Flesh very melting and juicy, somewhat buttery, with a rich and perfumed flavour. October and November.

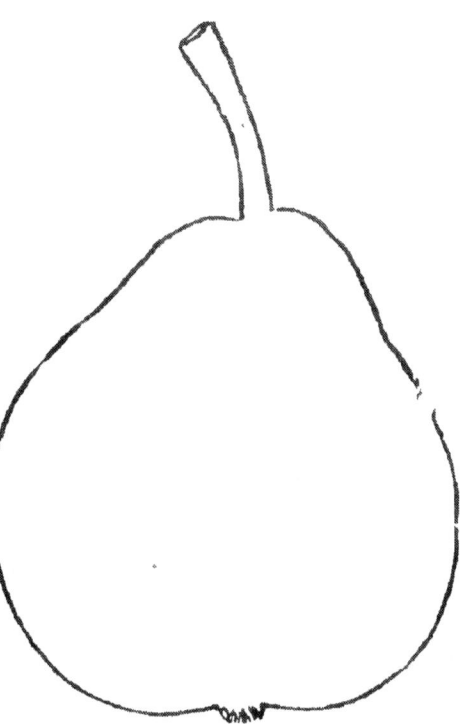

Fig. 164. *Dutchess of Mars.*

107. D'Amour.

Ah! Mon Dieu. *O. Duh. Lind.*
Mon Dieu.
D'Abondance.
Poire d'Amour.

This little French pear, once considerably esteemed, is now little cultivated. We have sometimes tasted it of very rich flavour. It is a very fruitful tree.

Fruit small, obovate, inclining to turbinate, the end tapering and swelling regularly into the stalk. Skin pale yellow, but nearly covered with red, which is sprinkled with numerous darker dots next the sun. Stalk an inch long, curved, set in a swollen base. Calyx small, nearly level, the shallow basin having a few plaits. Flesh white, very juicy, tender and melting, with a sweet, rich flavour.

108. De Louvain. Van Mons.

Poire de Louvain. *Nois. Lind.*

A pear of the finest quality, raised by Van Mons in 1827 while his "Nursery of Fidelity" was at Louvain.

Fruit of medium size, obovate, inclining to pyriform, and tapering to the stalk. Skin rather uneven, clear light yellow, a little marked with russet, and dotted with brown points, which take a ruddy tinge next the sun. Stalk about an inch long, stout, inserted obliquely without depression, or by the side of a fleshy lip. Calyx placed in a very narrow, shallow basin. Flesh white, buttery and melting, with a rich, perfumed, and delicious flavour. Ripens the last of September, and keeps till November.

Fig. 165. *De Louvain.*

109. Duchesse d'Orleans.

Latey received from France, where it has the reputation being a very handsome fruit, of the first quality, with precisely the flavour of the old, and much admired Gansel's Bergamot. Young wood light green.

Fruit large, long-pyriform. Skin golden yellow, dotted and streaked with a little russet. Flesh buttery, melting, rich, sugary and aromatic. Very productive, and ripens in October.

110. Délices d'Hardenpont. Thomp.

Délices d'Ardenpont. *Lind*

A melting, buttery pear, one of the new Flemish varieties, and raised by the counsellor Hardenpont, of Mons. It has borne for several seasons in this country, and proves of rich and excellent flavour. The tree is moderately thrifty; shoots upright, yellowish-brown.

Fruit of medium size, obtuse-pyriform, with its widest part above the middle, and a little uneven in surface. Stalk an inch long, curved, and set rather obliquely in a narrow, shallow cavity. Skin pale yellow, dotted with numerous small gray dots in the shade, and somewhat russetted in the sun. Calyx very small, closed, and placed in a small, uneven basin. Flesh buttery, melting, with an abundant, slightly perfumed, and rich juice. Middle of October.

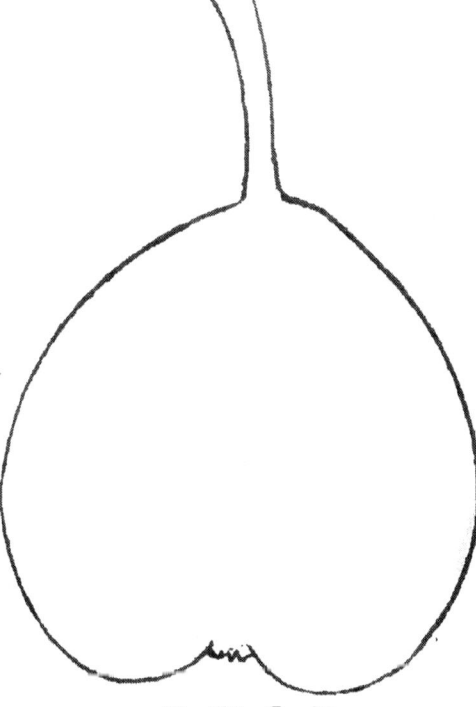

Fig. 166. *Dundas*

111. Dundas. § Van Mons. Man. in H. M.

A very brilliant coloured fruit, remarkably handsome for the dessert, and of rich flavour. It is a recent Belgian variety, sent to this country by Van Mons, in 1834.

Fruit medium size,

obovate, inclining to turbinate. Skin clear yellow, sprinkled
with greenish-black dots, and heightened by a very brilliant
red cheek. Stalk dark brown, an inch long, stout, inserted
without depression. Calyx small, placed at the bottom of a
deep round basin. Flesh yellowish-white, half buttery, melting,
with a rich, perfumed juice. First of October, and keeps
some time.

112. Elizabeth, Edwards'.   Wilder. Mss.

Edwards' Elizabeth is a seedling pear of great beauty, and
nearly, if not quite, of first rate quality, raised by ex-governor
Edwards, of New-Haven, Conn.

Fruit of medium size, often large, obtuse-pyriform, angular,
and oblique at the base, the stalk frequently planted in a fleshy
protuberance, like a fold. Skin smooth, pale lemon yellow,
very fine, and of a peculiar waxen appearance. Flesh
white, buttery, slightly sub-acid and good. October.

113. Elizabeth, Manning's.   Man. in H. M.

Van Mons. No. 154.

Manning's Elizabeth, a seedling of Dr. Van Mons', named by
Mr. Manning, is a very sweet and sprightly pear, with a peculiar flavour.

Fruit below medium size, obovate, shaped like the Julienne, or
a small White Doyenné. Skin smooth, bright yellow, with a
lively red cheek. Stalk one inch long, set in a shallow, round
cavity. Flesh white, juicy, and very melting, with a saccha
rine, but very sprightly, perfumed flavour. Last of August.

114. Edwards' Henrietta.

This is also one of Gov. Edwards' new Seedlings, raised at
New-Haven. It bears most profusely, is a very agreeable fruit,
and deserves a trial generally.

Fruit nearly of medium size, obovate, flattened at the base,
sloping to an obtuse point at the stalk. Skin smooth, pale yellowish-green, with few dots. Stalk an inch and a half long, inserted in a very slight depression. Calyx closed, and set in a
shallow, faintly plaited basin. Flesh melting, juicy, sub-acid
and rich. Middle and last of August.

115. Enfant Prodige.   Van Mons.

This is one of Dr. Van Mons' seedlings, which, from its name,
Enfant Prodige——*wonderful child*—must have been considered

one of his most remarkable. The fruit is often remarkably ugly, and at times remarkably good. The tree bears abundantly with us, and the pears vary much, both in shape and quality—sometimes indifferent, and at others first rate, with a rich sub-acid flavour, between a Brown Beurré pear, and a Banana.

Fruit of medium size, varying in form, obovate, always narrow at the stalk. Skin rough, and a little uneven, pale tawny yellow, a little russeted, and dotted with small specks, gray in the shade, and reddish gray on the sunny side. Stalk one and a half inches long, a little curved, and set in a very slight depression, or under a slight lip. Calyx closed, crumpled, set in a slight, narrow, furrowed basin. Flesh melting, full of rich, sub-acid, vinous juice, of very agreeable flavour. October, and will keep a month. Shoots diverging, dark-olive.

116. EYEWOOD. Thomp.

A seedling of Mr. Knight's, not yet fairly proved in this country, but coming to us from Mr. Thompson, as of first rate quality, the tree vigorous, hardy, and a sure bearer.

Fruit of medium size, oblate or flattened; skin much covered with russet. Flesh buttery, rich and excellent.

117. FLEMISH BEAUTY. § Lind. Thomp.

Belle de Flanders.	Impératrice de France.
Bouche Nouvelle.	Josephine. } incorrectly,
Bosch.	Fondant Du Bois. } of some.
Bosc Sire.	Boschpear.

In good soils and open situations, the Flemish Beauty is certainly one of the most superb pears in this climate. We have seen specimens, grown on the banks of the Hudson, the past summer, which measured 12 inches in circumference, and were of the finest quality. The tree is very luxuriant, and bears early and abundantly; the young shoots upright, dark brown. It should be remarked, however, that the fruit requires to be gathered sooner than most pears, even before it parts readily from the tree. If it is then ripened in the house, it is always fine, while, if allowed to mature on the tree, it usually becomes soft, flavourless, and decays soon.

Fruit large, obovate. Skin a little rough, the ground pale yellow, but mostly covered with marblings and patches of light russet, becoming reddish brown at maturity, on the sunny side. Stalk rather short, from an inch, to an inch and a half long, and pretty deeply planted in a peculiarly narrow, round cavity. Calyx short, open, placed in a small, round basin. Flesh yellowish-white, not very fine grained, but juicy, melting, very saccharine and rich, with a slightly musky flavour. Last of September.

Fig. 167. *Flemish Beauty.*

118. Fondante Van Mons. Thomp.

An excellent melting pear, raised by Dr. Van Mons, and first introduced by Mr. Manning. It bears abundantly.

Fruit nearly of medium size, roundish, a little depressed. Skin pale yellow. Stalk stout, an inch and a half long, planted in a rather deep cavity. Calyx set in a pretty deep basin. Flesh white, juicy, melting, sweet, and of very agreeable flavour. First of November.

119. Fondante d'Automne. § Thomp.

Belle Lucrative.* *Lind. Man. and of most American gardens,*

If we were asked which are the two *highest flavoured* pears

---

* This is the pear described by Lindley as Belle Lucrative. By some error, Mr. Thompson, in the last edition of the Catalogue of the London Horticultural Society, has made the two sorts distinct. They are identically the same.

known in this country, we should not hesitate to name the Seckel, and the Fondante d'Automne (*Autumn melting*.) It is a new Flemish pear, and no garden should be destitute of it. The tree is of moderate growth, the young shoots long, yellowish-gray.

Fruit medium size, obovate, narrow, but blunt at the stalk. Skin pale yellowish-green, slightly russeted. Stalk little more than an inch long, stout, often fleshy, obliquely inserted in a slight, irregular cavity. Calyx very short, open, with few divisions, set in a basin of moderate depth. Flesh exceedingly juicy, melting, sugary, rich and delicious. Last of September.

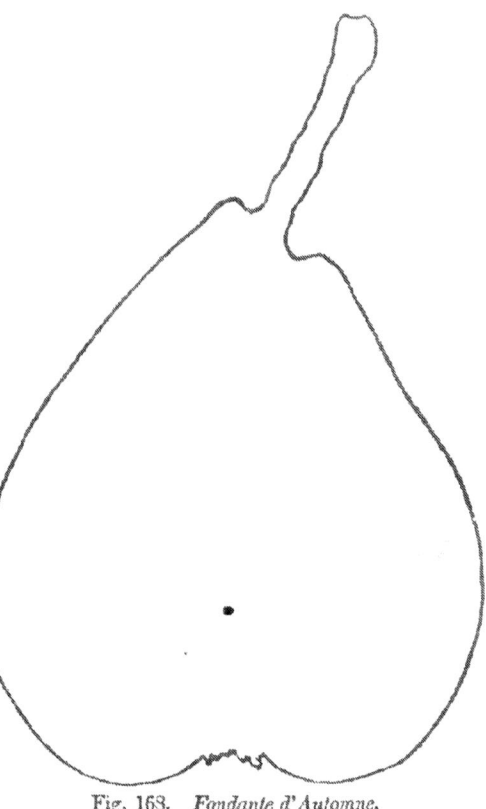

Fig. 163.   *Fondante d'Automne.*

120. FORME DE DÉLICES. Thomp.

A new Flemish pear, of excellent quality, received from the London Horticultural Society. Young shoots stout, upright, yellowish-green.

Fruit of medium size, obovate. Skin rough, yellowish, a good deal marked, or nearly covered with dull russet. Stalk an inch long, planted in a smooth, round cavity. Calyx wide, open, large, projecting. Flesh buttery, melting, somewhat dry, but sweet and good. Last of October.

121. FIGUE DE NAPLES. Thomp.

Comtesse de Frénol.   Beurré Bronzée, *incorrectly of some.*
De Vigne Pelone.   Fig Pear f N, i s Man.

A very good late autumn pear, but inferiour to several others It grows vigorously and bears well.

Fruit of rather large size, oblong-obovate. Skin near'y covered with brown, and tinged with red next the sun. Flesh buttery, melting, and agreeable. November.

122. FORELLE. Thomp. P. Mag. Lind.

Forellen-birne.
Poire Truite.
Trout pear.

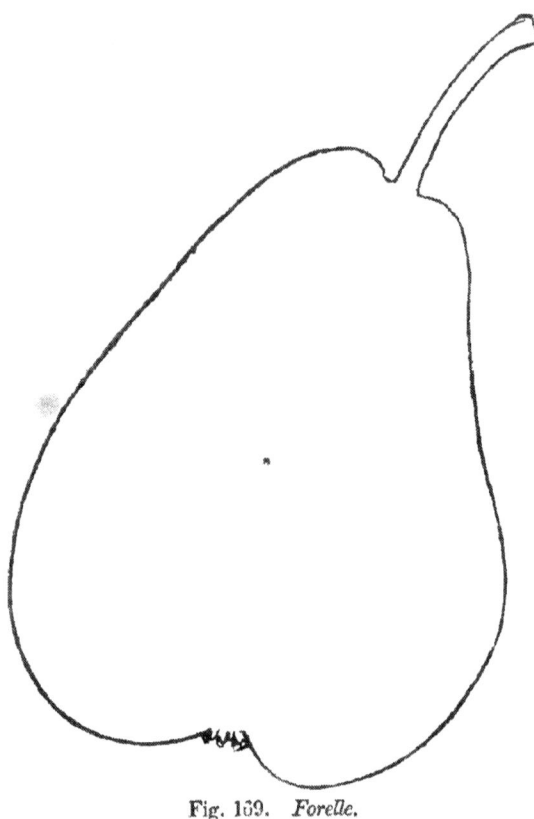

Fig. 169. *Forelle.*

This exquisitely beautiful German pear—called in that language Forellen-birne— i. e. *trout pear,* from its finely speckled appearance, is one of the most attractive dessert fruits. It requires a warm soil and exposure, and well deserves to be trained as an espalier. It does not appear to have succeeded well near Boston, but it fully sustains its high foreign character with us. Young shoots long, with few, and dark coloured branches.

Fruit oblong-obovate, inclining to pyriform. Skin smooth, at first green, but, when fully ripe, lemon yellow, washed with rich deep red on the sunny side, where it is marked with large, margined, crimson specks. Stalk about an inch long, rather slender, slightly curved, rather obliquely planted, in a shallow, uneven cavity. Calyx rather small, basin abruptly sunk. Flesh white, fine grained, buttery, melting, with rich, slightly vinous juice. Beginning of November, and may be kept, with care, till Christmas.

123. FRÉDÉRIC DE WURTEMBURG. § Van Mon. Nois.

Frederick of Wurtemburg.*

It is remarkable that this extremely handsome and very good
dessert fruit, originated by Van Mons in 1812, should not to this
day have found its way into the large collection of the London

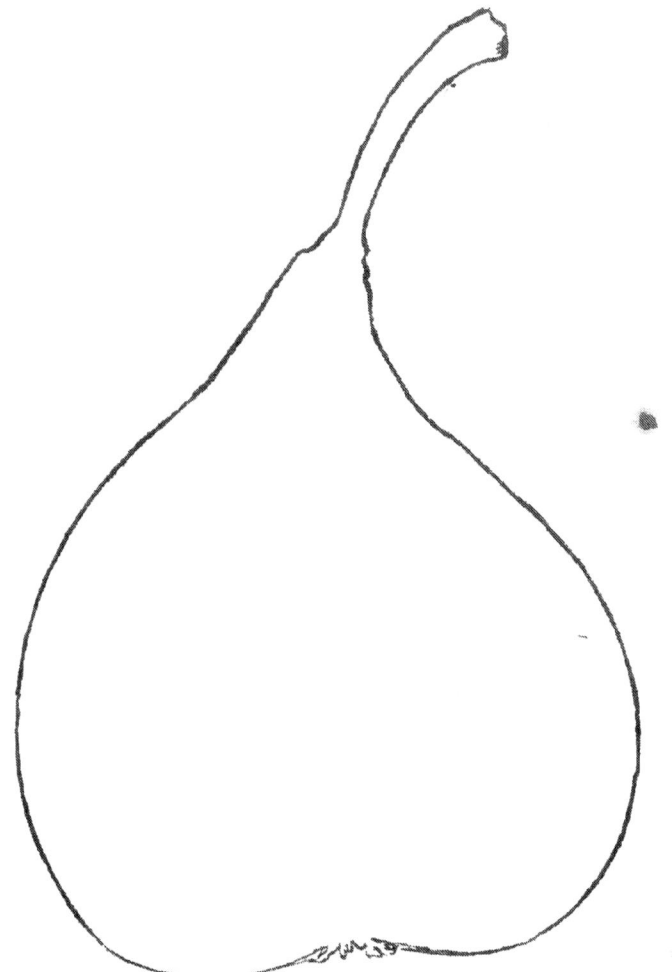

Fig. 170.   Frederick of Wurtemberg.

Horticultural Society.   It is very distinct from the Beurré Capiumont, with which it is sometimes confounded in this coun-

* The *Napoleon* is sometimes incorrectly received under the name of "Wurtemberg," and the *Glout Morceau* as "Roi de Wurtemberg," both of which names
have also been applied to this pear in America.

try—the latter being very smooth, with a prominent calyx, while this is rather uneven, with a somewhat sunken basin. The young wood is very stout and blunt, yellowish-brown, and the tree bears very young. (Part of the stock in this country seems stunted; it may be renovated by severe pruning back and grafting on thrifty stocks.) This is a pear that every amateur will cultivate.

Fruit large, one-sided, pyriform, rather uneven in its surface. Skin deep yellow at maturity, with a remarkably rich crimson cheek. Stalk quite stout, rather more than one inch long, curved, sometimes placed in a blunt hollow, but usually thickening into the fruit. Calyx open, large, set in a shallow, slightly furrowed basin. Flesh white, very juicy, melting and sweet; and when in perfection, buttery, and delicious. September.

124. Fulton. Man. Ken.

This American pear is a native of Maine, and is a seedling, from the farm of Mrs. Fulton, of Topsham, in that state. It is very hardy, and bears every year abundant crops o. nice, small, grayrusset pears, which, if picked pretty early and ripened in the house, are of very excellent quality. Ripened on the tree they are worthless. Young shoots rather slender, and reddish-brown.

Fruit below medium size, roundish, flattened. Skin, at first, entirely grayrusset in colour, but

Fig. 171. *Fulton.*

at maturity, of a dark cinnamon russet. Stalk one to two inches long, slender, planted in a narrow cavity. Calyx with long segments, sunk in an uneven hollow. Flesh half buttery, moderately juicy, with a sprightly, agreeable flavour. Seeds compressed, October and November.

125. GENDESHEIM. Thomp. Lind.

A Flemish pear, which has but lately come into bearing, **but** promises well.

Fruit large, obtuse-pyriform, a little irregular. Skin pale greenish-yellow, much dotted with gray, and marked with a little russet. Stalk an inch long, obliquely planted, in a slight cavity, which is sometimes swollen. Calyx small, set in a narrow, irregular depression. Flesh rather gritty near the core, elsewhere buttery, rich and excellent. October and November.

126. GREEN PEAR OF YAIR. Thomp.

Green Yair.

The green pear of Yair is an European fruit, which proves but little worthy of cultivation here. It bears abundantly.

Fruit of medium size, obovate ; skin green ; flesh very juicy, but not high flavoured or rich. September.

127. GREAT CITRON OF BOHEMIA. Man. in H. M.

Citronenbirne Böhmische grosse, punctirte. *Baum. Cat.*

This pear was imported some years ago, by Mr. Manning, from the nursery of the brothers Baumann of Bolwyller, on the Rhine. It has not yet fruited with us, or any where, that we can learn, except in Mr. M.'s garden. We therefore give his notes, with the remark that its merits will soon be fully tested here. Young shoots very stout, dark gray.

"Fruit large, oblong, yellow, spotted and tinged with red on the side of the sun ; stem one inch long ; flesh sugary, juicy, and very fine." The specimen we tasted was a little coarse grained. Ripens the last of September.

128. HARVARD. Man. Ken.

Boston Epargne.
Cambridge Sugar Pear.

The Harvard is one of the best and most profitable orchard pears, to plant in quantity for market purposes. It produces enormous crops of fine looking fruit, which is of fair quality, and commands the best prices. The tree is remarkably hardy and vigorous, its upright shoots forming a fine head. It originated at Cambridge, Mass., the seat of Harvard University.

Fruit rather large, oblong-pyriform. Skin russety olive-yellow, with a brownish red cheek. Stalk rather stout, inserted **rather** obliquely on the narrow summit or in a small cavity. **Calyx** set in a narrow basin. Flesh white, tender, juicy and melting, of excellent flavour, but liable, if not picked early, to rot at the core.   Beginning of September.

129. Henry the Fourth. § Lind.

Henri Quatre. *Thomp.*
Jacquin.

This little pear, perhaps not very attractive in appearance, being small, and of a dull colour, is one of our greatest favourites as a dessert fruit.   It always bears well—often too abundantly—and the very melting fruit abounds with delicious, high

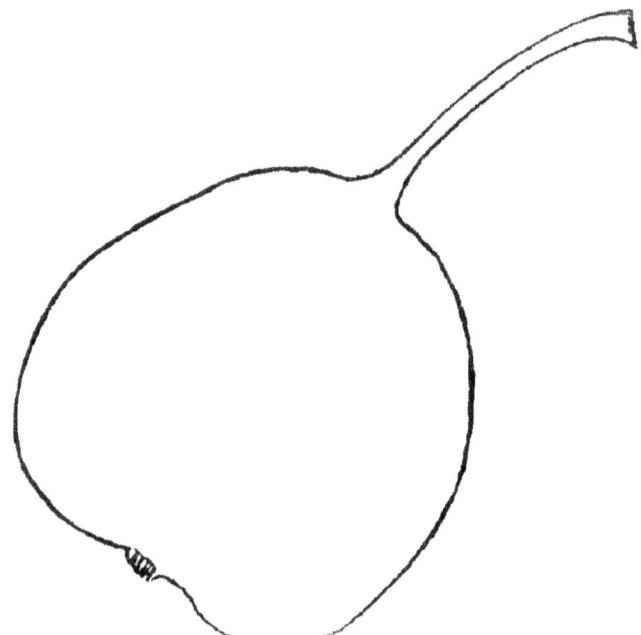

Fig. 172. *Henry IV.*

flavoured juice.   Every good collection of pears should comprise it.   The tree is hardy, and the branches, very thick of foliage, are a little pendant.   Young shoots diverging, yellowish-brown.

Fruit below medium size, roundish-pyriform.   Skin pale greenish-yellow, dotted with small gray specks.   Stalk rather more than an inch long, slender, bent, and obliquely planted on a slightly flattened prominence, or under a swollen lip.   Calyx small, placed in a shallow, abrupt basin.   Flesh whitish, not very fine grained, but unusually juicy and melting, with a rich, delicately perfumed flavour.   It should always be ripened in the house.   Early in September.

130. Héricart.   Van Mons.

A second rate, Belgian pear, with a pleasant, perfumed juice, ripening early in Autumn.

Fruit of medium size, obovate, often rather oblong and irregular. Skin pale green, slightly tinged with yellow, and dotted with many greenish and russety specks. Stalk an inch or more long, rather slender, set in a small cavity. Calyx set in a shallow basin. Flesh white, fine grained, buttery, not rich, but with a delicate, peculiar aroma. The fruit ripens from the last of August, for a month or more.

131.   Heathcot.   Man.

Gore's Heathcot.   Ken.

The heathcot, one of our most excellent native pears, will always compete with the best foreign ones, especially for orchard culture. It is a hardy, thrifty tree, bears abundant crops of fair fruit, which is always of good quality. It was originated on the farm of Governor Gore, in Waltham, Mass., by Mr. Heathcot, then a tenant, and the original tree came into bearing in 1824. Young shoots upright, reddish-brown.

Fruit of medium size, regularly obovate. Skin pale greenish-yellow, with very few dots, and a few russet streaks. Stalk an inch long, planted in a very small cavity. Calyx closed, and set in a rather narrow and shallow basin. Flesh white, buttery and melting, moderately juicy, with an agreeable, vinous flavour. Middle and last of September.

132. Hull.   Hov. Mag.

A new pear, which originated in the town of Swanzey, Mass. It received a premium and high commendation at the annual exhibition of the Massachusetts Horticultural Society, in 1843, when it was first presented.

Fruit of medium size, obovate. Skin yellowish-green, a good deal sprinkled with russet. Flesh white, a little coarse grained, but melting, juicy, with a sweet, slightly perfumed flavour.

133. Huguenot.

A fruit of second quality, originated by Mr. Johonnot, of Salem. It bears abundantly, but is rather dry, and not worthy of general cultivation. Young shoots strong, upright, yellowish-brown.

Fruit of medium size, roundish. Skin smooth, pale yellow, sprinkled with large round spots of bright red. Stalk rather

slender, curved, and inserted without depress on, on the slightly
flattened end. Calyx small, set in a nicely rounded basin. Flesh
white, fine grained, half breaking, sweet, but wanting in flavour
and juice. October.

134. HACON'S INCOMPARABLE. Lind. Thomp.

Downham Seedling.

A capital English fruit, of modern origin, raised by Mr.
Hacon, of Downham Market, Norfolk. It is a hardy, productive tree, with rather depending branches, and the fruit is of
the finest quality. Young shoots rather slender, diverging,
olive-coloured.

Fruit rather large, roundish, inclining to turbinate. Skin
slightly rough, pale, and dull yellowish-green, mixed with pale
brown, sprinkled with numerous greenish russet dots, and russet
streaks. Stalk an inch or more long, straight, inserted in a
broad, shallow depression. Calyx with many small divisions,
set in a wide, shallow basin. Flesh white, buttery, melting,
with a rich vinous flavour. October and November.

135. JOHONNOT. Man.

This excellent native pear, which we received from the late
Mr. Manning, originated in the garden of George S. Johonnot,
Esq., of Salem, Mass., and bore first in 1823. The fruit is of
medium size, of a roundish, and peculiar irregular form. Skin
very thin, dull yellowish-brown, and obscurely marked with
russet. Stalk short and thick, planted by the side of a swollen
protuberance. The flesh is fine grained, melting, buttery and
very goood. The tree is not very vigorous, but it bears good
crops, and is in perfection from the middle of September to the
middle of October.

136. JALOUSIE. Duh. Nois. Thomp.

A very unique looking, old French pear, with the richest
reddish-russet skin, admired by the curious amateur, but not
by the general cultivator. It makes a handsome appearance
on the table, but is only of second rate flavour, and soon rots
at the core. Young shoots stout, olive.

Fruit rather large, varying in form from roundish to obovate,
and more frequently pyriform. Skin rough, of the deepest
russet, ruddy in the sun, and singularly marked with conspicuous, lighter coloured specks, which are slightly raised. Stalk
an inch or an inch and a half long, planted in a very slight
cavity. Calyx small, set in a rather narrow basin. Flesh a

little coarse grained, soft, sweet, and of pleasant flavour. Last
of September.

137. JALOUSIE DE FONTENAY VENDÉE. § Man. in H. M.

This excellent French pear, was imported from Vilmorin, of
Paris. It is greatly superiour in flavour to the old Jalousie,
though having a little of its peculiar appearance. Young shoots
upright, long, brownish-yellow.

Fruit of me-
dium size, tur-
binate, or ob-
tuse – pyriform.
Skin dull yellow
and green, con-
siderably mark-
ed with russet
patches and dots,
and tinged with
a red cheek.
Stalk about an
inch long, set
obliquely, with-
out depression
on an obtuse
point. Calyx
with closed and
stiff segments,
set in a shallow,
round basin.
Flesh white, but-
tery, melting,
with a rich fla-
voured juice.
First of October.

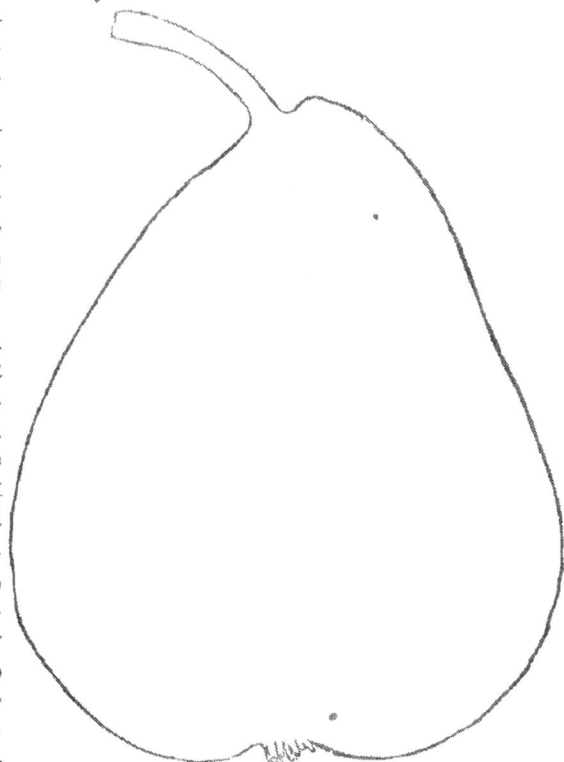

Fig. 173. Jalousie de Fontenay Vendée.

138. KING EDWARD'S. Thomp.

Jackman's Melting. *Man.*

King Edward's is a large, and very handsome fruit, which
was received from England, with a high reputation, but which
proves a very *uncertain* fruit in this climate. Occasionally, it
is of excellent flavour, but very often it is quite astringent and
indifferent. The tree is very thrifty. Young shoots stout, upright, dark brown.

Fruit large, pyriform, tapering gradually to the stalk, which is very short, and inserted without depression. Skin rather rough, yellow, a little mottled with patches of greenish russet, and marked with a fine red cheek. Calyx small, somewhat projecting, basin very slight. Flesh yellowish, buttery, melting and good, when the season is favourable. October.

139. LOUISE BONNE OF JERSEY. § Thomp.

Louise Bonne de Jersey.
Louise Bonne d'Avranches.
Beurré, or Bonne Louise d'Araudoré.
William the Fourth.

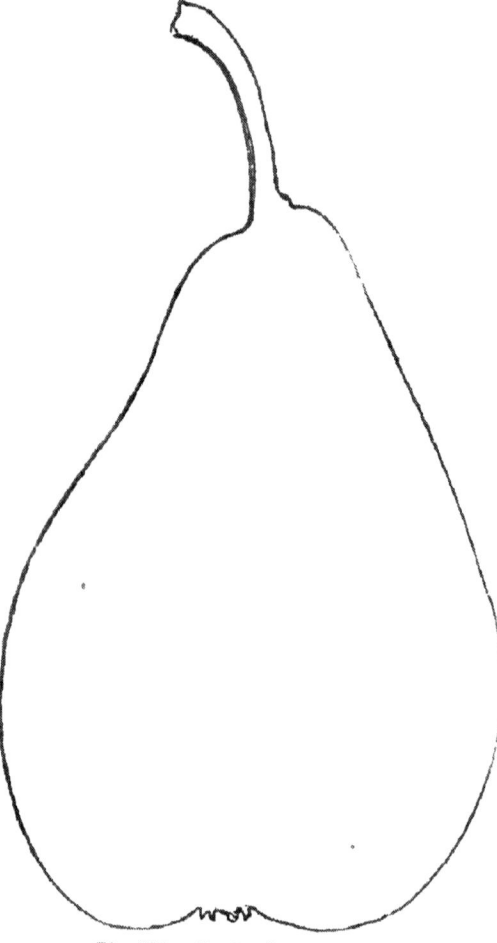

Louise Bonne, of Jersey, is one of the best new autumn pears, fair and glossy, exceedingly juicy, and well flavoured. It is claimed by English cultivators for the Isle of Jersey, and by the French for the neighbourhood of Avranches, and there is no doubt it originated in the latter place. The first fruit seen in England, was sent to the London Horticultural Society's exhibition, from the gardens of Gen. Gordon, of Jersey, in 1820. In this country it succeeds admirably, and will become a very popular fruit, being hardy and productive, the tree making fine upright shoots

Fruit large, pyriform, a little one-sided. Skin smooth and glossy, pale green in the shade, but overspread with brownish red in the sun, and dotted with numerous gray dots. Stalk about an inch long, curved, rather

Fig. 174. *Louise Bonne of Jersey.*

obliquely inserted, without depression, or with a fleshy, enlarged base. Calyx open, in a rather shallow, uneven basin. Flesh greenish-white, very juicy and melting, with a rich and excellent flavour. September and October. [This is very distinct from the old Louise Bonne, a green winter fruit, of third quality.

140. LODGE.   Ken.

The Lodge Pear is a native of Pennsylvania, and is understood to have originated near Philadelphia. It is a very agreeable sub-acid pear, and has so much of the Brown Beurré character, that we suspect it is a seedling of that fine old variety. Kenrick compares it to the Seckel, to which it has no points of resemblance.

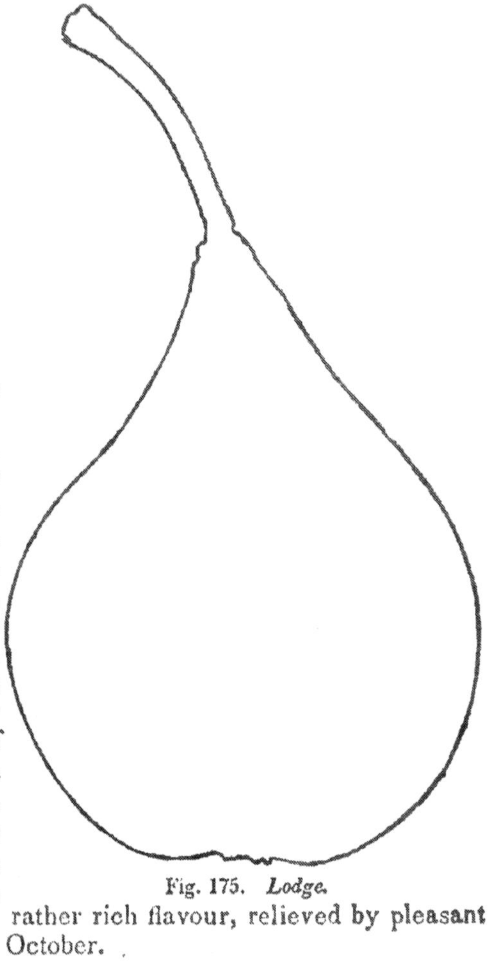

Fruit of medium size, pyriform, tapering to the stem, and one-sided. Skin greenish-brown, the green becoming a little paler at maturity, and much covered with patches of dull russet. Stalk an inch and a fourth long, obliquely planted at the point of the fruit, which is a little swollen there. Flesh whitish, a little gritty at the core, which is large; juicy,

Fig. 175.   *Lodge.*

and melting, with a rather rich flavour, relieved by pleasant acid. September and October.

141. MICHAUX.   Man. in H. M.

Compte de Michaux.

A fruit imported from the nursery of the Messrs. Baumann, of Bolwyller, France, by Mr. Manning. Young wood light green. It is of medium size, and nearly round. Skin light yellowish green, with a faint blush on the sunny side. Calyx open, slightly sunk. Stalk an inch and a half long, rather slender, inserted with little or no depression. Flesh white, half-buttery, juicy, sweet, but second rate. September and October.

142. MOOR-FOWL EGG. Lind. Thomp.

Little Swan's Egg.
Knevett's New Swan's Egg.

The Moor-fowl Egg is a Scotch pear, very hardy, and therefore, popular in that climate, which is cold and unfavourable for the pear. It is a third rate fruit, much like the Swan's Egg, and unworthy of cultivation in this country. [The Moor-fowl's Egg, of some Boston gardens, is the *Swan's Egg*.]

Fruit rather small, roundish. Skin dull green, washed with brown on the exposed side, and dotted with minute russet dots. Stalk long and slender, planted in a slight hollow, or by the side of a fleshy lip. Basin narrow, slightly sunk. Calyx open. Flesh yellowish-white, soft, a little gritty, juicy and sweet. September and October.

143. MARIE LOUISE. § P. Mag. Lind. Thomp.

Forme de Marie Louise.   Princesse de Parme.
Marie Chrétienne.   Braddick's Field Standard.

This truly delicious pear was originated from seed, by the Abbé Duquesne, of Belgium, in 1809, and its fruit was first sent to England by Van Mons, in 1816. It was introduced into this country, along with many other fine Flemish pears, about 15 years ago, and is every where held in the highest estimation, keeping for a long time in the house. The tree is hardy, but has an awkward, rather crooked, and declining habit, and very narrow leaves. In the nursery it is best, therefore, to graft it standard high, when it soon makes a good head. The young shoots are olive-gray. It is a pear for every garden, bearing very regularly.

Fruit pretty large, oblong-pyriform, rather irregular or one-sided in figure. Skin at first pale green, but at maturity, rich yellow, a good deal sprinkled and mottled with light russet, on the exposed side. Stalk an inch and a half long, obliquely planted, sometimes under a slightly raised lip, sometimes in a very small, one-sided cavity. Calyx small, set in a narrow somewhat plaited basin. Flesh white, exceedingly buttery and melting, with a rich, very saccharine, and vinous flavour Last **of September and middle of October.**

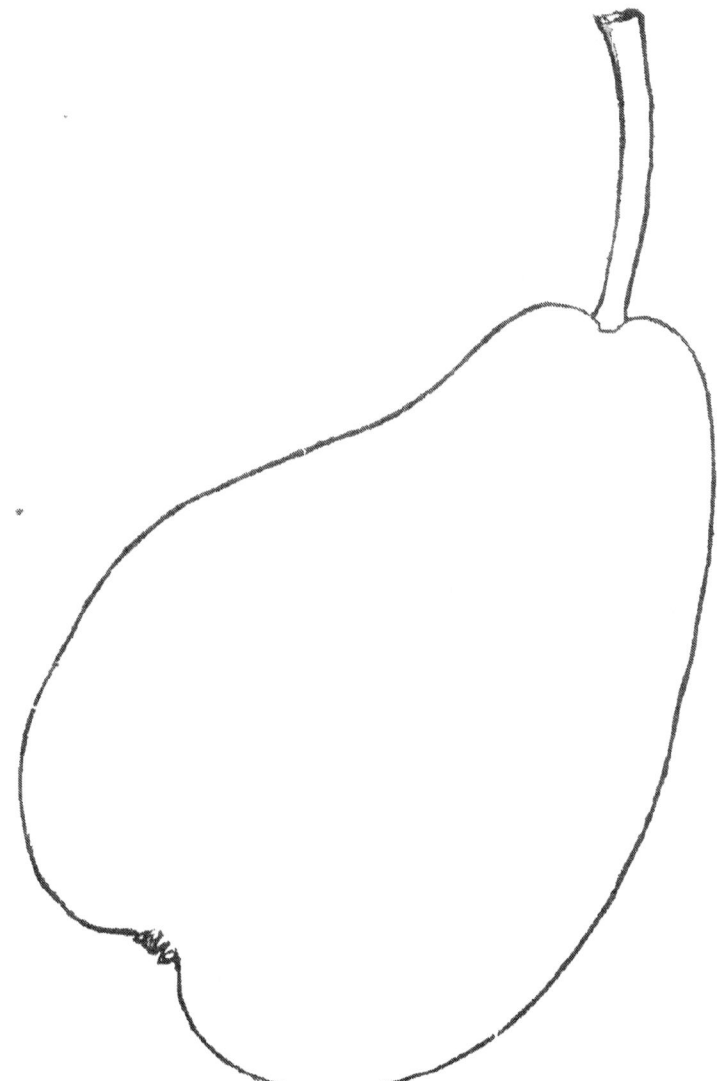

Fig. 176. *Marie Louise.*

144. MARIE LOUISE NOVA. Van Mons. Ken.

This variety, was sent by Van Mons to Mr. Manning. It will by no means bear a comparison with the Marie Louise, though in some seasons a very good fruit. Col. Wilder, of Boston, considers it " hardly second rate," while the Salem cultivators " think it an excellent, juicy, rich pear, though sometimes a little rough." It has borne two seasons with us, and is enormously productive, but, even with thinning the crop, it is an indifferent fruit. The wood is very strong, and dark coloured.

Fruit rather large, regular pyriform, tapering into the stalk. Skin smooth, yellow, with a brownish-red cheek. Stalk one to two inches long, rather slender and curved. Calyx set in a shallow depression. Flesh at first melting, juicy, and some times rich, but quickly decays. Last of September.

145. NIELL. Thomp. Van Mons.

Beurre Niell. *Man. in H. M.*　　Colmar Bosc.
Poire Niell. *Lind.*　　Fondante du Bois, (*incorrectly of some.*)

A large and handsome Belgian variety, raised by Van Mons, from seeds sown in 1815, and named in honor of Dr. Niell, of Edinburgh, a distinguished horticulturist, and man of science. The tree bears plentifully. Its quality is not yet fully ascertained, but specimens obtained here, promise well. Young wood stout, diverging, gray.

Fruit large, obovate, inclining to pyriform, rather shortened in figure on one side, and enlarged on the other—tapering to the stalk which is about an inch long, obliquely planted, with little or no cavity. Skin pale yellow, delicately marked with thin russet, finely dotted, and sometimes marked with faint red. Flesh white, buttery, sweet, with a plentiful and agreeable juice. Last of September.

146. NAPOLEON. Lind. P. Mag. Thomp.

Medaille.　　Charles d'Autriche. } *incorrectly*
Sucrée Dorée, (*of some.*) Wurtemberg.　　 } *of some.*
Roi de Rome

The Napoleon is a pear of many fine qualities. As a tree it is very hardy, thrifty, and bears abundant crops, even while very young; and its fruit is exceedingly juicy, melting, and agreeable in flavour. In poor soils, or in unfavourable exposures only, it is a little astringent. The leaves are broad, and the shoots are upright, and olive-coloured.

Lindley gives this as a seedling of Dr. Van Mons—but we believe, incorrectly, though Van Mons first sent it to England in 1816. It was raised from seed in 1808, by M. Liart, gardener at Mons; exhibited by him before the Horticultural Society of Mons, which decreed him a medal for it, [whence the synonyme Médaille;] the original tree was then purchased for 33 francs, by the Abbé Duquesne, who bestowed on it the name of Napoleon.

Fruit pretty large, obtuse-pyriform, (but varying more than almost any other pear in form.) Skin smooth, clear green at
34*

first, but be-
coming pale
yellowish-
green at ma-
turity, slight-
ly brighter
and darker
on its expo-
sed cheek.
Stalk vary-
ing from half
an inch to
an inch long,
pretty stout,
set in a slight
depression or
under a swol-
len lip. Ca-
lyx set in a
basin of mo-
derate depth.
Flesh white,
melting, re-
markably
full of juice,
which   is
sweet,
sprightly and
excellent.
Should be ri-
pened in the
house, when
it will be fit

Fig. 177. *Napoleon.*

for use in September, and may be kept for weeks.

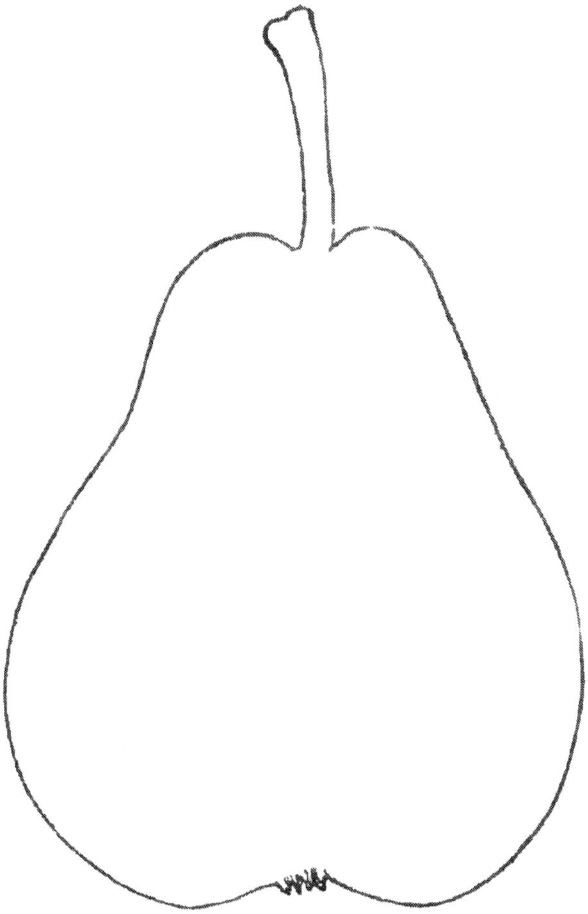

147. NAUMKEAG. Man.

A second rate fruit, a native of Salem, Mass. In wood and
leaf it resembles the Brown Beurré. Its appearance is ordinary, and it is often rather astringent. Fruit of medium size,
roundish. Skin yellow russet, marked with brown russet in
the sun. Stalk set in a very slight depression. Flesh juicy,
melting, but rather astringent in flavour. Bears abundantly.
October.

148. PARADISE D'AUTOMNE. Thomp.

A newly imported pear, and the few specimens that we have

seen here, so strongly resemble Beurré Bosc, as to lead us to suspect its identity. The following description is from a fruit of the present autumn.

Fruit large, pyriform, tapering into the stalk, which it joins by a fleshy base. Skin dull yellow, russeted, a good deal like the Brown Beurré. Calyx quite small, open, stiff, set in a shallow basin. Stalk an inch and a half long, curved. Flesh white, fine grained, buttery, with a high, rich flavour. Last of September.

149. Petré

An American pear, of the highest excellence. The original tree is growing in that interesting place, the old Bartram Botanic Garden, near Philadelphia. Col. Carr, the proprietor, who has disseminated this tree, informs us that in 1735, a seed was received by the elder John Bartram, from Lord Petré, of London, as being the seed of a fine butter pear. Twenty-five years after, ripe fruit was returned him from this seedling—called the Petre pear—which he pronounced superiour to that of the original tree.

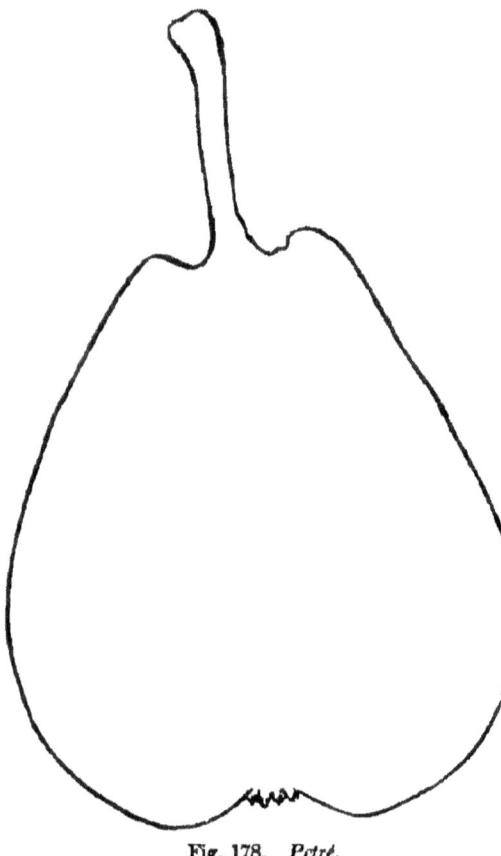

The tree is not a rapid grower, but produces very regular and abundant crops. The fruit has much of the quality of a fine Doyenné with a higher perfume. Young wood slender, yellowish-brown.

Fruit of medium size, or rather large, obovate. Skin very thin, pale yellow, (sometimes marked with greenish russet, and sprinkled with russet about the eye.) Stalk stiff

Fig. 178. *Petré.*

and strong, about an inch long, stout at the lower end, and set in a peculiar, abruptly flattened cavity. Caylx small, set in a narrow, but smooth basin. Flesh whitish, fine grained, buttery, and very melting; with a perfumed, slightly musky, high fla- vour. October, and if picked early, will keep a long time.

150. Pitt's Prolific.

Pitt's Surpasse Marie. *Ken.*
Surpass Maria Louise, (*incorrectly of some American gardens.*)

An English market fruit, introduced by Mr. Kenrick. It was raised from the seed of the Marie Louise, but is greatly *infe- riour* to it. Its principal merit seems to us, to be its beauty and surprising fertility, its long, thrifty branches being literally load- ed with fruit. It is handsome, but in flavour it is third rate, quite poor, and soon decays.

Fruit of medium size, oblong-pyriform, (sometimes turbinate,) usually shaped a little like a Jargonelle. Skin yellow, but nearly covered, in the sun, with brownish-red, and a little rus- setted. Stalk curved, fleshy at the base where it joins the fruit. Flesh juicy, soft, sweet, rather coarse, and of indifferent quality. September.

[The Surpasse Marie Louise of some European gardens, is the Compte de Lamy, a very fine pear.]

151. Paquency.

A new pear, introduced from France, by Col. M. P. Wilder, President of the Massachusetts Horticultural Society. It proves to be a fruit of the first quality.

Fruit of medium size, regularly pyriform. Skin green at first, becoming dull yellow at maturity, marked with patches of russet at both extremities, and dotted with the same. Stalk long, inserted without depression. Calyx stiff, open, set in a very shallow basin. Flesh white, buttery, with sweet, rich, and perfumed flavour. October to November.

152. Pennsylvania.

Smith's Pennsylvania.

The Pennsylvania is a seedling, originated by J. B. Smith, Esq., of Philadelphia, a well known amateur. It is a handsome and good pear, of second quality. Young shoots diverging, reddish-brown.

Fruit of medium size, obovate, a good deal narrowed towards the stalk. Skin brown russet, nearly covering a dull yellow ground, and becoming russet red on the sunny side. Stalk an

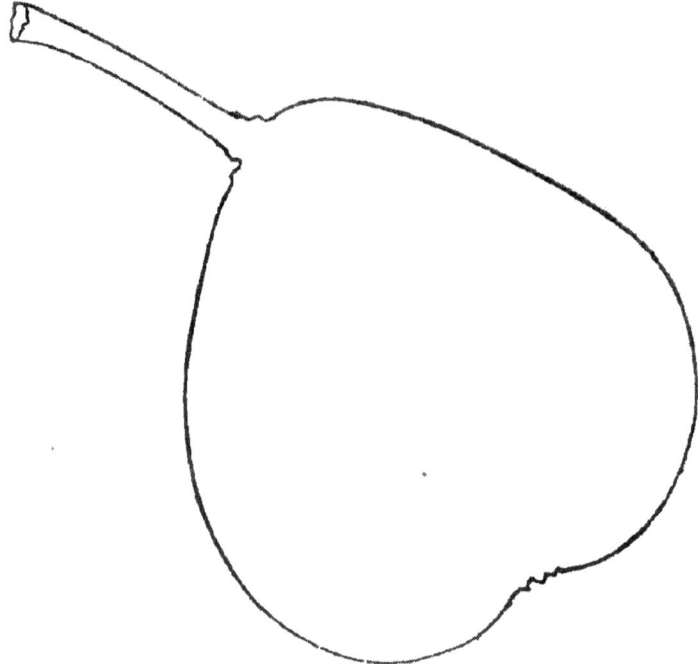

Fig. 179. *Pennsylvania.*

inch and a half long, obliquely planted, without depression, but
a fleshy base. Calyx small, basin very shallow. Flesh yellowish-white, not very
fine grained, juicy,
half melting, sweet
and rich, with a highly
perfumed, musky fla-
vour. Middle and last
of September.

153. PRINCESS OF
ORANGE. Lind.
Thomp. P. Mag.

Princesse d'Orange.
Princesse Conquéte.

The Princess of
Orange is a pleasant,
crisp, juicy pear, of
second quality. Its
long and upright shoots
bear, with us, very
regular crops of rich
looking, ruddy pears.

Fig. 180. *Princess of Orange.*

It is a Flemish variety, raised by the Count Coloma, in 1802. Young wood long, light olive.

Fruit of medium size, or a little less, roundish. Skin cinnamon russet in the shade, but nearly covered with bright reddish russet, mixed with a little orange, in the sun. Stalk an inch or more long, planted in a very slight cavity. Calyx small, in a shallow basin. Flesh pale yellowish-white, crisp, juicy, flavour vinous—sugary, relieved by acid, and when in perfection, excellent. October and November.

154. POPE'S SCARLET MAJOR.

We have discontinued the cultivation of this pear, as, though very handsome, it is quite inferiour. Fruit rather large, obovate, yellow, with a bright red cheek. Stalk long and thick. eye rather small. Flesh white, breaking, and rather dry, Last of August.

POPE'S QUAKER is another variety, a little better in quality, but not comparable to many other sorts of the same time. Fruit very fair, middle sized, oblong-pyriform, smooth yellow-russet, juicy, melting and pleasant. October. Both these pears are natives of Long Island, N. Y.

155. PAILLEAU. Van Mons. Man. in H. M.

A Belgian pear, of good quality, but rather coarse grained.

Fruit medium size, turbinate, inclining to pyriform. Skin rough, greenish-yellow, dotted with greenish gray dots, and marked with patches of russet. Stalk about an inch long, very stout, obliquely inserted with a fleshy base. Calyx in a basin slightly depressed. Flesh juicy, sweet and good. Early in September.

156. QUEEN OF THE LOW COUNTRIES. Ken. Man. in H. M.

Reine des Pays Bas. *Van Mons.*

This fine, large, and handsome fruit, was transmitted by Dr. Van Mons to Mr. Manning, with the assurance that it was " the most perfect of pears." Without, as yet, quite equalling this high character here, it proves worthy of extensive trial.

Fruit large, often very large, broad pyriform, tapering abruptly to the stalk. Skin in the shade, dull yellow, dotted and russetted around the eye, and overspread with fine dark red on the side next the sun. Stalk an inch and a half long, curved, and planted without depression. Calyx very small, and with few divisions, set in a pretty deep basin. Flesh white, buttery,

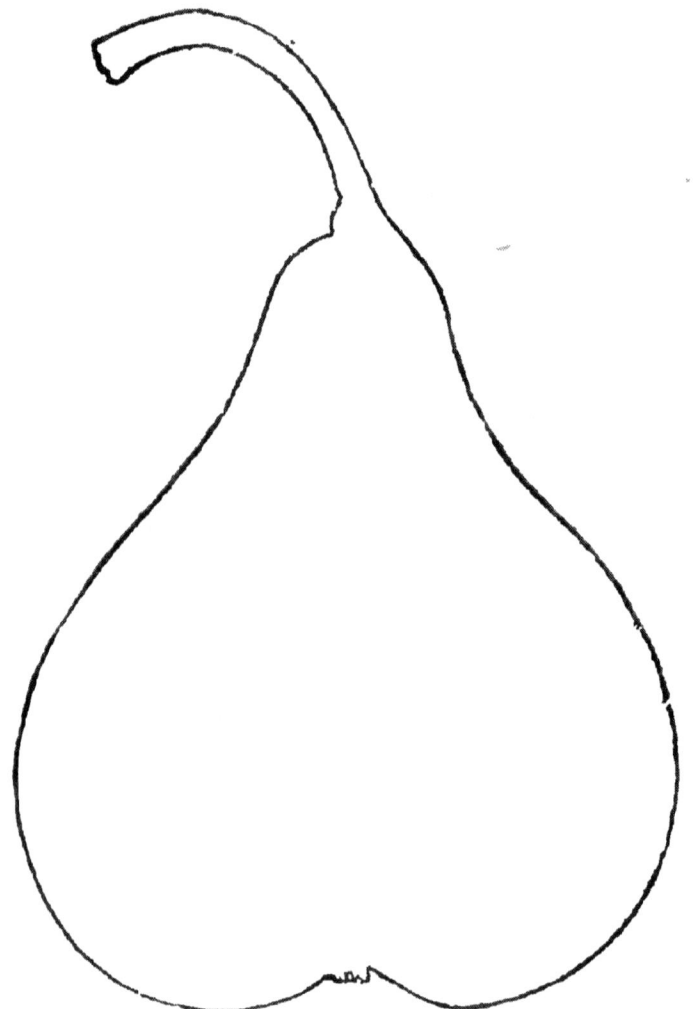

Fig. 181. *Queen of the Low Countries.*

melting and very juicy, with a rich, sub-acid, vinous flavour.
Early in October.

157. QUILLETETTE. Van Mons.

A new, and odd-looking, late autumn fruit, of the first qual.
ity, recevied from Van Mons, and which deserves a general
trial.

Fruit nearly of medium size, roundish, a little flattened.
Skin greenish, nearly covered with dull, iron-coloured russet.

Stalk about an inch and a half long, and set without depression, but with a peculiar fleshy swelling at its point of insertion. Calyx extremely small, sometimes abortive, set in a narrow, rather deep basin. The flesh is white, buttery, and melting, rich, sweet, and perfumed. November.

158. REINE CARO LINE. Thomp.

Queen Caroline.

A pretty looking, European pear, ripening late in autumn, but

Fig. 132. *Quilletette.*

coarse, and only fit for cooking. Fruit of medium size, narrow-pyriform. Skin smooth yellowish-green, becoming yellow at maturity, with a rich, brownish-red cheek. Stalk an inch long, curved, planted with little or no cavity. Flesh white, crisp, rather dry and indifferent in quality. November—and will keep for several weeks.

159. REINE DES POIRES. Thomp.

This French pear, with its fine name, unfortunately proves very poor and worthless. It is regularly formed, and handsome—quite distinct from the Cumberland, with which it is considered synonymous, by some. It bears abundantly.

Fruit rather large, varying from turbinate to obtuse-pyriform, regularly shaped. Skin smooth greenish-yellow, with rarely a very little red on its cheek. Stalk an inch and a fourth long, slender, inserted with little or no depression. Calyx set in a shallow basin. Flesh dry and poor. September and October

160. ROUSSELET DE MEESTER. Van Mons. Man. in H. M.

Ferdinand de Meester? *Nois.*

This is a seed-
ling of Dr. Van
Mons', and is a
very excellent
pear in this cli-
mate, the flesh
melting and su-
gary, though a
little rough.

Fruit of medi-
um size, roundish,
somewhat flatten-
ed. Skin pale
yellow, marked
with very light
russet dots, and
washed with pale
red next the sun.
Stalk an inch
and a half long,
rather slender,
and planted some-
what obliquely in,
or by the side of
the swollen, ab-
rupt end. Calyx
large, open, pla-
ced in a very
slight and irregu-
lar basin. Flesh

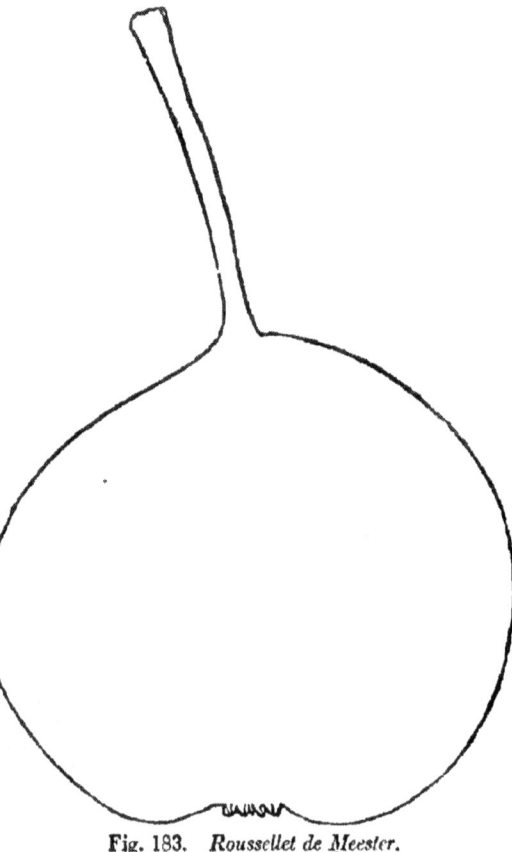

Fig. 183. *Roussellet de Meester.*

juicy, melting, sugary and rich, but a little rough, which does
not prevent its being of excellent flavour. October.

Rousselet de Meester is the name by which this fruit was received, but we suspect that it is the Ferdinand de Meester, a
larger and better pear than the former sort, which was named
by Van Mons after his gardener. [See *Annale's de la Societé
d'Horticulture.* Paris. Vol. 15, p. 362.]

161. RAYMOND. Man.

The Raymond is a native of Maine, and originated on the
farm of Dr. I. Wight, in the town of this name. It has a good
deal of the flavour of the White Doyenné, and is a productive
pear, often of the first quality, and if the tree were a little more

vigorous, would become a popular variety.   Young shoots very slender, dark yellowish-brown.

Fruit of medium size, obovate, shaped like the Doyenné Skin yellow, marked with russet near the stalk, and tinged with a little red towards the sun.   Stalk an inch or more long, inserted with little or no depression.   Calyx round, firm, open, set in a shallow basin.   Flesh white, buttery, melting, and very excellent.

162. ROSTIEZER.   Man.

The Rostiezer is, we believe, a German pear, and was received from the nursery of the brothers Baumann, of Bolwiller, on the Rhine.   It is likely to prove a capital variety.   It bears abundantly.

Fruit of medium size, oblong-pyriform.   Skin a dull yellowish-green, with a reddish-brown cheek, and whitish dots, light russet.   Stalk very long, nearly two inches, irregular, slender, set with very little depression.   Calyx open, but little sunk.   Flesh juicy, a little coarse, but very melting, sweet and delicious, with a rich perfume.   August and September.

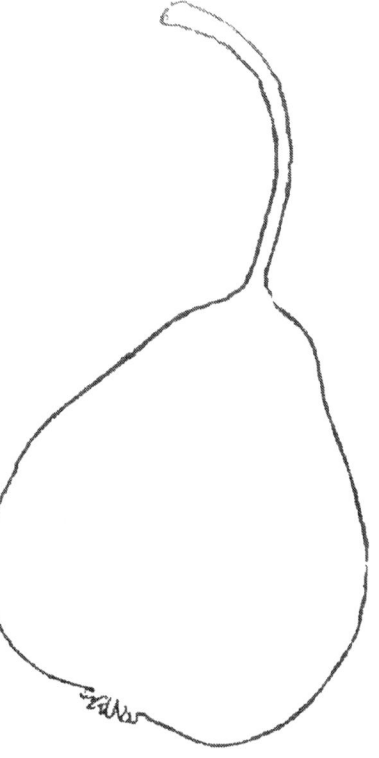

Fig. 184.   *Rostiezer*

163. ST. GHISLAIN. § Thomp.

A most excellent Belgian pear, recently originated by M. Dorlain, and introduced into the United States by S. G. Perkins, Esq., of Boston.   When in perfection, it is of the highest quality, but on some soils it is a little variable.   The tree is remarkable for its uprightness, and the great beauty and vigour of its growth.   Young shoots light brown.

Fruit of medium size, pyriform, tapering to the stalk, to which it joins by fleshy rings.   Skin pale clear yellow, with a few gray specks.   Stalk an inch and a half long, curved. Calyx rather small, open, set in a shallow basin.   Core small. Flesh white, buttery and juicy, with a rich, sprightly flavour.

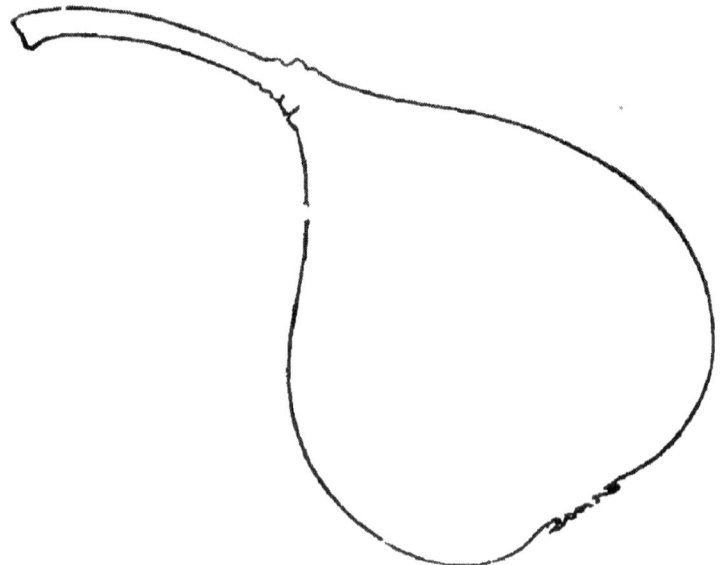

Fig. 185. *St. Ghislain.*

164. SUPERFONDANTE. Thomp.

The Superfondante is a fine French pear, of the same class as the White Doyenné, which indeed, it strongly resembles in appearance and flavour. Young shoots slender, yellowish-brown.

Fruit of medium size, obovate. Stalk an inch long, slightly inserted. Skin smooth, pale yellow, marked with a few dots, and sometimes marked with russet. Stalk an inch and a fourth long, set in a slight cavity. Calyx rather large, in a shallow basin. Flesh white, buttery, melting, and very good. October.

165. ST. ANDRÉ. Man. in H. M.

Imported by Mr. Manning, from the Brothers Baumann, of Bolwyller. A first rate variety.

Fruit medium size, obovate, shaped like Henry the 4th. Skin light greenish-yellow, somewhat dotted with red. Stalk about an inch and a quarter long. Calyx small. Flesh white, fine grained, buttery, melting, and excellent. Early in September.

166. SULLIVAN. Man. in H. M.

Van Mons, No. 889.

A second rate seedling, ser ' to this country by Van Mons, and named by Mr. Manning. Young shoots slender, diverging, reddish-brown. Fruit of medium size, oblong-pyriform. Skin pale greenish-yellow. Stalk an inch and a half long, stout, inserted at the tapering, pointed end. Flesh juicy, melting, sweet and pleasant. September.

167. STYRIAN. Thomp.

This very bright coloured and excellent pear, comes from England. We think it worthy of a general trial in the middle states. Like the Passe Colmar, it often produces a second crop of fruit, which, however, is seldom good.

Fruit rather large, pyriform, a little one-sided and irregular. Skin deep yellow, with a bright red cheek, and streaks of light russet. Stalk an inch and a half long, curved, slender, fleshy where it tapers into the fruit. Calyx large, open, and set in an irregular basin. Flesh yellowish, not very fine grained, crisp, with a rich, high-flavoured juice. October.

168. STEVENS' GENESSEE. § Man. Thomp.

Guernsey. *Pom. Man.*
Stephen's Genessee.

This admirable pear, combining in some degree, the excellence of the Doyenné and Bergamot, is reputed to be a seedling of Western New - York. It originated on the farm Mr. F. Stevens, of Lima, Livingston Co., N. Y. Altho' placed among Autumn pears, it frequently ripens here at the end of August, among the late Summer varieties. Young shoots diverging, dark-gray.

Fig. 186. *Stevens' Genessee.*

Fruit large, roundish-obovate, and of a yellow colour, resem, bling that of the Doyenné (or Virgalieu.) Stalk about an inch long, stout, thicker at the base, and set in a slight, rather one-sided depression. Calyx with short, stiff divisions, placed in a smooth basin of only moderate depth. Flesh white, half buttery, with a rich, aromatic flavour, somewhat like that of Gansel's Bergamot. First of September.

169. SYLVANGE. Nois. Thomp.

Bergamotte Sylvange.
Green Sylvange. *Lind.*

A pleasant, juicy pear, which is much esteemed by some persons, and always bears good crops with us. Young shoots stout, upright, dark olive.

Fruit roundish-obovate, shaped much like a bergamot. Skin rough, pale green, with a slightly darker green cheek, a good deal marked with dark dots. Stalk three-fourths of an inch long, slender, slightly inserted. Calyx small, set in a rather uneven, shallow basin. Flesh greenish-white, juicy, tender and melting, with a rich, sweet, agreeable flavour. October, and keeps a long time.

170. SHENKS.

A new native pear, from the eastern states. It soon grows mealy if left on the tree, but ripened in the house is remarkably juicy and sprightly. Fruit rather large, obovate, and shaped somewhat like Henry the 4th. Skin light yellowish-green. Stalk an inch long, slender. Calyx in a narrow, rather deep basin. Flesh white, tender and melting, with a juicy, and very sprightly flavour. October.

171. SIEULLE. Thomp.

Beurré Sieulle.

A new fruit, very lately received from the London Society's garden, and so far as it is yet proved, of very excellent character.

Fruit of medium size, roundish, flattened. Skin pale yellow, with a little red on the sunny side. Stalk an inch and a quarter long, set in a shallow cavity. Calyx closed, basin scarcely at all sunken. Flesh buttery, melting, rich, and very good. October

172. THOMPSON'S. § Thomp.

This new, and very rich flavoured pear, received by us from the Horticultural Society of London, was named in honour of

35*

Mr. Robert Thompson, the head of the fruit department, in the Society's garden, to whose pomological acumen, the horticultural world is so largely indebted. It is, appropriately, a fruit of high merit, having the qualities of the Passe Colmar and Doyenné somewhat combined, but with most of the richness of the former. It is very productive, and merits a place in every collection of pears. Young shoots diverging, yellowish-olive.

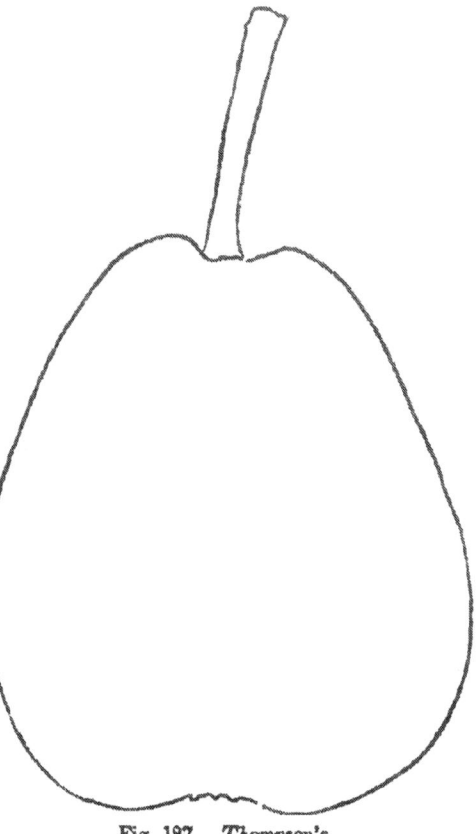

Fruit of medium size, obovate, slightly irregular in surface. Skin pale lemon yellow, with a few small, russetty dots and streaks. Stalk pretty stout, an inch or more long, inserted in a blunt, uneven cavity. Calyx open, stiff, often without divisions, basin slightly sunk. Flesh white, buttery, melting, with a rich, sugary, slightly aromatic flavour. October and November.

Fig. 187. *Thompson's.*

173. SWAN'S EGG. Thomp. Lind.

Moor-fowl Egg, *incorrectly of some Boston gardens.*

The Swan's Egg is an old English pear, valued in Britain, for its great hardiness and the large crops it bears as a standard, where comparatively few pears succeed without being trained. In this country it is little esteemed, for no man, where so delicious a fruit as the Seckel can be had merely for the trouble of planting, will care to retain so ordinary a kind as the Swan's Egg. Branches long, upright or waving, dark coloured.

Fruit small, oval, inclining to obovate. Stalk an inch or more long, slender, inserted with very slight depression. Skin

pale green, washed with pale brown on the sunny side, and dotted with brownish specks. Calyx small, set on the narrow
crown without being sunk. Flesh soft, juicy, with a swee
somewhat musky flavour. October.

174. Seckel. § Coxe. Lind. Thomp.

Seckle	Syckle.
Sickel.	Red Cheeked Seckel.
New-York Red Check.	

We do not hesitate to pronounce this American pear the richest and most exquisitely flavoured variety known. In its highly concentrated, spicy, and
honied flavour, it is not surpassed, nor indeed equalled,
by any European variety.
When we add to this, that the
tree is the healthiest and hardiest of all pear trees, forming
a fine, compact, symmetrical
head, and bearing regular and
abundant crops in clusters at
the ends of the branches, it is
easy to see that we consider
no garden complete without
it. Indeed we think it indispensable in the smallest
garden. The stout, short-
jointed olive-coloured wood,
distinguishes this variety, as

Fig. 183. *Seckel.*

well as the peculiar reddish-brown colour of the fruit. The
soil should receive a top-dressing of manure frequently, when
the size of the pear is an object. The Seckel pear originated on
the farm of Mr. Seckel, about four miles from Philadelphia.*

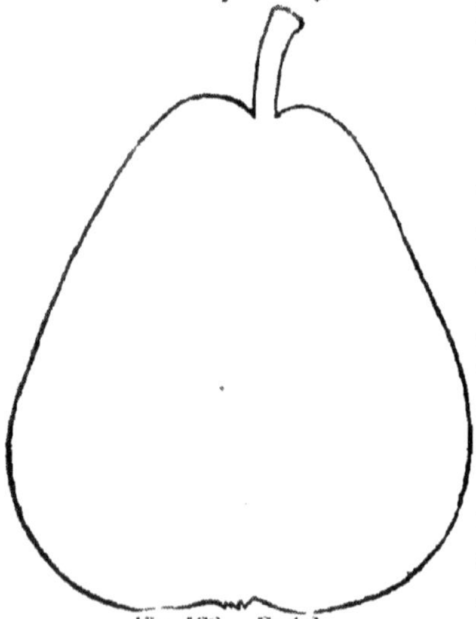

* The precise origin of the Seckel pear is unknown. The first pomologists of
Europe have pronounced that it is entirely distinct from any European variety,
and its affinity to the Rousselet, a well known German pear, leads to the supposition that the seeds of the latter pear having been brought here by some of the
Germans settling near Philadelphia, by chance produced this superiour seedling.
However this may be, the following *morceau* of its history may be relied on as au-
thentic, it having been related by the late venerable Bishop White, whose tenacity of memory is well known. About 80 years ago, when the Bishop was a lad,
there was a well known sportsman and cattle dealer in Philadelphia, who was
familiarly known as "Dutch Jacob." Every season, early in the autumn, on
returning from his shooting excursions, Dutch Jacob regaled his neighbors with
pears of an unusually delicious flavour, the secret of whose place of growth,
however, he would never satisfy their curiosity by divulging. At length the
Holland Land Company, owning a considerable tract south of the city, disposed
of it in parcels, and Dutch Jacob then secured the ground on which his favorite
pear tree stood, a fine strip of land near the Delaware. Not long afterwards, it became the farm of Mr. Seckel, who introduced this remarkable fruit to

It was sent to Europe by the late Dr. Hosack, in 1819, and the fruit was pronounced by the London Horticultural Society, exceeding in flavour the richest of their autumn pears.

Fruit small, (except in rich soils,) regularly formed, obovate. Skin brownish-green at first, becoming dull yellowish-brown, with a lively russet red cheek. Stalk half to three-fourths of an inch long, slightly curved, and set in a trifling depression. Calyx small, and placed in a basin scarcely at all sunk. Flesh whitish, buttery, very juicy and melting, with a peculiarly rich, spicy flavour and aroma. It ripens gradually in the house, from the end of August to the last of October.

175. Surpasse Virgalieu. § Man.

Surpasse Virgouleuse.

The precise origin of this very delicious fruit is not known. It was first sent out from the nursery of the late M. Andrew Parmentier, of Brooklyn, under this name, and is, perhaps an unrecognized foreign pear, so named by him in allusion to its surpassing the favourite Virgalieu, (White Doyenné) of New-York. We consider it one of the finest of Autumn pears, deserving extensive dissemination. It bears regularly and well. Young shoots long, upright, yellowish-brown.

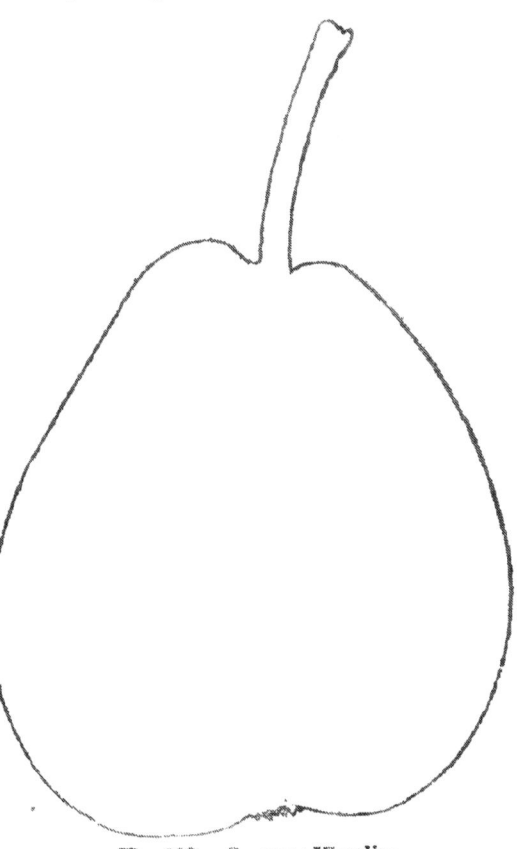

Fig. 189. *Surpasse Virgalieu.*

public notice, and it received his name. Aferwards the property was added to the vast estate of the late Stephen Girard. The original tree still exists, (or did a few years ago,) vigorous and fruitful. Specimens of its pears were, quite lately exhibited at the annual shows of the Pennsylvania Horticultural Society.

Fruit rather large, obovate, sometimes roundish-obovate. Skin smooth, pale lemon yellow, with a very few minute dots, and rarely a little faint red on the sunny side. Stalk rather more than an inch long, not deeply planted in a cavity rather higher on one side. Calyx rather small, and pretty firm, set in a slight, smooth basin. Flesh white, exceedingly fine grained and buttery, abounding with delicious, high flavoured, aromatic juice, different from that of the Doyenné. October.

176. URBANISTE. § Thomp. Lind.

The Urbaniste is a fruit for which we confidently predict the highest popularity in this country. In its delicious flavour it compares, perhaps, more nearly with the favourite old Doyenné or Virgalieu, than any other fruit, and adds, when in perfection, a delicate perfume, peculiarly its own. Its handsome size and appearance, and remarkably healthy habit, commend it for those districts where, from neglect or bad soil, the Doyenné does not flourish. The tree is a moderately vigorous grower, and though

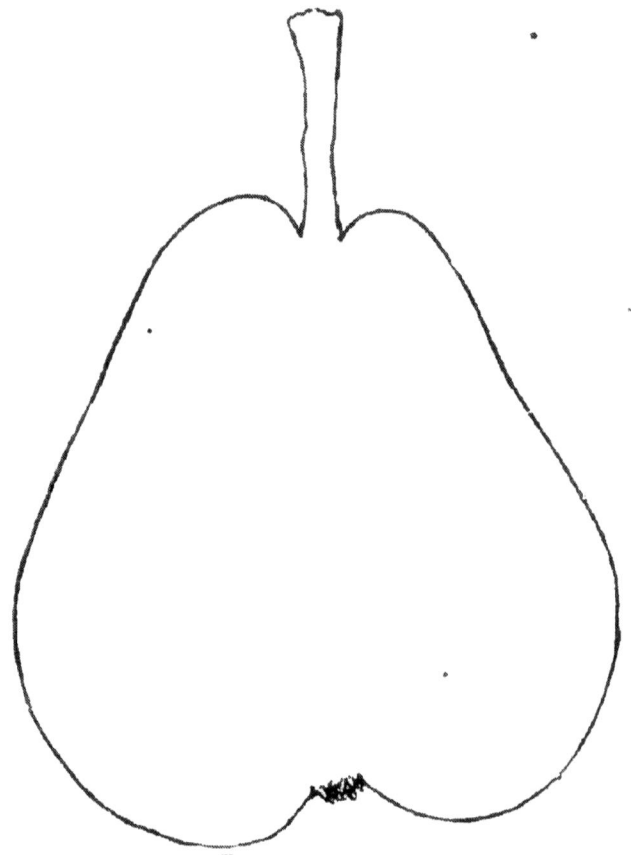

Fig. 190. *Urbanis.*

t does not begin to bear so early as some of the new varieties
t yields abundant and regular crops, and gives every indication
of a long-lived, hardy variety. For the orchard or garden in
the middle states, therefore, we consider it indispensable. With
so many other fine sorts, we owe this to the Flemish, it having
been originated by the Count de Coloma, of Malines. It was
first introduced into this country in 1823. Young shoots upright, short-jointed, grayish yellow.

Fruit of medium size, often large, pyramidal obovate. Skin
smooth and fair, pale yellow, with gray dots, and a few russet
streaks. Stalk about an inch long, rather stout, and inserted in
a well marked or rather broad depression. Calyx small, closed
and set in a narrow basin, which is abruptly and rather deeply
sunk. Flesh white, (yellowish at the core,) buttery, very melting and rich, with a copious, delicious juice, delicately perfumed. Ripens from the last of September till the end of November, if kept in the house.

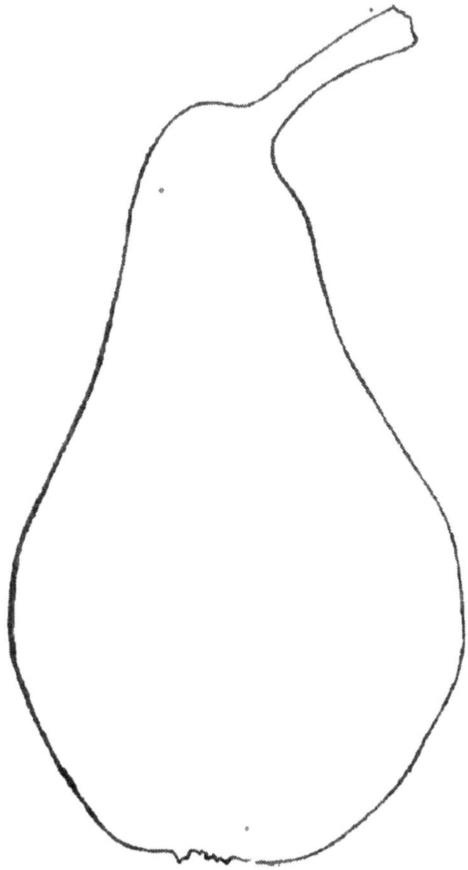

177. Verte Longue.
Duh. Lind. Thomp.

Long Green.
Mouth Water.
New Autumn.
Muscat Fleuré.

The Long Green, or Verte Longue, is an agreeable, refreshing fruit, remarkably juicy and sprightly. It also bears most abundant crops.

Fruit long-pyriform, narrowing a good deal from the middle towards both ends. Skin green even at maturity, with numerous minute dots. Stalk about an inch long, straight, planted

Fig. 191. *Verte Longue.*

a little on one side, and without depression. Calyx small, set
on the very narrow crown, which is scarcely hollowed. Flesh
white, very juicy, with a sweet, slightly perfumed, very excellent flavour. Last of September to middle of October.

There is a small and inferiour variety, known also as the Mouth Water.

VERTE LONGUE PANACHÉE, (*Verte longue, Suisse, Culotte de Suisse,*) or Striped Long Green, resembles the foregoing in all respects, except that the first is prettily striped with yellow and green It ripens at the same time.

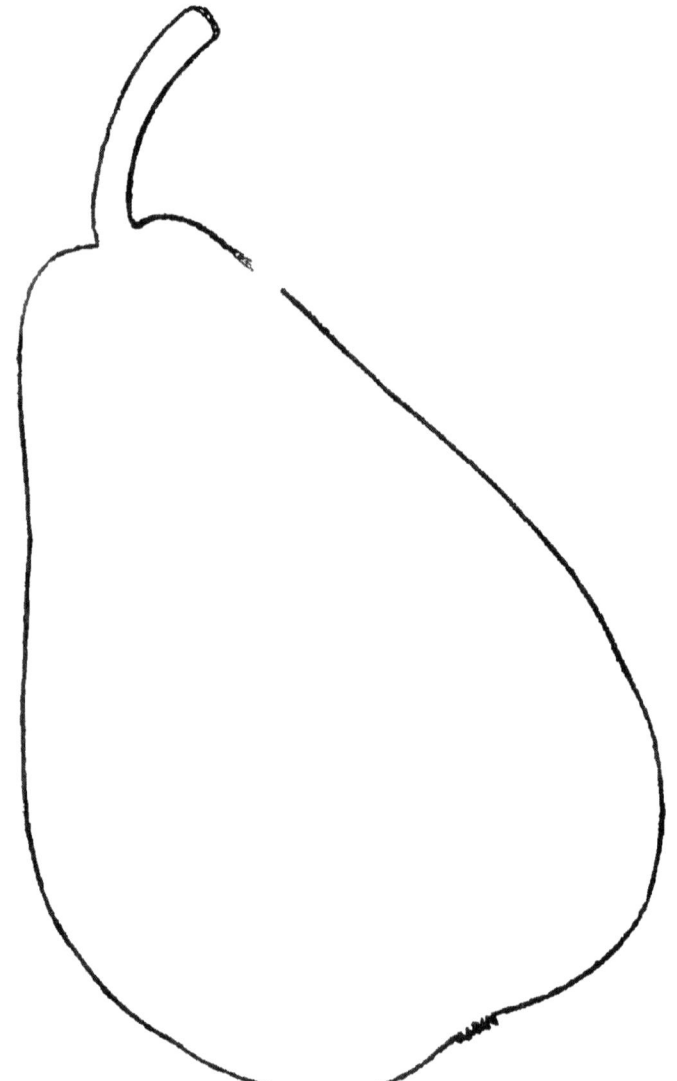

Fig. 192. *Van Mons Leon le Clerc.*

178. VAN MONS LÉON LE CLERC. § Thomp. in Gard. Mag.

This new fruit, which has of late created so much sensation

in the pomological world on both sides of the Atlantic, has borne
for the first time in this country, the past season, and is likely
to sustain its high character as one of the most delicious of Autumn Pears, "combining the properties of large size, handsome
appearance, and rich flavour." Our outline is from a specimen
just produced by Col. Wilder, of Boston, whose standard pears
are unrivalled in New-England.

Van Mons Léon le Clerc was originated by M. Léon le
Clerc, an amateur cultivator, of Laval, in France, who, in
naming it, desired to couple his own name, with that of his
friend, Dr. Van Mons—"le grand prêtre de Pomona." Its
shoots strong, upright, olive.

Dr. Van Mons himself, had previously raised a large *winter
pear* of tolerable quality, but very inferiour to this, which he
had named simply *Léon le Clerc.* [See Léon le Clerc in a
succeeding page.] As this was known by many as Van Mons's
Léon le Clerc, it was naturally confounded with the Van Mons
Léon le Clerc—the present variety, and when the latter came
into notice, and was sold in England at a guinea a plant, hundreds of the inferiour kind were sold under the same name, and
confounded with it. Incorrect grafts were also sent to this country, but the genuine kind has finally been obtained, and proved.

Fruit large, oblong-obovate. Skin yellowish, much mingled
with brown over nearly the whole surface, and slightly russeted near the stalk. Stalk an inch and a half long, rather stout,
obliquely inserted, with little depression. Calyx small, open,
set in a shallow basin. Flesh yellowish-white, buttery and
melting, with a rich, sugary flavour. October and November.

179. Van Buren. Wilder, Mss.

An American seedling, raised by Gov. Edwards of New-
Haven, for which we are indebted to Col. Wilder of Boston. It
is a most beautiful fruit, of second quality only for the table,
but very excellent for baking and preserving, and kitchen
use generally.

Fruit large, obovate, rather flattened at the eye. Skin clear
yellow, with a rich orange-red blush next the sun, regularly
dotted with conspicuous brownish specks, and slightly touched
with greenish and russet spots. Flesh white, crisp, sweet and
perfumed.

180. William Edwards'. Wilder. Mss.

This fruit is from the same source as the foregoing, and promises to take its place among the buttery, autumn pears of the
first quality.

Fruit of medium size, obtuse-pyriform, terminating rather abruptly at the stalk. Skin yellow, and at maturity, profusely dotted with red and russet points or dots on the sunny side. Flesh yellowish-white, buttery, melting, very sugary and rich. September.

181. WILBUR.

The Wilbur is a native fruit, which originated in Somerset, Mass., and has recently been brought into notice. It will not rank above second quality. Shoots slender, yellowish-brown.

Fruit of medium size, obovate. Skin dull green and and russeted. Stalk three-fourths of an inch long, inserted with little or no depression. Calyx prominent, basin scarcely sunk. Flesh melting, juicy, sweet and pleasant, but slightly astringent. September.

182. WILKINSON. § Man. Thomp.

This is a native pear, first brought into notice about 15 years ago. The original tree grows on the farm of Mr. J. Wilkinson, Cumberland, Rhode Island. In the middle states it proves a most excellent late pear, coming between the autumn and winter sorts, worthy of general cultivation. The tree is very thrifty, hardy, and a regular bearer. The shoots are long, upright, stout, greenish-yellow. The fruit is very fair. In the neighborhood of Boston, as a standard tree, it does not succeed so well.

Fig. 193. *Wilkinson.*

Fruit of medium size, obovate, inclining to oval. Skin smooth and glossy, bright yellow, dotted with brown points. Stalk an inch and a quarter long, rather stout, inserted with little or no depression. Calyx small, open, and firm, set in a shallow basin. Flesh very white, juicy, melting, sweet and rich, with a slight perfume. October to December.

183. Washington. § Man. Ken.

Robertson.

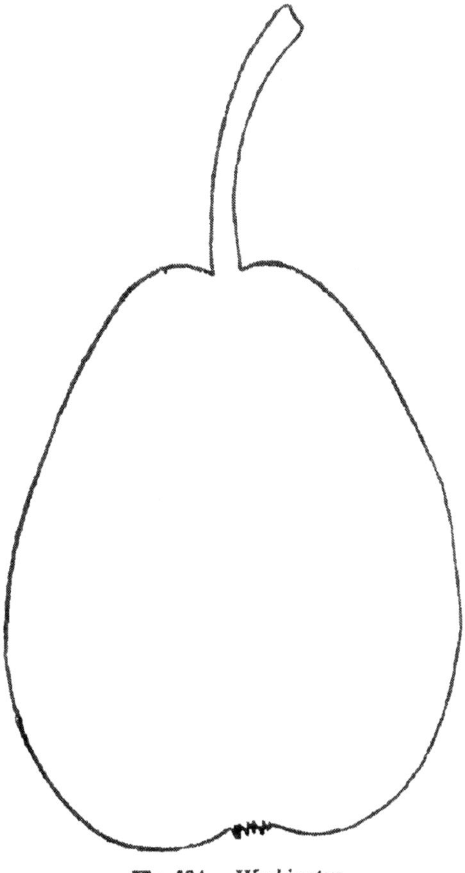

A beautiful oval American pear of very excellent quality, which is a native of Delaware. It was discovered there in a thorn hedge, near Naaman's creek, on the estate of Col. Robinson* about 50 years ago. It is one of the most attractive and distinct of our native dessert pears. Young shoots slender, diverging, reddish-brown.

Fruit of medium size, oval-obovate, regularly formed. Skin smooth, clear lemon-yellow, with a sprinkling of reddish dots on the sunny side. Stalk about an inch and a half long, inserted even with the surface, or with a slight depression. Calyx small, partly closed, and set in a shallow basin. Flesh white, very juicy, melting, sweet and agreeable. Middle of September.

Fig. 194. *Washington.*

184. Yat. Lind. Thomp.

Yutte.

A Dutch pear, recently introduced, which is said to be a very

* The original tree is said to be still standing, and bears 14 to 16 bushels annually.

excellent variety, and a very abundant bearer. The trees have slender, drooping branches.

Fruit rather small, turbinate, inclining to pyriform, and a little compressed on its sides. Skin dense brown russet, thickly sprinkled with round, gray specks. Stalk an inch long, slender, and planted obliquely, without depression. Calyx very small, set in a shallow basin. Flesh white, tender, juicy, with a sugary, perfumed flavour. September.

Class III. Winter Pears.

185. ANGORA.

This pear, recently introduced into the United States, purports to come from the town of Angora, near Constantinople; and it is said to be one of the largest and most delicious winter pears of the latter city. The fruit is said to weigh from two to five pounds, to be yellow, with a red cheek, to have a crisp flesh and sprightly flavour, and to keep till May. It will no doubt bear the coming season, and it is doubtful, taking into account the difference of climate in Turkey, whether it proves much more than a good cooking pear here.* Spurious sorts have been sold for the Angora—such as the Pound Pear and Catillac ; and we are inclined to believe that the latter sort is what has been received in this country as the true Angora.

186. BEURRÉ D'AREMBERG. § Thomp. Lind.

Duc d'Aremberg.	D'Aremberg Parfait.
Deschamps.	L'Orpheline.
Colmar Deschamps.	Beurré des Orphelines.

The Beurré d'Aremberg is certainly one of the first of winter dessert pears in our climate. It is a fine, large fruit, very high flavoured, bears most abundantly, and always keeps and matures, with perhaps less care than any other winter fruit in the house. Its flavour is of the rich *vinous* kind—sugar, mingled with acid—and, when in perfection, is not unlike that of the pine apple. This vinous flavour is not so agreeable to some persons as the sugary, and such will prefer the Winter Nelis and Glout Morceau to the present variety.

The Beurré d'Aremberg was raised, not long since, by the Abbé Deschamps, in the garden of the Hospice des Orphelines,

---

* We notice, since writing the above, that two sorts introduced into the Paris gardens from Constantinople under this name have borne, and both are very indifferent, one being the Catillac.

at Enghein. Noisette, the French nurseryman, having introduced, about the same time, another fine pear from the garden
of the Duke of Aremberg, gave it the name of Beurré d'Aremberg. This latter pear proved to be the Glout Morcean, and
hence arose the confusion, which still, in some measure, exists
between the English and French works respecting it—the
Beurré d'Aremberg of many French catalogues, being the
Glout Morceau. The two sorts are, however, easily distinguished. The fruit of the d'Aremberg has a short, or thicker
stalk, usually bent to one side ; its flavour is vinous, instead of
sugary, and its wood is stronger, with more deeply serrated
leaves. Branches clear yellowish-brown, dotted with pale
specks.

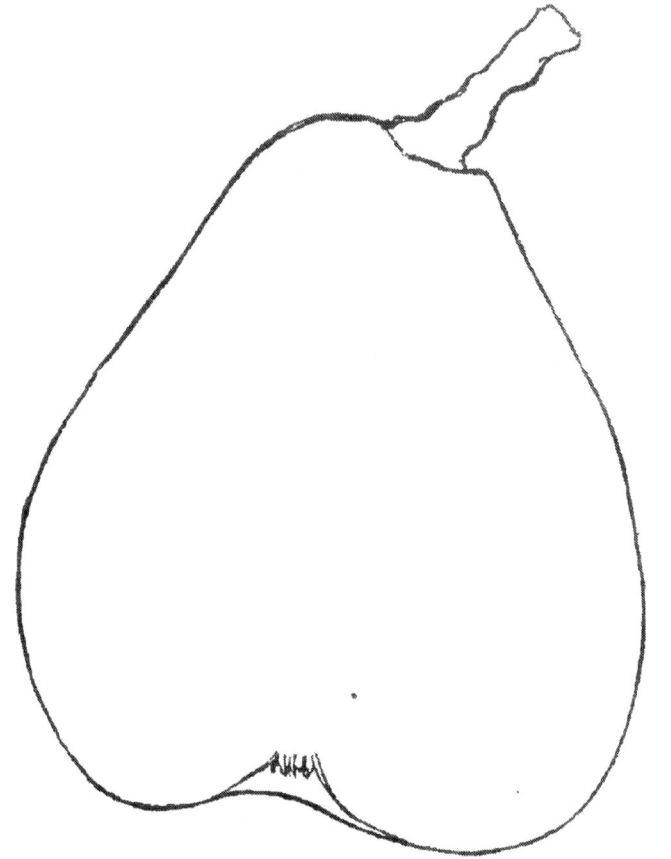

Fig. 195. *Beurré d'Aremberg.*

Fruit obovate, but narrowing a good deal to the stalk. Skin
thick, rather uneven, pale greenish-yellow, becoming yellow at
maturity, with many tracings and spots of light russet. Stalk
short, half an inch, to an inch long, thick, and very fleshy

especially where it joins the fruit, and usually planted very obliquely. Calyx short and small, set in a deep basin. Flesh white, buttery, and melting, with an abundant, rich, delicious vinous juice. December.

187. BEURRÉ, EASTER. P. Mag. Thomp.

Bergamotte de la Pentecôte.
Beurré de la Pentecôte.
Beurré d'Hiver de Bruxelles.
Doyenné d'Hiver.
Doyenné du Printemps.
Beurré Roupé.
Du Pâtre.

Beurré de Pâques
Philippe de Pâques.
Bezi Chaumontelle tres gros
Chaumontel tres gros.
Canning.
Seigneur d'Hiver.

The Easter Beurré is considered abroad, one of the very best late winter or spring pears. It seems to require a rather warmer climate than that of the eastern states, to arrive at full perfection, and has disappointed the expectation of many culti-

Fig. 196. *Easter Beurré*
36*

vators. It bears well here, but is rather variable in quality In good seasons, if packed away in boxes and ripened off in a warm room, it is a delicious, melting, buttery fruit. The tree grows upright, and thriftily, with reddish yellow shoots. It requires a warm exposure and a rich soil, to give fine fruit as an open standard tree.

Fruit large, roundish-obovate, often rather square in figure. Skin yellowish-green, sprinkled with many russetty dots, and some russet, which give it a brownish cheek in some specimens. Stalk rather short, stout, planted in an abruptly sunken, obtuse cavity. Calyx small, closed, but little sunk among the plaited folds of the angular basin. Flesh white, fine grained, very buttery, melting, and juicy, with a sweet and rich flavour.

188. BEURRÉ GRIS D'HIVER NOUVEAU.   Thomp.

A new variety, which comes to us from France, with a high reputation, as one of the best of all late pears It is just introduced into this country.

Fruit large, almost round. Skin rather smooth, entirely russeted and having a slight red tinge on the sunny side. Stalk very thick and short, inserted in a slight cavity. Calyx very small, basin slightly sunken. Flesh white, very melting and fine grained, with an abundant, sugary, slightly perfumed juice, rather richer, but somewhat resembling a fine Brown Beurré. February.

189. BEURRÉ, MOLLETT'S GUERNSEY.   Thomp.*

Mollet s Guernsey Chaumontelle.   *Ken.*

Mollett's Guernsey Beurré is a new English variety, raised by Charles Mollet, Esq., of the Island of Guernsey ; it has the reputation of a fruit of the highest quality, " very melting and buttery, with a very rich Chaumontel flavour." Its adaptation to our climate remains yet to be proved.

Fruit of medium size, oval-pyriform—there being often a remarkable extension, or prolonged neck of the fruit where it unites with the stalk. Skin rather uneven, yellow and yellowish-green, nearly covered on one side with dark cinnamon brown russet, in stripes and tracings. Stalk an inch long, pretty stout, and planted in the fleshy extended neck of the fruit. Calyx large, with widely expanded divisions, and placed in a shallow basin. Flesh yellowish, exceedingly melting and buttery, with a rich vinous flavour. December.

---

* In Gardener's Chronicle, 1842, p 37 and 85.

190. BEURRÉ RANCE. § Thomp.

Beurré Rance. *Lind.*	Beurré de Flandre.
Hardenpont du Printemps.	Josephine, *incorrectly of some.*
Beurré Epine.	Beurré de Ranz.

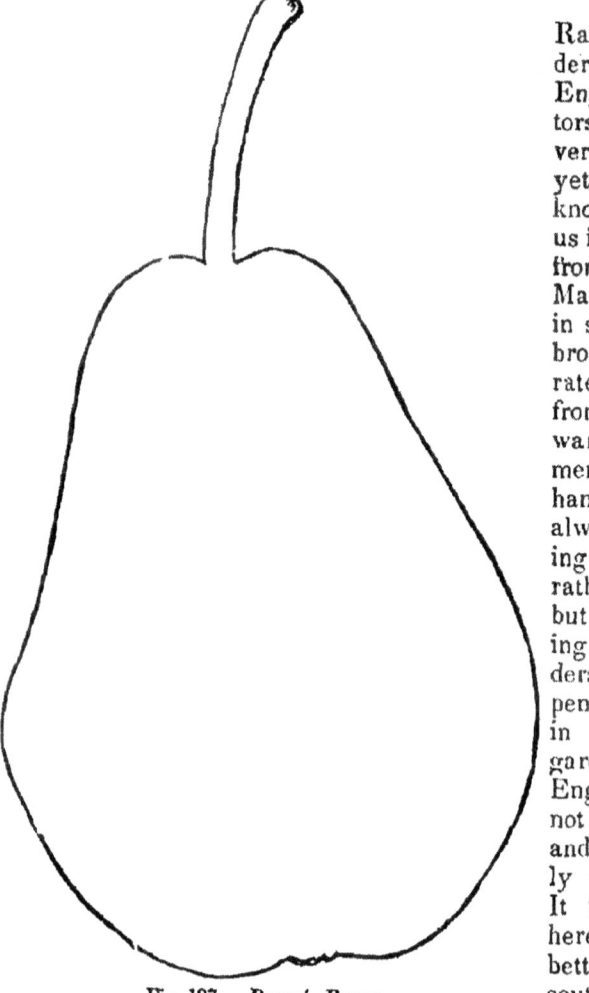

The Beurré Rance is considered by all English cultivators, the best very late pear yet generally known. With us it is in eating from March to May, ripening in succession if brought in separate parcels from a cool to a warm apartment. It is not a handsome fruit, always remaining green and rather rough, but its long keeping quality renders it an indispensable variety in every good garden. In New England it does not mature well, and is frequently second rate. It is excellent here, and still better farther south. The

Fig. 197. *Beurré Rance.*

wood is brownish-yellow, straggling in growth, and rather pendulous when in bearing, and when the tree has attained a moderate size it bears well.

Fruit of medium size, obtuse pyriform. Skin dark green, even at maturity, rather thick, and dotted with numerous russet specks. Stalk rather slender, an inch and a half long, set in a slight, blunt depression, or often without any cavity. Calyx quite small, and set in a basin very little sunk. Flesh greenish-white, melting, a little gritty at the core, full of sweet, rich juice, of excellent flavour.*

This is a Flemish pear, raised by M Haidenpont, of Mons. Its name is, properly, *Beurré de Rance*, from the name of the village in which it was raised, near Mons

191. BEURRÉ BRONZÉE.   Thomp.

This pear has as yet, only proved second rate with us. Fruit pretty large, roundish Skin rough-ish, greenish, nearly covered with dull russet, becoming red next the sun. Stalk an inch or more long, slightly inserted. Flesh white, crisp, juicy and sweet, of tolerable flavour.

[The Beurré Bronzée of some Boston gardens, is the Figue de Naples.]

192. BEZI VAET.   Thomp. Lind.

The Bezi Vaet has been considerably cultivated in this country, but is not generally considered more than a good second rate pear. The young shoots are upright, long, dark coloured.

Fruit of medium size, obovate, narrowing to the stalk. Skin rough-ish, pale green, becoming yellowish, with many russetty spots and a brownish cheek. Stalk an inch or more long, inserted in a slight cavity. Calyx set in a small basin. Flesh yellowish-white, melting, juicy, with a sweet, somewhat perfumed flavour. November to January.

193. BROOM PARK.   Thomp.

This new pear, a seedling of Mr. Knight's, comes to us with a high reputation, "partaking," says Mr. Thompson, "of the flavour of the melon and pine apple." Fruit of medium size, roundish. Skin brown, flesh white, juicy, melting, perfumed and delicious. Shoots strong, diverging, dark brown. December to January.

194. BEZI D'HÉRI   Thomp.

Bezi Royal.
Französische Rumelbirne.

This is a very excellent, winter stewing pear, which bears

---

* As we have stated before, a great deal depends on the mode of keeping winter pears. They are best when packed in small boxes or kegs, with layers of paper between them These boxes should be kept in a cool, dry cellar or garret, free from frost, till within two or three weeks of the season of their maturity, when they should be brought into a close or warm room of a warm temperature to ripen. In this way the fruit will attain a much higher flavour than if ripened in the ordinary way, and without shrivelling.

most abundantly. It is of no value for the dessert, but would probably prove a good market fruit. It derives its name from the forest of Héri in Bretagne.

Fruit of medium size, roundish. Skin greenish-yellow, with a reddish blush. Stalk an inch and a half long, slender, curved. Calyx open, slightly sunk. Flesh tender, juicy, free from grit, with an anise-like flavour. Fit for cooking from October to January.

195. BLACK WORCESTER. § Thomp.

Black Pear of Worcester. *Lind. Man.*
Parkinson's Warden.

A very profitable market fruit, bearing always heavy crops of kitchen pears, which are esteemed for cooking. The branches incline downwards with the weight of the fruit. Young shoots dark olive, diverging. Fruit large, obovate or oblong. Skin thick, rough green, nearly covered with dark russet. Stalk one half to an inch long, stout, planted with but little depression. Calyx small, and set in a moderate hollow. Flesh hard and coarse, but stews and bakes well. November to February.

196. BERGAMOT, EASTER.   Mill. Lind. Thomp.

Bergamotte de Pâques. *Duh.*	Winter Bergamot.
Bergamotte d'Hiver.	Paddrington.
Bergamotte de Bugi.	Royal Tairling.
Bergamotte de Toulouse.	Terling.
Robert's Keeping.	

The Easter Bergamot is a second rate, winter dessert pear, but it is one that we consider well worthy of cultivation. It bears, with us, very large crops of handsome pears, which are very tender, excellent stewing pears, all winter, and keep admirably till late in the spring, when they are agreeable for the table. It is much inferiour to the Easter Beurré for eating, and it is readily distinguished from that variety by the rounder form and lighter colour of its fruit, as well as the *greenish* hue of the young shoots. It is a thrifty old French variety.

Fruit medium to large, roundish-obovate, narrow at the stalk. Skin smooth, pale green, thickly speckled with conspicuous, light gray dots, and becoming pale yellowish at maturity. Stalk varying from three-fourths to an inch and a half in length, set in a very slight depression. Calyx small, and placed in a very shallow basin. Flesh white, crisp, juicy and melting at maturity, with a sprightly flavour. February to May.

197. Bergamotte d'Hollande.   Thomp. Duh.

Holland Bergamot. *Lind.*	Bergamotte de Fougére.
Beurre d'Allençon	Amoselle
Bergamotte d'Alleçnon.	Lord Cheeney's

An excellent kitchen fruit, which will keep sound till May or June, and becomes then of good second rate quality for the table.   Shoots stout, diverging, olive brown.

Fruit rather large, roundish.   Skin green, much marbled and covered with thin brown russet, but becoming yellowish at maturity.   Stalk an inch and a half long, slender, crooked, and planted in a rather shallow, one-sided cavity.   Calyx small, with few or no divisions, and set in a wide, rather deep basin.   Flesh white, crisp, with an abundant, sprightly, agreeable juice.

198. Bon Chrétien, Spanish. § Mill. Lind. Thomp.

Bon Chrétien d'Espagne.
Spina

The Spanish Bon Chrétien is a kitchen fruit of excellent quality, the handsome appearance of which, joined to its occasional good flavour when raised on warm soils, renders it worthy of a place among dessert fruits.

Fruit large, pyriform, rather irregular and one-sided in figure. Skin at maturity, deep yellow, with a brilliant red cheek, and dotted with reddish-brown specks.   Stalk an inch and a half long, bent, and slender, inserted on the narrowed end, and usually with very little depression.   Calyx small, placed at the bottom of a rather deep, narrow, irregular basin.   Flesh white, crisp, or half breaking, and of moderately rich, good flavour.

199. Bon Chrétien, Flemish.   Thomp.

Bon Chrétien Turc.

The Flemish Bon Chrétien is an excellent cooking pear.   The tree a most abundant bearer, and the fruit fair.   Young shoots diverging, gray.

Fruit of medium size, obovate.   Skin pale green, and brown on the side exposed to the sun.   Flesh crisp, juicy, and stews very tender.   November to March.

200. Columbia. §

Columbian Virgalieu.
Columbia Virgalouse.

This splendid American pear is one of the most excellent qualities, and will, we think, become more generally popular

Fig. 198. *Columbia.*

than any other early winter fruit. It is large, handsome, very productive, and has a rich, sugary flavour, resembling, but often surpassing, that of the Beurré Diel. The original tree grows on the farm of Mr. Casser, in Westchester co., 13 miles from New-York. Its productiveness may be judged of from the fact that a single graft, five years inserted, has borne over four bushels in a single season, and its value as a market fruit, from the pears having readily brought six dollars per bushel in the New-York market. The tree grows upright, with stout brownish-yellow shoots. This fine pear was first brought into notice a few years since, by Bloodgood & Co., of Flushing, Young wood stout, upright, yellowish-brown.

Fruit large, regularly formed, obovate, usually a little ob long, and always broadest in the middle. Skin smooth and fair, pale green in autumn, but when ripe, of a fine golden yellow

with occasionally a soft orange tinge on its cheek, and dotted
with small gray dots   Stalk rather more than an inch long,
slender, slightly curved, placed towards one side of a narrow
depression. Calyx of medium size, partially open, set in a
very shallow basin.   Flesh white, not very fine grained, but
melting, juicy, with a sweet, rich and excellent, aromatic fla
vour.   November to January

201. COMSTOCK

Comstock Wilding

A very handsome, bright coloured pear, crisp, and of good
second quality, and a very ornamental winter dessert fruit.   It
is a native of the town of Washington, Dutchess co , N. Y , and
was brought into notice by Mr. J. R. Comstock, an orchardist
there. Shoots long, upright, reddish-yellow.

Fruit of medium size, regularly formed, obovate. Skin
smooth and glossy, bright yellow, with a crimson cheek. Stalk
about an inch long, straight, inserted in a slight cavity. Calyx
set in a shallow basin   Flesh white, juicy, crisp, and if well
ripened, with a sweet and sprightly flavour. November to
January.

202. CATILLAC.   Mill. Duh. Thomp.

| Cadillac. | Groote Mogul. |
| Grand Monarque. | Katzenkopt. |

The Catillac is an old French baking and stewing pear, of
very large size and of good quality for these purposes, stewing
tender, and of a fine light red colour.   In rich soil the fruit is
often remarkably large and handsome.

Fruit very large, broadly-turbinate, (flattened top-shaped)
Skin yellow, dotted with brown, and having sometimes a
brownish-red cheek at maturity. Stalk stout, about an inch
long, curved, and placed in a very narrow, small cavity. Calyx
short and small, and set in a wide, rather deep plaited basin.
Flesh hard and rough to the taste.   November to March.

203. CROSS. Hovey's Mag.

Winter Cross.

A new and delicious melting winter pear, which originated on
the premises of Mr. Cross, of Newburyport, Mass.   The original tree is not more than 19 years old, and is an abundant
and constant bearer.   It will, no doubt, prove a very hardy variety.   It deserves a general trial in all parts of the country
Branches rather slender, grayish-yellow.

Fruit of medium
size, roundish.
Skin smooth, at first
pale, but ripening
to a deep yellow,
with a red cheek,
and marked with
numerous russet
dots, and patches of
russet around the
eye. Stalk three-
fourths of an inch
long, very thick,
planted in a slight
depression. Calyx
small, basin a good
deal sunk. Flesh
white, melting, jui-
cy, and sweet, with
a rich and perfu-
med flavour. In
eating from the last
of November to the
middle of Janua-
ry, but chiefly in December.

Fig. 199. *Cross.*

204. Chaumontel. § Lind. Thomp. Nois.

Bezi de Chaumontelle. *O. Duh. Poit.* .
Beurré d'Hiver. *Roz.*
Winter Beurré.
Oxford Chaumontel.

This grand old French pear, which takes its name from the
village of Chaumontelle, in France, is a very desirable variety,
where it can be cultivated to advantage—that is, in a warm rich
soil; as it is seldom seen in perfection in a cold climate, or indifferent soil. When grown in favourable positions it is an exceedingly rich and excellent fruit, of very large and magnificent appearance. Young shoots long, slender, dark brown.

Fruit large, varying from obovate to oblong, but usually oblong and irregular, largest in the middle, and narrowing each
way. Skin a little rough, yellowish in the shade, dotted with
many brownish russet dots and brownish-red or rich deep red in
the sun. Stalk about an inch long, inserted moderately deep, in
an angular cavity. Calyx placed at the bottom of a deep,
uneven, angular basin. Flesh buttery and melting, sugary, with
a peculiar and agreeable perfume. November to February.

37

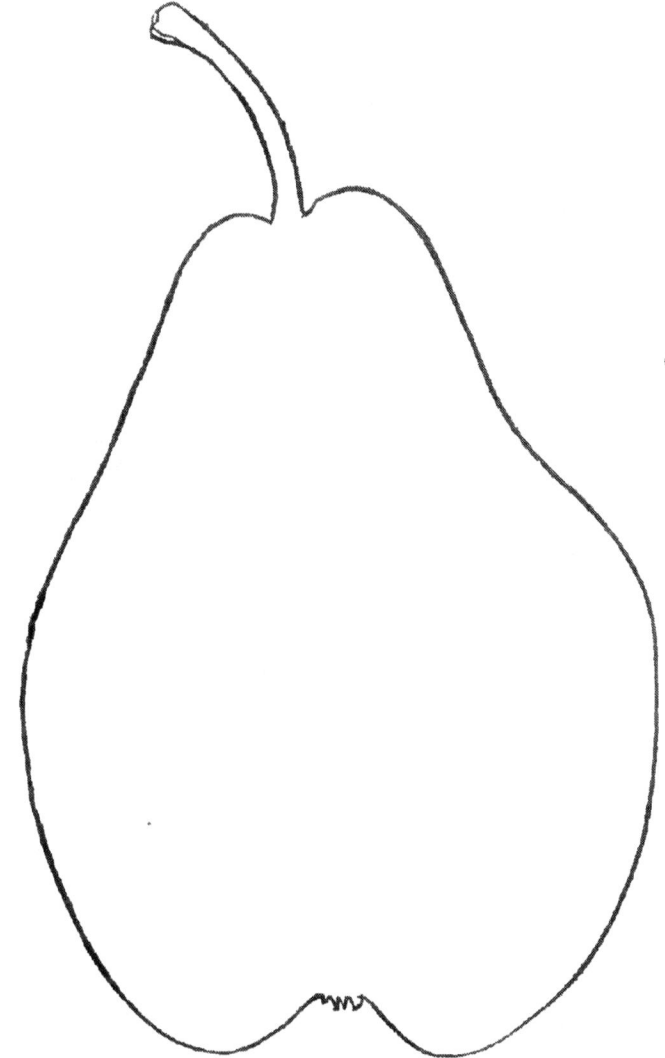

Fig. 200.   *Chaumontel.*

205. COLMAR.   O. Duh. Lind. Mill.

D'Auch.   Colmar Doré.
De Maune.   Incompɩrable.
        Winter Virgalieu, (*of some.*)

The place of this fine old variety, has of late been mostly
taken by the newer sorts—the Passe Colmar, Winter Nelis,
&c., which are not only superiour in flavour, but much hardier
trees.   Still it is a good variety, and well deserves a place in collections—more especially in the middle states.   The bark of this
tree is remarkably rough.

Fruit medium or large, obtuse-pyriform. Skin smooth, pale greenish-yellow, becoming light yellow at maturity, dotted with a few light gray specks. Stalk an inch or an inch and a half long, tolerably stout, bent, and planted in a cavity often one-sided and uneven. Calyx rather small, set in a wide deep basin. Flesh melting, half buttery, juicy, sweet, rich and excellent. December.

206. ECHASSERY.   O. Duh. Lind. Nois.

Echasserie. *Thomp.*	Bezi de Chasserie.
Bezi d'Echassey	Jagdbirne.

A rich, melting, French pear, which has been a good while in cultivation, but still holds its place as a first rate fruit. It is but little known in this country. The wood is rather weak, with crooked joints.

Fruit of medium size, roundish-oval. Skin smooth, pale green, yellowish at maturity, slightly dotted with gray. Stalk an inch and a half long, straight, somewhat uneven, planted in a narrow, irregular depression. Calyx open, with flat divisions, placed almost level. Flesh melting, buttery, with a sweet, perfumed and sugary flavour.

207. EMERALD.   Thomp.

A Belgian variety, recently introduced. It resembles very considerably in appearance the Glout Morceau, and is likely to prove a fine variety in the middle states. New-England may be too cold for it.

Fruit of medium size, obovate, rather square in figure, one-sided, and somewhat knobby. Skin green, dotted with brown, and having a pale brown cheek. Stalk an inch and a half long, planted obliquely in a slight cavity. Calyx with short, stiff divisions, and set in a rather narrow, plaited, irregular basin. Core large. Flesh melting, buttery, sweet and excellent. December.

208. FONDANTE DU BOIS.   Thomp.

This pear has not yet been proved in this country, the trees first received under this name having proved to be the Flemish Beauty. Mr. Thompson says it " resembles the Passe Colmar, is almost equal to it in quality, and keeps longer."

" Fruit of medium size, obovate ; skin greenish-yellow ; flesh juicy, melting, of first quality. Ripens from December to February."

209. Fortunée. Bon. Jard. Thomp.

La Fortunee de Parmentier.
La Fortunée de Paris
Beurré Fortunée.

A new, round, russet pear, raised by M. Parmentier, of
Enghein It came to us with the reputation of a fruit of the
first quality, and as keeping till June and July. It has fruited
the past season, and proves to be a small pear, of fair quality,
juicy and sprightly, but rather astringent, and in eating until
March or April. It deserves further trial.

Fruit below medium size, roundish, depressed. Skin covered with gray russet. Stalk short, with a fleshy base, tapering
abruptly into the fruit. Calyx small, in a round, smooth basin.
Flesh white, juicy and sprightly, but not high flavoured. December to April.

210. Franc Réal d'Hiver.   Thomp.

Franc Réal. *Lind O. Duh.*
Fin Or d'Hiver.

The Winter Franc Réal is a good cooking pear, which bears
abundantly with us, and is esteemed for stewing—as its flesh
becomes very tender, and takes a pretty, light purple colour.
It bears well, and grows upright, with wavy leaves.

Fruit of medium size, roundish. Skin yellow, speckled with
russet brown, and having a brownish cheek. Stalk an inch long,
set in a small cavity. Calyx small, set in a shallow basin.
Flesh crisp and firm. In use from December to March.

211. Gilogil   Lind. Thomp. '

Gile-o-gile   Garde d'Ecosse.
Poire à Gobert.   Jilogil.

A large, showy, globular French pear, only fit for cooking.
The French, we see, by recent accounts, esteem it highly for
preserving. It grows very strong and upright, and bears large
crops.

Fruit large, roundish. Skin thickly covered with russet,
with a reddish russet cheek. Stalk an inch and a half long,
set in an uneven cavity. Calyx large, set in a deep plaited
hollow. Flesh very firm and crisp. November to February.

143. Glout Morceau. Thomp. Lind.

Glou Morceaux.		Goulu Morceau.
Beurré d'Hardenpont.		Roi de Wurtemberg.
Hardenpont d'Hiver.	*of the*	Kronprinz Ferdinand.
Colmar d'Hiver.	*French.*	—————— von Oestreich.
Beurré d'Hiver Nouvelle.		Beurré de Cambron.
Linden d'Automne.		Got Luc de Cambron.
Beurré d'Aremberg, (*wrongly*.)		Hardenpont's Winterbutterbirne

Germans.

The Glout Morceau is universally admitted to be one of the most delicious of the recent Flemish winter pears ; and as it is

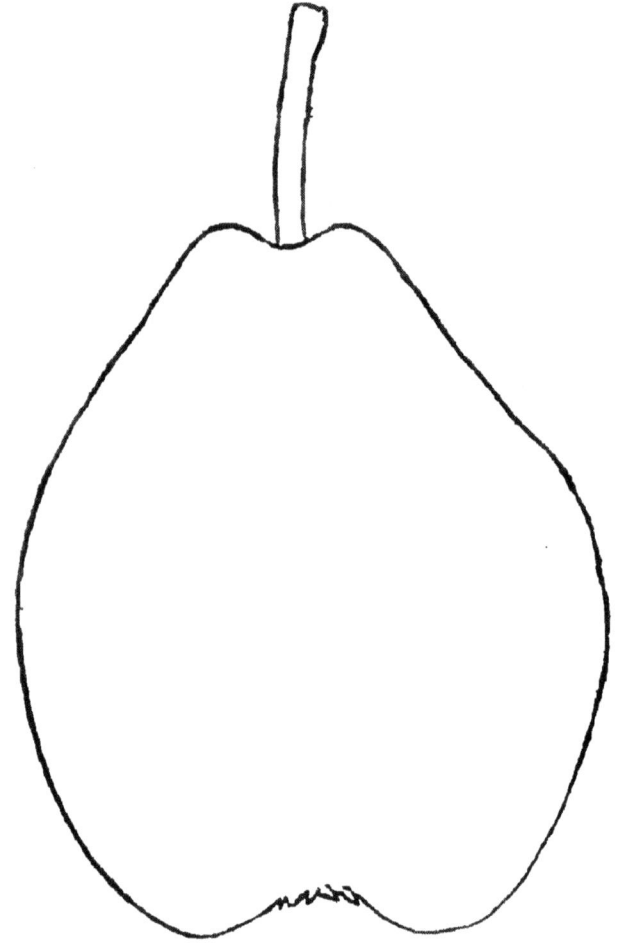

Fig. 201. *Glout Morceau.*

perfectly suited to our climate, bearing excellent crops, it should have a place in every good garden. It has been confounded with the Beurré d'Aremberg, as has already been explained,

37*

but is readily distinguished from that pear, by its sweeter, more sugary flavour, more oval figure, and more slender stalk.* The growth of the tree is also distinct, having dark olive shoots, spreading and declining in habit, with wavy leaves.

The signification of Glout Morceau, is *greedy morsel ;* but Mr. Thompson suggests that this or the synonyme Goulu Morceau is used (in the same sense as *pois goulu,* i. e sugar peas,) to signify honied, or sugared pear, which is most appropriately applied to the present fruit.

Fruit rather large, varying in form, but usually obtuse-oval, and wider towards the stalk than Beurré d'Aremberg. Skin smooth, thin, pale greenish-yellow, marked with small green dots, and sometimes with thin patches of greenish-brown. Stalk rather slender and straight, an inch or more long, planted in a small, regular cavity. Calyx usually with open divisions, set in a moderately deep basin. Flesh white, fine grained, and smooth in texture, buttery, very melting, with a rich, sugary flavour, with no admixture of acid. December.

213. GROOM'S PRINCESS ROYAL.   Thomp.

A new English fruit, not yet proved in America, but having the reputation of a variety of the first quality. It was raised by Mr. Groom, the famous tulip grower.

Fruit of medium size, roundish   Skin greenish-brown, with a tinge of brownish-red, and some russet tracings. Stalk short and thick, set in a very trifling depression. Calyx small, open, set in a shallow basin. Flesh buttery, melting, a little gritty near the core, but sweet, and high flavoured. January and February.

214. JAMINETTE.   Thomp.

Sabine.	Nois. and	Josephine.
D'Austrasie.	the French	Colmar Jaminette.
Beurré d'Austrasie	gardens	Hardenpont du
		printemps, (of some.)

The Jaminette (or Josephine, of American gardens,) is a very excellent winter pear, which grows strongly, produces abundant and regular crops, and is well worthy of general cultivation. It was raised from seed by M. Jaminette, of Metz.

Fruit of medium or large size, varying in form, but mostly obovate, a good deal narrowed at the stalk. Skin clear green, paler at maturity, considerably marked with russetty brown, especially near the stalk, and sprinkled with numerous brown

---

* Mr Hovey evidently figures the d'Aremberg for this pear in his Magazine, vol. ix. p 260.

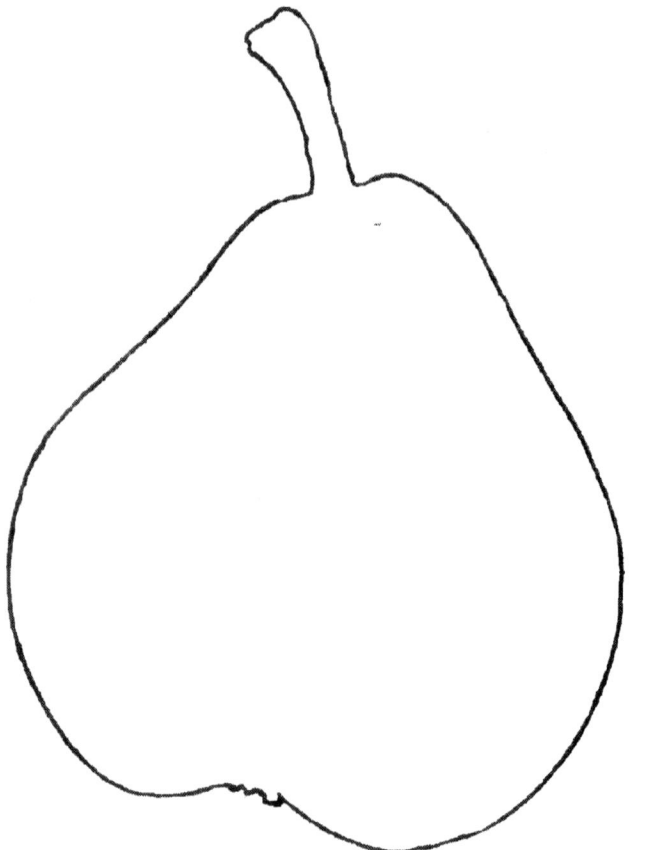

Fig. 202. *Jaminette.*

dots. Stalk scarcely an inch long, rather thick, and obliquely planted, without any depression. Calyx open and firm, set in a basin of moderate depth. Flesh white, a little gritty near the core, but very juicy and melting, with a sugary, aromatic flavour. November and December.

215. KNIGHT'S MONARCH. Thomp. .

This new and most delicious pear was originated from seed by the late Thomas Andrew Knight, Esq., of Downton Castle, England, to whom the horticultural world is so largely indebted. He called it the Monarch, because he considered it superiour to all others, and on account of its first perfecting its fruit in the first year of the reign of William IV. It seems likely to stand equally high in this country, and will, we hope, soon become widely disseminated. The tree is a strong grower and bears abundantly.

By some unlucky error, Mr. Knight transmitted to **this coun**

try, and disseminated partially in England, several years ago, grafts of a worthless sort for this fine pear, which in no way resembled it. The false sort was pretty largely propagated and distributed before the error was discovered. The two are readily distinguished by their wood. The true Monarch having *yellowish* or light olive shoots, the spurious, dark olive or violet.*

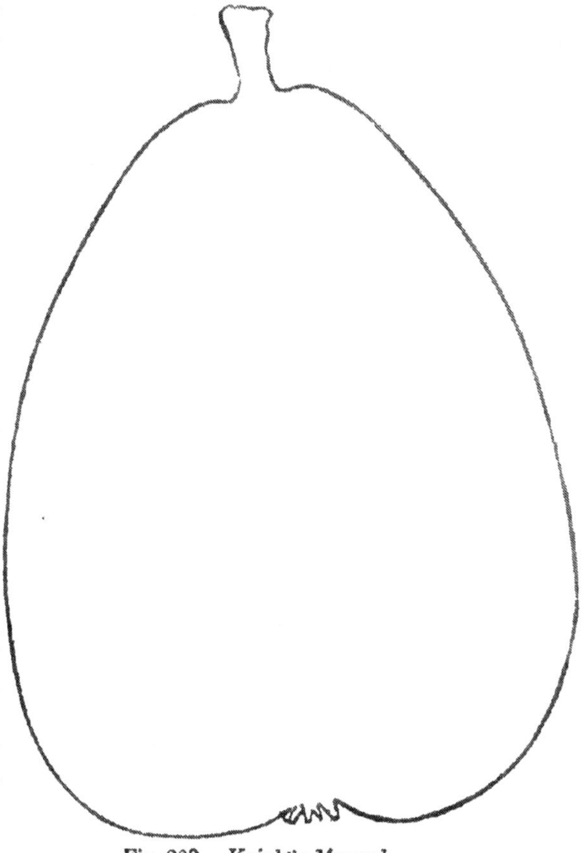

Fruit large, obovate. Skin yellowish-brown, tinged with red on the sunny side, and thickly dotted with pale, gray specks. Stalk remarkably short and thick, set with little or no depression. Calyx open, placed in a rather shallow basin. Flesh yellowish-white, buttery, melting, and very rich, with a slightly musky, and very delicious flavour. In perfection in January.

Fig. 203. *Knight's Monarch.*

216. Léon le Clerc. Thomp.

Léon le Clerc de Laval. *Nois.*

This is a good cooking pear, of large size, and very distinct from the celebrated " Van Mons Léon le Clerc," described in a foregoing page. In favourable seasons it is of tolerable quality for the table.

* Mr. Knight was deeply mortified at this accidental error, and is said to have remarked, that he would gladly have sacrificed £10,000 rather than it should have occurred. Would that some nurserymen were as conscientious!

Fruit large, obovate, but swollen at the crown, and narrow-ing a good deal at the stalk. Skin yellow, smooth, a little glossy, with russetty spots at either end, and some large dots. Calyx large, with long, straight, narrow divisions, and placed in a slight basin. Stalk an inch and a half long, pretty stout, swollen at its point of insertion. Flesh white, juicy, crisp, and rather firm, with a tolerably pleasant flavour. December to April.

217. LOUISE BONNE. O. Duh. Lind. Thomp.

Louise Bonne Réal.
St. Germain blanc.

An old French, winter pear, which bears regularly with us, but is so inferiour to many more newly originated, that we do not think it worthy of cultivation.

Fruit large, pyriform, a little rounded towards the stalk. Skin smooth, pale green. Stalk short, seldom an inch long, straight, a little swollen where it is set on the fruit. Calyx small, open, very slightly sunk. Flesh white, rather coarse grained, melting, sweet, and pretty good. December.

218. LEWIS. § Man. Ken. Thomp.

This is an excellent winter pear, which originated some thirty years ago, on the farm of Mr. John Lewis, of Roxbury, and was first described and brought into notice by that veteran and zealous amateur of fruits, Samuel Downer, Esq., of Dorchester, near Boston. It is a very profitable market fruit, bearing enormous crops; indeed, this is the chief fault of the tree, and the soil should therefore be kept rich, or

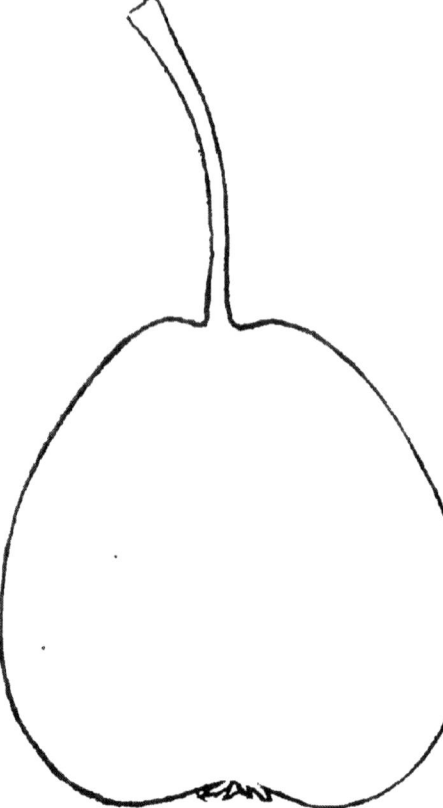
Fig. 204. *Lewis.*

the pears will necessarily be small. The fruit has the good quality of adhering closely to the tree, is not liable to be blown off or injured by early frosts, and should be allowed to remain on till late in the season. The tree grows vigorously, and has long, drooping branches, of dark olive colour.

Fruit scarcely of medium size, obovate. Skin thick, dark green in autumn, pale green at maturity, with numerous russetty specks. Stalk long and slender, inserted nearly even with the surface. Calyx large, with wide spread divisions, basin almost level. Flesh yellowish-white, rather coarse grained, melting, juicy and rich in flavour, with a slight spicy perfume. November to February.

219. LOCKE. Hov. Mag.

Locke's New Beurré

This is a new native fruit, very lately originated from seed by Mr. James Locke, an extensive orchardist in West Cambridge, Mass. From the few specimens we have tasted, we should judge it to be a fruit of excellent quality. The wood considerably resembles that of the St. Germain, from a seed of which Mr. Locke believes it to have been produced.

Fruit of medium size, roundish-obovate. Skin dull yellowish-green, slightly mottled with spots of darker green and bits of russet. Stalk an inch long, set without depression. Calyx small, closed, set in a shallow basin. Flesh greenish-white, very melting and juicy, with an excellent, sprightly, vinous flavour. November and December.

220. LAWRENCE.

The Lawrence pear is a new variety, which will, undoubtedly, take its place among those of the first quality. It is a seedling, which sprung up in Flushing, L. I, in the neighbourhood of two other pear trees only, the St. Germain and the White Doyenné, and bears some proofs, in its qualities, of being a natural cross between the two. Messrs. Wilcomb and King, nurserymen, of that place, first introduced this pear to notice; we learn from them that it produces regular and abundant crops, and the fruit is not inclined to rot or shrivel, commencing to ripen in October, and will keep till March. The tree is moderately vigorous, and has thorny, rather slender, light yellowish-brown shoots.

Fruit rather large, obovate, narrowing to an obtuse end, and a little irregular; pale, yellowish-green, marked with small patches of greenish-brown. Calyx set in a rather deep basin. Flesh yellowish-white, melting, juicy, with a very rich and sugary flavour.

221. MOCCAS. Thomp.

The Moccas is one of the many seedling fruits, originated by Mr. Knight. It has just begun to produce fruit in this country, and proves to be a winter pear of high quality.

Fruit of medium size, obovate. Skin pale green, or a little yellowish, with a brown cheek, and pretty thickly sprinkled with small brown russet dots and streaks. Stalk long, curved, and inserted without depression. Calyx short, partially closed, set in a narrow, rather shallow basin. Flesh whitish-yellow, juicy, melting, with a rich and excellent flavour. December.

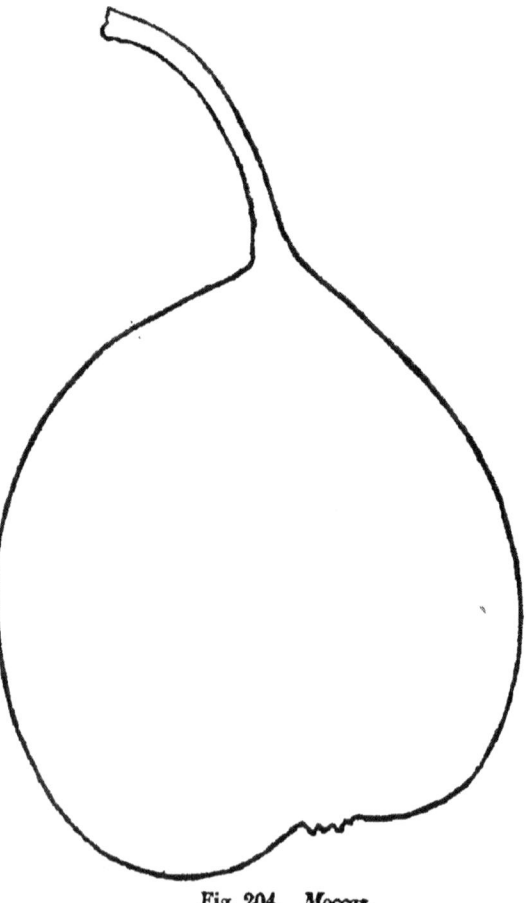

Fig. 204. *Moccas.*

222. MESSIRE JEAN. O. Duh. Mill. Thomp.

Monsieur Jean.	Messire Jean Doré.
Messire Jean Gris.	Mr. John.
Messire Jean Blanc.	John.

The Messire Jean is a rich, sugary, old French pear, but rather coarse grained and gritty, and therefore only of second quality, and not worthy of general culture. Shoots dark gray.

Fruit of medium size, turbinate, but narrowed a little towards the eye also. Skin somewhat rough, yellow, nearly covered with brown russet.   Stalk an inch long, inserted in a small wide cavity. Calyx small, open, set in a shallow, plaited basin. Flesh gritty, white, crisp, juicy, and breaking, with a very sweet, rich flavour. In deep, warm, and favourable soils, it is sometimes highly excellent. November and December.

223. Ne Plus Meuris.   Thomp.

This is a Belgian pear, one of Dr. Van Mons' seedlings, named in allusion to Pierre Meuris, his gardener at Brussels, when his garden there was about to be destroyed   It is an unprepossessing looking, uneven, dull russet fruit, but keeps admirably, and in February and March, is really of very fine flavour. The tree grows upright, has short-jointed, olive coloured shoots, and bears in thick bunches or clusters.

Fruit medium or rather small, roundish, usually very irregular, with swollen parts on the surface. Skin rough, dull yellowish-brown, partially covered with iron-coloured russet. Stalk quite short, set without depression, in a small cavity. Flesh yellowish-white, buttery, melting, with a sugary, and very agreeable flavour. January to March.

224. Passe Colmar.   § Lind. Thomp. P. Mag.

Passe Colmar Epineaux.		Colmar Hardenpont.
Colmar Gris.		Present de Malines.
Passe Colmar Gris.		Marotte Sucree Jaune.
Beurré Colmar Gris, dit précel.		Souverain
Précel.	ac. to	Colmar Souveraine.
Fondante de Panisel.	Thomp.	Gambier.
Fondante de Mons.		Cellite.
Beurré d'Argenson.		Colmar Preule
Regintin.		Colmar Doree.
Chapman's.		D'Ananas, (of some.)

The Passe Colmar is a Belgian pear of comparatively recent origin, raised by the counsellor Hardenpont. It is a fruit of the first quality ; and has become one of the most popular winter pear in the middle states, on account of its excellent flavour, vigorous growth, and abundant bearing. It grows indeed almost too thrifty, making long, bending shoots, and owing to this over-luxuriance, the fruit is often second rate on young trees. This should, therefore, be checked by occasional root-pruning, or cutting off the leading roots with a sharp spade. The young shoots are of a lively brownish-yellow, and the tree frequently bears a second crop of fruit on its after growth.* It is every way superiour to the old Colmar.

ᵗ   ⁓ ᵗᵒ ᵉⁿsure fine fruit of the Passe Colmar, prune or thin out half the fruit-
„   in the month of March.

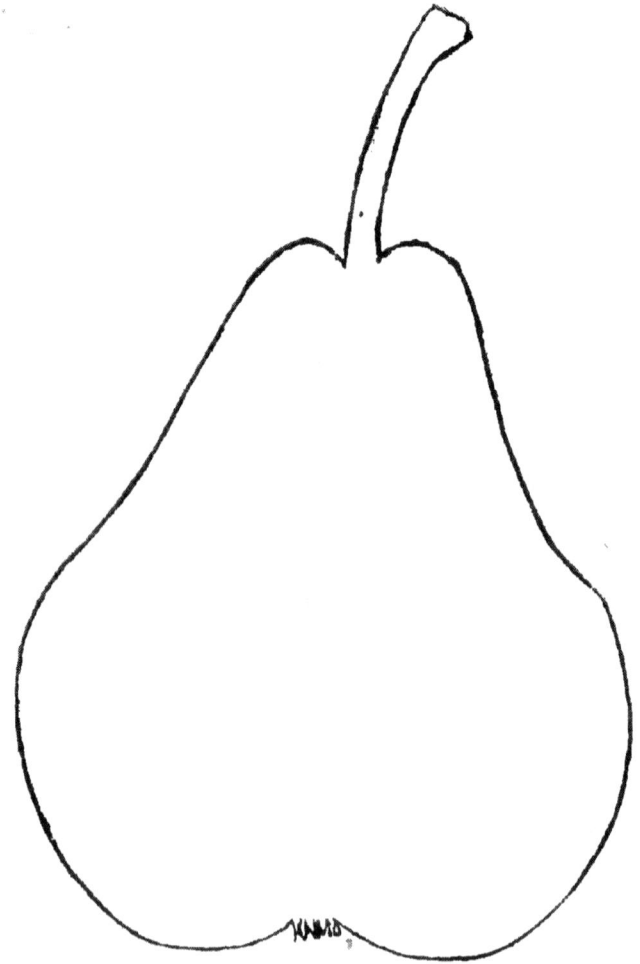

Fig. 205. *Passe Colmar.*

Fruit rather large, varying considerably, from obovate to obtuse-pyriform, but most usually as in Fig. 205. Skin rather thick, yellowish-green, becoming yellow at maturity, a good deal sprinkled with light brown russet. Stalk an inch and a half long, inserted in an obtuse uneven cavity, or sometimes without depression. Calyx open, basin shallow. Flesh yellowish-white, buttery and juicy, with a rich, sweet, aromatic flavour.

225. Pound. Coxe.

Winter Bell.
Bretagne le Cour.

ne round, or Winter Bell pear, valued only for **cooking**, is one of the most common fruits in the middle states.   Indeed, this and the Black Pear of Worcester, so common in New England, are the only two kitchen pears extensively grown in this country.   The pound pear is the larger of the two, often weighing a couple of pounds each.   It is also an abundant bearer, and a profitable orchard crop.   The trees are strong and healthy, with very stout, upright, dark coloured wood.

This is, no doubt, an old European pear, though it does not appear to be described in the books.   A Belgian pear under the name of Bretagne le Cour, which has fruited with us for three years past, appears to be identical with this.

Fruit large, pyriform, swollen at the crown, and narrowing gradually to a point at the insertion of the stalk. Skin yellowish - green, with a brown cheek, (yellow and red when long kept,) and sprinkled with numerous brown russet dots.   Stalk two inches or more long, stout, bent. Calyx crumpled, set in a narrow, slight basin.   Flesh firm and solid, stews red, and is excellent, baked or preserved.

226. St. Germain. O. Duh. Lind. Thomp.

St. Germain Gris.
Saint   Germain
   Jaune.
Inconnue la Fare.

This is a well known

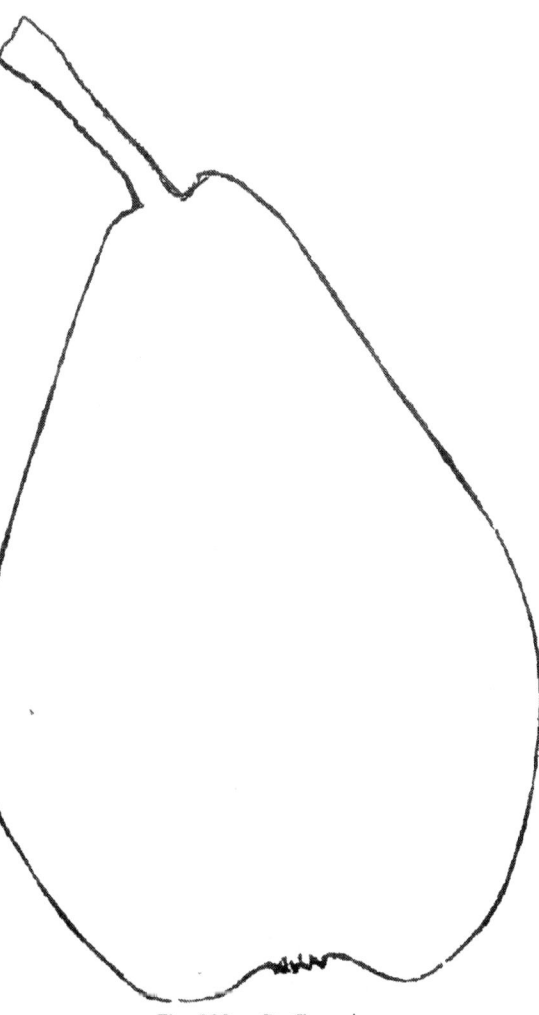

Fig. 206. *St. Germain.*

and capital old French variety, and when in perfection, is scarcely surpassed by any other juicy pear. Unfortunately, however, it is not a very hardy tree, and is therefore worth little, near the sea-coast. In the interiour, and in the warm, rich soils of the west, it is, on the contrary, highly deserving of general cultivation. The tree is rather a slow grower, with a dense head of foliage,—the leaves narrow, folded, and curved; the wood slender, and light olive coloured.

Fruit large, pyriform, tapering regularly from the crown to the stalk. Skin yellowish-green, marked with brownish specks on the sunny side, and tinged with a little brown when ripe. Stalk an inch long, strong, planted obliquely by the side of a small, fleshy swelling. Calyx open, set in a shallow basin. Flesh white, a little gritty, but full of refreshing juice, melting, sweet, and agreeable in flavour. November and December.

The STRIPED GERMAIN, (*St. Germain Panachée,*) is a pretty variety of this fruit, differing only in being externally striped with yellow.

227. St. Germain, Prince's. § Pom. Man. Thomp.

Brown St. Germain.
New St. Germain.

Fig. 207. *Prince's St. Germain.*

Prince's St. Germain is a seedling from the foregoing pear, raised at Prince's nurseries, at Flushing, about forty years ago. It is a most thrifty and hardy tree, with dark reddish brown shoots. The fruit keeps as well as a russet apple, is uniformly good, and is certainly one of the best late pears when under good cultivation. It is much more esteemed in the eastern states than the old St. Germain.

Fruit of medium size, obovate, inclining to oval. Skin nearly covered with brownish russet over a green ground, and becoming dull red next the sun   Stalk an inch or more long, a little curved, and placed in a slight, flattened depression. Calyx large, open, firm, and nearly without divisions, set in a smooth, nearly flat basin.   Flesh yellowish-white, juicy, melting, with a sweet, somewhat vinous and very agreeable flavour.   November to March.

228. SAINT GERMAIN, BRANDE'S.

This is a new variety, received, we believe, from England. It has fruited in Salem, Mass., and proves of the first quality.

Fruit of medium size, oval, narrowing towards both ends. Skin yellowish-green.   Stalk short, three-fourths of an inch long, thick, set obliquely on one side of the end of the fruit. Calyx small, stiff, placed on the narrow crown, mostly without a basin.   Flesh melting, juicy, with a rich and excellent flavour. November and December.

229. ST. GERMAIN, UVEDALE'S.   Mill. Lind. Thomp.

Uvedal's Warden	De Tonneau	} of the
Germain Baker.	Belle de Jersey.	} French
Lent St Germain	Piper.	
Pickering Pear.	Union.	
	Chambers' Large.	

Uvedale's St. Germain is a very large winter pear, only fit for cooking, for which it is very good.   It is an English variety, which has been 100 years in cultivation, and frequently grown to the size of three pounds in that country   In this country it is not so much planted as others, being less hardy.   It is very distinct from the pound pear.

Fruit very large, oblong-pyriform, obtuse at the end, and tapering to the eye.   Skin yellowish green at maturity, with a brown cheek.   Stalk an inch long, bent and planted in a rather deep, oblique, angular cavity.   Calyx large, set in a deep hollow. Flesh white, hard and astringent, but bakes and stews well.   In use from January to April.

230.   VICAR OF WINKFIELD.   Thomp.

Le Curé.	} of the
Monsieur le Curé.	} French.
Dumas.	
Bourgermester, incorrectly of Boston.	
Clion. Kenrick	

This large and productive pear was discovered not long since, as a natural seedling in the woods of Clion, France, by a French curate, whence it obtained in France, the familiar names of Le Curé, or Monsieur le Curé.   A short time after it became known at **Paris**, it was imported into England by the Rev. Mr. Rham, of Winkfield, Berkshire, and cultivated and disseminated from thence, becoming known in the neighbourhood of London as the *Vicar of Winkfield*. Now, although we think Mr. Thompson erred in adopting this English name instead of continuing the French title, yet for the sake of having some uniform standard, we shall follow him, considering, however, Le Curé as the genuine name.*

We should add that the same fruit was imported to Boston and here, a few years ago, under the erroneous name of *Bourgermester*, and considerably disseminated.

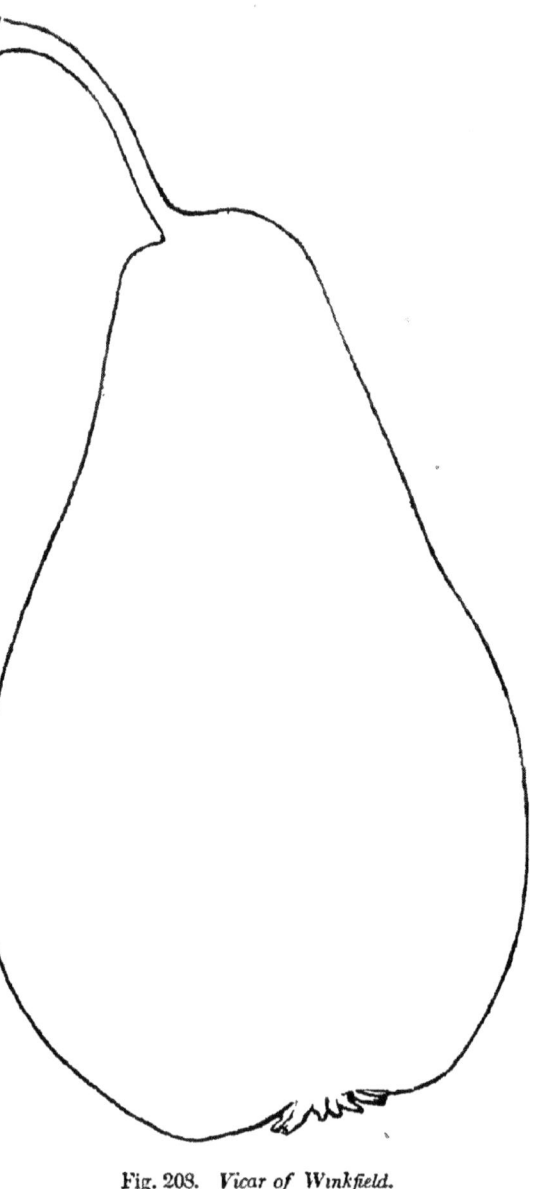

Fig. 208. *Vicar of Winkfield.*

With regard to its merits there is some difference of opinion—some persons considering it a fine fruit. It has borne very ad-

* The only reason that can be given for an English *re-christening*, is that the French (see *Bon Jardinier*, 1844,) confuse this pear, *Le Curé*, with the *St. Lezin*, an inferieur *firm* fleshed pear, fit *only* for stewing and cooking.

mirably with us for some years past.   It is always remarkably
large, fair and handsome.   We think it always a first rate baking
pear.   Occasionally we have tasted it fine as a table pear, but
generally it is astringent, and only third rate for this purpose.
If ripened off in a warm temperature however, it will generally
prove a good, second rate eating pear.   But its great productive
ness, hardiness, and fine size, will always give it a prominent
place in the orchard as a profitable, market, cooking pear.   The
tree grows thriftily, with drooping fruit branches.   Shoots diverging, dark olive.

Fruit large and long-pyriform, often six inches long, and a
little one-sided.   Skin fair and smooth, pale yellow, sometimes
with a brownish check, and marked with small brown dots.
Stalk an inch or an inch and a half long, slender, obliquely inserted without depression   Calyx large, open, set in a basin
which is very slightly sunk   Flesh greenish-white, generally
juicy, but sometimes buttery, with a good sprightly flavour.
November to January.

231. VIRGOULEUSE.   O. Duh. Poit. Thomp.

Poire-glace.
Chambrette
Bujaleuf.

An excellent old French variety, which, in consequence of
its indifferent crops, is scarcely cultivated in the middle states.
In the warmer and richer western states, it is well worthy of a
trial   The tree grows strongly.   It takes its name from Vir-
goulé a small French village—the place of its origin.   It is,
however, a very different pear from the *Virgalieu* of New-York,
which is the White Doyenné.

Fruit rather large, oval, obovate—handsomely rounded at
both ends   Skin very smooth, yellowish-green at maturity,
sprinkled with numerous gray or reddish dots.   Stalk about an
inch long, set in a very trifling depression.   Calyx small,
placed in a wide, shallow basin, sometimes scarcely at all
sunk.   Flesh white, buttery, melting, and of excellent flavour.
November to January.

232. WINTER NELIS.   § Lind. Thomp.

Nelis d'Hiver	La Bonne Malinoise.
Bonne de Malines.	Milanaise Cuvelier.
Beurré de Malines.	Etourneau

The Winter Nelis holds, in our estimation, nearly the same
rank among winter pears, that the Seckel does among the autumnal varieties   We consider it *unsurpassed* in rich, delicious
flavour, and indispensable to every garden, however small.   It

is a very hardy and thrifty tree, and bears regular crops of pears which always ripen well, and in succession. Branches diverging, rather slender, light olive.

It is a Flemish pear, and was originated, above twenty years since, by M. Nelis, of Mechlin.

Fruit of medium size, or usually a little below it, roundish-obovate, narrowed-in near the stalk. Skin yellowish-green at maturity, dotted with gray russet, and a good deal covered with russet patches and streaks, especially on the sunny side. Stalk an inch and a half long, bent, and planted in a narrow cavity. Calyx open, with stiff, short divisions, placed in a shallow basin. Flesh yellowish-white, fine

Fig. 208. *Winter Nelis.*

grained, buttery and very melting, abounding with juice, of a rich, saccharine, aromatic flavour. In perfection in December, and keeps till the middle of January.

233. WILHELMINE. Nois. Bon. Jard. Thomp.

Wilhelmina. *Ken.*

New, and lately received from France, where it has the reputation of being a late winter fruit of the first quality.

Fruit of medium size, obovate, rather narrowed-in towards the stalk. Skin greenish-yellow, dotted with distinct gray specks, and washed with a little red towards the sun. Stalk an inch and a quarter long, inserted in a slight, rather blunt depression. Calyx large, open, set level with the surface, or a little projecting. Flesh yellowish-white, buttery and melting, with an abundant, sugary, perfumed juice. February and March.

Selection of choice pears for a small garden, to ripen in succession from July to April. Madeleine, Bloodgood, Dearborn's Seedling, Bartlett, or William's Bon Chrétien, Andrews, Summer Franc Réal, White Doyenné, Seckel, Fondante d'Automne, Gray Doyenné, Urbaniste, Dunmore, Marie Louise, Van Mons Léon le Clerc, Beurré Bosc, Dix, Columbian, Winter Nelis, Beurré d'Aremberg, Knight's Monarch, and (for deep warm soil,) Beurré de Ranz.

Selection of very hardy and good pears for a cold climate. Fulton, Bloodgood, Seckel, Stevens' Genesee, Heathcot, Marie Louise, Beurré Bosc, Dix, Hacon's Incomparable, Buffum, Beurré Capiumont, Andrews, Bartlett, Washington, White Doyenné, Beurré Diel, Winter Nelis, Beurré d'Aremberg, Prince's St Germain.

Almost all the varieties do well in the interiour; the old French sorts usually better than with us, and the following sorts are generally finer in a warmer climate, say that of Maryland, than here; Beurré de Ranz, Glout Morceau, Easter Beurré, Messire Jean, St. Germain, &c.

Perry pears. These are little attended to in this country; perry being made from the most common varieties. The best English perry pears are the following; Oldfield, Barland, Longland, and Teinton Squash.

CHAPTER XXII.

THE PEACH.

Persica vulgaris, Dec ; *Rosaceæ,* of botanists.
Pêcher, of the French ; *Pfirschbaum,* German ; *Persickeboom,* Dutch ; *Persica,* Italian, and *Ll Melocoton,* Spanish.

THE peach tree is a native of Persia and China, and was brought from the former country to Italy by the Romans in the time of the Emperor Claudius. It was considerably cultivated in Britain as early as the year 1550, and was introduced to this country by the early settlers somewhere about 1680. From Persia, its native country, its name in all languages—Persico—Pêcher—Peach, has evidently been derived.

The peach is a rather small fruit tree, with narrow, smooth, serrated leaves, and pink blossoms. It is more tender, and of shorter duration than most other of the fruits usually grown in temperate climates. It is never raised in England, and not generally in France, without the aid of walls. Even at Montreuil, near Paris, a village whose whole population is mainly employed in cultivating the peach for market, it is grown entirely upon white-washed walls. China and the United States are, therefore, the only temperate countries where the peach and the apple both attain their highest perfection in the open orchard. The peaches of Pekin are celebrated as being the finest in the world, and of double the usual size.*

It is a curious fact in the history of the peach, that with its delicious flavour were once coupled, in the East, certain notions of its poisonous qualities. This idea seems vaguely to have accompanied it into Europe, for Pliny mentions that it was supposed that the king of Persia had sent them into Egypt to poison the inhabitants, with whom he was then at war. As the peach and the almond are closely related, it has been conjectured by Mr. Knight that the poisonous peaches referred to, were swollen almonds, which contain a considerable quantity of prussic acid. But it is also worth remarking that the peach tree seems to hold very much the same place in the ancient Chinese writings, that the tree of knowledge of the old scriptures, and the golden Hesperides apples of the heathens, do in the early history of the western nations. The traditions of a peach tree, the fruit of which when eaten conferred immortality, and which bore only once in a thousand years—and of another peach tree of knowledge, which existed in the most remote period on a mountain guarded by an hundred demons, the fruit of which produced death, are said to be distinctly preserved in some of the early Chinese writings. Whatever may have been the nature of these extraordinary trees, it is certain that, as Lord Bacon says, " not a slip or sucker has been left behind." We must therefore content ourselves with the delight which a fine peach of modern times affords to the palate and the eye.

We believe there is at the present time, no country in the world, where the peach is grown in such great quantities as in the United States.† North of a line drawn from the Mohawk river to Boston, comprising most of the eastern states, they do not indeed flourish well, requiring some artificial aid to produce

---

* The Horticultural world since our intercourse has been put upon a more favourable footing with the "Celestial Empire," are looking with great eagerness to the introduction of many valuable plants and trees, the Chinese being the most curious and skilful of merely practical gardeners.

† It will amuse our readers to read in McIntosh's work, "The Orchard," that " the Americans usually eat the clingstones, while they reserve the freestones for feeding the pigs !"

regular crops, but in all the Middle, Southern, and Western
States, they grow and produce the heaviest crops in every garden
and orchard. Thousands of acres in New-Jersey, Delaware
and Maryland, are devoted to this crop for the supply of the
markets of New-York and Philadelphia, and we have seen in
seasons of great abundance, whole sloop loads of fruit of second
quality, or slightly decayed, thrown into the North river in a
single morning. The market price usually varies from fifty
cents to four dollars per bushel, according to the abundance of
the crop, and to the earliness or lateness of the season at which
they are offered ; one hundred and fifty cents being considered
a good retail price. Many growers in New-Jersey have orchards of from 10,000 to 20,000 trees of different ages, and
send to market in good seasons as many bushels of fruit from
the bearing trees. When the crop is not universally abundant,
the profits are very large, if the contrary, they are often very
little. But, as in some districts, especially in New-Jersey,
peaches are frequently grown on land too light to produce good
crops of many other kinds, the investment is a good one in almost
all cases. Undoubtedly, however, the great peach growing district
of the United States, will one day be the valleys of the Ohio and
Mississippi. With an equally favourable climate, that portion
of the country possesses a much finer soil, and the flavour of its
peaches is unusually rich and delicious.

The very great facility with which the peach grows in this
country, and the numerous crops it produces, almost without
care, have led to a carelessness of cultivation which has greatly
enfeebled the stock in the eastern half of the Union, and, as we
shall presently show, has, in many places, produced a disease
peculiar to this country. This renders it necessary to give
some additional care and attention to the cultivation of the
peach, and with very trifling care, this delicious fruit may be produced in great abundance for many successive years.

Uses. Certainly no one expects us to write the praises of
the peach as the most delicious of fruits. " To gild refined gold,"
would be a task quite as necessary, and if any one doubts the
precise rank which the peach should take among the different
fruits of even that cornucopian month—September—and wishes
to convince us of the higher flavour of a Seckel or a Monarch
pear, we will promise to stop his mouth and his argument with
a sunny cheeked and melting "George the Fourth," or luscious
" Rareripe !" No man who lives under a warm sun will hesitate about giving a due share of his garden to peaches, if he have
no orchard, and even he, who lies north of the best Indian corn
limits, ought to venture on a small line of espalier, for the sake
of the peach. In pies and pastry, and for various kinds of preserving, the peach is every where highly esteemed. At the south
and west, where peaches are not easily carried to market, a con-

siderable quantity of peach brandy is annually distilled from them, but we believe, by no means so much as formerly. Hogs are fattened, in such districts, on the refuse of the orchard and distillery.

In Western New-York, and indeed in most parts of the country where peaches are largely cultivated, the fruit is dried, and in this state, sent to market in very large quantities. The drying is performed, on a small scale, in spent ovens ; on a large scale, in a small drying house heated by a stove, and fitted up with ventilated drawers. These drawers, the bottoms of which are formed of laths, or narrow strips sufficiently open to allow the air to circulate through them, are filled with peaches in halves. They are cut in two without being peeled, the stone taken out, and the two halves placed in a single layer with the skin downward. In a short time the heat of the drying house will complete the drying, and the drawers are then ready for a second filling. Farther south they are spread upon boards or frames, and dried in the sun merely ; but usually, with the previous preparation, of dipping the peaches, (in baskets,) for a few minutes in boiling water before halving them.

The leaf of the peach, bruised in water and distilled, gives the peach water, so much esteemed by many for flavouring articles of delicate cookery ; and steeped in brandy or spirits, they communicate to it the flavour of Noyeau. Indeed a very good imitation of the celebrated Noyeau is made in this way, by using the best white brandy, which, after being thus flavoured, is sweetened with refined sugar mixed with a small quantity of milk, and afterwards decanted.

PROPAGATION. The peach is the most easily propagated of all fruit trees. A stone planted in the autumn will vegetate in the ensuing spring,. grow three or four feet high, and may be budded in August or September. Two years from this time, if left undisturbed, it will, usually, produce a small crop of fruit, and the next season bear very abundantly, unless the growth is over-luxuriant.

In nursery culture, it is customary to bury the peach stones, in autumn, in some exposed spot, in thick layers, covered with earth. Here they are allowed to lie all winter. As early in the spring as the ground is in fine friable condition, the stones are taken out of the ground, cracked, and the kernels sown in mellow, prepared soil, in the nursery rows, where they are to grow. They should be covered about an inch deep. Early in the following September they will be fit for *budding*. This is performed with great care on the peach, and grafting is therefore seldom or never resorted to in this country. The buds should be inserted quite near the ground. The next season the stock should be headed back in March, and the trees will, in good soil, grow to the height of a man's head in one year. This is, by far, the best size for transplanting the peach—one year old from the bud.

For northern latitudes, for cold soils, and for training, the plum stock is much preferable to the peach for budding the fine varieties. In England the plum stock is universally employed. The advantage gained thereby is, not only, greater hardihood, but a dwarfer and neater habit of growth, for their walls. In France, some of the best cultivators prefer the almond stock, and we have no doubt, as it would check the over productiveness of the peach, it would be desirable to employ it more generally in this climate. Still, healthy peach stocks afford the most natural foundation for the growth of standard, orchard trees. At the same time we must protest against the indiscriminate employment (as is customary with some nurserymen,) of peach stones from any and every source. With the present partially diseased state of many orchards in this country, this is a practice to be seriously condemned. And, more especially, as with a little care, it is always easy to procure stones from sections of country where the *Yellows* is not prevalent.

For rendering the peach quite dwarf, the *Mirabelle* plum stock is often employed abroad.

SOIL AND SITUATION. The very best soil for the peach is a rich, deep sandy loam ; next to this, a strong, mellow loam, then a light, thin, sandy soil, and the poorest is a heavy, compact clay soil. We are very well aware that the extensive and profitable appropriation of thousands of acres of the lightest sandy soil in New-Jersey and Delaware, has led many to believe that this is the best soil for the peach. But such is not the fact, and the short duration of this tree in those districts, is unquestionably owing to the rapidity with which the soil is impoverished. We have, on the contrary, seen much larger, finer, and richer flavoured peaches, *produced for a long time successively*, on mellow loam, containing but little sand, than upon any other soil whatever.

It is a well founded practice not to plant peach orchards successively upon the same site, but always to choose a new one. From sixteen to twenty-five feet apart may be stated as the limits of distance at which to plant this tree in orchards—more space being required in warm climates and rich soils than under the contrary circumstances. North of New-York it is better always to make plantations in the spring, and it should be done pretty early in the season. South of that limit it may usually be done with equal advantage in the autumn.

In districts of country where the fruit in the blossom is liable to be cut off by spring frosts, it is found of great advantage to make plantations on the north sides of hills, northern slopes or elevated grounds, in preference to warm valleys and southern aspects. In the colder exposures the vegetation and blossoming of the tree is retarded until after all danger of injury is past.

Situations near the banks of large rivers and inland lakes are equally admirable on this account, and in the garden where we write, on the banks of the Hudson, the blossoms are not injured once in a dozen years, while on level grounds only five miles in the interiour, they are destroyed every fourth or fifth season.

With regard to the culture of peach orchards, there is a seeming disparity of opinion between growers at the north and south. Most of the cultivators at the south say, *never plough* or cultivate an orchard after it has borne the first crop. Ploughing bruises the roots, enfeebles the tree, and lessens the crop. Enrich the ground by top-dressings, and leave it in a state of rest. The best northern growers say, always keep the land in good condition,—mellow and loose by cultivation,—and crop it very frequently with the *lighter* root and field crops. Both are correct, and it is not difficult to explain the seeming difference of opinion.

The majority of the peach orchards south of Philadelphia, it will be recollected, grow upon a thin, light soil, previously rather impoverished. In such soils, it is necessarily the case, that the roots lie near the surface, and most of the food derived by them is from what is applied to the surface, or added to the soil. Ploughing therefore, in such soils, wounds and injures the roots, and cropping the ground takes from it the scanty food annually applied or already in the soil, which is not more than sufficient for the orchard alone. In a stronger and deeper soil, the roots of the peach tree penetrate farther, and are, mostly, out of the reach of serious injury by the plough. Instead of losing by being opened and exposed to the air, the heavier soil gains greatly in value by the very act of rendering it more friable, while at the same time it has naturally sufficient heart to bear judicious cropping with advantage, rather than injury, to the trees. The growth and luxuriance of an orchard in strong land, kept under tillage, is surprisingly greater than the same allowed to remain in sod. The difference in treatment therefore, should always adapt itself to the nature of the soil. In ordinary cases, the duration of peach orchards in the light sandy soil is rarely more than three years in a bearing state. In a stronger soil, with proper attention to the shortening system of pruning, it may be prolonged to twenty or more years.

PRUNING. It has always been the prevailing doctrine in this country that the peach requires no pruning. It has been allowed to grow, to bear heavy crops, and to die, pretty much in its own way. This is very well for a tree in its native climate, and in a wild state, but it must be remembered that the peach comes from a warmer country than ours, and that our peaches of the present day are artificial varieties. They owe their origin to artificial means, and require therefore, a system of culture to correspond.

In short, we view this absence of all due care in the management of the peach tree, *after it comes into bearing*, as the principal original cause of its present short duration, and the disease which preys upon it in many of the older parts of the country. We therefore earnestly desire the attention of peach growers to our brief hints upon a regular system of pruning this valuable tree. Of course we speak now of common standard trees, in the orchard or garden.

A peach tree, left to itself after being planted, usually comes into bearing the third or fourth year, and has a well shaped, rounded head, full of small bearing branches, and well garnished with leaves. It must be borne in mind that the fruit is only borne on the young shoots of the previous summer's growth. In a young tree these are properly distributed throughout. But in a couple of seasons, the tree being left to itself, the growth being mostly produced at the ends of the principal branches, the young shoots in the interiour of the head of the tree, die out. The consequence is, that in a short time the interiour of the tree is filled with long lean branches, with only young shoots at their extremities. [See Fig. 209.] Any one can see that such a tree can be provided with but half the number of healthy strong shoots for bearing, that one would have if filled throughout with vigorous young wood. The sap flows tardily through the long and rigid branches, and not half leaves enough are provided to secure the proper growth of the fruit. And, finally, all the fruit

Fig. 209. *A peach tree, without pruning, as commonly seen.*

which the tree yields being allowed to remain at the ends of the branches, they often break under its weight.

Now, we propose to substitute for this, what is generally known as the *shortening-in* system of pruning. We affirm, both from its constant success abroad, and from our own experience and observation in this country, that putting its two diseases out of the question, (which we will presently show how to avert,) the peach may be continued in full vigour and production in any good soil, for from ten to thirty years.

Let us take a healthy tree in the orchard or garden, in its first blossoming year. It is usually about 6 to 8 feet high, its well-shaped head branching out about three feet* from the

---

* We think *low* heads much preferable to high ones on many accounts. They shade the root, which insects are therefore much less liable to attack, and they are more within reach both for pruning and gathering.

ground. It has never yet been trimmed except to regulate any deformity in its shape, and this is so much the better.

At the end of February or as early in the spring as may be, we commence pruning. This consists only of *shortening-in*, i. e. cutting off *half the last year's growth* over the whole outside of the head of the tree, and also upon the inner branches. As the usual average growth is from one to two feet, we shall necessarily take off from six to twelve inches. It need not be done with precise measurement; indeed, the strongest shoots should be shortened back most, in order to bring up the others, and any long or projecting limbs that destroy the balance of the head should be cut back to a uniform length. This brings the tree into a well rounded shape. By reducing the young wood one half, we at the same moment reduce the coming crop one half in number. The remaining half, receiving all the sustenance of the tree, are of double the size. The young shoots which start out abundantly from every part of the tree, keep it well supplied with bearing wood for the next year, while the greater luxuriance and size of the foliage, as a necessary consequence, produces larger and higher flavoured fruit.* Thus, while we have secured against the prevalent evil, an over crop—we have

also provided for the full nourishment of the present year's fruit, and induced a supply of fruit bearing shoots throughout the tree, for the next season.

This course of pruning is followed regularly, every year, for the whole life of the tree. It is done much more rapidly than one would suppose; the pruned wounds are too small to cause any gum to flow; and it is done at the close

Fig. 210. *A peach tree, pruned by the shortening-in mode.*

of winter, when labour is worth least to the cultivator.

The appearance of a tree pruned in this way, after many years of bearing, is a very striking contrast to that of the poor skeletons usually seen. It is in fact, a fine object, with a thick low bushy head, filled with healthy young wood, [Fig. 210,] and in the summer with an abundance of dark green, healthy foliage, and handsome fruit. Can any intelligent man hesitate about adopting so simple a course of treatment to secure such valuable results? We recommend it with entire confidence to

* It is well, in shortening-back, to cut off the shoot close above a *wood-bud* rather than a blossom-bud. Few persons are aware how much the size and beauty of the fruit depends on the size and vigour of the leaves. We have seen wo peach trees of the same age side by side, one unpruned, and the other regularly *shortened-in*, and both bearing about four bushels. That of the latter was, however, of double the size, and incomparably finer

the practice of every man in the country that cultivates a peach tree. After he has seen and *tasted* its good effects, we do not fear his laying it aside.*

Training the peach tree against walls or espaliers is but little practised in this country, except in the neighbourhood of Boston Espalier training, on a small scale, is however, highly worthy of the attention of persons desiring this fruit in the colder parts of the country, where it does not succeed well as a standard. Every where in New-England excellent crops may be produced in this way. Full directions for training the peach with illustrations are given in page 38.

INSECTS AND DISEASES. For a considerable time after the peach was introduced into America, it was grown every where south of the 40° of latitude, we may say literally without *cultivation*. It was only necessary to plant a stone in order to obtain, in a few years, and for a long time, an abundance of fruit. Very frequently these chance seedlings were of excellent quality, and the finer grafted varieties were equally luxuriant. In our new western lands this is now true, except where the disease is carried from the east. But in the older Atlantic states, two maladies have appeared within the last twenty years, which, because they are little understood, have rendered this fine fruit tree comparatively short lived, and of little value. These are the *Peach borer*, and the *Yellows*.

The PEACH BORER, or Peach-worm (*Ægeria exitiosa*, Say.)

* While this is going through the press our attention is drawn to the following remarkable examples of the good effects of regular pruning, which we translate from the leading French Journal of Horticulture We ask the attention of our readers to these cases, especially after perusing our remarks on the Yellows and its cause

"M Duvilliers laid before the Royal Society of Horticulture, an account of some old peach trees that he had lately seen at the Chateau de Villiers, near Ferte-Aleps (Seine-et-Oise.) These trees, eight in number, are growing upon a terrace wall which they cover perfectly, and yield abundant crops The gardener assured M. Duvilliers that they had been under his care during the thirty years that he had been at the chateau, that they were as large when he first saw them as at present, and that he supposed them to be at least *sixty years old. We cannot doubt* (says the editor,) *that it is to the annual pruning that these peach trees owe this long life , for the peach trees that are left to themselves in the latitude of Paris never live beyond twenty or thirty years* M Duvilliers gave the accurate measurement of the trunks and branches of these trees, and stated, what it is more interesting to know, that although all their trunks are hollow, like those of old wil lows, yet their vigour and fertility are still quite unimpaired. (*Annales de la Societe d'Horticulture, tome* xxx. p 53)

In volume 25, p 67 of the same journal, is an account of a remarkable peach tree in the demesne of M Joubert, near Ville neuve-le Roi, (departement de l'Yonne.) It is trained against one of the wings of the mansion. covers a large space with its branches, and the circumference of its trunk taken at some dis tance from the ground, is two feet and a half *It is known to be, actually, of more than 93 years growth.* and is believed to be more than 100 years old It is still in perfect health and vigour. It is growing in strong soil, but it has been regularly subjected to an uniform and covere system of pruning, equivalent to our shortening-in mode Where can any peach tree of half this age, be found in the United States—naturally a much more favourable climat for it, than that of France?

does great mischief to this tree by girdling and devouring the whole circle of bark just below the surface of the ground, when it soon languishes and dies.

The insect in its perfect state is a slender, dark blue, four winged moth, somewhat like a wasp. It commences depositing its eggs in the soft and tender bark at the base of the trunk, usually about the last of June, but at different times, from June to October. The egg hatches and becomes a small white *borer* or grub, which eventually grows to three-fourths of an inch long, penetrates and devours the bark and sap wood, and, after passing the winter in the tree, it enfolds itself in a cocoon under or upon the bark, and emerges again in a perfect or winged form in June, and commences depositing its eggs for another generation.

It is not difficult to rid our trees of this enemy. In fact nothing is easier to him who is willing to devote a few moments every season to each tree. The eggs which produce the borer, it will be recollected, are deposited in the soft portion of bark just at the surface of the earth. Experience has conclusively proved that if a small quantity, say *half a peck* of air-slaked lime, is heaped around the trunk of each tree at the end of May and suffered to remain till October, the peach borer will not attack it. It has been tried most successfully in large orchards, where the protected trees have long remained sound, while those unprotected have been speedily destroyed by the borer. The remedy undoubtedly lies chiefly, in covering the most vulnerable portion of the tree from the attack of the insect; and therefore persons have been more or less successful with ashes, charcoal, clay, mortar, and other protectives. But we recommend for this purpose *air-slaked lime* or *ashes*,* because these more fully answer the purpose as protectives, and when spread over the surface, as they should be every autumn, they form the best fertilizers for the peach tree.

This is the easiest and the most successful mode, and it should not be neglected a single season. Many careful and rigid cultivators prefer a regular examination of the trees every spring and autumn. On removing the earth, for a few inches, the appearance of gum or castings quickly indicates where the borer has made his lodging. A few moments with the knife will then eradicate the insect for the season. This is a very effectual mode, but not, on the whole, so simple or so good as the other, because the tree is always left exposed to attack, and to consequent injury, before the insect is dislodged.

THE YELLOWS. This most serious malady seems to belong exclusively to this country, and to attack only the peach tree. Although it has been the greatest enemy of the peach planter for the last thirty years—rendering the life of the tree uncertain, and frequently spreading over and destroying the orchards

39*   * Bleached ashes.

of whole districts ; still, little is known of its nature, and nothing with certainty of its cause. Many slight observers have confounded it with the effects of the peach-borer, but all persons who have carefully examined it, know that the two are totally distinct. Trees may frequently be attacked by both the yellows and the borer, but hundreds die of the yellows when the most minute inspection of the roots and branches can discover no insect or visible cause. Still, we believe proper cultivation will entirely rid our gardens and orchards of this malady, and this belief is in part borne out by experiments under our own inspection. In order to combat it successfully it is necessary that the symptoms should be clearly understood.

Symptoms. The Yellows appears to be a constitutional disease, no external cause having yet been assigned for it. Its infallible symptoms are the following :

1. The production upon the branches, of very *slender wiry shoots,* a few inches long, and bearing starved, diminutive leaves. These shoots are not protruded from the extremities, but from latent buds on the main portions of the stem and larger branches. The leaves are very narrow and small, quite distinct from those of the natural size, and are either pale-yellow or destitute of colour.

2. The premature ripening of the fruit. This takes place from two to four weeks earlier than the proper season. The first season of the disease it grows nearly to its natural size ; the following season it is not more than half or a fourth of that size ; but it is always marked externally, (whatever may be the natural colour) with specks and large spots of purplish red. Internally, the flesh is more deeply coloured, especially around the stone than in the natural state.

Either of the foregoing symptoms (and sometimes the second appears a season in advance of the first,) are undeniable signs of the yellows, and they are not produced by the attacks of the worm or other malady. We may add to them the following additional remarks.

It is established beyond question, that the yellows is always propagated by budding or grafting from a diseased tree ; that the stock, whether peach or almond, also takes the disease, and finally perishes ; and that the seeds of the diseased trees produce young trees in which the yellows sooner or later break out. To this we may add that the peach budded on the plum or apricot is also known to die with the yellows.

The most luxuriant and healthy varieties appear most liable to it. Slow growing sorts are rarely affected.

Very frequently, only a single branch, or one side of a tree, will be affected the first season. But the next year it invariably spreads through its whole system. Frequently, trees badly affected will die the next year. But usually it will last, growing more and more feeble every year, for several seasons. The roots on digging up the tree, do not appear in the least diseased.

The soil does not appear materially to increase or lessen the liability to the Yellows, though it first originated, and is most de structive in light, warm, sandy soils. Trees standing in hard trodden places, as in, or by, a frequented side-walk, often outlive all others.

Lastly, it is the neai y universal opinion of all orchardists that the Yellows is a *contagious* disease, spreading gradually, but certainly, from tree to tree through whole orchards. It was conjectured by the late William Prince that this takes place when the trees were in blossom, the contagion being carried from tree to tree in the pollen by bees, and the wind. This view is a questionable one, and it is rendered more doubtful by the fact that experiments have been made by dusting the pollen of diseased trees upon the blossoms of healthy ones without communicating the Yellows.

We consider the contagious nature of this malady an unsetled point. Theoretically, we are disinclined to believe it, as we know nothing analagous to it in the vegetable kingdom. But on the other hand, it would appear to be practically true, and for all practical purposes we would base our advice upon the supposition that the disease is contagious. For it is only in those parts of the Atlantic states where every vestige of a tree showing the Yellows is immediately destroyed, that we have seen a return of the normal health and longevity of the tree.*

Cause of the Yellows. No writer has yet ventured to assign a theory, supported by any facts, which would explain the cause of this malady. We therefore advance our opinion with some diffidence, but yet not without much confidence in its truth.

We believe the malady called the Yellows to be a *constitutional taint* existing in many American varieties of the peach, and produced in the first place by bad cultivation, and the consequent

---

* The following extract from some remarks on the Yellows by that careful observer, Noyes Darling, Esq., of New-Haven, Ct., we recommend as worthy the attention of those who think the disease contagious. They do not seem to indicate that the disease spreads from a given point of contagion, but breaks out in spots. It is clear, to our mind, that in this and hundreds of other similar cases the disease was *inherent* in the trees, they being the seedlings of diseased parents.

"When the disease commences in a garden or orchard containing a considerable number of trees it does not attack all at once. It breaks out in *patches* which are progressively enlarged, till eventually all the trees become victims to the malady. Thus in an orchard of two and a half acres, all the trees were healthy in 1827. The next year two trees on the *west side* of the orchard, within a rod of each other, took the Yellows. In 1829, six trees on the *east side* of the orchard were attacked; five of them standing within a circle of four rods diameter. A similar fact is now apparent in my neighbourhood. A fine lot of 200 young trees, last year in perfect health, now show disease in two spots near the opposite ends of the lot, having exactly six diseased trees in each patch contiguous to each other; while all the other trees are free from any other marks of disease." *Cultivator*

exhaustion arising from successive over-crops. Afterwards it has been established and perpetuated by sowing the seeds of the enfeebled tree either to obtain varieties or for stocks.

Let us look for a moment into the history of the peach culture in the United States. For almost an hundred years after this tree was introduced into this country it was largely cultivated, especially in Virginia, Maryland, and New-Jersey, as we have already stated, in perfect freedom from such disease, and with the least possible care. The great natural fertility of the soil was unexhausted, and the land occupied by orchards was seldom or never cropped. Most of the soil of these states, however, though at first naturally rich, was light and sandy, and in course of time became comparatively exhausted. The peach tree, always productive to an excess in this climate, in the impoverished soil was no longer able to recruit its energies by annual growth, and gradually became more and more enfeebled and short-lived. About 1800, or a few years before, attention was attracted in the neighborhood of Philadelphia to the sudden decay and death of the orchards without sudden cause. From Philadelphia and Delaware the disease gradually extended to New-Jersey, where, in 1814, it was so prevalent as to destroy a considerable part of all the orchards. About three or four years later it appeared on the banks of the Hudson, (or from 1812 to 1815,) gradually, and slowly, extending northward and westward, to the remainder of the state. Its progress to Connecticut was taking place at the same time, a few trees here and there showing the disease until it became well known, (though not yet generally prevalent,) throughout most of the warmer parts of New-England.

It should be here remarked that, though the disease had been considerably noticed in the Maryland and Middle States, previously, yet it was by no means general until about the close of the last war. At this time wheat and other grain crops bore very high prices, and the failing fertility of the peach orchard soils of those states was suddenly still more lowered by a heavy system of cropping between the trees, without returning any thing to the soil. Still the peach was planted, produced a few heavy crops, and declined, from sheer feebleness and want of sustenance. As it was the custom with many orchardists to raise their own seedling trees, and as almost all nurserymen gathered the stones *indiscriminately* for stocks, it is evident that the constitutional debility of the parent tree would naturally be inherited to a greater or less degree by the seedlings. Still the system of allowing the tree to exhaust itself by heavy and repeated crops in a light soil was adhered to, and generation after generation of seedlings, each more enfeebled than the former, at last produced a completely sickly and feeble stock of peach trees in those districts

The great abundance of this fruit caused it to find its way, more or less into all the markets on the sea-coast. The stones of the enfeebled southern trees were thus carried north, and, being esteemed by many better than those of home growth, were every where more or less planted. They brought with them the enfeebled and tainted constitution derived from the parent stock. They reproduced almost always the same disease in the new soil and thus, little by little, the Yellows spread from its original neighborhood, below Philadelphia, to the whole northern and eastern sections of the Union. At this moment it is slowly, but gradually moving west; though the rich and deep soils of the western alluvial bottoms will, perhaps, for a considerable time, even without care, overpower the original taint of the trees and stones received from the east.

Let us now look a little more closely into the nature of this enfeebled state of the peach tree, which we call the Yellows.

Every good gardener well knows that if he desires to raise a healthy and vigorous seedling plant, he must select the seed from a parent plant that is itself decidedly healthy. Lindley justly and concisely remarks, " all seeds will not equally produce vigorous seedlings; but the healthiness of the new plant will correspond with that of the seed from which it sprang. For this reason it is not sufficient to sow a seed to obtain a given plant; but in all cases when any importance is attached to the result, the plumpest and healthiest seeds should be selected, if the greatest vigor is required in the seedling, and feeble or less perfectly formed seeds, when it is desirable to check natural luxuriance."*

Again, Dr. Van Mons, whose experience in raising seedling fruit trees was more extensive than that of any other man, declares it as his opinion that the more frequently a tree is reproduced *continuously* from seed, the more feeble and short-lived is the seedling produced.

Still more, we all know that certain peculiarities of constitution, or habit, can be propagated by grafting, by slips, and even by seeds. Thus the *variegated* foliage, which is a disease of some sorts, is propagated for ever by budding, and the disposition to mildew of some kinds of peaches, is continued almost always in the seedlings. That the peach tree is peculiarly constant in any constitutional variation, the *Nectarine* is a well known proof. That fruit tree is only an accidental variety of the peach, and yet it is continually reproduced with a smooth skin from seed.

Is it not evident, from these premises, that *the constant sowing of the seeds of an enfeebled stock of peaches would naturally produce a sickly and diseased race of trees*. The seedlings

* Theory of Horticulture

will at first, often appear healthy, when the parent had been only partially diseased, but the malady will sooner or later show itself, and especially when the tree is allowed to produce an over-crop.

That poor soil, and over-bearing, will produce great debility in any fruit tree, is too evident to need much illustration. Even the apple, that hardiest orchard tree, requires a whole year to recover from the exhaustion of its powers caused by a full crop. The great natural luxuriance of the peach enables it to lay in new fruit buds while the branches are still loaded with fruit, and thus, except in strong soil, if left to itself it is soon enfeebled.*

There are some facts, in our every day observation, which may be adduced in proof of this theory. In the first place, the varieties of this tree always most subject to this disease are the *yellow peaches ;* and they, it is well known, also produce the heaviest crops. More than nine-tenths of the victims, when the disease first appeared, were the yellow fleshed peaches. On the other hand, the white fleshed kinds (those white and red externally) are much more rarely attacked ; in some parts of the country never. They are generally less vigourous, and bear more moderate crops. And it is well worth remarking that certain fine old sorts, the ends of the branches of which have a peculiar, *mildewed* appearance, (such as the old Red Rareripe, the Early Anne, &c.,) which seems to check the growth without impairing the health, are rarely, if ever attacked by the Yellows. Slow growing, and moderately productive sorts, like the Nutmeg peaches, are almost entirely exempt. We know an orchard in the adjoining county, where every tree has gradually died with the Yellows, except one tree which stood in the centre. It is the Red Nutmeg, and is still in full vigour. It is certainly true that these sorts often decay and suddenly die, but we believe chiefly from the neglect which allows them to fall a prey to the Peach Borer. Indeed the frequency with which the Borer has been confounded with the Yellows by ignorant observers, renders it much more difficult to arrive at any correct conclusions respecting the *contagious* nature of the latter disease.

It may be said, in objection to these views, that a disease which is only an enfeeblement of the constitution of a tree, would not be sufficient to alter so much its whole nature and duration as the Yellows has done that of the peach. The answer to this is, that the debility produced in a single generation of trees, probably would not have led to such effects, or to any settled form of constitutional disease. But it must be borne in mind that the same bad management is to a great extent going on to this day, the whole country over. Every year, in the month of August,

---

* The miserably enfeebled state of some kinds of pears on the sea-coast, arising from unsuitable climate and the continual propagation by grafting from the same debilitated stock, is only a fair parallel to the Yellows in the peach tree.

the season of early peaches, thousands of bushels of fruit, showing the infallible symptoms of the Yellows—a spotted skin, &c., are exposed and sold in the markets of New-York, Philadelphia and Boston. Every year more or less of the stones of these peaches are planted, to produce, in their turn, a generation of diseased trees, and every successive generation is even more feeble and sickly than the last! Even in the north, so feeble has the stock become in many places, that an excessive crop of fine fruit is but too frequently followed by the Yellows. In this total absence of proper care in the selection both of the seed and the trees, followed by equal negligence of good cultivation, is it surprising that the peach has become a tree comparatively difficult to preserve, and proverbially short-lived!

Abroad, it is well known that the peach is always subjected to a regular system of pruning, and is never allowed to produce an over-crop. It is not a little singular, both that the Yellows should never have originated there, and that, notwithstanding the great number of American varieties of this fruit that have been repeatedly sent to England and are now growing there, the disease has never extended itself, or been communicated to other trees, or even been recognized by English or French horticulturists. We must confess these facts appear to us strong proofs in favour of our opinion as to the nature and origin of the malady.

Remedy for the Yellows. It may seem to many persons a difficult task to rid ourselves of so wide spread a malady as this, yet we are confident that a little perseverance and care will certainly accomplish it. In the present uncertainty with regard to its contagious nature, it is much the wisest course to reject "the benefit of the doubt," and act upon the principle that it is so. We know at the present moment several gardens, where the trees are maintained in good health by immediately rooting out and destroying every tree as soon as it shows marked symptoms of the malady.

1. We would therefore commence by exterminating, root and branch, every tree which has the Yellows. And another tree should not be planted in the same spot without a lapse of several years, or a thorough removal of the soil.

2. The utmost care should be taken to select seeds for planting from perfectly healthy trees. Nurserymen to secure this should gather them from the latest ripening varieties, or procure them from districts of the country where the disease is not known.

3. So far we have aimed only at procuring a healthy stock of rees. The most important matter remains to be stated—*how to preserve them in a healthy state.*

The answer to this is emphatically as follows; *pursue steadily, from the first bearing year, the shortening-in system of pruning,* already explained. This will at once secure your trees against

the possibility of over-bearing, and its consequences, and maintains them in vigour and productiveness for a long time.*   It
will, in short, effectually prevent the Yellows where it does not
already exist in the tree.   To whoever will follow these pre-
cautions, pursue this mode of cultivation, and adopt at the
same time the remedy for the Borer, already suggested, we
will confidently insure healthy, vigourous, long-lived trees, and
the finest fruit.   Will any reasonable man say that so fine a
fruit as the peach does not fully merit them?

Whether the system of shortening-in, and careful culture, will
prevent the breaking out of the Yellows when constitutionally
latent in the tree we will not yet undertake to say.   A few more
experiments will prove this.   In slight cases of the disease we
believe that it may.   Of one thing, however, we are certain; it
has hitherto failed entirely to reclaim trees in which the malady
had once broken out.   Neither do we know of any well attested case of its cure, after this stage, by any means whatever.†   Such cases have indeed been reported to us, and published in the journals, but, where investigated, they have
proved to have been trees suffering by the effects of the *borer*
only.

A planter of peach trees must, even with care, expect to see
a few cases of Yellows occasionally appear.   The malady is
too widely extended to be immediately vanquished.   Occasionally, trees having the constitutional taint will show themselves
where least suspected, but when the peach is once properly
cultivated, these will every day become more rare until the original health and longevity of this fruit tree is again established.

The Curl is the name commonly given to a malady which
often attacks the leaves of the peach tree.   It usually appears
in the months of May or June.   The leaves curl up, become
thickened and swollen, with hollows on the under, and reddish
swellings on the upper side, and finally, after two or three weeks,
fall off.   They are then succeeded by a new, and healthy crop
of foliage.   This malady is caused by the punctures of very
minute aphides, or plant lice, (*Aphis Persicæ?*), which attack the
under side of the leaves.   Although it does not appear materially to injure either the tree (or the crop,) yet it greatly dis-
figures it for a time.   In orchards, perhaps few persons will

* The following remarks, directly in point, are from London's last work.
"The effect of shortening the shoots of the peach is not merely to throw more
sap into the fruit, but to add vigour to the tree generally, by increasing the power
of the roots relatively to the branches. The peach being a short-lived tree, *it
has been justly remarked by Mr. Thompson, were it allowed to expend all its accu-
mulated sap every year, it would soon exhaust itself and die of old age.*" Suburban
Horticulturist.
† All the specific applications to the root of such substances as salt, ley, brine,
saltpetre, urine, &c., recommended for this disease, are founded on their good
effects when applied against the *borer*. They have not been found of any value
for the Yellows.

trouble themselves to destroy the insect, but in gardens, it is much better to do so. A mixture of whale oil soap or strong soft soap and water, with some tobacco stems boiled in it, and the whole applied to the branches from below, with a syringe or garden engine, will soon rid the tree of the insects for one or more years. It should be done when the leaves are a third grown, and will seldom need repeating the same season.

VARIETIES. The variety of fine peaches cultivated abroad is about fifty ; and half this number embraces all that are highly esteemed, and generally cultivated in Europe. Innumerable seedlings have been produced in this country, and some of them are of the highest excellence. One or two of our nurserymen's catalogues enumerate over an hundred kinds, chiefly of native origin. Half of these are second rate sorts, or merely local varieties of no superiour merit, and others are new names for old sorts or seedlings newly produced, and differing in no essential respects from old varieties. It is very desirable to reduce the collection of peaches to reasonable limits, because, as this fruit neither offers the same variety of flavour, or the extent of season as the apple and pear, a moderate number of the choicest kinds, ripening from the earliest to the latest is in every respect better than a great variety, many of which must necessarily be second rate.

It is worthy of remark that most of our American varieties, of the first quality, have proved second rate in England. This is owing to the comparative want of sun and heat in their climate. Indeed our finest late peaches will not ripen at all except under glass, and the early varieties are much later than with us. On the other hand many of the best European sorts are finer here than in England, and we have lately endeavoured to introduce all of the foreign sorts of high quality, both with the view of improving our collection, and because we believe they are generally purer and healthier in constitution than many of our own native kinds.

In the description of peaches and nectarines the form, and outlines, of many kinds are so nearly similar that we are obliged to resort to other characteristics to distinguish the varieties. The two most natural classes into which the kinds of this fruit are divided, are *free-stones,* and *cling-stones, (melters* and *pavies,* of the English ;) the flesh of the former parting freely from the stone, that of the latter adhering.

Next to this the strongest natural distinction is found in the *leaves* of the peach. At the base of the leaves of certain kinds are always found small *glands,* either round and regular, or oblong and irregular, while the leaves of certain other kinds have no glands, but are more deeply cut or *serrated* on the margin. These peculiarities of the foliage are constant, and they aid us greatly in recognizing a variety by forming three distinct

40

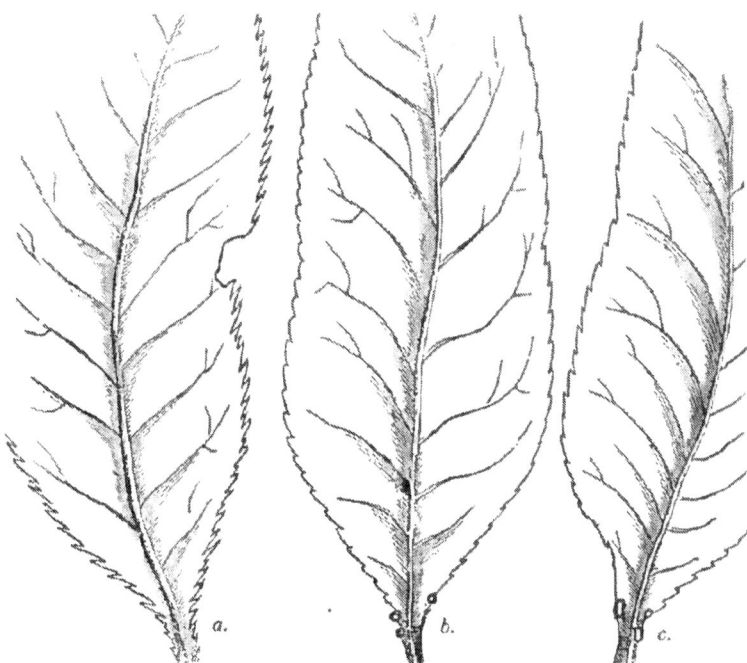

Fig. 211. *Characters in the leaves of peaches.*

classes, viz. 1. Leaves serrated and *without glands*, Fig. 211, *a*. 2. Leaves with small round, or *globose glands; b.* 3. Leaves with large irregular, *reniform glands; c.*

This distinction of leaves is valuable, because it not only as-sists us when we have the fruit before us, but it may be referred to, for the sake of verifying an opinion, at any time during the season of foliage.

There is also another class of characteristics to be found in the *blossoms* which is constant and valuable ; though not so much so as that of the leaves, because it can only be referred to for a few days in the spring. The blossoms afford two well marked sub-divisions ; 1st, Large flowers, always red in the centre, and pale at the margin ; 2d, small flowers, tinged with dark at the margin.*

The most desirable peaches for market growers in **this** country are very early, and very late kinds. These command double the price in market of kinds ripening at the middle sea-son. For New-England, and the north, only the earliest kinds are desirable, as the late ones seldom mature well.

We shall divide peaches into three classes. 1. *Freestone Peaches* with *pale flesh.* 2. *Freestone peaches* with *deep yellow flesh.* 3. *Clingstone Peaches.*

* Lindley makes a third division, embracing a few sorts with blossoms of **an** intermediate size. But it is of no practical value, as any doubt as to which of the two divisions any blossom belongs is immediately set at rest by the *colour* of the blossom.

Class I. Freestone Peaches, with pale flesh.

---

1. ACTON SCOTT. Lind. Thomp.

The Acton Scott, an English peach, raised by **Mr. Knight**, is one of his cross bred seedlings, between the Noblesse and the Red Nutmeg. It is an excellent early fruit, and will thrive and ripen well at the north.

Leaves with globose glands. Fruit of medium size, rather narrow and depressed at the top, with a shallow suture. Skin rather woolly, pale yellowish-white, with a marbled, bright red cheek. Flesh pale quite to the stone, melting, sugary and rich, with sometimes a slight bitter flavour. Middle of August. Flowers large.

2. ASTOR. Floy.

An American peach, which originated in New-York, twenty-five years ago. It is good, but hardly first rate.

Leaves with globose glands. Fruit large; rather flattened, or broad, and slightly sunk at the top, suture well marked. Skin pale yellowish-white, with a deep red cheek. Stone small. Flesh melting, very juicy, sweet, and of excellent flavour. Ripens the last week in August. Flowers large.

3. BELLEGARDE. § O. Duh. Lind. Thomp.

Galande.	*⎱ Nois. and the*	
Noir de Montreuil.	*⎰ French.*	
Violette Hâtive.	*⎫ of many*	Brentford Mignonne.
Violette Hâtive Grosse.	*⎪ English*	Ronald's Mignonne.
French Royal George.	*⎬ gardens.*	Large Violet.
Smooth leaved Royal George.	*⎭*	Early Garlande, (*of some.*)
Early Royal George.	*⎱ incorrectly of some*	
Red Magdalen.	*⎰ American gardens.*	

This very excellent French peach is the one most highly esteemed by the Montreuil growers, who supply the Paris markets, and it is equally valued by the English. It is also one of the handsomest and most delicious fruits here.

Leaves with globose glands. Fruit large, round and regular, the suture shallow, the top slightly hollowed, and having a little projecting point. Skin pale yellowish-green, with a rich red cheek, often streaked with darker purple. Flesh slightly marked with red at the stone, a little firm, but very melting, juicy, rich and high flavoured. Stone rather large. End of **August,** and first of September. Flowers small.

4. BREVOORT. §

Brevoort's Morris.
Brevoort's Seedling Melter.   *Floy*.

One of the richest and most delicious of American peaches, and one of the favourite sorts for garden cultivation. It was raised some years ago by Henry Brevoort, Esq., of New-York. Mr. Floy describes this, in his edition of Lindley, as a small fruit. It is almost always large on the Hudson river, and bears regular, moderate crops.

Leaves with uniform glands. Fruit medium or large, round and rather broad, with a distinct suture, deep at the top. Skin pale yellowish-white, often a little dingy, with a bright red cheek. Flesh rather firm, slightly red at the stone, rich, sugary and high flavoured. First of September. Flowers small.

5. BELLE DE VITRY. Duh. Lind. Thomp.

Admirable Tardive.
Bellis.   *Mill.*

This is not the Belle de Vitry of most of our gardens, which is the *Early Admirable*. It is quite distinct also, from the *Late Admirable ;* but is the Belle de Vitry, described by Duhamel, and is a very firm fleshed and excellent French variety, little known in this country.

Leaves serrated, without glands. Fruit middle size, rather broad, with a deep suture, the top depressed. Skin pale yellowish-white, tinged and marbled with bright and dull red. Flesh rather firm, red at the stone, melting, juicy and rich. Ripens here the last of September. Flowers small.

6. BARRINGTON. P. Mag. Thomp. Lind.

Buckingham Mignonne.
Colonel Ausleys.

A handsome, very fine, and very hardy English peach. The tree is vigorous and healthy. The fruit ripens at the medium season, about a week after the Royal George.

Leaves with globose glands. Fruit large, roundish, inclining to ovate, and rather pointed at the top, with a moderate suture on one side. Skin pale yellowish-white, with a deep red, marbled cheek. Flesh but slightly tinged with red at the stone, melting, juicy, very rich, and of the first quality. Stone rugged, dark brown. Beginning of September. Flowers large.

7. CLINTON.

A native variety, of second rate flavour.

Leaves with globose glands. Fruit of medium size, round-ish, a little depressed at the top, but nearly without suture. Skin pale yellowish-white, with a red cheek marked by broken stripes of dull red. Flesh scarcely stained at the stone, juicy and good. Last of August. Flowers large.

8. COLE'S EARLY RED.

A new American peach, which is a very fruitful and excellent variety, for market culture.

Leaves with globose glands. Fruit of medium size, round-ish, with but little suture. Skin pale in the shade, but nearly all covered with red, becoming dark red on the sunny side. Flesh melting, juicy, rich, and very sprightly. Beginning, to the middle of August. Flowers small.

9. COOLEDGE'S FAVOURITE.§ Man. Ken.

Cooledge's Early Red Rareripe

This most popular early New England peach, was raised from seed by Mr. J. Cooledge, of Watertown, Mass. It is unusually productive, and a very bright coloured, handsome peach, of excellent quality; and its hardiness renders it valuable at the north.

Leaves with globose glands. Fruit large, roundish (the suture prominent at the top only), but rather the largest on one side. Skin clear smooth white, with a fine crimson mottled cheek. Flesh very melting and juicy, with a rich, sweet, and high flavour. Middle of August. Flowers small.

10. CHANCELLOR. Mill. Lind. Thomp.

Chancellière, var. O. Duh.
Noisette.
Late Chancellor.

Stewart's Late Galande
Edgar's Late Melting.

The Chancellor is a celebrated French peach, long cultivated and highly esteemed abroad. It is said to have been originated by M. de Seguier, of Paris, then Chancellor of France.

Leaves with reniform glands. Fruit large, oval, with a well marked suture. Skin pale yellowish-white, with a dark crimson cheek. Flesh very deep red next the stone, melting, and possessing a rich, vinous flavour. Stone oblong. Middle of September. Flowers small.

40

11. Double Montagne.§ Lind. Thomp.

Double Mountain
Montagne.
Montauban.

A high flavoured and beautiful peach, much resembling the Noblesse. It is of French origin, and is a favourite variety with the English gardeners. We think it one of the finest peaches in this climate.

Leaves serrated, without glands. Fruit of medium size, roundish, but somewhat narrower at the top. Skin pale greenish-white, with a soft-red cheek, which is marbled with darker red at maturity. Flesh white to the stone, very delicate and melting, with a plentiful and high flavoured juice. Stone ovate and rugged. Middle of August. Flowers large.

12. Druid Hill.§

This new freestone peach, of splendid size, high flavour, and very late maturity, we think will prove one of the greatest acquisitions to our gardens. It was originated about six years ago, by Lloyd N. Rogers, Esq., of Druid Hill, near Baltimore, and we named the variety after his country seat, where may be found one of the largest collections, not only of peaches, but all other fine fruits, in Maryland. We know no other late freestone variety which equals it in flavour and size. The tree is unusually vigorous, the shoots and leaves very large, and it bears abundantly. The very late season of its maturity renders it valuable, as most of the luscious sorts are then gone.

Leaves with globose glands. Fruit very large, roundish, the cavity at the stalk rather narrow, the suture very slight, and the swollen point distinct, but scarcely prominent. Skin pale greenish-white, clouded with red on the sunny side. Flesh greenish-white, purple at the stone, very juicy, and melting, with an exceedingly rich, high vinous flavour. Stone long and rather compressed, much furrowed. Ripens from the 20th of September to the 1st of October. Flowers small.

13. Early Anne. Lind. Thomp.

Anne. *Lang. Forsyth.*
Green Nutmeg.

The Early Anne is an old and familiar English sort. It is the first peach of any value that ripens, the Red and White Nutmegs being too small, and of indifferent flavour; and the Early Anne, itself, is so inferior to the *Early Tillotson* (which ripens at the same time), that it will soon scarcely be cultivated, except by amateurs. The tree is of slender growth.

Leaves serrated, without glands. Fruit rather small, round. Skin white, with a faint tinge of red next the sun. Flesh white to the stone, soft, melting, sweet, and of pleasant flavour. Last of July, and first of August. Flowers large, nearly white.

14. EARLY TILLOTSON.§

The Early Tillotson is considered by many persons one of the best of the very early freestone peaches. It is a variety from central New York, first introduced to notice by our friend, J. J. Thomas, of Macedon, Wayne county. It is considered a native of that part of the State.

It ripens early in August. about the same time as the Early York, Royal George, and the other very choice early kinds, and only a few days after the Early Anne. It is much higher flavoured than any peach that ripens, except the true Early York, and as a garden variety, is entitled to considerable favour. The tree grows slowly when young, but freely and more vigorously afterwards, and is a great and constant bearer. It is very hardy, but a good deal inclined to mildew at the end of the shoots—a drawback to its culture.

Leaves deeply serrated, without glands. Fruit of medium size, round. Skin nearly covered with red, the ground-colour —pale yellowish-white, being thickly dotted with red, and the exposed cheek being a dark red. Flesh whitish, but red at the stone, to which, though a freestone. it partially adheres : melting, juicy, with a rich, highly excellent flavour. It ripens the middle of August. Flowers small.

15. EARLY YORK.

Large Early York.

The Early York has long been the most popular of early peaches in this country. It is at least a week earlier than the (true) Royal George, more melting and juicy, though not quite so rich, and deserves a place in every garden. In unfavourable soil, the ends of the branches are a little liable to mildew ; but the tree is very hardy and productive. There are one or two newer seedlings raised from this, and bearing the same name, in New Jersey, which are rather more thrifty for the orchard, but do not possess the high *flavour* of the old kind. They are easily known from it by the absence of glands in the leaves and by the large flowers of the true sort. It is quite distinct from the Red Rareripe, which is large, broader, deeply marked with a suture, later in ripening and richer flavoured.

Leaves serrated, without glands. Fruit of medium size, roundish, inclining a little to ovate, with a slight suture only. Skin very thin, pale red thickly dotted over a pale ground, in the shade, but quite dark red in the sun. Flesh greenish white, remarkably tender and melting, full of rich, sprightly juice. Ripens about the 18th of August. Flowers large.

16. EARLY NEWINGTON FREESTONE.§

Newington Peach, } *of many Am. gardens.*
Early Newington, }

This is a large, and exceedingly high-flavoured, early peach ; indeed, we consider it without a superior, at its season. It is quite distinct from the other Newingtons, which are clings, and rather late, while this is early, and generally parts from the stone, though it frequently happens that some of the fruit on the same tree adheres partially, or wholly to the stone ; and this peculiarity (common, so far as we know, to but one other kind) is one of its constant characteristics. It has been cultivated here and disseminated, for the last twenty years, and we suppose it to be an American variety. The tree is only a moderate bearer. Leaves with globose glands. Fruit rather large, round, with a distinct suture, and one-half the fruit always the larger. Skin pale yellowish-white, dotted and streaked with red, the cheek a rich red. Flesh white, but red at the stone, to which many particles adhere. If not fully ripe, it has the habit of a cling. Flesh juicy, melting, with a rich vinous flavour. Ripens directly after the Early York, about the 24th of August. Flowers small.

17. EARLY SWEET WATER.§ Floy. Thomp.

Sweet Water.
Large American Nutmeg

A very early, and very agreeable white peach, among the best of its season, as it ripens early in August, not long after the Early Anne, and ten days or more before the Early York. It is an American peach, raised from a stone of the Early Anne. It is so much larger and superior to the Early Anne, or any of the Nutmeg peaches, that it has almost driven them out of our gardens. The tree is thrifty and productive, with pale shoots, and nearly white blossoms.

Leaves with globose glands. Fruit of medium size, sometimes large, roundish, with a slight suture. Skin pale white, very seldom with a faint blush when fully exposed. Flesh white, slightly stained at the stone, melting, juicy, sweet,

and of very agreeable flavour.   Ripe about the 8th of August,
Stone small.   Flowers large.

18. EMPEROR OF RUSSIA. Floy. Thomp.

Cut-Leaved.	Serrated.
New Cut-Leaved.	Unique.

A very rich and fine-flavoured peach, raised by Mr. Floy, in
1812.   Its growth is slow, and its shoots are inclined to become mildewed.   It is rather a shy bearer here, but is an
admirable sort in the Western States.   The leaves are very
deeply cut, or serrated on the edges.   .
    Leaves serrated, without glands.   Fruit large, roundish, and
broad, with one-half more swollen than the other.   Skin downy,
dull yellowish-white, with a dark red cheek.   Flesh yellowish-
white, rather firm, rich and high flavoured.   Last of August.
Flowers small.

19. EARLY ADMIRABLE. Lind. Thomp.

Admirable.
L'Admirable.
Belle de Vitry, (*Bon Jardinier.*)

A very excellent French peach, wrongly known by many
in this country as the Belle de Vitry, which is a distinct
variety.   We find it early, and very prolific.
    Leaves with globose glands.   Fruit not quite round.   Skin
pale yellowish-white, with a lively red cheek.   Flesh red next
the stone, melting and juicy, with a good, rich, sweet flavour.
Middle of August.   Flowers large.

20. FAVOURITE. Coxe.

Favourite Red.

A capital orchard fruit, of large size, hardy and a most
abundant bearer.   It is a very good native peach, though not of
high flavour.
    Leaves with obscure globose glands, often with none.   Fruit
large, oblong or oval.   Skin white, rather downy, much covered with red, which becomes a very dark red, when fully exposed
in the sun.   Flesh red at the stone, a little firm, but juicy, with
a good, vinous, but not rich flavour.   Second week in September.   Flowers small.

21. FOX'S SEEDLING.

A good and productive late peach, a native of New-Jersey.

Leaves with globose glands. Fruit round, a little compressed, cavity at the stalk narrow. Skin white with a red cheek. Flesh melting, juicy, sweet and good. Middle of September Flowers small.

22. GEORGE THE FOURTH. § Floy. Lind. Thomp.

This is certainly the most popular peach for garden culture in the United States. It is large, bears regular and abundant crops, is of the highest flavour, and the tree is unusually hardy and vigorous, succeeding well in all parts of the country. No garden should be without it. The original tree stood, not long since, in the garden of Mr. Gill, Broad street, New-York.

Leaves large, with globose glands, often obscure. Fruit large, round, deeply divided by a broad suture, and one-half a little larger than the other. Skin pale, yellowish white, finely dotted with bright red, and deepening into a rich dark red cheek on one side. Flesh pale, marked with red at the stone (which is small), melting, very juicy, with a remarkably rich luscious flavour. Ripens the last of August. Flowers small.

23. GROSSE MIGNONNE. § O. Duh. Lind. Thomp.

Royal Kensington.		Vineuse de Fromentin
Grimwood's Royal George.		Mignonne.
—— New Royal George.		Veloutée de Merlet.
Large French Mignonne.	*Of various English, and French gardens, according to Thomp.*	Vineuse.
French Mignonne.		Pourprée de Normandie.
Swiss Mignonne.		Belle Beauté.
Purple Avant.		Belle Bausse.
Early Purple Avant.		La Royal (*of some.*)
Early May.		Pourprée Hâtive (*of some.*)
Early Vineyard.		Ronald's Seedling Galande.
Neil's Early Purple.		Royal Sovereign.
Johnson's Early Purple.		Superb Royal.

The Grosse Mignonne is certainly the " world renowned " of peaches. In France, its native country, in England, in America, in short everywhere, it is esteemed as one of the most delicious of varieties. It is a good and regular bearer, a large and handsome fruit, is a favourite for those who have to grow peaches under glass, and ripens the best crops even in a rather unfavourable climate, like that of Boston. The great number of names by which it is known abroad (and we have not quoted all) proves the universality of its cultivation.

Leaves with globose glands. Fruit large roundish, always somewhat depressed and marked with a hollow suture at the top. Skin pale greenish yellow, mottled with red, and having a purplish red cheek. Flesh yellowish white, marked with red at the stone, melting, juicy, with a very rich, high, vinous flavour. Stone small, and very rough. Middle of August, before the Royal George. Flowers large.

24. HAINES' EARLY RED.

An early peach, newly originated in New-Jersey, of very fine flavour, and so hardy and productive as to be a popular orchard fruit.

Leaves with globose glands, fruit of medium size, round, depressed at the top, with a well-marked suture extending round the fruit, one half larger than the other. Skin pale white marked with red, and nearly covered with deep red. Flesh greenish white, very juicy, melting, sweet and well flavoured. Middle of August. Flowers small.

25. KENRICK'S HEATH. Ken.

Freestone Heath.

A large, showy, oblong peach, often growing to the largest size, and a very hardy tree, but the quality of the fruit is only second rate. This sort, which is a native of New-England, is vigorous, and bears large crops. It is quite distinct from the celebrated Heath Cling.

Leaves with reniform glands. Fruit very large, oblong, with a slight suture, and a small swollen point at the top. Skin pale greenish white, with a purplish red cheek. Flesh greenish white, deep red at the stone, a little coarse, melting, quite juicy, with a pleasant sub-acid flavour. Middle of September. Flowers small.

26. LATE ADMIRABLE. § Lind. Thomp.

Royale. *O. Duh*	Téton de Venus.
La Royale.	French Bourdine
Pêche Royale.	Judd's Melting.
Bourdine.	Motteux's.
Boudin.	Pourprée Tardive. } *incorrectly*
Narbonne.	Late Purple. } *of some.*

"The Late Admirable," says Mr. Thompson, "is one of the very best of late peaches, and ought to be in every collection," an opinion in which we fully concur. It is one of those delicious sorts that, originating a long time ago in France, have received the approval of the best cultivators everywhere. It is hardy and productive in this climate.

Leaves with globose glands. Fruit very large, roundish, inclining to oval, with a bold suture dividing the fruit pretty
deeply all round, and a small, acute, swollen point at the top.
Skin pale yellowish green, with a pale red cheek, marbled with
darker red. Flesh greenish white, but red at the stone, very
juicy, melting, and of delicate, exquisite flavour. Middle of
September. Flowers small.

27. La Grange. §

The La Grange is a new white freestone peach, of very late
maturity, large size, and fine flavour. It was originated from
seed five or six years ago, in the garden of Mr. John Hulse,
Burlington, New-Jersey.

Its late period of maturity, its colour, its productiveness, and
size, have already given it quite a reputation among the extensive
growers of New-Jersey, and it is undoubtedly a most valuable
fruit, not only for the table but for preserving at the most
desirable period for this purpose—late in the season. Its flavour is remarkably rich and delicious, equalling, in this respect, almost any peach of its season of maturity. It was first
brought into notice and disseminated by Mr. Thomas Hancock.

Leaves with reniform glands. Fruit large, oblong, shaped
somewhat like the Heath Cling. Skin greenish white, with occasionally some red on the sunny side. Flesh pale, juicy,
melting, very rich, sweet, high flavoured and delicious. Last
of September, and beginning of October. Flowers small.

28. Morris's Red Rareripe.

Morris Red.
Red Rareripe.   } of some
Large Red Rareripe.

This very popular and well-known American peach, has the
reputation of having originally been disseminated from the garden of Robert Morris, Esq., of Philadelphia. It is everywhere
justly esteemed for its acknowledged good flavour, beauty, and
productiveness. Mr. Kenrick, and some other American writers, have erred in supposing it synonymous with the Grosse
Mignonne, which is quite different, both in the colour of its skin
and flesh as well as in its flavour and blossoms.

Leaves with small globose glands. Fruit large, roundish, a
little depressed at the top, with a moderately well-marked suture.
Skin fine pale greenish white, a little dotted, and with a lively,
rich red cheek. Flesh pale, greenish white, quite red at the
stone, very melting and juicy, with a sweet and rich flavour.
Last of August. Flowers small.

29. Morris's White Rareripe. §

Morris White.	*of vari-*	White Malacaton.
White Rareripe.	*ous Ame-*	Cole's White Malocoton.
Luscious White Rareripe.	*rican Gar-*	Freestone Heath.
Lady Ann Steward.	*dens.*	Morris White Freestone *Floy*

Morris's White Rareripe, a native, is the most popular and well-known white peach, and is everywhere cultivated in this country, either under this, or some of the other names quoted above. It is a rich fruit in a warm climate, but is not quite so high flavoured at the north or east. The tree is vigorous and healthy, and bears fair crops.

Leaves with reniform glands. Fruit rather large, oval; suture only of moderate depth, swollen point small. Skin rather downy, greenish white on all sides, at first, but white with a creamy tint when fully ripe; and when fully exposed, sometimes with a slightly purple cheek. Flesh white to the stone, a little firm, melting, juicy, sweet and rich. Middle of September. Flowers small.

30. Morrisania Pound. Thomp.

Hoffman's Pound. Floy.
Morrison's Pound.

very large and late variety, originated many years ago, Martin Hoffman, Esq., but first disseminated from the garden of Governor Morris, of Morrisania, near New York. It is a good fruit, but its place has been taken, of late, by other more popular sorts.

Leaves with globose glands. Fruit very large and heavy, nearly round. Skin, dull greenish white, with a brownish red cheek. Flesh, pale yellow, firm, juicy, sugary, and rich in flavour. Ripens the middle and last of September. Flowers small.

31. Madeleine de Courson. Thomp. Lelieur. Lind.

Red Magdalen (*of Miller*).	Madeleine Rouge, O. Duh
True Red Magdalen	Rouge Paysanne.
French Magdalen.	

The Red Magdalen, of Courson, is a favourite old French peach, very little known in this country; the Red Magdalen of many of our gardens being either a spurious sort, or the Royal George. It is an excellent, productive peach, hardy, and worthy of more general cultivation.

Leaves serrated, without glands. Fruit of medium size, or rather below it, round, flattened, with a deep suture on one side.

41

Skin pale yellowish white, with a lively red cheek. Flesh white, slightly red at the stone, juicy, and melting, with a rich vinous flavour. Middle and last of August. Flowers large

32. MALTA.§   Lind. Thomp. P. Mag.

Pêche Malte *O. Duh*	Italian.
Malte de Normandie	Belle de Paris

A most delicious, old European peach, of *unsurpassable* flavour. The tree is not a great bearer, but it is hardy and long lived, and richly deserves a place in every garden. There is a spurious sort sold under this name in the United States, which is easily known by its globose glands. The fruit of the Malta keeps well after being gathered.

Leaves serrated, without glands. Fruit of rather large size, roundish, flattened, with a broad, shallow suture, on one side. Skin pale, dull green, marked on the sunny side with broken spots, and blotches of dull purple. Flesh greenish, with a little dark red at the stone, very juicy and melting, with a peculiarly rich, vinous, piquant, and delicious flavour. Last of August. Flowers large.

The trees of the true Malta are remarkably free from the yellows, in this country, affording another proof of our theory regarding this disease, as they bear only moderate and regular crops.

33. NUTMEG, RED.   Mill. Lind. Thomp.

Avant Rouge. *O. Duh*	Brown Nutmeg.
Avant Pêche de Troyes	Early Red Nutmeg
Red Avant.	

The Red Nutmeg is a very small and inferior peach, which has long been cultivated, solely on account of its earliness. It is now seldom seen in our gardens, being abandoned for better sorts. Is is desirable, however, in a complete collection. Both this and the following are European varieties. The tree grows slowly, and is of dwarf habit.

Leaves small, with reniform glands. Fruit small, roundish, with a distinct suture, terminating in a small, round, swollen point at the top. Skin pale yellow, with a bright, rich red cheek. Flesh yellowish white, red at the stone, with a sweet and rather pleasant flavour. Middle and last of July. Flowers large.

34. Nutmeg, White. Mill. Lind. Thomp.

Avant Blanche. O. Duh.
White Avant.
Early White Nutmeg.

The White Nutmeg resembles the foregoing in its genera, habit, being dwarfish, and of slender growth. It is the smallest of peaches, the flavour is inferior, and it is only esteemed by curious amateurs as ripening a few days earlier than any other variety.

Leaves serrated, without glands. Fruit very small, rather oval, with a deep suture extending a little more than half round. Skin white, or rarely with a pale blush. Flesh white to the stone, with a sweet and slightly musky, pleasant flavour. Ripens about the 10th or 15th of July. Flowers large

35. Noblesse.§ Lang. Lind Thomp.

Vanguard.
Mellish's Favourite
Lord Montague's Noblesse

An English peach of the highest reputation, and which, in this country, is esteemed wherever known, as one of the largest, most delicious, and most valuable varieties. The tree is hardy and productive, and every cultivator should possess it. In England it is one of the favourite kinds for forcing and wall culture, yielding regular and abundant crops of beautiful, pale fruit.

Leaves serrated, without glands. Fruit large, roundish oblong, a little narrowed at the top, and terminated by an acute swollen point. Skin slightly downy, pale green throughout, marked on the cheek with delicate red, clouded with darker red. Flesh pale greenish white to the stone, melting, very juicy, with a very high and luscious flavour. Last of August. Flowers large.

36. Nivette. O. Duh. Lind. Thomp.

Nivette Veloutée.
Veloutée Tardive.
Dorsetshire.

The Nivette is an excellent French variety, much resembling the Late Admirable.

Leaves with globose glands. Fruit large, roundsh, inclining to oval, suture shallow, and the top slightly depressed. Skin pale green, with a lively red cheek. Flesh pale green, but deep red at the stone, juicy, melting, and very rich. Beginning, and middle of September. Flowers small.

37. Oldmixon Freestone. Pom. Man.

Oldmixon Clearstone. Coxe.

A large American peach, of late maturity and rich flavour. It was, we believe, raised either from a stone of the Catherine Cling or the Oldmixon Cling, the latter having been brought to this country many years ago, by Sir John Oldmixon. It bears good crops, and is a valuable variety.

Leaves with globose glands. Fruit large, roundish, or slightly oval, one side swollen, and the suture visible only at the top; cavity but slightly sunk at the stalk. Skin pale yellowish white, marbled with red, the cheek a deep red. Flesh white, but quite red at the stone, tender, with an excellent, rich, sugary and vinous flavour. Beginning of September. Flowers small.

38. President. P. Mag. Lind. Thomp.

One of the best of our peaches, and a capital variety, originated, several years ago, on Long Island.

Leaves with globose glands. Fruit large, roundish oval, the suture shallow. Skin very downy, pale yellowish green, with a dull red cheek. Flesh white, but deep red at the stone, very juicy, melting, rich and high flavoured. Stone very rough. Middle of September. Flowers small.

39. Pourprée Hative. O. Duh. Thomp. Lind.

Pourprée Hâtive à Grandes Fleurs.
Early Purple.

This is the *Early Purple* of Duhamel; what is often incorrectly called the Early Purple, being the Grosse Mignonne.

Leaves with reniform glands. Fruit of medium size, globular and depressed, and having a deep suture running across the top. Skin pale, light yellow, with a mottled purplish red cheek. Flesh pale, but red at the stone, melting, very juicy, with a high vinous flavour. Stone broad and rough. Middle of August. Flowers large.

The Pourprée Hative Veritable, of the French (Early Purple, True Early Purple, of some), with *globose* glands and large flowers, Thompson says, is "probably nothing different from the Grosse Mignonne."

40. ROYAL GEORGE.§ P. Mag. Lind. Thomp.

Early Royal George.	Red Magdalen.
Millet's Mignonne.	Madeleine Rouge à Petite Fleurs.
Lockyer's Mignonne.	French Chancellor. ⎫
Griffin's Mignonne.	Early Bourdine. ⎬ *Incorrectly, of some*
Superb.	Double Swalsh. ⎭

Few of the early peaches surpass in flavour and beauty the Royal George. It is one of the finest European varieties, and attains the highest flavour with us. The points of its shoots are a little inclined to mildew, which is entirely, in our climate, prevented by the shortening-in pruning. It is a regular and moderate bearer, and is one of the varieties indispensable to every good garden, ripening directly after the Early York.

The peach generally cultivated as the Royal George, Early Royal George, or Red Magdalen, in almost all parts of the United States, from Salem, Mass., to Baltimore (and described by Manning), is not the true Royal George, but the *Bellegarde*, or Smooth-leaved Royal George, which is rather later, not so rich, and has *globose* glands.

Leaves serrated, without glands. Fruit above the middle size, or rather large, globular, broad and depressed, the suture deep and broad at the top, and extending round two-thirds of the fruit. Skin pale, or white, thickly sprinkled with red dots, and the cheek of a broad rich, deep red slightly marbled. Flesh whitish, but very red at the stone, melting, juicy, very rich; and of the highest flavour. From the 20th to the last of August. Flowers small.

41 RED RARERIPE.§

Large Red Rareripe, *of some.*
Early Red Rareripe.

This remarkably fine early peach, is a very popular one with us, and has been cultivated for many years in this State. It strongly resembles the Royal George, and we believe it an American seedling from that variety, which is however distinct, and superior in flavour.

It must be observed that this is totally different both from the *Early York*, and *Morris' Red Rareripe*, with which it is often confounded by some nurserymen. The fruit is larger, broader, and a week later than the first; and its serrated leaves, and different flavour, separate it widely from the latter. Ends of the branches sometimes slightly mildewed.

Leaves serrated, without glands. Fruit rather large, globular, but broad, depressed, and marked with a deep broad suture, extending nearly round the whole fruit. Skin white, mottled,

41*

and marked with numerous red dots, and the cheek of a rich dark red. Flesh whitish, but red at the stone, melting, juicy, very rich and high flavoured. Middle and last of August. Flowers small.

42. RARERIPE, LATE RED.§

Prince's Red Rareripe.

This noble American fruit, the late Red Rareripe, is unquestionably one of the very finest of all peaches, even surpassing often the Late Admirable. Its large size, and great excellence, its late maturity, and its productiveness and vigour, all unite to recommend it to universal favour. We cannot praise it too highly. The rather *grayish* appearance of the fruit serves to distinguish it, at first sight, from all others.

Leaves with globose glands. Fruit large and heavy, roundish oval, suture depressed only at the top, where the swollen point is distinctly sunken. Skin downy, pale grayish yellow, thickly marbled and covered with reddish spots, the cheek dull deep red, distinctly mottled with fawn-coloured specks. Flesh white, but deep red at the stone; very juicy, melting, and of an unusually rich, luscious, high flavour, not surpassed by any other peach. First to the 10th of September. Flowers small

43. ROYAL CHARLOTTE.§   Thomp.

New Royal Charlotte, *Lind.* Grimwood's Royal Charlotte, Kew Early Purple, Lord Nelson's, Lord Fauconberg's Mignonne	*of the English.*	Madeleine Rouge Tardive, Madeleine Rouge à Moyenne Fleur. Madeleine à Petite Fleur.	*of the French.*

A very excellent peach, and a favorite variety with all European gardeners. Its leaves are more coarsely and deeply serrated than those of other varieties.

Leaves serrated, without glands. Fruit rather large, inclining to ovate, being rather broader at the base than at the top; the suture of moderate size. Skin pale greenish white, with a deep red marbled cheek. Flesh white, but pale red at the stone, melting, juicy, rich and excellent. Beginning of September. Flowers small.

44. SNOW.§

The Snow peach is a remarkably fair and beautiful fruit, of American origin, which has but lately made its appearance in our gardens. The fruit and blossoms are white, and the foliage and wood of a light green. It is a very hardy, productive, and desirable variety.

Leaves with reniform glands. Fruit large, globular; suture faintly marked except at the top. Skin, thin, clear beautiful white, on all sides. Flesh, white to the stone, juicy, and melting, with a sweet, rich, and sprightly flavour. Beginning of September. Flowers small.

45. Van Zandt's Superb. Pom. Man.

Waxen Rareripe.

A very bright-coloured and handsome peach, originated some years ago by Mr. Van Zandt, of Flushing, Long Island. It is one of the most beautiful dessert peaches, though only of medium size, and possesses very agreeable flavour.

Leaves with globose glands. Fruit of medium size, roundish, the suture slight, but one-half the fruit larger than the other. Skin white, with a beautifully sprinkled red cheek, on a yellowish white ground, the union of the two softened by delicate dotting of bright carmine red. Flesh whitish, but tinted with red at the stone, melting, juicy, sweet, and of good flavour. Stone deeply furrowed. First of September. Flowers small.

46. Scott's Early Red.

Scott's Early Red is a new variety, of very excellent flavour, and a prolific bearer, which we have lately received from New Jersey.

Leaves with obscure globose glands. Fruit of medium size, roundish, a little depressed, the suture distinctly marked, but not deep. Skin, pale greenish white, but much covered with red, which is mottled with fawn-coloured dots. Flesh whitish very juicy, with a rich and luscious flavour. Middle of August. Flowers small.

47. Strawberry

Rose.

The strawberry peach we received from Mr. Thomas Hancock, of Burlington, proprietor of one of the most respectable and extensive nurseries in New Jersey. It is esteemed one of the very finest early varieties for orchard culture in that State. It is quite distinct from the Early York.

Leaves with reniform glands. Fruit of medium size, oval, the cavity at the stem deeply sunk, the suture extending half round. Skin marbled with deep red over almost the whole surface. Flesh whitish, melting, juicy, rich, and of very delicious flavour. Middle of August. Flowers small.

48. WASHINGTON. Floy.

Washington Red Freestone. Ken.

The Washington is a handsome and very delicious peach, of American origin. It was named, and first introduced to notice, by Mr. Michael Floy, nurseryman, New York, about forty years ago. The fruit ripens late; the tree is vigorous hardy, and productive, and it is altogether a valuable variety.

Leaves with globose glands. Fruit large, broad, depressed with a broad deep suture extending nearly round it. Skin very thin, yellowish white, with a deep crimson cheek. Flesh pale yellowish white, very tender, juicy, and melting, with a sweet, rich, and luscious flavour. It often adheres slightly to the stone, which is quite small. Middle of September. Flowers small.

49. WALTER'S EARLY. Ken.

Walter's Early is esteemed as one of the most popular, early varieties for orchards in New Jersey, where it originated. It is remarkably well adapted to the light sandy soil of that State, bearing abundant crops of excellent fruit. At the north it is much inferior to the White Imperial, and the Royal George.

Leaves with globose glands. Fruit large, roundish. Skin white, with a rich red cheek. Flesh whitish, a little touched with red at the stone, melting, juicy, sweet, and of very agreeable flavour. Ripens about the 20th of August.

50. WHITE IMPERIAL.§

The White Imperial is a new early fruit, of most estimable quality. We consider it quite a valuable variety for every garden north of New York, as its flavour is very excellent. it is extremely hardy and vigorous, it bears good and regular crops without the bad habit of overbearing, and its fruit is uniformly excellent in all seasons.

This fine peach originated (it is believed, from the Noblesse) in the garden of David Thomas, of Cayuga county, N. Y., so long known for his skill and science as an amateur horticulturist. It was first made known to us by his son, J. J. Thomas, of Macedon, N. Y. Leaves with globose glands. Fruit rather large, broad, depressed, hollowed at the summit; with a wide, deep cavity at the stem; the suture moderately deep, and the fruit enlarged on one of its sides. Skin yellowish white, with only a slight tinge of red next the sun. Flesh nearly white, very melting and juicy, of a very delicate texture, and the flavour sweet and delicious. Ripens among the earliest, a few days after the Early York, about the 25th of August. Flowers small.

51. WHITE-BLOSSOMED INCOMPARABLE. P. Man. Thomp.

White-Blossom.
Willow Peach.

This is a native fruit of second quality, much inferior, both in flavour and appearance, to the Snow peach. Its seeds very frequently produce the same variety. The flowers are white, the leaves are of a light green, and the wood pale yellow, Leaves with reniform glands. Fruit large, oval. Skin fair, white throughout. Flesh white to the stone, melting, juicy, sweet and pleasant. Beginning of September. Flowers large, white.

---

*Class II. Free-Stone Peaches with deep yellow flesh.**

52. ABRICOTÉE. Thomp. O. Duh.

Yellow Admirable.   Admirable Jaune, *O. Duh. Nois.*
Apricot Peach.   D'Abricot.
Grosse Jaune Tardive.   'Orange. (Orange Peach. *Ken.*)

The Apricot-Peach (or *Yellow Admirable*, as it is more frequently called), is an old French variety, but little cultivated in this country, though deserving of attention in the Middle States. It ripens very late, and is thought to have a slight apricot flavour. It grows with moderate vigour, and bears abundantly.

Leaves with reniform glands. Fruit large, roundish oval, with a small suture running on one side only. Skin clear yellow all over, or faintly touched with red next the sun. Flesh yellow, but a little red at the stone, firm, rather dry, with a sweet and agreeable flavour. Stone small. Ripens at the beginning of October. Flowers large.

---

* Nearly all this class are of American origin, and the Yellow Alberge of Europe is the original type. They are not so rich as Class 1, and require our hot summers to bring out their flavour. In a cold climate, the acid is always prevalent. Hence they are inferior in England, and at the northern limits of the peach in this country.

53. Bergen's Yellow.§

Bergen's Yellow is a native, we believe, of Long Island.   It is very large, and of very delicious flavour.   It 's darker coloured, more depressed in form, rather finer flavoured, and ripens some days later than the Yellow Rare-Ripe, which it much resembles. It is a moderate, but good bearer.   It is earlier, and much superior to the Malacoton, and its glands distinguish it, also, from that variety.

Leaves with reniform glands.   Fruit large (often measuring nine inches in circumference), globular, depressed, and broad ; the suture well marked, and extending more than half round. Skin deep orange, dotted with some red, and with a very broad, dark red check.   Flesh deep yellow, melting, juicy, and of rich and luscious flavour.   Ripens at the beginning of September.   Flower small.

54. Baltimore Beauty.

A very good, and remarkably handsome peach, of native origin, ripening very early, which we received from Lloyd N. Rogers, Esq., of Baltimore.

Leaves with globose glands.   Fruit rather small, roundish oval.   Skin deep orange, with a rich brilliant red cheek.   Flesh yellow, but red at the stone, sweet and very good—a little mealy if over-ripe.   Ripens early in August.   Flowers large.

54. Crawford's Early Melocoton.§

Early Crawford.   Ken
Crawford's Early.

This is the most splendid and excellent of all early, yellow-fleshed peaches, and is scarcely surpassed by any other variety in size and beauty of appearance.   As a market fruit, it is perhaps the most popular of the day, and it is deserving of the high favour in which it is held by all growers of the peach.   It was originated a few years ago, by William Crawford, Esq., of Middletown, New Jersey.   The tree is vigorous and very fruitful.

Leaves with globose glands.   Fruit very large, oblong, the swollen point at the top prominent—the suture shallow.   Skin yellow, with a fine red cheek.   Flesh yellow, melting, sweet, rich and very excellent.   It ripens here the last week in August.   Flowers small.

55. Crawford's Late Melocoton.§

Crawford's superb Malacatune.

Crawford's Late Melocoton, from the same source as the foregoing, is one of the most magnificent American peaches. We think it unsurpassed by any other yellow-fleshed variety; and deserving of universal cultivation in this country. As a splendid and productive market fruit, it is unrivalled, and its size, beauty and excellence, will give it a place in every garden.

Leaves with globose glands. Fruit very large, roundish, with a shallow but distinct suture. Skin yellow, with a fine dark red cheek. Flesh deep yellow, but red at the stone, juicy and melting, with a very rich and excellent vinous flavour. Ripens from the 20th to the last of September. Flowers small.

56. Columbia. Coxe.

The Columbia is a singular and peculiar peach. It was raised by Mr. Coxe, the author of the first American work on fruit trees, from a seed brought from Georgia. It is a very excellent fruit, which every amateur will desire to have in his garden. The tree is not a very rapid grower and bears only moderate crops, being, of course, all the less subject to speedy decay. The young wood is purple.

Leaves with reniform glands. Fruit large, globular, broad and much depressed, the suture distinct, extending half way round. Skin rough and rather thick, dull dingy red, sprinkled with spots and streaks of darker red. Flesh bright yellow, of the texture, as Coxe remarks, of a very ripe pine apple, rich, juicy, and of very excellent flavor. Ripens from the beginning to the middle of September.

57. Poole's Large Yellow. Ken.

Poole's late Yellow Freestone.

A very large and handsome peach, of the Melocoton family, which is worthy of general orchard cultivation. It lately originated near Philadelphia and bears the finest crops.

Leaves with reniform glands. Fruit large, roundish, with a suture extending from the base to the top. Skin deep yellow, with a dark red cheek. Flesh yellow, but red at the stone, rich, juicy, and of excellent flavor. Ripens last of September.

CH

58. RED CHEEK MELOCOTON.* Pom. Man.

Malagatune.	
Malagatune.	Yellow Malagatune.
Hogg's Melocoton	Red Cheek Malocoton. *Cove.*
Yellow Malocoton.	

The Melocoton (or Malagatune, as it is commonly called) is almost too well known to need description. Almost every orchard and garden in the country contains it, and hundreds of thousands of bushels of the fruit are raised and sent to market in this country, every year. It is a beautiful and fine fruit, in favorable seasons, though in unfavorable ones the acid frequently predominates somewhat in its flavor. It is an American seedling, and is constantly reproducing itself under new forms, most of the varieties in this section having, directly or indirectly, been raised from it; the finest and most popular at the present time, being Crawford's Early, and Late, Melocotons, both greatly superior, in every respect, to the original Melocoton.

Leaves with globose glands. Fruit large, roundish oval, with a swollen point at the top. Skin yellow with a deep red cheek. Flesh deep yellow, red at the stone, juicy, melting, with a good, rich vinous flavour. First of September. Flowers small.

59. SMOCK FREESTONE. Ken.

St. George.

A variety which ripens late, and is much esteemed for orchard culture. It was originated not long since, by Mr. Smock, of Middletown, New Jersey, the centre of extensive peach cultivation.

Leaves with reniform glands. Fruit large, oval, narrowed towards the stalk, and rather compressed on the sides. Skin light orange yellow, mottled with red, or often with a dark red cheek, when fully exposed. Flesh bright yellow, but red at the stone, moderately juicy and rich. Ripens last of September and first of October.

60. YELLOW ALBERGE. Thomp.

Alberge Jaune. *O. Duh*	Purple Alberge. *Lind*
Pêche Jaune.	Red Alberge
Gold Fleshed	Golden Mignonne
Yellow Rareripe, of *many Am. Gardens.*	

* *Melocoton* is the Spanish for peach.

The Yellow Alberge is an old French variety, and one of the earliest of the yellow fleshed peaches. It is, no doubt, the original sort from which our Melocotons and Yellow Rareripes have sprung in this country. It has only a second rate flavour, except in rich warm soils, and is not comparable to the Yellow Rareripe in size or quality.

Leaves with globose glands. Fruit of medium size, roundish, with a well marked furrow running half round. Skin yellow, with a deep purplish red cheek. Flesh yellow, but deep red at the stone, soft, juicy, sweet, with a pleasant vinous flavour. Middle of August. Flowers small.

The ROSANNA (Lind. Thomp.), *Alberge Jaune* of many French gardens, and Yellow Alberge of some gardens here, differs from the above only in having reniform glands, and ripening ten or twelve days later. Flavour second rate.

61. YELLOW RARERIPE.§

Large Yellow Rareripe.
Marie Antoinette

One of the finest very early yellow fleshed peaches. It is an American seedling, produced about a dozen years ago, and well deserves the extensive cultivation it receives, both in the orchard and garden.

Leaves with globose glands. Fruit large, roundish, the suture slightly depressed, extending more than half round; the swollen point at the top small.

Skin deep orange yellow, somewhat dotted with red, the cheek rich red, shaded off in streaks. Flesh deep yellow, but red at the stone, juicy, melting, with a rich and excellent vinous flavour. Ripens from the 25th to the 30th of August. Stone small. Flowers small.

There is an inferior and older sort, very commonly known as the Yellow Rareripe and Yellow Malagatune, the fruit of which is scarcely of medium size, dull yellow, with very little red, and of a flavour very inferior to the true kind just described.

Class III. *Clingstone Peaches (or Pavies).*

62. BLOOD CLINGSTONE. Floy.

Claret Clingstone.
Blood Cling.

The Blood Clingstone is a very large and peculiar fruit, of

no value for eating, but esteemed by many for pickling and preserving—the flesh very red, like that of a beet. This is an American seedling, raised many years ago, from the French Blood Clingstone,—SANGUINOLE À CHAIR ADHÉRENTE. It is a much larger fruit than the original sort, which has large flowers, otherwise they are the same in all respects.

Leaves with reniform glands. Fruit often very large, roundish oval, with a distinct suture. Skin very downy, of a dark, dull, clouded, purplish red. Flesh deep red, throughout, firm and juicy—not fit for eating. September to October. Flowers small.

There is a FRENCH BLOOD FREESTONE (*Sanguinole, Sanguine, Cardinale, or Betrave,* Duh. Thomp.) of the same nature, and used for the same purpose as this, but smaller in size, and not equal to it for cooking. Leaves without glands.

63. CATHERINE. Lang. Lind. P. Mag. Thorp.

The Catherine cling is a very fine, old English variety, of excellent quality, but not, we think, equal to the *Large White Clingstone,* a native seedling, so much esteemed in the Middle States.

Mr. Manning, and, after him, Mr. Kenrick, have remarked that "the Catherine, the old Newington, and old Mixon Clingstone, cannot be distinguished from each other." This is an error, probably from not having seen together, the genuine sorts, as they are quite distinct fruits, and the glands of the leaves—that unerring characteristic—different in each variety.

Leaves with reniform glands. Fruit large, roundish oval, more swollen on one side than the other, and terminated by a small swollen point at the top. Skin pale yellowish green, much sprinkled with red dots, the exposed cheek of a bright lively red, streaked with darker red. Flesh firm, yellowish white, but dark red at the stone, to which it adheres very closely. juicy, rich and excellent. Middle and last of September. Flowers small.

64. HEATH. § Coxe.

Heath Clingstone
Fine Heath.
Red Heath.

The most superb and most delicious of all late Clingstones. It seldom ripens in New England, but here, and to the southward, it is one of the most valuable kinds, of very large size, and the very finest flavour.

Coxe informs us that this is a seedling produced in Maryland from a stone brought by Mr. Daniel Heath from the Mediterranean ; and it is frequently still propagated from the stone, without variation, in that State. The tree is vigorous, long lived, and moderately productive; with the *shortening-in* mode of pruning, the fruit is always large and fine, otherwise often poor. This tree is well deserving of a place on the espalier rail or wall, at the north.

Leaves nearly smooth on the edges, with reniform glands. Fruit very large, oblong, narrowing to both ends, and terminating at the top with a large swollen point: the suture distinct on one side. Skin downy, cream-coloured white, with a faint blush or tinge of red in the sun, or a brownish cheek. Flesh greenish white, very tender and melting, exceedingly juicy, with the richest, highest, and most luscious flavour, surpassed by no other variety. It adheres very closely to the stone. It ripens in October, and frequently keeps for a month after being gathered. Flowers small.

BAYNE'S NEW HEATH, is a recent seedling, very similar in all respects, originated lately by Dr. Bayne, of Alexandria, D. C It is considered rather finer by some.

65. INCOMPARABLE. Lind. Thorp.

Pavie Admirable. *Bon. Jard. Ken.*
Late Admirable Cling.

Larger than the Catherine, which it resembles. It is inferior to it and several others in flavour, and is only worthy of cultivation for market.

Leaves with reniform glands. Fruit large, roundish, one side enlarged. Skin pale yellowish white, light red on the exposed side. Flesh yellowish white, red at the stone, juicy, melting, and of agreeable flavour. Last of September. Flowers small.

66. LARGE WHITE CLINGSTONE. §

New York White Clingstone. Floy.
Williamson's New York.
Selby's Cling.

The Large White Clingstone is by far the most popular of this class of peaches in this State, and in New England. We think it superior to the Catherine, and old Newington, and only surpassed in flavour by the old Mixon cling, and the Heath cling.

This variety was raised about forty years ago by David Williamson, a nurseryman, in New York, and was first described by Floy as the *New York Clingstone*. But as it is universally known now by the present title, we have placed the original names as synonymes. The light colour, and excellen quality of this fruit, render it the greatest favourite for preserving in brandy or sugar. The tree is remarkably hardy and long lived ; rarely, if ever, being attacked by the yellows. It bears regular and good crops.

Leaves with globose glands. Fruit large, round ; the suture slight, and the swollen point at the top small. Skin white (inclining to yellow only when over ripe), dotted with red on the sunny side, or with a light red cheek when fully exposed. Flesh whitish, tender, very melting, full of juice, which is very sweet, luscious, and high flavoured. Beginning and middle of September. Flowers small.

67. LEMON CLINGSTONE. § Floy. Thomp.

Kennedy's Carolina. *Pom. Man.*	Long Yellow Pine Apple. *Coxe.*
Kennedy's Lemon Clingstone.	Pine Apple Clingstone.
Largest Lemon.	Yellow Pine Apple.

The Lemon Clingstone is one of the largest, and most beautiful of all the yellow fleshed clings, and though of course inferior in flavour to the white fleshed, is deserving of its universal popularity. It is originally a native of South Carolina, and was brought from thence by a Mr. Kennedy, of New York, before the war of the Revolution. There are now many seedlings reproduced from it, but none superior to the original. This is a very productive, hardy tree.

Leaves long, with reniform glands. Fruit large, oblong, narrowed at the top, and having a large, projecting, swollen point, much like that of a lemon. Skin fine yellow, with a dark brownish red cheek. Flesh firm, yellow, slightly red at the stone, adhering firmly, with a rich, sprightly, vinous, subacid flavour. Middle and last of September. Flowers small.

68. LATE YELLOW ALBERGE. Pom. Man.

October Yellow.
Algiers Yellow.
Algiers Winter.

A very late Clingstone Peach, entirely yellow, scarcely good for eating, but esteemed by some for preserving. It was originally introduced from the south of France, and has been considerably cultivated here, but we have abandoned it. The Heath cling is in every way greatly its superior.

Leaves with reniform glands. Fruit of medium size, roundish oval, with a small distinct suture. Skin downy, green till the last of September, but at maturity being yellow. Flesh yellow to the stone, very firm, rather juicy, sweet. October. Flowers large.

70. OLDMIXON CLINGSTONE. § Coxe

Oldmixon Cling.
Green Catherine, of the Americans *Thomp.*

The Oldmixon Clingstone is certainly one of the highest flavoured of all peaches known in this country, where it is raised
in perfection, and should have a place in every good garden.
Indeed we consider this, the large White Cling, and the Heath
Cling, as being the sorts among the most desirable of this class of
peaches for small collections.

This fruit is quite distinct from the Catherine cling of Europe,
or the old Newington, as a single glance at its leaf glands will
show, to say nothing of its superior flavour. It can scarcely
be the "Green Catherine of the Americans" of the London Horticultural Society's Catalogue, as that is said to be a poor fruit.
We are not familiar with it. Coxe says the Oldmixon cling
was introduced by Sir John Oldmixon, from Europe. It is
more probable that he introduced the stone only.

Leaves with globose glands. Fruit large, roundish oval, the
suture distinct only at the top, on one side of which the fruit is
slightly enlarged. Skin yellowish white, dotted with red, or
with a red cheek, varying from pale to lively red. Flesh pale
white, very melting and juicy, with an exceedingly rich, luscious, high flavour. First of September. Flowers small.

71. ORANGE CLINGSTONE.

The Orange Cling is a very large, handsome, and excellent
fruit, somewhat resembling the Lemon Cling in colour, but globular in form, rather richer in flavour, and quite a distinct sort.

Leaves large, serrated, without glands. Fruit large, round,
the suture distinctly marked, and extending nearly round the
fruit—swollen point at the top, none. Skin deep orange, with
a rich dark red cheek. Flesh dark yellow, rather firm, juicy
with a rich vinous flavour. September. Flowers small.

72. OLD NEWINGTON. Lang. Lind. Thomp.

Newington. *Parkinson.* (1629.)
Large Newington. *Coxe*

A celebrated English clingstone which has been in cultivation more than 200 years, and still is perhaps the best in the
English climate. Although excellent, it is not so generally esteemed here as the Large White Cling, and Oldmixon Clingstone.

Leaves serrated, without glands. Fruit large, roundish, the
suture slight. Skin pale yellowish white, with a fine red cheek,
42*

marked with streaks of darker red. Flesh pale yellowish white, deep red at the stone, to which it always adheres very firmly; melting, juicy, and rich. Ripens about the 15th of September. Flowers large.

73. PAVIE DE POMPONE. Bon. Jard. Lelieur. Thomp.

Monstrous Pomponne. } Lind.	Pavie Rouge de	
Monstrous Pavie.	Pompone. *O. Duh*	
Pavie de Pomponne Grosse.	Pavie Camu.	
Pavie Monstrueux.	Gros Mélecoton.	
	Gros Persique Rouge	

A very large and magnificent old French clingstone, not so well known in this country as it deserves. The fruit is very solid in flesh, and much sweeter here than in France. The tree is of very strong growth.

Leaves with reniform glands. Fruit very large, roundish oval, with a well marked suture extending to the top, and terminating there in an obtuse swollen point. Skin yellowish white, a good deal covered with the broad, very deep red colour of its cheek. Flesh firm, yellowish white, deep red at the stone, to which it adheres very firmly, and which is rather small; juicy, flavour sweet and good. First of October. Flowers large.

74. SMITH'S NEWINGTON. Lind. Thomp.

Early Newington.	} *Of the*	
Smith's Early Newington.	} *English*	
Early Newington.	*Coxe.*	

This is one of the best Early Clingstone Peaches. It is of English origin, and is little cultivated in this country. The Early Newington of our gardens as generally known (see Early Newington Freestone), is earlier and a very much finer variety, with *reniform* glands, being a partial clingstone, but most frequently parting from the flesh, has quite supplanted it.

Leaves serrated, without glands. Fruit middle sized, rather oval, narrower at the top, and one half a little enlarged. Skin pale straw colour, with a lively red cheek streaked with purple. Flesh firm, pale yellow, but light red at the stone, to which it adheres closely; juicy, and of very good quality. Last of August. Flowers large.

What Mr. Thompson calls "*Newington of the Americans*" is a seedling cling with *globose* glands, and of second quality; quite distinct from our Early Newington Freestone.

75. Tippecanoe.

Hero of Tippecanoe.

A new, very large, and handsome clingstone, originated by Mr. George Thomas, of Philadelphia, and first exhibited before tne Horticultural Society there in 1840. Its lateness and beauty render it a valuable kind.

Leaves with reniform glands, the shoots dark purplish red. Fruit very large, nearly round, a little compressed on the sides. Skin yellow, with a fine red cheek. Flesh yellow, juicy, with a good vinous flavour. It ripens from the 20th to the last of September. Flowers small.

76. Washington Clingstone. §

An American variety, remarkably juicy and sweet. Although Thompson finds it third rate in England, it is here scarcely surpassed. To use the expressive words of one of our friends in Maryland, a good judge of fruit, "there is nothing better than this peach out of paradise." It is neither handsome nor prepossessing externally.

Leaves with reniform glands. Fruit of medium size, roundish. Skin yellowish green, marked with grey specks, and with a slight tinge of red on the sunny side. Flesh very juicy, tender, and melting, with a very sweet and luscious flavour. Last of September. Flowers small.

Curious, or Ornamental Varieties.

77. Double Blossomed. Thomp.

Double Flowering Peach.	Pécher à Fleurs Doubles. *Bon. Jard.*
Rose Flowering	Pécher à Fleurs Semi-Doubles. *O. Duh*

The Double Blossomed Peach is, when in full bloom, one of the gayest and most beautiful of fruit trees, and blooming with its lovely companion, the Double Flowering Cherry, finds a place in all our pleasure grounds and ornamental plantations. Its flowers are three times the size of those of the common peach, of a lively rose colour, nearly full double, and so thickly disposed on the branches as to be very striking and showy. They are produced at the usual season or a few days later

This sort is rendered more dwarf for shrubberies, by budding it upon the Mirabelle, or the Cherry Plum stock.

The leaves have reniform glands. The fruit, which is sparingly produced, is roundish oval, pale greenish yellow, faintly tinged with red, freestone, and of indifferent flavour.

78. FLAT PEACH OF CHINA. Lind. Thomp.

Chinese Peach.
Java Peach.
Peen To.

A very singular variety, from China, where the gardeners affect all manner of vegetable curiosities. The fruit is of small size, about two inches in diameter, and so much flattened at the ends that only the skin and the flat stone remains, the fleshy part being crowded on either side. The tree is of rather dwarfish habit, and holds its leaves very late. The fruit is of very good flavour, and is well worthy of a place in the gardens of the curious.*

Leaves with reniform glands. Fruit small, so much flattened as to form a deep hollow at both ends, having at the top a singular broad, rough, five-angled eye. Skin pale yellowish green, mottled with red on one side. Flesh pale yellow, with a circle of red round the stone (from which it separates), sweet, juicy, with a slight noyeau flavour. Beginning of September. Flowers large.

79. WEEPING PEACH.

Reid's Weeping Peach.

A peculiar variety, with pendant, weeping branches, and a habit much like that of the weeping ash. It was lately originated by Mr. William Reid, the skilful nurseryman at Murray Hill, near New York. To display itself to advantage, it should be grafted six or eight feet high, on the clean stem of a peach or plum stock. Reniform glands. Flowers large.

Selection of choice peaches for a small garden, to furnish in succession. *Freestones ;* Early York, White Imperial, Early Newington Freestone, Royal George, Grosse Mignonne, George IV., Crawford's Early, Bergen's Yellow, Noblesse, Brevoort, Malta, Late Red Rareripe, Druid Hill. *Clingstones ;* Large white Clingstone, Oldmixon, and Heath.

---

* This variety has been several times imported to this country and lost on the way. Should any one of our amateurs now possess it, we shall be much gratified to receive buds of it.

Selection of hardy and excellent sorts, for a northern latitude. George the Fourth, Yellow Rareripe, Early York, Morris Red Rareripe, Grosse Mignonne, Noblesse, White Imperial, Crawford's Early, Favourite, Bellegarde, Brevoort, Cooledge's Favourite, Morris', White Rareripe, Large White Clingstone.

The best varieties for forcing, are the Grosse Mignonne, Noblesse, Bellegarde, Royal George White Imperial, Royal Charlotte, and Barrington.

CHAPTER XXIII.

THE NECTARINE

Persica vulgaris (v.) *Lævis*. Dec. *Rosaceæ of botanists.*

THE Nectarine is only a variety of the peach with a smooth skin (*Peche lisse*, or *Brugnon* of the French). In its growth, habit, and general appearance, it is impossible to distinguish it from the peach tree. The fruit, however, is rather smaller, perfectly smooth, without down, and is one of the most wax-like and exquisite of all productions for the dessert. In flavour, it is perhaps scarcely so rich as the finest peach, but it has more piquancy, partaking of the noyeau or peach leaf flavour.

The Nectarine is known in Northern India, where it is called *moondla aroo* (smooth peach). It appears to be only a distinct, accidental variety of the peach, and this is rendered quite certain, since there are several well known examples on record of both peaches and nectarines having been produced on the same branch*—thus showing a disposition to return to the natural form. Nectarines, however, usually produce nectarines again on sowing the seeds,—but they also occasionally produce peaches. The Boston Nectarine originated from a peach stone.

The Nectarine appears a little more shy of bearing in this country, than the peach, but this arises almost always from the destruction of the crop of fruit by the *curculio*, the destroyer of all smooth-skinned stone fruit in sandy soils. It is quite hardy here wherever the peach will thrive, though it will not generally bear large and fine fruit unless the branches are *shortened-in* annually, as we have fully directed for the peach tree.

* See London Gardener's Magazine, Vol. 1, p. 471 ; Vol 14, p. 53.

With this easy system of pruning, good crops are readily obtained, wherever the curculio is not very prevalent.

Where this insect abounds, we must recommend the steady annual application of salt, spread over the surface of the ground, the surface being first made hard and firm. This should be done when the punctured fruit commences to drop. (See the Plum for further remarks on this insect.) And we would, as a preventive to the attacks of the insect, recommend rags, dipped in *coal tar*,* to be hung in the branches for two or three weeks after the fruit is formed. The coal tar should be renewed occasionally, as soon as it loses its powerful smell.

The culture of the nectarine is, in all respects, precisely similar to that of the peach, and its habits are also completely the same. It is longer lived, and hardier, when budded on the plum, but still the nurserymen here usually work it on the peach stock.

Class I.   *Freestone Nectarines.* (Pêches lisses, *Fr.*)

[The same characters are used as in describing peaches, for which the reader is referred to that part].

1.   Boston.   § Thomp.

Lewis'
Perkins' Seedling. } *Ken.*

This American seedling is the largest and most beautiful of all nectarines. It was raised from a peach stone by Mr. T. Lewis of Boston. The original tree was, when full of fruit, destroyed by boys, but the sort had been preserved by that most skilful cultivator, S. G. Perkins, Esq., and soon in his hands attracted attention by the uncommon beauty of its fruit. In 1821, this gentleman transmitted trees of this variety to the London Horticultural Society, of which he is a corresponding member, together with a very accurate drawing of the fruit grown by him, measuring eight and a half inches round, and " so beautiful, that its correctness was doubted abroad," until Mr. Knight showed specimens grown there in 1823.   The fruit, though not of high flavour, is excellent, the tree very hardy and productive, and one of the best for general standard culture. Mr. Perkins' seedling, raised from the original Lewis tree, is quite identical, and we adopt the name of " Boston " nectarine, as the standard one.   Three trees of this sort covering fifty-five feet of wall at his place at Brookline, are now very beautiful objects.   [See Broomfield Nectarine.]

---

* To be had very cheap at the city gas works

Leaves with globose glands. Fruit large and handsome, roundish oval. Skin, bright yellow, with very deep red cheek, shaded off by a slight mottling of red. Flesh yellow to the stone (which is small and pointed), sweet, though not rich, with a pleasant and peculiar flavour. First of September. Flowers small.

2. Duc du Tellier's. § Lind. Thomp.

Du Tilliers.	Duke de Tilley.
Du de Tello.	Du Tilly's.

A very excellent Nectarine, considerably resembling the Elruge, but a much greater bearer.

Leaves with reniform glands. Fruit rather large, roundish oblong, being slightly narrowed at the top, and broad at the base or stalk. Skin pale green, with a marbled purplish-red cheek. Flesh greenish white, pale red at the stone, melting, juicy, sweet and good. Last of August. Flowers small.

3. Downton. Thomp.

The Downton is a seedling, raised by Mr. Knight. It is in quality, appearance, and season, an intermediate variety, between the Violette Hâtive and the Elruge, ripening a few days earlier than the latter.

Leaves with reniform glands. Fruit large, roundish oval. Skin pale green, with a deep violet-red cheek. Flesh pale green, slightly red at the stone, melting, rich, and very good. Ripens about the 25th of August. Flowers small.

4. Elruge. § Thomp.

Common Elruge.	} Lind.	Anderson's.	} of some
Claremont.		Temple's.	} English gardens.
Oatlands.			
Spring Grove.		Peterborough.	} incorrectly of many American gardens.

The Elruge is everywhere esteemed as one of the very finest Nectarines. It is an English variety which has been a good while cultivated, and, with the Violet Hâtive, is considered indispensable in every collection. In this country, when the young wood is annually *shortened-in*, it bears good crops on standard trees, which ripen finely.

Without this precaution, like almost all other nectarines, the fruit is small, poor, and ripens imperfectly.

Leaves with reniform glands. Fruit of medium size, round.

ish-oval, the suture slight, except at the top, where it is distinctly marked. Skin with a pale green ground, but when fully exposed, it is nearly covered with deep violet, or blood red, dotted with minute brownish specks. Flesh pale green to the stone, or slightly stained there with pale red ; melting, very juicy, with a rich high flavour. Stone oval, rough, of a *pale* colour. Last of August and beginning of September. Flowers small.

5. FAIRCHILD's Lind. Thomp.

Fairchild's Early.

A very small, indifferent sort, only valued for its earliness, and scarcely worth cultivating when compared with the following.

Leaves with reniform glands. Fruit small, about an inch and a fourth in diameter, round, slightly flattened at the top. Skin yellowish green, with a bright red cheek. Flesh yellow to the stone, rather dry, with a sweet, but rather indifferent flavour. Beginning of August. Flower small.

6. HUNT's TAWNY. § Thomp.

Hunt's Large Tawny. ⎫ Lind.
Hunt's Early Tawny. ⎭

This is the best, very early Nectarine. It is a very distinct sort, with serrated leaves, and was originated in England about thirty years ago. It is worthy of general cultivation, as it is not only early, but hardy, and an abundant bearer.

Leaves serrated, without glands. Fruit nearly of medium size, roundish-ovate, being considerably narrowed at the top, where there is a prominent swollen point ; and the fruit is slightly enlarged on one side of the suture. Skin pale orange, with a dark red cheek, mottled with numerous russety specks. Flesh deep orange, juicy, melting, rich, and very good It ripens from the 5th to the 15th of August Flowers small.

(The accidental variation of this sort, described as *Hunt's Large Tawny*, does not seem to have been permanently different from this.)

7. HARDWICKE SEEDLING. Thomp.

Hardwicke's Seedling.

A comparatively new variety. of high reputation, which we have lately received from Mr. T. Rivers. It was raised at Hardwicke House, in Suffolk, England, and has the reputation of being " one of the best and hardiest of nectarines, and a very excellent bearer."

Leaves with reniform glands. Fruit very large, roundish, inclining to oval, and resembling the Elruge. Skin pale green, with a deep, violet-red cheek. Flesh pale green, slightly marke with red at the stone, juicy, melting, rich, and high flav ured. End of August.

8. MURREY. Ray. Thomp.

Murry. Lind.
Black Murry.

The Murrey is an old English Nectarine, which, though of good quality, is rather a poor bearer, and is little known or cultivated in this country.

Leaves with reniform glands. Fruit of medium size, roundish-ovate, slightly swollen on one side of the suture. Skin pale green, with a dark red cheek. Flesh greenish white, melting, sweet, and of good flavour. Stone almost smooth. Ripens about the 20th of August. Flowers small.

9. NEW WHITE. Thomp.

Neat's White. Lind.
Flanders.
Cowdray White.
Emerton's New White.
Large White.

The New White is the finest light skinned variety, and is a beautiful, hardy, and excellent nectarine, bearing abundant crops, and is well worthy to be generally planted. It is an English seedling, raised by the Rev. Mr. Neate, near London, fifty years ago, from the seed of the following variety.

Leaves with reniform glands. Fruit rather large, nearly round, skin white, with occasionally a slight tinge of red when exposed. Flesh white, tender, very juicy, with a rich, vinous flavour. The stone is small. Ripens early in September. Flowers large.

10. OLD WHITE. Lind. Thomp.

This nectarine is supposed to have been introduced from Asia into England, about sixty years ago. It is much like the foregoing in flavour, perhaps a little richer, but it is less hardy and productive.

Leaves with reniform glands. Fruit rather large, roundish

43

oval. Skin white, slightly tinged with red. Flesh white, tender, juicy and rich. Early in September. Flowers large.

11. PITMASTON'S ORANGE. Lind. Thomp.

William's Orange.
William's Seedling.

The Pitmaston Orange, which is considered the best *yellow* fleshed nectarine, was raised in 1816, by John Williams of Pitmaston, near Worcester, England. It is yet but little known, but will prove one of the best sorts for general cultivation in this country. The tree is vigorous.

Leaves with globose glands. Fruit large, roundish ovate, the base (towards the stalk) being broad, and the top narrow, and ending in an acute swollen point. Skin rich orange yellow, with a dark, brownish red cheek, streaked at the union of the two colours. Flesh deep yellow, but red at the stone; melting, juicy, rich, sweet, and of excellent flavour. The stone is rather small. Ripens middle and last of August. Flowers large.

12. PETERBOROUGH. Mill. Lind. Thomp.

Late Green.
Vermash (*of some*).

This is the latest nectarine known. It is rather small, and of inferior quality, and scarcely deserves cultivation except to make complete a large collection. It was brought by Lord Peterborough, from Genoa to England.

We doubt if this fruit is now in this country. All the specimens that we have seen under this name, from different districts, being only the Elruge imperfectly grown.

Leaves with reniform glands. Fruit rather small, roundish. Skin mostly green, or slightly tinged with dingy red on the sunny side. Flesh greenish white to the stone, somewhat juicy and of tolerable flavour. It ripens early in October. Flower small.

13. VIOLETTE HÂTIVE. Lind. Thomp.

Early Violet.		Petite Violet Hâtive. O Dh
Violet *P. Mag*		Brugnon Hâtif.
Early Brugnon.	*Of various*	Violette Angervillières.
Brugnon Red at the Stone.	*European gardens,*	Violette Musquée.
Hampton Court.	*ac. to Thomp.*	Lord Selsey's Elruge.
Large Scarlet.		Violet Red at the Stone.
New Scarlet.		Violet Musk.
Aromatic.		

The Violette Hâtive, or Early Violet Nectarine, everywhere takes the highest rank among nectarines. It is of delicious flavour, fine appearance, hardy, and productive. Externally, the fruit is easily confounded with that of the Elruge, but it is readily distinguished by its dark coloured stone, and the deep red flesh surrounding it. The fruit is usually rather darker coloured. It is of French origin, and has been long cultivated.

Leaves with reniform glands. Fruit rather large, roundish, narrowed slightly at the top, where it is also marked with a shallow suture. Skin pale yellowish-green, in the shade, but, when exposed, nearly covered with dark purplish red, mottled with pale brown dots. Flesh whitish, but much rayed with red at the stone. The latter is roundish, the furrows not deep, and the surface reddish brown. The flesh is melting, juicy, rich, and very high flavoured. It ripens about the last of August. Flowers rather small.

The VIOLETTE GRÒSSE (Thomp.) resembles the foregoing in leaves and flowers, and general appearance. The fruit is, however, larger, but not so richly flavoured.

Class II.—Clingstone Nectarines, (Brugnons, *Fr.*)

14. BROOMFIELD.

Lewis, (*incorrectly, of some.*)

A handsome clingstone nectarine, of second quality. It is an accidental seedling, which sprung up in the garden of Henry Broomfield, Esq., of Harvard, Mass., and was first named and disseminated by S. G. Perkins, Esq. of Boston, thirty-five years ago.

Leaves with obscure, reniform glands. Fruit large, roundish. Skin rather dull yellow, with a dull or rather dingy red cheek. Flesh yellow, and adheres closely to the stone, juicy, rather pleasant, but not high flavoured. First to the middle of September. Flowers small.

15. GOLDEN. Lang. Mill. Thomp.

Orange.
Fine Gold Fleshed.

A very handsome looking nectarine, but of decidedly indifferent quality, when compared with many others. Its waxen appearance, when fully ripe, is very beautiful. It is an old English variety.

Leaves with reniform glands. Fruit of medium size, roundish, ovate. Skin of a fine bright, waxen yellow colour, with a small scarlet cheek. Flesh orange-yellow, firm, juicy, sweet, and tolerably good. It ripens about the 10th of September. Flowers small.

PRINCE'S GOLDEN NECTARINE is of much larger size. It ripens about a week later, but is also only of second quality. Leaves with reniform glands. Flowers large.

16. NEWINGTON. Lang. Mill. Thomp.

Scarlet Newington. Lind.	Anderson's.
Scarlet.	Anderson's Round
Old Newington.	Rough Roman
Smith's Newington.	Brugnon de Newington
French Newington	D'Angleterre.
Sion Hill.	

A very good clingstone nectarine, of English origin. It should be allowed to hang on the tree till it begins to shrivel, when the flavour is much improved.

Leaves serrated, without glands. Fruit rather large, roundish. Skin pale greenish-yellow, nearly covered with red, marbled with dark red. Flesh firm, pale, but deep red next the stone, juicy, sweet and rich, with an excellent vinous flavour. Ripens about the 10th of September. Flowers large

17. NEWINGTON, EARLY. § Lind. Thomp.

Early Black Newington.	Lucombe's Black.
New Dark Newington.	Lucombe's Seedling.
New Early Newington	Early Black.
Black	

The Early Newington is one of the best of clingstone nectarines. It is not only a richer flavoured fruit than the old Newington, but it is larger, dark coloured, and earlier.

Leaves serrated, without glands. Fruit large, roundish, ovate, a little enlarged on one side of the suture, and terminating with an acute swollen point at the top. Skin pale green in its ground, but nearly covered with bright red, much marbled and mottled with very dark red, and coated with a thin bloom. Flesh greenish white, but deep red at the stone, juicy, sugary, rich and very excellent. Beginning of September. Flowers large.

18. RED ROMAN. § Forsyth. Lind. Thomp.

Old Roman.
Roman.
Brugnon Violette Musquée. **O. Dul.**
Brugnon Musquée.

The Red Roman is a very old European variety, having been enumerated by Parkinson, in 1629. It is still esteemed, both in Europe and this country, as one of the richest and best of clingstone nectarines. The tree healthy and productive.

The Newington is frequently sold for the Red Roman in this country, and the true Roman is comparatively scarce.

Leaves with reniform glands. Fruit large, roundish, a little flattened at the top. Skin greenish yellow, with a brownish, muddy, red cheek, which is somewhat rough, and marked with brown russetty specks. Flesh firm, greenish yellow, and deep red at the stone, juicy, with a rich, high vinous flavour. Ripening early in September. Flowers large.

Selection of choice hardy Nectarines, for a small Garden.— Early Violet, Elruge, Hardwicke Seedling, Hunt's Tawny, Boston, Roman, New White.

CHAPTER XXIV.

THE QUINCE.

Cydonia vulgaris, Dec.; *Rosaceæ*, of Botanists.
Coignassier, of the French; *Quittenbaum*, German; *Kivepeer*, Dutch; *Cotogno*, Italian; and *Membrillo*, Spanish.

THE Quince is a well-known, hardy, deciduous tree, of small size, crooked branches, and spreading, bushy head. It is indigenous to Germany and the south of Europe; and it appears first to have attracted notice in the city of *Cydon*, in Crete or Candia—whence its botanical name, Cydonia. The fruit is of a fine golden yellow, and more nearly resembles that of the orange than any other. It was even more highly esteemed by the Greeks and Romans, for preserving, than by us. "Quinces," says Columella, "not only yield pleasure, but health."

The Quince seldom grows higher than fifteen feet, and is usually rather a shrub than a tree. Its large white and pale pink blossoms, which appear rather later than those of other fruit trees, are quite ornamental; and the tree, properly grown, is very ornamental when laden in October and November with its ripe golden fruit.

USES.—The Quince is, in all its varieties, unfit for eating raw. It is, however, much esteemed when cooked. For preserving, it is everywhere valued, and an excellent marmalade is also made from it. Stewed, it is very frequently used, to

43*

communicate additional flavour and piquancy to apple-tarts, pies, or other pastry. In England, wine is frequently made from the fruit, by adding sugar and water, as in other fruit wines; and it is a popular notion there, that it has a most beneficial effect upon *asthmatic* patients. Dried Quinces are excellent.

In this country, large plantations are sometimes made of the Quince; and as it is, in good soil, a plentiful bearer, it is considered one of the most valuable market fruits. The Apple quince is the most productive and saleable; but as the Pear quince ripens, and can be sent to market much later, it frequently is the most profitable.

PROPAGATION.—The Quince is easily propagated from seed, layers, or cuttings. From seeds the quince is somewhat liable to vary in its seedlings, sometimes proving the apple-shaped and sometimes the pear-shaped variety. Cuttings, planted in a shaded situation, early in the spring, root very easily, and this is perhaps the simplest and best way of continuing a good variety. The better sorts are also frequently budded on common seedling quince stocks, or on the common thorn.

Quince *stocks* are extensively used in engrafting or budding the Pear, when it is wished to render that tree *dwarf* in its habit.

SOIL AND CULTURE.—The Quince grows naturally in rather moist soil, by the side of rivulets and streams of water. Hence it is a common idea that it should always be planted in some damp neglected part of the garden, where it usually receives little care, and the fruit is often knotty and inferior.

This practice is a very erroneous one. No tree is more benefited by manuring than the quince. In a rich, mellow, deep soil, even if quite dry, it grows with thrice its usual vigour, and bears abundant crops of large and fair fruit. It should, therefore, be planted in deep and good soil, kept in constant cultivation, and it should have a top-dressing of manure, every season, when fair and abundant crops are desired. As to pruning, or other care, it requires very little indeed—an occasional thinning out of crowding or decayed branches, being quite sufficient. Thinning the fruit, when there is an over-crop, improves the size of the remainder. Ten feet apart is a suitable distance at which to plant this tree.

The Quince, like the apple, is occasionally subject to the attacks of the borer, and a few other insects, which a little care will prevent or destroy. For their habits we refer the reader to the apple.

VARIETIES.—Several varieties of the common Quince are enumerated in many catalogues, but there are in reality only three distinct forms of this fruit worth enumerating, viz:

1. Apple-shaped Quince. Thomp.

Orange Quince,
Cydonia v. Maliformis, *Hort. Brit.*
Coignassier Maliforme, *of the French.*

This is the most popular variety in this country. It bears large roundish fruit, shaped much like the apple, which stews quite tender, and is of very excellent flavour. It also bears most abundant crops. Leaves oval.

There are several inferiour varieties of the apple quince. The true one bears fruit of the size of the largest apple, fair and smooth, and a fine golden colour.

2. Pear-shaped Quince. Thomp.

Oblong Quince.
Coignassier pyriforme, *of the French.*
Cydonier sub. v. pyriform, *Hort. Brit.*

The pear-shaped quince is dryer and of firmer texture than the foregoing. It is rather tough when stewed or cooked, the flesh is less lively in colour, and it is therefore much less esteem-ed than the apple-shaped variety. The fruit is of medium size, oblong, tapering to the stalk, and shaped much like a pear The skin is yellow. The leaves are oblong-ovate. It ripens about a fortnight later, and may be preserved in a raw state considerably longer.

3. Portugal Quince. Thomp.

Cydonia Lusitanica. *Hort. Brit.*
Coignassier de Portugal, *of the French.*

The Portugal quince is rather superior to all others in quality, as it is less harsh, stews much better, and is altogether of milder flavour, though not fit for eating raw. For marmalade and baking it is much esteemed, as its flesh turns a fine purple or deep crimson when cooked.

The leaf of the Portugal Quince is larger and broader than that of the common quince, and the growth of the tree is stronger. It is therefore preferred by many gardeners for stocks on which to work the pear.

The fruit is of the largest size, oblong. The skin is in colour not so deep an orange as that of the other sorts.

· The Portugal Quince is unfortunately a shy bearer, which is the reason why it has never been so generally cultivated as the Apple Quince.

Ornamental Varieties.—There are two or three ornamental varieties of the quince, which are natives of China and Japan, and are now among the most common and attractive of our garden shrubs. They are the following —

4. JAPAN QUINCE.

Cydonia Japonica. *Dec*
Pyrus Japonica. *Thunberg*

The Japan Quince is a low thorny shrub, with small dark green leaves. It is the most brilliant object in the shrubbery, during the month of April, the branches being clothed with numerous clusters of blossoms, shaped like those of the quince, but rather larger, and of the brightest scarlet. The fruit which occasionally succeeds these flowers, is dark green, very hard, and having a peculiar and not unpleasant smell. It is entirely useless.

The WHITE, or BLUSH JAPAN QUINCE (*C. jap. fl. albo*), resembles the foregoing, except that the flowers are white and pale pink, resembling those of the common apple-tree.

5. CHINESE QUINCE.

Cydonia Sinensis *Dec*

We have had this pretty shrub in our garden for several years, where it flowers abundantly, but has, as yet, produced no fruit. The leaves are oval, somewhat like those of the common quince, but with a shining surface. The flowers are rosy red, rather small, with a delicate violet odour, and have a very pretty effect in the month of May, though much less showy than those of the Japan Quince. The fruit is described as large. egg-shaped, with a green skin and a hard dry flesh, not of any value for eating. The leaves assume a beautiful shade of red in autumn.

CHAPTER XXV.

THE RASPBERRY AND BLACKBERRY

1. THE RASPBERRY

Rubus Idæus, 4: *Rosaceæ*, of botanists
Framboisier, of the French; *Himbeerstrauch*, German; *Framboos* Dutch, *Rova idea*, Italian; and *Frambueso*, Spanish.

THE Raspberry is a low deciduous shrub, which in several forms is common in the woods of both Europe and America

The large fruited varieties most esteemed in our gardens have all originated from the long cultivated *Rubus idæus*, or Mount Ida bramble, which appears first to have been introduced into the gardens of the South of Europe from Mount Ida. It is now quite naturalized in some parts of this country. Besides this, we have in the woods the common black raspberry, or thimble-berry (*Rubus occidentalis*, L.), and the red raspberry (*Rubus strigosus*, Michx.), with very good fruit.

The name raspberry (*Raspo*, Italian) is probably from the rasping roughness of prickly wood. The term *raspis* is still used in Scotland.

Uses.—The raspberry is held in general estimation, not only as one of the most refreshing and agreeable sub-acid fruits for the dessert, but it is employed by almost every family in making preserves, jams, ices, sauces, tarts and jellies; and on a larger scale by confectioners for making syrups, by distillers for making raspberry brandy, raspberry vinegar, &c. Raspberry wine, made in the same way as that of currant, is considered the most fragrant and delicious of all home-made wines.

Succeeding the strawberry at the beginning of summer, when there is comparatively little else, this is one of the most invalu-able fruits, and, with the strawberry, generally commands the attention of those who have scarcely room for fruit trees. It is, next to the strawberry, one of the most wholesome berries, and not being liable to undergo the acetous fermentation in the stomach, it is considered beneficial in cases of gout or rheu-matism.

Propagation.—The raspberry is universally propagated by suckers, or offsets, springing up from the main roots. Seeds are only planted when new varieties are desired. The seedlings come into bearing at two or three years of age.

Soil and Culture.—The best soil is a rich deep loam, rather moist than dry, but the raspberry will thrive well in any soil that is rich and deep, provided it is fully exposed to the sun and air.

In making a plantation of raspberries, choose, therefore, an open sunny quarter of the garden, where the soil is good and deep. Plant the suckers or canes in rows, from three to four feet apart, according to the vigour of the sort. Two or three suckers are generally planted together, to form a group or *stool*, and these stools may be three feet apart in the rows.

The plantation being made, its treatment consists chiefly in a single pruning, every year, given early in the spring. To perform this, examine the stools in April, and leaving the strong-est shoots or suckers, say about six or eight to each stool, cut away all the old wood, and all the other suckers (except such as are wanted for new plantations). The remaining shoots should have about a foot of their ends cut off, as this part of the wood is feeble and worthless. With a light top-dressing of manure, the ground should then be dug over, and little other care will be requisite during the season.

When very neat culture and the largest fruit are desired, more space is left between the rows, and after being pruned, the canes are tied to long lines of rods or rails, like an espalier, by which means they are more fully exposed to the sun and light, and the ground between the rows is kept cropped with small vegetables.

A fine late crop of raspberries is readily obtained by cutting down the canes over the whole stool, in the spring, to within a few inches of the ground. They will then shoot up new wood, which comes into bearing in August or September.

We have found a light application of salt given with the top-dressing of manure in the spring, to have a most beneficial effect on the vigour of the plants, and the size of the fruit.

A plantation of raspberries will be in perfection at the third year, and after it has borne about five or six years, it must be broken up, and a new one formed, on another plot of ground.

In New England, and the northern part of this State, the Antwerp raspberries are often liable to be killed to the ground by severe winters. In such situations, it is customary to prune them in fall, after which the canes are bent down, and covered lightly with earth or branches of evergreens till spring. Here, and to the south of this place, this is not necessary.

VARIETIES.—The finest raspberries in general cultivation for the dessert, are the Red and the White Antwerp. The Franconia is a fine, large, and productive variety, greatly esteemed at the North and East, as being hardier and later in ripening than the Antwerp. The Fastolff is a new and uncommonly fine fruit, which deserves a place in every garden. The common American Red is most esteemed for flavouring liqueurs or making brandy, and the American Black is preferred by most persons for cooking. The Ever-bearing and the Ohio Ever-bearing, are valuable for prolonging the season of this fruit till late frosts.

1. ANTWERP, RED.§   P. Mag. Thomp.

New Red Antwerp	Burley
True Red Antwerp	Knevet's Antwerp.
Howland's Red Antwerp	Framboisier à Gros Fruit.

The Red Antwerp is the standard variety for size, flavour, and productiveness, wherever it is known. It is a Dutch sort, originally from Antwerp city. It bears early and abundantly with us, and is one of the most profitable native fruits.

Fruit very large, conical, dull red ; flavour rich and sweet.

Canes moderately strong, yellowish green, becoming pale brown early in autumn, covered below with dark brown bristles; but the upper portions, especially, of the bearing wood, nearly smooth. Leaves large, plaited. The fruit commences ripening about the 10th of July, rather before the other varieties.

The COMMON RED ANTWERP, as known in this country, is a very inferior variety of the foregoing, with fruit half the size, less conical, and canes stronger, and more inclined to branch. It is not worth cultivating when compared with the foregoing, though it is almost universally known as the Red Antwerp, in this country—whence we are often obliged to call the foregoing the true, or New Red Antwerp, to prevent its being confounded with the common and inferior sort.

2. ANTWERP, YELLOW.§ Thomp. Lind.

White Antwerp.
Double Bearing Yellow.

The Yellow Antwerp is the largest and finest light coloured raspberry, and indispensable to every good garden.

Fruit large, nearly conical, pale yellow, sweet and excellent. Canes strong and vigorous, light yellow, with many bristles or spines. On successive suckers, which shoot up, this raspberry will frequently continue somewhat in bearing for months.

3. AMERICAN RED.

Common Red.
English Red (*of some*).
Rubus Strigosus (*Michx*).*

The Common Red Raspberry is a native of this, and all the middle states. It ripens nearly a week earlier than the Antwerps, bears well, and though inferior in flavour and size to these sorts, is esteemed by many persons, particularly for flavouring liqueurs.

Fruit of medium size, roundish, light red, pleasant sub-acid in flavour. Shoots very vigorous, long, upright, and branching, grows from six to ten feet high. Light shining brown, with purplish spines. Leaves narrow, light green.

4. AMERICAN BLACK.

Common Black-cap.
Black Raspberry.
Thimble-berry.
Rubus Occidentalis

* This strongly resembles the Common Red Raspberry of Europe, *R. Idœus*, but according to Torrey and Gray is quite distinct.

This raspberry, common in almost every field, with long rambling purple shoots, and flattened small black berries, is everywhere known. It is frequently cultivated in gardens, where, if kept well pruned, its fruit is much larger and finer Its rich acid flavour renders it, perhaps, the finest sort for kitchen use—tarts, puddings, &c. It ripens later than other raspberries.

The AMERICAN WHITE resembles the foregoing in all respects, except in the colour of its fruit, which is pale yellow or white.

5. BARNET. P. Mag. Thomp.

Cornwall's Prolific.
Cornwall's Seedling.
Lord Exmouth's.
Large Red.

The Barnet is a very large and fine English variety. considerably resembling the Red Antwerp ; it ripens early, and is very productive, though not so good a market fruit, as it does not bear carriage well.

Fruit very large, roundish-conical, bright transparent purplish red, flavour very rich and agreeable. Canes long, yellowish green, branching much more, especially towards the ground, than the Red Antwerp, and covered with numerous slender bristles, which are stronger towards the top of the cane. They become dull brown early in autumn. Bearing shoots nearly smooth.

6. BRENTFORD CANE. Thomp

A pretty good fruit, though much inferior to the best. Fruit of medium size, oval-conical, dark dull red Canes strong, branching, with purplish prickles.

7. CRETAN RED. Pom. Man.

A rather late variety, of good quality, introduced some years ago from the Mediterranean. Its lateness renders it valuable, but it is inferior to the Franconia, which has taken its place in most of our gardens. It is a hardy sort.

Fruit of medium size, globular, inclining to conical, deep purplish-red, sub-acid and good Canes upright, branches dark grey, with few bristles. Leaves rather narrow ; dark green, but very light coloured on the lower side. It ripens about two weeks after the White Antwerp, and continues several weeks in perfection.

8. DOUBLE BEARING.   Thomp.

Perpetual Bearing.
Siberian.
Late Cane.

A very good variety of the Antwerp Raspberry, chiefly es-
eemed for its habit of bearing late in the season. A finer crop,
which will continue ripening till late frosts, is obtained by cut-
ing down the shoots to within a few inches of the ground, every
spring. It is a hardy variety.

There is a TWICE BEARING Raspberry known in some gardens
in this country, which is an inferior small fruit, and bears
sparingly.

9. FRANCONIA.§

The hardiest large Raspberry, very productive, and very
excellent. It was imported from Vilmorin, of Paris, under this
name (which does not appear in any foreign catalogues) by S.
G. Perkins, Esq., of Boston, some years ago. It flourishes admirably in New England, and north of us, where the climate is
too cold for the Antwerps, and is by far the finest variety for a
northern latitude. Its crops are abundant, the fruit is firm,
and bears carriage to market well, and it ripens about a week
or ten days later than the Red Antwerp. It is perhaps the
finest sort for preserving.

Fruit very large, obtuse conical, dark purplish red, of a rich
acid flavour, more tart and brisk than that of the Red Antwerp.
Canes strong, spreading, branching, yellowish brown, with
scattered, rather stout, bristles. Leaves rather narrow, and
long, deep green.

10. FASTOLFF.§

The Fastolff Raspberry is a new English variety of the
highest reputation. It derives its name from having originated
near the ruins of an old castle, so called, in Great Yarmouth.
It fruited with us last season, and fully sustained its character
as the finest Red Raspberry known. The fruit is of the richest
flavour, and is borne for a long time in succession. It ripens
about the same time as the Red Antwerp.

Fruit very large, obtuse, or roundish conical, bright purplish
red, very rich and high flavoured. Canes strong, rather erect,
branching, light yellowish brown, with pretty strong bristles.

44

11. Knever's Giant.

A capital English Raspberry, a variety of Red Antwerp, ripening among the very earliest. Its canes are very strong, and quite hardy. The fruit is very large, conical, deep red, and of excellent flavour

12. Nottingham Scarlet.

An excellent variety, introduced from England by Col. Wilder, of Boston. He considers it the richest in flavour of any of the older varieties. The fruit is red, obtuse-conical, of medium size.

13. Ohio, Everbearing.

Ohio Raspberry. *Ken.*

This is a native of Ohio, and was first made known to Eastern cultivators by Mr. Longworth, of Cincinnati, though, we believe, it had been cultivated for some time previous, at a Quaker settlement, in Ohio. It is precisely like the American Black Raspberry, or Black-cap, in all respects, except that it has the valuable property of bearing abundant crops of fine fruit, till late in the season. We have seen a quart gathered from a single plant, on the 1st day of November. It deserves a place in every large garden.

14. Victoria.

A new English seedling of high reputation, not yet fairly tested here. It is said to resemble and fully equal the Red Antwerp, in size and flavour, and to be everbearing in its habits —producing an abundant crop from July to December, on numerous side branches which it throws out, from eighteen inches to two feet long. Its value will soon be fully proved in this country.

II. The Blackberry.

There are several species of the Bramble indigenous to this country, which produce eatable fruit, but the two best for the table, or for cooking, are the Low Blackberry, a trailing shrub, and the High Blackberry, a bush about four or five feet high.

The fruit is larger than that of the Raspberry, with fewer and larger grains, and a brisker flavour. It ripens about the last of July, or early in August, after the former is past, and is much used by all classes in this country. The sorts are seldom cultivated in gardens, as the fruit is produced in such great abundance in a wild state; but there is no doubt that varieties of much larger size, and greatly superiour flavour, might be produced by sowing the seeds in rich garden soil, especially if repeated for two or three successive generations.

1. Low Blackberry.

Trailing Blackberry.
Dewberry.
Rubus Canadensis. *Lin.*

A low, trailing, prickly shrub, producing large white blossoms in May, and very large roundish-oblong black fruit in midsummer. Leaflets from three to five in number. The fruit, when in good soil, and fully exposed to the sun, is high flavoured, sweet, and excellent.

2. High Blackberry.

Bush Blackberry.
Rubus Villosus. *Tor. and Gray.*

This is an erect growing blackberry, the stems tall, and more or less branching. In its foliage it resembles the foregoing, but its flowers, which are white, are smaller. The fruit is also smaller, rounder, not so dark coloured (being reddish-black), and though good, is seldom so juicy or high flavoured.

There is a variety, cultivated abroad, with *white* fruit.

Ornamental Varieties. The Double-White-Blossomed, *and* Double Pink-blossomed Brambles, are beautiful climbing shrubs, of remarkably luxuriant growth, which may be trained for a great length in a season, and are admirably adapted for covering walls and unsightly buildings. The flowers are like small double roses, and are produced in numerous clusters in June, having a very pretty effect. North of New York these climbers are rather tender in severe winters.

The Rose Flowering Bramble (*Rubus odoratus*) is a very pretty native shrub, with large broad leaves, and pleasing rose-coloured flowers, and groups well with other shrubs in ornamental plantations.

CHAPTER XXVI.

THE STRAWBERRY.

Fragaria (of species) L   *Rosaceæ,* of botanists.
Frasier, of the French, *Erdoeerpflanze,* German, *Aadbezie,* Dutch;
Pianta di Fragola, Italian; and *Fresa,* Spanish.

THE Strawberry is the most delicious and the most wholesome
of all berries, and the most universally cultivated in all gardens
of northern climates. It is a native of the temperate latitudes
of both hemispheres,—of Europe, Asia, North and South America; though the species found in different parts of the world
are of distinct habit, and have each given rise, through cultivation, to different classes of fruit—scarlet strawberries, pine
strawberries, wood strawberries, hautbois, &c.

The name of this fruit is popularly understood to have arisen
from the common and ancient practice of laying straw between
the plants to keep the fruit clean. In the olden times the variety of strawberry was very limited, and the garden was chiefly
supplied with material for new plantations from the woods. Old
Tusser, in his "Five Hundred Points of Good Husbandry,"
points out where the best plants of his time were to be had, and
turns them over, with an abrupt, farmer-like contempt of little
matters, to feminine hands :—

> "Wife, into the garden, and set me a plot
> With strawberry roots, of the best to be got,
> Such growing abroad, among thorns in the wood,
> Well chosen and picked, prove excellent good."

The strawberry belongs properly to cold climates, and though
well known, is of comparatively little value in the south of
Europe. Old Roman and Greek poets have not therefore sung
its praises; but after that line of a northern bard,

> " A dish of ripe strawberries, smothered in cream,"

which we consider a perfect *pastoral idyl* (as the German
school would say), in itself, nothing remains to be wished for.
We have heard of individuals who really did not, by nature,
relish strawberries, but we confess that we have always had
the same doubts of their existence as we have of that of the
unicorn.

Ripe, blushing, strawberries, eaten from the plant, or served with sugar and cream, are certainly Arcadian dainties with a true paradisiacal flavour, and fortunately, they are so easily grown that the poorest owner of a few feet of ground may have them in abundance.

To the confectioner this fruit is also invaluable, communicating its flavour to ices, and forming several delicate preserves. In Paris a cooling drink, *bavaroise à la grecque*, is made of the juice of strawberries and lemons, with the addition of sugar and water.

The strawberry is perhaps the most wholesome of all fruits, being very easy of digestion, and never growing acid by fermentation as most other fruits do. The often quoted instance of the great Linnæus curing himself of the gout by partaking freely of strawberries—a proof of its great wholesomeness—is a letter of credit which this tempting fruit has long enjoyed, for the consolation of those who are looking for a bitter concealed under every sweet.

PROPAGATION AND SOIL. The strawberry propagates itself very rapidly by runners* which are always taken to form new plantations or beds. These are taken off the parent plants early in August, and either planted at once where they are to grow, or put out in nursery beds, or rows, to get well established for the next spring planting. When the parent plants have become degenerated, or partially, or wholly barren, we should avoid taking the runners from such, and choose only those which grow from the most fruitful ones. In order to be sure of the latter point it is only necessary to mark the best bearing plants by small sticks pushed into the bed by the side of each when the fruit is in perfection. Some varieties, as the Prolific Hautbois, the English wood, and the Large Early Scarlet, are not liable to this deterioration, and therefore it is not necessary to select the runners carefully; but others, as the Pine strawberries, and some of the Scarlets, are very liable to it, and if the runners are taken and planted promiscuously, the beds, so made, will be nearly barren.

The best soil for the strawberry is a deep, rich, loam. Deep it must be, if large berries and plentiful crops are desired; and the wisest course, therefore, where the soil is naturally thin, lies in trenching and manuring the plot of ground thoroughly, before putting out the plants. But even if this is not necessary it should be dug deeply, and well enriched with strong manure beforehand.

The best exposure for strawberries is an open one, fully exposed to the sun and light.

* Excepting the *Bush* Alpines, which have no runners, and are propagated by division of the roots.

44*

CULTURE IN ROWS. The finest strawberries are always ob
tained when the plants are kept in *rows*, at such a distance apart
as to give sufficient space for the roots, and abundance of light
and air for the leaves.

In planting a plot of strawberries in rows, the rows should be
two feet apart, and the plants, of the large growing kinds, two
feet from each other in the rows; of the smaller growing kinds,
from one foot to eighteen inches is sufficient. The runners must
be kept down by cutting them off at least three times a year, and
the ground must be maintained in good order by constant dressing. During the first year a row of any small vegetables may
be sown in the spaces between the rows. Every autumn, if the
plants are not luxuriant, a light coat of manure should be dug
in between the rows; but if they are very thrifty it must be
omitted, as it would cause them to run too much to leaf.

A light top-dressing of leaves, or any good compost, applied late
in the fall, though not necessary, greatly promotes the vigor of
the plants, and secures the more tender kinds against the effects
of an unusually cold winter. Before the fruit ripens, the
ground between the rows should be covered with straw, or light
new-mown grass, to keep it clean.

A plantation of this kind in rows, will be found to bear the
largest and finest fruit, which, being so fully exposed to the
sun, will always be sweeter and higher flavoured than that
grown in crowded beds. A plantation in rows is generally
in full perfection the third year, and must always be renewed
after the fourth year.

CULTURE IN ALTERNATE STRIPS. A still more easy and economical mode is that of growing the strawberry in alternate
strips.

Early in April, or in August, being provided with a good
stock of strong young plants, select a suitable piece of good
deep soil. Dig in a heavy coat of stable manure, pulverizing
well and raking the top soil. Strike out the rows, three feet
apart, with a line. The plants should now be planted along
each line about a foot apart in the row. They will soon
send out runners, and these runners should be allowed to take
possession of every alternate strip of three feet—the other strip
being kept bare by continually destroying all runners upon it,
the whole patch being kept free of all weeds. The occupied
strip or bed of runners will now give a heavy crop of strawberries, and the open strip of three feet will serve as an alley from
which to gather the fruit. After the crop is over, dig and prepare this alley or strip for the occupancy of the new runners
for the next season's crop. The runners from the old strip will
now speedily cover the new space allotted to them, and will perhaps require a partial thinning out to have them evenly distributed. As soon as this is the case, say about the middle of

August, dig under the whole of the old plants with a light coa.; of manure. The surface may be then sown with turnips or spinage, which will come off before the next season of fruits.

In this way the strips or beds, occupied by the plants, are reversed every season, and the same plot of ground may thus be continued in a productive state for many years.

Both of the above modes are so superior to the common one of growing them more closely in *beds*, that we shall not give any directions respecting the latter.

It may be remarked that the Alpine and European Wood strawberries will do well, and bear longer in a rather shaded situation. The Bush-Alpine, an excellent sort, having no runners, makes one of the neatest *borders* for quarters or beds in the kitchen garden, and produces considerable fruit till the season of late frosts. If the May crop of blossoms is taken off, they will give an abundant crop in September, and they are, therefore, very desirable in all gardens.

To accelerate the ripening of early kinds in the open garden it is only necessary to plant rows or beds on the south side of a wall or tight fence. A still simpler mode, by which their maturity may be hastened ten days, is that of throwing up a ridge of soil three feet high, running east and west, and planting it in rows on the south side. (The north side may also be planted with later sorts, which will be somewhat retarded in ripening.) The best early sorts for this purpose are Duke of Kent, and Large Early Scarlet.

Staminate and Pistillate Plants.—A great number of experiments have been made, and a great deal has been written lately, in this country, regarding the most certain mode of producing *large crops* of this fruit. On one hand it is certain that, with the ordinary modes of cultivation, many fine kinds of strawberries have disappointed their cultivators by becoming barren; on the other, it is equally certain, that, by the mode of cultivation practised at Cincinnati, large crops may be obtained every year.

The Cincinnati cultivators divide all Strawberries into two classes, characterized by their *blossoms*. The first of these they call *staminate* (or male), from the stamens being chiefly developed; the second are called *pistillate* (or female), from the pistils being chiefly developed.

The first class, to which belong various sorts, as Keen's Seedling, British Queen, etc., usually in this climate bear uncertain crops, from the fact that only a part of the blossoms develop the pistils sufficiently to swell into perfect fruit.

The second class, to which belong various other sorts, such as Hovey's Seedling, Black Prince, etc., producing only pistil-bearing flowers, do not set fruit at all when grown quite apart by themselves; but when grown near a proper number of staminate plants, so as to be duly fertilized by them, they bear much larger crops, of much more perfect berries, than can be produced in this climate in any other way.

This is no longer a matter of theory, for the market of Cincinnati, in which are sold six thousand bushels of strawberries annually, is supplied more abundantly and regularly than perhaps any other in the world, by this very mode of culture.

In planting strawberry beds, it is important, therefore, to the cultivator, to know which are the *staminate,* and which the *pistillate,* varieties—as they are found to be permanent in these characters. We have, accordingly, designated these traits in the descriptions of the varieties which follow.

Upon the relative proportion of *staminate* to pistillate plants, cultivators are not absolutely agreed. Where, however, such hardy sorts as the Large Early Scarlet, or the Duke of Kent, are chosen for *staminates,* it is sufficient to plant *one-fourth* as many of these as of *pistillates,* to insure a full crop of the latter. When staminate sorts, like Keen's Seedling, or like less hardy kinds, are chosen, then the proportion should be *one-third* to two-thirds of pistillates.

Thus, in planting in the *alternate strip* mode, let every twelve feet of each strip be planted with Hovey's Seedling, (*pistillate,*) and the succeeding four feet with Large Early Scarlet. A very little trouble, bestowed when the runners are extending across the open spaces, will preserve the proportion good from year to year. The appearance of a plat, planted in this way, will be as follows : S representing *staminate,* and P *pistillate,* varieties.

In planting in beds, the same course may be adopted, or, what is perhaps better, every third or fourth bed may be entirely staminate, and the rest pistillate sorts (the beds in this case being supposed to be side by side).

Nothing is easier than to distinguish the two classes of strawberries when in blossom. In one, the *staminate,* the long yellow anthers (*a*), bearing the fine dust or pollen, are abundant ; in the other, the *pistillate,* only the cluster of pistils (*b*), looking like a very minute green strawberry, is visible—(that is to the common observer, for the wanting organs are merely *rudimentary,* and not developed).

Fig. 211. *Strawberry Blossoms.*

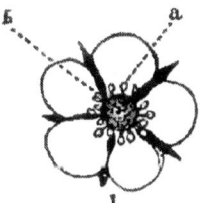  

Perfect blossom.   Staminate blossom.   Pistillate blossom

Besides these, there is really a third class, quite distinct, the blossoms of which are regularly hermaphrodite, or *perfect*, in themselves, and which always bear excellent crops—though not perhaps so large as some of the most prolific of the pistillates do when fertilized. To this belong the common English Wood Strawberries and the Alpines. Hence, these old inhabitants of the gardens have, from their uniform productiveness, long been favourites with many who have not understood the character and habits of the larger staminate and pistillate varieties. Fig. 211 (*d*) shows the blossom of this class of strawberries.

VARIETIES.—The varieties of this fruit are very numerous, indeed quite unnecessarily so for all useful purposes. They have chiefly been originated abroad within the last thirty years. The different species from which the varieties have been raised, have given a character to certain classes of Strawberries, pretty distinctly marked. Thus, from our own Wild Strawberry, or Virginia Scarlet, as it is called abroad, have originated the Scarlet Strawberries; from the Pine or Surinam Strawberry has been raised the class called Pines. From the common Wood Strawberry of Europe, another class, comprising the Woods and Alpines. Beside, there are the Hautbois, from a sort, a native of Bohemia, the Chili Strawberries, from South America, the Green Strawberries, and the Black Strawberries.

Of these the Pines and the Scarlets are the largest and highest flavoured. The Wood and Alpine Strawberries are valuable for bearing a long time, and parting freely from the hull or stalk, in picking.

Class I. Scarlet Strawberries.

[Flowers small. Leaves rather long, of thin texture, and rather light colour, with sharp serratures; the fruit of a bright colour, and a sub-acid flavour: the seed sunk in ridged intervals. Fruit medium or large, acid or sub-acid.]

1. BISHOP'S ORANGE.§

Bishop's New.
Orange Hudson Bay:

A handsome and very highly flavoured variety, which has proved of the finest quality, in the Middle States, when planted in rich, deep, sandy soils. The fruit is a beautiful light scarlet, somewhat approaching orange—of large size, very regularly shaped, conical, borne in large clusters lying on the surface. Flesh firm. Flavour very high. Leaves hairy. Ripens rather late, and bears well. Pistillate.

### 2. BLACK ROSEBERRY.	Thomp.

A good, nearly round Strawberry, of rather large size, and a fine, dark, purplish-red colour. Flesh firm, with an excellent, rather peculiar flavour. Only a moderate bearer.

3. DUNDEE.§

A capital Scotch variety, extensively cultivated here, and esteemed for its great productiveness and hardiness. Leaves very long, foot-stalks and fruit also, supported on long stalks in large clusters. Fruit pretty large, roundish oval, regularly formed, and of a fine light scarlet. Flesh firm, and of a rich acid flavour. It ripens pretty late—at the same season as the Hudson Bay. Pistillate.

### 4. DUKE OF KENT'S SCARLET.	Thomp.

Austrian Scarlet, *Lind.*	Globe Scarlet.
Nova Scotia Scarlet	Early Prolific Scarlet, &c

We have long cultivated this, which is the earliest of all Strawberries. The fruit is rather small, and the sort is altogether inferior to the large Early Scarlet which ripens a week later. Still, it is valuable where the earliest fruit is desired. Fruit small, varying from roundish, to long conical; bright scarlet: flavour sharp and good. Ripens here in the middle or last of May. Flowers staminate.

5. GROVE END SCARLET. Thomp.

Atkinson Scarlet.

A very handsome English Strawberry, but not esteemed here so much as the Large Early Scarlet. Leaves very widely serrated. Fruit of medium size, very bright vermillion scarlet, globular and flattened. Seeds slightly imbedded. Flesh of a pleasant, mild flavour. Ripens pretty early. Staminate.

6. HUDSON'S BAY. Thomp.

Hudson.	American Scarlet. (*of some.*)
Late Scarlet.	York River Scarlet. *etc.*

The Hudson Strawberry is perhaps more celebrated than any other for the markets of Philadelphia and New-York. Its great firmness enables it to bear carriage well, and its deep acid flavour, and the late season at which it ripens, have made it the most popular sort for preserving.

Fruit pretty large, ovate (with a neck), of a rich dark shining red. Seeds deeply imbedded. Flesh very firm, of a high, but brisk acid flavour. It should therefore be allowed to hang late Ripens late, after most of the scarlets are gone. Hudson's Bay.

7. LARGE EARLY SCARLET. Pom. Man.

The finest of all very early Strawberries, a regular, very abundant, and excellent bearer and indispensable in every garden. The flowers generally perfect. It is an American variety, the leaves rather broad, and the flowers larger than the most of its class. It is so superiour to the *Old Scarlet* as to entirely supersede it wherever known.

Fruit pretty large, roundish ovate, regularly formed, handsome light scarlet, seeds deeply imbedded. Flesh tender, of a rich, excellent flavour. Ripens before all the other sorts, but Duke of Kent's Scarlet. Staminate.

8. METHVEN'S SCARLET. Thomp.

Methven Castle.
Southampton Scarlet.
Warren's Seedling.

An immense fruit, but hollow and of rather coarse flavour. The leaves are very broad. Fruit of the largest size, roundish or cockscomb shaped, rather dull scarlet. Flesh soft, and of indifferent flavour. Seeds not deeply imbedded. Ripens at medium season.

[About Philadelphia, this sort was, a year or two ago, pretty generally cultivated as the Keen's Seedling, a very different fruit.]

9. MELON

A very good Scotch variety of dwarfish habit, and quite productive Fruit of medium size, roundish, of very darkish colour; flavour rich and good.

10. OLD SCARLET. Thomp

Original Scarlet.		Scarlet.
Virginia Scarlet		Early Scarlet.

This is the common wild strawberry of this country, and is the type of the class. It is here quite supplanted by the Large Early Scarlet. Fruit roundish-conical, bright scarlet, and deeply imbedded; flesh of good flavour. It ripens pretty early, three or four days after the Large Early Scarlet. Staminate.

11. ROSEBERRY.

Aberdeen.
Roseberry
Scotch Scarlet

A very good Strawberry not so much liked here as the Dundee, another Scotch variety. The fruit-stalks are short. It ripens gradually in succession, with a very short neck, dark red. Flesh firm, of tolerably good flavour. Ripens at a medium season. Flowers pistillate.

Class II. Pine Strawberries.*

[Flowers large, leaves rather broad, dark green with obtuse serratures; seeds prominent, on a smooth surface, fruit large, rich and sweet.]

12. BLACK PRINCE. Thorp.

Black Imperial.

The Black Prince which we imported a few years since from England, proves a variety of rare merit for this climate. The plants are very hardy, the fruit very handsome and large, always very dark polished red—almost black, roundish, or ovate

* We include in this class the small class of BLACK STRAWBERRIES of the English authors, which we do not think need really be considered distinct from the Pines, to which they have so much affinity.

depressed ; seeds slightly imbedded ; flesh firm, very rich and high flavoured. It always bears heavily almost without care with us. It is highly worthy of a general trial in different sections of the country. Flowers pistillate.

13. BREWER'S EMPEROR.

A recent English variety. It may be compared in size and flavour to Keen's Seedling, with the great superiority for our climate, of being quite hardy and an abundant bearer. Fruit large, ovate, dark red, excellent. Medium season. Staminate.

14. DOWNTON. Thomp.

Knight's Seedling.

A very rich flavoured late Strawberry, but so uncertain in its crops as to have been nearly abandoned by our cultivators. The leaves are small and light green, but with the coarse serratures of this class. Fruit-stalks very long and upright. Fruit pretty large, with a neck, ovate, or cockscomb-shaped, dark purplish scarlet ; grains not deeply imbedded ; flesh firm, very rich and aromatic. Flowers staminate.

15. ELTON. Thomp.

Elton Seedling. Lind.

A very delicious, and very late Strawberry, ripening some time after most varieties have passed by. The plants are rather tender, and north of Philadelphia, require a slight covering of straw in winter, which the amateurs will not grudge so excellent a sort. Leaves rather smaller and paler than in most of this class.

Fruit large, ovate, most frequently cockscomb-shaped ; glossy, light red at first, but when fully ripe, dark red ; flesh rather firm, with a very rich flavour. Flowers staminate.

45

16. HOVEY'S SEEDLING. § Hov. Mag.

This splendid Strawberry was raised, in 1834, by Messrs. Hovey, seedsmen, of Boston, and is undoubtedly, for this climate, one of the finest of all varieties. The vines are unusually vigorous and hardy, producing very large crops, and the fruit is always of the largest size and finely flavoured. It is well known at the present moment throughout all the states, and has everywhere proved superior, for all general purposes, to any other large-fruited kind. The leaves are large, rather light green, and the fruit-stalk long and erect.

Fruit very large, roundish oval, or slightly conical, deep shining scarlet, seeds slightly imbedded; flesh firm, with a rich, agreeable flavour. It ripens about the medium season, or a few days after it. Flowers pistillate.

17. KEEN'S SEEDLING. Thomp.

Keen's Black Pine.
Murphy's Child.

This Strawberry, raised in 1821 by Keen of Isleworth, the celebrated English strawberry grower, has, ever since its introduction, enjoyed in England the highest reputation for productiveness and excellence. In this country, though of the finest quality, it proves too tender for general cultivation, and has been supplanted by Ross' Phœnix, a perfectly hardy sort, fully equal to it, and by Hovey's Seedling.

Fruit very large, roundish, usually a little depressed, often cockscomb-shaped, dark purplish scarlet, surface polished, seeds slightly imbedded, flesh firm, with a rich, high flavour. It ripens pretty early. Spurious sorts, especially the Methven Scarlet, are often sold for this, in this country. Staminate.

18. MYATT'S BRITISH QUEEN. Thomp.

The largest, finest, and most productive, of all the new Strawberries that have lately been originated in England. The fruit is borne on tall footstalks, and the leaves are large. Its qualities for general culture are not generally tested yet in different parts of the country ; but unfortunately it proves rather tender in our winters.

Fruit of monstrous size, roundish, occasionally of cockscomb shape, rich scarlet colour, flavour rich and excellent. It ripens pretty early. Flowers staminate.

19. MYATT'S PINE. Thomp.

A very large and splendid fruit of the richest flavour, but difficult of cultivation and usually a shy bearer. It requires a deep rich soil, rather light and warm, and the bed to be renewed every year. The fruit is large, round, bright scarlet, supported high, on stout footstalks. Flowers staminate.

20. MYATT'S DEPTFORD PINE.§

The Deptford Pine is a superb new English variety which we have just proved in this country. It is quite hardy, far more so than the British Queen, and will therefore be much more esteemed here. The leaves are very downy underneath ; the fruit is of extraordinary size, wedge shaped, of a clear bright scarlet. Flesh firm and solid, with a rich and excellent flavour. Ripens at the medium season, and is likely to prove hardy and productive. Flowers staminate.

21. MYATT'S ELIZA.

One of the new sorts, second-rate in flavour, but hardy, though the plants make few runners   Fruit large, handsome and juicy.

22. PRINCE ALBERT.

A very large and showy new English variety and a good bearer, but of second rate flavour as compared with Ross' Phœnix or Hovey's Seedling.   Fruit of the largest size, ovate, rich scarlet; flesh rather soft and not high flavoured.   Staminate.

23. OLD PINE, OR CAROLINA.   Thomp.

Pine Apple.	Old Carolina.
Carolina.	Blood Pine.
Old Scarlet Pine.	Grandiflora.

The Old Pine or Carolina Strawberry is believed to have been carried from Carolina to England many years ago, and nearly all this class of strawberries have been directly or indirectly raised from it.   It is one of the very richest flavoured sorts.   Still, it is only rarely seen in our gardens, as it requires a rich soil and a considerable degree of care to get crops of fruit

Fruit large, conical, with a longish neck, sometimes cockscomb shaped ; uniform bright scarlet, grains slightly imbedded ; flesh solid, juicy, and very rich in flavour.   Ripens at the middle of the season.   Flowers staminate.

24. Ross' Phœnix.

Ross' Phœnix appears to be suited only to particular soils. In such, it certainly has all the good qualities of the celebrated Keen's Seedling, and is more hardy than that excellent old variety. It appears to demand a *deep loamy* soil; in such we have seen this sort succeed with the commonest culture, and produce fine crops of truly splendid fruit in gardens where the finest English Pines generally failed with much greater care. It is a native seedling, raised in 1837, by Mr. Alexander Ross, of Hudson, N. Y., from the Keen's Seedling, which it most resembles, but the leaves are broader, very dark green, with very coarse serratures, and lie close to the ground. The clusters of fruit are very large.

Fruit very large, generally cockscomb-shaped, or compressed,
45*

of a very dark purplish red, with a polished surface. Flesh firm, of the richest pine flavour. Ripens about the medium season. **Flowers staminate.**

25. SWAINSTONE'S SEEDLING. Thomp.

A new variety, from England, which fruited well in this country last season, and gives promise of being a very hardy and valuable sort. It ripens quite early, but the fruit matures a long time in succession, and sometimes a second crop is borne in autumn. It grows very strongly, the foliage and flowers are large, and the footstalks long. Fruit large, ovate, of a beautiful light, glossy scarlet, flavour very delicious. Staminate.

Class III. *Alpine and Wood Strawberries.*

[Flowers rather small. Leaves quite small, light green, and quite thin. Fruit small, roundish in the Wood Strawberries, and conical in the Alpines, parting more readily from the stalk than other sorts, with very tender sweet flesh.]

26. RED WOOD. Thomp.

English Red Wood.
Common Rouge.
Des Bois à Fruit Rouge.

This is the wild strawberry of Europe (F. vesca), long more commonly cultivated in our gardens than any other sort, and still, perhaps, the easiest of cultivation, and one of the most desirable kinds. It always bears abundantly, and though the fruit is small, yet it is produced for a much longer time than that of the other classes of strawberries, and is very sweet and delicate in flavour. Flowers always perfect.

Fruit red, small, roundish-ovate. Seeds set even with the surface of the fruit. It ripens at medium season.

27. WHITE WOOD. Thomp.

This is precisely similar in all respects to the foregoing, except in its colour, which is white. It ripens at the same time.

28. RED ALPINE. Thomp.

Red Monthly Strawberry.
Des Alpes à Fruit Rouge.
Des Alpes de Tous les Mois à Fruit Rouge, &c.

The common Red Alpine or monthly bearing strawberry, a native of the Alps. and succeeds well with very trifling care in this country. The A.pines always continue bearing from June till November; but a very fine autumnal crop is secured, by cutting off all the spring blossoms. The plant resembles the Red Wood, and the fruit is similar in flavour and colour, but long-conical in form. Flowers always perfect.

29. WHITE ALPINE. Thomp.

White Monthly,
Des Alpes à Fruit Blanc.
Des Alpes de tous les mois à Fruit Blanc, &c.

Precisely similar to the Red Alpine, except in colour. Fruit conical, white.

30. RED BUSH ALPINE.§ Thomp.

Monthly, without Runners.
Buisson.
Commun sans Filets.
Des Alpes sans Filets

The Bush Alpines are remarkable among strawberries for their total destitution of runners. Hence they always grow in neat compact bunches, and are preferred by many persons for edging beds in the kitchen garden. The fruit is conical, and the whole plant, otherwise, is quite similar to common Alpines. We think it one of the most desirable sorts, and it bears abundantly through the whole season. The Bush Alpines were first introduced into the United States by the late Andrew Parmentier, of Brooklyn. To propagate them the roots are divided. Flowers always perfect.

31. WHITE BUSH ALPINE.§ Thomp.

White Monthly, without Runners.
Buisson des Alpes Blanc, &c.

This differs from the foregoing only in the colour of the fruit, which is conical and white.

Class IV. Hautbois Strawberries.*

[Leaves large, and crumpled, pale green, supported on tall stalks. Fruit stalk tall and erect. Fruit, pale at first, dull purplish at maturity.]

32. PROLIFIC, OR CONICAL.§ Thomp.

Musk Hautbois.	Double Bearing
French Musk Hautbois.	Caperon Royal
Caperon Hermaphrodite.	

* *Haut-bois*, literally *high-wood*, that is, wood strawberries with high leaves and fruit stalks.

This is a cap.tal variety, and the only one of this class that we consider worth cultivating here.   Its strong habit, and very large, usually perfect, flowers, borne high above the leaves, distinguish it.   The fruit is very large and fine, dark coloured, with a peculiarly rich, slightly musky flavour.   It bears, most abundant crops.   Fruit large, conical, light purple in the shade dark blackish purple in the sun, seeds prominent, flesh rather firm, sweet and excellent   It ripens tolerably early, and some. times gives a second crop.   Staminate.

The COMMON HAUTBOIS, GLOBE, LARGE FLAT, &c., are scarcely worthy of cultivation here.

Class V. Chili Strawberries.

[Originally from Chili.   The leaves are very hairy, the leaflets thick and obtusely serrated ; the fruit of monstrous size, pale colour, and rather insipid flavour.   They are too tender to withstand our cold winters well]

33. TRUE CHILI.   Thomp.

> Patagonian
> Greenwell's new Giant
> Greenwell's French.

Fruit very large, bluntly conical or ovate, dull red, seeds dark brown, projecting, flesh very firm, hollow-cored, of a rather indifferent, sweet flavour.   Ripens late.

34. WILMOT'S SUPERB.   Thomp.

An English seedling, raised from the foregoing—very showy in size, but indifferent fruit and a poor bearer.   Fruit roundish, sometimes cockscomb shaped, surface pale scarlet, polished, seeds projecting, flesh hollow and of only tolerable flavour.   Medium season.

35. YELLOW CHILI.   Thomp.

Fruit very large, irregular in form, yellow with a brown cheek, seeds slightly imbedded.   Flesh, very firm, rather rich.

Class VI. Green Strawberries.

[Little valued or cultivated, being more curious than good.   They resemble, in general appearance, the Wood strawberries.   Leaves light green, much plaited.   Flesh solid.   There are several sorts grown by the French, but the following is the only one of any value, and it is a shy bearer]

36. GREEN STRAWBERRY. Thomp.

Green Pine.   Fraisier Vert.
Green Wood.   Powdered Pine.
Green Alpine.

Fruit small, roundish or depressed, whitish green, and at maturity, tinged with reddish brown on the sunny side. Flesh solid, greenish, very juicy. with a peculiar, rich, pineapple flavour. Ripens late.

Selection of the finest strawberries for a small garden. Large Early Scarlet, Hovey's seedling, Black Prince, Hudson's Bay, British Queen, Prolific Hautbois, Red, and White Alpine.

Selection of sure bearing and very hardy kinds for the North. Large Early Scarlet, Hovey's seedling, Black Prince, Prolific Hautbois, Red Wood, White Wood.

Varieties requiring care, but very fine in deep rich soils. Bishop's Orange, Elton, Myatt's Pine, Old Pine, Downton.

CHAPTER XXVII.

Cucumis Melo, L. *Cucurbitaceæ*, of botanists.
Melon, of the French: *Melona*. German ; *Meleon*, Dutch ; *Melone*, Italian ; and *Melon*, Spanish.

THE Melon (or musk melon) is the richest and most luscious of all herbaceous fruits. The plant which bears this fruit is a trailing annual, supposed to be a native of Persia, but which has been so long in cultivation in all warm climates that it is quite doubtful which is its native country.

The climate of the Middle and Southern States is remarkably favourable for it—indeed far more so than that of England, France, or any of the temperate portions of Europe. Consequently melons are raised as field crops by market gardeners, and in the month of August the finest citrons or green-fleshed melons may be seen in the markets of New York and Philadelphia in immense quantities, so abundant in most seasons as frequently to be sold at half a dollar per basket, containing nearly a bushel of the fruit. The warm dry soils of Long Island and New Jersey are peculiarly favourable to the growth of melons, and even at low prices the product is so large that this crop is one of the most profitable.

CULTURE.—The culture of the melon is very easy in all, except the most northern portions of the United States. Early in May, a piece of rich, light soil is selected, well manured and thoroughly dug, or prepared by deep ploughing and harrowing.

Hills are then marked out, six feet apart each way. These hills are prepared by digging a foot deep, and two feet across, which are filled half full of good, well-rotted manure. Upon the latter are thrown three or four inches of soil, and both manure and soil are then well mixed together. More soil, well pulverized, is now thrown over the top, so as to complete the hill, making it three inches higher than the surface. Upon this, plant eight or ten grains of seed, covering them about half an inch deep.

When the plants have made two rough leaves, thin them so as to leave but two or three to each hill. Draw the earth nicely around the base of the plants with the hoe. And to prevent the attack of the *striped cucumber bug* (*Galereuca vittata*), the great enemy of the melon and cucumber plants, sprinkle the soil just beneath the plants, as soon as they come up, with *guano*. The pungent smell of this manure renders it an effectual protection both against this insect and the *cucumber flea beetle*, a little black, jumping insect, that also rapidly devours its leaves in some districts; while it also gives the young plants a fine start in the early part of the season.

As soon as the runners show the first blossom buds, stop them, by pinching out the bud at the extremities. This will cause an increased production of lateral shoots, and add to the size of the fruit. Nothing more is necessary but to keep the surface free from weeds, and to stir the soil lightly with the hoe, in field culture. In gardens, thinning the fruit, and placing bits of slate, or blackened shingles under each fruit, improve its size and flavour.

To retain a fine sort of melon in perfection, it should be grown at some distance from any other sort, or even from any of the cucumber family, otherwise the seeds of the next generation of fruit will be spoiled by the mixture of the pollen.

VARIETIES.—More than seventy varieties are enumerated in the catalogue of the London Horticultural Society's garden, but many of these do not succeed without extra care in this country, which their quality is not found to repay. Indeed what is popularly known as the *Citron* melon, one of the finest of the green fleshed class, is the greatest favourite with all American gardeners. It is high flavoured, uniformly good, very productive, and in all respects adapted to the climate.

Melons may be divided into three classes—the *Green-Fleshed*, as the citron, and nutmeg; *Yellow-Fleshed*, as the cantelopes; and *Persian Melons*, with very thin skins and the most melting honey-like flesh, of delicious flavour. The Green-Fleshed melons are of very rich flavour and roundish form; the Yellow-Fleshed are large, usually oval, and of second rate flavour:

the Persian melon, the finest of all, but yet scarce with us, requiring much care in cultivation, and a fine warm season.*

Class I.   Green-Fleshed Melons.

1. CITRON.   This is much the finest melon for general culture.   Fruit rather small, roundish, flattened at the end, regularly ribbed and thickly netted; skin deep green, becoming pale
greenish yellow at maturity; rind moderately thick, flesh green,
firm, rich, and high flavored.   Ripens pretty early and bears a
long time.

2. NUTMEG.   An old variety, often seen impure, but when in
perfection, very melting and excellent.   Fruit as large again as
the foregoing, roundish oval; skin very thickly netted, pale
green, slightly but distinctly ribbed; rind rather thin, flesh pale
green, very melting, sweet and good, with a high musky flavour.
Medium season.

3. FRANKLIN'S GREEN-FLESHED.   Very excellent and productive.   Fruit rather large, roundish; skin very slightly netted, greenish yellow when ripe; flesh green, exceedingly tender and rich.

4. IMPROVED GREEN-FLESH.   A new English variety, of exquisite flavour.   Fruit pretty large, roundish, not ribbed, slight

---

* We hope to see the Persian melon more common in our gardens,
as its exquisite flavour richly repays the additional care it requires
It almost always requires in this country the aid of a slight hot-bed to forward the plants in the spring, and needs the use of the glass frequently
even in summer, during cold nights and stormy weather.   The following treatment will produce fine Persian melons in this latitude, and south
of this probably less care will be necessary.

About the middle of April prepare a slight hot-bed, not more than three
feet wide, and as long as may be desired.   Cover the manure of the hot-
bed with a mixture of two thirds fresh loamy soil taken from just below
the turf on the road sides, and one third sand, mixing with the whole
guano, or pigeon dung—the best manure for the melon, at the rate of half a
peck of guano, or a peck of pigeon dung, to a bed ten feet long.   Give the
plants as much air as possible, consistent with vigorous growth, till the last
of June—taking off the sashes altogether during a few hours in the middle
of very warm bright days.   All this time the soil must be kept pretty
moist by frequent watering, which should be applied on the surface of
the ground, and not over the leaves of the plants.

After the first of July, if the summer is a warm one, the glass may be
taken off almost entirely during the day—or only restored to it in cold
stormy weather, or in sudden changes of temperature.   If the season should
not be as warm and fine as ordinary, the beds may be kept partially covered to ripen the fruit.   It should be borne in mind that the Persian melon
requires a very dry, warm atmosphere, and a very moist soil.   In Persia
the beds are irrigated by small streams of water running between them, and
when it is practicable this should be put in practice here, or otherwise the
soil should be regularly watered.   It is best to lay some light branches over
the surface, on which to train the vines.

ly netted; skin thin, pale yellow at maturily; flesh thick, green, and of very delicious flavour.

5. BEECHWOOD. One of the very best of this class. Fruit of medium size, oval, netted, skin greenish yellow; flesh pale green, rich and very sugary. Ripens early.

Class II.   Yellow, or Orange-Fleshed Melons.

6. EARLY CANTELOUP. Early and productive—its chief merits. Fruit small, nearly round, skin thin, smooth, ribbed nearly white; flesh orange colour, of sweet and pleasant flavour. The first melon ripe.

7. NETTED CANTELOUP. The best flavoured of this class, often quite rich. Fruit rather small, round, skin pale green, closely covered with net-work; flesh dark reddish-orange, flavour sugary and rich.

8. BLACK ROCK (or Rock Canteloup). A very large melon, frequently weighing 8 or 10 pounds, and of pretty good flavour. Fruit round, but flattened at both ends, covered with knobs or carbuncles; skin dark green, thick; flesh salmon coloured, sweet, but not rich. Ripens rather late.

Class III.   Persian Melons.

9. KEISING. One of the very finest and most delicate flavoured of melons. Fruit rather large, egg-shaped, skin pale lemon colour, regularly netted all over; flesh nearly white, high flavoured, and "texture like that of a ripe Beurré pear."

10. GREEN HOOSAINEE. One of the best for this climate, and bears well. Fruit egg-shaped, of medium size, skin light green, netted; flesh pale greenish white, tender and abounding with sugary, highly perfumed juice. Seeds large.

12. SWEET ISPAHAN. The most delicious of all melons. Fruit large oval; skin nearly smooth, deep sulphur colour; flesh greenish white, unusually thick, crisp and of the richest and most sugary flavour. Ripens rather late.

13. LARGE GERMEK. Eally, good bearer, and very excellent. Fruit of large size, roundish, flattened at the ends, and ribbed, skin green, closely netted; flesh greenish, firm, juicy, rich and high flavoured.

Besides the foregoing there are *Winter Melons* from the South of Europe, very commonly cultivated in Spain, which, if suspended in a dry room, may be kept till winter. The GREEN

VALENCIA and the DAMPSHA are the three principal sorts; they are oval, skin netted, flesh white, sugary and good.

CHAPTER XXVIII.

THE WATER-MELON.

Cucurbita citrullus, L. *Cucurbitaceæ*, of botanists.
Pasteur, of the French; *Wasser Melone*, German; *Cocomero*, Italian

THE water-melon is a very popular and generally cultivated fruit in this country. The vine is a training annual of the most vigorous growth, and the fruit is very large, smooth, and green, with a red or yellow core. Though far inferior to the melon in richness, its abundant, cooling juice renders it very grateful and refreshing in our hot midsummer days. Immense fields of the water-melon are raised in New Jersey and Long Island, and their culture is very easy throughout all the middle and southern states.

The cultivation of the water-melon is precisely similar to that of the melon, except that the hills must be eight feet apart. The finest crops we have ever seen, were grown upon old pieces of rich meadow land, the sod well turned under with the plough at the last of April, and the melons planted at once.

The following are its best varieties.

1. IMPERIAL. A remarkably fine flavoured and very productive sort, from the Mediterranean. Fruit of medium size, nearly round. Skin pale green and white, marbled, rind remarkably thin, flesh solid to the centre, light red, crisp, rich, and high flavoured. Seeds quite small, light brown.

2. CAROLINA. The large common variety. Fruit very large, oblong, skin dark green and white marbled, rind thick, flesh deep red, hollow at the centre, sweet and good, seeds large black.

There is also a sub-variety with pale yellow flesh and white seeds.

3. SPANISH. A rich and very excellent water-melon. Fruit large, oblong; skin very dark blackish-green, slightly marbled, rind moderately thick, flesh red, solid, rich, and very sweet.

THE CITRON WATER-MELON is a small, round, pale green, marbled sort, ripening late, and esteemed by many for preserving.

CHAPTER XXIX.

THE ORANGE FAMILY.

Citrus, L. *Aurantiaceæ*, of botanists

THE Orange family includes the common orange, (*Citrus aurantium ;*) the Lemon, (*C. limonum ;*) the Lime, (*C. limetta ;*) the Shaddock, (*C. decumana ;*) and the Citron, (*C. Medica ,*) all different species, with the same general habit.

The Orange, a native of Asia, is the most attractive and beautiful of fruit trees, with its rich, dark evergreen foliage, and its golden fruit ; and it may well therefore enjoy the reputation of being the golden apple of the Hesperides. When to these charms we add the delicious fragrance of the blossoms, surpassing that of any other fruit tree, it must be conceded that, though the orange must yield in flavour to some other fruits, yet, on the whole, nothing surpasses an orange grove, or orchard. in its combination of attractions—rich verdure, the delicious aroma of its flowers, and the great beauty of its fruit.

The south of Europe, China, and the West Indies, furnish the largest supplies of this fruit. But it has, for a considerable time, been cultivated pretty largely in Florida, and the orange groves of St. Augustine yield large and profitable crops. Indeed, the cultivation may be extended over a considerable portion of that part of the Union bordering on the Gulf of Mexico ; and the southern part of Louisiana, and part of Texas, are highly favorable to orange plantations. The bitter orange has become quite naturalized in parts of Florida, the so-called wild orange seedlings furnishing a stock much more hardy than those produced by sowing the imported seeds. By continually sowing the seed of these wild oranges, they will furnish stocks suited to almost all the Southern States, which will in time render the better kinds grafted upon them, comparatively hardy.

North of the latitude. where, in this country, the orange can be grown in groves, or orchards, it may still be profitably cultivated with partial protection. The injury the trees suffer from severe winters, arises not from their freezing—for they will bear, without injury, severe frost—but from the rupture of sap-vessels by the sudden thawing. A mere shed, or covering of boards, will guard against all this mischief. Accordingly, towards the south of Europe, where the climate is pretty severe, the orange is grown in rows against stone walls, or banks, in terraced gardens, or trained loosely against a sheltered trellis; and at the approach of winter they are covered with a slight moveable shed or frame of boards. In mild weather, the sliding doors are opened and air is admitted freely—if very severe, **a** few pots of charcoal are placed within the enclosure. **This** covering remains over them four or five months, and in this **way** the orange may be grown as far north as Baltimore.

SOIL AND CULTURE.—The best soil for the orange is a deep rich loam. In propagating them, sow, early in the spring, the seeds of the naturalized or wild bitter orange of Florida, which gives much the hardiest stock. They may be budded in the nursery row the same season, or the next, and for this purpose the earliest time at which the operation can be performed (the wood of the buds being sufficiently firm), the greater the success. Whip, or splice grafting, may also be resorted to early in the spring. Only the hardiest sorts should be chosen for orchards or groves, the more delicate ones can be grown easily with slight covering in winter. Fifty feet is the maximum height of the orange in its native country, but it rarely forms in Florida more than a compact low tree of twenty feet. It is better therefore to plant them so near as partially to shade the surface of the ground.

INSECTS.—The orange plantations of Florida have suffered very severely within a few years, from the attacks of the scale insect (*Coccus Hisperidum*), which, in some cases, has spread over whole plantations and gradually destroyed all the trees. It is the same small, oval brownish insect so common in our greenhouses, which adheres closely to the bark and under side of the leaves. All efforts to subdue it in Florida have been nearly unavailing.

A specific, however, against this insect has lately been discovered in England. It is the use of the common *Chamomile.* It is stated that merely hanging up bunches of fresh chamomile herb in the branches, destroys the scaled insect, and that cultivating the plants at the roots of the trees is an effectual preventive to the attacks of this insect. Where the bark and leaves are much infested, we recommend the stem and branches to be well washed with an infusion of fresh chamomile in water, and the foliage to be well syringed with the same. Repeating this once or twice, will probably effectually rid the trees of the scaled insect.

Another very excellent remedy for this and all other insects that infest the orange, is the *gas liquor*, of the gas works, largely diluted with water, and showered over the leaves with a syringe or engine. As this liquor varies in strength and is sometimes very strongly impregnated with ammonia, it is difficult to give a rule for its dilution. The safest way is to mix some, and apply it at first to the leaves of tender plants; if too strong, it will injure them; if properly diluted it promotes vegetation, and estroys all insects.

VARIETIES.—From among the great number of names **that**

figure in the European catalogues, we select a few of those really deserving attention in each class of this fruit.

I. THE ORANGE.

THE Orange (*Oranger*, French ; *Pomeranze*, German ; *Arancio*, Italian ; and *Naranja*, Spanish) is on the whole the finest tree of the genus. Its dark green leaves have winged foot-stalks, its fruit is round with an orange coloured skin. It is one of the longest lived fruit trees, as an instance of which we may quote the celebrated tree at Versailles, called "the Grand Bourbon," which was sown in 1421, and is at the present time in existence, one of the largest and finest trees in France.

The fruit of the orange is universally esteemed in its ripe state. The bitter orange is used for marmalades ; the green fruits, even when as small as peas, are preserved, and used in various ways in confectionary ; the rind and pulp are used in cooking ; and the orange flowers distilled, give the orange flower water, so highly esteemed as a perfume and in cookery.

Besides the COMMON SWEET ORANGE, the most esteemed sorts are the MALTESE, and the BLOOD-RED, both of excellent flavour with *red* pulp. The MANDARIN Orange is a small, flattened fruit, with a thin rind separating very easily from the pulp, frequently parting from it of itself, and leaving a partially hollow space. It comes from China, and is called there the Mandarin, or noble orange, from its excellent quality. The flesh is dark orange coloured, juicy and very rich.

The ST MICHAEL's orange is a small fruit, the skin pale yellow, the rind thin, the pulp often seedless, juicy, and lusciously sweet. It is considered the most delicious of all oranges, and the tree is a most abundant bearer.

The SEVILLE, or bitter orange, is the hardiest of all the varieties, enduring very hard frosts without injury. It has the largest and most fragrant flowers : the pulp, however, is bitter and sharp, and is valued chiefly for marmalades. The *Double Bigarde* is a French variety, of this species, with fine double blossoms.

The BERGAMOT orange has small flowers, and pear-shaped fruit. The leaves, flowers, and fruit, being peculiarly fragrant, it is highly esteemed by the perfumer, and yields the bergamot essences. "The rind, first dried and then moistened, is pressed in moulds into small boxes for holding sweetmeats, to which it communicates a bergamot flavour."

Besides the above, the *Fingered, Sweet-skinned, Pear-shaped*, and *Ribbed* oranges, are the most striking sorts, all chiefly cultivated by curious amateurs.

II —Lemons.

The Lemon (*Limonier,* of the French and German ; *Limone,* Italian ; *Limon,* Spanish) has longer, paler leaves than the orange, the footstalks of which are naked or wingless ; the flowers tinged with red externally, and the fruit is oblong, pale yellow, with a swollen point, and usually an acid pulp. Its principal use is in making lemonade, punch, and other cooling acid drinks.

Besides the common Lemon, there is an Italian variety, called the Sweet Lemon, the pulp of which is sweet and good.

III.—THE LIME.

The Lime (*Limellier,* of the French) differs from the Lemon by its smaller, entirely white flowers, and small, roundish, pale yellow fruit, with a slight protuberance at the end. The acid, though sharp, is scarcely so rich and high as that of the lemon, and is used for the same purposes. The green fruit is more esteemed than any other for preserving. The Italians cultivate a curiously marked variety called *Pomo d'Adamo,* in which Adam is said to have left the marks of his teeth.

IV.—THE CITRON.

The Citron (Cidratier of the French ; *Citronier,* German ; *Cedrato,* Italian) is one of the finest growing trees of this family, with large, oblong, wingless leaves, and flowers tinged with purple externally. The fruit, shaped like that of the lemon, is much larger, of a yellow colour, warted and furrowed externally. The rind is very fragrant, and very thick, the pulp is subacid, and is used in the same way as that of the lemon. It is chiefly valued however for the rich sweetmeat or preserve, called *citron,* made from the rind.

The Madras citron is considered the largest and best variety.

V.—THE SHADDOCK.

The Shaddock (*Pampelmous,* French ; *Arancio massimo,* Italian) may be considered a monstrous orange, with a comparatively tasteless pulp. It is a native of China and Japan, and has its name from Dr. Shaddock, who first carried it to the West

46*

Indies. The leaves are winged, like those of the orange, the flowers white, and the fruit globular. Its size is very large. as it often weighs six or eight pounds. The pulp is sweetish, or sub-acid, and the juice is rather refreshing. It is, however, more showy than useful, and certainly makes a magnificent appear-ance in a collection of tropical fruits.*

CHAPTER XXX.

THE OLIVE.

Olea Europea, L , *Oleinæ*, of botanists.
Olivier, of the French , *Oehlbaum*, German , *Ulivo*, Italian ;
Olivo, Spanish

The Olive, which, as Loudon justly remarks, furnishes, in its invaluable oil, the cream and butter of Spain and Italy, will undoubtedly one day be largely cultivated in our Southern States. Already small plantations of it have been formed by a few spirited gentlemen in Georgia and Mississippi, and its adapta-tion to the Southern parts of the Union near the sea-coast, tested. The apathy of Southern planters generally, respecting all pro-ducts but cotton and rice, is the only reason for the tardy man-ner in which this and other valuable trees are introduced into cultivation there.

The uses and value of the olive-oil are still comparatively unknown in this country. In the South of Europe it is more valuable than bread, as, to say nothing of its wholesomeness, it enters into every kind of cookery, and renders so large a quantity of vegetable food fit for use. A few olive trees will serve for the support of an entire family, who would starve on what could otherwise be raised on the same surface of soil ; and dry crevices of rocks, and almost otherwise barren soils in the deserts, when planted with this tree, become flourishing and valuable places of habitation.

The olive is a native of the temperate sea-coast ridges of Asia and Africa ; but it has, time out of mind, been cultivated in the South of Europe. It is a low evergreen tree, scarcely twenty feet high, its head spreading, and clothed with stiff, nar-row, bluish green leaves. Its dark green or black fruit is oval,

---

* To those of our readers who desire to pursue this branch of the sub-ject, we recommend that splendid work, the *Histoire Naturelle des Orangers*, of Risso and Poiteau, with superb coloured plates of every variety Paris, folio, 1818.

the hard fleshy pulp enclosing a stone. In a pickled state the fruit is highly esteemed. The pickles are made by steeping the unripe olives in ley water, after which they are washed and bottled in salt and water, to which is often added fennel, or some kind of spice. The oil is made by crushing the fruit to a paste, pressing it through a coarse hempen bag, into hot water, from the surface of which the oil is skimmed off. The best oil is made from the pulp alone : when the stone also is crushed, it is inferiour.

PROPAGATION AND CULTURE.—A very common mode of propagating the olive in Italy, is by means of the *uovoli* (little eggs). These are knots or tumours, which form in considerable numbers on the bark of the trunk, and are easily detached by girdling them with a pen-knife, the mother plant suffering no injury. They are planted in the soil like bulbs, an inch or so deep, when they take root and form new trees. It is also propagated by cuttings and seeds. The seedlings form the strongest and thriftiest trees ; they are frequently some months in vegetating, and should therefore be buried an inch deep in the soil as soon as ripe.

The wild American olive (*Olea Americana*, L.) or Devil-wood, a tree that grows more or less abundantly as far North as Virginia, will undoubtedly prove a good stock, on which to engraft the European olive. It is of a hardier habit, and though worthless itself, may become valuable in this way.

The olive-tree commences bearing five or six years after being planted. Its ordinary crop is fifteen or twenty pounds of oil per annum, and the regularity of its crop, as well as the great age to which it lives, renders an olive plantation one of the most valuable in the world. With respect to its longevity, we may remark, that there is a celebrated plantation near Terni, in Italy, more than five miles in extent, which, there is every reason for believing, has existed since the time of Pliny.

The olive is not a very tender tree. It will thrive farther north than the orange. The very best sites for it are limestone ridges, and dry, crumbling, limestone, rocky regions always produce the finest oil. The tree, however, thrives most luxuriantly in deep, rich, clayey loams, which should be rendered more suitable by using air-slacked lime as manure. It requires comparatively little pruning or care, when a plantation is once fairly established.

VARIETIES.—There are numberless varieties enumerated in the French catalogues, but only a few of them are worth the attention of any but the curious collector. The common European olive is, on the whole, much the best for general cultivation, yielding the most certain and abundant crops.

The sub-variety most cultivated in France is the LONG-LEVAED OLIVE (*Olea, e. longifolia*), with larger and longer leaves; the fruit nearly of the same size as that of the common olive.

The favorite sort in Spain is the BROAD-LEAVED OLIVE (*Olea e. latifolia*). Its fruit is nearly double the size of the common olive, and yields an abundance of oil, but the latter is so strong in flavour as to be more relished by the Spaniards than by strangers.

The OLIVIER A FRUIT ARRONDI (*Olea spherica*, N. Duh.) is a hardy French variety, which, in a moist rich soil, yields most abundant crops of fine oil.

The OLIVIER PLEUREUR (*Olea eranimorpha*, N. Duh), or weeping olive, is one of the largest and finest trees. Its branches are pendant, its fruit excellent, and the oil pure and abundant. It is a very hardy sort, and grows best in damp valleys.

The OLIVIER PICHOLINE (*Olea oblonga*, N. Duh.) yields the fruit most esteemed for pickling. It grows quite readily in any tolerable soil, and is one of the hardiest varieties.

There are two varieties of the olive, which are said to have been found not long since in the Crimea, lat. 45° and 46°, which bear abundant crops of fine fruit, and the trees endure a temperature in winter, of zero of Fahrenheit. These sorts have not yet been introduced into this country, and though it is a desideratum to obtain them and test them at the South, yet it is not unlikely that, in common with many trees similarly reported, they may prove little different from the common olive.

CHAPTER XXXI.

THE POMEGRANATE.

Punica granatum, L , *Granatacea*, of botanists
Grenadier, of the French , *Granatenbaum*, German ; *Melagrano*,
Italian ; *Granado*, Spanish

THIS unique fruit, the most singularly beautiful one that ever appears at the dessert, is a native of China and the South of Europe. It grows and bears very readily in this country, as far North as Maryland and the Ohio river, though the fruit does not always mature well north of Carolina, except in sheltered places. It is even hardy enough to stand the winter here, and will bear very good fruit, if trained as an espalier, and protected in winter.

The fruit is as large as an apple. Its skin is hard and leathery, of a yellowish orange colour, with a rich red cheek. It is crowned in a peculiar manner with the large calyx, which remains and increases in size after the flower has fallen. There is a pretty bit of mythological history told by Rapin, the French poet, respecting this fruit. Bacchus once beguiled a lovely Scythian girl, whose head had been previously turned by the diviners having prophesied that she would some day wear a crown, and who therefore lent a willing ear to his suit. The fickle god, however, not long after abandoned her, when she soon died of grief. Touched at last, he metamorphosed her into a pomegranate tree, and placed on the summit of its fruit, the crown (calyx), which he had denied to his mistress while living.

The fruit of the common pomegranate is acid, but the cultivated variety bears fruit of very agreeable sweet flavour. The interior of the fruit consists of seeds enveloped in pulp much like those of the gooseberry, but arranged in compartments, and of the size and colour of red currants. Medicinally it is cooling and much esteemed, like the orange, in fevers and inflammatory disorders.

The tree is of low growth, from twelve to twenty feet, with numerous slender twiggy branches, and is very ornamental in garden scenery, either when clad with its fine scarlet flowers or decked with fruit, which hangs and grows all summer, and does not ripen till pretty late in the season. It is well worthy of a choice sheltered place at the north, on a wall or espalier rail, where it can be slightly protected with mats or straw in winter; and it deserves to be much more popular than it now is in every southern garden. If raised in large quantities there, it would become a valuable fruit for sending to the northern cities, as it is now constantly sent from the south of Europe to Paris and London. Hedges are very often made of it near Genoa and Nice.

PROPAGATION AND CULTURE.—This tree is readily propagated by cuttings, layers, suckers or seeds. When by seeds, they should be sown directly after they ripen, otherwise they seldom vegetate. Any good rich garden soil answers well for the Pomegranate—and, as it produces little excess of wood, it needs little more in the way of pruning, than an occasional thinning out of any old or decaying branches.

VARIETIES.—There are several varieties. The finest, viz.:

1. THE SWEET-FRUITED Pomegranate (*Grenadier à Fruit. Doux*), with sweet and juicy pulp.
2. THE SUB-ACID FRUITED Pomegranate; the most common variety cultivated in gardens.
3. THE WILD, or ACID-FRUITED Pomegranate, with a sharp acid flavour; which makes an excellent syrup.

Besides these, there are several double-flowering varieties of the Pomegranate which are very beautiful, but bear no fruit.

They are also rather more tender than the fruit-bearing ones. The finest are the DOUBLE RED Pomegranate, with large and very splendid scarlet blossoms, and the DOUBLE WHITE Pomegranate, with flowers nearly white.   There are also the rarer varieties, the YELLOW-FLOWERED and the VARIEGATED FLOWER-ED Pomegranate—seldom seen here except in choice green-house collections.

APPENDIX.

~~~~~~~~~~~~

REMARKS ON THE DURATION OF VARIETIES OF FRUIT TREES.

It was, for a long time, the popular notion that when a good variety of fruit was once originated from seed, it might be continued by grafting and budding, for ever,—or, at least, as some old parchment deeds pithily gave tenure of land—"as long as grass grows, and water runs."

About fourteen years ago, however, Thomas Andrew Knight, the distinguished President of the Horticultural Society of London, published an Essay in its Transactions, tending entirely to overthrow this opinion, and to establish the doctrine that all varieties are of very limited duration.

The theory advanced by Mr. Knight is as follows: All the constitutional vigor or properties possessed by any variety of fruit are shared at the same time by all the plants that can be made from the buds of that variety, whether by grafting budding, or other modes of propagating. In simpler terms, all the plants or trees of any particular kind of pear or apple being only parts of one original tree, itself of limited duration, it follows, as the parent tree dies, all the others must soon after die also. "No trees, of any variety," to use his own words, "can be made to produce blossom or fruit till the original tree of that variety has attained the age of puberty;* and, under ordinary modes of propagation, by grafts and buds, all become subject, at no very distant period, to the debilities and diseases of old age."

It is remarkable that such a theory as this should have been offered by Mr. Knight, to whose careful investigations the science of modern horticulture is so deeply indebted—as, however common it is to see the apparent local decline of certain sorts of fruit, yet it is a familiar fact that many sorts have also been continued a far greater length of time than the life of any

---

* This part of the doctrine has of late been most distinctly refuted, and any one may repeat the experiment. Seedling fruit trees, it is well-known, are usually several years before they produce fruit. But if a graft is inserted on a bearing tree, and after it makes one season fair growth, the grafted shoot is bent directly down and tied there, with its point to the stock below, it will, the next season—the sap being checked—produce flower-buds, and begin to bear, long before the parent tree

one parent tree. Still the doctrine has found supporters abroad and at least one hearty advocate in this country.

Mr. Kenrick, in his new American Orchardist, adopts this doctrine, and in speaking of Pears, says. "I shall, in the following pages, designate some of these in the class of old varieties, once the finest of all old pears whose duration we had hoped, but in vain, to perpetuate. For, except in certain sections of the city, and some very few and highly favoured situations in the country around, they (the old sorts) have become either so uncertain in their bearing—so barren—so unproductive—or so miserably blighted—so mortally diseased—that they are no longer to be trusted; they are no longer what they once were with us, and what many of them are still described to be by most foreign writers."

Mr. Kenrick accordingly arranges in separate classes the *Old* and *New* Pears; and while he praises the latter, he can hardly find epithets sufficiently severe to bestow on the former poor unfortunates. Of the Doyenné he·says: "This most eminent of all Pears has now become an outcast, intolerable even to sight;" of the Brown Beurré, "once the best of all Pears—now become an outcast." The St. Germain "has long since become an abandoned variety," &c., &c.

Many persons have, therefore, supposing that these delicious varieties had really and quietly given up the ghost, made no more inquiries after them, and only ordered from the nurseries the new varieties. And this, not always, as they have confessed to us, without some lingering feeling of regret at thus abandoning old and tried friends for new comers—which, it must be added, not unfrequently failed to equal the good qualities of their predecessors.

But, while this doctrine of Knight's has found ready supporters, we are bound to add that it has also met with sturdy opposition. At the head of the opposite party we may rank the most distinguished vegetable physiologist of the age, Professor De Candolle, of Geneva. Varieties, says De Candolle, will endure and remain permanent, so long as man chooses to take care of them, as is evident from the continued existence, to this day, of sorts, the most ancient of those which have been described in books. By negligence, or through successive bad seasons, they may become diseased, but careful culture will restore them, and retain them, to all appearance, for ever.

Our own opinion coincides, in the main, with that of De Candolle. While we admit that, in the common mode of propagation, varieties are constantly liable to decay or become comparatively worthless, we believe that this is owing not to natural limits set upon the duration of a variety; that it does not depend on the longevity of the parent tree; but upon the **care** with which the sort is propagated, and the nature of the climate or soil where the tree is grown.

It is a well established fact, that a seedling tree, if allowed to grow on its own root, is always much longer lived, and often more vigorous than the same variety, when grafted upon another stock; and experience has also proved that in proportion to the likeness or close relation between the stock and the graft is the long life of the grafted tree. Thus a variety of pear grafted on a healthy pear seedling, lasts almost as long as upon its own roots. Upon a thorn stock it does not endure so long. Upon a mountain ash rather less. Upon a quince stock still less; until the average life of the pear tree when grafted on the quince, is reduced from fifty years—its ordinary duration on the pear stock—to about a dozen years. This is well known to every practical gardener, and it arises from the want of affinity between the quince stock and the pear graft. The latter is rendered dwarf in its habits, bears very early, and perishes equally soon.

Next to this, the apparent decay of a variety is often caused by grafting upon unhealthy stocks. For although grafts of very vigorous habit have frequently the power of renovating in some measure, or for a time, the health of the stock, yet the tree, when it arrives at a bearing state, will, sooner or later, suffer from the diseased or feeble nature of the stock.

Carelessness in selecting scions for engrafting, is another fertile source of degeneracy in varieties. Every good cultivator is aware that if grafts are cut from the ends of old bearing branches, exhausted by overbearing, the same feebleness of habit will, in a great degree, be shared by the young graft. And on the contrary, if the thrifty straight shoots that are thrown out by the upright extremities, or the strong limb-sprouts are selected for grafting, they ensure vigorous growth, and healthy habit in the graft.

Finally, unfavourable soil and climate are powerful agents in deteriorating varieties of fruit-trees. Certain sorts that have originated in a cold climate, are often short-lived and unproductive when taken to warmer ones, and the reverse. This arises from a want of constitutional fitness for a climate different from its natural one. For this reason the Spitzenburgh apple soon degenerates, if planted in the colder parts of New England, and almost all northern sorts, if transplanted to Georgia. But this only proves that it is impossible to pass certain natural limits of fitness for climate, and not that the existence of the variety itself is in any way affected by these local failures.

Any or all of these causes are sufficient to explain the apparent decay of some varieties of fruit, and especially of pears, over which some cultivators, of late, have uttered so

47

many lamentations, scarcely less pathetic than those of Jere-
miah.

Having stated the theories on this subject, and given an
outline of our explanation, let us glance for a moment at the
actual state of the so-called decayed varieties, and see whether
they are really either extinct, or on the verge of annihilation.

Mr. Knight's own observations in England led him to consider the English Golden Pippin and the Nonpareil, their two
most celebrated varieties of apple, as the strongest examples
of varieties just gone to decay, or, in fact, the natural life of
which had virtually expired twenty years before. A few years
longer he thought it might linger on in the warmer parts of
England, as he supposed varieties to fall most speedily into
decay in the north, or in a cold climate.

Lindley, however, his contemporary, and second to no one in
practical knowledge of the subject, writing of the Golden Pippin,*
very frankly states his dissent as follows. "This apple is considered by some of our modern writers on Pomology, to be in a
state of decay, its fruit of inferior quality, and its existence
near its termination. I cannot for a moment agree with such
an opinion, because we have facts annually before our eyes
completely at variance with such an assertion. In Covent
Garden, and indeed in any other large market in the southern
or midland counties of England, will be found specimens of
fruit as perfect, and as fine, as have been figured or described
by any writer, either in this or any other country whatever.
Instead of the trees being in a state of "rapid decay" they may
be found of unusually large size, perfectly healthy, and their
crops abundant; the fruit, perfect in form, beautiful in colour,
and excellent in quality." And the like remarks are made of
the Nonpareil.

Certain French writers, about this time, gladly seized
Knight's theory as an explanation of the miserable state into
which several fine old sorts of pears had fallen, about Paris,
owing to bad culture and propagation. They sealed the death-
warrant, in like manner, of the Brown Beurré, Doyenné, Chaumontel, and many others, and consigned them to oblivion in
terms which Mr. Kenrick has already abundantly quoted.

Notwithstanding this, and that ten or fifteen years have since
elapsed, it is worthy of notice that the repudiated apples and
pears still hold their place among all the best cultivators in
both England and France. Nearly half the pear-trees annually introduced into this country from France, are the Doyenné
and Beurré. And the "extinct varieties" seem yet to bid de-
fiance to theorists and bad cultivators.

But half the ground is not yet covered. How does the theory

*Guide to the Orchard, by George Lindley.

work in America ? is the most natural inquiry. In this country, we have soil varying from the poorest sand to the richest alluvial, climate varying from frigid to almost torrid—a range wide enough to include all fruit trees between the apple and the orange.

We answer that the facts here, judged in the whole, are decidedly against the theory of the extinction of varieties. While here, as abroad, unfavourable soil, climate, or culture, have produced their natural results of a feeble and diseased state of certain sorts of fruit, these are only the exceptions to the general vigour and health of the finest old sorts in the country at large. The oldest known variety of pear is the Autumn Bergamot—believed by Pomologists to be identically the same fruit cultivated by the Romans in the time of Julius Cesar—that is to say, the variety is nearly two thousand years old. It grows with as much vigour, and bears as regular and abundant crops of fair fine fruit in our own garden, as any sort we cultivate. Whole orchards of the Doyenné (or Virgalieu) are in the finest and most productive state of bearing in the interior of this State, and numberless instances in the western states—and any one may see, in September, grown in the apparently cold and clayey soil near the town of Hudson, on the North River, specimens of this " outcast," weighing three fourths of a pound, and of a golden fairness and beauty of appearance and lusciousness of flavour worthy of the garden of the Hesperides,— certainly we are confident never surpassed in the lustiest youth of the variety in France. The same is true of all the other sorts when propagated in a healthy manner, and grown in the suitable soil and climate. Wherever the *soil is not exhausted of the proper elements* the fruit is beautiful and good. The largest and finest crops of pears regularly produced in our own gardens, are by a Brown Beurré tree, only too luxuriant and vigorous. Of the Golden Pippin apple, we can point out trees in the valley of the Hudson, productive of the fairest and finest fruit, and the St. Germain Pears grown by a neighbour here, without the least extra care, are so excellent, that he may fairly set them against any one of the newer varieties of Winter fruit.

On the other hand, we candidly admit that there has been for some time a failure of many sorts of pear and apple in certain parts of the country. All along the sea-coast *where the soil is light, and has been exhausted, by long cultivation, of lime, potash, and phosphates,* the inorganic elements absolutely necessary to the production of fine pears, many varieties that once flourished well, are now feeble, and the fruit is often blighted.*

The apparent decline in these districts is owing to the lightness

---

* The symptoms of the decline or decay in the pear are chiefly these

of the soil, which in this climate, under our hot sun (as we have already remarked), lays the foundation of more than half the diseases of fruit-trees—because, after a few years, the necessary sustenance is exhausted by the roots of a bearing tree, and every one knows how rarely it is re-supplied in this country. We can from our own observation on the effects of soil, take a map and mark out the sandy district on the whole sea-board, where certain sorts of pears no longer bear good fruit; while within a few miles, on strong deep loams, the fruit is fair and beautiful—the trees healthy and luxuriant.

Nothing is more convincing, on this point, than to compare the vigour and productiveness of the old pears, at the present moment, in the new soils of Rochester and Syracuse, abounding, not merely with vegetable matter, but with the necessary *inorganic food*, with the same sorts grown along the sea-board, in light soils, where the latter elements are no longer present in sufficient abundance. In the former localities, it is as common to see trees of the old varieties bearing from ten to twenty bushels of unblemished fruit annually, as it is in the latter to see them bearing only crops of blighted pears.

Recent experiments have proved, that it is not sufficient to bring healthy trees of the old varieties from the interior to the sea-board to insure, in the latter localities, fair and excellent crops. But, on the other hand, the complete renovation of blighted trees in light and exhausted soils, by the plentiful use of wood-ashes, bone dust, lime, and blacksmith cinders, along with common manure, shows us distinctly that it is not the *age* of these varieties of fruit which causes their apparent decline, but a want of that food absolutely necessary to the production of healthy fruit.

But there is another interesting point in this investigation. Do the newly originated soils really maintain in the unfavourable districts the appearance of perfect health? Are the new pears uniformly healthy where the old ones are always feeble?

Undoubtedly this question must be answered in the negative. Some of the latest Flemish pears already exhibit symptoms of decay or bad health in these districts. Even Mr. Kenrick, with

---

The tree, apparently healthy in the spring, blossoms, and sets a crop of fruit. Towards midsummer its leaves are disfigured with dark or black spots, and except a few at the ends, fall from the branches. The fruit is covered with black specks, often ceases growing when at half its size, and in the worst cases the skin becomes hard, cracks, and the fruit is entirely worthless. This rusty and diseased state of the skin, is caused by the attack of a minute species of fungi (*Uredo, Puccinia*, etc.), which fasten upon, or are generated in vegetable surfaces in a languid state of health.

all his enthusiasm for the new sorts, is obliged to make the following admission respecting the Beurré Diel pear, the most vigorous and hardy here of all, "I regret to add that near Boston this noble fruit is liable to crack badly." We predict tha many of the Flemish pears originated by Van Mons will become feeble, and the fruit liable to crack, in the neighbourhood of Boston, in a much less time than did the old varieties.

And this leads us to remark here, that the hardness of any variety depends greatly upon the circumstances of its origin. When a new variety springs up accidentally from a healthy seed in a semi-natural manner, like the Seckel, the Dix, and other native sorts, it will usually prove the hardiest. It is, as it were, an effort of nature to produce a new individual out of the materials, in a progressive state, which garden culture has afforded. Cross-bred seedlings—one parent being of a hardy nature, and both healthy—such as Knight's own seedlings, the Monarch and Dunmore Pears—are next in hardiness. Lastly, we rank varieties reared by Van Mons' method—that of continually repeated reproductions. This, as Van Mons distinctly states, is an *enfeebling* process—without any compensating element of vigour. Hence it follows as a matter of course, that seedlings of the fifth or sixth generation, as are some of his varieties, must in their origin be of feeble habit. Van Mons himself was fully aware of this, and therefore resorted to " grafting by copulation"—in fact, root grafting—well knowing that on common stocks these new varieties would in light soils soon become feeble and decayed. It is needless for us to add that hence we consider the Belgian mode of producing new varieties greatly inferior to the English one—since it gives us varieties often impaired in health in their very origin.

If any further proof of this is desired, we think it is easily found by comparing the robust vigour and longevity of many native pear trees, to be found in the United States—some of them 80 or 100 years old, and still producing large crops of fruit—with the delicate trees of several new varieties now in our gardens, from Europe. These varieties are delicate not only with respect to their constitutional vigour, but they are also more susceptible to injury from the severity of our winter's cold and summer's sun.

There are great advantages, undoubtedly, for soils naturally unfavourable, and for small gardens, in grafting the pear upon quince stocks ; yet, as it diminishes the vigour of the tree, it is not impossible that continued propagation from dwarf trees may somewhat lessen the vital powers and the longevity of a given variety.

The decay of varieties of the Apricot, or Peach, much shorter lived trees by nature, we seldom or never hear of. Varieties of both are now in cultivation, and in the most perfect vigour of 200 years' duration. This, probably, is owing to the

47*

more natural treatment these trees receives generally. Varieties of the vine are said never to degenerate. and this is
perhaps owing to their having very rarely been propagated by
grafting.*

We are not without remedy for varieties that have partially
decayed in a certain district If the trees have once been productive of excellent fruit, and are still in a sound condition,
though enfeebled, a thorough renewal of their powers will
again restore them to health. To effect this, the soil about the
roots should be replaced by new, enriched by manure or peat-
compost, and mixed with the mineral substances named in the
preceding page. The bark of the trunk and large branches
should be well scraped, and, as well as all the limbs, thoroughly
washed with soft soap The head should be moderately pruned.
And finally the tree should be suffered to bear no fruit for the two
following seasons After this it will generally bear excellent
fruit for several years again.†

In making plantations of fine old varieties, in districts where
the stock has become feeble, something may be gained by procuring grafts or trees from more favourable localities, where the fruit
is still as fair as ever—and care should be exercised in selecting
only the healthiest grafts or trees. Nurserymen in unfavourable districts should endeavour to propagate only from trees of
healthy character, and if those in their own variety are
diseased, they should spare no pains to bring into their nurseries and propagate only such as they feel confident are healthy
and sound. On them, next to the soil, depends very considerably
the vigour or debility of the stock of any given variety in the
country around them.

In Mr. Knight's original essay on the decay of varieties, he
clearly stated a circumstance that most strongly proves what
we have here endeavoured to show—viz · that the local decline

* We do not deny that in any given soil there is a period at which a variety of tree or plant exhibits most vigour, and after having grown there
awhile it ceases to have its former luxuriance The same is true of wheat
or potatoes, and accordingly, farmers are in the habit of "changing their
seed " The nutriment for a given variety is after a time exhausted from
the soil, and unless it is again supplied the tree must decline. In light soils
this speedily happens In strong, clayey or rocky soils, the natural decom-
position of which affords a continual store of lime, potash, etc , the necessary supply of inorganic food is maintained, and the variety continues
healthy and productive.

† It is not uncommon to hear it said that the Newtown pippin—that finest
of all apples—is degenerating rapidly The solution of this is easy More
than any other apple does this one need lime, and high culture In proof,
we may state that *never* have there been finer Newtown pippins raised, or
in so large quantities, as at the present moment on the Hudson River. One
gentleman's orchards supply hundreds, we may say thousands of barrels to
the London markets of the fairest, largest, and highest flavoured fruit we
have had the pleasure of seeing or tasting If any one will turn to page
62, he will speedily see *why* this variety has not fallen into decay at Pelham farm

of a variety is mainly owing to neglect, and to grafting on bad stock. We allude to the fact repeatedly verified, that healthy young shoots taken from the *roots* of an old variety in apparent decline, produce trees which are vigorous and healthy. "The decay," says he, "of the powers of life in the roots of seedling trees is exceeding slow, comparatively with that in the branches. Scions (or shoots) obtained from the roots of pear trees two hundred years old, afford grafts which grow with great vigour, and which are often covered with thorns like young seedling stocks; whilst other grafts taken at the same time from the extremities of the branches of such trees present a totally different character, and a very slow and unhealthy growth. I do not conceive that such shoots possess all the powers of a young seedling, but they certainly possess no inconsiderable portion of such powers."

This is nothing more, in fact, than going back to the roots, the portion of the tree least exhausted, for the renewal of the health of a variety when the branches of the tree have been exhausted by overbearing, etc. It is a simple and easy mode of increasing the vigour of a sort of delicate habit, to take scions from young root suckers for grafting anew. This can of course only be done with trees that grow on their own roots—or have not been grafted. And we suggest it as worth the attention of those interested in gardening to graft feeble sorts on pieces of roots, with a view to establishing them finally on their own roots; or to raise them from *layers*, a more simple mode of attaining the object.

Mr. Knight's idea that old varieties first decay in the north, while they yet remain comparatively good in warmer and more southern districts, is by no means borne out by the existing facts in America. On the contrary the decline here, as we have already stated, is almost entirely along the sea-board, and to the southward. In the interior, and to the north, the same sorts are universally fair and excellent, except in cases where a diseased stock has been obtained from the sea-board, and has not recovered its health by removal. The whole middle and western sections of the country abound, more or less, with the finest pears, of sorts that are in a state of decline on Long Island, in portions of New Jersey, or near Boston. But *the influence of the soil*, so far as our own observations extend, is, after a certain time, always the same. In this light soil the pear and the apple soon become feeble, because the sustenance afforded by it is, after a time, insufficient to keep the tree in a continual healthy, bearing state. The moisture afforded by it is not great enough to answer the demand made upon the leaves by our hot summer sun. Unless this is remedied by skilful culture, these fruits must, more speedily fail in health in such districts, while in more favourable ones they will remain as sound and healthy as ever.

From these remarks, it will be perceived how important it is in all exhausted soils to supply the *necessary food* to varieties that have "run out" from the want of it, and how unwise we believe to be to reject such incomparable fruits as the Newtown pippin, and the Doyenné pear, because *in certain local districts*, from causes easily explained, they have become feeble and diseased.

Note.—*To prevent mice or rabbits from girdling trees.*—Great injury is done to young orchards in some districts by the *meadow mouse.* This little animal always works *under cover,* and therefore does its mischief in winter when the snow lies deeply upon the ground. A common and effectual mode of deterring it is that of treading down the snow firmly about the stem directly after every fall of snow. But this is a very troublesome affair.

The following mixture will be found to be an effectual prevention. Take one spadeful of hot slaked lime, one do. of clean cows-dung, half do. of soot, one handful of flowers of sulphur, mix the whole together with the addition of sufficient water to bring it to the consistency of thick paint. At the approach of winter paint the trunks of the trees sufficiently high to be beyond the reach of these vermin. Experience has proved that it does no injury to the tree. A dry day should be chosen for its application.

English nurserymen are in the habit of protecting nurseries of small trees from the attacks of *rabbits,* simply by distributing through the squares of the nursery coarse matches made by dipping bunches of rags, or bits of tow, in melted sulphur, and fastening these in split stakes a couple of feet high. The latter are stuck into the ground, among the trees, at from 12 to 20 feet apart, and are said completely to answer the purpose.

Note.—*Wash for the trunks and branches of fruit trees.*—The best wash for the stems and branches of fruit trees is made by dissolving two pounds of *potash* in two gallons of water. This is applied with a brush at any season, but, perhaps, with most effect in the spring. One, or, at most, two applications will rid the stem of trees of the bark louse, and render it smooth and glossy. It is far more efficacious than whitewash, as a preservative against the attacks of insects, while it promotes the growth of the tree, and adds to the natural lively colour of the bark.

The *wash of soft soap* is also a very good one for many purposes. Though not equal for general purposes to the potash wash, it is better for old trunks with thick and rigid bark, as a portion of it remains upon the surface of the bark for some time, and with the action of every rain is dissolved, and thus penetrates into all the crevices where insects may be lodged, destroying them, and softening the bark itself.

NOTE.—*Key to French standard names of Fruit.*—To meet the wants of some of our farming friends, in various parts of the country, who are zealous collectors of fruit, but at the same time are more familiar with plough-handles than with the sound of *Monsieur Crapaud's* polite vernacular, we have prepared the following little key to the pronunciation of such French names as are necessarily retained among the standard varieties.

So long as these sorts must retain their foreign names, it is very desirable that they should be correctly pronounced. To give to these French terms what appears to merely English readers the proper sound is often as far as possible from the true pronunciation. A skilful Hibernian gardener puzzled his employer, a friend of ours, during the whole month of September with some pears that he persisted in calling the "Lucy Bony," until after a careful comparison of notes, the latter found he meant the *Louise Bonne.*

We have, therefore, in the following, eschewed all letters with signs, and given, as nearly as types alone will permit us, the exact pronunciation of the French names.

KEY TO FRENCH NAMES.

APPLES

Court Pendu Plat.—Coor Pahn du Plah.
Drap d'Or—Drah dor.
Fenouillet Gris—Fen-nool-yai Gree.
Male Carle.—Mal Carl.
Pomme de Neige.—Pum de Naije.
Reinette Blanche d'Espagne.—Ren-ett-Blansh d'Espagl.
Reinette Triomphante.—Ren-ett Tre-ome-fant.

APRICOTS.

Albergier.—Al-bare-je-ai.
Briançon.—Bre-ahn-sohn.

CHERRIES.

Belle de Choisy.—Bel de Shwoi-sey
Belle Magnifique.—Bel Man-gne-feek
Bigarreau —Be-gar-ro.
Bigarreau Rouge.—Be-gar-ro Rooje
Bigarreau Couleur de Chair —Be-gar-ro Coo-lur de Shair
Bigarreau Gros Cœuret —Be-gar-ro Gro Keur-ai.
Bigarreau Tardif de Hildesheim —Be-gar-ro Tar-deef de Hildeshein.
Gros Bigarreau Rouge —Gro Be-gar-ro Rooje
Griotte d'Espagne.—Gre-ote Des-pan

GRAPES.

Chasselas Musqué —Shah-slah Meus-kay
Chasselas de Fontainebleau.—Shah-slah de Fone-tane-blo
Ciotat —Se-o-tah
Lenoir.—Lun-war.

NECTARINES.

Brugnon Violet Musqué —Brune-yon Ve-o-lay Meus-kay.
Brugnon Musqué.—Brune-yon Meus-kay.
D'Angleterre —Dahn-glet-are
Duc du Tellier —Deuk du Tel-yay.

PEACHES.

Abricotée.—Ab-re-co-tay.
Belle de Vitry.—Bell de Ve-tree
Grosse Mignonne.—Groce Mene-yon
Madeleine de Courson —Mad-lane de Coor-son
Pavie de Pompone.—Pah-vee de Pom-pone.
Pourprée Hâtive —Poor-pray Hat-eve.
Sanguinole à Chair adhérente.—Sahn-gwe-nole ah Shair Ad-hay-rout

PEARS.

Amiré Joannet —Am-e-ray Jo-ahn-nay.
Ananas —An-an-ah.
Ananas d' Eté.—An-an-ah Da-tay.
Angleterre.—Ahn-glet-are.
Beurié —Bur-ray.
Belle de Bruxelles —Bel-de Broos-ell.
Belle et Bonne —Bel-a-Bun.
Belle Lucrative —Bel-lu-crah-teve
Beurré de Capiumont.—Bur-ray de Cap-u-mohn
Beurré d'Amalis —Bur-ray Dah-mah-lee.
Beurré Gris d'Hiver Nouveau.—Bur-ray Gree Dee-vair Noo-vo.
Beurré Diel —Bur-ray De-ell.
Beurré Bronzée.—Bur-ray Brone-zay.
Bezi d'Heri —Ba-zee Daree
Bezi Vaet.—Bazee Vah-ai
Beurré Crapaud —Bur-ray Crah-po
Bezi de Montigny —Bay-zee de Mon-teen-gnee.
Bon Chretien Fondante —Bone Cray-ti-an Fone-donte.
Boucquia —Boo-kiah.
Calebasse Grosse —Cal-bass Groce.
Capucin —Cap-u-san.
Chaumontel très Gros.—Sho-moné-tell tray Gro.

Compte de Lamy.—Conte de Lah-me.
Colmar Epine.—Cole-mar A-peen.
Crassanne.—Cras-sahn.
Cuisse Madame.—Kuees Mah-dam.
D'Amour.—Dam-oor.
De Louvain.—Dul-oo-van
Délices d'Hardenpont.—Day-lece Dar-dahn pone.
Doyenné d'Eté.—Dwoy-on-nay Day-tay.
Doyenné Panaché.—Dwoy-on-nay Pan-ah-Shay.
Dumortier.—Du-mor-te-ay.
Duchesse d'Angoulême.—Du-shess Dong-goo-lame.
Duchesse d'Orléans.—Du-shess Dor-lay-on.
Enfant Prodige.—On-font Pro-deeje.
Epine d'Eté.—A-peen day-tay.
Figue de Naples.—Feeg de Nah-pl.
Fondante d'Automne.—Fone-donte do-tonn.
Forme de Délices —Form de Day-lece.
Forelle.—Fo-rel.
Fondante du Bois.—Fone-dont du Bwoi.
Fortunée.—For-tu-nay.
Franc Réal d'Hiver.—Fronk Ray-ahl Dee-vair.
Glout Morceau.—Gloo Mor-so.
Héricart.—Hay-re-car.
Jalousie.—Jal-oo-zee.
Jalousie de Fontenay Vendée.—Jal-oo-zee de Fone-ten-ai Von-day.
Léon le Clerc.—Lay-on le Clair.
Limon.—Lee-mohn.
Louise Bonne.—Loo-eze Bun.
Madeleine, or Citron des Carmes.—Mad-lane, or Cee-trone day Carn
Marie Louise.—Mah-re Loo-eze.
Michaux.—Me-sho.
Passans de Portugal.—Pah-sahn de Por-tu-gal.
Pailleau.—Pahl-yo.
Paradise d'Automne —Par-ah-deze do-tonn.
Passe Colmar.—Pass Col-mar.
Quilletette.—Keel-tet.
Reine Caroline.—Rane Car-o-lene
Reine des Poires.—Rane day Pwore.
Rousselet Hâtif.—Roos-lay Hat-eef.
Sanspeau.—Sahn-po
Sieulle.—Se-ull.
Sucrée de Hoyerswarda.—Seu-cray de Hoyersworda.
Surpasse Virgalieu.—Seur-pass Vere-gal-yu.
St. Germain.—Sau Jare-man.
Sylvange.—Seel-vonje.
Vallée Franche —Vol-lay Fronsh.
Verte Longue.—Vairt Longh.
Verte Longue Panachée.—Vairt Longh Pan-ah-shay.
Virgouleuse.—Vere-goo-leuz.
Wilhelmine.—Wil-el-meen.

PLUMS.

Abricotée Rouge.—Ab-re-co-tay Rooje.
Diaprée Rouge.—De-ah-pray Rooje.
Drap d'Or.—Drah-dor.
Jaune Hâtive.—Jaun Hat-eve.
Mirabelle.—Me-rah-bell.
Précoce de Tours.—Pray-cose de Toor.
Prune Suisse.—Prune Su-ece.
Royale Hâtive.—Rwoy-al Hat-eve.

INDEX TO THE DIFFERENT FRUITS.

[The standard names are in Roman letters   The synonymous names in *Italic*]

ALMONDS

	Page
Amande Commune	150
Amandier Commun	150
Amandier à petit fruit	150
Amandier à gros fruit	150
Amandier à gros fruit dur	150
Amandier à coque tendre	150
Amandier des dames	150
Amande Princesse	150
Amande Sultane	151
Amandier Sultane	151
Amande Pistache	151
Amandier Pistache	151
Amandier Pêcher	151
Bitter Almond	152
Common Almond	150
Common Sweet	150
Doux à coque tendre	150
Dwarf Double-Flowering Almond	152
Long Hard-Shell Almond	150
Ladies' Thin Shell	150
Large Double-Flowering Almond	152
Pistachia Sweet Almond	151
Peach Almond	151
Pêcher	151
Peach Almond	151
Soft-Shell Sweet Almond	150
Sultan à coque tendre	150
Sultana Sweet Almond	151
Sultan	151

APPLES

	Page
Alexander	79
Alfriston	97

	Page
American Mammoth	110
American Newtown Pippin	118
Amber Crab	147
American Summer Pearmain	70
American Red Juneating	73
American Pippin	98
Aporta	79
Arbroath Pippin	75
Aurore	129
Autumn Pearmain	80
Autumn Seek-no-further	96
Baltimore	110
Balgone Pippin	112
Boyfordbury Golden Pippin	112
Bay Apple	71
Baldwin	98
Belle-Fleur	102
Belle-Fleur Rouge	102
Bedfordshire Foundling	107
Benoni	70
Beauty of Kent	81
Beauty of the West	81
Bell's Scarlet Pearmain	96
Bell-Flower	100
Black Detroit	106
Black Apple	106
Blenheim Pippin	81
Blenheim Orange	81
Black Apple	99
Black American	99
Boston or Roxbury Russet	133
Borovitsky	70
Bonne de Mai	71
Bough	71
Borsdorffer	99
Borsdorff	99
Brabant Belle Fleur	102
Brandy Apple	111
Bread and Cheese Apple	92

	Page		Page
Burlington Greening	128	Duchess of Oldenburgh	83
Catshead	103	Duc d'Arsel	120
Catshead Beaufin	120	Dutch Codlin	83
Cathead Greening	103	Dutch Mignonne	107
Calville Blanche d'Hiver	102	Dyer	83
Calville Rouge d'Hiver	103	Early Summer Pearmain	70
Calville Rouge	103	Early Summer Pippin	71
Capendu	105	Early Harvest	72
Cayuga Red Streak	140	Early French Reinette	72
Canada Reinette	129	Early Red Margaret	73
Canadian Reinette	129	Early Red Juneating	73
Campfield	144	Early Strawberry Apple	73
Carthouse	144	Early Crofton	74
Catline	82	Early Sweet Bough	74
Chandler	104	Easter Pippin	109
Charles Apple	116	Edmonton's Aromatic Pippin	88
Chalmer's Large	83	Edler Winter Borsdoffer	99
Claygate Pearmain	122	Eighteen Ounce Apple	140
Copmanthorpe Crab	107	Elizabeth	129
Cornish Gilliflower	102	Elton Pippin	82
Cornish July-flower	102	Embroidered Pippin	109
Cos or Caas	103	Emperor Alexander	79
Court Pendu Gris	109	English Codlin	91
Court Pendu Plat	105	English Golden Pippin	112
Court Pendu	105	English Nonpareil	120
Court Pendu Plat Rougeatre	105	English Pippin	129
Court Pendu Extra	105	English Russet	132
Court Pendu Rond Gros	105	English Golden Russet	132
Court Pendu Rose	105	Epse's Sweet	108
Court Pendu Musqué	105	Esopus Spitzenburgh	138
Coriander Rose	105	Eve Apple	73
Court of Wick	105	Fall Pippin	130
Court of Wick Pippin	105	Fall Harvey	84
Court de Wick	105	Fall Pippin	84
Court Pendu Doré	129	Fameuse	91
Cobbett's Fall Pippin	130	Fallawater	109
Cooper's Russeting	144	Fenouillet Gris	110
Cole	71	Fenouillet Jaune	109
Cornish Aromatic	81	Fenouillet Rouge	109
Cranberry Pippin	106	Flower of Kent	83
Crimson Pippin	106	Flint Russet	93
Cumberland Spice	101	Flushing Spitzenburgh	139
Dainty Apple	113	Forest Styre	146
Danver's Winter Sweet	108	Formosa Pippin	131
De St. Julian	108	Fox Whelp	146
Detroit	101	Fry's Pippin	105
Detroit	106	French Pippin	121
De Bretagne	129	French Crab	109
D'Espagne	130	Franklin's Golden Pippin	83
Devonshire Quarrenden	71	Frank Rambour	94
De Witt	107	Garnon's Apple	105
Doctor	107	Ganet Pippin	99
Domine	107	Gates Apple	142
Downton Pippin	82	Gilpin	144
Downton Golden Pippin	82	Gloria Mundi	110
Downy	113	Glazenwood Gloria Mundi	110
Drap d'Or	71	Glace de Zelande	78
Drap d'Or	109	Glory of York	131
Dundee	129	Golden Drop	105

	Page.		Page.
Golden Ball....	111	*Knight's Codlin*	97
Golden Harvey	111	*Koening's Pippelin*	112
Golden Pippin	112	*Large Black*	106
Golden Reinette	129	*Large Fall Pippin*	130
Golden Russet	131	Ladies' Sweeting	136
Golden Sweet	84	Lady Apple	115
Gray Apple	124	Large Red Siberian Crab	147
Green Bell-flower	101	*Large White Juneating*	72
Green Newtown Pippin	118	Large Yellow Bough	74
Green Winter Pippin	118	*Large Yellow Summer*	75
Grise	124	*Le Grand Bohemian Bors-*	
Gross Reinette d'Angleterre	129	*dorffer*	99
Gregson Apple	82	Lemon Pippin	115
Gravenstein	83	*London Golden Pippin*	112
Grave Stije	85	Longville's Kernel	90
Grand Sachem	86	*Lord Guydr's Newtown Pip-*	
Grindstone	98	*pin*	97
Grosser Casselar Reinette	107	*Loveden's Pippin*	120
Grune Reinette	120	*Lyman's Large Summer*	75
Hartford Sweeting	136	*Lyscom*	89
Harrison	145	*Lyman's Pumpkin Sweet*	89
Hagloe Crab,	145	*Male Carle*	116
Hawthorden	86	*Maclean's Favorite*	117
Hampshire Yellow	85	*Margil*	117
Hay's Winter	143	*Margaret, or Striped Juneat-*	
Herefordshire Golden Pippin.	112	*ing*	73
Herefordshire Pearmain	121	*Margaretha Apfel*	73
Hewe's Virginia Crab	145	Maiden's Blush	90
Herefordshire Red Streak	146	*Mela di Carlo*	116
Hinckman	121	*Mela Carla*	116
Hoary Morning	113	*Menagère*	117
Hollow-cored Pippin	101	*Megginch Favorite*	129
Holland Pippin	86	*Milton Golden Pippin*	112
Hubbardston Nonsuch	113	Minister	116
Hunt's Nonpareil	120	Michael Henry Pippin	118
Hutching's Seedling	76	*Monstrous Bell-flower*	101
Irish Peach Apple	74	*Monstrous Pippin*	110
Irish Russet	134	Mouse Apple	117
Ironstone	109	*Moose Apple*	117
Jonathan	113	*Munche's Pippin*	117
Januarea	129	Murphy	118
Jersey Greening	128	*New York Gloria Mundi*	110
Jersey Sweeting	87	Newtown Spitzenburgh	139
July Pippin	72	*New Scarlet Nonpareil*	120
Juneating	78	*Never-Fail*	117
Kentish Fill-basket	114	Newtown Pippin	118
Keswick Codlin	87	Newark King	121
Kenrick's Autumn	87	Newark Pippin	121
Kerry Pippin	88	*Newark Sweeting*	144
King Philip	113	Nonpareil	120
Kirke's Lord Nelson	114	Northern Spy	120
Kirke's Lemon Pippin	115	*Norfolk Pippin*	123
Kirk's Golden Reinette	129	Norfolk Beaufin	120
Kilham Hill	87	Nonsuch	91
King of the Pippins	88	*Nonsuch*	91
King George the Third	99	*Ohio Favorite*	101
King	99	*Old Golden Pippin*	112
Knightwick Pippin	105	Old English Codlin	91
Knight's Golden Pippin	82	*Oldaker's New*	97

	Page		Page
Old Nonpareil	120	Ramsdell's Red Pumpkin, Sweet	137
Orange Sweeting	84	Ramsdell's Sweeting	137
Ortley Apple	142	Read's Baker	120
Ortley Pippin	142	Red Belle-Fleur	102
Original Nonpareil	122	Red Winter Calville	103
Oslin	75	Red Calville	103
Osgood's Favorite	89	Red Letroit	106
Owen's Golden Beauty	78	Red Doctor	107
Ox Apple	110	Red or Black Gilliflower	134
Oxford Peach	96	Red Pumpkin Sweet	137
Paternoster Apfel	107	Red Streak	146
Parmin Royal	121	Red Quarrenden	71
Parmain d'Eté	80	Red Juneating	73
Pepin d'Or	112	Red Astrachan	75
Petersburgh Pippin	118	Red Ingestrie	95
Pennock's Red Winter	125	Reinette blanche d'Espagne	130
Pennock	125	Reinette Triomphante	130
Pearson's Plate	126	Reinette d'Angleterre	112
Peck's Pleasant	126	Reinette du Canada Blanche	129
Pennington's Seedling	127	Reinette Grosse du Canada	129
Peach Pond Sweet	91	Reinette du Canada à Cortes	129
Pecker	98	Reinette d'Aix	129
Petit Api Rouge	115	Reinette Dorée	107
Philip Rick	113	Reinette d'Hollande	86
Phillip's Reinette	105	Reinette Bâtarde	99
Pie Apple	86	Reinette de Misnie	99
Pine Apple Russet	93	Rhode Island Greening	128
Pomme d'Api Rouge	115	Ribston Pippin	131
Pompey	141	Rival Golden Pippin	105
Pomme Grise	124	Round Catshead	103
Pomme de Caractère	109	Royal Pearmain	121
Pomme Royale	83	Royale d'Angleterre	121
Pomme Rose	115	Roxbury Russeting	133
Pound Royal	124	Rode Wyn Appel	77
Pomme Regelans	102	Royal Pearmain	80
Pomme de Berlin	105	Roman Stem	131
Pomme d'Anis	110	Romanite	93
Pomme d'Or	112	Ross Nonpareil	95
Pomme de Charles	116	Russian	105
Pomme Finale	116	Russet Golden Pippin	112
Pomme de Laak	107	Russian Emperor	79
Pound	127	Saint Julian	108
Pomme de Caen	129	Sam Rawlings	113
Portugal	129	Sam Young	134
Pomme de Neige	91	Sack Apple	71
Porter	92	Sapson	77
Princesse Noble Zoete	105	Sam's Crab	90
Priestley	126	Sanguineus	91
Priestley's American	126	Scudamore's Crab	146
Prince's Harvest, or Early French Reinette	72	Scarlet Perfume	71
Pumpkin Russet	93	Scarlet Pearmain	96
Pumpkin Sweet	93	Scarlet Nonpareil	120
Putnam Russet	132	Seek-no-further	93
Queen's	99	Seek-no-further	98
Rambo	93	Sheep Nose	131
Rambour Franc	94	Siberian Bitter Sweet	146
Rambour d'Eté	94	Siberian Crab	147

	Page.
Sine-qua-non	76
Sops of Wine	77
Smithfield Spice	83
Spencer Sweeting	136
Sturmer Pippin	135
Styre	146
Styre	146
Striped Juneating	73
Stroat	97
Straat	97
Stal cubs	141
Surprise	134
Sugar Loaf Pippin	76
Summer Rose	77
Summer Queen	77
Summer Golden Pippin	77
Summer Pearmain	80
Summer Hagloe	146
Summer Pippin	86
Summer Rambour	94
Summer Sweet Paradise	96
Swaar	131
Sweet Russet	93
Sweet Pearmain	123
Sweet Harvest	74
Tart Bough	72
Tewksbury Winter Blush	140
Tolman Sweeting	137
Travers	131
Twenty ounce Pippin	140
Tetofsky	78
Transparent Pippin	105
Transparent de Moscovie	78
True Spitzenburgh	138
Twenty Ounce	140
Twenty ounce Apple	140
Vandyne	142
Warter's Golden Pippin	112
Victuals and Drink	141
Vandevere	141
Victorious Reinette	130
Vrai drap d'or	71
Watson's Dumpling	142
Whare Reinette	129
Watson's Dumpling	142
Waxen Apple	112
White Apple	142
Woolman's Long	142
Week's Pippin	105
Wells's Sweeting	140
Westfield Seek-no-further	96
White Bell-Fleur	101
White Bellflower	101
White Detroit	101
White Winter Calvi'le	103
White Calville	103
White Spanish Reinette	130
White Juneating	78
White Astrachan	78

	Page
White Hawthornden	89
Winter Pearmain	80
Winter Queen	144
Winter Queening	144
Wine Apple	143
Wine Sap	143
Wine Sop	143
White Apple	142
Williams's Favourite	79
Wollaton Pippin	105
Woolman's Long	142
Winter Sweet Paradise	124
Wood's Huntingdon	105
Woolman's Harvest	77
Woodstock Pippin	81
Woodstock	83
Wormsley Pippin	97
Woodpecker	98
Wyker Pippin	129
Wygers	129
Yellow	105
Yellow Newtown Pippin	119
Yellow Pippin	121
Yellow German Reinette	129
Yellow Siberian Crab	147
Yellow Harvest	72
Yellow Belle Fleur	100
Yellow Bell-flower	100
Young's Long Keeping	109

APRICOTS

Abricot Pêche	157
Abricot Commun	157
Abricot Précoce	158
Abricot Hatif Musqué	158
Abricot Hatif	158
Abricotier	158
Abricot blanc	159
Abricotier blanc	153
Albergier	153
Alberge	153
Amande Aveline	154
Ananas	154
Angoumois	154
Anson's Imperial	157
Blotched Leaved Turkey	159
Black	154
Blotched Leaved Roman	157
Blenheim	158
Blanc	159
Breda	154
Brussels	155
Brown Maseuline	158
Briançon	159
D'Alexandrie	156
De Hollande	154
De St. Jean	155

	Page		Page.
De St. Jean Rouge	155	Common Red	160
De Nancy	155	Mahonia	161
De Nancy	157	Nepal	161
De Nancy	159	Seedless	161
Double flowering Apricot	160	Stoneless	161
Du Pape	154	Vinetier Sans Noyeau	161
Dunmore	155		
Dunmore's Breda	155	**CHERRIES.**	
Du Luxembourg	157		
Early Orange	156	À Courte Queue de Provence	193
Early Masculine	158	Allen's Sweet Montmorency	193
Early White Masculine	159	Allerheiligen Kirsche	200
Früher Muscateller	158	American Amber	167
Germine	157	Amber Gean	168
Gros Précoce	155	Amber Heart	173
Gros d'Alexandrie	155	Amber à petit fruit	178
Gros Frühe	155	American Heart	178
Grosse Germine	157	Amber or Imperial	179
Hasselnussmandel	154	Ambrée de Choisy	190
Hemskirke	155	Ambrée à Gros Fruit	190
Hunt's Moorpark	155	Ansell's Fine Black	169
Large Early	155	Anglaise Tardive	191
Large Turkey	159	Apple Cherry	187
Moorpark	155	Arden's Early White Heart	173
Musch-Musch	156	Armstrong's Bigarreau	181
Noir	154	Arch Duke	189
Oldaker's Moorpark	155	Baumann's May	168
Orange	156	Belle de Rocmont	182
Persique	154	Belle de Rocmont	183
Persian	156	Belle de Choisy	190
Peach	157	Benham's Fine Early Duke	191
Pêche	157	Belle Magnifique	193
Pêche Grosse	157	Belle et Magnifique	193
Pfirsche	157	Bigarreau de Mai	168
Purple	154	Bigarreau	179
Red Masculine	158	Bigarreau Royal	179
Royal	158	Bigarreau Gros	179
Roman	157	Bigarreau Tardif	179
Royal Peach	157	Bigarreau Blanc	180
Royal Persian	156	Bigarreau Rouge	181
Royal Orange	156	Bigarreau d'Hollande	181
Royal George	156	Bigarreau Couleur de Chair	183
Shipley's	158	Bigarreau à Gros fruit Blanc	182
Shipley's Large	158	Bigarreau de Rocmont	182
Sudlow's Moorpark	155	Bigarreau Lauermann	183
Temple's	155	Bigarreau Gros Cœuret	183
Transparent	157	Bigarreau Gros Monstrueux	183
Turkey	159	Bigarreau à Gros Fruit Rouge	183
Violet	154	Bigarreau Tardif de Hildesheim	184
Walton Moorpark	155	Bigarreau Marbrée de Hildes-	
White Masculine	159	heim	184
White Apricot	159	Bigarreau Blanc Tardif de	
White Algiers	159	Hildesheim	184
Wurtemburg	157	Bigarreau Noir	185
		Bigarreau Gros Noir	188
		Bigarreautier à Feuilles de	
BERBERRIES.		Tabac	189
		Bigarreautier à Grandes Feu-	
Black Sweet Magellan	161	illes	189

48*

	Page.		Page
Bloodgood's Amber	167	Cluster	194
Bloodgood's Honey	167	Common English	171
Bloodgood's New Honey	167	Corone	172
Black Heart	169	Couronne	172
Black Caroon	169	Coroun	172
Black Russian	169	Cœur de Pigeon	189
Black Eagle	170	Coularde	191
Black Circassian	170	Commune à Trochet	194
Black Tartarian	170	Common Red	196
Black Russian	170	Commune	196
Black Mazzard	171	Common Red	197
Black Honey	171	Common Sour Cherry	197
Black Orleans	172	Common Morello	198
Bleeding Heart	171	Crown	194
Black Bigarreau	185	Davenport's Early	172
Black Bigarreau of Savoy	185	Davenport	172
Bowyer's Early Heart	171	Davenport's Early Black	172
Bouquet Amarelle	194	De Hollande	191
Bristol Cherry	171	D'Espagne	191
Bullock's Heart	176	Downton	172
Buttner's Yellow	185	Downer's Late	173
Buttner's Wdch's--Knorpel		Downer	173
Kirsche	185	Downer's Late Red	173
Buttner's Gelbe-Knorpel		Downing's Red Cheek	186
Kirsche	185	Double Volgers	195
Buchanan's Early Duke	191	Double French Cherry	199
Buttner's October Morello	193	Double Flowering Kentish	200
Buttner's October Zucker		Dredge's Early White Heart	173
Weichsel	193	Dutch Morello	197
Busch Weichsel	191	Dwarf Double Flowering	200
Buschel Kirsche	194	Early Black	169
Carnation	194	Early White Heart	173
Cerise Ambrée	179	Early Purple Guigne	174
Cerisier de 4 à livre	189	Early Purple Griotte	174
Cerise Doucette	190	Early Duke	191
Cerise de la Palembre	190	Early May	195
Cerise à Noyeau Tendre	190	Early Richmond	196
Cerise Guigne	191	Elton	186
Cerise Nouvelle d'Angleterre	191	Elkhorn	188
Cerise de Portugal	191	Elkhorn of Maryland	188
Cerise à Bouquet	194	English Weichsel	195
Cerise à Trochet	194	English Morello	197
Cerisier Nain à Fruit Rond	195	Ever Flowering Cherry	200
Cerisier Nain à Fruit Rond	195	Flesh-Colored Bigarreau	182
Cerisier Nain à Fruit Précoce	195	Florence	187
Cerise à Courte Queue	195	Flemish	195
Cerise du nord	197	Four to the Pound	189
Cerisier à fleurs Doubles	200	Fraser's Black Tartarian	170
Cerise de la Toussainte	200	Fraser's Black Heart	170
Cerise Tardive	200	Fraser's Black	170
Cerisier Pleurant	200	Fraser's Tartarische	170
Cerise de St. Martin	200	Fraser's White Tartarian	178
Cerisier de Virginie	201	Fraser's White Transparent	178
China Bigarreau	184	Fruhe Kleine Runde Zwerg	
Chinese Heart	184	Weichsel	195
Cherry Duke	190	Gascoigne's Heart	174
Cherry Duke	191	Gean Amber	168
Chevreuse	194	Gobet à Courte Queue	195
Chinese Double Flowering	200	Grosse Schwarze Herz Kirsche	169

	Page.
Graffion	179
Groote Princesse	179
Grosse Bigarreau Couleur de Chair	182
Gros Bigarreau Blanc	182
Gros Cœuret	183
Gros Bigarreau Rouge	183
Gridley	187
Grosse Schwarze Knoorpel	188
Griotte de Portugal	189
Griotte Grosse Noir	191
Griotte d' Espagne	191
Griotte Précose	191
Grosse Cerise Rouge Pâle	194
Griottier Rouge Pâle	194
Griotte de Villennes	194
Griottier à Bouquet	194
Griottier Nain Précoce	195
Gros Gobet	195
Griotte Ordinaire du Nord	197
Guinier à Fruit Noir	169
Guigne Grosse Noir	169
Guigne Rouge Hâtive	171
Guigne Noir Tardive	188
Guignier à Feuilles de Tabac	189
Guignier à Rameaux Pendans	200
Harrison Heart	180
Hâtive	195
Herefordshire Black	172
Herefordshire Heart	174
Hildesheimer ganz Spâte Knorpel Kirsche	184
Hildesheimer Spâte Herz Kirsche	184
Hildesheim Bigarreau	184
Honey	175
Hollandische Grosse	179
Holland Bigarreau	181
Holman's Duke	192
Hyde's Red Heart	175
Italian Heart	179
Jeffrey's Duke	190
Jeffrey's Royal	190
Jeffrey's Royal Caroon	190
Kentish	195
Kentish	196
Kentish	196
Kentish Red	196
Kentish Red	197
Knevett's Late Bigarreau	187
Knight's Early Black	175
Kentish	197
Large Wild Black	172
Large Honey	175
Large White Bigarreau	180
Large Heart-Shaped Bigarreau	182
Lauermann's Kirsche	183
Lauermann's Grosse Kirsche	183

	Page
Lauermann's Herz Kirsche	183
Large Heart-Shaped Bigarreau	183
Large Red Bigarreau	183
Lady Southampton's Yellow	187
Lady Southampton's Duke	187
Lady Southampton's Golden Drop	187
Large Black Bigarreau	188
Late Arch Duke	189
Late Duke	189
Late Duke	191
Large Mayduke	191
Late Kentish	197
Late May Duke	192
Large Morello	197
Late Morello	197
Large Double-Flowering	199
Lion's Heart	176
Manning's Early Black Heart	169
Mazzard	171
Manning's Mottled	176
Maccarty	187
Madison Bigarreau	187
Manning's Late Black	188
Manning's Late Black Heart	188
May Duke	191
May Cherry	195
Martin's Weichsel	200
Merry Cherry	171
Merisier à petit fruit	171
Merisier à petit fruit noir	171
Merisier à fruit blanc	175
Merisier à fleurs Doubles	199
Millett's Late Heart Duke	191
Milan	197
Mottled Bigarreau	176
Morris' Early Duke	191
Montmorency	195
Montmorency à gros fruit	195
Montmorency	196
Montmorency à longue queue	196
Montmorency	196
Morello	197
Monat's Amarelle	200
Muscat de Prague	196
Napoleon Bigarreau	183
Nain Précoce	195
New Large Black Bigarreau	185
Ochsen Herz Kirche	176
Ox Heart	176
Petite Cerise Rouge Précose	195
Pie Cherry	196
Pie Cherry	197
Plumstone Morello	198
Portugal Duke	189
Portugal Duke	191
Prinzessin Kirsche	179
Prince's Duke	194

	Page.			Page
Précoce	195		West's White Hear	179
Red Heart	174		Weichsel mit gauzkurzen stiel.	195
Remington	188		Weeping or All Saint's	200
Remington White Heart	188		White Mazzard	171
Remington Heart	188		Whixley Black	171
Rivers' Early Heart	177		White Heart	173
Rivers' Early Amber	177		White Transparent	173
Ronald's Large Black Heart	170		White Tartarian	178
Ronald's Heart	170		White Bigarreau	179
Robert's Red Heart	176		White Bigarreau	180
Royale	190		White Ox Heart	180
Royale Ordinaire	190		Wilder's Bigarreau de Mai	168
Royal Hâtive	191		Wild English Cherry	171
Royal Duke	192		Wild Black Fruited	171
Royal Anglaise Tardive	192		Wild Cherry	201
Ronald's Large Morello	197		Yellow Honey	175
Rumsey's Late Morello	199		Yellow Spanish	179
Schwarze Herz Kirsche	170		Yellow or Golden	187
Schöne von Choisy	190		Yung To	200
September Weichsel Grosse	197			
Serrulated leaved Cherry	200		CURRANTS.	
Small Double-Flowering	200			
Small May	195		Black English	204
Small Wild Black	171		Black Naples	205
Spanish Black Heart	169		Cassis	204
Sparkhawk's Honey	177		Champagne	204
Sparrowhawk's Honey	177		Common Black	204
Spotted Bigarreau	181		Groseillier Rouge à Gros Fruit	203
Späte Hildesheimer Marmor			Groseillier à fruit couleur de	
Kirsche	184		Chair	204
Spanish Yellow	187		Knight's Large Red	204
St. Martin's Amarelle	200		Knight's Early Red	204
Superb Circassian	170		Knight's Sweet Red	204
Sussex	196		Large Red Dutch	203
Sweet Montmorency	193		Large Bunched Red	203
Tartarian	170		Long Bunched Red	203
Thompson's Duke	191		May's Victoria	204
Tobacco Leaved	189		Missouri Currant	205
Transparent Guigne	177		Morgan's Red	203
Transparent Gean	177		Morgan's White	203
Transparent	177		New Red Dutch	203
Tradescant	180		New White Dutch	203
Tradescant's Black Heart	188		Pheasant's Eye	204
Tradescant's	188		Red Dutch	203
Trauben Amarelle	194		Red Grape	203
Très Fertile	194		Reeve's White	203
Turkey Bigarreau	179		Red Flowering Currant	205
Turkey Bigarreau	180		Striped Fruited	204
Very Large Heart	176		Grosse Weiss und Rothge-	
Vier auf ein Pfund	189		streifte Johannisbeere	204
Virginian May	196		White Dutch	203
Virginian Wild Cherry	201		White Crystal	203
Virginisch Kirsche	201		White Leghorn	203
Waterloo	178			
Wax Cherry	194			
Werder's Early Black Heart	169			
Werder's Early Black	169		FIGS.	
Werdersche Frühe Schwarze				
Herz Kirsche	169		Angelique	211

	Page.		Page
Bayswater	209	Early Green Hairy	216
Black Naples	209	Edwards's Jolly Tar	216
Black Ischia	210	Farrow's Roaring Lion	215
Blue Ischia	210	Glenton Green	216
Black Genoa	210	Gorton's Viper	216
Bordeaux	211	Green Walnut	217
Brunswick	209	Hartshorn's Lancashire Lad	216
Brown Hamburg	209	Hapley's Lady of the Manor	217
Brown Turkey	210	Hepburn Green Prolific	217
Brown Italian	210	Hill's Golden Gourd	216
Brown Naples	210	Keen's Seedling	216
Brown Ischia	210	Leigh's Rifleman	216
Chestnut	210	Massey's Heart of Oak	217
Chestnut-coloured Ischia	210	Melling's Crown Bob	216
Clementine	209	Miss Bold	216
Concourelle Blanche	211	Part's Golden Fleece	216
Early Forcing	210	Parkinson's Laurel	217
Figue Blanche	212	Pitmaston Green Gage	217
Ford's Seedling	212	Prophet's Rockwood	216
Green Ischia	212	Red Warrington	216
Hanover	209	Saunder's Cheshire Lass	217
Italian	210	Taylor's Bright Venus	217
Large Blue	210	Wainman's Green Ocean	217
Large White Genoa	212	Wellington's Glory	217
Lee's Perpetual	210	White Honey	217
Madonna	209	Woodward's Whitesmith	217
Malta	211	Yellow Champagne	216
Marseilles	212	Yellow Ball	216
Mélitte	211		
Murrey	210		
Nerii	212	GRAPES.	
Pocock	212		
Pregussata	212	Alicant	237
Red	209	Alcatica du Po	240
Small Brown	211	Aleppo	246
Small Brown Ischia	211	Alexander's	253
Violette	211	Amber Muscadine	242
Violette de Bordeaux	211	Amiens	212
White Marseilles	212	American Muscadine	258
White Naples	212	Ansell's large Oval Black	238
White Standard	212	Auverne	236
White Ischia	212	Auvernat	236
		Auvernas Rouge	236
		August Traube	239
GOOSEBERRIES.		Black Cluster	236
		Black Morillon	236
Berry's Greenwood	216	Black Burgundy	236
Boardman's British Crown	215	Black Frontignan	236
Buerdsill's Duckwing	216	Black Frontignac	236
Capper's Top-Sawyer	215	Black Constantia	236
Capper's Bunker's Hill	216	Blue Frontignan	237
Capper's Bonny Lass	217	Black Hamburgh	237
Champagne	215	Blue Trollinger	237
Cleworth's White Lion	217	Black Prince	237
Collier's Jolly Angler	216	Black Spanish	237
Cook's White Eagle	217	Black Valentia	237
Crompton Sheba Queen	217	Black Portugal	237
Early Sulphur	216	Black Lisbon	237

	Page.		Page
Black Lombardy	238	*Fleish Traube*	237
Black Morocco	238	*Flame Colored Tokay*	247
Black Muscadel	238	*Fox Grape*	258
Black St. Peter's	238	*Franc Pineau*	236
Black Palestine	238	*Frankendale*	237
Black Muscat of Alexandria	238	*Frankenthaler*	237
Black Tripoli	239	*Frankenthaler Gros Noir*	237
Black Grape from Tripoli	239	*Fromenté*	240
Black Muscadine	239	*Frontiac of Alexandria*	243
Black Chasselas	239	*Genuine Tokay*	244
Black Sweetwater	239	*Gibraltar*	237
Blanc de Bonneuil	241	*Golden Chasselas*	242
Blacksmith's White Cluster	242	*Grove End Sweetwater*	241
Bland	253	*Gray Tokay*	244
Bland's Virginia	253	*Grosser Riessling*	245
Bland's Madeira	253	Grizzly Frontignan	246
Bland's Pale Red	253	*Grizzly Frontignac*	246
Bourdales des Hautes Pyrenées	236	*Grauer Muscateller*	246
Boston	237	*Hampton Court Vine*	237
Brown Hamburgh	237	*Hardy Blue Windsor*	240
Burgunder	236	*Hudler*	237
Burgunder	239	Isabella	253
Bull or Bullett	258	*Jacob's Traube*	239
Cambridge Botanic Garden	237	*Jews*	247
Cannon Hall Muscat	244	*Jerusalem Muscat*	241
Cape Grape	253	*July Grape*	238
Catawba	254	*Kleiner Rissling*	245
Catawba Tokay	254	Knight's Variegated Chasselas	247
Chasselas noir	239	*Kummel Traübe*	246
Chasselas Musqué	241	*Languedoc*	237
Chadsworth Tokay	244	*Le Cœur*	238
Chasselas Doré	242	*Le Meunier*	240
Chasselas Blanc	242	*Le Cœur*	241
Chasselas de Fontainebleau	242	*Le Melier*	241
Chasselas Précoce	244	Lenoir	256
Chasselas Royal	244	Lombardy	247
Chasselas Panaché	246	*Longworth's Ohio*	257
Chasselas Rouge	247	*Lunel*	243
Ciotat	240	*Madeleine*	239
Clifton's Constantia	253	*Madeleine Noir*	239
Clarence	256	*Malmsey Muscadine*	240
Cumberland Lodge	240	*Madeira Wine Grape*	243
D'Arbois	242	*Madeira*	253
De St. Jean	239	*Malaga*	243
Diana	255	Malaga	243
Dutch Hamburg	237	*Maurillan Panaché*	246
Dutch Sweetwater	241	*Maurillan noir Panaché*	246
Early Black	236	*Melier Blanc*	241
Early Black July	239	Miller's Burgundy	240
Early White Malvasia	241	*Miller Grape*	240
Early Chasselas	241	Missouri	256
Early White Teneriffe	242	*Missouri Seedling*	256
Early White Muscadine	241	*Morillon Noir*	236
Early Sweetwater	244	*Mohrendutte*	237
Elsinburgh	255	*Money's*	238
Elsenborough	255	*Morillon Hâtif*	239
Esperione	240	*Morillon Tacconné*	240
Farineux Noir	240	*Morone Farinaccio*	**240**

	Page.		Page.
Morna Chasselas	241	Reissling	245
Mornain Blanc	241	Red Frontignan	246
Moschata Bianca	244	Red Constantia	246
Moscado Bianco	244	Rhenish Red	247
Moscatel Common	244	Roanoke	258
Muscat Noir Ordinaire	236	Rother	236
Muscat Noir de Jura	236	Royal Muscadine	242
Müller	240	Rössling	245
Mulleorebe	240	Rudesheimerberg	245
Musk Chasselas	241	Salisbury Violet	237
Muscat d'Alexandrie	243	Saint Peter's	238
Muscat Blanc	244	Sauvignien noir	240
Muscat Blanc de Jura	244	Schwarzer Frühzeiteger	239
Muscateller	244	Scotch White Cluster	242
Muscat Rouge	246	Schloss Johannisberg	245
Muscat Gris	246	Schuylkill Muscadell	253
Muscado Rosso	246	Schuylkill Muscadine	253
Muscat Noir	236	Scuppernong	258
Nepean's Constantia	244	Schwarzer	236
Noirin	240	Segar-Box Grape	257
Norton's Virginia	256	Shurtleff's Seedling	257
Norton's Seedling	256	Sir William Rowley's Black	236
Ohio	257	Sir A. Pytche's Black	237
Oldaker's West's St. Peter's	238	Small Black Cluster	236
Parsley-leaved	240	Smart's Elsingburg	253
Parsley-leaved Muscadine	240	Spring Mill Constantia	253
Passe longue Musqué	243	Steward's Black Prince	237
Passe Musqué	243	Stillward's Sweetwater	244
Petit Riessling	245	Striped Muscadine	246
Pineau	236	Sumpter	256
Pitmaston White Cluster	241	Switzerland Grape	246
Pocock's Damascus	237	Syrian	242
Poonah	238	Tasker's Grape	253
Powell	253	Tottenham Park Muscat	243
Pond' Seedling	255	Tokai Blanc	244
Purple Frontignan	236	To Kalon	254
Purple Constantia	236	Troller	237
Purple Hamburg	237	Trollinger	237
Pulverulenta	240	True Burgundy	236
Raisin de Bourgugne	236	Turner's Black	240
Raisin des Carmes	238	Valentine's	237
Raisin de Cuba	238	Variegated Chasselas	246
Raisin d'Espagne	238	Variegated Chasselas	247
Raisin Précoce	239	Verdelho	243
Raisin d'Autriche	240	Verdilhio	243
Raisin de Champagne	242	Verdal	245
Raisin de Frontignan	244	Victoria	237
Raisin Suisse	246	Warner's Black Hamburgh	237
Raisin d'Alep	246	Water Zoet Noir	239
Red Frontignan	246	Water Zoete Blanc	244
Red Grape of Taurida	247	Wantage	247
Red Chasselas	247	Warren	258
Red Muscadine	247	Welscher	237
Red Scuppernong	253	Weissholziger Trollinger	237
Red Muncy	251	West's St. Peter's	238
Red Hamburgh	237	White Parsley-Leaved	240
Red Muscat of Alexandria	238	White Melier	241
Red Frontignan of Jerusalem	238	White Chasselas	242

	Page
White Muscat of Alexandria	213
White Muscat	213
White Muscat of Lunel	213
White Frontignan	211
White Constantia	211
White Frontinac	211
White Sweet Water	211
White Muscadine	211
White Tokay	211
White Hamburgh	215
White Lisbon	215
White Portugal	215
White Raisin	215
White Nice	215
White Rissling	215
Winne	253
Wilmot's New Black Hamburgh	237
Weisser Muscateller	214
Weisse Muscaten Traube	214
Zebibo	213

MELONS

	Page
Beechwood	540
Black Rock	540
Citron	539
Dimpsha	541
Early Canteloup	540
Franklin's Green Fleshed	539
Green Hoosainee	540
Green Valencia	540
Improved Green Flesh	539
Keising	540
Large Germek	540
Netted Canteloup	540
Nutmeg	539
Rock Canteloup	540
Sweet Ispahan	540

MULBERRIES.

	Page
Black or English	260
Johnson	260
Red	259

NECTARINES.

	Page
Anderson's	508
Anderson's (of some)	503
Anderson's Round	508
Aromatic	506
Black	505
Black Murry	505
Boston	502
Broomfield	
Brugnon Hâtif	506
Brugnon Red at the Stone	508

	Page
Brugnon de Newington	508
Brugnon Musqué	508
Brugnon Violette Musquée	508
Claremont	503
Common Elruge	503
Cowdray White	505
D'Angleterre	508
Downton	503
Duc du Tellier's	503
Duc de Tilly	503
Duc de Tello	503
Du Tilley's	503
Early Violet	506
Early Brugnon	506
Early Newington	508
Early Black Newington	508
Early Black	508
Elruge	503
Emerton's New White	505
Fairchild's	504
Fairchild's Early	504
Fine Gold-Fleshed	507
Flanders	505
French Newington	508
Golden	507
Hardwicke Seedling	504
Hampton Court	506
Hunt's Tawny	504
Hunt's Large Tawny	504
Hunt's Early Tawny	504
Large White	505
Late Green	506
Large Scarlet	506
Lewis	502
Lord Selsey's Elruge	506
Lucombe's Black	508
Lucombe's Seedling	508
Murrey	505
Murry	505
New White	505
Neal's White	505
New Scarlet	506
Newington	508
New Dark Newington	508
New Early Newington	508
Oatland's	503
Old White	505
Old Newington	508
Old Roman	508
Orange	507
Perkins' Seedling	502
Peterborough (of some)	503
Peterborough	506
Petite Violette Hâtive	506
Pitmaston Orange	506
Red Roman	508
Roman	508
Rough Roman	508
Scarlet Newington	508
Scarlet	508

	Page.		Page.
Zion Hill	508	POMEGRANATES.	
Smith's Newington	508		
Spring Grove	503	Double Red	550
Temple's	503	Double White	550
Vermash (of some)	506	Grenadier à Fruit Doux	549
Violette Hâtive	506	Sweet Fruited	549
Violet	506	Sub-acid Fruited	549
Violette Angervillières	506	Variegated Flowered	550
Violette Musquée	506	Yellow Flowered	550
Violet, red at the stone	506	Wild, or Acid-Fruited	549
Violet Musk	506		
Williams' Orange	506		
Williams' Seedling	506	PEACHES.	
		Abricotée	489
NUTS.		Acton Scott	471
Chestnut	262	Admirable Tardive	472
Chinquepin	262	Admirable	477
Cosford Filbert	261	Admirable Jaune	489
European Walnut	260	Alberge Jaune	492
Filbert	261	Algiers Yellow	496
Frizzled Filbert	261	Algiers Winter	496
Hickory Nut	261	June	474
Northhamptonshire Prolific		Apricot Peach	489
Filbert	262	Astor	471
Red Filbert	262	Avant Rouge	482
White Filbert	262	Avant Pêche de Troyes	482
		Avant Blanche	483
		Barrington	472
OLIVES.		Baltimore Beauty	490
		Bellegarde	471
Broad-Leaved Olive	548	Belle de Vitry	472
Common Olive	547	Bellis	472
Long-Leaved	547	Belle Beauté	478
Olivier à fruit arrondi	548	Belle de Vitry	477
Olivier Pleureur	548	Belle Bausse	478
Olivier Picholine	548	Belle de Paris	482
Wild American	547	Bergen's Yellow	490
		Betterave	494
		Blood Clingstone	493
ORANGE FAMILY.		Blood Cling	493
		Blood Freestone	494
1. Oranges.		Bourdine	479
Bergamot	544	Boudin	479
Blood Red	544	Brevoort	472
Common Sweet	544	Brevoort's Morris	472
Fingered	544	Brevoort's Seedling Melter	473
Maltese	544	Brown Nutmeg	482
Mandarin	544	Buckingham Mignonne	472
Pear-Shaped	544	Cardinale	494
Ribbed	544	Catherine	494
Seville	544	Chancellor	473
St. Michael's	544	Chancellière	473
Sweet-Skinned	544	Chinese Peach	500
2. Lemons.		Clinton	473
Common	545	Claret Clingstone	493
Sweet	545	Cole's Early Red	473
3. Limes.		Cooledge's Favourite	473
Common	545	Cooledge's Early Red Rareripe	473
Pomo d' Adamo	545	Colonel Ansley's	473

	Page.		Page
Cole's White Malocoton	481	Grosse Persique Rouge	498
Columbia	491	Haine's Early Red	479
Crawford's Late Melocoton	491	Heath Clingstone	491
Crawford's Early	490	Heath	494
Crawford's Early Melocoton	490	Hero of Tippecanoe	499
Crawford's Superb Malaca-		Hoffman's Pound	481
tune	491	Hogg's Melocoton	492
Cut-Leaved	477	Incomparable	495
D' Abricot	489	Italian	482
Double Montagne	471	Jura	500
Double Mountain	474	Johnson's Early Purple	478
Dorsetshire	483	Judd's Melting	479
Double Swalsh	485	Kenrick's Heath	479
D'Orange	489	Kew Early Purple	486
Double Blossomed	499	Kennedy's Carolina	496
Double Flowering	499	Kennedy's Lemon Cling	496
Druid Hill	474	Late Chancellor	473
Early Anne	474	Large Early York	475
Early Tillotson	475	Large American Nutmeg	476
Early York	475	L'Admirable	477
Early Newington Freestone	476	Large French Mignonne	478
Early Newington	476	La Royale	478
Early Sweet-Water	476	La Royale	479
Early Admirable	477	Late Admirable	479
Early Purple Avant	478	Late Purple	479
Early May	478	La Grange	480
Early Vineyard	478	Large Red Rareripe	485
Early Red Nutmeg	482	Large Red Rareripe	480
Early White Nutmeg	483	Lady Ann Steward	481
Early Purple	484	Late Red Rareripe	486
Early Royal George	485	Lady Gallatin	492
Early Bourdine	485	Large Yellow Rareripe	493
Early Red Rareripe	485	Late Admirable Cling	495
Early Crawford	490	Large White Clingstone	495
Early Newington Cling	498	Late Yellow Albarge	496
Edgar's Late Melting	473	Largest Lemon	496
Emperor of Russia	477	Large Newington	497
Favourite	477	Lemon Clingstone	496
Favourite Red	477	Lord Montague's Noblesse	483
Flat Peach of China	500	Lockyer's Mignonne	485
Fox's Seedling	478	Lord Nelson's	486
French Mignonne	478	Lord Fauconberg's Mignonne	486
French Royal George	471	Long Yellow Pine Apple	496
French Magdalen	481	Luscious White Rareripe	481
Freestone Heath	479	Madeleine de Courson	481
French Bourdine	479	Madeline Rouge	481
Free-stone Heath	481	Malta	482
Galande	471	Malte de Normandie	482
George the Fourth	475	Madeleine Rouge à Petites	
Gold Fleshed	492	Fleurs	485
Golden Mignonne	492	MadelineRouge Tardive	486
Green Nutmeg	471	Madeleine Rouge à Moyennes	
Grosse Mignonne	478	Fleurs	486
Grimwood's Royal George	478	Madeleine à Petites Fleurs	486
Grimwood's New Royal George	478	Malagatune	492
Griffin's Mignonne	485	Malacatune	492
Grimwood's Royal Charlotte		M Antoinette	493
Grosse Jaune Tardiv		Mrs Lisa's Favorite	483
Green Catherine		Mignonne	478
Gros Malecaton		Millet's Mignonne	485

	Page		Page
Montague	474	Red Nutmeg	482
Montauban	474	Red Avant	482
Motteux's	479	Red Cheek Melocoton	492
Morris's Red Rareripe	480	Red Magdalen	485
Morris Red	480	Red Cheek Malocoton	492
Morris White Rareripe	481	Red Alberge	492
Morris White	481	Red Heath	494
Morris White Freestone	481	Reid's Weeping Peach	500
Morrisania Pound	481	Royal Kensington	478
Morrison's Pound	481	Ronald's Seedling Galande	478
Monstrous Pavie	498	Royal Sovereign	478
Monstrous Pompone	498	Royale	479
Narbonne	479	Rouge Paysanne	481
Newington Peach	476	Royal George	485
New Cut-leaved	477	Royal Charlotte	486
Neill's Early Purple	478	Rose	487
New Royal Charlotte	486	Rosanna	493
New York White Clingstone	495	Sanguinole à Chair Adhérente	494
Newington	497	Scott's Early Red	487
Nivette	483	Serrated	477
Nivette Veloutée	483	Selby's Cling	495
Noisette	473	Smock Freestone	492
Noblesse	483	Smith's Newington	498
Noir de Montreuil	471	Smith's Early Newington	498
October Yellow	496	Smooth-leaved Royal George	471
Oldmixon Freestone	484	Snow	486
Oldmixon Clearstone	484	Stewart's Late Galande	473
Oldmixon Clingstone	497	Strawberry	487
Old Newington	497	St. George	492
Orange Clingstone	497	Superb Royal	478
Orange Peach	480	Superb	485
Pavie Admirable	495	Sweet Water	476
Pavie de Pompone	498	Swiss Mignonne	478
Pavie de Compone Grosse	498	Têton de Venus	479
Pavie Rouge de Compone	498	Tippecanoe	499
Pavie Caum	498	True Red Magdalen	481
Pavie Monstreux	498	Unique	477
Pêche Royale	479	Vanguard	483
Pêche Malte	482	Van Zandt's Superb	487
Pêche Jaune	492	Veloutée Tardive	483
Pêche à Fleurs Doubles	499	Veloutée de Merlet	478
Pêche à Fleurs Semi-Doubles	499	Violette Hâtive	471
Peen-To	500	Vineuse	478
Pine-Apple Clingstone	496	Vineuse de Fromentin	478
Pourprée de Normandie	478	Waxen Rareripe	487
Pourprée Hâtive	478	Washington	488
Pourprée Tardive	479	Washington Red Freestone	488
Pourprée Hâtive à Grandes Fleurs	484	Walter's Early	488
Pourprée Hâtive	484	Washington Clingstone	499
Poole's Large Yellow	491	Weeping Peach	500
Poole's Late Yellow Freestone	491	White Rareripe	481
President	484	White Malacaton	481
Prince's Red Rareripe	486	White Nutmeg	483
Purple Avant	478	White Avant	483
Purple Alberge	492	White Imperial	488
Red Rareripe	480	White Blossomed Incomparable	489
Red Rareripe	485	White Blossom	489
Red Magdalen	481	Willow Peach	489
		Williamson's New York	495

	Page
Yellow Admirable	489
Yellow Malocoton	492
Yellow Malagatune	492
Yellow Alberge	492
Yellow Rareripe	492
Yellow Rareripe	493
Yellow Pine Apple	496

PEARS.

	Page
Ah! Mon Dieu	383
Alpha	348
Althorpe Crassaune	352
Amiré Joannet	330
Ambrosia	331
Amory	349
Amande Double	353
Amanda's Double	353
Amoselle	430
Andrews	349
Ananas	349
Ananas d'Eté	350
Ananas	350
Angleterre	351
Angora	423
Archiduc d'Eté	330
Aston Town	351
Autumn Colmar	353
Autumn Bergamot	366
Bartlett, or Williams' Bonchré-tien	331
Bartlett	331
Badham's	357
Belle de Bruxelles	334
Belle d'Août	334
Beau Présent	337
Bellissime d'Eté	339
Bellissime Suprême	339
Bellissime Jargonelle	339
Belmont	353
Belle et Bonne	353
Beurré Haggerston	333
Beurré d'Angleterre	351
Beurré Boucquia	355
Beurré de Capiumont	357
Beurré Gris	357
Beurré Rouge	357
Beurré d'Or	357
Beurré Dorée	357
Beurré d'Amboise	357
Beurré du Roi	357
Beurré	357
Beurré d'Anjou	357
Beurré d'Anjou	360
Beurré Vert	357
Beurré Bosc	358
Beurré d'Yelle	358
Beurré d'Yelle	360
Beurré d'Amalis	360

	Page
Beurré d'Amaulis	360
Beurré d'Amanlis	360
Beurré Diel	360
Beurré Royale	360
Beurré Magnifique	360
Beurré Incomparable	360
Beurré Knox	361
Beurré Kenrick	362
Beurré Duval	363
Beurré Preble	363
Beurré Colmar	363
Beurré Colmar d'Automne	363
Beurré de Beaumont	364
Beurré Van Mons	364
Beurré Romain	364
Beurré de Ranz	427
Beurré Rance	427
Beurré Epine	427
Beurré de Flandre	427
Beurré Bronzée	428
Beurré d'Alençon	430
Beurré d'Hiver	433
Beurré Fortunée	436
Beurré d'Hardenpont	437
Beurré d'Hiver Nouvelle	437
Beurré d'Aremberg	437
Beurré de Cambron	437
Beurré d'Austrasie	438
Beurré Colman Gris, dit Précel.	444
Beurré d'Argenson	444
Beurré de Malines	450
Beurré Van Marum	365
Beurré Spence	365
Beurré Crapaud	365
Beurré Picquery	365
Beurré Beauchamps	367
Beurré Romain	368
Beurré Blanc de Jersey	368
Beurré Curté	371
Beurré de Payence	374
Beurré Plat	375
Bergaloo	378
Beurré Blanc	378
Beurré Rouge	380
Beurré Bronzée	383
Beurré or Bonne Louise-d'Araudoré	397
Beurré Niell	401
Beurré Sieulle	413
Beurré d'Aremberg	423
Beurré des Orphelins	423
Beurré de la Pentecôte	425
Beurré d'Hiver de Bruxelles	425
Beurré Roupé	425
Beurré de Pâques	425
Beurré Gris d'Hiver Nouveau	426
Belle de Brussels	353
Bezi Vaet	429

	Page.		Page.
Bezi d'Héri	428	Bujaleuf	450
Bezi Royale	428	Caillot Rosat d'Eté	345
Bergamotte de Pâques	429	Capiumont	357
Bergamotte d'Hiver	429	Calabasse Bosc	358
Bergamotte de Bugi	429	Cabot	370
Bergamotte de Toulouse	429	Capsheaf	374
Bergamotte d'Hollande	430	Calebasse	374
Bergamotte de Fouégre	430	Calebasse Double Extra	374
Bergamot d'Eté	333	Calebasse d'Hollande	374
Bergamotte d'Angleterre	333	Calebasse Grosse	374
Bergamotte Suisse	367	Capucin	375
Bergamotte Cadette	367	Capuchin	375
Bergamotte Crassane	375	Claire	375
Bergamotte Sylvange	413	Calhoun	376
Bergamotte de la Pentecôte	425	Cambridge Sugar Pear	392
Bezi de Chaumontelle	433	Canning	425
Bezi d'Echassey	435	Catillac	432
Bezi de Chasserie	435	Cadilloc	432
Belle de Jersey	448	Collite	444
Beauchamps	367	Chelmsford	370
Bezi de Montigny	368	Charles of Austria	376
Bezi de la Motte	368	Charles d'Autriche	376
Bein Armudi	368	Charles d'Autriche	401
Belle de Flanders	356	Chaumontel très gros	425
Belle Lucrative	387	Chaumontel	433
Bezi Chaumontelle très gros	425	Chapman's	444
Bishop's Thumb	389	Chambers' Large	448
Bloodgood	332	Chambrette	450
Bleeker's Meadow	355	Citron	336
Black Worcester	429	Citron des Carmes	341
Black Pear of Worcester	429	Citron de Septembre	378
Bon Chrétien d'Eté	346	Citronenbirne Bömische Grosse	
Bonne de Keingheim	347	Punctirte	392
Boucquia	355	Clara	375
Bosc's Flaschenbirne	358	Clinton	376
Bonne Rouge	366	Clion	448
Bon Chrétien Fondante	370	Common Bergamot	366
Bonne-ente	378	Compte de Lamy	371
Bouche Nouvelle	386	Comprette	371
Bosch	386	Commodore	372
Bosch Sire	386	Copea	373
Bosch Pear	386	Colmar Epine	376
Boston Epargne	392	Colmar Neill	376
Bon Chrétien d'Espagne	430	Comtesse de Frêsnol	388
Bon Chrétien Turc	430	Compte de Michaux	398
Bourgermester	448	Colmar Bosc	401
Bonne de Malines	450	Colmar Deschamps	423
Brougham	354	Columbia	430
Brown Beurré	357	Columbian Virgalieu	430
Brocas Bergamot	366	Columbian Virgalouse	430
Braddock's Field Standard	398	Comstock	432
Broom Park	428	Comstock Wilding	432
Bretagne le Cour	415	Colmar	434
Brown St. Germain	417	Colmar Doré	434
Brande's St. Germain	448	Colmar d'Hiver	437
Buffam	356	Colmar Jaminette	438
Buffum	356	Colmar Gris	444
Burnett	370	Colmar Hardenpont	444
Butter Pear	378	Colmar Souveraine	444

49*

	Page		Page
Colmar Preule	414	Duchesse de Mars	382
Colmar Dorée	414	Duchesse d'Orleans	384
Crawford	335	Dundas	384
Croft Castle	372	Duc d'Aremberg	423
Cross	432	Du Pâtre	425
Crassane	375	Dumas	448
Crésane	375	Early Sugar	330
Cuisse Madame	339	Early Beurré	331
Cuisse Madame	347	Early Beurré	332
Cushing	373	Early Bergamot	333
Cumberland	375	Early Queen	341
Culotte de Suisse	419	Early Chaumontelle	341
Cyprus Pear	343	Early Catherine	343
D'Ambre	341	Early Rousselet	343
D'Amour	383	Easter Beurré	425
D'Abondance	383	Easter Bergamot	429
D'Aremberg Parfait	423	Echassery	435
D'Auch	431	Echasserie	435
D'Austrasie	438	Edward's Elizabeth	385
D'Ananas	444	Edwards' Henrietta	385
Dearborn's Seedling	336	Edwards' William	420
De Vallée	347	Ellanrioch	333
De Keinzheim	347	Emerald	435
Des Trois Tours	360	English Red-Cheek	330
De Melon	360	English Beurré	351
Dean's	378	English Bergamot	360
Dechantsbirne	378	English Autumn Bergamot	360
De Louvain	383	Enfant Prodige	355
Délices d'Hardenpont	384	Epargne	337
Délices d'Ardenpont	384	Epine Rose	345
De Vigne Pelone	338	Epine d'Eté Couleur Rose	345
Deschamps	423	Epine d'Eté	345
De Maune	431	Epine d'Eté	346
De Tonneau	448	Etourneau	350
Die Sommer Christebirne	346	Eyewood	386
Diel's Butterbirne	360	Ferdinand de Meester	409
Diel	360	Fingal's	333
Dillen	360	Figue de Naples	385
Diamant	366	Fig Pear of Naples	385
Dingler	371	Fin Or d'Hiver	436
Dix	378	Fleur de Guignes	345
Dorothée Royale	360	Flemish Beauty	386
Doyenné d'Eté	336	Flemish Bon Chrétien	433
Doyenné	378	Fondante	344
Doyenné Blanc	378	Fondante du Bois	386
Doyenné Panaché	380	Fondante Musquée	346
Doyenné Galeux	380	Fondante Van Mons	357
Doyenné Boussouck	380	Fondante d'Automne	357
Doyenné Gris	380	Fondante du bois	401
Doyenné Rouge	380	Fondante du Bois	435
Doyenné Roux	380	Fondante de Panisel	444
Downham Seedling	395	Fondante de Mons	441
Doyenné d'Hiver	425	Forme de Délices	388
Doyenné du Printemps	425	Forelle	389
Doyenné d'Automne	380	Forellen-birne	389
Dumortier	378	Forme de Marie Louise	399
Dunmore	380	Fortunée	436
Duchesse d'Angoulême	381	Frauenschenkel	337
Duchess of Mars	382	Frédéric de Wurtemburg	390

	Page.		Page.
Frederick of Wurtemburg....	390	Heathcot....................	394
Französische Rumelbirne.....	428	Hooper's Bilboa..............	363
Franc Réal d' Hiver..........	436	Holland Bergamot..........	430
Franc Réal d' Eté...........	344	Hull......................	394
Franc Réal.................	436	Huguenot..................	394
Fulton.....................	391	Impératrice de France.......	386
Gansel's Bergamot...........	366	Incomparable..............	434
Garde d' Ecosse............	436	Inconnue la Fare............	446
Gambier...................	444	Isambert.... :.............	357
Gendesheim................	392	Isambert le Bon............	357
Germain Baker.............	448	Ives' Bergamot............	366
Gibson....................	349	Jargonelle, English........	337
Gil-o-gile.................	436	Jargonelle, French.........	339
Gil-o-gil..................	436	Jacquin..................	393
Glout Morceau.............	437	Jalousie..................	395
Gloux Morceaux...........	437	Jalousie de Fontenay Vendée .	396
Golden Beurré............	357	Jackman's Melting	396
Golden Beurré of Bilboa.....	362	Jagdbirne.................	435
Gore's Heathcot...........	394	Jaminette.................	438
Goulu Morceau...........	437	Jilogil...................	436
Got Luc de Cambron.......	437	Joannette	336
Green Chisel.............	337	Johonnot................	395
Green Chisel....	341	Josephine................	366
Green Sugar............	337	Josephine	427
Grosse Cuisse Madame.....	337	Josephine	438
Gros Micet d' Eté.......	344	John....................	443
Gratioli................	346	July Pear...............	344
Gratioli d' Eté.........	346	Julienne................	339
Gratioli di Roma........	346	Kattern	343
Gracieuse...............	353	Kaiserbirne.............	378
Grey Beurré............	357	Kaiser d'Automne.........	378
Grosse Dorothée........	360	Katzenkopt	432
Grosse Dillen..........	360	King Edward's...........	396
Gray Doyenné..........	380	Knevett's New Swan's Egg ..	399
Gray Butter Pear........	380	Knight's Monarch..........	439
Gray Deans............	380	Konge..................	347
Green Pear of Yair........	392	Kronprinz Ferdinand......	437
Green Yair.............	392	Kronprinz Von Oestreich...	437
Great Citron of Bohemia.....	392	Large Summer Bergamot.....	333
Green Sylvange.........	413	Large Sugar.............	346
Grand Monarque.........	432	Large Seckel............	355
Groote Mogul...........	432	La Fortunée de Parmentier...	436
Groom's Princess Royal.....	438	La Fortunée de Paris......	436
Gurle's Beurré..........	366	Lawrence...............	442
Guernsey...............	412	La Bonne Malinoise........	450
Harvest Pear...........	330	Léon le Clerc.............	440
Hampden's Bergamot........	333	Léon le Clerc de Laval......	440
Hazel..................	337	Lewis..................	441
Harvard...............	392	Lent St. Germain.........	448
Hacon's Incomparable.......	395	Le Curé.........	448
Hardenpont du Printemps....	427	Limon..................	340
Hardenpont d' Hiver........	437	Little Muscat.............	340
Hardenpont's Winter Butter-		Little Musk........	340
birne..................	437	Little Swan's Egg.	399
Hardenpont du Printemps....	438	Linden d'Automne	437
Hessel...	337	Lodge..................	393
Henry the Fourth..........	393	Long Green.............	418
Henri Quatre.............	393	L'Orpheline.............	423
Héricart..................	394	Lord Cheney's.............	430

	Page.		Page
Louise Bonne de Jersey..	397	Parkinson's Warden	429
Louise Bonne of Jersey........	397	Paddington	429
Louise Bonne d'Avranches ...	397	Passe Colmar....··	444
Louise Bonne...., ...	441	Passe Colmar Epineaux...	444
Louise Bonne Réal	441	Passe Colmar Gris..........	444
Locke.......	442	Perdreau..	343
Locke's New Beurré	442	Petit Muscat..............	340
Madeleine, or Citron des Carmes	341	Petit Rousselet............	343
Madeleine	341	Petre	403
Magdalen..	341	Pennsylvania	404
Manning's Elizabeth	355	Philippe de Pâques..........	425
Marianne Nouvelle..........	358	Pine Pear................	378
Marie Louise Nova	371	Pitt's Prolific.	404
Marie Louise the Second.....	371	Pitt's Surpasse Marie	404
Marie Louise	399	Pickering Pear	418
Marie Chrétienne............	399	Piper...	448
Marie Louise Nova..........	400	Poire Guillaume.....	334
Marotte Sucré Jaune	444	Poire des Tables des Princes .	337
Melon de Kops	360	Poire à la Reine.......... ...	341
Médaille	401	Poire de Chypre	343
Messire Jean	443	Poire Sans Peau............	345
Messire Jean Gris...... ..	443	Poire de Rose.......... ...	345
Messire Jean Blanc..........	443	Poire Ananas	349
Messire Jean Dorée	443	Poire d'Amboise............	357
Michaux	398	Poire de Cadet......	367
Milanaise Cuvelier..... .	450	Poire de Simon.............	378
Mon Dieu..............	353	Poire Neige.............	378
Moor-Fowl Egg........	399	Poire de Seigneur............	378
Moor-Fowl Egg...........	414	Poire Monsieur....	378
Mouth Water.	418	Poire d'Amour	383
Mollett's Guernsey Beurré.....	426	Poire de Louvain..	383
Mollett's Guernsey Chaumon-		Poire Truite...............	359
telle....	426	Poire-Glace....	450
Moccas	443	Poire Niell.............	401
Monsieur Jean	443	Poire à Gobert............	436
Monsieur le Curé	418	Pope's Scarlet Major	406
Mr John................	413	Pope's Quaker................	406
Muscat Petit.....	340	Pound.................	445
Muscat Robert....., ...	341	Primitive.	340
Muscat Fleuré..	418	Prince's Sugar............	344
Musk Robine	341	Prince's Sugar-Top....	344
Muscadine	342	Princesse de Parme........	399
Musk Summer Good Christian	346	Princess of Orange..	405
Napoleon	401	Princesse d'Orange.	405
Naumkeag.................	402	Princesse Conquête..........	405
New York Red Cheek....	415	Précel	441
New Autumn	418	Présent de Malines.....	444
Ne Plus Meuris..	444	Prince's St Germain..	447
New St Germain	447	Queen's Pear....	341
Nélis d'Hiver	450	Queen of the Low Countries...	406
Niell	401	Queen Caroline.	408
No 8 of Van Mons	333	Quilletette..	407
Ognon..................	345	Raymond.....	409
Ognonet	367	Real Jargonelle...	337
Oxford Chaumontel..........	433	Red Muscadel	339
Passans du Portugal.........	342	Red Cheek	339
Paquency.................	404	Red Beurré..............	357
Pailleau	441	Red Doyenné	380
Paradise d'Automne..........	402	Red Beurré............. ..	380

	Page.		Page
Reine des Pays Bas	406	Striped Germain	447
Reine Caroline	408	*Striped Long Green*	419
Reine des Poires	408	*Staunton*	366
Red-cheeked Seckel	415	*Sugar Pear*	330
Regintin	441	Sugar Top	344
Rousselet Hâtif	343	Summer Bergamot	333
Rousselet de Rheims	343	*Summer Bergamot*	333
Rousselet	343	*Summer Doyenné*	336
Rosenbirne	345	*Suprême*	339
Roi de Rome	401	Summer Beauty	339
Roi de Wurtemberg	437	*Summer Portugal*	342
Rousselet de Meester	409	Summer Franc Real	344
Rostiezer	410	Summer Rose	345
Robertson	422	Sucrée de Hoyerswerda	346
Royal Tairling	429	Sugar of Hoyerswerda	346
Robert's Keeping	429	*Summer Thorn*	346
Saint Sampson	337	Summer Bon Chrétien	346
Saint Lambert	337	*Summer Good Christian*	346
Sabine d'Eté	339	Summer St. Germain	347
Sanspeau or Skinless	345	*Summer Bell*	347
Satin Vert	346	*Sucrée Dorée*	401
Saint Germain de Martin	347	Superfondante	411
Sabine	438	Sullivan	411
Saint Germain Jaune	446	*Surpasse Marie Louise*	401
Scotch Bergamot	333	Surpasse Virgalieu	416
Schöne und Gute	353	*Surpasse Virgouleuse*	416
Sept-en-gueule	340	*Swiss Bergamot*	367
Seckel	415	*Sweet Summer*	337
Seckle	415	Swan's Egg	414
Seigneur d'Hiver	425	*Sylvanche Vert d'Hiver*	360
Short's Saint Germain	347	Sylvange	413
Shenks	413	*Syckle*	415
Sieulle	413	*Terling*	429
Skinless	345	*Thorny Rose*	345
Sickel	415	Thompson's	413
Smith's Pennsylvania	404	*Trouvé de Montigny*	368
Snow Pear	378	*Trout Pear*	389
Sommer Apothekerbirne	346	Union	448
Sommer Gute Christenbirne	346	Urbaniste	417
Souverain	444	Uvedale's St. Germain	448
Spanish Bon Chrétien	430	*Uvedale's Warden*	448
Spice or Musk Pear	343	Vallée Franche	347
Spina	430	*Van Mons, No. 1218*	372
St. Jean	330	*Valencia*	378
St. John's Pear	330	*Van Mons, No. 154*	385
St. Jean Musquée Gros	341	*Van Mons, No. 889*	411
St. Germain d'Eté	347	Van Buren	420
St. Michael	378	Van Mons Léon le Clerc	419
St. Michel	378	*Van Mons, No. 1238*	376
St. Michel Doré	380	*Vermillion d'Eté*	339
St. Ghislain	410	Verte Longue	418
St. André	411	*Verte Longue Suisse*	419
St. Germain Blanc	441	Verte Longue Panachée	419
St. Germain	446	*Virgalieu*	378
St. Germain Gris	446	*Virgaloo*	378
St. Germain Panachée	447	Vicar of Winkfield	448
Styrian	412	Virgouleuse	450
Stevens' Genessee	412	*Warwick Bergamot*	376
Stephen's Genessee	412	Washington	422

	Page.		Page
Weisse Herbst Butterbirne	378	*Brignole*	287
White Doyenné	378	Brevoort's Purple	289
White Beurré	378	*Brevoort's Purple Bolmar*	289
White Autumn Beurré	378	*Brevoort's Purple Washington*	289
Williams' Bon Chrétien	334	*Brignole Violette*	290
Windsor	347	Buel's Favorite	272
Williams' Early	345	*Bury Seedling*	273
William the Fourth	397	Byfield	272
Wilbur	421	*Catalonian*	279
Wilkinson	421	*Caledonian*	300
Winter Bergamot	429	*Caledonian*	306
Winter Cross	432	Cherry	294
Winter Beurré	433	Cheston	295
Winter Virgalieu	434	Chickasaw Plum	263
Winter Bell	445	Coe's Golden Drop	273
Winter Nelis	450	*Coe's Imperial*	273
Wilhelmine	451	Cooper's Large	291
Wilhelmina	451	*Cooper's Large Red*	291
Wurtemberg	401	*Cooper's Large American*	291
Yat	422	Columbia	292
Yellow Butter	378	*Columbian Gage*	292
York Bergamot	366	Corse's Admiral	293
Yutte	422	Corse's Field Marshal	293
		Corse's Nota Bene	293
		Coe's Late Red	295
		Common Damson	297
PLUMS.		*Common Quetsche*	310
		Common English Sloe	316
Abricotée de Tours	272	*Coetche*	310
Abricotée	272	*Cruger's Scarlet*	293
Abricot Vert	276	*Cruger's*	293
Abricotée Rouge	289	*Cruger's Seedling*	293
Agen Datte	309	*Cruger's Scarlet Gage*	293
Amber Primordian	279	Dana's Yellow Gage	275
American Yellow Gage	287	*Damas Vert*	276
American Wheat	289	*Dauphine*	276
Apricot	272	*D'Avoine*	279
Apricot Plum of Tours	272	*Dame Aubert*	286
Autumn Gage	271	*Dame Aubert Blanche*	286
Austrian Quetsche	311	*Dame Aubert Jaune*	286
Azure Hâtive	289	*D'Amérique Rouge*	294
Beekman's Scarlet	303	*Damson*	297
Beach Plum	263	*Damas d'Italie*	302
Bingham	272	*D'Agen*	309
Bleecker's Gage	273	*Damas Violet*	310
Blue Gage	289	*Damask*	310
Black Perdrigon	289	*Damas Gros*	310
Blue Perdrigon	290	*Damas Violet Gros*	310
Blue Imperatrice	290	*Dame Aubert Violette*	312
Blue Perdrigon	307	*De Virginie*	294
Black Damson	297	Denniston Red	296
Blue Holland	301	Denniston's Albany Beauty	275
Bleecker's Scarlet	303	Denniston's Superb	275
Black Morocco	306	*Denyer's Victoria*	315
Black Damask	306	Diamond	295
Bolmar	284	*Diaprée Violette*	295
Bolmar's Washington	284	Diamond	295
Bruyn Gage	276	*Diaprée Rouge*	308
Bradford Gage	276	*Die Violette königinnClaudie*	308
Brugnon Gage	276	Downton Imperatrice	274

	Page.		Page.
Domine Dull..	296	*Imperial Diadem*	293
Double-Flowering Sloe........	316	*Impératrice Violette*........	310
Double-Blossomed Plum......	316	*Imperatrice Violette Grosse*..	310
Drap d'Or....................	274	*Imperial Violet*.............	312
Dutch Prune................	296	*Impériale Violette*..........	312
Dutch Quetzen..............	296	*Impériale Rouge*............	312
Duane's Purple French.......	297	*Impériale*..................	312
Dwarf Texas Plum...........	263	*Isleworth Green Gage*.......	276
Early Yellow...............	279	Isabella.....................	305
Early Scarlet..............	294	*Italian Damask*.............	306
Early Damson..............	297	Italian Damask..............	302
Early Orleans...............	304	*Jaune Hâtive*...............	279
Early Morocco.............	306	*Jaune de Catalogue*.........	279
Early Black Morocco.......	306	Jefferson...................	279
Early Damask..............	306	*Jenkins's Imperial*..........	306
Early Tours................	307	*Keyser's Plum*..............	277
Early Violet...............	307	Kirke's.....................	306
Early Royal................	313	*Knights' Large Drying*......	281
Egg Plum..................	286	*Knights No. 6*..............	302
Elfrey......................	299	Lawrence's Favorite..	280
Elfry's Prune..............	299	*Lawrence's Gage*...........	280
Emerald Drop...............	275	Large Green Drying..........	281
Fair's Golden Drop.........	273	*Large Early Damson*........	301
Flushing Gage.............	278	*Large Long Blue*...........	309
Florence...................	312	*Late Yellow Damson*........	287
Fotheringham...............	299	*La Délicieuse*..............	291
Franklin...................	284	*La Royale*..................	311
Frost Gage..................	300	*Leipzic*.....................	310
Frost Plum..................	300	*Little Queen Claude*........	288
German Gage................	273	*Little Blue Gage*...........	289
German Prune..............	296	Lombard....................	303
German Prune..............	310	Long Scarlet................	303
Ghiston's Early.............	276	*Louis Philippe*.............	306
Golden Gage...............	273	Lucombe's Nonsuch.........	281
Gonne's Green Gage........	288	*Magnum Bonum*............	286
Golden Cherry Plum.........	295	*Maitre Claude*.............	287
Goliath.....................	300	*Matchless*.................	295
Green Gage.................	276	Manning's Long Blue Prune...	309
Grosse Reine Claude........	276	*Manning's Long Blue*.......	309
Grosse Reine..............	276	*Mirabelle Double*..........	274
Grosse Luisante...........	286	*Mirabelle Grosse*...........	274
Grove House Purple........	299	*Mirabelle*.................	282
Grimwood's Early Orleans...	301	*Mirabelle Petite*............	282
Gwalsh......................	301	*Mirabelle Jaune*............	282
Hampton Court.............	301	*Miser Plum*................	294
Holland.....................	301	*Mimms*....................	298
Holland Prune.............	301	*Miriam*....................	313
Horse Plum.................	301	*Monsieur*..................	304
Howell's Early..............	302	*Monsieur Ordinaire*........	304
Howell's Large.............	306	*Monsieur Hâtif*............	304
Hudson Gage...............	277	*Monsieur Hâtif de Montmo-*	
Huling's Superb............	277	*rency*.....................	304
Ickworth Imperatrice........	302	*Monsieur Tardif*...........	314
Imperial Ottoman...........	278	Morocco	306
Imperial Gage..............	278	Mulberry...................	282
Imperatrice Blanche........	285	Myrobolan..................	294
Impériale Blanche..........	286	*Myrobolan*	294
Impératrice................	290	*New Golden Drop*..........	273
Impératrice Violette........	295	*New Washington*	**284**

	Page
New York Purple.	289
New Early Orleans	301
New Orleans	301
Nectarine	306
Noire Hative.	307
Old Orleans	301
Orleans	301
Orange	252
Orange Gage	252
Petite Reine Claude.	288
Peach Plum	306
Peach Plum	306
Peoly's Early Blue	309
Perdrigon Rouge.	312
Perdrigon Blanc	287
Perdrigon Violette	290
Perdrigon Violet	307
Pigeon's Heart.	310
Pond's Seedling	309
Pond's Purple	309
Prince's Imperial.	278
Prune de St. Barnabé	279
Prince's Yellow Gage	287
Prune Pêche	306
Précoce de Tours.	307
Prune de la St Martin	295
Prune d'Agen	309
Prune d'Ast.	309
Prune de Brignole.	309
Prune d'Allemagne	310
Prune d Œuf.	312
Prune d'Altesse.	314
Prune Suisse.	311
Purple Damson	297
Purple Favorite	307
Purple Gage	308
Purple Egg	312
Purple Magnum Bonum	312
Quetsche or German Prune	310
Quetsche Grosse.	310
Quetsche d'Allemagne Grosse.	310
Queen Victoria	315
Queen Mother	310
Reine Claude	276
Reine Claude Violette	308
Reine Claude Blanche	288
Reine Claude petite espèce	288
Red Gage	313
Red Gage	303
Red Damask	301
Red Magnum Bonum	301
Red Queen Mother	310
Red Perdrigon	312
Red Magnum Bonum	312
Red Imperial.	312
Rivers' Early	311
Roe's Autumn Gage	271
Roche Corbon	288
Robe de Sergent	308

	Page
Royale	311
Royale de Tours	313
Royal Tours	313
Royale Hâtive	313
Saint Martin's Quetsche	283
Saint Catherine	283
Saint Martin	295
Saint Martin Rouge	295
St Maurin	309
St James Quetsche	311
Saint Cloud	300
Schuyler's Gage	276
Scarlet Gage	303
Semiana	291
Shailer's White Damson	287
Shropshire, or Prune Damson	297
Shea	299
Sharp's Emperor	315
Siamese	284
Simiana	311
Small Green Gage	288
Smith's Orleans	301
Steer's Emperor	306
Sucrin Vert	276
Superior Green Gage	278
Suisse	311
Sweet Damson	297
Sweet Damson	301
Sweet Prune	310
Swiss Plum	311
Thomas	315
True Large German Prune	310
Turkish Quetsche	310
Vert Bonne	276
Véritable Impératrice	290
Violet Perdrigon	290
Violette	290
Violet Diaper	295
Violet Perdrigon	304
Violette Hative.	307
Violet de Tours	307
Violet Queen Claude	309
Virginian Cherry	294
Virgin.	315
Washington	281
Wentworth	286
White Gage	278
White Primordian	279
White Imperatrice	285
White Empress	285
White Magnum Bonum	286
White Mogul	286
White Imperial	286
White Holland	286
White Egg	286
White Damson	287
White Prune Damson	287
White Damascene	287
White Perdrigon	287

	Page.
White Gage	287
Wilmot's Green Gage	276
Wilmot's New Green Gage	276
Wilmot's Late Green Gage	276
Winter Damson	297
Wilmot's Late Orleans	300
Wilmot's New Orleans	304
Wild Red or Yellow Plum	263
Yellow Apricot	272
Yellow Perdrigon	274
Yellow Magnum Bonum	286
Yellow Egg	290
Yellow Gage	288
Zwetsche	310

QUINCES.

Apple-Shaped	511
Chinese	512
Japan	512
Oblong	511
Orange	511
Pear-Shaped	511
Portugal	511

RASPBERRIES AND BLACKBERRIES.

1. RASPBERRIES.

American Red	515
American Black	515
American White	516
Barnet	516
Black Raspberry	515
Brentford Cane	516
Burley	514
Common Red Antwerp	515
Common Red	515
Common Black-Cap	515
Cornwall's Prolific	516
Cornwall's Seedling	516
Cretan Red	516
Double Bearing	517
Double-Bearing Yellow	515
English Red, of some	515
Ever-Bearing Ohio	518
Fastolff	517
Franconia	517
Framboisier à Gros Fruit	514
Howland's Red Antwerp	514
Knevet's Antwerp	514
Knevet's Giant	518
Large Red	516
Late Cane	517
Lord Exmouth's	516
New Red Antwerp	514
Nottingham Scarlet	518
Ohio Raspberry	518

	Page
Perpetual Bearing	517
Red Antwerp	514
Siberian	517
Thimble Berry	515
True Red Antwerp	514
Twice Bearing	517
Victoria	518
White Antwerp	515
Yellow Antwerp	515

2. BLACKBERRIES.

Bush Blackberry	519
Dewberry	519
Double White-blossomed Bramble	519
Double Pink-blossomed Bramble	519
High Blackberry	519
Low Blackberry	519
Rose Flowering Bramble	519
Trailing Blackberry	519

STRAWBERRIES.

Aberdeen	528
American Scarlet	527
Atkinson Scarlet	527
Austrian Scarlet	526
Bishop's Orange	526
Bishop's New	526
Black Prince	528
Black Imperial	528
Blood Pine	532
Black Roseberry	526
Brewer's Emperor	529
Buisson	535
Carolina	532
Caperon Royal	535
Caperon Hermaphrodite	535
Common Hautbois	536
Commun Sans Filets	535
Commun Rouge	534
Des Alpes à Fruit Rouge	534
Des Alpes à Fruit Blanc	535
Downton	529
Double-Bearing	535
Dundee	526
Duke of Kent's Scarlet	526
Early Scarlet	528
Early Prolific Scarlet	526
Elton	529
Elton Seedling	529
English Red Wood	534
Fraisier Vert	537
French Musk Hautbois	535
Globe Scarlet	526
Green Strawberry	537
Green Alpine	537
Green Pine	53?

	Page.		Page
Green Wood	537	*Patagonian*	536
Greenwell's New Giant	536	*Pine Apple*	532
Grove-End Scarlet	527	Prince Albert	532
Hovey's Seedling	530	Prolific, or Conical Hautbois	535
Hudson's Bay	527	Red Bush Alpine	535
Hudson	527	Red Alpine	534
Keen's Seedling	531	*Red Monthly*	534
Keen's Black Pine	531	Red Wood	534
Knight's Seedling	529	Roseberry	528
Large Early Scarlet	527	Ross Phœnix	533
Late Scarlet	527	Scarlet	528
Melon	528	*Scotch Scarlet*	528
Methven Scarlet	527	*Southampton Scarlet*	527
Methven Castle	527	Swainstone Seedling	534
Monthly, without Runners	535	True Chili	536
Murphy's Child	531	*Virginia Scarlet*	528
Musk Hautbois	535	*Warren's Seedling*	527
Myatt's British Queen	531	Wilmot's Superb	536
Myatt's Pine	531	White Alpine	535
Myatt's Deptford Pine	531	White Bush Alpine	535
Myatt's Eliza	532	*White Monthly*	535
Nova Scotia Scarlet	526	*White Monthly, without Run-*	
Old Scarlet	528	*ners*	535
Old Pine	532	White Wood	534
Orange Hudson's Bay	526	Yellow Chili	536
Original Scarlet	528	*York River Scarlet*	527

GENERAL INDEX.

~~~~~~~~~

Almond, its history and uses, page 149; cultivation, 149; varieties of, 150; ornamental varieties, 152.

American Blight, 66.

Amelioration of Fruits, 1.

Apple, history of, 56; its uses, 56; criterion of qualities in, 58; propagation, and soil and situation for, 59; grafting the trees, 17; pruning, 62; cultivation of orchards of the, 61; the bearing year of, to alter, 61; insects injurious to, and modes of destroying, 62; gathering and keeping, 67.

Apple Borer, to destroy, 63.

Apricot, its history, uses, and cultivation, 152; diseases of, 153; varieties of, 153; ornamental sorts, 159; selection of choice varieties, 160

Aspect of fruit trees, 48; effects of hills and valleys, 50

Bark Louse, to destroy, 66, 560.

Bending the limbs, to induce fruitfulness, 34.

Berberry, its uses, culture, and varieties, 160.

Birds, destroyers of insects, 55.

Blackberry, its culture and varieties, 518.

Black Gum, on the plum tree, 269.

Black Walnut, 261.

Butternut, 261.

Budding, the theory and practice of, 19; its advantages, best season for, 20; shield and American shield budding, 21; after treatment of the buds, 22; reversed shield, and annular, 23.

Canker Worm, its habits, 64; best modes to destroy, 65.

Caterpillar, to destroy, 63.

Chestnut, its varieties, 262

Cherry, history and uses, 162; planted for avenues in Germany, 163; soil and situation for, 163; propagation of, 164; classification of, and its varieties, 165; ornamental varieties, 199; selections of choice sorts, 201.

Chamomile, used to destroy insects, 54; for the scale insect on the orange tree, 543.

Cider, to make, 68.

Citron, the, 545.

Coal-Tar, to prevent mice from girdling trees, 560.

Codling Moth, 66.

Composition for wounds in fruit trees, 32.

Crab, the type of the apple, wild species of, 57.

Cranberry, its habits and culture, 205.

Cross-Breeding, to obtain new varieties, 9

Curl, in Peach trees, 469

Curculio, its habits, 266, to destroy, 268.

Currant, its history, 201; uses and culture, 202; varieties, 203; ornamental sorts, 205.

Cuttings, propagation by, 24

Duration of varieties of Fruit-Trees, 551

De Candolle, his remarks on the decay of varieties, 552

Eyes, or Buds, propagation by, 27.

Fig, its history, 207, propagation and culture, 208, to hasten the ripening of the fruit, and its varieties, 209

Filbert, its varieties and culture, 261

Fire-Blight, its nature, 322

French Standard Names, key to the pronunciation of, 561

Frozen-Sap Blight, in the pear tree, 324.

Fruitfulness, induced by root-pruning, 32; by bending the limbs, and by disbarking, 31; by salts of lime, 35.

Grafting, its influence on varieties, 5, 553; its uses, 12; proper time for 13; its limits, 14; splice and tongue-grafting, 15; cleft-grafting, 17; saddle-grafting, 18.

Graft, its influence on the stock, 26.

Grafting-clay, 19.

Grafting-wax, 19.

Grape, its history, 218, soil and propagation, 219; culture of the foreign, 220; vinery culture, 222; insects and diseases of, 235, foreign varieties, 236, culture of the native, 247, vineyard culture of, 250, selection of choice sorts, 259.

Grape-Beetles, 252.

Gooseberry, its habits and uses, 213, propagation and culture, 214, varieties, 215; selection of choice, 217.

Hickory Nut, 261

Hybridising plants, 9, its limits, 10

Inoculating, or Budding Fruit-Trees, 19

Insect Blight, in the pear, 322.

Insects, general remarks on, 51, to destroy by hand-picking, to kill in the grub state, 52, to kill in the winged state, 53, sorts injurious to the apple, 62; to the grape, 235 and 252, to the plum, 266; to the pear, 322, to the peach, 460; to the melon, 538; to the orange, 513

Knight, his mode of raising new varieties, 9; his theory on the decay of varieties, 551.

Knots, on the plum, 269

Layers, propagation by, 28.

Laying-in-by-the-heels, 47.

Lemons and Limes, 545.

Longworth, on vineyard culture, 250.

Manure for fruit-trees, 45

Madeira Nut, 260.

Melon, its history and culture, 537, insects affecting, 538, culture of the Persian, 538; varieties, 539.

Mice, to deter from girdling trees, 560

Mildew, on the grape, 252

Moths, to destroy, 54.

Mulberry, its habits and varieties, 259.

Mulching newly-planted trees, 45.

Nectarine, its habits and culture, 501; insects affecting, 502; varieties 502; selection of choice sorts, 509.

Nuts, description of, 260; European Walnut, Butternut, 261; Filberts of various sorts, 261; Chestnuts, 262.

Orange, its history and uses, 542; soil and culture, 543; scale insect on, 543; its varieties, 543.

Olive, its history and uses, 546; propagation, culture, and finest varieties, 547.

Peach, its history, 452; its uses, 454; propagation, 455; soil and situation for, 456; pruning, 457; insects and diseases of, 460; the Yellows in, its cause and remedy, 461; destruction in the leaves of, 470; varieties, 471; ornamental varieties, 499; selection of choice sorts of, 500; tongue-grafting the, 15.

Peach Borer, 460.

Pear, its history, 316; uses; and remarkable trees of, 318; gathering and keeping, 319; propagation, 320; soil and culture, 321; diseases of, blight, etc., 322; forms and character of varieties, 330; selection of choice sorts, 452.

Planting deep, ill effects of, 45.

Plum, its history and uses, 262; propagation and culture, 264; best soil for, 265; insects and diseases of, curculio, etc., 266; varieties, 271; ornamental varieties, 315; selection of choice sorts, 316.

Pomegranate, its history and uses, 548; propagation and culture 549; varieties, 550.

Potash Wash for the Stems of Fruit-Trees, 560.

Position of Fruit-Trees, 48.

Preparing the Soil for Fruit-Trees, 43.

Propagation, by grafting, 12; by budding, 19; by cuttings, 26; by eyes, 27; by layers, 28; by suckers, 29.

Prunes, to make, 263.

Pruning, to promote growth, 29; theory of, 30; to induce fruitfulness, 32; root pruning, 32; transplanted trees, 46; shortening-in, 458

Qenouille training, 36.

Quince, its history and uses, 509; propagation, culture, and varieties, 510; ornamental varieties, 512.

Rabbits, to prevent their girdling trees, 560.

Raspberry, its habits, 512; uses, culture, and varieties, 513.

Renewal Training of the Vine, 221.

Ringing and Disbarking, 34.

Rivers' Remarks on Root-Pruning, 33.

Root-grafting, Dr. Van Mons' remarks on, 17.

Root-pruning, its advantages, 32.

Rust and cracking of the fruit of the Pear-tree, 556.

Salt, to destroy insects generally, 53; to destroy the curculio, **269.**

Scions, to select, 13.

50*

Seedlings, to raise, 5.

Sea Air, its effects on fruit-trees, 555

Shaddock, 515

Shellac, composition for wounds in trees, 32

Shortening-in, mode of pruning the peach, 458.

Smells. their power of driving away insects, 53.

Soil, the best for fruit-trees, 48, gravelly loam, sandy loam, clayey loam, 49; its effect on the health of the trees, 49.

Soft-Soap, for the stems of fruit-trees, 560.

Species of Fruit-Trees, 3, reproduce themselves, 3.

Slug-worm on the Pear, 325.

Spurring-in, training the vine, 221.

Stools, for propagation, 29

Stocks, for grafting on, 13, their influence on the graft, 24; bad ones cause the decay of varieties, 553.

Strawberry, its history and uses, 520; propagation and soil for, 521; culture in rows and in strips, 522, fertile and barren plants of, 523; varieties, 525, selections of choice sorts, 536.

Taking-up trees, 42.

Thorn, the, as stocks for the pear, 320

Tobacco-water, for insects, 54

Toads, destroyers of insects, 56.

Transplanting, directions for, 41; preparing places for 43

Training, general remarks on, 35; its objects, 36; conical standards, and quenouille training, 36; fan training, 38; horizontal, 40, renewal of grapes, 221

Vallies, effects of, 50

Varieties, to produce new, 3; their tendency to change, 4; do not produce the same, 4; influence of grafting on, 4; Van Mons' mode of raising new, 5; raising new, by crop breeding, 9; propagation of, 12; remarks on the duration of, 551; Knight's theory on the decay of, 552; effects of climate on, 555; to restore decayed, 558.

Vine, grafting the, 18, culture of, 221.

Vinery, cheap mode of building, 222, for fire heat, 226; diary of culture in the, 228.

Vineyard Culture, 250.

Wash for the Stems of Fruit-Trees, 560.

Water Melon, its uses, culture, and varieties, 541.

Whale oil soap, to destroy insects, 54.

Yellows, a disease of the Peach, 462; its symptoms, 462; its cause 463, remedy for, 467

Lightning Source UK Ltd.
Milton Keynes UK
UKOW05f2055040416

271547UK00009B/235/P